ACADIE
Then and Now

ACADIE
Then and Now

Warren A. Perrin

Mary Broussard Perrin

Phil Comeau

ISBN 978-0-9768927-3-1

Printed in the United States of America

General Editor: Phil Comeau
Cover design / Map illustrations: Megan Barra
Interior text design: André Andrepont
Revisions: Ryan Bernard, Jennifer Ritter Guidry
Printer: Andrepont Publishing, LLC

Cover art: George Rodrigue
Spinning Cotton in Erath (1977)
Of this painting, artist George Rodrigue (1944-2013) recalled, "General Curney J. Dronet Sr. of Erath, Louisiana, brought me a photograph some 35 years ago of his grandmother and great-grandmother. The photograph was taken about 1939. Dronet asked me to consider a painting of this important slice of Acadian history. I saw immediately that this was an iconic image, and I reinterpreted it in my Cajun style."

Cover photos of authors: (top row left to right) Zachary Richard, Michel Bastarache, Françoise Euguehard, Herménégilde Chiasson, Barry Ancelet. (Second row left to right), Jean-Marie Nadeau, Marvonne Le Gac, Alexandre Riopel, Gisèle Faucher, Georges Arsenault.

Back cover photos of directors : (left to right) Warren Perrin, Mary Broussard Perrin, Phil Comeau

Photographer credits: Julien Faugere (Z. Richard), Philip Gould (B. Ancelet), Mathieu Léger (H. Chiasson), Acadie-Nouvelle (J-M. Nadeau), Kermit Bouillion (M. Broussard Perrin), Ed Broussard (W. Perrin).

The photo credits not included are photos courtesy of the authors.

Andrepont Publishing, LLC
5043 Interstate 49 South
Opelousas, LA 70570
(800) 738-2500 / (337) 942-6385

Contents

III. REMARKABLE ACADIE

IV. DIGNITY OF A PEOPLE

V. ACADIAN REGIONAL HISTORIES

VI. EPILOGUE

MAPS

THE "THEN" MAPS

THE "NOW" MAPS

The locations of settlements, physical features, and other information portrayed on these maps have been compiled from a variety of sources, including 17th and 18th century maps, and through consultations with Acadian historians. The spelling of French names is based on contemporary usage. The maps were researched and compiled by Phil Comeau and illustrated by Megan Barra.

Prologue

Shane K. Bernard

A common misunderstanding persists, at least where I reside, that the entire population of Acadian exiles came to south Louisiana to start life anew after being forcibly removed by the British from Nova Scotia some 260 years ago. This, of course, is untrue. Not only did about one-third of the Acadian exiles die from disease, starvation, exposure, shipwrecks, and violence during the exile, but the survivors ended up strewn along the margins of both the Old and New Worlds.

Nothing drives home this point for the uninitiated as effectively as the familiar wall poster, *Acadie: The Odyssey of a People*, issued by Parks Canada in conjunction with the Center for Acadian Studies at the *Université de Moncton*. The poster reveals the complexity of the expulsion in graphic detail. The exiles did not simply board a single vessel and sail from "here" to "there." On the contrary, they were (to borrow from the title of Dr. Carl A. Brasseaux's book on the subject) "scattered to the wind."

The convoluted arrow lines and lines of the poster reflect the brutal chaos of the expulsion—a purposeful attempt to destroy the Acadian people by dispersing them across a sizable wedge of the earth. Driven from their homeland by what Dr. John Mack Faragher calls the first episode of European state-sponsored ethnic cleansing against a European people in North American history, the exiles found themselves in such varied locations as the British colonies of North America, England, France, Saint Pierre and Miquelon, New Brunswick, Saint-Domingue (modern-day Haiti), Martinique, French Guiana, and even the Falkland Islands (about 7,000 miles from Nova Scotia). The British scheme failed—as this book itself proves. Not merely in one or two places, but in many, the Acadian identity survives.

Preface

Darrell Bourque

One of the crucial decisions we make as human beings is what to remember and what to forget. This crossroad comes upon us whether we invite it or not. Memory and how we utilize it is a defining element of personal life, culture, identity, citizenship, and participation in every aspect of commerce and communication with other humans we encounter, locally and globally.

This memory experience is as old as we are. As recounted in stories of ancient belief, a person passing into the afterlife drank from the river Lethe if they wanted to forget the pains of their past lives and from the pool of Mnemosyne if they wanted to remember the lessons of the past life in order not to repeat the pain and mistakes in future reincarnations.

In Western literature, we find this memory experience in the story of the Olympian Zeus and the Titan goddess Mnemosyne (Memory). According to legend, an anxious Zeus went to this daughter of Gaia (Earth) and Uranus (Heaven) with concerns about how his great godly experiences would be remembered. Her solution was to sleep with him for nine consecutive nights from which they produced the nine muses which were to be the vessels of remembrance: one vessel for the epic exploits (Calliope); one for history (Clio); love poetry (Erato); music (Euterpe); tragedy (Melpomene); dance (Terpsichore); sacred song (Polyhymnia); comedy (Thalia); and astronomy (Urania). In short, a remembrance vessel for the way we read the skies and make music; for the woes and the silliness of being human; for expressions of love and songs of divine nature; and for how we move and how we travel through time in our histories.

In *Acadie Then and Now: A People's History,* the authors use the vessel of Clio (history) to relate the experiences of a remarkable and resilient people. The Acadians, then and now, are funny, reverent dancers who were forced to read the sky and other nearly impossible texts in order to survive. They place the tragic story of the Acadians inside an on-going saga punctuated by revelations of brilliance and a talent for endurance that goes far beyond simple survival.

This history, divided into five sections, includes a brief summary of the arrival of the French settlers in the early 1600s into the pre-Canadian territories, their experiences with ruling authorities, and their experiences with the Amerindians (primarily the Mi'kmaq). It traces the movements that lead to the Deportation Order of 1755, and the subsequent brutalities, as well as the various resistance efforts and the great dispersal, including one of the early "migrations" led by Joseph Beausoleil Broussard from Halifax to Louisiana, as well as the other efforts at erasure which brought these Acadians to what Warren Perrin calls in his article, "far-flung ports." The history concludes with the observation that it is still being written and that a significant part of that history is being experienced in the *Congrès mondial acadien* (CMA), which began in 1994 and continues in the *Congrès* of 2014.

This book also addresses the geography needed to understand the story of the Acadians: where they came from and where they settled. The book identifies the dominant regions of France from where these people emigrated, but reminds us that nearly every part of France claims to be a contributor to what became the New World Acadian communities and settlements. The major regions of historic pre-Canada and present-day Canada are presented in the story of the Acadians as well as settlements in the U.S. Mainland and other world locations.

Also highlighted in the history are details of the important syntheses in Acadian history and culture worldwide, but predominantly in Louisiana and Canada, beginning with racial mixes which produce the rich Black and Creole cultures prevalent in Louisiana and Texas (but not exclusively so). The history continues with a look at Cajun music, Royal Proclamation issues and events, the Amerindian experiences, Acadians in England, the cattle culture, the Grand-Pré story, Canadian and Louisiana searches for shared past(s), visual arts, the birth of the world reunions, music, folk practices, cinema, literature, minority rights, and the story of Beausoleil Broussard, an Acadian hero.

In this book, the authors have done what all historians and cultural activists can do if they do not want their work to be a static document or an academic exercise. They have compiled a lively and challenging human story in which they see history as both a report *and* an inquiry, as both a record of wrongs, in this case, but also as a projection of hope. They see history as an inquiry that clarifies but also complicates simple stories. In this book they have created a work of dedication and love of who they are and of who we are as Acadians.

This book is a call to everyone to see culture as textured and precious, to see how, in reporting the history of one group of people, we are able to understand the larger human picture and the responsibilities of world citizenship. This book is an enlargement of history in every sense of the word: it tells of a people who remain unknown to many who live in the mainstream of their own cultures, but it also reveals the remarkable triumph of a people who have much to contribute to our understanding of history, folkways, politics, world music, art in all its genres, to say nothing of human rights and respect for the lives and histories of people we might see as *other* or *minor*. It is a reminder that all our histories count and all our histories are guidebooks of a sort for responsible and compassionate human behavior. It reminds us that the godly and the profane, the extraordinary and the humble, all deserve an accurate telling of their stories.

FOREWORD

Mary Broussard Perrin

Addressing the many aspects of the Acadian Deportation at the hands of the British, and of the Acadians' re-establishment in faraway places, is a complex endeavor. The violent upheavals of the *Grand Dérangement* rendered thousands of Acadians homeless as the deportation order was relentlessly carried out from one Acadian settlement to the next in an inexorable march across Acadie. Families were torn apart, in many cases never to be reunited again.

Most of the Acadians who survived the brutal upheaval ended up in unfamiliar and far-flung places throughout the Western World. The Acadie of our forebears gave way to many smaller Acadies, some more permanent than others. Regrettably, much of the history of these subsequent Acadies still has not been documented. A contemporary history of the Acadian people is not complete without an authentic understanding of the trials, successes, and failures of the Acadies and Acadians throughout the world.

Today, many of the myths and legends surrounding the exile have been considerably debunked. As more archaeological, civil, religious, and personal documentation becomes available in well-researched historical works, the mysterious and anonymous are now being revealed, obtaining names, personalities, occupations and family connections.

In the last 75 years, the most visible and documented manifestation of contemporary Acadian life in the United States has been the Cajun culture of Louisiana, which has blossomed to an unprecedented prominence. From its inception until about the mid-20th century, this was a culture existing in the shadows. Cajun music, dance, food, folklore, and traditions, plus the bounty of Louisiana's nature have all been significant factors in exposing this Acadian identity to the world.

The transformation of Acadians to Cajuns actually began in Europe, Canada, and various regions of the American colonies. Before Louisiana became a major sanctuary for displaced Acadians, nine regions on the Eastern Seaboard of the present-day United States whose populace was still seeking an English identity were forced to give asylum to 7,000 French-speaking refugees exiled from Nova Scotia by the British. Imagine the impact of these deportees, dropped off in lightly-populated areas in numbers such as these: Massachusetts (700-900 exiles); Virginia (1,500); Maryland (900); South Carolina (900); Connecticut (700); Pennsylvania (450); Georgia (400); New York (350); and North Carolina (50).

There had always been the question of why the supposedly Christian colonists did not treat the Acadians with more charity—or at least sympathy. Now we know that the situation was more complex and convoluted than was presupposed, as vividly described by Christopher Hodson in his book *The Acadian Diaspora* (New York: Oxford University Press, 2012). According to Hodson, the trauma of the exiled Acadians, coupled with the demands on provincial governments and private citizens, stirred a myriad of emotions and raised many complicated new questions of justice and prejudice. The English colonists were generally fearful of the French due to recent skirmishes between the English and the French that served as a prelude to the French and Indian War. It is often stated that the exiles were not welcome in the colonies, and that they were left hungry and destitute while the legislatures, influential planters, sheriffs, and the mostly Protestant populations of the few established towns sought to accommodate or else rid themselves legally of the unexpected influx of French-speaking Catholic exiles. While much of this may be true, it must also be stated that many colonists were unprepared for the experience and distracted by their own problems, including economic downturns and fear of invasion by French armies with whom the Acadians might take sides. Ironically, to add even more complexity to the situation, just weeks before Acadians arrived in Maryland, the region was hit by an earthquake that caused considerable destruction and chaos.

The colonists were also conflicted by the Christian admonition to feed the hungry and give shelter to the homeless, although it often seemed that they were more influenced by practical considerations, political realities, and even cultural bigotry. One horrific example personifies the situation: in 1755, selectman Elisha Stoddard of Woodbury, Connecticut, placed the apparently orphaned children of Acadians Paul Landry and his wife into indentured servitude but refused to give them back to the Landrys when they appeared, ragged, vermin-ridden, wraithlike, and starving after having searched for their offspring for two years on foot in often frigid conditions. The selectmen of Woodbury stolidly refused a reunification of the family despite the herculean efforts put forth by the Landrys to locate and reclaim their lost children. The reasons they cited were the parents' indigent circumstances and the crucial "business" of child labor. Two days later the Landrys were forcefully spirited out of town. Landry then petitioned the Connecticut General Assembly to reclaim his children, now seven- and five-years-old, but the response of that assembly has not survived.

There was also the case of the 1,500 Acadians who were deported by ship to Virginia. Upon arrival, they were not allowed to disembark while their future was being determined and debated, but instead were forced to remain in the bowels of the filthy and disease-ridden ships for four hellish months. Finally, it was decided that they were to be deported again, this time to England. From there, in 1763, the survivors—by then only about half of the original group—were finally sent to France, which to them was as foreign a country as England.

On July 28, 2013, in Princess Anne, Maryland, with the support of the Maryland Historical Trust, the first historical marker was unveiled to commemorate the 913 Acadians who were exiled to Maryland. While most of those Acadians eventually moved on to places with more of a French presence such as Louisiana, a few of them stayed and eventually anglicized their names to better fit into local society. This chapter of Acadian history is documented by Gregory A. Wood in his book *Acadians in Maryland* (Baltimore: Gateway Press, Inc., 1995). The marker recognizes the footprint that the Acadians made as they passed through the area, part of the path they took in looking to establish communities of their own. The event was organized by Marie Rundquist of Maryland, a descendant of these Acadians, and was attended by Cajuns Martin "Marty" Guidry and Warren Perrin of Louisiana, who made presentations on Acadian history and donated a Louisiana Acadian flag to the Maryland delegation. I also attended the event, accompanied by our niece Melanie Perrin of Washington, D.C.

The connection we felt with the place and the local citizens was moving, and the event made us optimistic that our Acadian culture, both past and present, will continue to find ways to express itself by enduring, as well as developing, in areas around the world in the 21st century and beyond.

Director's Note

Warren A. Perrin

In August 2012, I was invited—along with Kermit Bouillion, Director of the Acadian Museum of Erath's Living Legend program, and south Louisiana's Chef Pat Mould—to attend the *Festival Acadien de la Nouvelle-Acadie* in the Lanaudière region near Montreal, Quebec. Here, we were warmly hosted by festival president Évangeline Richard and her husband Raymond Gaudet. Having heard that budget cuts had been made in Louisiana, they, with the able assistance of Vera-Ann Petley, organized a fundraiser for our French programming at home.

Although I had been a passionate student of Acadian culture and history for most of my life, I was stunned to learn that there was such a large Acadian presence in that region. At a lunch meeting organized by Petley and local historian Alexandre Riopel, the idea came to me to do a book, which would attempt to provide a short history with photos of Acadian communities in the world. The next day I had talks with my Canadian editor and publisher Roger Leger, historian Sylvain Gaudet, and filmmaker Phil Comeau, director of the film series *Les Acadiens du Quebec*. They pledged their support and encouraged me to go forward with the project.

After my wife Mary agreed to co-direct the book (after all, she is the writer in the family), I immediately started working on an outline. Jean-Robert Frigault from CODOFIL provided the initial information, which was later expanded by nearly 100 writers, historians, educators, and museum directors from around the world.

As the deadline of having to send our book manuscript to the publisher for both English and French editions of the book grew closer, I needed to bring fresh eyes to the project. After all, I had been involved in the project for over two years. In January 2014, Mary and I invited Phil Comeau to dinner in order to discuss the book. Phil was in Lafayette at the time for the *Cinema on the Bayou Film Festival* presenting two of his new films and a retrospective of some of his Acadian films.

Having known Phil for over 25 years, I knew he was truly passionate about our Acadian history and contemporary life. He seemed to be the best man to edit and pull this book together in a professional way. Phil had also travelled to most of the Acadian areas in the world and was a strong believer in our people's potential to continue progressing from our diaspora. I felt he would bring to the project a needed Canadian and French Acadian perspective.

Happily, Phil accepted our proposal to work with us on the book. A published author and writer of some 70 scripts, including 35 scripts on Acadian subjects, Phil gathered ten new articles for the book from new geographical areas and also convinced new authors to write about unique subjects. Due to his dedicated work, we now have a total of 65 articles in our book.

Since he is fully bilingual, I knew Phil would be best-suited to coordinate the translation of the 21 original French language articles to English, and the 43 original English language articles to French. Temporarily putting aside his film script writing, he worked full time on the book for over five months, even working weekends and often late into the night to meet our publishing deadline. Phil, after all, is a self-admitted "workaholic." Mary and I are very grateful for his insight and vision, and for helping us to reach our goal of launching this book at the *Congrès mondial acadien*, which we all hope will work to educate, inform, and reach Acadians worldwide. I hope that this book will provide a better understanding of our Acadies, both past and present.

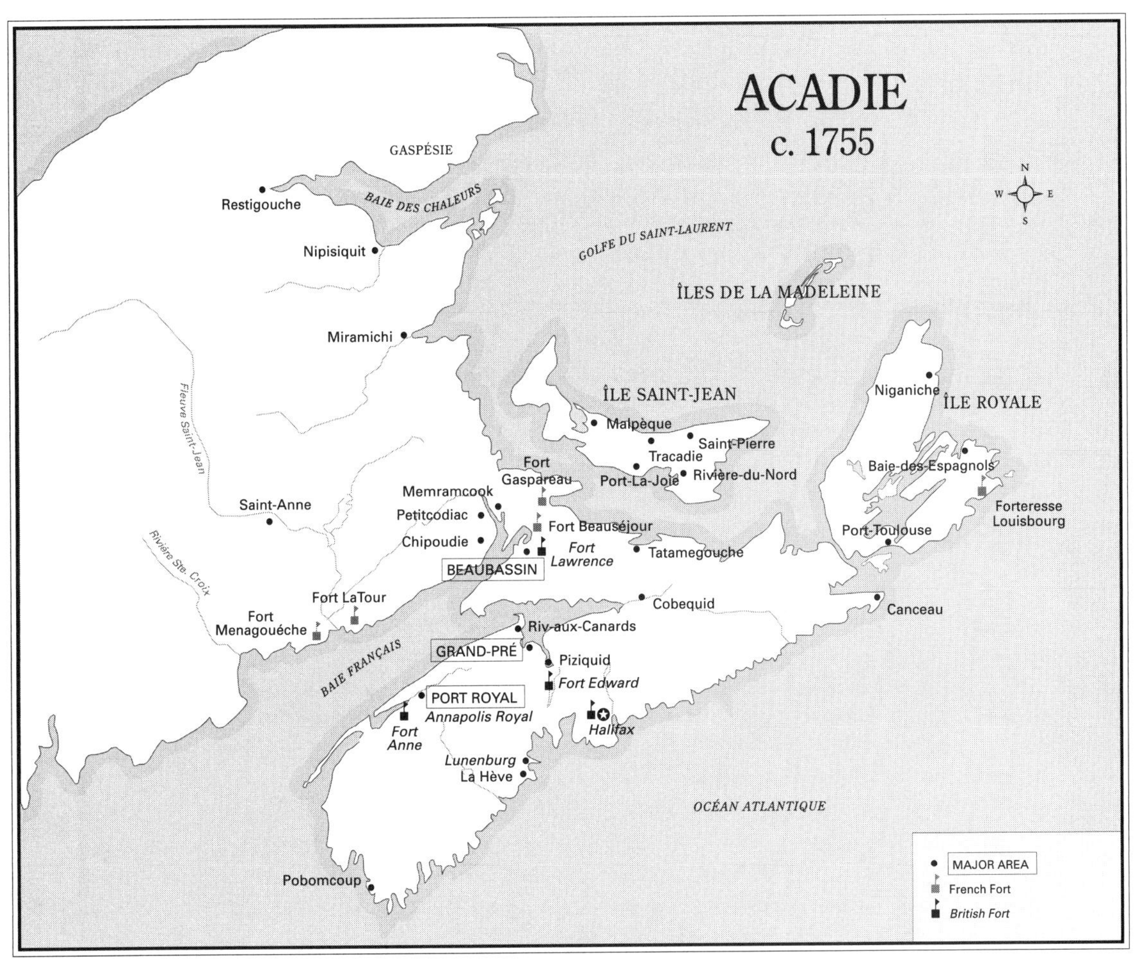
ACADIE
c. 1755
N
W
E
S
GASPÉSIE
Restigouche
BAIE DES CHALEURS
Nipisiquit
GOLFE DU SAINT-LAURENT
ÎLES DE LA MADELEINE
Miramichi
Fleuve Saint-Jean
ÎLE SAINT-JEAN
Malpèque
Saint-Pierre
Tracadie
Port-La-Joie
Rivière-du-Nord
Niganiche
ÎLE ROYALE
Baie-des-Espagnols
Forteresse
Louisbourg
Port-Toulouse
Fort
Gaspareau
Memramcook
Petitcodiac
Chipoudie
Fort Beauséjour
Fort
Lawrence
Tatamegouche
Saint-Anne
Rivière Ste. Croix
BEAUBASSIN
Fort LaTour
Fort
Menagouéche
Cobequid
Canceau
Riv-aux-Canards
GRAND-PRÉ
Piziquid
Fort Edward
BAIE FRANÇAIS
PORT ROYAL
Annapolis Royal
Fort
Anne
Halifax
Lunenburg
La Hève
OCÉAN ATLANTIQUE
Pobomcoup
MAJOR AREA
French Fort
British Fort

PROVINCES OF ACADIAN ORIGINS IN FRANCE
ENGLAND
Artois
Flandre
Hainaut
Picardie
ÎLE-DE-FRANCE
PARIS
Normandie
Champagne
Lorraine
Alsace
Bretagne
Maine
Orléanais
Bourgogne
Anjou
Touraine
Franche-
Comté
Berry
Poitou
Bourbonnais
Aunis
Marche
Angoumois
Lyonnais
Saintonge
Limousin
Savoie
Auvergne
ATLANTIC OCEAN
Guyenne
Dauphiné
Gascogne
Comtat
Venaissin
Comté
de Nice
Languedoc
Provence
Béarn
Comté de
Foix
Roussilon
MEDITERRANEAN SEA
SPAIN
N
W
E
S
Poitou: 50% of settlers to Acadie
Other provinces with many settlers

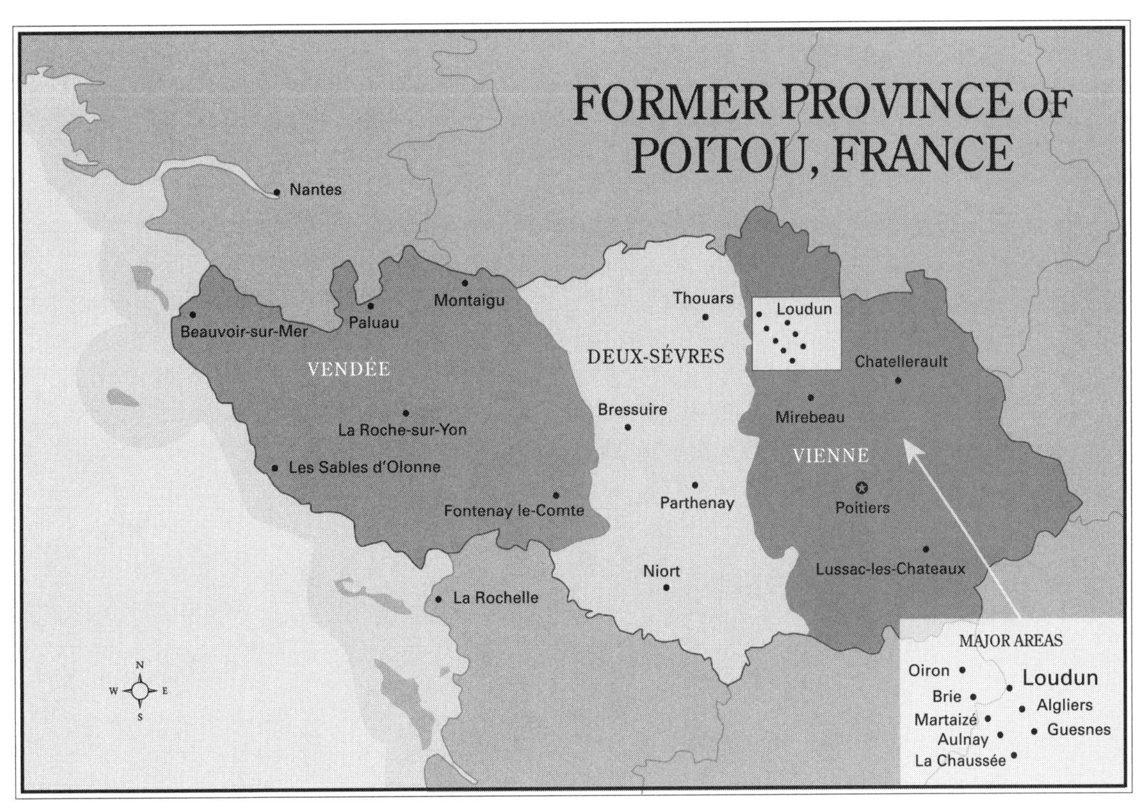
FORMER PROVINCE OF POITOU, FRANCE
Nantes
Montaigu
Paluau
Beauvoir-sur-Mer
VENDÉE
La Roche-sur-Yon
Les Sables d'Olonne
Fontenay le-Comte
La Rochelle
Thouars
DEUX-SÉVRES
Bressuire
Parthenay
Niort
Loudun
Chatellerault
Mirebeau
VIENNE
Poitiers
Lussac-les-Chateaux
MAJOR AREAS
Oiron
Loudun
Brie
Algliers
Martaizé
Guesnes
Aulnay
La Chaussée
N
W
E
S

I

World Acadie

Acadie

Zachary Richard

The first time that I went to Acadie was the summer of 1975. I had already toured France (1973) and Quebec (1974), so the musical-spiritual journey to my ancestral homeland was the cherry on my francophone sundae. Somehow, a message had made it through the centuries, calling me back. This epic journey came only weeks after my appearance at the second *Festivals Acadiens et Créoles* in Lafayette, where I had managed to alienate the pro-French elite with my singing of "Réveille (Wake Up)" and the unfurling of two "Acadian Power" flags. One flag had a live oak on a field of white with a blue ribbon of bayou and the gold star of Acadie in the corner, shining on the words *Solidarité et Fierté* (Solidarity and Pride). Between the words, a red drop of blood had been strategically placed to symbolize our Catholic past and serve as a reminder that nothing great comes without a cost.

I do not remember how it was that I received an invitation to attend the *Frolic Acadien*, an Acadian music festival, on August 15, 1975. Somehow it had arrived, possibly via Quebec. I do remember sewing the flags, or participating when they were being hand-sewn by the nimble fingers of young *Québécoises*.

It was there that earlier, I met my first *Acadien du Nord* (Acadian from the North). This would have been *chez* Kenneth Richard in the hills overlooking Cankton, Louisiana, where we would gather to play music and make plans for the revolution. Donald Doiron had hitchhiked from Miramichi, New Brunswick, because he had heard that French-speaking teachers were needed to teach in the public schools of South Louisiana. Through Donald, I discovered that it was not a myth, and that the Acadian people did in fact exist. And Donald was one of them, although, with his long hair and hippie clothes, he fit right in with our crowd. In fact, he was easily mistaken for one of us, until his New Brunswick English accent gave him away. His French, however, sounded like the Cajun French that was spoken all around me.

The message that arrived from New Brunswick was an invitation to attend the second *Frolic Acadien*. A "Frolic" is a big celebration which follows a communal task. In a very persistent Acadian-Cajun tradition, a mutually undertaken project was always followed by a celebration. Usually this concerns harvesting, or barn raising or a *boucherie* (the slaughtering of a cow or pig) or some such. In this case, however, the thing being built was *La Nation Acadienne!* (the Acadian Nation!). That was my kind of deal. Count me in.

I am not sure where my sense of Acadian identity came from. Certainly as a child speaking French with my grandparents, aunts and uncles, it was obvious to me that something unique was happening. The language that we spoke was certainly not the American English that I spoke at school or with my classmates or heard on the radio or television. I was acutely, if not somewhat nonchalantly, aware that I was part of something "different," of a culture that was special and distinctly our own. However, no one in my family ever did nor could they have explained to me the exact nature of our *différence.*

I do not know when I first heard of *Le Grand Dérangement* (the Great Nuisance). This is the term that the Acadians use to refer to the agonizing period in our history that immediately preceded and followed the Acadian Deportation of 1755. In a very tongue-in-cheek fashion, the deported Acadians referred to their forced removal (read "ethnic cleansing") from the homeland that they had developed in present-day Nova Scotia for over 120 years as a "Big Nuisance." *Dérangement* is simply a nuisance like a mosquito or a barking dog. Had my grandparents ever spoken to me of *Le Grand Dérangement?* Perhaps, but unfortunately, if in fact they did, I was so young that I cannot remember, and so will never really know. It is more likely that I learned of the term through reading Dudley LeBlanc's monumental, though somewhat romanticized, history of the Acadians of Louisiana, *The Acadian Miracle,* published in 1927. Regardless of where I first learned of it, I was deeply moved by the story of the forced removal of my ancestors from their home in Acadie and the years of strife that preceded their ultimate arrival in Louisiana.

I am Zachary à Joseph Eddie à Fergus à Sylvain à Anaclet à Pierre à Pierre à Alexandre à Martin à Michel Richard. My first North American ancestor arrived in Acadie in 1641 from Saintonge, home of Samuel de Champlain and one of the main venues of France's incessant 17th-century religious wars. My ancestor Pierre à Alexandre was the first to arrive in Louisiana. He, along with 192 other exiles (including my direct ancestor on my mother's side, Olivier Boudreau[x]), arrived in the port of New Orleans in February 1765 led by resistance leader Joseph Broussard, who the Acadians called "Beausoleil." Beausoleil's mother was Catherine à Michel Richard. My ancestor and Beausoleil were cousins (and hard heads—apparently a family trait).

Somehow, in spite of the indifference of the Anglo-American-Centro-historical bias of my native country, as well as the institutionalized policy of assimilation to which my community was and continues to be subjected, the story of the Deportation somehow made it to me. Now, in the summer of 1975, I was being invited to the original homeland to participate in a musical festival dedicated to the creation of *La Nation Acadienne.* I would have crawled there if I had to.

The show was outdoors on a hill called La Butte à Napoléon not far from Cap Pelé, New Brunswick, overlooking La Baie Verte, with Île Saint-Jean (Prince Edward Island) just over the horizon. I would later learn that my ancestor Alexandre à Martin had fled to Île Saint-Jean from Beaubassin to escape the troubles already plaguing pre-dispersal Acadie in Nova Scotia. But in the summer of 1975, I was concerned with genealogy only in its widest sense.

What struck me, as they say in Evangeline Parish, *entre l'oeil et la corne* (between the eye and the horn–a bovine reference), was the astounding similarity between the people of Acadie and us of Acadian descent in *Louisiane*. Everybody has the same last name: Arsenault, Boudreau, Cormier, Comeau, etc., and everybody looks the same (limited gene pool). But more striking is the worldview, which animates both the Acadian society of the Canadian Maritimes, and that of South Louisiana. Both communities are rural, with agricultural farming and fishing economies. Both have strong family traditions. Both are steeped in the Roman Catholic religion. And both communities have had to maintain themselves in the face of intolerance, prejudice, and contempt.

Once I had finished my performance, accompanied by Roy Harrington, my faithful partner of many years and native of Pecan Island, Louisiana, I was approached by an older Acadian woman. Not only did she resemble my grandmother, Sarah Sonnier, but she also spoke like my grandmother, in that deliciously thick and soothing accent of Cajun Louisiana. She began by asking me if there were in fact Acadians living in Louisiana. When I replied that there were, she asked me how we lived, what we ate, how we enjoyed ourselves. They were all very basic questions regarding daily life that my grandmother would have also asked. She told me her family name was LeBlanc, and left me saying that she would pray for me. I still get choked up every time I think about it.

How is it that this sense of identity and this feeling of kinship persist over 250 years after the Deportation? And how is it that the bond between the Acadian communities of the Canadian Maritimes and those of South Louisiana are stronger now than they have been for decades, if not centuries? How has this notion of identity persisted in the face of relentless pressure to assimilate? Maybe because we're still pissed off.

During my first visit to Acadie, I made some very strong friendships, one of which was with the Acadian poet Gérald LeBlanc. It was during my stay in Moncton following the Frolic that Gerald and I were told to leave a restaurant because we refused to speak English. "Speak white or leave," we were told. This was only a few years (February 1968) after Mayor Jones of Moncton, a notorious francophobe, had been presented with a roasted pig's head during a meeting of the municipal counsel the day after he had refused to recognize a French Acadian–speaking student delegation. For the first time in my life, I was the victim of ethnic prejudice. The sentiment that this episode provoked was a potent stimulus for the development of a militant francophone attitude with which I am not unhappy to be associated.

The Acadian community of New Brunswick particularly, but that of Nova Scotia and Prince Edward Island as well, has come a very long way since I first visited in 1975. The *Sommet de la Francophonie* (World Francophone Summit) of 1999, which was held in Moncton, proved, not only to the Anglo New Brunswickers but also to the Acadians themselves, the value of their language. However, the primary watershed event that gave great impetus to the nascent cultural pride of the Acadian community of Canada was the first *Congrès mondial acadien* of 1994. I get chills when I remember singing "Réveille" and having tens of thousands of Acadians singing along with me. In a real way, the circle had been rejoined: a Louisiana descendant of the Acadian exiles had returned to the homeland after more that 260 years to sing a song inspired by the Deportation. The challenge for us today in Louisiana is to import that feeling and, in the words of Dewey Balfa after the Newport Folk Festival of 1964, to let the Cajun people "hear the echo of the applause."

The Birth of a People –1604 to 1755

Warren A. Perrin

This article is a synopsis of the first 150 years of the common history of all Acadians. In 1604, Frenchman Pierre Dugua de Mons led the failed first attempt to settle on Ile Sainte-Croix (today on the New Brunswick/Maine border), on the northern side of the Bay of Fundy. In 1605, he sought a better location on the mainland across the Bay of Fundy and chose a spot on the northern side of the present-day Annapolis Basin, opposite Goat Island, which became Port Royal.

French nationals first settled Port Royal in what was to become Acadie in 1605, 15 years before 41 Pilgrims on the *Mayflower* docked off the coast of Plymouth, Massachusetts. Samuel Argall of Virginia raided and burned Port Royal in 1613. He then raided and destroyed the new settlement of St. Sauveur on Mount Desert Island (today in Maine). Argall felt threatened by Acadie, as all of their shipping had to pass nearby. Surprisingly, Acadie also claimed to extend all the way south to what is now Philadelphia, making it an immense territory.

This destruction put Acadie in the hands of the English until 1632, including the territory that the Pilgrims would settle on, and this commenced 150 years of warfare between the English and French in North America. On November 4, 1620, King James I of England laid claim to Acadie. Either by military campaign or by negotiated treaties, the colony of Acadie changed ownership several times between 1604 and 1710, and would be lost in 1713. The actual New Brunswick, Prince Edward Island, and Cape Breton areas where Acadians lived (and considered French territory) would only be lost to the British in 1763 at the Treaty of Paris.

In 1636, the Acadian capital of Port Royal was physically moved from the north shore of the Dauphin River to the actual Annapolis Royal town site, where the legendary "*sakmow*" (grand chief) Membertou of the Mi'kmaq First Nations tribe had once made his summer home. It remained the capital until Halifax was settled by British Gov. Edward Cornwallis in 1749.

The first French pioneer families crossed the Atlantic to the New World on the *Saint-Jehan*, departing for Acadie on April 1, 1636. More than 50 percent of Acadians were originally from the Poitou region of France. Others were mostly from the surrounding provinces (see map on page xii), though historians contend every province of France contributed at least one future Acadian toward the establishment of Acadie. The immigrant families succeeded French adventurers in the colony. From that year until the year 1714, many more French families migrated to Acadie. Due to frequent changes in European control over their colony, these early settlers sought with great diligence to remain neutral during anticipated clashes between France and England.

On October 7, 1690, England made Acadie part of Massachusetts. On June 14, 1691, Sir Robinau de Villebon seized Port Royal away from the English and was appointed the new French governor of Acadie. On September 26, 1697, the Treaty of Ryswick officially gave Acadie to France.

On September 18, 1710, an English fleet under the command of Francis Nicholson laid siege to Port Royal once again and, despite a gallant defense, capitulation was signed on October 13, 1710. Port Royal was renamed Annapolis Royal in honor of Queen Anne of Great Britain, and since then Acadie has been called Nova Scotia by the British.

The Treaty of Utrecht was signed in 1713, putting an end to the war of the Spanish Succession, a conflict that arose out of the disputed succession to the throne of Spain but included Queen Anne's War in North America. At this time, Acadie was definitively ceded to England. Article 14 of the treaty stated: "It is expressly provided ... that such of the French inhabitants ... as are willing to remain there, and to be subject to the Kingdom of Great Britain, are to enjoy the free exercise of their religion according to the usage of the Church of Rome as far as the laws of Great Britain do allow the same." Therefore, Acadians who remained in Nova Scotia—thus becoming British subjects—were granted the right to maintain their Catholic faith.

Moreover, Queen Anne of England decreed the following in a letter to then-Gov. Nicholson dated June 23, 1713: "Whereas ... we being willing to show by some mark of our favor towards his subjects ... and are willing to continue our subjects, to retain and enjoy [the Acadians'] said lands and tenements without any molestation, as fully and freely as our other subjects do or may possess their lands or estates, or to sell the same, if they shall rather choose to remove elsewhere." Therefore, conforming to "Good Queen Anne's" decree, the Acadians were guaranteed rights equal to other subjects of the British Crown. In 1714, having been assured of their rights and encouraged by the Annapolis Royal English authorities, the vast majority of the Acadian families decided to remain on their native soil as a part of the new regime. Unfortunately for them, Queen Anne died an early death at age 49 on August 1, 1714, to be succeeded by George I.

The new king's governors tried to make the Acadians take an unqualified oath of allegiance to the British Crown. Their tenuous control of the colony was compacted by the smaller British population, thus the attempt to hold the Acadians to an iron-clad declaration of allegiance to King George.

Acadians refused to take the oath. It contained restrictions implying the renunciation of rights accorded to them by the 1713 Treaty of Utrecht, and contradicted a right granted by Queen Anne's decree to decide whether to remain or to move to French territory. Further, they feared retaliation from the First Nations people who before had treated them as "blood brothers." Finally, Acadians strongly feared that an oath of outright allegiance to Great Britain could leave them liable to be called upon to bear arms against their French relatives in future wars.

In the early 1700s, Paul Mascarene, a Huguenot originally from France, became Gov. Samuel Vetch's principal intermediary to the Acadian and Native American inhabitants. In 1714, he negotiated a treaty with the Mi'kmaq, Abenakis, and Maliseets, obligating all parties to live in peace. This was in part in a response to an incendiary letter presented to the government by the "Mi'kmaq chiefs of Minas," which stated, "We are masters, and dependents of no one."

On January 13, 1716, 36 Acadians signed a conditional oath of allegiance to King George I. Gov. Richard Philipps arrived in Nova Scotia with much fanfare and display of British power at Annapolis Royal in April 1720. On December 28, 1720, the Colonial Office in London directed Gov. Philipps: "... you are not to attempt their [Acadians'] removal without His Majesty's positive order for that purpose ... let them stay where they are."

Gov. Philipps' goal was to obtain the allegiance of the Acadians. He referred to them as "neutral subjects of another prince." Shortly after his arrival, the Acadians sent a delegation, led by Fr. Justinien Durand, to explain why they could not swear allegiance: "they were sure of having their throats cut by the Indians whenever they became Englishmen." Over the ensuing years Philipps tried to win them over by degrees but, for the *first* time, the Acadians expressed the notion that they had a *right* to be there. This novel idea shows that the Acadians had determined that they were their own masters—with inherent rights.

In October 1727, as George II ascended to the British Throne, the Acadians gave consent to the oath of allegiance, with conditions. However, on November 13, 1727, the Annapolis Royal Council declared the deal null and dishonorable because of the restrictions on their neutral status.

On January 3, 1730, Gov. Philipps wrote to authorities in London, saying that Acadians "of all parishes have taken the oath of allegiance." What Philipps did not include in his report was the fact that he had enticed them to sign granting the Acadians the neutral status they had sought for such a long time.

Thereafter, the Acadians became known to London authorities as French Neutrals, and were therefore assured of the free exercise of their Catholic religion and the possession of their lands. Now British subjects, they scrupulously respected the conditional pledge that they had taken towards the British Crown.

Alexandre Bourq, the notary, made a notation of Philipps' concession. A copy of the document was sent to French officials and another kept by Bourq. From that time forward until 1755, the Acadians were exempted from bearing arms or fighting in wars against the French or First Nations people. By convincing them to accept the oral amendment to the oath, Philipps played upon their belief that a given word was the most sacred pledge. As stated by Dr. John Mack Faragher, author of *A Great and Noble Scheme* (2005), the Acadians had held out and finally won from the British governor recognition of their neutrality. The Acadians' new-found status was acknowledged both in Halifax and in London.

The 1730s were years of Acadian prosperity. Overcrowding led to land disputes; thus many Acadians relocated to lands on tidal rivers, including the Chipoudy, Petitcodiac, and Memramcook rivers in today's New Brunswick. There, no government exercised control over them. In 1740, Joseph Beausoleil Broussard and his brother Alexandre, who had married two Thibodeau sisters, moved and settled on the Petitcodiac and established Beausoleil Village. After the deportations began in 1755, they would become leaders of the Acadians' resistance against the British.

The War of Austrian Succession in 1741 broke the long period of peace between France and England. In light of this new development, the new Gov. Paul Mascarene, a man who showed goodwill and patience towards the Acadians, wrote to the British Secretary of War on July 2, 1744, "The Acadians ... have kept hitherto in their fidelity, and in no ways joined with the enemy ... they helped in the repairing of our works [on] the very day preceding the attack."

Writer Jon Tattrie stated in his book, *Cornwallis–The Violent Birth of Halifax* (2013), that, "on June 21, 1749, Gov. Edward Cornwallis set foot in three places at once. The next step he took would determine the destiny of tens of thousands of people stretched across half a continent. To the Mi'kmaq people, the British governor general stood on their ancestral home of Mi'kma'ki, the millennial-old name for the Seven Districts that comprised the main Mi'kmaq government in what is today Nova Scotia, New Brunswick, Prince Edward Island, and parts of Maine. For France, Cornwallis was entering Acadie, heartland of New France's territorial ambitions on the New World. For Cornwallis and the British crown he represented, it was Nova Scotia–territory France ceded to Britain on paper in 1712, and a land he intended to dominate with his massive influx of soldiers and settlers."

Further, Cornwallis' actions over the next three years would set in motion events that would determine the future of not only Nova Scotia, but of the vast land that would become Canada. Steeped in a brutal militaristic philosophy learned in the bloody fields of Scotland's Battle of Culloden, Cornwallis devised a plan to force both Acadians and Mi'kmaq to bend to the will of the British Crown through threat of forced removal or massacre.

His conquest of Nova Scotia laid the groundwork for the expulsion of the Acadians and created the conditions that allowed his colleague Major Gen. James Wolfe to claim a final British victory over France on the Plains of Abraham in Quebec City, a decade later. It also pushed the Mi'kmaq toward the brink of extinction. Mi'kmaq historian Daniel Paul stated, "Gov. William Shirley, the British governor of Massachusetts, like Cornwallis, also issued proclamations for the scalps of First Nations men, women, and children." After a series of unresolved disputes with the London Board of Trade, Cornwallis resigned in the summer of 1752.

Following this suppression, Peregrine Hopson was named governor of Nova Scotia on August 3, 1752. In December 1753, believing that the Acadians were destined to become satisfactory British subjects, he ordered the commandants of Grand-Pré and Piziquid (today Windsor) to "deal with the Acadians in the same manner as with the other subjects of His Majesty..." During his short reign of power, he showed compassion and understanding to the Acadians. Unfortunately, due to ill health, Gov. Hopson left the colony and was in England immediately preceding and during the deportation of the Acadians and, as Faragher stated, "putting the leadership of the province in the hands of Lt.-Col. Charles Lawrence, president of the Governor's Council, a man cast in the mold of Cornwallis rather than the accommodating Mascarene."

Regardless, the reality throughout 1753 was that tensions between the British and French had been steadily increasing in both Europe and North America. Critical importance was attached to control of the "continental cornice," as historian John Brebner named it—the region running northeast of Maine and southeast of New France, embracing the lands of present-day southern New Brunswick, Prince Edward Island, and Nova Scotia. According to historian N.E.S. Griffiths in *From Migrant to Acadian* (2005), this region became one of the most important areas in North America for the military strategies of both powers. The Acadians had used the ingenious system of *aboiteaux* (dikes) to convert their salt-water marshes into fertile farmland, which was coveted by New Englanders. However, the Acadians occupied these lands and their loyalty was to their land; their allegiance belonged only to their tightly-knit community of the interconnected families, not the military powers.

In 1754, the new lieutenant-governor of Nova Scotia was Charles Lawrence, a man of violent character. He had the type of military personality that was not suited to the situation, which called for subtlety. Richard Bulkeley, aide-de-camp to Cornwallis, described Lawrence as one who was feared for his assertive methods and who had no tolerance for compromise or accommodation.

As a harbinger of what was to come, on August 1 of that year, Lawrence wrote to his supervisors in London, "As they possess the best and largest tracts of land in this Province, it cannot be settled with any effect while they remain in this situation ... I cannot help being of the opinion that it would be much better ... that they were away."

In November of 1754, Lawrence began planning an unauthorized deportation with Massachusetts Gov. William Shirley, commander-in-chief of British forces in New England, and an unabashed supporter of British supremacy in North America. It is believed, based upon historical data, that they created a fake threat from the French in the region that allowed them to gain the support of the Massachusetts militia which then amassed troops, and in April of 1755, about 2,000 men from New England arrived at the Isthmus of Chignecto, the land mass connecting Nova Scotia with what is now New Brunswick. Supporters of the ethnic cleansing of the colony hauntingly referred to the plan as a "great and noble scheme."

Sec. of State Thomas Robinson demonstrated that the British authorities were alarmed by the drastic measures advocated by Lawrence when he wrote, "It cannot therefore be too much recommended to you to use the greatest caution and prudence in your conduct toward these Neutrals ... that they may remain in the quiet possession of their settlements under proper regulations...."

Under English law, Nova Scotia Gov. Lawrence did not have the authority to ignore Queen Anne's Edict of 1713 and the prior policies set forth by Gov. Hopson. Nevertheless, Lawrence ignored the laws, as well as the Conventions of 1730 in which Gov. Phillips verbally granted them the status of French Neutrals. In particular, he dispensed with the part of the law prohibiting the confiscation of the Acadians' boats and weapons, and furthermore placed restrictions upon their movements.

In 1755, the year the ethnic cleansing began, no English law of the time carried provisions for the confiscation of the properties of a father of a family or the punishment of his wife and children for an offense that could have been committed by the father. The law provided severe sanctions for political crimes and acts of treason, but never—not for any motive whatsoever—the confiscation of the lands or any other possessions of an entire group of persons and their banishment.

Nevertheless, on July 28, 1755, the new Chief Justice Jonathan Belcher, totally unfamiliar with the provinces' history and people, published a poorly documented brief stating that Acadians could no longer be tolerated in Nova Scotia. His decision was rendered without allowing the Acadians to have a hearing or even appear before a judge. This was palpably contrary to Great Britain's law providing that subjects could not be proven guilty without being formally accused before a court of justice. And on September 14, 2004, in a speech in Fredericton, New Brunswick, former Supreme Court Justice of Canada Michel Bastarache said as much when he opined that the deportation was an illegal act for two reasons: it was against British public law and it passed without a vote of the assembly. [For a more detailed discussion on this topic, see Bastarache's article on page 196.]

In his ruling Judge Belcher found that the Acadians were indeed British subjects, yet he ignored long-established British law and jurisprudence. To wit: Article III of the Petition of Right (1628) states that no British subject may be exiled except by "lawful judgment of his peers ... and whereas also by the statute called 'The Great Charter of the Liberties of England,' it is declared and enacted, that no freeman may be taken or imprisoned or be disseized of his freehold or liberties, or his free customs, or be outlawed or exiled, or in any manner destroyed, but by the lawful judgment of his peers, or by the law of the land." Moreover, Article IV of the Petition of Right provides, "And in the eight-and-twentieth year of the reign of King Edward III, it was declared and enacted by authority of parliament, that no man, of what estate or condition that he be, should be put out of his land or tenements, nor taken, nor imprisoned, nor disinherited nor put to death without being brought to answer by due process of law."

According to N.E.S. Griffiths, a distinguished scholar of Acadian history and professor emeritus of the Department of History at Carleton University, the Deportation was different from every other similar government action in four ways. First, the possibility of removing the Acadians had been discussed for a long time, whereas other deportations—like the 1745 Scottish exile—were the immediate consequences of particular actions to a recent problem. Second, the pressure for action came not from within the government but from the neighboring territory of Massachusetts; London had consistently argued against such action. Third, the enterprise itself was significantly different from other deportations such as those following the Monmouth and Jacobite rebellions. These had been organized after battles had been fought and where the number of deportees was only a fraction of the communities involved, whereas the Acadian deportation was the attempted removal of an entire population, which had been judged collectively—not by a court of law. Fourth, the Acadians had been permitted by both a governor and a queen to retain their cultural identity. Throughout their history they had made their own decisions to shape their lives based upon the belief that they were a distinct people. This belief continues into the 21st century.

The first military action started at the beginning of June 1755, before war was declared, when some English troops and many from Massachusetts led by Lt. Col. Robert Monckton captured Fort Beauséjour, located on the western side of the Missaguash River on the present-day border of Nova Scotia and New Brunswick. Over 400 Acadians were captured and imprisoned at the French fort, renamed Fort Cumberland, and later imprisoned at Halifax. Troops from Halifax and Fort Edward in Piziquid (today Windsor, Nova Scotia) began preparing to carry out one of the most brutal and successful military campaign ever executed by British forces. They were also ordered to seize the arms of the Acadians of the Grand-Pré region. On July 31, 1755, Lawrence gave detailed instructions to Lt. Col. Monckton, commanding officer at Beauséjour. Britain and France were not yet at war on this date.

The world's first truly global war is referred to as the Seven Years' War in Europe but in North America as the French and Indian War. It was not declared until May 18, 1756. Thus, the deportation had begun ten months earlier, during a time of peace, by paranoid military officials in charge of the British colony. Civil laws still in effect were ignored. The campaign was carried out with merciless efficiency by a group of British regulars and 2,000 men of the Massachusetts militia. On October 10, 1755, the first Acadians were deported from the Chignecto Region.

In Grand-Pré, under the leadership of Col. John Winslow on September 5, 1755, Acadian men and boys over ten years of age were lured to their church under the pretext of a meeting, and then imprisoned inside. Next, Winslow began carrying out the rest of Lawrence's instructions as submitted to Lt. Col. Monckton. All Acadians were arrested. Their properties were burned and their crops were destroyed so that Acadians who escaped by fleeing into the woods would either perish during the winter months or eventually be forced to surrender.

On October 27, 1755, 14 transports carrying 1,600 Acadians from the Grand-Pré region and about 1,300 from Piziquid and Cobequid (today Truro, Nova Scotia) joined ten transports in the Bay of Fundy loaded with approximately 1,900 Acadian prisoners from the Beaubassin area. A few months later when the next transport ships arrived, the British would deport another 600 Acadians from Grand-Pré. The Acadians were cruelly banished from lands that they had cultivated for 150 years and were plunged into immediate and abject poverty.

Thus began, during the course of the Seven Years' War (1756-1763), seven years of forced Acadian migrations to the Anglo-American Atlantic seaboard colonies, to England, and finally France. And thereafter followed 40 years of migrations and resettlements in Quebec, French Guiana, the Falkland Islands, the Maritime Provinces of Canada, France (including St. Pierre and Miquelon), the Caribbean Antilles, and Louisiana.

Genealogist Stanley LeBlanc has made an important observation of an often overlooked distinction between Nova Scotia with Prince Edward Island (Isle St. Jean) and New Brunswick. While most tend to consider these areas as being parts of Acadie, there is an important distinction regarding the exile of the Acadians. Those in Nova Scotia were deported beginning in 1755 and sent to the British American Colonies and to England, the reason being that England could not send them to France because they were no longer French subjects but now considered British citizens. When the British captured Fortress Louisbourg in Île Royale (today Cape Breton) and Prince Edward Island, in accordance with protocols of the period, most of the Acadians and the other non-Acadian French inhabitants were repatriated to France because they had been living in French territory.

Some Acadians on Prince Edward Island managed to escape and settle in Quebec. But, among the deportees from this island, there were three ships (*Duke William, Violet*, and *Ruby*) that tragically sank with the loss of some 865 deportees in 1758, while being transported to France.

The 1,100 Acadians who had been exiled to England in 1755, after the colony of Virginia refused to accept them, were repatriated to France when the war ended in 1763. The French from Prince Edward Island and Louisbourg (Cape Breton) who had married Acadians were allowed to go to Louisiana in the migrations of 1785.

The war against the Acadians had no positive ground of justice. Indeed, historian Edouard Richard in his *Missing Links in a Lost Chapter of American History* (1895) said, "the expulsion of the Acadians by Lawrence in 1755 had plunder for its object."

At the time of the 1763 Treaty of Paris, there was no longer a homeland for the Acadians. Cape Breton, New Brunswick, and Prince Edward Island had all been successively ceded to England, but the Acadians, having fallen into the ambush of 1755–"the great trouble" as they called it–never coined a term of hatred to designate their persecutors even though they had first been imprisoned, then robbed, and finally "scattered to the four winds," as American poet Henry Wadsworth Longfellow wrote in his 1847 poem *Evangeline—A Tale of Acadie*. In 1755, according to the early French historian Edme Rameau de Saint-Père, the Acadians numbered about 18,000. However, nine years later, as shown by a March 22, 1764, missive to the Lords of Trade in London, Gov. Montagu Wilmot could find only 1,700 in Nova Scotia.

The Acadians were victims of a tragic fate. It is believed that about one-third of the total population died in the historic tragedy. According to Faragher, the Acadian Deportation was similar to modern ethnic cleansing operations, and in this case many of the exiles died as a result—directly or indirectly—of their uprooting. Historian Fred Anderson, in *Crucible of War* (2000), described the expulsion as "chillingly reminiscent of modern ethnic cleansing operations ... executed with a coldness and calculation rarely seen in other wartime operations."

The French settlers, now a people who had acquired a new ethnicity, were scattered all over the Atlantic world. When one examines all of the horrors that have taken place in North America, the exile of the Acadians may appear less egregious when compared to what the United States did to the Native Americans and Africans, but it nevertheless reverberates profoundly.

The Seven Years' War was driven by the antagonism between Great Britain and France, the result of overlapping interests in their colonial and trade empires. In the end, Great Britain expelled its French and Spanish rivals in the contested territories, gaining the bulk of New France in Eastern Canada, Spanish Florida, and some Caribbean islands.

In the ensuing peace treaties, both the Acadians and many of the Native American people were excluded and therefore unable to return to their former lands, thus requiring that they find a new home. Article 37 of Vaudreuil's Capitulation of Montreal (1760) stipulated that "no Frenchman remaining in Canada shall be afterwards transported to England or to English colonies." However, Gen. Jeffrey Amherst wrote on the margin: "Granted, except as regards the Acadians."

There is a similar restriction to Article 54, which proposed that the officers of the militia, the militiamen, and the Acadians who were prisoners in New England be sent back to their lands. The document again says: "Granted except as to the Acadians." In the end, all parties who participated in the war were allowed, without restriction, to return peaceably to their homes—except the Acadians. They were eventually permitted to return to what had been their homeland provided they took the oath of allegiance. Unable to resettle their fertile ancestral farms, which had already been given away to Protestant settlers from New England, those who returned or remained were forced to start clearing the land and rebuilding all over again in distant corners of today's Canadian Maritime Provinces.

Having been expelled headlong to many distant ports, the Acadians unknowingly became connected in many ways to historically significant concepts and events: imperialism, attempts at resettlement, depopulation, overpopulation, slavery, and most notably the American Revolution—in which they actively participated. Even today, the Acadian story is still being written as the long and wandering journey that continues to be impacted by the realities of modernity. In a continuing effort to maintain their cultural identity as well as a spiritual connection, the Acadians of the world have been reuniting at the *Congrès mondial acadien* (CMA) since 1994. This two-and-a-half week event, held every five years in various areas with a large Acadian presence, is a major celebration of Acadian culture and history. In 2014, the *Congrès* was held in the region known as the Acadie of the Lands and Forests, an area on the triple border of New Brunswick, Quebec, and the state of Maine.

Bibliography

Primary sources for the above article are Bona Arsenault, *History of the Acadians* (Ottawa, 1988); Dr. Carl A Brasseaux, *The Founding of New Acadia: The Beginnings of Acadian Life In Louisiana, 1765-1803* (Louisiana State University Press, 1987); Dr. John Mack Faragher, *A Great and Noble Scheme* (New York, W.W. Norton and Co. Inc., 2005); and Christopher Hodson, *The Acadian Diaspora* (Oxford University Press, 2012).

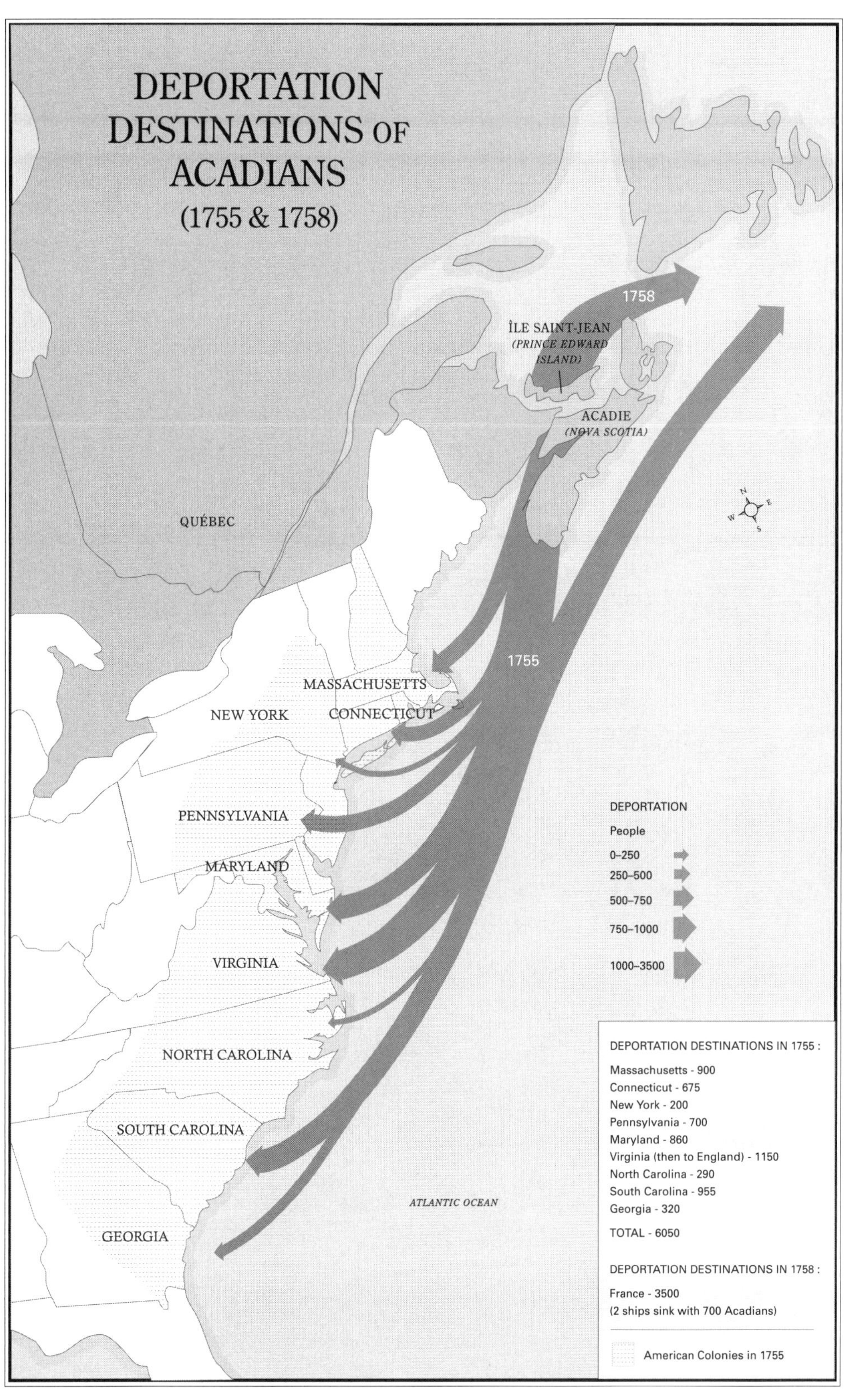
DEPORTATION DESTINATIONS OF ACADIANS
(1755 & 1758)
1758
ÎLE SAINT-JEAN
(PRINCE EDWARD ISLAND)
ACADIE
(NOVA SCOTIA)
QUÉBEC
1755
MASSACHUSETTS
NEW YORK
CONNECTICUT
PENNSYLVANIA
MARYLAND
VIRGINIA
NORTH CAROLINA
SOUTH CAROLINA
GEORGIA
ATLANTIC OCEAN
DEPORTATION
People
0–250
250–500
500–750
750–1000
1000–3500
DEPORTATION DESTINATIONS IN 1755 :
Massachusetts - 900
Connecticut - 675
New York - 200
Pennsylvania - 700
Maryland - 860
Virginia (then to England) - 1150
North Carolina - 290
South Carolina - 955
Georgia - 320
TOTAL - 6050
DEPORTATION DESTINATIONS IN 1758 :
France - 3500
(2 ships sink with 700 Acadians)
American Colonies in 1755

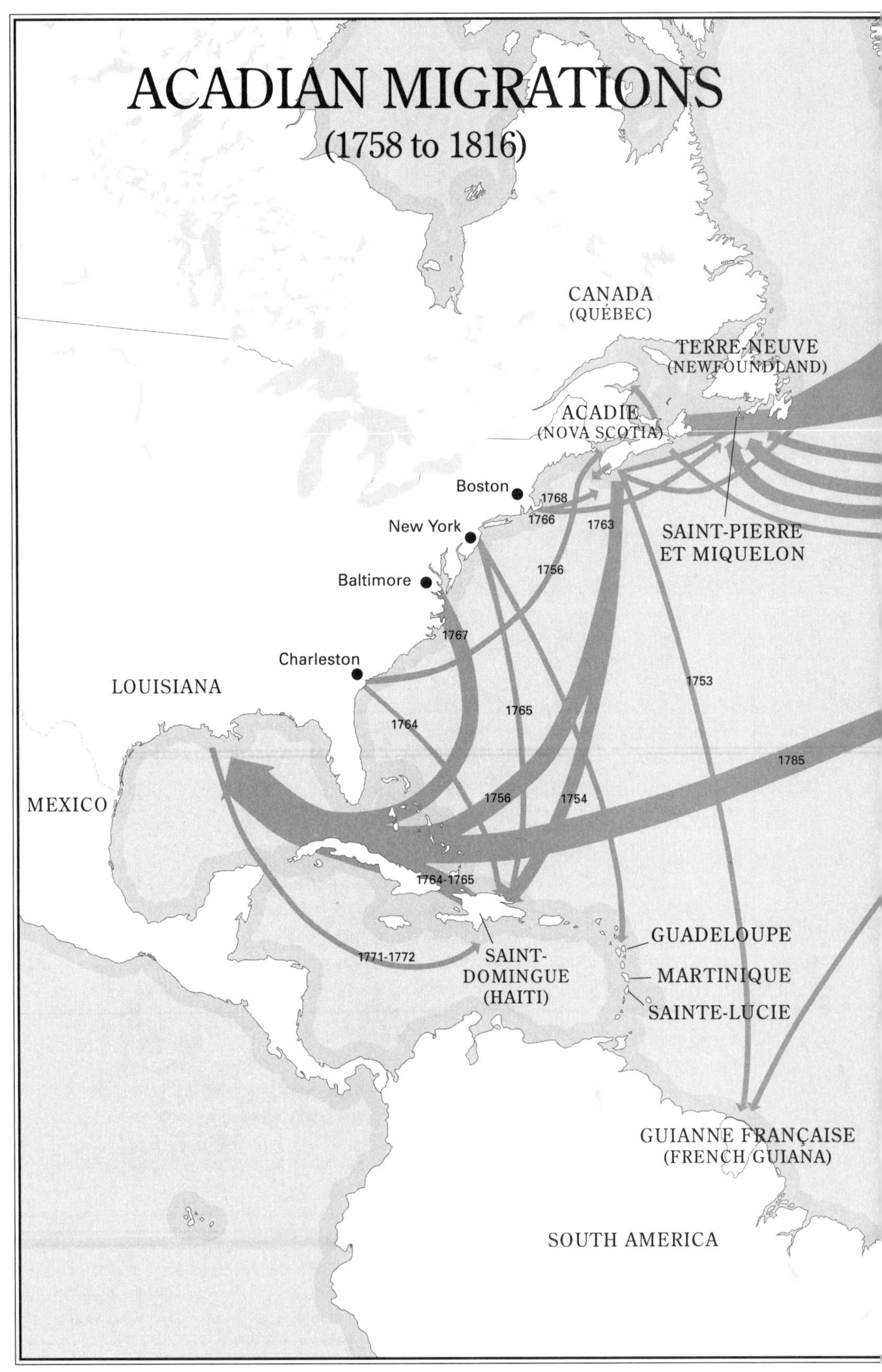
ACADIAN MIGRATIONS
(1758 to 1816)
CANADA
(QUÉBEC)
TERRE-NEUVE
(NEWFOUNDLAND)
ACADIE
(NOVA SCOTIA)
Boston
New York
Baltimore
Charleston
1768
1766
1763
1756
SAINT-PIERRE
ET MIQUELON
1767
LOUISIANA
1753
1765
1764
1785
MEXICO
1756
1754
1764-1765
GUADELOUPE
MARTINIQUE
SAINTE-LUCIE
1771-1772
SAINT-
DOMINGUE
(HAITI)
GUIANNE FRANÇAISE
(FRENCH GUIANA)
SOUTH AMERICA

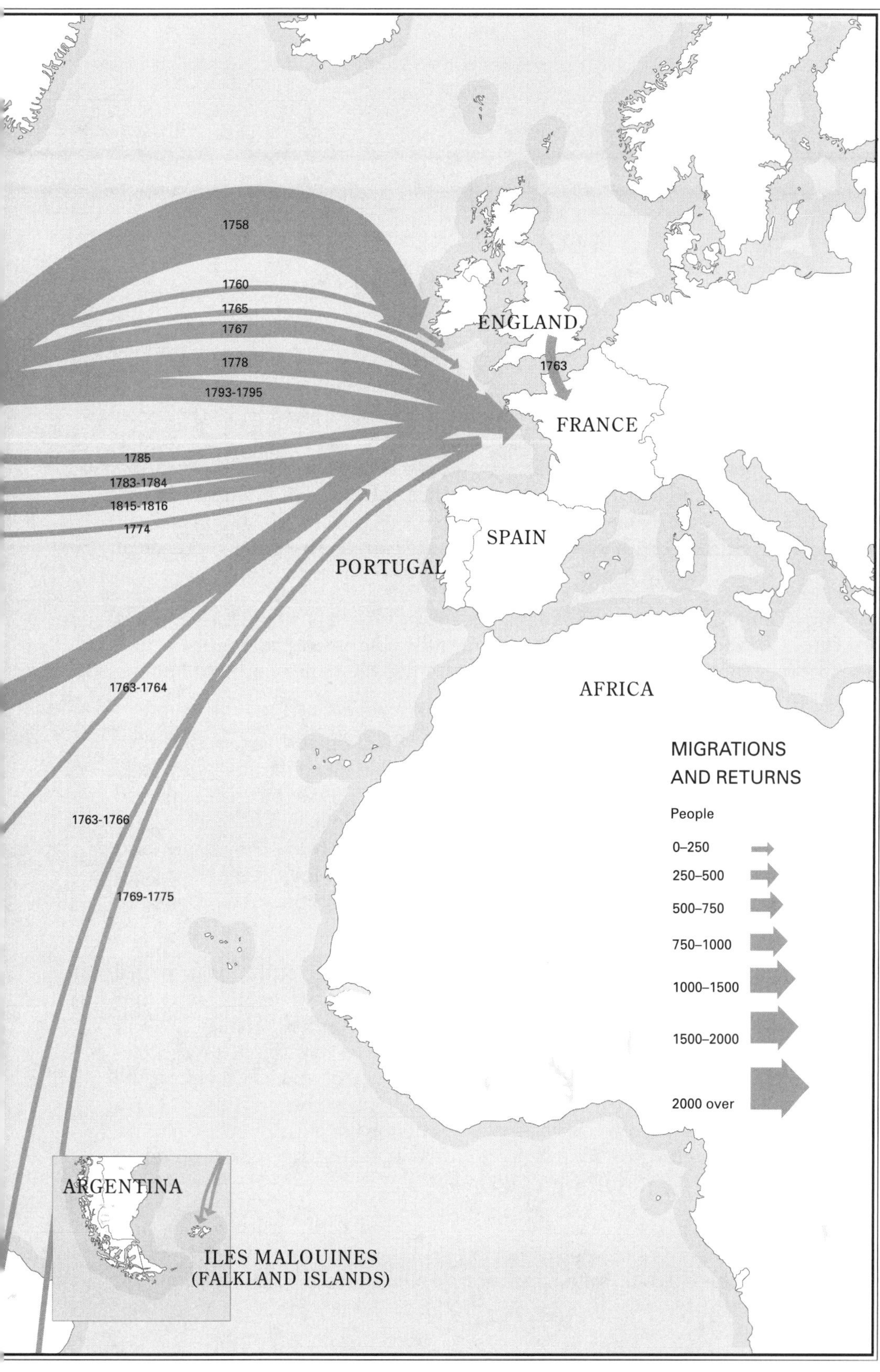
1758
1760
1765
1767
1778
1793-1795
ENGLAND
1763
FRANCE
1785
1783-1784
1815-1816
1774
SPAIN
PORTUGAL
AFRICA
1763-1764
MIGRATIONS
AND RETURNS
People
0–250
250–500
500–750
750–1000
1000–1500
1500–2000
2000 over
1763-1766
1769-1775
ARGENTINA
ILES MALOUINES
(FALKLAND ISLANDS)

The Acadians' Remarkable Demographic History

Warren A. Perrin

The Acadians had an extremely high population growth rate–the highest in North America. The stability of the people and the availability of a stable and nutritious food source for children were important factors in determining why Acadians had such large and healthy families. Also, having many children was essential to the management and expansion of agricultural enterprises. In the 1730s, Nova Scotia Gov. Richard Philipps noted that, "the great increase of the Acadians ... like Noah's progeny, is spreading over the province."

According to the Evangeline myth, all Acadian girls were chaste, pure, and virtuous. In reality, they were liberated, individualistic, pragmatic, industrious, and very fertile. Passion and fertility are not the same concepts but the Acadians obviously had plenty of both.

In early Acadie, illegitimacy was a fact of life. Records exist that document claims brought by women against men for the establishment of paternity. A notable case was *l'Affaire Broussard.* Marie Daigle asked the council to declare that a married man, Joseph Beausoleil Broussard, husband of Agnes Thibodeau, was the biological father of her daughter's child. Daigle accused Broussard of committing fornication with her daughter Mary, who then gave birth to a daughter. Marie Daigle acted as her daughter's representative before the council.

The midwife who attended the birth was put under oath and testified that, when the girl was in her most violent pains of delivery, she declared that Joseph Broussard was the real father of her child. The council ruled in favor of Daigle and ordered Beausoleil to pay child support. Two months after the verdict, Beausoleil's mother, Catherine Richard, successfully appeared before the council to request a reduction of the child support. Jeanne Dupuis, wife of Guillaume Blanchard, volunteered to care for the child for five shillings per month. Finally, Mary Daigle–faced with the possibility of losing her child–opted to keep her baby without receiving any child support.

Frequent intermarriage was very common in Acadie, with nearly half of the marriages requiring dispensation by the Catholic Church. Historians have proven that the need for a dispensation often stemmed from a premarital pregnancy.

The infant mortality rate within Acadian families was low, with about three-fourths of all children reaching adulthood compared to about one-half in other parts of North America and France. The knowledge of natural contraception allowed for the timing of birth rates to warmer times of the year, thus increasing the chances of the child's survival. Acadians had large families and yet several generations lived under the same roof, allowing everyone to work together and support each other. Most Acadian houses had only one room, but the parents always had a *cabinet à coucher* (sleeping cabinet) for privacy. The long Canadian winters exposed the Acadians to very cold temperatures–an atmosphere conducive to spousal intimacy–and the resulting large numbers of offspring provided a work force for the family. Moreover, Catholic priests encouraged large families in order to "spread the word of God." This resulted in Acadians outnumbering the British population, thus sparking fear in London.

Victory in the French and Indian War (1756-1763) worked to minimize the concern the British had over their depopulation problems. The French in Europe, during a period of surging nationalism, decided that their problem was rooted in a lack of fecundity resulting in depopulation, which was caused by everything from the Catholic Church to the French army.

Fecundity generally refers to the ability to reproduce. In demography, fecundity is the potential reproductive capacity of an individual or population. Fecundity is determined by both genetic and environmental factors and is the major measure of fitness. To many, the answer to depopulate was in emulation, and they looked to the Acadians' as one of near legendary proportions. According to historian Christopher Hodson, the poet Dièreville wrote this verse to emphasize their amazing ability and capacity to procreate:

All that remains is to people the world;
Which is, in any case, what they do best,
Never dividing their tenderness,
From the first transports of callow youth,
They have many children well into old age.

Post-exile, all believed that the Acadians had the secret to solve the problem of the seemingly impotent Frenchmen. According to Hodson, the focus then became how best to accomplish the obvious solution. Some policy makers sought to send the 4,000 Acadian refugees to settle in French colonies–like French Guiana, Saint-Domingue (Haiti), and the Malouines (Falkland Islands)–while others wanted them re-settled in French cities. Still others like Abbé Gabriel-Francois Coyer proposed that they be sent to cultivate available farmland, thus hoping to increase not only crop yields, but also population.

The French Minister of State Étienne François, duc de Choiseul wanted to establish an Acadian colony at Belle-Île-en-Mer, an island off the French coast of Brittany, which had been taken by the British during the war, but was given back to France in exchange for the Mediterranean island of Minorca. The powerful minister was quoted in the granting of leniency to one charged with a serious crime that "His Majesty [King Louis XV] accords a special protection to all the Acadians."

Interestingly, Acadians were now seen as virtuous people to be looked up to and respected, not only for their fertility, but also for their work ethic and prior loyalty to their French heritage. In the end, all of these ideas were attempted with results ranging from catastrophic to mere failures, and all due to such things as poor planning, lack of financial support, intolerable climates, and poor soil. Just as the Acadians had done in Acadie, they used their new-found status to achieve their ultimate goal: a return to North America to build a New Acadie.

In pre-exile Acadie, the Mi'kmaq influence on the Acadian ethnicity and population growth cannot be overstated. The first settlers were men so they took advantage of the Mi'kmaq's relative sexual freedom among the young unmarried females. The record indicates that many of the early French settlers in Acadie also married Mi'kmaq women, a testament to their mutual respect and shared knowledge of the surrounding natural resources.

There were six rules of marriage set by the Mi'kmaq. First, the boy had to ask the family for permission; second, the boy had to reside in the family lodge; third, the boy had to hunt and trap exclusively for the family; fourth, the boy would stay with the family for one year; fifth, intimate relations were not permitted until after the marriage; and sixth, the boy had to demonstrate his ability to support a family. It is believed that these native customs were generally adopted by the Acadians and provided for stable marriages, thus producing many children and at the same time teaching them to survive in an alien land.

Miscegenation created what is called Métis (Mi'kmaq and Acadian). Some report that an Acadian became chief of a tribe by marrying the chief's daughter. These relations between the Mi'kmaq and the Acadians made the British authorities suspicious of the Acadians and, therefore, a law was passed against "consorting with Indians." According to Mi'kmaq historian Daniel Paul, such laws were never rescinded and therefore still exist today.

Miscegenation with the "noble savage" created more casual attitudes about sexual customs. For example, if a Mi'kmaq saw a child born to a girl out of wedlock, this was seen as proof of the woman's fertility and thus was a positive thing, making her desirable. Acadians were the first Europeans to respect Native American culture. Sadly, as noted by Dr. John Mack Faragher in *A Great and Nobel Scheme* (2005), the Acadian Deportation in 1755 destroyed possible long-term benefits which would have resulted from their continued close association. Paul opines that the Acadians and the Mi'kmaq were in the process of "marrying up" much of the best of their two worlds. Had this been allowed to continue, it is believed that the relationships between the Europeans and the Native Americans in other parts of North America would have been different in a positive way.

Professor Amy H. Sturgis, PhD, author and scholar on Native Americans, was featured in a series of short documentary films produced for the Institute of Human Studies. In one of them, *The Expulsion of the Acadians* (2012), she noted that the Deportation was important for two reasons: first, to date, it is one of the only European state-sponsored ethnic cleansings on the continent of North America. Acadians had created much wealth, and the British simply took by force what they wanted. The event pre-dates the United States of America but it set the stage for later atrocities against human rights such as the Trail of Tears in 1830 against Native Americans.

Secondly, the Acadian Deportation marked the end of a possible altered history. Acadians had an economy based upon trade, not raid. They understood they were on the border between two great powers and they took advantage of trade with both, thus becoming prosperous. Like the Mi'kmaq, they realized they had some intrinsic rights, which no government could take from them. They became neutrals, thereby de facto revolutionaries ahead of their time. This small idea led to big ideas and set the stage for the American colonists to declare independence from England in 1776. Acadians had become classical republicans–against any form of tyranny, whether monarchic or democratic–and based upon the concept of common civility.

Professor Muriel K. Roy of the University of Moncton, in her article "Settlement and Population Growth in Acadia" in *The Acadians of the Maritimes*, noted another important factor in population growth: nuptiality, which is the frequency of marriage within a population. Nuptuality varies with the age of the first marriage common in a society and with the age structure of the population.

Obviously, nuptiality will be lower in an aging population than in a very young one. It is a major factor in fertility. In the European historical experience, nuptiality patterns played a very significant role in the development of low fertility. Late marriage and widespread celibacy provided one of the mechanisms by which fertility rates were reduced. Therefore, Acadian population growth was high when compared to Europe. Acadian girls married at a relatively young age. The mean age for girls was 21, while in France the mean age was 25.

There is much proof of the progressive attitudes of the Acadian women. This was very different from the Pilgrims of the 18th century. Acadian girls enjoyed dancing and even drinking with men "after dark," and taverns remained open on Sundays even during the celebration of Mass. On New Year's Day, men and boys went from house to house kissing women. This tradition was called the "new beginning."

According to Daniel Paul, the Mi'kmaq also adopted this custom and they all enjoyed it immensely. Women loved songs and social interactions that reflected their attitudes toward men. Some song lyrics were lascivious and often referred to saucy Acadian women. Women were also active in social and political affairs of the community. As noted in *l'Affaire Broussard*, women played most major community roles. According to famed Acadian novelist, playwright, and scholar Antonine Maillet, women were sometimes profane and definitely more sensual than their counterparts in other frontier societies of the time.

Finally, isolation and a constant fresh food supply were important factors in the excellent health of the Acadians. Prof. Roy observed that Acadie seems to have avoided the scourges of war, famine, and epidemics, having only two in more than 150 years. The Acadians' good health not only promoted fertility but also allowed them to live to an advanced age. The desire and pride in having a large family was continued long after the Acadians came to Louisiana. At Louisiana's 1938 Crowley Rice Festival, a $50 award was given to the largest family that attended the festival.

In *Scattered to the Wind* (1991), Dr. Carl Brasseaux published a projected Acadian growth rate from 1750 to 1975. Based on the population rate doubling every 25 years, he projected that, had the 1755 Acadian Deportation not happened, there would be some 7,680,000 Acadians by 1975. Today, it is generally agreed that there are approximately three to four million Acadians in the world. Clearly, the ethnic cleansing carried out against the Acadians by the British in the mid-18th century is still having ramifications in the 21st century.

Although increasing assimilation has cast a cloud over the culture, the interest of young people in maintaining their unique Acadian heritage is increasing. About 30 years ago, Professor Roy wrote that in the past, the Acadians' collective resources, will, and tenacity did not fail them. Why should the future belie the past? Rest assured the same rings true today.

Five Famous Acadian Women

Madeleine LeBlanc

Madeleine LeBlanc was an Acadian heroine from Grand-Pré, and was among the first settlers of the Baie Sainte-Marie region and one of ten children of Pierre LeBlanc and Marie Madeleine Babin (m. 1745 in Grand-Pré). The family was later deported in 1755 to Salem, Massachusetts. Eight years after the Treaty of Paris, in 1771, the LeBlanc family returned to Nova Scotia, along with the François Doucet family. Discovering English settlers on their Grand-Pré lands, they found refuge in the isolated southwestern end of the province, known as Baie Sainte-Marie. Upon arrival on the island of Séraphin, they were disheartened because the area was densely forested and because they had lost so many family and friends to the Deportation.

Inspiring the group, the courageous young Madeleine grabbed an axe and proceeded to cut down the first tree. The young heroine defiantly announced to all, "We've cried enough, now let's build a shelter for the night." These simple words emboldened the returning Acadians and after a concerted effort, they constructed a place of refuge.

Remembering the fearless encouragement they received from Madeleine, the first Acadians continued on and eventually obtained ownership of 1,735 arpents of land four years later in 1775. Therefore, the first families to successfully settle Pointe-de-l'Église (Church Point) were the LeBlanc and Doucet families. In 1975, a group of women in Baie Sainte-Marie, Nova Scotia, founded an association named in her honor. In 2000, the association received official status as the *Société Madeleine LeBlanc*. In the early 1980s, a slate gravestone was erected in her memory in the Sainte-Marie cemetery, near the tallest wooden church in North America. Today, Pointe-de-l'Église is also the site of the *Université Sainte-Anne*, the only Acadian university in Nova Scotia.

Marguerite Thibodeau Cyr

Marguerite Blanche Cyr (born Thibodeau), called "Tante Blanche" (1738-1810), was an Acadian heroine originally from Rivière-aux-Canards, near Grand-Pré. She later settled in the village of Grande Rivière (today Saint-Leonard in New Brunswick). The granddaughter of René LeBlanc, notary of Grand-Pré, she married François-Joseph Cyr at age 20 in 1758.

After many years as fugitives during the deportation years, they settled near Ekoupag, a First Nations mission. She gave birth to 13 children, nine of whom survived to adulthood. They left their land again in 1785 because of an influx of Loyalists in their area. The Acadian community went north along the St. John River and founded St. David (today in Maine).

During the 1797 *misère noir* (black famine), which occurred 12 years after the founding of the settlement, Tante Blanche distinguished herself among all others at age 59. In mid-winter, the settlement was running out of food because an early onset of cold weather had destroyed their crops the previous autumn. The men organized a hunting party but a huge storm raged, forcing animals into hiding and stranding the men for several days. Tante Blanche knew that some families had food and others did not, so she took up the responsibility of gathering up what food was left and redistributing it. She went from house to house in the raging storm, making sure each family had something to eat and tending to the sick. Tante Blanche was an aunt to many because she was married to a Cyr. The seven Cyr brothers made up about half of the settlement; they had 120 children among them. Fortunately, all of the residents managed to survive until the hunting party returned with meat and the colony was saved. As a result, Tante Blanche was revered like a saint. Her admirers sought her advice on all matters. She helped those who sought her aid and comfort, was a healer, and mediated disputes among residents. She died in 1810, and was buried in the St. Basile cemetery in New Brunswick. There is a museum in St. David, Maine, dedicated to her life.

Antonine Maillet

Born in 1929 in Bouctouche, New Brunswick, Antonine Maillet is an Acadian novelist, playwright, and scholar. Publicly recognized as the most renowned "unofficial" Acadian ambassador, she has traveled the world making public appearances to speak about her culture.

Maillet received her BA from the *Université de Moncton*, followed by an MA from the same institution. She then received her PhD in literature in 1970 from the *Université Laval* in Quebec City. Between 1971 and 1976, she taught literature and folklore at the *Université Laval*, and then in Montreal. She has written over 30 books on Acadians.

The famous fictional character in her radio-turned-theatrical play *La Sagouine,* gained her fame in both North America and Europe, and the book has been translated into eight languages. In the 40 years since writing this one-woman play, it has been presented nearly 3,000 times by famous Acadian actress Viola Léger.

A tourist village installation in Bouctouche called *Le Pays de la Sagouine* is among New Brunswick's most visited sites. In 1979, Maillet's fiction book, *Pélagie-la-Charrette,* which was inspired by the Acadian exile and return, won 15 awards including the prestigious *Prix Goncourt*, making Maillet the first person to receive it who was not a citizen of France. The book has been translated into 12 languages.

Maillet has received many honors, including Companion of the Order of Canada, the Order of New Brunswick, and the Royal Society of Canada's Lorne Pierce Medal. In France, she was made an Officer of *l'Ordre de la Légion d'Honneur*, Officer of *L'Ordre des Arts et des Lettres,* and Commander of *l'Ordre National du Mérite*. She has received 29 honorary doctorates from universities in Canada, the U.S., and France. From 1989 to 2000, she served as chancellor of the *Université de Moncton*, the first woman to hold this post. A Montreal street is named Rue Antonine-Maillet.

Edith Butler

Born in 1942 in Paquetville, New Brunswick, Edith Butler is a renowned Acadian singer-songwriter and ethnologist, who is often described as the "Mother of Acadian Music."

Since her debut in the popular television show *Sing Along Jubilee* with Anne Murray and John Allen Cameron, she has performed in many folk festivals in the U.S., appearing on-stage with such legends as Bob Dylan, Joni Mitchell, Gordon Lightfoot, and Buffy St. Marie. She has performed in Japan (500 shows), France, Switzerland, Belgium, the U.S., and Canada.

Butler's recording career includes 28 solo albums with nearly two million copies sold, gaining her five gold and three platinum albums. Her latest album, called *Le Retour* (The Return), is rich with tenderness and draws from episodes of her life, dreams, and aspirations. A fascinating storyteller, Butler recalls with passion and humor the tragic history of her Acadian people. She received many honors and distinctions such as the Order of Canada, the

Grand Prix of Académie Charles Cros in Paris, the Dr. Helen Creighton Life Achievement Award, the Governor General's Prize for Excellence in the Arts, as well as a Felix and a Nellie Award for Best Performance on stage and radio. Butler has also received three honorary doctorates from Canadian universities. Her work has made tremendous contributions to Acadian culture. To quote Antonine Maillet: "Edith Butler gives us an aspect of the world that otherwise we would have missed forever."

Aldéa Landry

Born in 1945 in Sainte-Cécile, New Brunswick, Aldéa Landry is a politician, lawyer, and public servant who served as president of the New Brunswick Liberal Association and became a trusted advisor, along with her husband Fernand, to Frank McKenna upon his election as leader of the party in 1985.

She was elected to the legislature in 1987 and served as deputy premier, Minister of Intergovernmental Affairs, and interim Minister of Fisheries under Premier Frank McKenna. She was the key point person for McKenna on the Meech Lake Accord and served as New Brunswick president of the Council for Canadian Unity. McKenna later appointed her to co-chair a Royal Commission on education in New Brunswick.

In 1997-1999, Landry served as Chairman of the Atlantic Provinces Economic Council. In 2004, Landry received an honorary doctorate in Humane Letters from Mount Saint Vincent University. She later served as a director of the Bank of Canada and, on June 24, 2005, she was appointed to the Security Intelligence Review Committee and the Queen's Privy Council for Canada.

On November 21, 2006, she was named a member of an advisory committee established by Prime Minister Stephen Harper to determine options for renewal and the future of the public service. She is the first woman named Chancellor of the *Université Ste-Anne* in Church Point, Nova Scotia. In 2006, she was honored with the Order of Canada.

Five Famous Cajun Women

Scholastique Breaux

Scholastique "Picou" Breaux, (1796-1846) founded the town of Breaux Bridge when she was 33 years old. A determined Cajun woman, Breaux drew up the *Plan de la Ville du Pont des Breaux* (the plan for the Village of Breaux Bridge), which included land for a school, church, and a detailed map of the area, including her late husband's bridge. She then proceeded to sell lots, resulting in Breaux Bridge's founding date of August 5, 1829. A bronze sculpture of Scholastique Breaux by sculptor

Celia Guilbeau Soper (great-great-granddaughter of Breaux) was installed in 1997 in City Park, in Beaux Bridge, Louisiana.

Cléoma Breaux Falcon

Cléoma Breaux Falcon (1906-1941) was a musician and singer who recorded the first Cajun record with her husband Joseph Falcon on April 27, 1928, in New Orleans. The song was called "Lafayette," also known as "Allons à Lafayette," and it sold well, leading to other recordings by Cajun musicians.

Though she played an impressive variety of instruments, Cléoma made her major contributions to Cajun music as a guitarist and singer. Her emotional singing and rhythmic guitar style set standards in Cajun music that are still in effect today. According to historians Ryan Brasseaux and Kevin Fontenot, she was embracing the era of the 1920s and the new roles for women that had prevented them from being able to work outside the home.

Sister Helen Prejean

Born in Baton Rouge in 1939, Sister Helen Prejean is a respected advocate for the abolition of the death penalty. In 1957, she joined the Sisters of Saint Joseph of Medaille (now Congregation of St. Joseph). In 1962, she received a Bachelor of Arts in English and education from St. Mary's Dominican College in New Orleans. In 1973, she earned a Master of Arts in religious education from Saint Paul University in Ottawa, Canada. Prejean has been the Religious Education Director at St. Frances Cabrini Parish in New Orleans, the Formation Director for her religious community, and has taught junior and senior high school.

Her efforts in death row ministry began in New Orleans in 1981, when an acquaintance asked her to correspond with convicted murderer Elmo Patrick Sonnier, who was sentenced to death by electrocution. She visited him at the Louisiana State Penitentiary and agreed to be his spiritual adviser in the months leading up to his execution. The experience gave Prejean greater insight into the process involved in executions, and she began speaking out against capital punishment.

At the same time, she also founded Survive, an organization devoted to counseling the families of victims of violence. Prejean has since ministered to many other inmates on death row and witnessed several more executions. She served from 1993 to 1995 as national chairperson of the National Coalition to Abolish the Death Penalty. She is also the subject of the 1995 film *Dead Man Walking,* a crime drama starring Susan Sarandon and Sean Penn.

Helen Boudreaux

Born in 1939 in Catahoula, Louisiana, Helen Boudreaux is a noted Cajun singer and composer. Boudreaux, the daughter of a sharecropper, worked the fields to help earn her family's living. Self-taught on the guitar, she has been writing and singing Cajun music all of her life. She sings many songs in Cajun French and is a selfless volunteer who works with young Cajun musicians.

Boudreaux has been nominated five times by the Cajun French Music Association (CFMA) as Female Vocalist of the Year and won three awards. She has also received the CFMA Association's Lifetime Achievement Award. Active in the preservation and promotion of the Cajun French language, Boudreaux is the mother of eight children, grandmother of 23, and great-grandmother of 12. For many years, she worked as an over-the-road line/haul truck driver. She has written her autobiography and recorded four Cajun and country albums. Boudreaux was named a Living Legend by the Acadian Museum of Erath, Louisiana.

Kathleen Babineaux Blanco

Kathleen Babineaux Blanco, born in 1942 in New Iberia, Louisiana, is a former governor of the state of Louisiana. The first woman to be elected to the office, she was the 54th governor of Louisiana, serving from January 2004 until January 2008.

Blanco took the oath of office in both English and French. From 1996 to 2004, while serving two terms as lieutenant governor, she helped to expand Louisiana's relationship with the French-speaking world, and in 1999 hosted the second *Congrès mondial acadien* in Louisiana. In 2004, she attended the third *Congrès mondial acadien* in Nova Scotia.

Despite the consecutive upheavals of Hurricanes Katrina and Rita, by the end of her term she had met all of her initial goals, most notably prioritizing education investment from pre-kindergarten to universities. She recruited a number of businesses to Louisiana and also provided proper funding and policies to lay a foundation for coastal Louisiana's recovery.

Bibliography

Dr. John Mack Faragher, *A Great and Nobel Scheme* (New York, W.W. Norton and Co. Inc., 2005); Muriel K. Roy, article "Settlement and Population Growth in Acadia" in *The Acadians of the Maritimes: Thematic Studies*, edited by Jean Daigle (1985); Ryan Brasseaux, PhD and Kevin Fontenot, article "Cleoma Breaux Falcon" in *Louisiana Women* (2009).

THE CONTEMPORARY EFFECTS OF THE ACADIAN DIASPORA

Barry Jean Ancelet

Diasporas are strange things. They represent the scattering of a human community due to tragic, catastrophic causes. Yet they often end up producing valuable new communities, along with social and cultural hybrids that survive and even thrive, in no small part because of the innovation and adaptation that are required for that survival.

New Orleans has experienced such a diaspora caused by Hurricane Katrina (2005) and its messy aftermath, when residents evacuated to places like Phoenix, Salt Lake City, and Cape Cod. There have been other massive migrations (forced and unforced) that have affected the culture and social structure of this nation. The fact that there are people of so many races and ethnicities on this continent is the result of the long-term immigration of Europeans, Africans, and Asians.

After the Revolutionary War, the descendants of those who first established the original 13 colonies headed west across the Appalachians, displacing the Native Americans who lived there. After the Louisiana Purchase and the War of 1812, new waves of people poured into the middle of the country.

The Indian Removal Act of 1830 was used to force untold numbers of Native Americans from their homelands to strange lands across the continent, including the Cherokee, who were sent down the infamous Trail of Tears to Oklahoma, where they retooled themselves as cowboys.

After the Civil War, untold numbers of former slaves headed north, while many in the rest of the country headed west. After the Great Flood of 1927, Southerners again headed north. During the Great Depression, people from the dust bowls and the South once again headed out in all directions. After World War II, rural folks headed into cities.

Each time, those who were migrating brought with them aspects of their culture. They influenced and were influenced by their new contexts in ways that eventually came to be part of the ever-evolving cultural scene. For example, places like Chicago and New York became important centers for new versions of imported blues and jazz, Detroit eventually produced Motown, and Bakersfield and Austin became the homes of fascinating country music alternatives.

More specifically to Louisiana, Cajuns and Creoles[1] flocked to southeast Texas and Houston and the Bay Area of California in the early part of the 20th century, establishing dancehalls and restaurants that featured music and food from South Louisiana with new twists and twangs. During the oil bust of the 1980s, Cajuns and Creoles sought employment and shelter in urban centers such as Atlanta and Denver, where they also continued to celebrate their music and food.

In one sense, Acadian and Cajun cultures have survived on the margins by resisting change. In another, they have thrived on the margins based on a surprisingly strong sense of identity, and on a clever survival strategy that incorporated and integrated change. There are reasons for this. According to my colleague, Carl A. Brasseaux, between 60 and 70 percent of the French peasants who eventually became the Acadians came from a 20-mile radius around Loudun in northern Poitou province (Brasseaux 1987).

This demographic fact, determined after an exhaustive examination of early colonial records, helps to explain the intensely resilient cultural and social identity of the Acadians. When the British exiled them from Nova Scotia in 1755, it was with the expressed intent of dispersing them among the British colonies so that they might be absorbed and acculturated. This did not happen. Instead of eliminating the Acadian identity, the exile galvanized it.

Those Acadians who arrived in Louisiana between 1764 and 1788 were expected to dissolve into French Creole society. This did not happen. They preserved their cultural and social specificity well past the French and Spanish periods. Under pressure from the fierce nationalism that accompanied World War I, they were expected to melt in the American pot. This did not happen. Cajuns found ways to negotiate the mainstream and continue to celebrate their traditions and language. Those living in the southwestern parishes recently affected by Hurricane Rita were there because they returned and rebuilt after Audrey.

On a related note, consider the following story: Boudreaux was hosting a couple of his old Army buddies for a few days, one from New York and the other from Missouri. While he was showing them around the old homestead that he had just inherited from his dad, they found themselves in an old abandoned barn. One of the visitors pried open a door and saw an old antique tractor in there, frozen in rust and covered with cobwebs. The guy from New York said, "Let's call a museum." The guy from Missouri said, "Let's call an antique shop." Boudreaux called his brother-in-law instead. Three days later, he was bush-hogging his pasture.[2]

When France sold Louisiana to the young United States in 1803, the federal government, as well as the government of the new Louisiana Territory and a few years later the state of Louisiana, began systematic efforts to Americanize us, including the replacement of our native French language with English, the language of the future. This was designed to eradicate the tenacious sense of identity forged by our Acadian ancestors in the cauldron of the New World beginning in the early 17th century and galvanized by a number of other social traumas, including the *Grand Dérangement* and a chronic succession of hurricanes, floods, droughts, economic depressions, and wars. Add to this the

Americanizing effects of various agriculture-, oil-, and war-economy related booms, improved transportation, and public education.

Recently, some scholars from historians (Shane Bernard) to anthropologists (Marc David) have suggested that these factors affected contemporary Cajun identity far more directly than the events of 1755, and that there is little evidence of traditionally transmitted Acadian identity among the Cajuns. This may be, *et pourtant,* here we are, now in the beginning of the 21st century, still self-identifying as Cajuns and Acadians.

There is undeniably considerable renewed interest in the Cajun/Acadian connection, through any number of factors that evolved in the 20th century. The filming in Louisiana of the 1929 silent movie *Evangeline* reinforced and expanded the effects of Longfellow's 19th-century poem into a nascent cultural tourism industry.

The 1955 bicentennial commemoration of the exile brought Acadian issues back to the fore and brought Cajuns into contact with Acadians in ways that would continue to develop through the first *Colloque sur l'acadie* and the subsequent *Congrès mondial acadien* series.

At the same time, it is also undeniable that contemporary Cajun culture has evolved from Acadian to Cajun in its own way over the centuries as historian Carl A. Brasseaux has made clear in his studies. During the first *Congrès mondial Acadien 1994,* held in the southeastern Acadian region of New Brunswick, far-flung representatives from the Acadian Diaspora gathered to celebrate our enduring identity. The emotional reunions initially led many to focus on our commonalities, including last names, language features, and social co-op patterns. But rather quickly it became apparent that in many ways (music and cuisine, for example), Acadian and Cajun cultures had evolved beyond their common origins.

Like twins separated at adolescence and later reunited, participants in scholarly conferences and family reunions alike have come to understand that both our similarities and differences are important and interesting to consider. What we have in common despite centuries of separation must be powerfully important to our cultural DNA. The ways we have come to differ also reflect important influences acquired in our various contexts. It is nature and nurture on a societal scale. The connections that have been made through these Acadian gatherings have renewed, or perhaps more accurately, reinvented real, affective ties in the spirit of what Louder and Waddell described as *l'archipel retrouvé.*

If we have survived more or less well, it may be because we have learned to negotiate the margins by constantly adapting and innovating solutions to the pressures from the dominant cultures in our contexts. With all due respect to the fictional yet ubiquitous Evangeline, her long-suffering, passive reaction is hardly the model for what got us to this point. Our own real-life ancestors recreated a society with the meager resources they had available, deftly negotiating a way through good times and bad. Their quietly heroic efforts are much more representative of what has worked, based on both the persistence and resistance that have sometimes been direct, but more often indirect, and characterized by a sort of socio-cultural judo.

Experts have consistently predicted our imminent demise via acculturation and assimilation since 1755. Yet, here in Louisiana, our culture survived the 1803 Louisiana Purchase from France, the War of 1812, the Civil War, and World War I. It survived after 1916, when the state banned the use of French in its new compulsory public education system, after the 1921 revision of the state constitution eliminating the legal status of French, and after the 1927 flood, which brought a deluge of aid and English language influence from the national level reinforced by another round of national aid and influence after the economic crash of 1929. It survived the development of the oil industry in the 1930s, which generated another flood of money and Americanizing influences, and World War II, which produced yet another layer of Americanization.

And yet, after all this, some of us are still standing, disrupting the predictions of linguists, sociologists, and politicians by our simple stubborn presence. Reporters and scholars alike frequently ask me how much chance there is, realistically, for French to survive into the future. I have come to think that the real question is how could it be that there is any left at all in the present, after all those well-organized and systematic efforts? *Et pourtant, on est encore là, moins qu'avant, mais néanmoins encore là malgré tout.* (However we are still there, fewer than before, but nevertheless still here, in spite of everything.) Never mind helping us, I sometimes wonder what might happen if they would just stop hindering us.

This spirit of adaptation at the heart of our survival is evident in any number of cultural and social expressions. Consider the contemporary evolution of Cajun house types and foods, such as porches and peppers, both of which reflect ongoing input from our constantly evolving context. So-called Acadian houses feature practical responses to the drastically different climate found in South Louisiana by the newly-arrived exiles, the most important of which were inspired by African Creoles. Houses were made drier and cooler by raising them off the ground on piers, porches kept the sun off the outside walls and provided breezy outdoor living space, and windows and doors were designed to provide as much cross-ventilation as possible within the simple living spaces of early houses.

Some of these features have become stylized in what are now considered and called Acadian-style houses. Sometimes the Acadian connection is only nominal, as Cajuns live in townhouses, apartment complexes, trailer parks, and ritzy subdivisions.

It is ironic that some of the most iconic foods now associated with Cajun culture, gumbo and rice and gravy, both owe their existence in Louisiana to African Creole culture. A popular joke suggests that a true Cajun is someone who can look over a rice field and determine how much gravy it will take to cover it. Gumbo has often been used as a metaphor for the cultural blending process that has occurred in South Louisiana. This process is responsible for the houses we live in, the foods we eat, the stories we tell and the music we dance to.

The term "Cajun" is useful to describe the results of this creolization on Acadian culture. And this process continues to produce new culinary innovations, such as crawfish eggrolls, crawfish tamales, microwave roux, and some things that strain the imagination. All the while, we can also enjoy hamburgers and fried chicken with iced tea and Dr. Pepper, without feeling that we are betraying our Cajun-ness.

Another important version of cultural creolization is in Cajun music, which I will take some time to examine as an extended example of Cajun cultural negotiation. Here we have not only survived on the margins; we have actually thrived by dancing on them and through them, integrating influences from outside sources and improvising new styles from within. For this to work best, the process must be organic and continuous, preserving and creating in the same motion, producing music that is at once surprisingly new and reassuringly connected. As Dewey Balfa so eloquently put it, "Tradition is not a product, but a process. It's like a tree. One must water the roots so that the tree can support new growth. Both are critically important."

Ultimately, the Acadian Diaspora scattered our ancestors to far away places, where they would learn to evolve in order to survive. This process has produced versions of Acadian culture that could be viewed as assimilated. Richard Guidry made considerable waves in 1978 at the *Conférence sur l'Acadie* at the ironically named *Université de Moncton* (General Monckton deported the Acadians from that area) when he pointed out that language loss was not the only form of assimilation, suggesting that Acadians in Quebec might be at least as assimilated as Louisiana Cajuns.

Despite the differences in the communities that Acadians of the diaspora have developed, there does seem to be a remarkable resiliency in Acadian self-identification and in their systems of social cooperation. It may be true, as Maurice Basque and others from the Canadian Maritimes have insisted, that Acadie must be located in a political geography in order to truly exist. Nevertheless, I would suggest that the enduring Acadian identity in most of the places where we have ended up may be our ultimate victory over those who tried to eliminate us as a people in what scholar John Mack Faragher has described as nothing short of ethnic cleansing. Instead of uprooting the Acadian nation, it turns out that they inadvertently spread its seeds in a rich variety of evolved forms in many places.

This positive spin on our history is true only if we continue to recognize and embrace each other in our similarities and our differences. It is also important to remember that we can revive and enhance our understanding of our past without jeopardizing our respective contemporary realities.

Bibliography

Helen Hunt Jackson, *A Century of Dishonor: A Sketch of the United States Government's Dealings with Some of the Indian Tribes* (New York: Harper & Brothers, 1881, rev. 1885, rpt. Norman: University of Oklahoma Press, 1995).

Endnotes

1. "Creole" historically refers to descendants of the earliest French settlers in Louisiana, and to French-speaking blacks who immigrated to Louisiana via the West Indies and Hispaniola. The Creole culture developed its own cuisine and its own unique version of French.

2. "Bush hog" is a common local term for a large mowing apparatus that is pulled by a tractor.

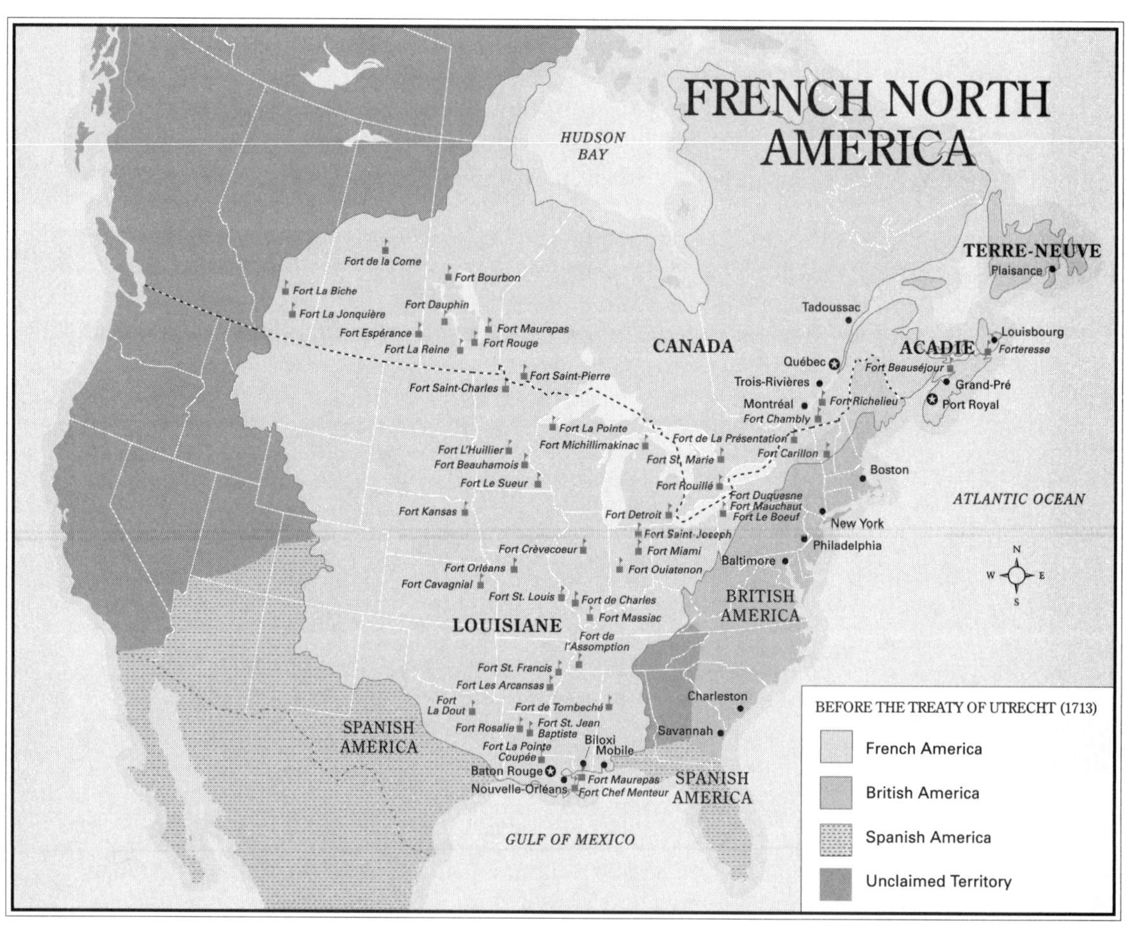
FRENCH NORTH AMERICA
HUDSON BAY
TERRE-NEUVE
Plaisance
Tadoussac
CANADA
ACADIE
Louisbourg
Forteresse
Québec
Fort Beauséjour
Trois-Rivières
Grand-Pré
Montréal
Fort Richelieu
Port Royal
Fort Chambly
Fort de La Présentation
Fort Carillon
Boston
ATLANTIC OCEAN
Fort de la Come
Fort Bourbon
Fort La Biche
Fort La Jonquière
Fort Dauphin
Fort Espérance
Fort Maurepas
Fort La Reine
Fort Rouge
Fort Saint-Pierre
Fort Saint-Charles
Fort La Pointe
Fort L'Huillier
Fort Michillimakinac
Fort Beauhamois
Fort St. Marie
Fort Le Sueur
Fort Rouillé
Fort Duquesne
Fort Mauchaut
Fort Le Boeuf
Fort Kansas
Fort Detroit
New York
Fort Saint-Joseph
Fort Crèvecoeur
Fort Miami
Philadelphia
Fort Orléans
Baltimore
Fort Ouiatenon
Fort Cavagnial
Fort St. Louis
Fort de Charles
BRITISH AMERICA
Fort Massiac
LOUISIANE
Fort de l'Assomption
Fort St. Francis
Fort Les Arcansas
Charleston
Fort La Dout
Fort de Tombeché
SPANISH AMERICA
Fort Rosalie
Fort St. Jean Baptiste
Savannah
Fort La Pointe Coupée
Biloxi
Mobile
Baton Rouge
Fort Maurepas
Nouvelle-Orléans
Fort Chef Menteur
SPANISH AMERICA
GULF OF MEXICO
N
W
E
S
BEFORE THE TREATY OF UTRECHT (1713)
French America
British America
Spanish America
Unclaimed Territory

The French Language and the Acadians in North America

Alain Troubat

I've always been passionate about the history of Acadie, Louisiana, and New France. Canada and more than half of the United States once belonged to France. What remains today of this heritage? Eight million Canadians speak French, including seven million in Quebec and nearly ten million Americans speak French, but when they were asked on the 2000 census about their ethnic and linguistic heritage, 20 million stated that they have French ancestors.

In this article, I will focus on the French language of Acadians and Cajuns. In Atlantic Canada, 300,000 Acadians (besides the 500,000 of Acadian ancestry) share French as a common language but are dispersed throughout the provinces of New Brunswick, Nova Scotia, Prince Edward Island, and Newfoundland-and-Labrador. In Louisiana, more specifically in "Cajun country," which includes the 22 parish area known as Acadiana, there are 800,000 Cajuns, but only 200,000 still speak French. Of the approximately 200,000 Cajuns who live in Texas, only 50,000 speak French. In Quebec, one million people have an Acadian surname (poll by Groupe Léger, 1988), but it is also important to emphasize that three million francophones in this province have Acadian ancestors (demographic study, UQAM, 2008).

In Louisiana, many grandparents still speak French, but its use in schools was banned in 1921 by the state constitution, and students who were caught speaking French were harshly punished. An entire generation was forced to conform and was nearly assimilated by mandating the use of the English language. Today, children rarely converse with their grandparents in French, but there has been a revival in Louisiana, and more and more children are learning French in schools. Since 1968, the *Conseil pour le développement du français en Louisiane* (CODOFIL) has been fighting to preserve the French language in Louisiana. The School Act on Teaching French (Act 408) was passed shortly before the Act to Establish CODOFIL (Act 409); both were signed by Gov. John McKeithen. The first French immersion class was offered in 1984 in Baton Rouge, and today 30 French immersion schools located in southern Louisiana offer French classes to more than 4,000 pupils up to grade eight. Universities also offer degrees in Francophone Studies. In Louisiana today, descendants of the Acadians who settled in the state remain proud of their French origins, despite the difficulties they have had in the past to achieve recognition. The realm of Cajun influence is centered on the city of Lafayette, located in the heart of the Acadiana region. Cajuns have an expression, "*lâche pas la patate*" (don't drop the [hot] potato), which is a good summary of their determination to survive as a distinct people.

New England is home to nearly a million descendants of Acadians. Those who are descended from the groups who were deported in 1755 have been assimilated into the English-speaking population, but the second wave of Acadians who came to the region to work in textile factories during the second half of the 19th century have fought to maintain their French. Their ancestors came as part of families from Acadie and Quebec who spoke no English. Until the end of the Second World War, they were clustered together in French-speaking areas and had French-language schools. In the next generation, many of their adult children migrated to other regions and almost entirely lost their ability to speak French.

In 1903, *La Société mutuelle de l'Assomption* was founded in Waltham, Massachusetts; four years later it already had 58 branches. This company is now *Assomption Vie* and has its headquarters in Moncton, New Brunswick. Early on, it made it possible for the French-speaking population in the area to meet regularly, to work together to promote French-language education, to protect the Catholic religion, Acadian culture, and the French language.

In the state of Maine, in the northeastern region (Aroostook County), approximately 25percent of Acadians out of a population of 75,000 speak French. Further south, in Androscoggin County, 15percent of the population of 103,000 speak French.

This is the current situation in the main areas in which Acadians live in North America. Since I belong to the *France-Canada* and *France-Louisiane* organizations, I have spent time in all of these places.

The Acadian Renaissance began in 1881 at the first Acadian convention. The date of August 15th was chosen as the Acadian national holiday. In 1884, a flag was chosen to represent the Acadian people; inspired by France's red, white and blue flag, it bears a gold star on a blue background. In 1969, New Brunswick became the only officially bilingual province of Canada. The *Université de Moncton,* with three campuses in Moncton, Shippagan, and Edmunston, celebrated its 50th anniversary in 2013. In 1978, bilingual schools were replaced by unilingual francophone schools. In 2003, in Nova Scotia, the *Université Sainte-Anne* and the six campuses of the *Collège de l'Acadie* merged to ensure better access to post-secondary education in French. Today, in the Atlantic provinces, French-speaking Acadians form 32percent of the population of New Brunswick, 5percent of that of Nova Scotia, their original home, and 4percent of Prince Edward Island.

In the Maritimes, our original Acadie, there is room for optimism. Canada is bilingual; the three provinces that are home to the majority of Acadians are located next to Quebec which is 90percent francophone; and as in many parts of North America, there is an active movement to protect Acadian identity. Although Acadie ceased to exist as a colony in North America three centuries ago, Acadians throughout the continent remain inspired by the Acadian flag, which symbolizes the French heritage to which Acadians have remained strongly attached for 410 years.

THE BIRTH OF THE CONGRÈS MONDIAL ACADIEN (CMA)

Jean-Marie Nadeau

While compiling this wonderful book on the Acadians of the world that my good friend Warren A. Perrin was working on collegially, he asked me to write an article about how the *Congrès mondial acadien* (CMA) came about and first got started. How could I resist Warren's plea? Impossible! So I enthusiastically embraced the exercise.

It is always difficult to zero in on the genesis of an idea, but easier to locate the moment when the idea was expressed or publicly exposed for the first time. In fact it was in May 1988, at the meeting of the foundation of the *Association acadienne de l'Alberta*, held in Edmonton, Alberta, where I had been invited as a conference speaker, that I expressed the idea for a *Congrès mondial acadien*. It was a magical moment; the proposal was welcomed with much enthusiasm.

But what led to this idea? As the secretary general of the *Société nationale de l'Acadie* (SNA) from 1985 to 1989, I had the great privilege of traveling the world meeting Acadians wherever they lived, whether in Louisiana, Texas, Maine, New England, Quebec, or in France. Each of these meetings was filled with emotion and solidarity. At every meeting, I was asked how local, provincial, national organizations, and even individuals could become members of the SNA. I had to answer that the SNA was a Canadian organization of the Acadian people, bringing together the representative associations of the four Atlantic provinces: the SANB (*Société de l'Acadie du Nouveau-Brunswick*), the FANE (*Fédération acadienne de la Nouvelle-Écosse*), the SSTA (*Société Saint-Thomas d'Aquin*) of Prince Edward Island, and the FFTNL (*Fédération des francophones de Terre-Neuve et du Labrador*). In 1988, the four provincial associations of Acadian youth also became full-fledged members of the SNA organizational structure. We were obviously overwhelmed. I hated to, but I had to reject all of these new membership requests from other parts of the world.

So, after considerable travel in France, Louisiana, and elsewhere with Father Léger Comeau, then-president of the SNA, and after having participated in the meetings of the foundations of the associations of the *Fédération acadienne du Québec* in 1987 and that of Alberta in 1988, I decided to launch the CMA idea so that Acadians from around the world could meet and decide how to empower each other to help ensure Acadian continuity and growth. But how is such an idea born? Was it from the late Philippe Rossillon (president of *Les*

Amitiés acadiennes in Paris, France), from Maryvonne LeGac (in Belle-Ile-En-Mer, France), or from Roger Léger (in Montreal, Quebec), or from others? I don't really know. All I know is that the great idea emerged because other exiled peoples around the world unite: Jews, Palestinians, Irish, Scottish, Armenians, etc. I thought: "Why not us?"

Getting this idea off the ground was not easy, particularly from a personal perspective. Even though the CMA idea was considered excellent and promising, the SNA board of directors felt that it already had enough on its plate dealing with issues related to ensuring the continuity of the Acadian people in Acadie of Atlantic Canada (that I called metropolitan Acadie) and that it didn't want to attenuate efforts to provide for the continuity of the Acadian people around the world. It seemed to me that this approach was narrow-minded and devoid of generosity and ambition; I was even ordered not to get involved in the matter anymore, at least formally, as secretary general of the SNA. Of course, at the time, Mulroney, Thatcher, and Reagan were in power: the watchword was to cut anything related to the social or cultural realm. This scared many. And, because I'm a bit of a rebel along the lines of Beausoleil Broussard, nobody could stop me from doing what I wanted in my spare time outside of work.

Meanwhile, I was under pressure from the late Acadian André Boudreau of Alberta to write a substantial text to clarify and develop the idea. It is very difficult to say "no" to André Boudreau. Just ask a few ministers of the day –like Bernard Valcourt at the federal level or Denis Losier at the provincial level–about it. André Boudreau wanted a text for a first CMA organizational meeting that he had planned for November 21, 1988, in Toronto. So, under pressure, I quickly drafted it in Cap-Pelé, New Brunswick, just prior to leaving for an SNA mission to Europe. This text can be read in my last book, *L'Acadie possible* (*Éditions de la Francophonie*, 2009).

Given that my board of directors didn't want me to get involved in the matter, and that I didn't have the personal finances to go to this meeting in Toronto, my heart was heavy. However, I knew that the project was in good hands, with the first Acadian knights in place to see the project through. These Acadians were André Boudreau, Daniel Arsenault, Yvon Samson, Pierre Laforest, Serge Martin, Jean Cormier, Denis Jean, Robert Frenette, and Raymond Lanteigne. Several of these people played an important role in the organization of the four CMAs that followed. We should thank them all and salute them with all due honor.

It should also be mentioned that, in addition to the reservations of the SNA vis-à-vis the CMA, several Acadians from political and artistic circles of Atlantic Canada were also somewhat put off by the idea. For them, as with the SNA, there was but one Acadie, one true Acadie, that of the four Atlantic provinces. Some strongly believed that the Acadie of the Diaspora was just folklore and should no longer be a concern. The years have eased these tensions. Those who were against the CMA in the beginning have changed their minds, and several of these individuals have been able to take advantage of it artistically and politically. Today, everybody wants to be in the photo, which is all for the best.

An international CMA corporation was created in 1990, and its executive did me the great honor of selling me the first membership card: 0001. I was touched by this special attention.

After leaving my job of secretary general at the SNA in 1989, I worked as editor for the New Brunswick newspaper *Acadie Nouvelle*, and then after a little over a year there, I left the country until mid-1991, so I was not involved in the organization of the first CMA of 1994 to be held in Moncton and southeast New Brunswick. Indirectly, I was sometimes consulted on how to reduce certain conflicts and power struggles.

Even if I had wanted to be more involved, certain people in high places didn't want to see me there. The initiator of the project, André Boudreau, even confided in me that an Acadian minister under McKenna had told him that the government of New Brunswick would put money into the CMA as long as I had no official role either as a volunteer or employee. As a known Acadian militant, they were afraid that I would use the CMA to create an autonomous global Acadian political movement. To be frank, I must admit that the idea crossed my mind at the time, but it did not justify the ostracism that I then endured. What was most important to me was that a first CMA be held reuniting the Acadians from worldwide.

At the opening ceremonies of the first CMA in August of 1994 in Cap-Pelé, I was one of few people associated with the CMA's beginnings who were not admitted with a VIP pass into the inner circle of dignitaries. Thankfully, out of embarrassment and probably shame, the 1994 CMA organizers quickly had a change of heart and offered me such a pass. The only time I didn't have to beg for an official pass to take part in the Acadian Congress was at the 2009 CMA in Caraquet and the Acadian Peninsula, in New Brunswick. But, it should be noted that at the time I was the president of the SANB, and even if some had wanted to avoid me, it would have been a political sting.

What's extraordinary is that this activity was so brilliantly held the first time in southeast New Brunswick in 1994, and then reproduced four times every five years with as much class: the 1999 CMA in Louisiana, the 2004 Nova Scotia CMA, the 2009 Northeast New Brunswick CMA, and finally in the 2014 Northwest New Brunswick CMA. This last CMA was held in three bordering territories, including the state of Maine, and the provinces of Quebec and New Brunswick. This region is called "Acadie's Lands and Forests" as it is not an ocean-bordering Acadian region like the other Canadian regions, and is the much-treasured area of my childhood. It was a blessing and gift to participate.

Historians will wrestle for years with evaluating the qualitative and quantitative scope of the CMAs with respect to its effects on building Acadian identity. But many of us feel that the CMA of 1994 raised the bar of Acadian identity in southeastern New Brunswick. It also boosted Acadian musical productions. In 1994, it was the first time in our history that the Acadian people organized an international event. Without the CMA's global impact, the *Sommet international de la Francophonie* (World Francophone Summit) of 1999 would not have been in held Moncton.

By mentioning this, I do not want to minimize the importance of the first three national conventions held over a hundred years ago. Some 5,000 Acadians from all over the world participated in the first Acadian National Convention at Memramcook, New Brunswick in 1881, then at Miscouche, Prince Edward Island in 1884, and many also attended the one in Church Point, Nova Scotia in 1890. I remain an unconditional admirer of these first events that were of great importance for Acadie's future. But it will be important for researchers–historians, sociologist, and others–to take into consideration how these present CMAs have influenced the vitality of the Acadian people. What I do know is that all these important Acadian reunions boosted our self-worth while creating crucial business opportunities. And of course, they are major parties! From an emotional standpoint, the reaction has been very favorable.

An individual idea without collective management is useless. Whether as participants or organizers, all who turned the idea of the *Congrès mondial acadien* into a reality are now its trustees. Some even now feel that the CMA is getting carried away in its organization, at least financially, similar to the Olympics. This needs to be seriously evaluated. For the moment, it does not appear to be a problem for the organizers of the CMA 2019, which will be a "twinning" of Prince Edward Island and Southeastern New Brunswick. Among the regions that hope to hold the next Congress, we can include the Acadians from the Trois-Rivières area of Quebec and the Acadians from the Poitou-Charentes region of France. But they must now start developing the idea if they wish to succeed.

The CMAs that we have seen up to this point have primarily been big family reunions (Acadian genealogists have counted almost 400 Acadian family surnames). Today, the CMAs are starting to include "extended families," beyond the strict ethnic family, which is great. Finally, Acadie is increasingly inclusive, and it is largely due to its springboard of CMAs. If I have any regrets vis-à-vis the various CMAs, it is only that there has not yet been enough space for the exchange of ideas and debates apart from the first 1994 CMA. Of course, there have always been meetings of youth, women, and business people at CMAs, but with no defined scope.

Finally, the other idea that I had which has not yet materialized is to create a World Acadian Development Fund to foster the economic growth of the Acadians of the Atlantic provinces (the original Acadie) and its identity-based growth, while building on Acadie here and elsewhere through different exchanges. Thankfully, the SNA has recently created the *Fonds national de l'Acadie*, and I hope that we will use this tool to build on our people's financial foundation. If, one day, French is no longer spoken among Acadians in the Atlantic provinces, there will no longer be an Acadie for anyone anywhere.

It is interesting to see how time and history sort things out. Whereas the SNA did not readily accept the idea of the *Congrès mondial acadien* in 1988, it was proud to take charge of the responsibility of providing for the future of the CMAs in the late 1990s. This eased the heartache of the beginning of this process. It was as if I had been redeemed. The CMAs of the future will be able to act as barometers for measuring the health of our wonderful people.

Up to this point, I have taken part in all of the CMAs, and I intend to continue as long as my health allows me to do so. I hope for all of us that CMAs will continue to be held for hundreds of years to come. Long live the CMAs, long live Acadie of the Atlantic provinces, and of the world!

Acadian Genealogical Research Resources

Stanley LeBlanc

Beginning in 1755, the Acadians were uprooted from Acadie and scattered throughout the world, yet Acadians have nevertheless been able to trace their roots back to their Acadian progenitors. This is possible because of the vast number of records that were preserved prior to, during, and after the exile.

This article addresses the research material that is available, but no article on Acadian genealogy would be complete without giving special recognition to Louisiana State Sen. Dudley J. LeBlanc, aka "*Cousin*" Dud (1894-1971). He was a great-great-grandson of René LeBlanc, who arrived in New Orleans in February 1765 as a young orphan with resistance leader Joseph Broussard *dit* Beausoleil.

LeBlanc was totally dedicated in his efforts to reconnect Cajuns in Louisiana with their Acadian relatives in Canada and France. In August 1936, he brought his "Evangeline Girls"–young women dressed in costumes evoking the heroine in Longfellow's poem *Evangeline*–to Lanaudière, Quebec. He also wrote *The True Story of the Acadians*, which was later re-issued as *The Acadian Miracle* (1966).

Photo©Evangeline Richard

Sen. Dudley J. LeBlanc is shown in the center of the front row. Standing to his right is Msg. Joseph-Arsène Richard, who developed the Acadian community in the Verdun district of Montreal.

Bona Arsenault (1903-1993), a former Minister of the Canadian Parliament, and originally from the Acadian area of Bonaventure, Quebec, has contributed greatly in uncovering many misplaced Acadian registers and genealogy sources, and after ten years of research, he published the impressive *Histoire et Généalogie des Acadiens* in 1965 (rev. 1978), in two volumes containing 1,178 pages. The English book editions were published in 1966 (rev. 1971).

It would take hundreds of pages just to list the titles and sources of the Acadian research material that is available; therefore this article will address only the major categories of records.

Census Records of Acadie, Prior to the Exile

The first census of Acadie was taken in 1671, followed by censuses in 1686, 1693, 1695, 1698, 1700, 1701, 1703, 1707, 1708, 1714, 1716, 1751, and 1752. The census of 1751 was mistakenly shown as 1732, and was a census of the Acadians who had moved and settled in current-day New Brunswick and along the St. John River. The last two years contain especially valuable information.

Sacramental Records from *St. Charles Aux Mines*, Smuggled Out of Acadie

When the Acadians were rounded up in 1755, many thought that they would be released soon, therefore they buried the church registers and other documents. Unfortunately, they did not return soon and these records have been lost to history. However, the registers of the *St. Charles Aux Mines* Catholic Church at Grand-Pré for 1707-1748 were smuggled out by the Acadians exiled to Maryland.

No mention was made of the registers either by the Acadians in Maryland or after some of them arrived in Louisiana in 1767. There was, however, one entry made on June 29, 1773, [not a Sunday] for the baptism of Marguerite Alein [*sic*]. This indicates that the registers had been in the possession of the Allain family, at least while they were in Maryland. They were discovered in 1895 in the archives of St. Gabriel Church in Iberville Parish, Louisiana. These extremely valuable records were microfilmed and a copy was sent to Canada. Extract cards were made from the microfilm and published in the Diocese of Baton Rouge Catholic Church Records, Acadian Records, 1707-1748, Volume 1(a) revised.

Acadian Censuses in 1760 and 1761; Prisoner Lists in Acadie

Some Acadians exiles gained control of the ship *Pembroke* and returned to the St. John River. Most of them ended up in Quebec, but some joined the Acadians who had escaped to the Restigouche River and the Gaspé Peninsula. There was a census taken on October 24, 1760, of the Acadians on the Restigouche River, and one dated July 31, 1761, of the Acadian refugees at the various locations on the Gaspé Peninsula. There were several Acadian leaders resisting the exile, but they were ultimately forced to surrender. They were imprisoned at Forts Beauséjour, Edward, and Halifax. There are prisoner lists for these three locations.

At the end of the French and Indian War in 1763, these prisoners were offered the opportunity to remain if they took an oath of allegiance. They refused, and in November 1764, a group left with Joseph Broussard *dit* Beausoleil. They went to Saint-Domingue (now Haiti), where they changed ships and went on to New Orleans, arriving in February 1765. A second group left Halifax in early 1765 and arrived in Louisiana (also via Saint-Domingue) in May 1765. The first Acadian group settled in the Attakapas Territory, however, some left because of numerous deaths and joined a group of Acadians settled on the Mississippi River in the present-day St. James and Ascension parishes.

Ship Records, Prisoner Lists, Census and Sacramental Records in Exile

There are records for the Acadians sent to the British Colonies, England, and France. There are census records of those in the British Colonies in 1763, and at the various locations in England. There are ship lists for those repatriated from England to France in 1763 and for those sent to France between 1755 and 1785. One especially valuable set of records are the Belle-Île-en-Mer notarial declarations made by the heads of households that traced ancestries back to the Acadian progenitors. Brittany had the Acadians record their origins in France. The pastors recorded recitations of their genealogy and history, which have been published in Reiders' *The Acadians in France,* V. II.

In 1785, some of the Acadians in France were allowed to go to Louisiana on seven ships for which there are passenger lists. For those Acadians who remained in France after 1785, there are some records of financial aid given them and also a few census records.

Canadian Records, After the Exile

Some Acadians returned to Nova Scotia and Prince-Edward Islands after 1763, but most ended up in New Brunswick. Some of the Acadians who had fled to Quebec remained there. Thus, there are civil and church records in all of the locations in which they settled.

Louisiana Records

a. Censuses, Militia Rosters, and Sacramental Records in Louisiana

According to *History of the Acadians* (1988) by former member of the Canadian Parliament Bona Arsenault, the largest number of exiled Acadians migrated to Louisiana; therefore, the civil and sacramental records recorded in Louisiana are very important. There is a list of 32 exiles who arrived with Joseph Broussard *dit* Beausoleil in February of 1765, and who signed for the exchange of card money in New Orleans. The first census and militia roster prepared after the Acadians arrived in Louisiana was in April 1766. Additional censuses were taken before the Acadians in France arrived in 1785: 1769-1770 (some completed in 1771); 1774, and 1777. The first census taken after the Acadians arrived from France in 1785 was the one of 1788. Additional ones were taken in 1791, 1792, 1795, 1797, and 1798. Louisiana became a territory of the United States in 1803 and there was a census taken of the Attakapas Territory in 1808 that lists the age and location of the residents.

Militia rosters were normally completed when the censuses were taken. There are special records for the period during Bernardo Galvez's governorship of the colony of Louisiana, from 1777 to 1785. Galvez, later the viceroy of New Spain, aided the 13 colonies in their quest for independence from Britain, defeating British forces at Pensacola and reconquering Florida for Spain. With the aid of the Acadians, he also defeated the British at the battles of Manchac, Baton Rouge, and Natchez.

Church officials, under both the French and the Spanish regimes, prepared sacramental records for births, marriages, and deaths. Marriage dispensations, which showed relationships back to grandparents and beyond, are also available. The sacramental records are available in the Archdiocese of New Orleans [ADNO]; the Diocese of Baton Rouge [DOBR]; the Southwest Louisiana Records; and the South Louisiana Records by Fr. Donald Hebert. Beginning in 1970 until his death in 2000, Father Hebert compiled dozens of volumes of Catholic Church records in south Louisiana. His first volume was published in 1974, and he went on to publish 96 more.

b. Marriage Contracts and Land Records, Including Successions and Tutorships in Louisiana

Marriage contracts, imported to Louisiana by Spanish laws, were made with the commandant, who was both the chief civil official and the military commander of a district. These contracts were used to alter the normal regime of community property and establish a system whereby spouses maintained their assets separately.

Land records (grants, sales, conveyances, and estate divisions) were kept for all transactions and now provide invaluable information. Successions, the body of law concerning the distribution of a person's property after his or her death, also had to be prepared for all estates. When minors were involved, tutors and undertutors had to be appointed. Thus, these records provide helpful information on spouses, children, and other relatives.

Records in other U.S. States

Some Acadians remained in the colonies to which they had been exiled. Later, other Acadians migrated to the United States. For example, beginning in 1780, Acadians migrated to Madawaska (today Maine), where there are records existing for this group. Many of those who remained in the colonies anglicized their surnames so that tracing their family lines is more difficult; for example, LeBlanc became White, and Dupuis became Wells.

Finally, there are many genealogical societies and associations in the Unites States, in Canada, and in France that can also assist in the search of Acadian ancestry.

II

Cultures of Acadie

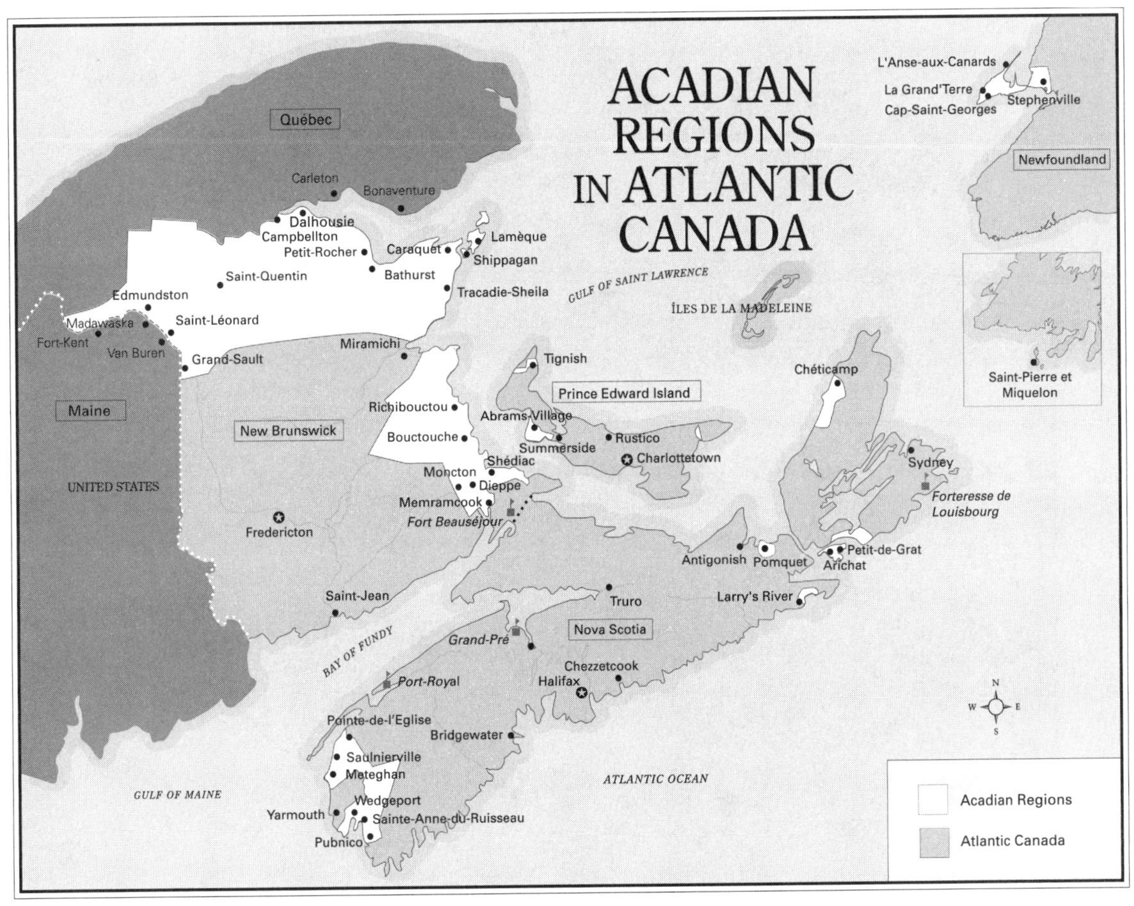
ACADIAN REGIONS IN ATLANTIC CANADA
Québec
Carleton
Bonaventure
Dalhousie
Campbellton
Petit-Rocher
Caraquet
Lamèque
Shippagan
Bathurst
Saint-Quentin
Tracadie-Sheila
Edmundston
Madawaska
Fort-Kent
Saint-Léonard
Van Buren
Grand-Sault
Miramichi
Maine
UNITED STATES
New Brunswick
Richibouctou
Bouctouche
Moncton
Shédiac
Dieppe
Memramcook
Fort Beauséjour
Fredericton
Saint-Jean
GULF OF SAINT LAWRENCE
ÎLES DE LA MADELEINE
Tignish
Prince Edward Island
Abrams-Village
Summerside
Rustico
Charlottetown
Chéticamp
Sydney
Forteresse de Louisbourg
Antigonish
Pomquet
Petit-de-Grat
Arichat
Larry's River
Truro
Nova Scotia
BAY OF FUNDY
Grand-Pré
Port-Royal
Halifax
Chezzetcook
Pointe-de-l'Eglise
Bridgewater
Saulnierville
Meteghan
Wedgeport
Yarmouth
Sainte-Anne-du-Ruisseau
Pubnico
GULF OF MAINE
ATLANTIC OCEAN
L'Anse-aux-Canards
La Grand'Terre
Cap-Saint-Georges
Stephenville
Newfoundland
Saint-Pierre et Miquelon
N
W
E
S
Acadian Regions
Atlantic Canada

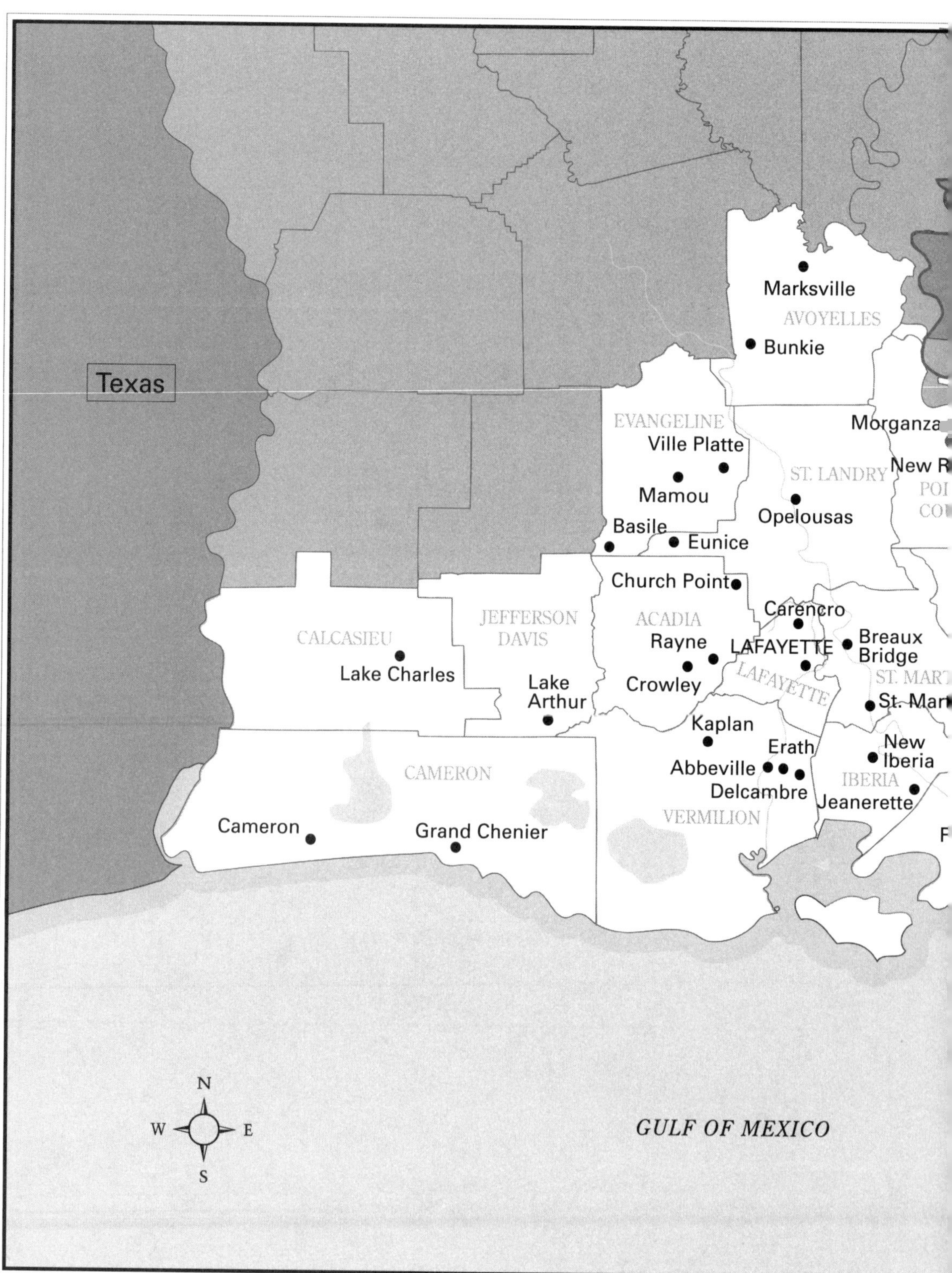
Texas
Marksville
AVOYELLES
Bunkie
EVANGELINE
Ville Platte
Mamou
Basile
Eunice
ST. LANDRY
Opelousas
Morganza
Church Point
Carencro
CALCASIEU
Lake Charles
JEFFERSON DAVIS
Lake Arthur
ACADIA
Rayne
Crowley
LAFAYETTE
LAFAYETTE
Breaux Bridge
Kaplan
Erath
Abbeville
Delcambre
New Iberia
IBERIA
Jeanerette
CAMERON
Cameron
Grand Chenier
VERMILION
GULF OF MEXICO
N
W
E
S

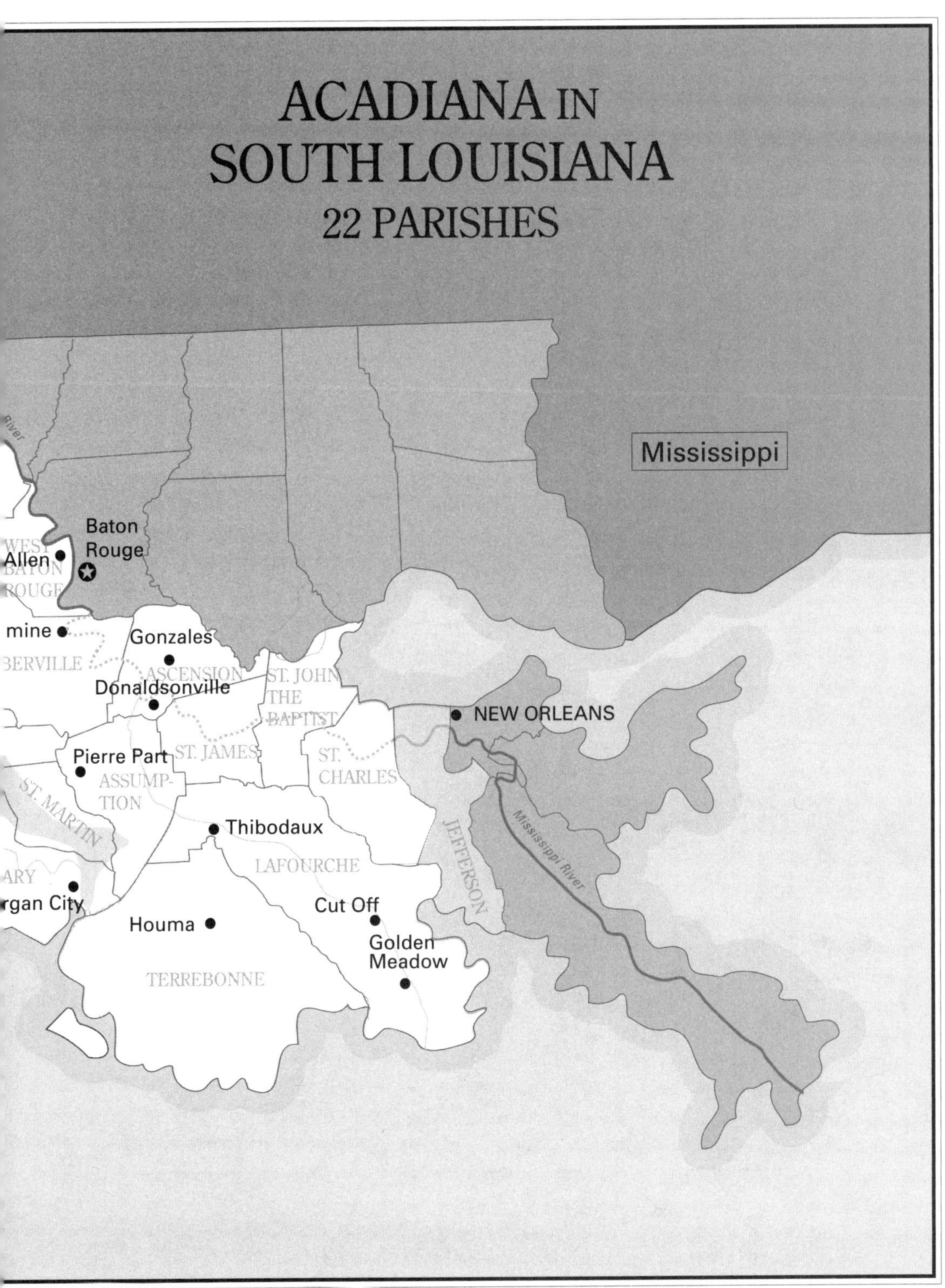
ACADIANA IN SOUTH LOUISIANA
22 PARISHES
Mississippi
River
Baton Rouge
WEST BATON ROUGE
Allen
mine
Gonzales
BERVILLE
ASCENSION
Donaldsonville
ST. JOHN THE BAPTIST
NEW ORLEANS
Pierre Part
ST. JAMES
ST. CHARLES
ASSUMPTION
ST. MARTIN
Thibodaux
JEFFERSON
Mississippi River
LAFOURCHE
ARY
rgan City
Cut Off
Houma
Golden Meadow
TERREBONNE

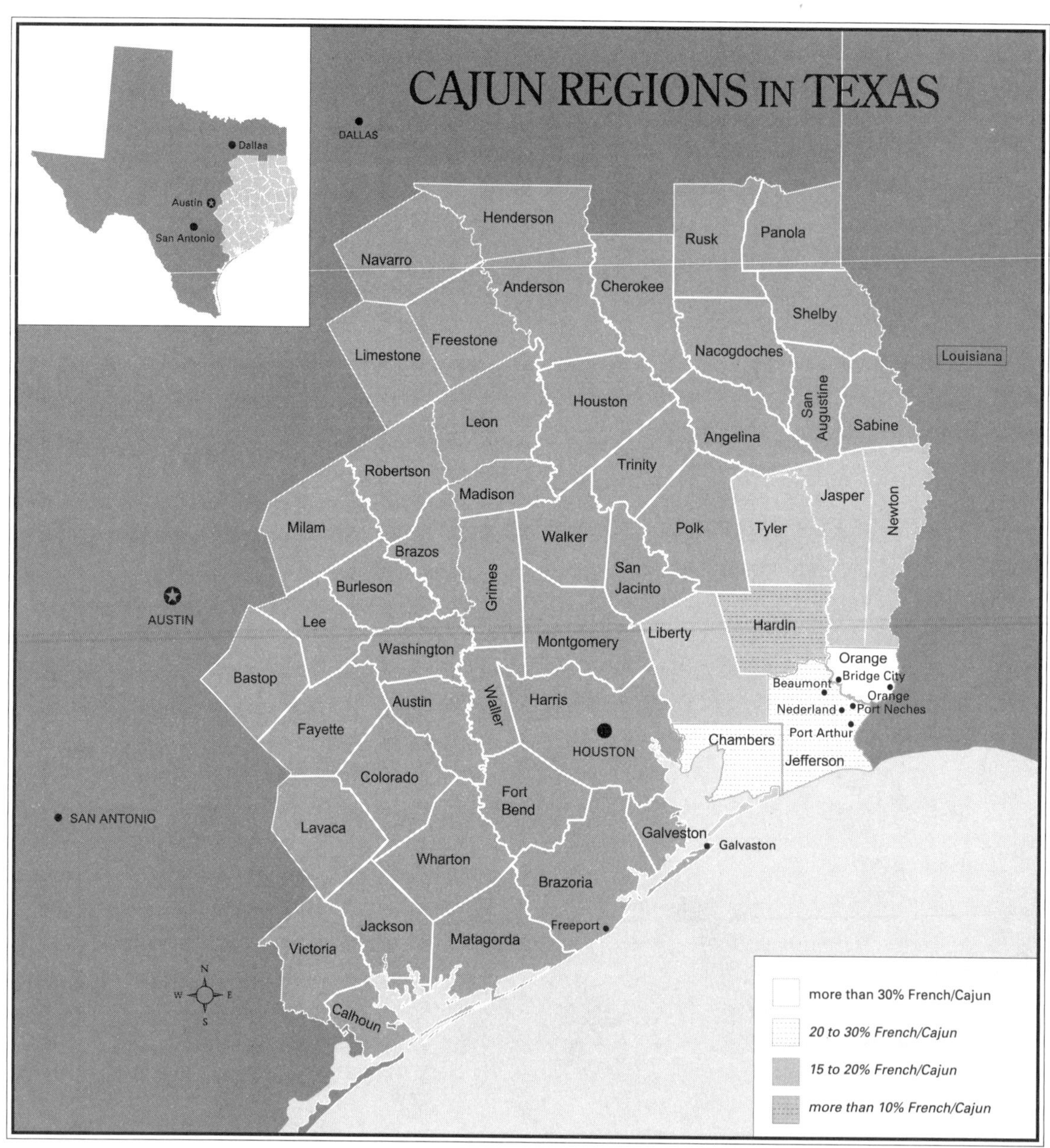
CAJUN REGIONS IN TEXAS
Dallas
Austin
San Antonio
DALLAS
AUSTIN
SAN ANTONIO
HOUSTON
Louisiana
Henderson
Navarro
Anderson
Cherokee
Rusk
Panola
Shelby
Limestone
Freestone
Nacogdoches
San Augustine
Sabine
Houston
Leon
Angelina
Trinity
Robertson
Madison
Jasper
Newton
Milam
Walker
Polk
Tyler
Brazos
San Jacinto
Burleson
Grimes
Lee
Hardin
Liberty
Washington
Montgomery
Orange
Bastop
Bridge City
Beaumont
Orange
Austin
Waller
Harris
Nederland
Port Neches
Fayette
Port Arthur
Chambers
Jefferson
Colorado
Fort Bend
Lavaca
Galveston
Galvaston
Wharton
Brazoria
Jackson
Freeport
Victoria
Matagorda
Calhoun
N
W
E
S
more than 30% French/Cajun
20 to 30% French/Cajun
15 to 20% French/Cajun
more than 10% French/Cajun

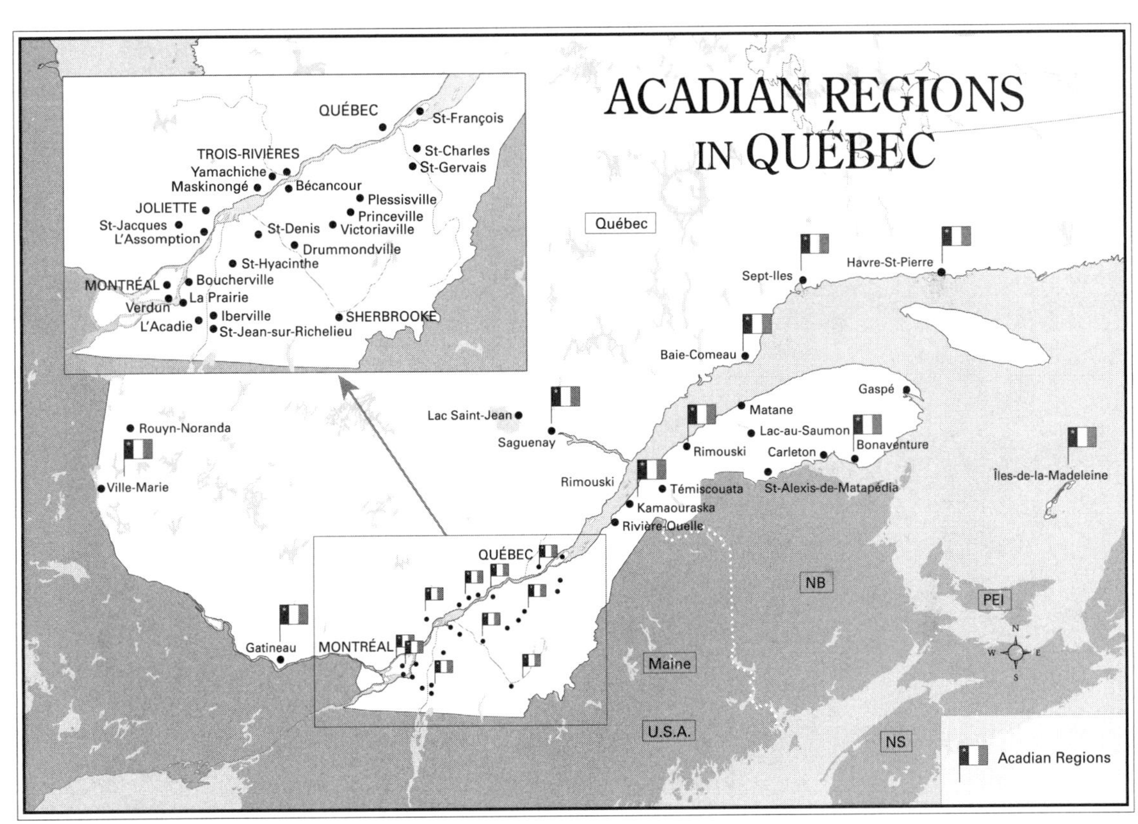
ACADIAN REGIONS
IN QUÉBEC
QUÉBEC
St-François
TROIS-RIVIÈRES
St-Charles
St-Gervais
Yamachiche
Maskinongé
Bécancour
Plessisville
JOLIETTE
Princeville
St-Jacques
St-Denis
Victoriaville
L'Assomption
Drummondville
St-Hyacinthe
MONTRÉAL
Boucherville
La Prairie
Verdun
Iberville
SHERBROOKE
L'Acadie
St-Jean-sur-Richelieu
Québec
Sept-Iles
Havre-St-Pierre
Baie-Comeau
Gaspé
Lac Saint-Jean
Matane
Rouyn-Noranda
Saguenay
Lac-au-Saumon
Rimouski
Carleton
Bonaventure
Îles-de-la-Madeleine
Ville-Marie
Rimouski
Témiscouata
St-Alexis-de-Matapédia
Kamaouraska
Rivière-Ouelle
QUÉBEC
NB
PEI
Gatineau
MONTRÉAL
Maine
U.S.A.
NS
Acadian Regions

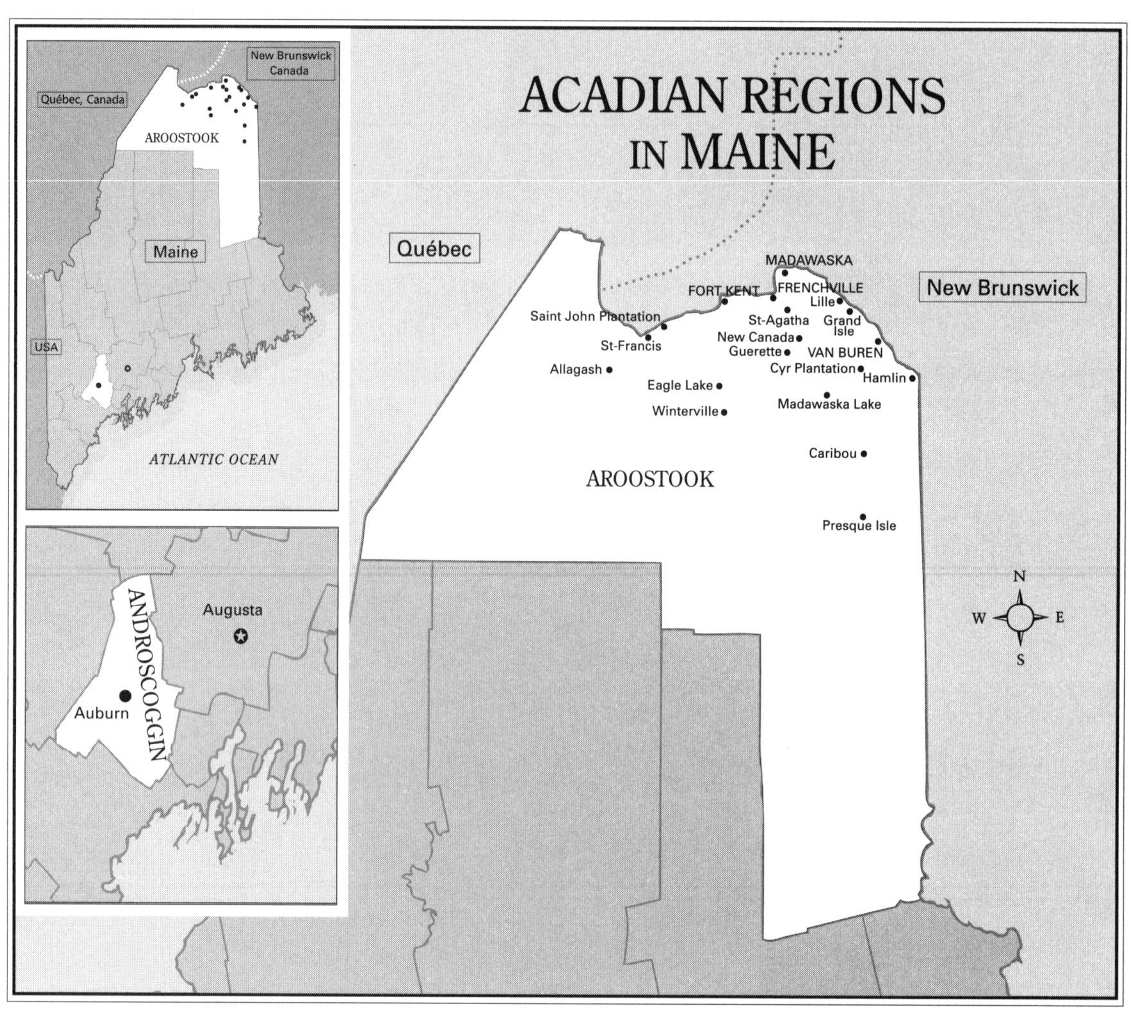

ACADIAN REGIONS IN MAINE
Québec, Canada
New Brunswick Canada
AROOSTOOK
Maine
USA
ATLANTIC OCEAN
ANDROSCOGGIN
Augusta
Auburn
Québec
New Brunswick
MADAWASKA
FORT KENT
FRENCHVILLE
Lille
Saint John Plantation
St-Agatha
Grand Isle
St-Francis
New Canada
Guerette
VAN BUREN
Allagash
Cyr Plantation
Hamlin
Eagle Lake
Madawaska Lake
Winterville
Caribou
AROOSTOOK
Presque Isle
N
W
E
S

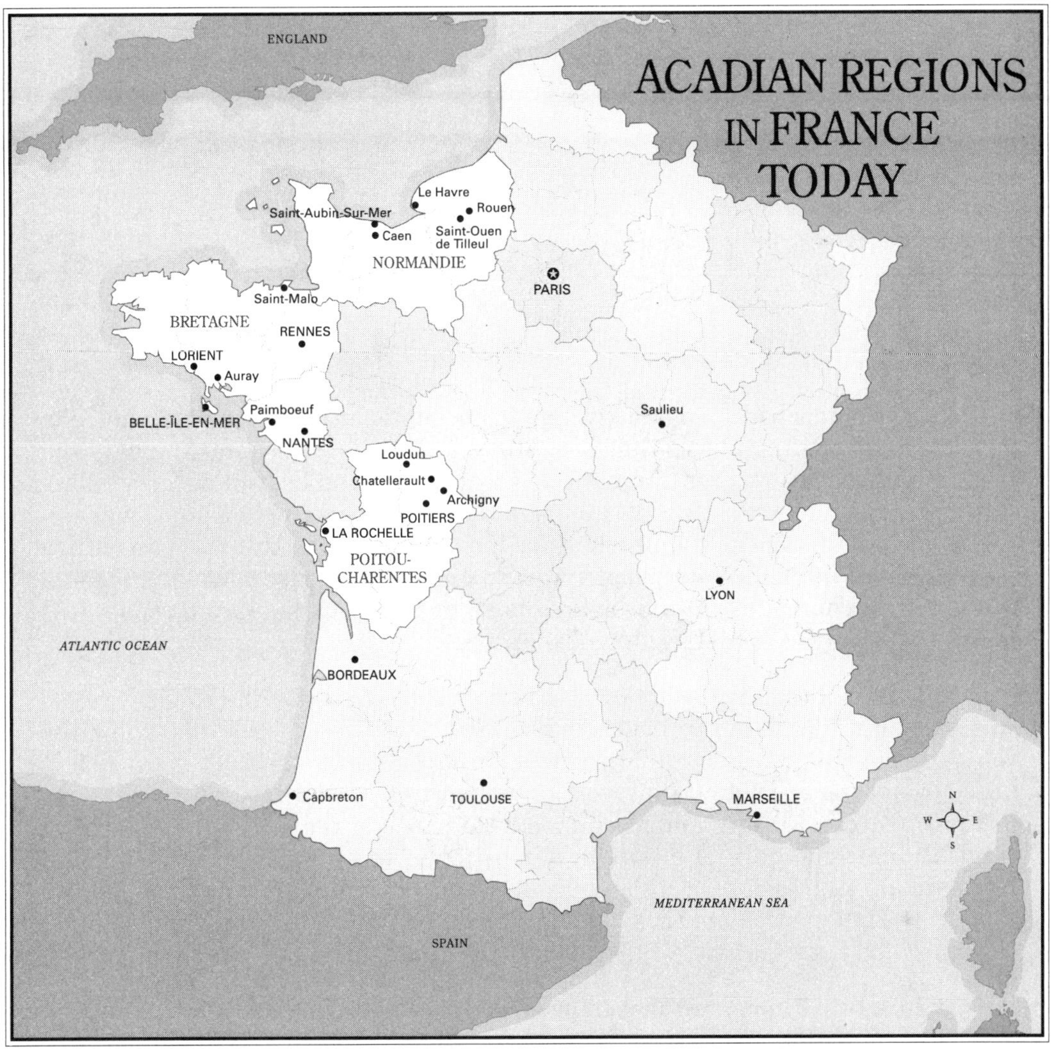

ACADIAN REGIONS IN FRANCE TODAY
ENGLAND
Le Havre
Rouen
Saint-Aubin-Sur-Mer
Caen
Saint-Ouen de Tilleul
NORMANDIE
PARIS
Saint-Malo
BRETAGNE
RENNES
LORIENT
Auray
Paimboeuf
BELLE-ÎLE-EN-MER
NANTES
Saulieu
Loudun
Chatellerault
Archigny
POITIERS
LA ROCHELLE
POITOU-CHARENTES
LYON
ATLANTIC OCEAN
BORDEAUX
Capbreton
TOULOUSE
MARSEILLE
N
W
E
S
MEDITERRANEAN SEA
SPAIN

POITOU-CHARENTES
LOUDUN
La Chaussée
CHATELLERAULT
Leigné
Monthoiron
Archigny
POITIERS
La Puye
LA ROCHELLE
Île d'Aix
ROCHEFORT
Jaulde
Brouage
Royan
Angoulême
Chalais

BELLE-ÎLE-EN-MER
Triboutoux
Borderun
Chubiguer
SAUZON
LE PALAIS
Kergoyet
Antoureau
BANGOR
Kerguénolé
Kernest
Bortémont
Calastren
LOCMARIA
Le Grand-Cosquet
Kerzo

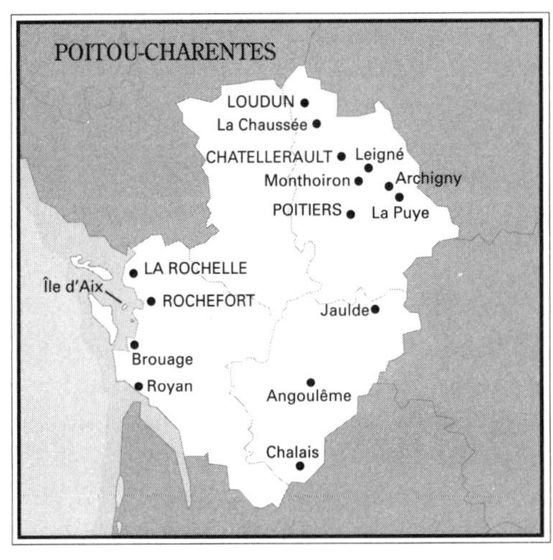

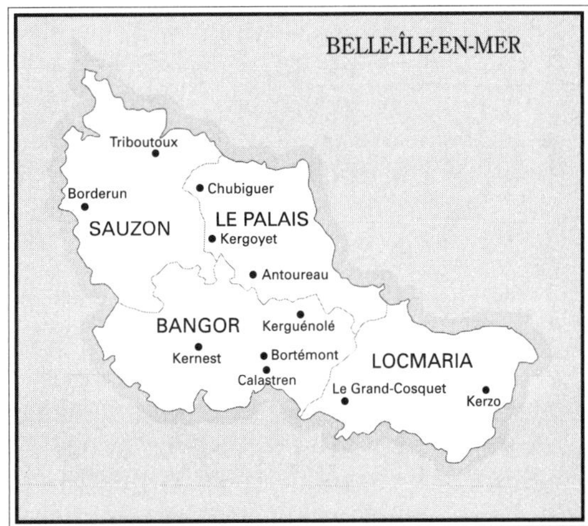

Acadian and Cajun Cultural Tourism

Barry Jean Ancelet

Tourism is based on a fairly simple phenomenon: people leaving home to go elsewhere, visiting places that are different. We like to see, taste, hear, and feel things that are different from what is usually around us. Change, therefore, is a critical factor in tourism. We appreciate being out of our element: the mountains, for coastal people, the beaches, for mountain people, the city, for country people, the country, for city people, and so on. You can also have a change of scenery by a change of culture or language, or by a journey into the past—as noted, for example, in historic towns of interest.

Cultural tourism is based on the notion that people like to visit people who are different, and see how others might live (speak, sing, eat, view the world). For Acadians, cultural tourism is perhaps a little different, because it is based in part on the notion that we like to visit people who are quite similar, so as to recognize a kinship and a common heritage—yet these people are interestingly different because of events in our history. We are right away fascinated by common features: family names, faces, aspects of language, and so on, but we quickly become just as fascinated by the nuances that vary from one Acadie to the other: food, architecture, other aspects of language, and so forth.

In many areas, cultural tourism has become popular; it is considered an ideal driving force for economic development, with the added advantage that it does not pollute the environment. To establish such undertakings, in order to present ourselves well, we must first discover ourselves. The best cultural tourism demands accuracy. If it rings false, it rings loudly. The best lure comes from word of mouth, and for this to occur consistently, authentic experience must be provided. The cultural tourist is interested in discovering the real trails, not artificial theme-park tours. To present oneself well, one must know one's self well, through solid research and knowledge. Details count for a lot. For example, serving meals at Louisbourg *Forteresse* without forks (because there were none at the time) can, in a subtle but essential way, add to the experience of an imaginary journey into the past.

It's one thing to visit history. There are well-defined boundaries that clearly show visitors what you want them to see. In today's cultural tourism, visitors are invited to visit us in our actual setting, where the boundaries are often not as clear. Indeed, in this kind of tourism, you're selling yourself. One must then be very careful not to sell one's self too short. It is important to create ways to conduct visitors to where we would like them to be and prevent them from going where we might not want them to go. It is also necessary to maintain one's dignity by negotiating the visits, so that we avoid becoming mere commodities. When we sell ourselves, we also run the danger of ruining our culture for ourselves. If we present ourselves in a tourist/folklore way long enough, we may end up believing that that's what we really are. Moreover, the pressure of tourists competing for the same lobster, the same scallops, the same strawberries, the same blueberries, and eventually the same rooms and the same houses ... that can raise the prices of these things for the locals.

Care must also be taken so that the culture does not become an exaggerated caricature of itself just to meet the tourists' expectations. Typically, one of the first signs of caricature is the "traditional" costume, which implies that people are there to play a role for the public. This is not necessarily a bad thing. Authentic historical costumes add to the experience of interpretive centers, as seen at the *Habitation* at Port Royal and the *Forteresse* in Louisbourg, both in Nova Scotia. When you are greeted by someone in costume at the entrance, it helps transport you to the past. But a costume can also be tacky, especially if it is an outfit designed to present an imagined "traditional" image. Dressing as a 17th- or 18th-century Acadian at a historical site is one thing, but to dress "in Acadian" is something else. And if that costume were historically accurate, why is there such a big difference between it and those in historical Acadian villages such as in Caraquet, New Brunswick, and Lafayette, Louisiana? We've been stereotyped enough from the outside; we should especially not endorse the phenomenon from the inside.

In Louisiana, we had this problem when the University of Louisiana's sports teams began calling themselves the Ragin' Cajuns. To create a visual rendition of the mascot, the teams had to decide what a Ragin' Cajun looks like. The first efforts were very stereotypical, with fishing or hunting outfits, rubber boots, and so on. But there are just as many Cajuns who wear suits. Then they dressed the mascot as a crawfish and an alligator, thus contributing to a different kind of caricature. Still trying to correctly visualize it, their latest effort is a man dressed as a cayenne pepper, based on yet another stereotype of our traditional cuisine. And on it goes.

Directly related to this costume issue is the phenomenon of Evangeline. It is clear that this character has played and still plays an important role in cultural tourism in all the Acadies. A product of mythical heritage from the American writer Henry Wadsworth Longfellow, Evangeline ends up lending her name to a variety of businesses (as so well sung by Angèle Arsenault) as well as providing a costume and a mythical identity for our festivals and our fancy. She represents a version of the Acadian story as appreciated by Anglo-Canadians and Americans.

I do not want to take anything away from a story revered by many, but there is still a problem of identity hidden therein. Evangeline was a victim. She did not resist. Her story was not problematic, nor was it threatening, as indeed it was for real-life resistance hero Beausoleil Broussard. It is a beautiful love story and, of course, an admirable symbol of loyalty and devotion. In the story, Evangeline leaves without a trace. She even ended her days in Philadelphia. I am not suggesting that we should dump her; we should simply reserve a special place for her and then discover and add other stories—our own stories—which embody our real experiences and our true past. There are historical figures who make us proud, such as resistance fighter Beausoleil Broussard and Joseph and Marie Dugas, who were the first Acadian couple to courageously settle along the rocky Baie Sainte-Marie shore in post-Deportation Nova Scotia. And there are also famous fictional Acadian characters, such as Rosalba and *La Sagouine.*

La Sagouine, created by *Prix Goncourt*–winning author Antonine Maillet and defined on stage and screen by actress Viola Léger, is now immortalized in *Le Pays de la Sagouine*, a tourist visitors' center in Bouctouche, New Brunswick. These Acadian icons should be part of the way we see ourselves, the way we characterize ourselves, balancing out our history with people who have done lasting things and who have left something of value—beyond loyalty—that will inspire future generations to follow.

I find particularly inspiring, for example, the story of Madeleine LeBlanc, from Baie Sainte-Marie, Nova Scotia. After the deportation years, when the LeBlanc family arrived there, they were disheartened to see the difficult conditions facing them. Prior to the deportation they were successful farmers, but they quickly realized that the fertile harvests they had known before the deportation would be impossible in this wooded and rocky region. But it is said that young Madeleine got up and grabbed an axe, saying: "We cried enough. Now it's time to cut wood and build a new home." Here is a heroine for all times. It is this very attitude that allowed Acadians everywhere to survive the events of the deportation and of their recovery in Acadies everywhere. We should learn about Madeleine LeBlanc and celebrate her in Louisiana, New Brunswick, Quebec, New England, as well as in Nova Scotia—wherever there are Acadians today.

Visiting Cajun Louisiana

Cultural tourism has been in Louisiana for some time, inspired largely by nature (the state is known as the Sportsman's Paradise) and by the same *Evangeline*, whose story is told here somewhat differently. That she came through here is one thing, but some in Louisiana had the idea to rewrite history to have her remain among us. Author (and judge) Felix Voorhies fabricated a "true *Evangeline* story," just as fictitious as that of Longfellow, in which she was called Emmeline Labiche and Gabriel was called Louis Arceneaux.

There is a Labiche family in Louisiana, but if there was an Emmeline Labiche it was through the imitation of fiction. There really was a Louis Arceneaux, but he was born in Louisiana, son of Pierre Arceneaux, one of the deportees who settled along the Mississippi at Cabanocey. The story of Emmeline and Louis was no more historical than the story of Evangeline and Gabriel, but it was much more useful for our tourism needs. Because this version of the story unfolded primarily in Louisiana, a tree could be identified in St. Martinville, for tourism purposes, under which she would have waited, hoping to meet her beau.

We're on our third tree. The first Evangeline Oak was struck by lightning and burned. Then information came up showing that this first oak wasn't the right one after all and that the real one was near the Bayou Teche. This second one was a little too close to the bayou; it fell in following high water that had eroded the bank. So then more information came up, showing that this too was not the right oak and that the real one was yet another, close enough to the bayou to be visited, but not too close. It is this one that we now show to visitors, but a few years ago, it was vandalized by youths, and now it's in danger of dying.

And would you believe it, more information has recently come up to indicate that this is not the right oak after all and that the real one is behind a nearby historical building; it is surrounded by a fence where it can be visited, but it's protected. I suggest that if this process continues, we will end up with an oak that wouldn't be as old as the story, and in that case, Emmeline or *Evangeline* might have incubated the acorn for it to hatch.

After playing the title role in the 1929 movie *Evangeline*, shot on location, the actress Delores del Rio, to thank the locals for their warm welcome, gave the village of St. Martinville a statue of herself dressed as Evangeline. It did not take long for this statue of the heroine, placed right next to the church and near its cemetery, to become her tomb, where she was buried after dying of a broken heart upon discovering that Louis, who had given up hope of finding her, was married to another. The real Louis, without having abandoned any Emmeline or Evangeline, married a young girl named Anne; they had a wonderful life and a wonderful family at their home, which Louis called Beaubassin, named after the land of his ancestors (reasoning that his ancestral land had been stolen, but not his memory). I know this because he was one of my ancestors. If he had done as Gabriel, I wouldn't be here today either.

We've had at least as many businesses named for Evangeline as the other Acadies. But for us, the story fades a bit, over time. Fewer and fewer people come to visit her statue. At the same time, a new interpretive center for Acadian history in Louisiana was opened in St. Martinville, where cultural tourism has long been linked to the phenomenon. Some young researchers, including anthropologist Marc David, even wonder if this affection for the history of the Acadians wasn't artificially resurrected and preserved, since there is virtually no direct trace of it in Cajun oral history with regard to events of the deportation.

Yet, there are more and more people who come to Louisiana to listen and dance to our music and enjoy our cuisine, which presents a whole new challenge in contemporary tourism. For a long time, we had a small tourism economy, but with the economic collapse caused by the oil bust of the 1980s, we began to seriously seek out economic alternatives. We looked around us for something to sell, and what we found was our culture and ourselves. On the one hand, it was very convenient; the media, who were just becoming interested in our distinctiveness, were driven by a search for an example of survival and resistance at the sociocultural and linguistic levels in America. This interest was reinforced at the same time by the curiosity of journalists overflowing from the Republican convention in New Orleans, who were looking for stories on local color.

The efforts of the Council for the Development of French in Louisiana (CODOFIL) to preserve and restore French in Louisiana had attracted much attention in a country fascinated by people who speak languages other than English, and who eat food other than hamburgers, hotdogs, and fried chicken. We saw the arrival of more and more tourists wanting to visit French and Cajun Louisiana. We needed something to show them. Restaurants like Mulatte's and Prejean's began presenting Cajun musicians every night of the week, because tourists couldn't wait for the weekend to look for music. This seriously affected the regional music scene, which before had revolved around weekend dances.

We also saw the development of tourist attractions like Acadian Village and Vermilionville, which sought to interpret our past with authentic old buildings collected together at the tourist sites. My grandmother commented that she had never before seen old houses so close to one another. The Jean Lafitte interpretive centers were developed from national and state resources (by the National Park Service). After decades of research by a team of academics and others, these centers produced films and museum exhibits interpreting the history and culture. Also, they all have presentations of living culture, such as music, cooking, oral tradition, and traditional crafts. This has not stopped the development of many other private tourism ventures that interpret the history and culture as suited to their needs.

Pressure from tourism can sometimes produce strange and potentially disruptive effects: Witness the latest "traditional" dances developed here in response to the tourist's demand for more and more sophistication. Then there are the tour buses that stop regularly at what were once small fishing ports along the Atchafalaya Basin, where they drop off hundreds of tourists who take the new guided tours in Louisiana's version of *bateaux-mouches*.

I had the dishonor of being the first to have the idea of bringing a tour bus down the basin levee to give the tourists a little ride in the swamps. If I hadn't done it, someone else would surely have had the idea, but I regret this contribution to cultural tourism whenever a boat full of tourists goes by my boat when I'm in one of my favorite spots, quietly fishing with my kids.

Today, busloads of tourists also arrive from time to time at dance halls and jam sessions. Not only does this disturb the regulars, it also disrupts the owner's idea of what constitutes success. We also saw the proliferation of caricatures for the tourists, with the production, to the point of absurdity, of alligator and crawfish souvenirs.

Today, there are Cajun brands for a whole range of products. You can go fishing in a Cajun boat with a Cajun cooler, filled with Cajun ice and Cajun bait, ad nauseam. For a while we had Cajun beer, made, of course, in Milwaukee. A reporter once asked musician Marc Savoy, "Are you sorry that the Cajuns have been discovered?" Savoy replied, "I'm sorrier that the Cajuns have discovered themselves."

Northern Acadians are faced with several challenges when coming to visit Louisiana. First of all, it's hot down here. The oppressive summer heat immediately rules out a quarter of the year when our cousins could visit. However, if you omit the Louisiana summer, you're missing out on a key aspect of tropical Acadie. On the other hand, it might be a little difficult to find Cajuns even when we are in full view. Then there's New Orleans, where, because of the established tours, many visitors tend to begin their Louisiana visit. It's a great city, with a French name and a great tourist reputation, but even if there are some Cajuns there, this is not exactly what you might call Cajun country. Moreover, up until not too long ago, this Creole city would never have thought of calling itself a Cajun destination. But if enough tourists demand something, we end up supplying it. There are now enough Cajun musicians and restaurants there to meet that demand.

Even if you eventually realize that Lafayette is where you have to go, it's still an urban center with a population of about 150,000 that is greatly affected by the oil and gas industry as well as other influences. In addition to Cajuns, there are also descendants of French Creoles, African Creoles, Spaniards, Germans, and Anglo-Americans. There are also Italians, Lebanese, Chinese, Vietnamese, Thais, and Cambodians. And the Cajuns are influenced by all these neighbors. One can easily find a Babineaux and a Thibodeaux eating cannelonis or kibbes or sushi or shish kebabs or mei fung. It's just as easy to find merguez as it is to find boudin.

It's easier to find people who identify themselves as Cajuns if you go to the smaller towns, but even there it's complicated. People who identify themselves as Cajuns have names like Comeaux, Cormier, Guidry, Thibodeaux, Boudreaux, LeBlanc, Landry, Broussard, and Arceneaux; but they can also be Fontenots, Vidrines, Fusiliers, or Menards (of French and Quebec origins), Romeros, Seguras, Manuels (of Spanish origin), Abshires, Walkers, Clarks, Putnams, or McGees (whose origins are obvious), or even Touchet (of Czech origin)! These people almost always have Lejeunes, Bernards, Moutons, Babins, Landrys, and so on, perched on the branches of the family tree, but it is not always apparent.

Finally, once you've made contact with all these people, they may or may not speak French, may or may not love Cajun music, may or may not even eat okra. That depends on their own experiences and their own response to the efforts made to eliminate the language and culture. And then there is the challenge of nature: one can't forget the alligators and snakes. There is, however, one consistency: mosquitoes.

Visiting Acadian Nova Scotia

The irony of Acadian tourism in Nova Scotia is simply that the historic sites and the sites of present-day Acadian communities are not in the same locations, because the Acadians were expelled from their original farmlands. The purpose of the deportation was to seize the best quality lands from the Acadians in the fertile valley between Grand-Pré and Port Royal. Therefore, to tell the Acadian story here, room must be made inside an area deemed psychologically and symbolically hostile.

It is not at all impossible. The new interpretive center at Grand-Pré succeeds quite well at making proper usage of this historic site. But in order to show an Acadian presence, the Grand-Pré Centre and the *Habitation* at Port-Royal are forced to import Acadians from the actual Acadian regions in the province. And to properly celebrate Acadian Days in Grand-Pré, people from the regions have to travel several hours to stay but a few hours. Yet, for visitors looking for a cultural catharsis, there are other ways to tap into the powerful potential of these places.

From my own experience, I added another dimension for several of my friends on a visit to Lookoff, on top of the Blomidon mountain, overlooking the ancestral Acadian lands of Grand-Pré. I asked them, if the events of 1755 had never occurred, what piece of land in Grand-Pré Centre did they think could be theirs?

Perhaps your guests could visit the Old Burying Grounds in Wolfville (the town neighboring Grand-Pré) to contemplate the graves of the people who replaced their ancestors in the area, at which time you could explain to them that they cannot visit old Acadian cemeteries because they've been plowed under and covered over a long time ago, to wipe out any trace. Or they could visit nearby Horton Landing, to walk on the same grounds as did the deportees just before they were loaded on the boats; while they were there, another kind of tourist would come to visit the monument to the New England Planters.

Or they could visit Fort Anne's Gardens in Annapolis Royal (this town once carried the name of Port Royal, when the old 1605 capitol site of Acadie was moved here in 1636), not so much for the flowers or even the interesting thatch-roofed Acadian cottage for tourists, as for the reeds and dikes established by the predeportation Acadians, which are still there today.

It must be said that the government has nevertheless provided some great opportunities to relate this story via the sites at Louisbourg *Forteresse*, the Port Royal *Habitation*, and the Grand-Pré National Historic Site, recently recognized by UNESCO as a World Heritage Site. Also, with Acadian help, the government is currently developing Melanson Settlement near Port Royal, and they've announced plans for a new site in Beaubassin, on the present border between Nova Scotia and New Brunswick—an impressive list of sites to commemorate a difficult history. The irony is that non-Acadian areas of Wolfville, Annapolis Royal, Amherst, Louisbourg, and other places associated with Acadian history, are obliged to learn how to present such a tour if they are going to develop the affective potential of cultural tourism. We're seeing the signs.

At the *Congrés mondial acadien* in Nova Scotia in 2004, for the first time there were Acadian flags all around the valley between Grand-Pré and Port Royal. I asked some English Canadians, "Why all the Acadian flags?" One answered, "Well, you know, the Acadians are coming." "Back?" I added. He didn't answer.

One of the Acadians working in Grand-Pré told me a similar story. One of her English neighbors in Wolfville told her she was leaving the area during the Congress so as not to have to put up with all the commotion. The Acadian lady from Meteghan Station shared with me that, in the past, she probably would have apologized for disturbing, but this time she had quite another reaction, answering instead, "Leave your keys. We may need the room." I made her laugh when I suggested another response could be, "Remember to take with you only what you can carry, and we'll have a boat waiting for you at Horton Landing."

Dating back to 1605, Annapolis Royal is described as one of the oldest European settlements in North America; but it should be pointed out that Annapolis Royal is still a phenomenon of English culture. The date 1605 goes back to the French, who settled on the other side of the river at the *Habitation* (now rebuilt by the Canadian government and open as a historical park). The English Captain Samuel Argall and his men destroyed this settlement in 1613, and the English did not arrive at the new site of Port Royal (Annapolis Royal) until much later. This is a detail, but failing to clarify it muddles two histories just to claim an early date.

With historical tourism there is the danger of getting stuck in a romanticized past. Acadian Historic Village installations, whether in Pubnico, Nova Scotia, or in Caraquet, New Brunswick, are very interesting and are a very effective way to provide the visitor with a unique experience, but should we rely solely on history to represent us? Visitors could have a pretty good idea of who we were, but what do we do with who we are? What can we do outside of historical villages?

The communities of Nova Scotia where Acadians live today are quite interesting to visit—whether in the communities of Baie Sainte-Marie (Clare Municipality), Par-en-bas (Argyle Municipality), or in Chéticamp and Île-Madame on Cape-Breton Island, among others—and visiting them is essential to understanding the Acadians as they have evolved into contemporary times. Many Cajuns have already visited Nova Scotia (and the reverse), especially during the previous *Congrès mondial acadien.* In Baie Sainte-Marie alone, Jean-Douglas Comeau, former director of the summer French-immersion courses offered at the *Université Sainte-Anne*, in Church Point, estimates that approximately 1,000 Cajuns have studied there since 1989. And during their stay, many of their families have come to visit them and the region.

How do we meet the challenge of contemporary cultural tourism? First, we must identify areas of potential interest and then use them while taking care not to pollute the natural, social, and cultural environments. There are many beautiful lakes in the Baie Sainte-Marie area, where there could be tours, but we should be very careful not to ruin these lakes for the residents who have built cottages and houses there specifically because it is quiet and secluded. Imagine the popular restaurant *La Cuisine Robichaud,* in Saulnierville, which specializes in traditional and contemporary Acadian fare, with only Quebeckers and Americans for a whole summer. Thursday night at a local *"bootleggeux's"* (private home where alcohol is served) would never be the same if a tour bus came to visit. And then there is the pressure that can come from visitors looking to experience linguistic tourism.

There is also a great potential for nature-based tourism in the Acadies. The clean, open ocean and the lakes of northern Acadie are incredibly beautiful for Louisiana Cajuns, who are impressed by the clear water. Likewise, the

Louisiana bayous and swamps, with their Spanish moss–covered trees growing in the water, seem to fascinate northern Acadians. But be careful what you wish for because it might come true. Do we really want local versions of *bateaux-mouches* everywhere?

There is also great potential in the Northern Acadies for sea excursions. There are lobster fishermen who are otherwise not busy in the summer and who would possibly be available to offer sightseeing tours. Recently I had the opportunity to take a wonderful trip in the Tusket Islands (south of the Acadian village of Wedgeport, Nova Scotia), where fishermen relocate during lobster season to fish and sleep in their pittoresque island shanties for weeks at a time. I am sure that many Cajun tourists would pay good money for a trip like that. Captain Victor LeBlanc offered me this trip free of charge simply because he wanted to show me the beauty that is dear to him. Cajuns are fascinated by whales; Acadians are fascinated by alligators.

The woods have potential here, as do the grasslands back home, for horse trail rides or birding trips. But tourism is a business, and that changes everything. There are endless regulations for passenger safety. Then there is the problem of Bay of Fundy fog in southwestern Nova Scotia. And in Louisiana, heat is a problem. In all the Acadies, there are the problems of mosquitoes and black flies. If we decide to develop anything, it would be better to go slowly and think about the potential impact.

The transportation issue to Nova Scotia can be challenging for Cajuns and others. By car, from Louisiana, it takes 36 hours. By plane, you have to land in Halifax and then you need to rent a car and drive for another three hours before making it to any of the Acadian regions. Once you're there, not many hotels are available. B&Bs are starting to grow a little; they can be preferable to the local hotels because they offer a warmer contact. The reverse trip, for Acadians of the north visiting Louisiana's Cajun regions, obviously offers some of the same challenges. A dream come true would be to have direct flights between Lafayette and Moncton or between New Orleans and Halifax. In the meantime, never mind the distance and time it takes to get there, the visits are definitely worthwhile.

Conclusion

At the end of the day, the greatest asset of Acadian cultural tourism is the people who allow, on their own terms and without costumes, contact with real Acadian life. My parents came with me one summer. In Baie Sainte-Marie, they had the chance to meet Arcade Comeau at *La Forêt Acadienne* and Camille Maillet at the *Vieux Moulin* in Bangor. An immediate friendship grew, based on an affinity and a real interest in exploring their ties. They exchanged stories and gifts and plans for the future.

Camille and my father discovered that they were the same age, and for hours they exchanged stories from their younger days. They'd still be there if we had not had to leave. They immediately understood each other well, and this was based not on shared experiences but on a way of understanding life, and how their experiences were made similar by the conditions that shaped them. As much as my father and my friend were impressed by the saw mill and the woods, what they enjoyed most were Camille and Arcade. The greatest strength of this kind of cultural tourism is not in the places but in the faces; less in nature and more in human nature.

There is plenty of potential for building relationships between the Acadies. I know more and more Cajuns who are interested in spending "air-conditioned" summers in the north. And if you go to visit one part of northern Acadie, you may as well travel all over. And right away you understand that you have to come back more than once. All the elements are certainly in place for building good business, but this should be done in a careful and respectful manner.

And by the way, back home in Louisiana, the winters are a lot less cold, and we seriously celebrate *Mardi Gras* around March, which is, for us, the beginning of spring. Being a dispersed people could have advantages after all—enough to make former British Gov. Charles Lawrence spin like a top in his grave—if we learn to become a migratory people, even if only for vacation.

CAJUN COOKING 101

Mary Broussard Perrin

What is the nature of Cajun food? The books will tell you that it's a rustic and spicy *mélange* (mixture) of the cuisines of many ethnicities—Cajun, African, Spanish, German, Native American, and Caribbean—and produced with mostly local ingredients. And although it is a rustic, rural fare, I can unequivocally say that it is among the tastiest cuisines in the world. Growing up as only half-Cajun with a mother who was Irish and German, I ate mostly "American" food. But my father, being a Broussard, could not live long without the staples of the kind of home cooking he grew up with: gumbo, jambalaya, rice and gravy, *sauce piquant.*

My mother had to learn everything she knew about the Cajun dishes that he loved from her mother-in-law in quick lessons, because Grandmère lived an hour and a half away. I guess Mom was a fairly good student, because my first memory of Cajun cooking was of gumbo, a thick, spicy soup consisting of chicken and sausage or shellfish, seasoning, vegetables, and a thickener called *roux* (a browned oil and flour mixture). It is a delectable and comforting dish, but chicken gumbo was a messy one for a child. I was usually lucky enough to get a meaty drumstick in my bowl, but it had to be picked up to be eaten—at least by a child—with the fingers, and invariably the juice from the broth ran down my hand all the way to my elbow. Gumbo, as we Cajuns know, is a warm, comforting, and aromatic winter dish, but in winter we wore long sleeve shirts and sweaters to the table—and thus a lot of juice soaked into a lot of fabric! It was definitely a two-napkin dish. The "ick" factor there was large.

And even ickier was chicken and okra gumbo, okra being a pod-like vegetable brought over from Africa with the slaves centuries ago. The ick factor in okra gumbo, as I remember it, was a stringy, virulent slime which oozed from the pod once sliced. An experienced cook knows to smother down a tomato or two along with what we call the Holy Trinity of Cajun seasoning vegetables—onions, celery, and bell pepper—and the acid from tomatoes will cut the okra's slime. But an inexperienced Cajun cook like my mother somehow missed this important lesson and seemed content to eat the slimy stuff anyway. I was not a picky eater myself so I would usually give it a go, but gumbo was not one of my top ten favorite foods.

But then, like all children, I did grow up. I fell in love with my soon-to-be husband Warren, and also with Warren's family, and especially with his mother who was an excellent Cajun cook. Her rice and gravy was to die for. I had never tasted anything like it. She used a big cast iron pot to brown her meat; this rendered the gravy as thick and dark as liquid ebony. I could eat a large soup bowl of nothing but this humble but finely crafted dish and be completely satisfied. Her gumbo was also good, excellent in fact—once I got past the shock of being served my first bowl, which contained a chicken foot still attached to the drumstick. I am quite sure I gasped inadvertently when I discovered this ingredient, but my mother-in-law calmly took a big cooking spoon, removed it from my bowl and put it back in the pot. "Chicken feet," she instructed, "impart a wonderful flavor to the gumbo, but usually they never leave the pot. I'm sorry about that," she said. "That was just a slip up." But I have never been quite sure that it was. I believe it to have been a test to see how I would stack up as a future daughter-in-law—a city girl, and worse yet, one who was studying art in college. After all, I was the only person at the table to have been served a chicken foot in my bowl. "And of course," she added smugly, "I did cut the toenails off." I had to let that tidy tidbit of information soak in for a minute, but to my credit, I did get past it and learned to enjoy her thick, fragrant gumbo served over rice with a delicious side of potato salad.

But chicken feet in gumbo was certainly not my only hurdle to overcome on my road to becoming a true connoisseur of Cajun cooking—and a passable daughter-in-law. My next "task" was to learn to love a dish called *débris* (in English this means "trash"). *Débris* was a thick stew also served over rice and containing quite good cuts of beef, but also a whole slew of organ meats: kidneys, liver, heart, and my all-time least favorite, spleen, a spongy organ that required a whole lot of chewing before it was in any shape to be swallowed. It was definitely an unattractive dish full of thick, bouncy arteries and veins and other more anonymous chunks—not pretty to look at, but with an unexpected buttery taste, smooth and spicy, and chock-a-block with flavor.

In summertime, after a big heavy meal at Warren's parent's house, we would wait a couple of hours to let our food digest and then we would have dessert. And what a dessert it was! Thick and heavenly homemade vanilla ice cream served up in big soup bowls rather than dainty dessert bowls. The "cream" in this ice cream came straight from the cow and, only having had store-bought ice cream up to this point in my life, I had never tasted anything so rich and fabulous. I wasn't sure I could get through such a huge serving, however, but I soldiered on, groaning just a bit towards the end. "What?" said Mrs. Perrin, "*Chère,* that was only the first flavor." Still to come was the strawberry and then the peach, and sometimes the ice cream was served atop warm *gateau syrop* (syrup cake). Might I humbly add that none of these people was fat.

I went on to get married and, like my mother, knew more about eating Cajun food than cooking it. We were on a strict budget in those early days because Warren was in law school and I was bringing home a teacher's salary. So it was a special treat the day he came home with a sack of *boudin.* I had eaten boudin (a sausage-like dish containing a spicy rice and meat mixture) in other places but had never actually "owned" any myself. Neither Warren nor I knew one vital piece of information about boudin: Did it come from the store already cooked or was it still raw? We decided to be on the safe side and cook it gently in a pot of simmering water. Of course, as we later learned, boudin came ready to eat, and our savory special treat turned into a pot full of watery rice dressing, the casing having completely disintegrated in the hot water. I went on to correct this and many other Cajun cooking disasters, such as tomato sauce does not go well with crawfish, and shrimp turn to mush if you cook them for more than five minutes.

But Cajun cuisine, once mastered, is simple to cook, with crawfish *étouffée*, a dish fit for a king, being one of the simplest and most attractive dishes I know. The bounty provided by the land and the waterways of South Louisiana, combined with our great ethnic diversity, has provided the lucky residents of Acadiana with a true feast for the senses. And although Cajun cooking was once a well-kept secret served up only in rural south Louisiana kitchens and at your grandmère's house on Sunday, there are now Cajun restaurants around the world. But if you are in Alabama or Georgia in the wintertime and see gumbo on the menu, ask the waiter if it is made with a *roux*. If he twangs, "A what?" just say, "Never mind."

Louisiana's Cultural Gumbo

May Gwin Waggoner

South Louisiana is a study in contrasts and contradictions. Moss grows in the air, swamp maples turn red in the spring, and bayous flow in two directions. Until recently, the region's public radio station devoted Saturday mornings to zydeco music and Saturday afternoons to live broadcasts from the Metropolitan Opera. Four-year-olds play accordion, and older couples who can hardly walk nonetheless manage a turn on the dance floor. From the hot, muggy days when slaves' work songs rang out in the humid Louisiana sky, to the cold winter nights when early Acadians gathered around the fireplace to sing and dance, through physical suffering and exile and isolation and neglect and economic hardship and war, music has been one constant, a way to keep the past alive, to mark events, to mourn and rejoice.

History books tell us that during the 17th and 18th centuries, the New World afforded opportunities to explorers and colonists who built a nation. These books neglect, however, the fact that the nation was also built by unwilling immigrants. Among them were two very dissimilar groups transported to the nascent colonies against their will and undergoing similar hardships. Thousands of miles apart, Africans and Acadians alike were forced into the holds of overcrowded ships, their families divided and destroyed.[1] The bodies of those who died of illness or dehydration or starvation were thrown overboard.[2] After weeks and months at sea, the human cargo was unloaded in the colonies. The Africans, in chains, were treated as commodities; the Catholic Acadians were shunned as pariahs. In some southern colonies, the Acadians were taken directly from the boats to the fields, where as indentured servants they worked alongside the slaves. In some northern colonies, many died in the streets, neglected by those who had fled religious intolerance in England. The slaves and the exiles eventually found a home in Louisiana. Their parallel experiences produced two different musics, "separate but equal," each imbued with its own flavor.

To outsiders, the word Louisiana conjures up exotic images of moss-draped live oaks, bayous, alligators, and accordions. The terms "Cajun," "Creole," and "zydeco" are often used interchangeably, and misconceptions abound. Restaurants in the United States and in Europe advertise as "Cajun" or "Creole" food that is merely charred or peppered, and New Orleans advertises the Cajun identity as its own. Those who "discovered" Cajun music in the 1970s celebrate the resurrection of a phenomenon that never died; those who discovered zydeco at the same time ignore three centuries' worth of tradition. The story of Louisiana dance is not the story of a series of dances but rather the story of one long dance, a river that swept up the new and deposited the superfluous at every bend.

It is tempting to compartmentalize Louisiana dances neatly into Cajun and zydeco. However, the truth is more complicated. Though an awareness of a black style existed as far back as the 1920s, black and white musicians all played what they called "French music." There was no detailed nomenclature; blacks often referred to their style as "lala" or Creole music.

The Cajun culture is in many ways atypical of the Protestant anglophone Deep South; however, in one essential way the two cultures are similar. Though Southern segregation was imposed by law, blacks and whites worked side by side in the fields and learned from one another for two centuries. Unlike the situation in the North, where laws promoted interaction but where de facto segregation separated the races, a camaraderie born of familiarity developed in Louisiana and all over the South. Custom transcended laws; music crossed artificial barriers. Musicians of both races performed together, and contacts and friendships encouraged the exchange and incorporation of ideas and musical styles. The radio made no racial distinctions. Just as an anglo-American boy from Tupelo synthesized his unique style from white popular music, blues, rock, R&B, and what was known in the 1950s as "hillbilly" music, descendants of slaves and exiles contributed to one another's musical styles. Lawrence Levine's characterization of zydeco as "a hybrid with a strong African base" can be applied equally well to Cajun music.[3]

A definition of terms is definitely in order. The word Cajun derives from the American pronunciation of the word *Acadien*, which refers to settlers who colonized the Canadian Maritime Provinces beginning in the early 17th century. The name zydeco has given rise to debate and disagreement,[4] but the term generally refers to music created by Louisiana's black Creoles after World War II, when the a cappella *juré* tradition was instrumentalized and used as dance music.[5] The term Creole has the most definitions, often contradictory. The word comes from the Spanish *criollo*, "native to America." The first definition refers to descendants of Old World stock born in the New World but kept "pure" of New World blood. The second definition is just the opposite; it describes that which has adapted to the climate of Louisiana and includes creole tomatoes and creole horses which were suited to the Louisiana climate. Later, the term served to differentiate French-speaking black people, called Creoles of color, from anglophone African Americans.[6] Today's white and black Creoles are conscious of their shared French heritage. Although this South Louisiana communality may create confusion in the minds of outsiders, it is the very mixing of traditions that has ensured their cultural survival.

For the past 50 years, an enthusiasm for taxonomy has artificially compartmentalized dance music into pop, rock, R&B, blues, swamp pop, jazz, soul, hip-hop, rap, gospel, rock 'n' roll, heavy metal, country, reggae, and others and has differentiated Cajun from zydeco.[7] This fragmentation may satisfy ethnomusicologists but not musicians, who have always vigorously resisted labels. Canray Fontenot, for example, supposedly disparaged the term zydeco, stating "I don't play that zodiac music."[8] At a time when Yo-Yo Ma records Appalachian folk music with other classical musicians and jazz violin is a recognized instrument, perhaps we, too, should refuse artificial musical boundaries. Like a Venn diagram, traditions overlap; the descendants of musicians of both races who worked together centuries ago in the fields now play together onstage.

Any cultural manifestation must adapt or die. Creolization, or adaptation to New World conditions, infused a hybrid vigor to contemporary Cajun and zydeco dances. Innovation was a means to cultural survival. The theories of creolization and retention can be applied equally to Louisiana; dances adapted to Louisiana continue to carry their European past in them. What forms the unique character of social dance in contemporary Louisiana is the ethnic blending that continues to redefine the culture.

The Cajuns and Their Dances

In a culture obsessed by food, South Louisianans like to describe their culture as a gumbo. This thick, spicy soup begun with a French roux includes fowl and game from the Louisiana bayous and prairies, rice and garlic from Spain, and okra from Africa, often spiced with Caribbean tasso and peppers and washed down with German beer! In contrast to European cultures in the United States that either assimilated or isolated themselves, the Acadians' very survival depended on cooperation and interaction. Those hardy souls from Poitou and the Vendée who arrived in Acadie (Nova Scotia, Canada) in 1604 were joined 30 years later by colonists from other regions of France and Europe. Freed from feudal constraints, they experienced their first taste of personal freedom and depended on one another and on the indigenous Mi'kmaq. At the time of their brutal expulsion four generations later, the only things they shared with France were their language and their religion. Ironically, these first northern Europeans to settle North America were also the first victims of ethnic cleansing there. The term ethnic cleansing is not too strong: Acadie simply disappeared. By 1765 when the Acadians arrived in Louisiana, now a Spanish possession, the dominant French culture of New Orleans absorbed the new arrivals from Malaga and the Canary Islands more easily than it accepted the Acadians.[9] New Orleans white Creoles, descendants of colonists who arrived as early as 1699, cherished their ties to France and considered themselves superior to the rural Acadian peasants. As the result of generous land grants, the Acadians settled along the Mississippi River in what would be called the Acadian Coast.[10] Many Spanish colonists moved westward with the Acadians; families named Romero and Miguez settled in the town of New Iberia. After the 1803 Louisiana Purchase and Louisiana's transformation to statehood in 1812, the Acadians continued to live along the bayous and on the prairies in relative isolation and were even fairly uninvolved in the Civil War.[11]

Substantial immigrant waves at the end of the 17th century and during the 19th century added new ethnicities to Louisiana. An Afro-Creole population arrived in Louisiana as early as 1791 as a result of a revolution in the island of Saint-Domingue, and a group of refugees from Cuba doubled the population of New Orleans in 1809.[12] A number of Napoleon III's soldiers settled in Avoyelles Parish after their disastrous defeat in Mexico in 1862, French journalists sought refuge in New Orleans after the revolutions of 1830 and 1848, young men left Germany to avoid forced conscription at the time of the Franco-Prussian War in 1870, Irishmen fled starvation, and other hardy souls sought their fortunes in the New World. And the Louisiana Cajuns continued to plow their fields, set their traps, live simply off the land, and quietly absorb new settlers with names like McGee, McCauley, Reed, Schexnayder, Huber, and Dubcek.[13] In the prairies and swamps, they lived as they had lived since their arrival, despite the social upheavals engendered by the war. Their dances reflected their European heritage; many a couple courted to a waltz, a quadrille, a square dance, a Virginia reel, a polka, or a "put-your-foot-right-there."[14]

Meanwhile, in New Orleans and surrounding areas, the French language languished for 50 years after the War of Secession before its death in the early years of the 20th century. The military occupation of the South, ironically referred to as "Reconstruction," destroyed both the francophone and anglophone economies of the region.[15] Both blacks and whites realized that their children's economic security depended on their knowledge of English and embraced the language of the anglophone conquerors. By World War I, despite efforts to preserve it, the French language was breathing its last in the New Orleans area.

As the 20th century dawned, the Louisiana Cajuns' isolation began to evaporate due to Teddy Roosevelt's melting-pot philosophy, the discovery of oil in 1901, and American military service. In 1916, a federal law established mandatory schooling to be effected in English. The Great Depression saw the exodus of many Louisiana Cajuns to East Texas, where they worked in the shipyards and the oil industry. There they spoke English, were called "Cajuns," and were exposed to new music. Louisiana soldiers returned from World War II with a broader worldview and a more sophisticated musical ear.

Mandatory schooling in English dealt a blow to the French language. The social stigma attached to children who failed first grade because they could not understand their teachers added to the humiliation of being Cajun, and at least two generations of parents refused to teach French to their children. As in New Orleans, many parents stopped using French at home, believing that success for their children depended on their assimilation. Ironically, the Cajuns were exiled in the very region they had claimed 150 years before.

The intrusion of the outside world into the Acadian community resulted in a series of changes in music and dance on several levels. The first change was social. Nineteenth-century *fais-do-do*, or *bals de maison* (house dances), had been family affairs held in private homes where behavior was closely monitored.[16] These house dances disappeared in the 1920s as public dance halls opened. There, young people were less supervised, and group dances gave way to couple dances.

The second change was a natural simplification in the dance tunes and steps that European peasants had brought to America. In a loose cultural application of Gresham's law, either the simpler Cajun steps drove complicated figures out of existence or the dances were modified as different ethnic groups sought a common denominator on the dance floor.[17] Circle dances became couple dances, complicated figures disappeared, the polka evolved into the familiar two-step, and the mazurka was influenced and modified by the waltz.

The third change was one of musical structure. Like their European ancestors, the Acadians had generally separated dance music and vocal music except during Lent, when they interpreted the Catholic church's ban on "music" as a ban on orchestral music alone and danced to a cappella vocal melodies.[18] In contrast, traditional African music present in Louisiana for two centuries had always combined movement with vocals. As the 20th century dawned, these European and African traditions began to blend, and in the 1930s, musicians started alternating verses with instrumental interludes. Elements from the blues tradition entered the mix, and dance bands eventually adopted a sixteen-bar instrumental bridge from popular and bluegrass music.

The fourth change occurred as musicians added instruments from their own musical traditions. The traditional Acadian band composed of fiddle, triangle, and sometimes harmonica grew to include Spanish guitar, African and Caribbean percussion, and German diatonic accordion. A more complex timbre resulted. At the same time, the accordion's limits in keys and notes resulted in simpler and less chromatic tunes. Because the accordion's volume made it the dominant instrument, vocalists were forced to sing in its key and on a higher pitch in order to be heard.

The fifth change of the twentieth century was technological. With electric amplification, the fiddler no longer had to bear down on the strings, and the style became less forced. The electric guitar and the steel guitar entered the orchestra from country-western music; the drum set reinforced strong African rhythms. Elements of rock 'n' roll and the new sounds of bluegrass, rhythm and blues, jitterbug, rock, and pop blended into what became known as "swamp pop."

The Festival that Started a Revolution

Cajun dances would no doubt have remained simple, and perhaps would have been lost, had it not been for a shift in the region's cultural equity, defined by folklorist Alan Lomax as the balance between preservation and innovation. In the middle years of the twentieth century, innovation, tradition, and fortunate circumstances combined in a serendipitous way to alert the outside world to the existence of a lively regional music that defied classification. Rooted in music, the consequences of this new awareness extended far beyond dance halls, and repercussions were felt even 40 years later as far away as Buckingham Palace.

The *Newport Folk Festival* of 1964 was a turning point in Cajun music and dance. The overwhelming success there of both black and white musicians not only made the outside world take notice of South Louisiana's vibrant sound, it also awakened its own citizens to the unique music they had always taken for granted and had sometimes disparaged as "chanky chank." A grassroots return to original heritage music followed, and the rest of the country responded. Tourism increased. Area restaurants began to feature Cajun bands every night.[19] Cajun French activists pressured the state legislature to establish the Council for the Development of French in Louisiana in 1968 to preserve the French language, to add it to school curricula, and to restore it as an official language of the state.[20] Francophone militants established Cajun French as a literary language by writing poetry and producing plays for the French-speaking population.[21] In addition, one Louisiana attorney's thirteen-year campaign against the British Crown finally resulted in the formal acknowledgement on December 9, 2003, by Queen Elizabeth II of the role Britain had played in the exile of the Acadians.[22]

Anyone listening to Dewey Balfa recordings from before this festival and afterward will notice a distinct fiddling-style change toward complexity, as the musicians responded to audience attention and interest. As bands experimented with complex sounds and timbres, young dancers' movements followed suit. Most had grown up with traditional French and German dances, several had learned folk dances from other cultures or festivals, and all of them knew swing, pop, jitterbug, and rock 'n' roll. Unconcerned with the lofty mission of preserving old traditions, they simply wanted to dance. They invented new movements and steps on the dance floors of newly opened restaurants and dance halls, incorporating arm movements from German traditional dances as well as from swing and jitterbug, giving rise to the arm pyrotechnics seen in some of today's Cajun dances.

An interesting anecdote concerns the invention of the dance now known as *la patte cassée* or "crippled chicken." In the early 1970s, newly formed bands like Coteau and Beausoleil performed at dance halls and student hangouts close to the campus of the University of Southwestern Louisiana (now the University of Louisiana at Lafayette). One evening, a particularly talented young dancer arrived with a sprained ankle. He took to the dance floor anyway but favored one leg. One observer likened him to a chicken with a broken leg, and several other couples joined in, laughing at themselves. The next week, these dancers were astonished to see couples executing the crippled chicken. This dance, basically a variation of the jitterbug, remained popular and is now a mainstay of the Cajun repertoire, though it is a pure invention, an example of Stephen J. Gould's punctuated evolution on the dance floor![23]

Another dance was invented at this time, as young dancers provided entertainment for the tourists who came to see dancing turned into a performance. In the *danse à trois*, one man dances with two women using twirls, turns, and intricate arm movements. Many Cajuns today would swear that this dance is traditional, though it would have been ludicrous to dance it in the past, when the point of social dance was to meet one-on-one.[24]

It was in the 1970s and 1980s that the Cajun jig, yet another example of hybrid vigor, entered the dance scene. This jig was influenced by the Irish jig, which in turn is based on step dancing as opposed to complicated figures.[25] It combined the two-step, swing, and jitterbug, which are all in duple meter. As opposed to the traditional waltz and two-step, the couple is connected by only one hand and dances apart as in the traditional jig.

Nowadays in dance halls almost anything goes. Certain bands are more traditional, others more country-western, others incorporate rock 'n' roll. Savvy dancers know which band is playing at which dancehall on which night. The traditional Cajun repertoire includes smooth waltzes, zydeco, jigs, line dances, and two-steps played by instruments that come from Cajun, country-western, and zydeco traditions. Southwest Louisiana may be one of the few regions in the country where a woman buys new boots to go dancing!

Never has Cajun music been so varied, so open to innovation. Musicians like David Greely are determined to find their voice inside the harmonies and instruments of the culture itself. Other bands, like Beausoleil, start from old sources but add Caribbean rhythms. New songs appear in Cajun French, normative French, English, or all three, influenced by musical trends. A band now based in Austin, Poor Man's Fortune, combines elements of French, Acadian, Louisiana, and Breton music. Some compositions resemble Cajun music in little but their instrumentation. These are all perfectly legitimate ways to create.

Zydeco: A "joyous work in progress"[26]

Like the music of the Cajuns, the origins of zydeco were drawn from three continents, creolized and tempered by the flames of hardship and exile. It is common knowledge that African Americans in the bayou country are the descendants of slaves brought from Africa and the West Indies. What is not generally known, however, is that many slaves were freed well before the Civil War, some because of military service, some as a reward for faithful employment, some according to a Spanish ban on native slaves, and some at their owners' deaths. In 1788, 1,701 freed slaves were registered in the census of lower Louisiana.[27] Free black communities all over South Louisiana and extending eastward and including New Orleans were home to people of mixed race, known as *gens de couleur libres*, or free people of color.

Like branches of the same tree, Cajun and zydeco traditions are rooted in the same soil; the music of one has its origins in the traditions of the other.[28] The creators of both traditions shared the same experiences in the early and middle years of the 20th century; young speakers of French or Creole at home were equally marginalized at separate segregated anglophone schools. Both Cajun and zydeco music were first performed in private homes. Both fell into disuse as "old folks' music" in the 1960s,[29] and the leap into public consciousness affected them equally. Simple instruments appear in both traditions; the Cajun *'tit fer* (triangle) is fashioned from the tines of a harrow, the percussive zydeco *frottoir* from the ordinary washboard,[30] and both traditions may incorporate spoons and bones. A cappella vocal lines appear in the form of *musique à bouche* and the *danses rondes* from the Cajuns, field hollers and *juré* from the Afro-Creoles.[31] The beat was provided by feet of the *musique à bouche*, by claps and shouts in *juré*.

However, these branches separate and grow in different directions. Instrumentation is similar but not identical. Though the accordion is the dominant instrument in both, Cajun music is usually played on a diatonic accordion, whereas zydeco favors the chromatic piano accordion that can play flatted, bluesy notes. The Cajun fiddle is usually absent in zydeco music, which may even use saxophone or trumpet. The Cajun *'tit fer* is replaced by the zydeco *frottoir*. One could say that the melody dominates Cajun music, whereas the rhythm, often syncopated, dominates Creole music.[32] Zydeco music is more often duple than triple; Cajun may be both. Zydeco is linked more directly to courtship and its results than its Cajun counterpart, this characteristic may shock those who make their first visits to zydeco clubs in the area. Historically, African dances celebrated fertility, and the African dancers were considered less inhibited than white dancers. Some slave owners banned the *kalinda*. Early zydeco, with less stylized complexity than Cajun dances, was a sexy dance. It was toned down in the 1930s and 1940s to conform to community expectations, but following societal changes in the 1980s and 1990s that permitted more open expression of sexuality, it returned to its roots.[33]

Elements of the Delta Stomp are present in zydeco from the beginning but appear in Cajun dances only later from rock 'n' roll. Cajun dancing is smooth and horizontal, with emphasis on forward movement and an erect upper body carriage. Zydeco's more vertical movements involve the whole body.[34] Arms may be held up and stiff. Unlike contemporary Cajun dances, no simplification was involved in zydeco. Its steps were always simple; there were no stylized figures that disappeared.

Could zydeco have been born anywhere else but in French Louisiana? Conditions favored a synthesis of social and musical elements from three continents, in a region where Africans and Cajuns had known and respected one another for more than two centuries. In nowhere else but South Louisiana could French have been a vehicle to unite the two with the Mississippi Delta's blues tradition serving as catalyst. Perhaps the best we can do is to state that zydeco is poised at the confluence of rock 'n' roll, rhythm and blues, Cajun, and *juré*. Who knows where the currents will take it.

Let me return to the favorite South Louisiana preoccupation with food. If two people are given the same ingredients and asked to create a meal, chances are that those meals will be different. Today's Cajun and zydeco dances continue to evolve, as diverse as the myriad traditions that formed them. This is good; whatever does not evolve dies. The evolution of dance is an organic one. Artificial controls are both useless and ludicrous.[35] Tradition is a process, not a product. Despite individual efforts to control or dominate them, Cajun and zydeco will become what they become.

Endnotes

1. Every schoolchild learns of the nightmare of slavery. Slaves were imported into Louisiana as early as 1719, along with smugglers, inmates of debtor prisons, indentured servants, and colonists. One must also remember that the Native Americans were also enslaved. The history of the Acadians is less well known. The expulsion of unarmed civilians resulted in the deaths of one-third of the Acadians and the forced resettlement of thousands more. For more on this history, see Barry Ancelet et al., *Cajun Country* (Jackson, MS: University Press of Mississippi, 1991); Carl Brasseaux, *Scattered to the Wind: Dispersal and Wanderings of the Acadians, 1755–1809* (Lafayette: Center for Louisiana Studies, University of Southwestern Louisiana, 1991); Glenn Conrad, ed., *The Cajuns: Essays on Their History and Culture* (Lafayette: Center for Louisiana Studies, University of Southwestern Louisiana, 1978); James Dormon, ed., *Creoles of Color of the Gulf South* (Knoxville: Univer-

sity of Tennessee Press, 1996); and Gwendolyn Midlo-Hall, *Africans in Colonial Louisiana: The Development of Afro-Creole Culture in the Eighteenth Century* (Baton Rouge: Louisiana State University Press, 1992).

2. Usually typhus or smallpox; Brasseaux, *Scattered to the Wind*, 9.

3. Lawrence Levine, *Black Culture and Black Consciousness: Afro-American Folk Thought from Slavery to Freedom* (Oxford: Oxford University Press, 1977), 24.

4. For a discussion of the terms, see Barry Ancelet, "Zydeco/Zarico: The Term and the Tradition," in *Creoles of Color of the Gulf South*, 126–144.

5. The word *juré* refers to a tradition of songs sung to the accompaniment of hands and feet. Alan Lomax called *juré* "the most African sound I found in America;" Ben Sandmel, *Zydeco!* (Jackson: University Press of Mississippi, 1999), 34. Some juré songs drew inspiration from the Cajun repertoire. Sandmel, *Zydeco!*, 33.

6. Another definition concerns Creole languages, which grew up as lingua francas between slave traders and their cargo. There are Dutch Creoles and English Creoles; Louisiana Creole is based on French. The word "Creole" does not necessarily imply racial mixing; the sine qua non for la créolité is adaptation.

7. The coining of the name "zydeco" was a part of this trend. The term was first used in 1960 by Mack MacCormack, a record producer in Houston; Barry Ancelet, *Cajun and Creole Folktales: The French Oral Tradition of South Louisiana* (Oxford: University Press of Mississippi, 1994), xix.

8. Susan Kiefer, personal interview with the author, July 26, 2005.

9. Wrought iron appeared on New Orleans balconies, architectural styles changed, and rice, olive oil, and green peppers appeared in New Orleans cuisine. The famous French Market beignets are plainly Spanish sopapillas!

10. The Acadian Coast comprises the present-day parishes (counties) of Ascension and St. James to distinguish the settlements from those of the German coast and present-day St. Charles and St. John the Baptist parishes, which were settled as part of John Law's colonization scheme. "German" referred to the entire Holy Roman Empire; May Waggoner, *Le plus beau païs du monde: Completing the Picture of Proprietary Louisiana, 1699–1722* (Lafayette: Center for Louisiana Studies, University of Louisiana at Lafayette, 2005), 19.

11. Many exiles eagerly fought the British during the American Revolution and the War of 1812. Fifty years later, however, they merely wanted to farm, and their loyalties lay neither with the Confederacy nor with the Union, both alien cultures. Desertion rates were high.

12. As an interesting digression, many of the Cubans came from the Oriente Province and brought with them a love of red beans, their national dish. The recipe is part of the New Orleans culinary iconography.

13. Some Cajuns refer to themselves today as "Swamp Irish." Just as earlier Rodriguez and Dominguez families had become Rodrigue and Domingue, many German family names were Gallicized: Huber to Oubre, Dubcek to Touchet, Himmel to Himel.

14. Corinne Saucier, *Traditions de la paroisse des Avoyelles en Louisiane* (Philadelphia: American Folklore Society, 1956), 52.

15. Other important Louisiana Creole settlements included Donaldsonville and St. Martinville, where descendants of old families still boast of aristocratic ancestors fleeing the French Revolution.

16. The origin of the term *fais do-do* to describe a party lies in this tradition. Parents brought their children and babies to the house dances, put them all together in one room, and told them *fais do-do* (go to sleep), so the parents could dance.

17. Gresham's law, formulated in the 16th century, states that bad money drives good money out of circulation.

18. These circle dances were referred to as *danses rondes*. Women also sang narrative songs and ballads during *veillées*, evenings spent with friends. An older tradition was the *musique à bouche*, an a cappella solo vocal line accompanied only by foot taps to mark the rhythm. This *bottine souriante* is also present in Quebec music. When the Acadian exiles arrived in St. Domingue on their way to Louisiana, the Acadian exiles are reported to have danced to *reels à bouche*, wordless dance music made by their voices alone; Ancelet et al., *Cajun Country*, 164.

19. Traditional dance halls had been open only on weekends.

20. Beginning with the 1864 state constitution, the use of French had eroded in legal documents. The 1921 constitution was amended to prohibit the use of all languages other than English in education; Carl Brasseaux and James Wilson, personal interviews with the author, July 13, 2005.

21. See also explanation in May Waggoner, *Une fantaisie collective: Anthologie du drame louisianais cadien* (Lafayette: Center for Louisiana Studies, University of Louisiana at Lafayette, 1999); Jean Arceneaux, *Cris sur le bayou* (Quebec: Les Editions Intermède, 1980); Jean Arceneaux et al., *Acadie tropicale* (Lafayette: Center for Louisiana Studies, University of Southwestern Louisiana, 1983).

22. Warren Perrin, *Acadian Redemption: From Beausoleil Broussard to the Queen's Royal Proclamation* (Erath, LA: Acadian Heritage and Cultural Foundation, 2004), 115.

23. Punctuated evolution, or punctuated equilibrium, states that most morphological evolution occurs during relatively brief episodes of rapid change that punctuate much longer periods of stasis.

24. Barry Ancelet, personal interview with the author, Lafayette, LA, June 29, 2005.

25. Simone Voyer, *La gigue: Danse de pas* (Sainte Foy, QC: Les editions GID, 2003), 13.

26. Sandmel, Zydeco!, 168.

27. Carl Brasseaux, "Creoles of Color in Louisiana's Bayou country," in *Creoles of Color of the Gulf South*, 67–68.

28. For example, one of the most popular of the Cajun songs, "Allons danser Colinda," probably refers not to a woman named Colinda but to an African dance, the kalinda.

29. Sandmel, *Zydeco!*, 12.

30. The washboard has been redesigned to be worn over the shoulder.

31. See note 5 for the definition of *juré* and note 17 for definitions of *musique à bouche* and *danses rondes*. Hollers were used in the fields to transmit information; the rhythm derived from clapping, foot stomping, or occasional shouting.

32. This syncopation derives from hambone syncopation (juba), a type of body percussion in a 3–3–2 rhythm in which the chest and thighs are slapped to keep the beat. Hambone syncopation also appears in the related Delta Stomp.

33. Barry Ancelet, "Zydeco/Zarico: The Term and the Tradition," in Dormon, *Creoles of Color of the Gulf South*, 138.

34. Levine, *Black Culture and Black Consciousness,* 16.

35. One well-intentioned South Louisiana organization dedicated to the preservation and promotion of Cajun music even voted in the 1990s to outlaw the Cajun jig as "inauthentic." Needless to say, the dance is still a popular one, and the artificial controls were as effective as the suggestion by some feminists during the 1970s that the plural of the word "woman" be changed to "womyn" to remove the offensive syllable "men."

Cajun Musics of the 21st Century

Joshua Clegg Caffery

Like the shifting waterways of the Louisiana coast, or the equally fluctuating geography of the Atchafalaya Basin, the musical styles of the Acadiana region are complex, changeable, and resistant to facile geography. Even within the domain of Cajun music, niggling questions of definition immediately arise: Do we mean a precisely ethnic music: the music of a people known as Cajuns, who may or may not identify with the historical narrative of the 18th century Acadian genocide and diasporic reconfiguration in Louisiana? Or do we mean a stylistic category defined by certain instrumentation, rhythmic proclivities, language, and harmonic structure?

The question, thus posed, is a bit like asking someone to describe Louisiana's Cow Island. This seems an easy enough task, though anyone familiar with the Atchafalaya Basin or the Louisiana coast will be confused: do we mean the Cow Island just south of Butte la Rose, or the one just off the Intracoastal Canal in St. Mary Parish, or the area near Nunez in Vermilion Parish? These are very different Cow Islands, and they are called islands for very different reasons. In the same way, in an essay about Cajun music in the 21st century, we really must speak about Cajun "musics."

A variety of musical styles and their practitioners identify, or have become identified, as Cajun for a variety of reasons. That said, a general category might be defined in this way: an accordion and fiddle-based music played primarily by white people from South-central Louisiana, often, though not always, sung in Cajun French. Although neat divisions are never perfect, I propose four descriptive categories that might be useful in situating major currents in the Cajun music of the 21st century: 1) dancehall/restaurant music, 2) zydecajun and its descendants, 3) folk revivalists and the neo-traditionalists, and 4) eclectic wildcards.

As the focus of a social event in dancehalls and restaurant/dance halls, Cajun music appears very much as it did in the last two decades of the 20th century. Although the heyday of the large dancehall has long since passed, venues such as *La Poussière* in Breaux Bridge and Whiskey River Landing in Henderson continue to host dances on both weekend evenings and Sunday afternoons. Some restaurant/dancehalls or Cajun-themed restaurants, such as Prejean's and Randol's in Lafayette, feature nightly Cajun dance bands. At such venues, bands tend to perform in a standard dancehall configuration: drums, bass, guitar (either electric, acoustic, or both), and fiddle, often led by an accordionist/vocalist. While such bands may occasionally introduce original material, such songs are often in a traditional vein, and most bands generally hew to the large body of traditional francophone Cajun songs composed at various times throughout the 20th century.

The second broad category might be considered the 21st-century legacy of Wayne Toups, who popularized a fusion of zydeco, rock, and Cajun music, dubbed *zydecajun*. Featuring blistering and often distorted electric guitar, electric keyboard, and a considerable percentage of songs in English, Toups developed a large following of younger anglophone, blue-collar Cajuns, and he continues to pack large venues into the 21st century. Though Toups' music often eschewed canonical Cajun songs, using accordion and fiddle to impart a Cajun atmosphere to rock and pop songs, he kept one foot in the more traditional realm, occasionally performing acoustic sets and often playing headlining slots at the *Festival de Musique Acadienne et Créole*, the Acadiana region's major festival devoted to Cajun and Creole music.

In the 21st century, other bands continued to find success in the same way. Two notable examples are Travis Matte and Jamie Bergeron, who both developed devout followings by doing what Toups did best: combining elements of Cajun instrumentation with a full rock band configuration, all while incorporating elements of more contemporary zydeco and often singing in Cajun-inflected English. Though Matte in particular attracted the ire of more traditionally-minded Cajun music enthusiasts, he attracted a large and devoted audience of Cajun people throughout the South Louisiana parishes of Acadiana. Like Toups, Matte began his career in a traditional vein, and he continued to record and perform songs from the standard repertoire, releasing, in 2013, the album *Old Time Cajun Songs*, which was largely devoid of his trademark fusion of Cajun rock and hip-hop infused zydeco.

A third distinct strand of 21st century Cajun music involves the continued work of tradition-minded musicians who came of age during the American folk revival of the 1960s and the subsequent surge of interest in traditional francophone Cajun music and culture in the 1970s, often called the Cajun Renaissance. In the first decade of the 21st century, the vanguard of this generation, notably Marc and Ann Savoy and Beausoleil avec Michael Doucet (who had performed together as the Savoy-Doucet Cajun Band and continue to do so), grew into respected elders of the music, while a new generation, which might be considered neo-traditionalist, arose.

Like their predecessors, the neo-traditionalist bands of the early 21st century looked back to early commercial and archival recordings. While these musicians harkened back to earlier eras for inspiration, they were, however, not necessarily purists. Unlike Toups and Matte, they tended to combine vintage sounds with other American roots genres or even other strains of global ethnic music, rather than pop and rock. For instance, the Red Stick Ramblers and the Lost Bayou Ramblers mixed Cajun two-steps and waltzes with 1940s-era Cajun swing, as well as bluegrass and honky-tonk.

In many cases, bands in a more neo-traditional vein had direct family ties to the previous generation of traditional standard-bearers: Marc and Ann

Savoy's sons Joel and Wilson, for instance, were key members of the Red Stick Ramblers and the Pine Leaf Boys, respectively, and Christine Balfa perpetuated her father Dewey Balfa's legacy in the group Balfa Toujours. Like their predecessors, these groups also plied the national and international folk festival circuit as ambassador of the region's cultural music.

These three major strands of 21st century Cajun music obviously cannot neatly include all of the various permutations of Cajun represented by each individual band that identifies as Cajun, but it does provide a frame of reference. Many bands incorporate characteristics from all three strands with their own unique emphases and modes of creativity. Zachary Richard, for instance, combines an ethos rooted in the Cajun Renaissance with elements of French Canadian pop and folk music. In live performances, he incorporates occasional English lyrics and elements of zydeco music, much in the manner of Wayne Toups.

The band Feufollet, similarly, garnered acclaim in the first decade of the 21st century for a lush reworking of archival recordings, while also writing songs in rock and indie-pop veins; never failing to mix in fairly conservative accordion and fiddle-based two-steps and waltzes in a dancehall style. In the same way, Steve Riley and the Mamou Playboys combine eclectic original songwriting with dancehall Cajun music, as well as elements of zydeco, songs in English, and close harmony singing indebted to the style of the Balfa Brothers, not to mention venerable fiddle tunes propelled by drums and electric bass.

In a general sense, then, Cajun music in the 21st century is particularly robust in that it draws on a panoply of 20th century styles that have all developed into dynamic sub-traditions. As Wilson Savoy puts it, "All folk music that's remotely popular has influences from 'modern day' music. Cajun music has been [borrowing from] Country music and melding the two together for decades. Younger bands continue to meld other styles of music into Cajun music from rock 'n roll, R&B, blues, even punk."

This diversity of what might be called "sub-traditions" allows for a range of creative endeavors and individual expression, as well as a mode and precedent for interaction with (and acceptance of) new elements churned up in pop culture. In the 20th century, we often reminded each other not to "drop the potato." Now, let me suggest that there is more than one potato, and that Cajun musicians have become skilled at juggling.

The Cultural Influences in Cajun Music

Barry Jean Ancelet

Recent analyses of historical and contemporary Cajun music lyrics, made possible by the acquisition of early fieldwork collections, especially the Lomax collection from 1934, have shown that oral poetics have evolved from unaccompanied ballads to dance music lyrics, condensing the format while preserving the essence of the messages. I have found no direct references to the exile experience anywhere in traditional Cajun music lyrics, not counting those developed consciously by contemporary performers such as Zachary Richard. Yet, much of Cajun music poetics seem to refer to the effects of that trauma, including loneliness, estrangement from home, being alone on the road, broken families, and lost loves.

As any living tradition, Cajun music has undergone several stylistic shifts over the last century. Some of these have been due to the creativity of individual artists, as in the case of Amédé Ardoin, Dennis McGee, Harry Choates, and Iry Lejeune, among others. There are other stylistic shifts owing to a change in the context of the music. These changes can be social, as in the evolution from house dances to public dance halls. They can also be technological, as heard in the effects of amplifying what had necessarily been an acoustic tradition, or in the effects of recording what had been a highly innovative tradition, and broadcasting what had been a highly local tradition.

Another important shift occurred with the development of festivals and concerts, in the effects of performing for people who are sitting and listening rather than dancing and courting; performing for crowds much larger than any in previous experience, on a four-foot high stage outdoors rather than on a one-foot high bandstand indoors. The stylistic shifts that resulted from these contextual changes can be heard by comparing the earliest commercial recordings from 1928 to 1938 with those that followed World War II. One hears such changes as the development of individual lead instrumental solos and the addition of electrically-based instruments such as the steel guitar.

Traditional performers instinctively renegotiate their performances according to context in ways that are not entirely unrelated to the contextualist approach as described by scholars such as Roger Abrahams, Robert Georges, and Kenneth Goldstein. For a specific example, compare Ralph Rinzler's field recordings of Dewey Balfa and the Balfa Brothers before their appearances at the Newport Folk Festival and the Smithsonian's Festival of American Folklife to what the group recorded commercially afterwards, and clearly you can hear stylistic changes including fancier fiddling, tighter arrangements, and the addition of high harmonies.

Performing on the same stage as the likes of Bill Monroe, Vassar Clements, and Tommy Jarrell, the Balfas learned several things about how to play before a festival crowd, including an intensified, fancier fiddle style, and simple high harmonies that added to the texture of their performances. They learned about visual dynamics and communicating to the crowd, previously unimportant when performing before a few hundred couples in a dancehall where everyone was primarily dancing and courting. They also learned about song selection and a sense of closing.

Traditional dances always ended with a waltz to give courting couples one last close dance together, but they found that festival performances end better with a rousing two-step. Songs such as "T'en as eu, t'en auras plus," The Bosco Stomp, "Les veuves de la coulée", or "Les flammes d'enfer" were more likely to generate a rousing burst of applause and maybe an encore; concepts that were unknown in the dancehalls.

The experience that groups such as the Balfa Brothers, the Ardoin Family, and McGee and Courville had gained on the folk festival circuit was deliberately used by organizers of the first *Tribute to Cajun Music* in Lafayette, Louisiana, in 1974. These festival veterans ironically had much more experience in this new context than the region's most popular dance bands of the time, such as Blackie Forrestier's Cajun Aces and Belton Richard's Musical Aces.

The generation of young Cajun and Creole musicians that was led back to its roots was attracted, at least initially, by means of the festival-influenced sound. In addition to the obvious extensions of the Balfa family tradition–Christine Balfa's Balfa Toujours and grand-nephew Courtney Granger–many young bands such as Michael Doucet and Beausoleil obviously learned more than music from the Balfas. Michael also learned Creole licks from the Ardoin Family Band's fiddler Canray Fontenot. In later Beausoleil recordings, Michael Doucet's brother David joined the band after a foray into bluegrass and old-time country, flat-picking Cajun melodies in a style clearly influenced by another of Ralph Rinzler's discoveries, Doc Watson.

The effects of contextual shifts are clearly evident today in the music of young bands, such as Steve Riley and the Mamou Playboys, who have continued to experiment. Their early sound was clearly a self-conscious preservation of Balfa-influenced fiddling and repertoire. They were hailed as an example of hope for the future of traditional music, of how young musicians could continue to be interested in playing the old stuff.

Soon enough, however, their youth caught up to their love of tradition. In order to stay interested as musicians who have taken to the road full-time, they began to experiment. Initially, these experiments were organic, taking place within the tradition. That is, style was shifting within the traditional repertoire. They redid traditional standards in four-part harmony and re-arranged openings for crowd effect.

Later, in a search for challenging complexity, they added new tunes that they encountered on the road in other parts of the francophone world, such as "Pointe-au-Pic," which they learned in Quebec. They strung together two or more traditional tunes in tour-de-force medleys, and re-arranged songs for obvious dramatic effect. These strategies have influenced the next generation, as is evident in the arrangements of the younger Cajun music group Feufollet.

Eventually, fiddler David Greely learned to play a swamp pop-style saxophone to accompany accordionist Steve Riley's forays into zydeco. Riley's early Savoy-influenced accordion licks have also been clearly affected by Clifton Chenier's zydeco, and Wayne Toups' southern rock and *zydecajun* fusion. When they revealed these changes, after pulling a big red chromatic accordion out of the bag onstage at the *Cajun Music Festival* in 1994, the South Louisiana crowd experienced a moment not unlike the one experienced by the Newport Folk Festival crowd in 1965 when Bob Dylan plugged in an electric guitar to play his ballad, "Like a Rolling Stone."

When festival producers heard their new licks, there was general consternation and concern that traditional Cajun music's fair-haired band was sliding toward the progressive side. It may have been a natural progression from Aldus Roger's take on Clifton Chenier's signature song. A remarkable exchange of emails with Peter Schwarz–the band manager, bassist, and Dewey Balfa student–demonstrated that band members were keenly aware of issues such as the effects of changing contexts, changing audience expectations at home and on the road, and the tensions between artistic and cultural integrity.

Perhaps the most important contemporary contextual change had to do with the shift from primarily French-speaking audiences to primarily English-speaking ones. On the one hand, whereas zydeco has readily translated itself into English in the last 20 years (often with dire lyrical results), there has been the persistent notion that French lyrics are an integral feature of Cajun music. It may be impossible to preserve enough cultural specificity while changing something as fundamental as its language of expression. However, some sort of evolution seems inevitable, for better or worse. Some, who could fairly be considered traditionalists, including the Mamou Playboys, have experimented with the process, more or less satisfactorily. These experiments have produced interesting music. That music's attachment to Cajun tradition is up for debate.

There can be a sense of cultural guilt that accompanies such efforts. Nevertheless, one can only wonder how long singers will continue to sing words they don't understand for audiences who increasingly don't understand them either. One of their recent albums, *Happytown*, otherwise filled with revivals of old Lomax material as well as original material in French, also features the ultra-modern, all-English radio hit, "Seems to Me", which includes modern trappings such as synthesized vocal tracks.

Those who measure the durability of the French base of this musical tradition by how devoted the performers are to preserving it may have underestimated the importance of changing contexts and audience, as well as the tradition's drive to survive by any means necessary. Yet they followed this with *Bon Rêve,* which represents a remarkable return to the tradition and to the concept of creating within it, including exclusive French lyrics; as in Sam Broussard's original "Bon Rêve," an impressionistic evocation of Creole fiddler Canray Fontenot's life, and the band's *a capella* version of "La chanson des Savoy" from the 1934 Lomax collection in four part harmony that closed the album. "Dominos," their latest effort, continues in this vein with original songs such as Steve Riley's "Elise" (named for his daughter) and his "Pays des étrangers"–all remarkably evocative of consistent Acadian concerns of being separated from one's home and loved ones.

Musicians from the so-called Louisiana French Renaissance generation, such as Michael Doucet and Zachary Richard, continue to create new songs and recycle old ones that reflect traditional and contemporary values. Wayne Toups recently came back from several forays into swamp pop and R&B to record traditional and original songs in French on *Little Wooden Box* and *Reflections of the Past.* It appears that key players continue to perceive that Cajun music needs to be in French, but this does not mean that there is a lack of innovation.

Groups such as the Pine Leaf Boys, the Lost Bayou Ramblers, Feufollet, Bonsoir Catin, the Lafayette Rhythm Devils, Acadien, and many others continue to produce new songs and revitalize old ones in a seamless integration of ancient and thoroughly modern sounds and styles. A few, including Kirby Jambon, have even explored the possibilities of Cajun hip-hop. They continue to produce music that is as playful and challenging as we expect young music to be. At the same time, it is as respectful and grounded as we hope it would be.

This young Cajun music is a perfect example of what Dewey Balfa meant when said that he wanted to preserve not the music itself but the process that produces the music, so that musicians will continue to innovate and improvise new forms that both surprise us and reassure us at the same time. To those who nevertheless think that there is little hope for the future, I say I would not want the responsibility of telling that to all these talented young Cajuns.

Keeping Cajun Music Alive In Texas

Jason Theriot

Les Johnson, known as Pe-Te, was born in 1934 in Grand Taso, near Eunice, Louisiana. His ancestors are direct descendants of the French Acadians expelled from Nova Scotia in the mid-18th century. His family name, Johnson, is the Americanized version of Jeansonne. He moved to Texas in 1959, to where many other Cajuns already had moved and others were still moving there for work. Pe-Te has been a radio host and promoter of Cajun music for over 30 years in Texas.

As a youth, Pe-Te served in the U.S. Air Force during the Korean War and was stationed in Chateauroux, France. For two-and-a-half years, he served as a valuable interpreter when the military opened a new base there in 1953. During that time, he did his first radio show at the V.A. hospital in Alexandria, Louisiana. After completing his service, Pe-Te moved to Beaumont, Texas. He worked at Wyatt's Cafeteria, then in 1961, he moved to Houston. Here, he became an inspector for the Arco Petrochemical Plant where he made more money selling barbeque sandwiches for lunch than his job paid. In 1979 he opened Pe-Te's Cajun BBQ House across from Ellington Field in Friendswood. The restaurant and dancehall remained a favorite of pilots, astronauts, cosmonauts, celebrities, and Cajuns.

People came from across the region and the world to eat, dance, and listen to music at Pe-Te's Cajun BBQ House on Galveston Road. Celebrity autographs, over 4,000 license plates, and 3,000 golf balls decorated the 7,000-square foot facility.

In 1981, even though the restaurant kept him busy, Pe-Te accepted an offer to start a local Cajun music radio show at KTEK. Two years later the program moved to listener-supported KPFT. In 2013, he celebrated his 30th year as the radio host of "Pe-Te's Cajun Bandstand."

Photo©Debbie Z. Harwell

Every Saturday morning Pe-Te awoke at 3:30 a.m. to make the drive in to the KPFT station in Montrose. At the controls with his dog Shaggy by his side, he organized his music, requests, and announcements for the three-hour program.

Pe-Te has arguably been the most influential public figure in promoting Cajun and zydeco music in the Houston region. The following excerpts are from a conversation with Pe-Te Johnson. He tells us what life was like in Texas then and today.

Cajun Immigration to Texas

Pe-Te: I've got a first cousin, and his family and they moved over here in the late 1940s, in Katy, to harvest rice fields. Still in Katy and he's 89. He was in the service during World War II ... I do remember some of the farmers that moved over to the Port Arthur and Beaumont areas to harvest crops, rice mostly, and a lot of them with very little education moved to work in the plants.

JT: Where did most of the Cajuns migrate from?

Pe-Te: From the Eunice area in Louisiana. Some were from Opelousas, Ville Platte, Basile, and Elton. There's also a lot of them who moved from Lake Charles to the plants in Beaumont and Port Arthur back then, because that's where they paid higher wages ... Because back then, you was lucky to make 50 cents a day down home, but if you went to work at the plants, you might make a dollar and a quarter an hour. So that was a lot of difference.

JT: Some of the things that make our people unique are our connections to close kinship ties, marriage within the community, the Roman Catholic faith, and our French language. Those things were hard to come by for the Cajuns who migrated over here to Texas. How do you think most of these families were able to cope with moving to a city like Beaumont or Houston?

Pe-Te: It was very hard on them, because I can remember several couples that got married and they moved out of town, out of state, and the women, especially the women, they couldn't cope with it. Within a month or less, they'd be back home again, and the next thing you know, there'd be divorces. They just couldn't cope with it ; almost like a new world. If you moved out of, say, Eunice and you came to Houston, my God, that was something that they just couldn't understand, all the people and all the traffic and different bylaws and so on and so forth. They just couldn't cope with it ... Now, if they were moving to, say, Port Arthur or where other Cajuns was, they would pick up with other families and friendship, and it was more comfortable. But some of them would move into an area where there wasn't any Cajuns. And a lot of them didn't have the education; some of the husbands could barely read or write that would go to work in the plants. It was hard for them to go to a bank and want to make a loan or whatever because they didn't speak fluent English, it was broken English, and so they wouldn't be understanding all the new laws in a different community or state. So it made it rough on those people.

JT: How surprised were you when you moved to Beaumont in 1959 to find such a large population of French-speaking Cajuns there?

Pe-Te: I was surprised. As a matter of fact, I worked for Wyatt's Cafeteria at the time, and when customers would come in, I could pick up the dialect. I knew where they were from. So I just automatically started speaking in French or asked them a question or say something in French, and, boy, they'd get all excited. So it was quite a treat, to find a lot of Cajuns that spoke French ... You have a lot of them that was raised in Louisiana, from Eunice or whatever, and a lot of them never did speak any Cajun anymore. They were taught at school, "Well, no, you don't want to speak that foreign language. You want to be high-class."

JT: How did that compare to Houston, where few Cajuns lived, when you moved there?

Pe-Te: I almost lost my French on account of that. I didn't have nobody to speak to. That was my biggest problem, so I went back home maybe once a month ... It went for a long time before I ran into somebody that did speak French in Houston.

In 2007 Jo-El Sonnier (right), Cajun singer-songwriter who performs both country and Cajun music, presented Pe-Te with an award for Outstanding Achievement for his contributions to Cajun music and culture. Sonnier's 34th record album was released in 2013, The Legacy, *an all-French production with classic accordion style of music.*

Cajun Dances and Music

Pe-Te Johnson brought the first "Cajun Dance" to the Houston area in 1980. Saturday night Cajun dances were (and still are) a traditional form of cultural and ethnic expression, where local Cajun French musicians performed at homes or on front porches. These dances pre-dated the amplification of musical instruments.

Pe-Te: I was the first one that had Cajun dances here in the Houston area. When I started the barbeque place, my dream was to have Cajun dances. So not even a year after we opened the barbeque place, we had our first Cajun dance there and I think we had about 40 people. It was supposed to only hold about 15. [Laughs.] But I brought a band in all the way from Louisiana. Oh, yeah. Lisa Cormier and the Sundown Playboys, and they played at the barbeque place for, God ... seven, eight years, I guess...

Shown are Paula Baltera, who assisted Pe-Te by listing the artists and songs played on the Cajun Bandstand, *Pe-Te with "co-host" Shaggy, and J.B. Adams, who hosted the* Zydeco Pas Salé *program on KPFT, Sunday mornings from 3:00 a.m. to 6:00 a.m.*

Photo©Debbie Z. Harwell

JT: Why do you like music so much?

Pe-Te: We used to have house dances when I was a kid, and matter of fact, they'd have a house dance at one house one Saturday night, then next week or two weeks later, they'd have another one at somebody else's house. Back then there was only a couple of musicians, and Amédé Ardoin that played the accordion. I was only about three years old and he played at my house. Back then they'd say, "Fais dodo," and they'd put the kids in the back room in the bed and everything, and you was supposed to stay in there and go to sleep. Man, that accordion music, it was in my blood. [Laughs.] And I'd drift out of there. Finally, after about the third time of getting a whoopin', they'd just leave me there and I'd just sit right there by his feet while he played.

Then later on, they had a fiddle player join him. Either Sady Courville or Dennis McGee would join him. But like I said, they'd move around. Then pretty soon a guitar player would come in. Different people would start, like Amédé Breaux or Joe Falcon. They would start putting bands together and everything. That's where all the dances would start, and pretty soon somebody opened a dancehall and then it went from there and pretty soon every town had a dancehall.

But all the music has changed so much. I remember when the zydeco was first started because we had some black folks that lived down the road from us in the country and they'd invite us to go out there. The Saturday, they would spend all day picking up the green beans, snap beans. Then on the Sunday, they'd come over in the afternoon when it was cool and they'd all bring their instruments and everything. While the women was out there snapping the green beans, they'd be playing their music ... I was just a little kid, but I'd go out there and break snap beans just for the heck of it and listen to the music. They had an old washtub turned over with a little rope tied to it to make some sound, and pots and pans they'd beat on, and it'd make some pretty good music. They had a few bottles of homemade brew and everybody would take a few little drinks. When I was maybe eight or nine, I'd go over there and while they wasn't looking, I'd get me a little sip and everything.

JT: Was there ever any integration between the zydeco musicians and the Cajun musicians at these house dances?

Pe-Te: Oh, yes. Matter of fact, Amédé Ardoin, he was black and Dennis McGee was white. Poor Amédé, he was killed, I guess about a month after he had played at one of our house dances ... Back then there wasn't no air conditioning, they'd just open all the windows and try to let the fresh air come in. This was like in June, July, August, and it was so hot in there, you'd be wringing wet all the time. He'd be just a-sweating; sweat would just run in his face while he was trying to play. One of the white women would get up there with a handkerchief and try to wipe his brow because the sweat was running down his eyes. In the 1950s and the early 1960s, until, oh, say, probably the early 1970s, Cajun music just about died altogether. Everybody started moving towards big bands like Bob Wills and started playing the country music, like Jimmy C. Newman who went from Cajun to country. Then probably in the middle of the 1970s, Cajun music started to come back up again. You had Nathan Abshire and a bunch of the other big bands like Steve Riley and some of those.

At the 2008 Bayou City Cajun Festival, Pe-Te presented then 17-year-old Hunter Hayes, now a very popular American country music singer and songwriter, with a "baby" accordion, knowing the country star had started playing accordion at age two. After playing D.L. Menard's The Back Door *on the tiny instrument, Hayes then autographed it for KPFT to auction in a fundraiser.*

JT: What do you think has been the influence on Cajun music of the record studios particularly here in Houston, like in 1946 with Harry Choates and 1947 with Iry LeJeune and Clifton Chenier? It's kind of ironic if you think about the song, "Jolie Blonde". The lyrics are about a woman who leaves a Cajun guy for somebody in Texas, and here you've got a man from Acadia Parish,

Harry Choates, who moves to the Golden Triangle [Beaumont, Orange, and Port Allen] to work in the shipyards and plays the fiddle at night, and he's the first to record the popularized version of "Jolie Blonde" by a Houston record studio. What we think of "Jolie Blonde" today is really a Texas version recorded here, played here.

Pe-Te: Right. But I guess what I want to try to say is the melody is just something that just gets into your system and makes you move. I don't know what it is about fiddle music, I mean, or the accordion. It's just something, once that sound comes out, it just sticks to you and you just want to keep listening to it ... Matter of fact, they've got two Louisiana national anthems. You've got the song "Jolie Blonde" and then "You Are My Sunshine." That's two. I guess I get just as many requests for "Jolie Blonde" as I do for "You Are My Sunshine" on Saturday mornings. There are very, very few recordings where they sing the "Jolie Blonde" in English. Now, some of them that will sing it bilingual; they'll sing it in French and then the next line they'll repeat it in English or French or whatever. I've even heard some of the Chicano bands do it in Spanish, and it tickles me. But as soon as you hear the music, you know what it is. You know the words regardless—well, if you don't understand French, you can pick it up pretty fast.

JT: So, Pe-Te, you would agree that it's really the music that is kind of the main attraction here?

Pe-Te: It's not really the food that brings them in; it's the music. The crawfish and the étouffée and so on, they'll go for it, but you mention Steve Riley and the Mamou Playboys is going to be there or Geno Delafose, you might as well get ready for a crowd, because you going to have a crowd.

Cajun fan favorite was "Pee Wee" Kershaw.

Cajun Radio

Through his many contacts, Pe-Te found several advertisers to help launch the new Cajun program that would be broadcast on Saturday mornings from 7:00 to 11:00 a.m. When Pe-Te asked who would be the disc jockey, the manager said, "You are." Pe-Te contacted some friends in the radio business and they encouraged him to do it. One DJ from Beaumont said, "Man, we need some more Cajun music in Houston." A year later, the radio station sold to a religious station and Pe-Te needed a new home for his Cajun music. He met with Huey P. Meaux at KPFT 90.1 FM who introduced him to the station manager and they agreed to bring Pe-Te's show to KPFT on Saturday mornings, airing from 6:00 to 9:00 a.m.

Pe-Te with record producer Huey P. Meaux (center) and singer-songwriter Jim Olivier (right) on New Years Eve, 1981.

Pe-Te: One Saturday morning, trail riders are coming through, and one of the trail riders was the general manager for KTEK in Alvin, Texas. I had an eight-track player set up and I was playing Cajun music on it at the barbeque place. He come in and he got all excited about it and he wanted to know who was Cajun and so I told him. Inside of a week, he asked me to come to his radio station.

Photo©Debbie Z. Harwell

Pe-Te brought his music into the studio in a large wooden crate on wheels to offer his listeners a wide array of Cajun musical favorites.

JT : Why did you want to bring in Cajuns into radio ?

Pe-Te: It's my culture, so, you know, hey, that's part of me. And so many Cajuns are still coming in and we get phone calls from all over the world. I even had a phone call from the space station, from the astronauts up there. So I enjoy it. I love it. Put it that way ... More Cajuns are moving into the Houston area. Pretty soon, if Houston don't watch out they'll be calling the city *Ti Mamou* (Little Mamou) ... You got Cajun entertainment every weekend over here in the Houston area and periodically during the week.

JT: You see what you started? [Laughs]

Pe-Te: But I've enjoyed every minute of it. Somebody asked me here last week, "Pe-Te, you're going on 27 years. We thought you were going to quit whenever you done 25." Every time I get up to a level, I said, "I think I'm going to try and make 30 now." [Laughs]

JT: How would you like to be remembered as a radio host?

Pe-Te: I'd like for them to remember me as I was and what I enjoyed doing to promote the Cajun heritage. If you want to do something for me, do it while I'm still alive, don't wait till I'm six feet under. Don't send me no flowers while I'm dead, in other words. [Laughs.]

Pe-Te's Cajun Bandstand still airs on Saturdays from 6:00 a.m. to 9:00 a.m. on listener-sponsored KPFT 90.1 FM. You can listen to past broadcasts anytime at http://archive.kpft.org/index.php.

Pe-Te and Jennie married on January 31, 1964. She was his partner in love, business, and life for 49 years until she passed away in 2013.

Acknowledgement

Reprinted with permission, *Houston History*, Vol. 11, No.1, Fall 2013

THE IMPORTANCE OF MUSIC IN ACADIE

Jeannita Thériault

Our Acadian ancestors have had difficult times throughout their history. The grim period of the 1755 Expulsion notwithstanding, they enjoyed moments of joy with music and family parties where the fiddle and dancing played an important role. In the past, almost all Acadian families had a fiddle or a pump organ set up in a prominent place, and furniture would be moved out of the way at the drop of a hat so everyone could dance in the kitchen. These gatherings created an atmosphere for relaxing, togetherness, friendship, and conversation despite uncertain social, economic, and political circumstances.

Large house parties in Acadie are not as popular today; the family unit has shrunk. Many of our young people have left to attend school, while some young couples must travel elsewhere to find work. Many of our senior citizens are also leaving their houses to live in nursing homes. Although the traditional Acadian family is undergoing transformation, all is not lost. Happily, music is thriving in Acadie, and we have homegrown artists sharing their talents and reminding us that we have a history, here and outside Canada.

At the beginning of the century, two great Acadian musicians brought musical fame to Acadie: Anna Malenfant and Arthur LeBlanc. Opera singer Anna Malenfant (1902–1988), born in Shédiac, had an extensive career across Canada, and also in Boston, New York, and Paris; a school in Dieppe has been named after her. Violinist Arthur LeBlanc (1906–1985), of Saint-Anselme (now Dieppe), joined the Montreal Symphony Orchestra in 1935. Acclaimed by critics after a New York concert, LeBlanc signed a major contract with Columbia Records and gave more than 300 performances in the United States, even playing at the White House in 1941 at the request of Franklin Roosevelt.

LeBlanc obtained the prized *Des Rosier* Stradivarius violin, which he played in Paris and across Europe. A string quartet called *Quatuor Arthur-Leblanc* was founded at the *Université de Moncton* and is now in permanent residence at *Université de Laval à Quebec.*

In the 1960s, new musicians began conquering the public beyond our borders: Edith Butler, Angèle Arsenault, Georges Langford, Calixte Duguay, Rose-Marie Landry, Raymond Breau, Donat Lacroix, and Ronald Bourgeois. All have readily assumed the role of ambassadors for Acadie.

For several years, we have seen an extraordinary explosion of young Acadian singers and musicians on the scene. They follow in their predecessors' footsteps but in a wider variety of musical genres: Roch Voisine, Marie-Jo Thério, Denis Richard, Lina Boudreau, Marc Beaulieu, Michel Thériault, Monique Poirier, Natasha St-Pierre, Sandra Lecouteur, Suzie LeBlanc, Roger Lord, Joseph Edgar, Pascal Lejeune, Jean-François Breau, Wilfred LeBouthilier, Annie Blanchard, Fayo (Mario LeBlanc), Jason Guerette, Jean-Marc Couture, Danny Boudreau, Cayouche, Herb LeBlanc, Isabelle Cyr, Dominique Dupuis, Lisa LeBlanc, and Caroline Savoie. Many of these artists have become well known internationally.

Still striking a chord today are two Acadian bands that were formed in the 1970s: 1755 and Beausoleil Broussard. Other bands followed in their footsteps including Cabestran, Zéro degrés Celsius, Les Païens, Les Suroit, La Virée, Blou, Radio-Radio, Les Hôtesses d'Hilaire, and Les Hay Babies.

In the area of music education, the nuns *at Notre-Dame-du-Sacré-Cœur* have always taught piano and singing. Many young Acadians developed their voices and learned choral singing under the direction of Sisters Florine Després, Élodie LeBlanc, and Lorett Gallant, among others. The music department of the *Université de Moncton* also offers excellent professional courses.

Nadine Hébert is keeping choral music alive with the Jeunes Chanteurs de l'Acadie. Professors Monique Richard and Monette Gould are among the excellent choral directors in Acadie. Male choirs have flourished under Neil Michaud and Léandre Brault with their passion for Gregorian chant as well as classical and traditional music. Neil Michaud has directed his choir, Les chanteurs du Mascaret, on many tours performing for our Louisiana cousins. This choir is still based in Moncton and now is under the direction of Martin Waltz, former music teacher.

I must apologize, in closing, for not having mentioned all our artists—there are just too many to list. This growing number of musicians and singers are living proof that Acadians have constantly held all genres of music dear to their hearts and souls. Music has helped put the Acadian people on the map, not only here, but around the world, wherever our artists perform. Music continues to be enormously significant in Acadie!

ACADIAN CINEMA IN CANADA

Phil Comeau

Acadians have appeared on our television and movie screens, and more recently on the Web, for quite a while now. To chronicle this history, we will examine three types of motion picture production: documentary, fiction and animated films. I will mostly use the original titles for the Acadian films mentioned, although there are English versions for at least 25 percent of them.

The first film dealing with Acadians, *An Acadian Elopement*, came out in 1907. This fiction film was shot in black and white by the American company Biograph Films and recounts the story of a couple who honeymoon in Acadie. In 1913, the first Canadian feature film, *Évangeline*, was shot. The script/story was inspired by Longfellow's poem, the tale of two lovers separated during the Expulsion of the Acadians. Directed by Edward P. Sullivan and William Cavanaugh for Halifax's Canadian Bioscope Company, the film was shot in the Annapolis Valley, home to many of our Acadian ancestors. Unfortunately, this first Acadian feature has disappeared, and only stills from the film survive. In the United States and Canada, six films of varying lengths based on the mythical figure Evangeline were made between 1908 and 1929. The last one was shot in Louisiana. In 1928 and 1931, a series of documentaries on historical Acadie called *Land of Evangeline* was made.

It was not until 1948 that images of Acadians again came to the screen in the feature film *Louisiana Story*, from American filmmaker Robert Flaherty. Shot in southern Louisiana with real people in the roles, the film is now considered a classic. In 1949, the Toronto company Crawley Films produced the short documentary *Les Acadiens*.

The 1950s and 60s

In 1952, Montreal filmmaker Roger Blais directed two Acadian documentaries for the National Film Board of Canada (NFB). His short films, *Voix d'Acadie* and *Chanteurs d'Acadie*, detailed the popularity of the Saint Joseph College choir from Memramcook, New Brunswick. In 1955, he again focused on the Memramcook Acadians in his film *Les Aboiteaux*, from a script written by Acadian Léonard Forest.

In 1954, Léonard Forest became an in-house director at the NFB. His first Acadian film, *Pêcheurs de Pomcoup* (1956), shot with actual fishermen in Pubnico, Nova Scotia, highlighted their profession and day-to-day lives. He then directed the feature-length documentary, *Les Acadiens de la Dispersion* (1967), about the Acadian culture on an international level: in France, Louisiana, and the Maritime Provinces. Another documentary, *Acadie Libre* (1969), looked at the Acadian socioeconomic situation.

In this same period, Québec directors Pierre Perrault and Michel Brault (a Québécois of Acadian origin), shot *Éloge du chiac* (1969) in Moncton, a film about a schoolteacher explaining the issues surrounding the use of *chiac* (a linguistic mix of French Acadian and English) to her students. The feature-length documentary *L'Acadie, l'Acadie?!?* (1971) traces student movements at the *Université de Moncton* from 1968 to 1969. Considered a documentary masterpiece, the film continues to inspire filmmakers today.

The 1970s

Léonard Forest's hundred or so films written or produced in the 1970s during his time at the NFB in Montreal include a few Acadian films. In 1971, he directed the first feature-length docudrama on Acadians, *La Noce est pas finie*, which used actual fishermen in various roles and featured music by Acadian Madelinot Georges Langford. The action, un-scripted, takes place in a fictional Acadian village. The film is a parable of cultural transformation in Acadie. It is interesting to note that his last major Acadian film was shot in color. His documentary short film, *Un soleil pas comme ailleurs* (1972), looks at the socioeconomic situation on New Brunswick›s Acadian Peninsula. He showed Acadians who were angry with a government that was trying to move them into the city.

Robert Awad, a director from Kedgwick, New Brunswick, made the short *Truck* (1975), a comedy about the terrible state of the roads in New Brunswick, for the NFB in Montreal. His film combined documentary style and animation. In 1976, filmmaker Michel Brault returned to Acadie, this time with André Gladu, to shoot a wonderful series on francophone music, *Le son des français d'Amérique*. Some episodes were shot in Louisiana. André Gladu returned to Acadie several years later to shoot his documentary *Tintamarre*.

Léonard Forest played an important role in developing a cinema industry for Acadians and by Acadians. Because of the pressure he applied and with support from the NFB, a film studio was opened in Moncton in 1974. This decentralization program was originally called *Régionalisation Acadie*, but it changed names several times and will be called *Studio ONF Acadie* in this article. This program became the heart of Acadian cinema: it provided Acadians with the opportunity to talk about their interests, their concerns, their culture and their distinctiveness. Since it opened 40 years ago, the *Studio* has generated more than 130 productions and co-productions, making the *Studio ONF Acadie* the largest producer and co-producer of Acadian documentaries to date. The studio has also produced several fiction and animated films.

The first in-house producer at *Studio ONF Acadie* was Acadian Paul-Eugène LeBlanc. He produced a dozen films from 1974 to 1980. His films examine themes such as language, culture, history, poetry, traditional music, religion, fishing, youth and others. Notable among these films are *Une simple journée* (Charles Thériault), *Abandounée* (Anna Girouard), *La Cabane* and *Les Gossipeuses* (Phil Comeau), *La Confession* and *Souvenir d'un écolier* (Claude Renaud), and *Au boutte du quai* (Robert Haché). Some documentaries were made by a group of directors: *La nuit du 8, Y'a du bois dans ma cour, Le Frolic* and *cé pour ayder* and *Kouchibouguac.*

In the beginning, some of the dozen young Acadian directors at the *Studio ONF Acadie* chose to express themselves through fiction grounded in real issues: an alienating and suffocating religion, inter-generational communication, and ownership of a new Acadian identity forged in the fire of an arduous history. The fear of seeing their identity and culture disappear haunts those who want to express the Acadian experience in images. During the 1970s, the *Studio ONF Acadie*'s fiction and documentary films became the voice of a dissident generation in New Brunswick and Nova Scotia who were breaking taboos. From the very beginning, the *Studio* has helped provide stable careers for many filmmakers such as Charles Thériault and Phil Comeau, and cameramen who have become directors, such as Denis Godin and Rodolphe Caron.

The 1980s

In 1980, the second in-house producer at *Studio ONF Acadie* was Acadian Rhéal Drisdelle. He produced three documentaries: *Armand Plourde, une idée qui fait son chemin* (Denis Godin), *J'avions 375 ans* (Phil Comeau), and *Arbres de Noël à vendre* (Denis Morissette). His time as an NFB producer was not without problems. In 1980, the federal government imposed major budget cuts on NFB French productions and threatened to close the Moncton studio. Acadian filmmakers and technicians took to the barricades to assure the survival of their production centre. But in Montreal, pressure from some Québec directors who were not happy to see their production budgets shrink convinced those in charge of NFB French productions to move the Acadian production budget back to Montreal and close the Moncton studio. Maritime Acadian filmmakers worked together until 1982 in a long campaign to re-open the *Studio ONF Acadie.*

At the same time, Acadian filmmakers started forming the first independent production houses so that they could continue to make films. *Les Productions Godin* in Moncton coproduced the documentary *C'est nice de parler les deux manières* (Denis Godin) with Bayou Films. *Les Productions L. LeBlanc* in Moncton made the documentary *La musique nous explique* (Phil Comeau). *Les Productions Ciné-Baie* from Baie Sainte-Marie in Nova Scotia produced four documentaries: *Les pêcheurs aux homards, Margo un village de bûcherons, La Pointe à Pinkney,* and *Acadiennes de Clare* (Phil Comeau). The three production houses were soon faced with a lack of distribution and broadcast outlets, a sector of the industry that would take some time to develop.

The film cooperative *Cinémarévie Coop,* established in Edmunston, survived nearly 25 years and, from 1980 to 2005, produced the documentaries *Monsieur Lude, Avec le cœur, Le champion (*Rodolphe Caron*), La Bagosse* (Benoit Bérubé), *Je danse ma vie* (France Gallant), and *Mon grand-père me racon-*

tait (Denise d'Astous); the fiction films *Par un bon matin (*Rodolphe Caron*), Quand on est vache (*Hélène Daigle*), Le doute de Thomas* and *Au bout du chemin* (Samuel Caron); and the animated films *L'avertissement* and *Les joies de Noël* (Anne-Marie Sirois).

The NFB crisis was settled in January 1982 following constant pressure from filmmakers and lobbying by the *Société nationale de l'Acadie.* The *Studio ONF Acadie* re-opened, giving Acadian film production its second wind, and Éric Michel from France was appointed in-house Studio producer. However, during this two-year cinema "coma," most Acadian-trained directors had abandoned their profession. Other, more dissident filmmakers, particularly Phil Comeau, Robert Awad and Denis Godin, had to leave for Montreal to make films in the private sector. Phil Comeau directed *Le Tapis de Grand-Pré,* the first Acadian children's film, with *Via le Monde Productions.*

At the *Studio ONF Acadie*, producer Éric Michel offered new talent the opportunity to develop their skills. He produced the fiction films *Sorry Pete* and *De l'autre côté de la glace* (Serge Morin), and two docudramas, *Toutes les photos finissent par se rassembler* and *Le grand Jack* (Herménégilde Chiasson). He also produced the documentaries *Bateau bleu, maison verte* (Bettie Arseneault), *Une sagesse ordinaire, Une faim qui vient de loin, Femmes aux filets* and *Crab-O-Tango* (Claudette Lajoie-Chiasson), and his first animated film, *Maille Maille* (Anne-Marie Sirois). *Massabielle* (Jacques Savoie) was also added to the list. Savoie then moved to Montreal where he made his mark as a film and TV scriptwriter.

We soon saw new independent production companies appearing in New Brunswick. The company *Ciné-Est en Action* was founded with Lawrence Carota producing. Among the films they made were the features *Cap Lumière* and *Madame Latour* (Herménégilde Chiasson). The company would close their doors a few years later.

In 1986, producer Jean-Claude Bellefeuille created *Tel-Vision Productions* (now *Bellefeuille Productions*). The company started producing magazine shows, but eventually switched to documentaries. Jean-Claude Bellefeuille produced the documentaries *Migrations* and *Tour de magie* (Roger LeBlanc), *L'éloge du chiac Part 2* (Marie Cadieux), *Le matois* (Paul Arseneau), *Kouchibouguac, l'histoire de Jackie Vautour et des expropriés* (Jean Bourbonnais), *Le chant du phare* (Julien Cadieux), and the series *Les couleurs de mon accent* (Phil Comeau) and *1755* (Ivan Vanhecke).

In 1987, the *Festival international du cinéma francophone en Acadie* (FICFA) was created. The company *Film Zone* has been organizing the festival every year since 1992. This international festival's mission is to promote francophone cinema and make it accessible to Atlantic Acadians while introducing Acadian Cinema to Acadie and Canadian and international francophone communities. Its goal is to develop and promote the Acadian cinema industry; bring francophone films to the attention of the francophone and francophile communities in New Brunswick and the Atlantic provinces; foster an interest for francophone cinema in schools; and cultivate partnerships with other francophone festivals. During its 25-year history, FICFA has made a name for itself and enjoyed growing popularity because of its programmer, Marie-Renée Duguay. Many Acadian filmmakers have become known outside the region because of the festival's broad reach.

In 1988, a major independent production house was founded in Moncton: *Productions Phare-Est* (now *Phare-Est Média*). With a lot of determination and talent, the company has found a way to endure while making documentaries and fiction films. Cécile Chevrier, Ginette Pellerin, Herménégilde Chiasson, and Marc Paulin founded the company. For more than 25 years, this production house—now owned by producer Cécile Chevrier—has been very successful. It has won more festival awards and Gemini nominations in fiction and documentary than any other Acadian production company.

Productions from *Phare-Est Média* include *Belle-Baie* (written and directed by Renée Blanchar), co-produced with Montreal's Cirrus Communications. This series was an extremely popular show on national broadcaster Radio-Canada. Other fiction and documentaries that should be mentioned are: *Anna Malenfant d'Acadie* (Ginette Pellerin), *Les années noires* (Herménégilde Chiasson), *Acadie Liberté* (Tim Radford), *1604* (Renée Blanchar), *La Voisine* (Pam Gallant), *Un bon gars* (Laurence Véron), and the children's series *Lunatiques* (Chris LeBlanc and Paul Bossé). *Phare-Est Média*'s documentaries include *Grand-Pré – Écho de l'UNESCO* (Anika Lirette), *De Moncton à Kinshasa* (Paul Arseneau), *Naufrages* (Paul-Émile d'Entremont), *Frédéric Back – grandeur nature (*Phil Comeau), *Plus grand que la mer (*Marc Savoie), *PHOQUES le film* (Raoul Jomphe), *Le souvenir nécessaire* and *Le temps X* (Renée Blanchar), and the documentary series *Trésors Vivants* (collective). It also produced the series *L'Acadie de la mer* (various), *Chroniques de l'Atlantique* (various) and the documentaries *Durelle* (Ginette Pellerin), *Ceux qui attendent* (Herménégilde Chiasson) and *À cheval sur une frontière* (Rodolphe Caron) with the NFB.

In 1988, Québécois Michel Lemieux was appointed producer at *Studio ONF Acadie.* He produced the documentaries *Robichaud* (Herménégilde Chiasson) and *L'option cooperative* (Marc Paulin). Lemieux also co-produced some of the documentary series mentioned above with *Phare-Est.*

Francophone communities occupy a very small place in Canadian television content. To address this disparity, the *Fédération culturelle canadienne-française* founded the *Regroupement des arts médiatiques* (RAM) in 1988. RAM is a volunteer collective of directors, producers and screenwriters who work in a minority francophone environment.

In 1989, Prince Edward Island film director Pamela Gallant established her own company in Moncton, *Les productions bouteilles vides* where she directed *A la lumière des joueurs* and *Cent ans d'île.* In 1990, Paul-Marcel Albert created *Productions du Fado* in Caraquet and co-produced a short fiction film, *Le violon d'Arthur* (Jean-Pierre Gariépy, written by Jacques Savoie) with the NFB, and *Films de l'isle* in Montreal.

That same year, Acadian artists founded the *Association acadienne des artistes professionel.le.s du Nouveau-Brunswick* (AAAPNB) to represent all disciplines before the government and to offer information, promotion, and training services. Each art form is represented in the AAAPNB and Acadian filmmakers, actors and technicians come under the media arts discipline. The association defends artists' rights, helps improve their socioeconomic situation, and is presently elevating the status of artists in New Brunswick in a manner similar to that which exists in Quebec.

The 1990s

From 1991 to 1997, producer Pierre Bernier, formerly an Acadian film editor, became the fifth producer at the *Studio ONF Acadie*. With the weight of seasoned directors behind him, he and *Phare-Est Média* co-produced the documentaries *Acadie à venir* and *L'Acadie retrouvée* (Herménégilde Chiasson), and on his own produced the documentaries *Évangeline en quête* and *Mathilda la passionaria acadienne* (Ginette Pellerin), *De retour pour de bon* (Bettie Arseneault), *Vocation ménagère* (Renée Blanchar), *Épopée* (Herménégilde Chiasson), and *Cigarette* (Monique LeBlanc). Monique LeBlanc had shot the documentary *Le lien acadien* for the NFB in Halifax a few years previously.

In 1994, director Phil Comeau released his fiction film, *Le secret de Jérôme* (Jerome's Secret), the first independent Acadian feature film. Shot in Caraquet, the film won 15 awards at Canadian and international festivals, including three at the *Festival international du film francophone* in Namur, Belgium. The film was co-produced by Barry Cowling from Citadel Communications (New Brunswick), Gilles Bélanger from Atlantica Productions (New Brunswick) and Marie-Andrée Vinet from *Ciné-Groupe* (Québec).

1995 heralded the opening of new production houses by directors wanting more artistic freedom. A case in point is Rodrigue Jean, who set up Transmar Films in Caraquet. He produced and directed the documentary *La mémoire des rivières*. In 1999, he directed and co-produced his first feature film, *Full Blast* with Montreal's *Les films de l'isle*. The film went on to win the award for Best Canadian Feature Film at the Toronto International Film Festival. The Jutra for best actor went to Marie-Jo Thério for her role in *Full Blast*. Two feature films followed with an Acadienne singer as the main character: *Yellowknife* (2002) and *Long Song* (2008). That same year, Renée Blanchar and Didier Maigret founded Ça Tourne Production and produced the documentaries *Qui a tué l'Enfant Jésus?* (Renée Blanchar) and *André Lapointe, espaces (ré)créatifs* (Didier Maigret).

In 1995, spurred on by pressure from producers and directors, the provincial government set up Film NB, a film development agency similar to the one in Nova Scotia. This organization would help the province's filmmakers make the documentary and fiction films they wanted to make. It was also felt that having more work in the region would encourage filmmakers and technical crews to stay in the province to earn their living.

The following year, 1996, the *Association des producteurs du Nouveau-Brunswick* (now Média NB) was set up. It was mandated to represent all francophone and anglophone film and TV producers in New Brunswick.

In 1997, director Diane Poitras became the *Studio ONF Acadie* in-house producer. She chose to train the new generation of filmmakers and produced the documentaries *Seuls, ensemble* (Paul-Émile d'Entremont), *Les émotions ivres* (Hélène Daigle), *À demain chères prunelles* (Aube Giroux), *Plus grand que nature* (Jonathan Snow), and *L'Éternité? ou la disparition d'une culture* (Marie-Claire Dugas). She also worked with a few experienced filmmakers on the documentaries *Fripes de choix, guenilles de roi* (Bettie Arseneault), *Abegweit, le pont de la Confédération* (Serge Morin), and the animated film *Joséphine* (Anne-Marie Sirois).

In 1997, Moncton producer François Savoie started Connections Productions. The company specialized in documentary series and musical variety shows, producing the documentary series *Francophonies d'Amérique* (various), *Tournants de l'histoire* (various), *L'Acadie en chanson* (various), *Profils* (various), and *Passeport musique* (various). They co-produced the animated series *Animacadie* (various) with the NFB. As for fiction, the company produced the series *La Sagouine* (Phil Comeau) and co-produced the children's feature film *La gang des hors-la-loi* (Jean Beaudry) with Montreal's *Les Productions La Fête.*

The *Alliance des producteurs francophones du Canada* (APFC) was created in 1999 to answer the need for discussion on a national level. Many New Brunswick producers are members. The producers wanted to give a voice to their communities, providing them with a mirror that accurately reflects their authentic reality and represents them in the national television landscape. The *Alliance* represents its members with governments, institutions and organization to support the development, production and distribution of francophone works created outside of Quebec. It also promotes its members' work.

In 1999, Monique LeBlanc opened *CinImages Productions.* Specializing in documentary films, the company produced several series including *Petites vues de chez-nous* (various), *Artiste dans l'âme* (various), *Bazart* (various), and *Les Acadiens du Québec* (Phil Comeau). It produced the documentaries *La Petitcodiac une rivière renaît* (Renée Morel) and *Roméo Savoie, la peinture au corps* (Monique LeBlanc). It co-produced *Les chemins de Marie* (Monique LeBlanc) with the NFB.

The 2000s

In 2000, producers Jacques Lévesque and Colette Mallais opened Cojak Productions in Tracadie. They made the fiction shorts *La légende Bricklin, Les bootleggers d'Atlantique* and *Les larmes du Lazaret,* and the documentaries *Libérateur libéré* and *Désoriental* (all by Chris LeBlanc), *Fortunat* and *Pêcheurs de Lamèque* (Raynald Basque), *McGraw et le cercle des chefs* (Suzanne Chiasson), and the fiction series *La famille Basque* (Chris LeBlanc and Raynald Basque). Producer Sam Grana, former Film NB executive director, created *Productions Grana.* Although he worked mainly on English-language productions, he produced the Acadian fiction series *Samuel et la mer* (Pierre Gang).

That same year, Jacques Turgeon was appointed producer at *Studio ONF Acadie.* He breathed new life into the animated film sector by creating the *AnimAcadie* program, which co-produced *Faire le saut* (Anne-Marie Sirois), *Télé-Vision* (Jean-Pierre Morin), *Pimp ma botte* (Marc Daigle), *La balade de Marco* (Philippe Lanteigne), *Voodoo* (André Guy Landry), and *La plume et l'éléphant* and *Timine et Brossette* (Réal O'Neil). He also produced the documentaries *Kacho Komplo* and *U.S. Assez* (Paul Bossé), *Bonnes vacances* (Louiselle Noël), *Dis-moi ce que tu manges* (Aube Giroux), *Reema allers-retours* and *Le confessionnal réinventé* (Paul-Émile D'Entremont), *Raoul Léger la vérité morcelée* (Renée Blanchar), and *L'extrême frontière, l'œuvre poétique de Gérald Leblanc* (Rodrigue Jean). The Studio also co-produced documentaries with four production houses, *CinImage*, Ça tourne, *Ameri'ka* and *Appalaches*.

In 2001, Suzette Lagacé and Maurice Aubin opened Mozus Productions in Moncton. They produced the documentaries *Cayouche, le temps d'une bière* and *Aujourd'hui on est pu en '68* (Maurice Aubin), *Au-delà des apparences* (Suzette Lagacé), *Bonnes vacances* (Louiselle Noël), *Du stir en Acadie* and *Hâvrer à la Baie* (Joël Robichaud), and the documentary series *Peu importe l'âge* (various) and *Les sceaux d'Utrecht* (Paul Bossé).

In 2004, when the film co-op *Cinémarévie* closed, Rodolphe Carin and France Gallant set up *Productions Appalaches.* They co-produced three films with the NFB: *Pour la cause, Marie Hélène Allain en dialogue avec la pierre,* and *Léonard Forest cinéaste et poète* (Rodolphe Caron). They also finished *Au bout du chemin* (Samuel Caron), a feature film that had been started by *Cinémarévie.*

In 2004, independent Acadian filmmakers joined with other Canadian francophone filmmakers to form a national association, *Le Front des réalisateurs indépendants du Canada* (FRIC). This collective of francophone directors represents their members' interests in Canadian political and cultural arenas. The association focuses on professional development and getting its directors known to a larger audience.

Private industry was growing rapidly, so a local post-production house seemed desirable. In 2006, Marc Savoie set up PostMan in Moncton for video finishing. Two years later, Marcel Gallant's Storytellers and sound mixer Chris Goguen's *Studio Révoluson* joined PostMan for sound finishing. PostMan did the post-production on hundreds of films and TV shows. Today it belongs to Marc Savoie and Chris Goguen and is still the largest post-production house east of Montreal.

In 2007, Jacques Turgeon was promoted to the position of executive director at the NFB for all francophone regions beyond Montreal. He was replaced at the *Studio ONF Acadie* by Acadian producer Murielle Rioux-Poirier. Under his leadership, the *Tremplin* program was created to nurture new filmmakers. This new generation of filmmakers made the documentaries *Habiter la danse* (Julien Cadieux), *Ils eurent treize enfants* (Anika Lirette), *La trappe* (Mathieu D'Astous), *La dernière batture* (Lina Verchery), *Voleuse de Poussière* (Marie-Thérèse François), *Infusion* (Amélie Gosselin), *Un dimanche à 105 ans* and *Les inséparables* (Daniel Léger), and the fiction *Drôle de chapeau* (Mélanie Léger). The animated films *Le secret de Moustafa* (Joline Robichaud) and *Tic Tac* (Marc Daigle) were made possible under the *AnimAcadie* program. Web series saw the light of day with *Ta parole est en jeu* (various), *PIB* (various), *Chez soi* and *Ça tourne dans ma tête* (Louiselle Noël). A few films were produced with seasoned directors, including the documentaries *Une dernière chance* (Paul-Émile d'Entremont), *Ron Turcotte, jockey légendaire* (Phil Comeau), and the co-production *Éloge du chiac*, part 2 (Marie Cadieux).

In short time, seven new independent production houses cropped up in New Brunswick. In 2007, Ginette Pellerin and Pauline Bourque created Ameri'Ka Productions. They would co-produce the documentary *Antonine Maillet, les possibles sont infinis* (Ginette Pellerin), and produce the short fiction film *Le cowboy et les sauvages,* and the documentary *La cathédrale* (Ginette Pellerin). In 2008, Daniel Omer LeBlanc founded an animation company to produce his comedy series *Acadieman* (Dano LeBlanc). Following its popular success (it was broadcast for three seasons) and numerous awards, he produced and directed the feature animation *Acadieman vs. le C.M.A.*

In 2010, after Cojak Productions closed, René Savoie and Colette Mallais set up *Productions du Milieu.* They made the fiction series *Rural.com* (Pat Gauvin) in New Brunswick's Acadian Peninsula. Director Jean-Pierre Desmarais founded Imagique Productions where he produced and directed the sci-fi film *Terra Mars* and the short fiction *S.W.I.T.C.H.* (Jean-Pierre Desmarais). In Fredericton, Donovan Richard and Danny Thebeau set up Redleaf Productions so that they could produce and direct the historical fiction *Délivrance* together. In Moncton, director Gilles Doiron joined brothers Jean-Marc and Martin Goguen to create Botsford Productions. They made *La spare part* et *Aller-retour* (Gilles Doiron). And then, in Lamèque, director Patrick Gauvin created *Bosco Médias,* where he produced and directed the documentary *Lamèque en mouvement* and produced the first Web fiction series *Pirate* (Pat Gauvin).

In 2011, producer Maryse Chapdelaine, who had previously co-produced the latest films by Murielle Rioux-Poirier, became the new producer at *Studio ONF Acadie.* The *Tremplin* competition was rekindled to uncover new talent resulting in the production of these first documentaries: *Une affaire de famille* (Justin Guitard), *Emma fait son cinéma* (Mélanie Léger), and *Ma radio, mon amie* (Karine Godin). The Studio is now part of the NFB's *Studio de la francophonie canadienne* under executive producer Dominic Desjardins. This former Zazie Films director and producer directed an Acadian feature film, *Le divan du monde* (2009) and was president of the *Front des réalisateurs indépendants du Canada* for two years.

Acadian Cinema is Alive and Well

Since 1974—40 years now—the *Studio ONF Acadie* has accomplished a great amount. The *Studio* has produced or co-produced 130 films from dozens of filmmakers who left their mark by revealing their stories, hopes and fears, affiliations and differences. They have also expressed a very personal viewpoint of the Acadian experience that includes an interest in universal themes. *Studio ONF Acadie* has proved its worth in the Canadian film landscape and has supported the formation of talented filmmakers by generating steady work for them. *Studio* films have received more than 30 awards and special mentions in national and international festivals.

Private industry works hard to finance and produce high-quality films. The Acadian film industry is currently going through a difficult period. Production houses, including experienced directors, have to deal with increasingly smaller budgets that do not even cover the basics. And getting a broadcast license from a national network such as Radio-Canada is a daunting task. The arrival in 2014 of a new national network, TV5-UNIS, may provide more outlets for the Canadian francophonie. New distribution opportunities via the Internet offer other possibilities.

Despite the challenges and pitfalls, Acadian cinema has survived and has a devoted audience. Some Acadian production houses that were founded a long time ago are still active, notably Phare-Est Média, Connections Productions, Bellefeuille Productions, and CinImage Productions. Acadian production, although particularly rich in documentaries, has opened the door to fiction and animated films as well.

Acadian cinema has developed greatly since filmmaker Leonard Forest blazed the trail. Today, filmmakers from the following generation are still active, particularly Rodolphe Caron, Phil Comeau, Renée Blanchar, Ginette Pellerin, Paul-Émile D'Entremont, Chris LeBlanc, Rodrigue Jean, Roger LeBlanc, Paul Arseneau, and Anne-Marie Sirois. For a dozen years now, a third generation of filmmakers, including an increasing number of women, has been emerging to ensure the continuity of the industry. Together, male and female directors and producers continue to show Acadie and the whole world the stuff we are made of and where we are going. To be continued...

Bibliography

Josette Déléas, *Images d'Acadiens et de Cadjens de 1908 à 1994 : filmographie acadienne*, Moncton, *Centre d'études acadiennes*, 1995; Roland Brideau, *Culture de l'Acadie-Cinéma* in *L'Encyclopédie canadienne,* 1996; Maurice Rainville, *Cent ans de cinéma acadien,* Moncton, N.B., 2006; *Studio ONF Acadie* Website and archives, Moncton, N.B. (www.onf.ca); *Festival international du cinéma francophone* and *international du cinéma francophone en Acadie* Website and archives, Moncton, NB. (www.ficfa.com).

Websites

Front des réalisateurs indépendants du Canada (www.fricanada.org); *Alliance des producteurs francophones du Canada* (www.apfc.info); and *Association acadienne des artistes professionnel.le.s* (www.aaapnb.ca).

Cajuns in Films

Barry Jean Ancelet

Over the years, South Louisiana, described by anthropologist C. Paige Gutierrez as "south of the South," has been portrayed in films as an exotic wilderness with clear cultural, ethnic, and linguistic boundaries, a region that has what it apparently takes to produce a Hollywood stereotype: the Cajuns are Catholics in the Bible Belt; many speak French in this English-speaking country; and in a land dominated by genteel, even Puritan standards, they are consistently described as drinking, dancing, brawling gamblers. Cajun country was "discovered" by Hollywood early on in the development of the film industry. The first Tarzan movie was filmed near Morgan City, and in the 1920s, Dolores del Rio starred in a film adaptation of Longfellow's *Evangeline.* Since then, a few dozen films have been set among Louisiana's Cajuns, with results ranging from curious and haunting to bizarre and threatening.

The Cajuns made it onto Hollywood storyboards as a people among whom a hero can get into exotic trouble, thus providing an interesting alternative to the third world, with two fringe benefits: film crews don't need passports or electrical current adapters; and this alternative will not yet get them in trouble. Unlike Blacks, Jews, American Indians and other cultural and ethnic groups, the Cajuns are concentrated in a relatively small region and they have not learned to complain as a group. Portrayals of the Cajuns invariably are built around violence, racism, xenophobia, alcoholism, ignorance, isolation and inbreeding. Traditional occupations, such as trapping and fishing, are almost exclusively used as the context for Cajun characters and thus set them in a rural, rustic, isolated, underdeveloped, and extremely wet world.

The swamp is a hauntingly beautiful, photogenic landscape. Except for *Casey's Shadow* (1977), about a Cajun horse trainer on the prairies, and *The Big Easy* (1987), about an Irish/Cajun cop in New Orleans, the Cajuns have been portrayed as swamp dwellers in documentaries as well as features. In fact, if one were to believe the silver screen, one would think that most of South Louisiana is under water. *Louisiana Story* takes place in the swamp around Bayou Petit Anse. *Thunder Bay* is set in a Gulf Coast fishing village and offshore, *Live and Let Die* uses dry land as little more than a hurdle for James Bond in a speedboat. In *Southern Comfort,* errant National Guardsmen find themselves lost in a seemingly endless swamp. In *No Mercy,* Richard Gere and Kim Bassinger jump from a dock along the Mississippi River in Algiers into a nearby swamp (an interesting trick in the New Orleans metropolitan area). Bassinger incidentally finds ingenious ways to remain wet through most of the movie, partly because of her physique, and partly, one supposes, because of her Cajun background. These are just a few examples.

Robert Flaherty's 1948 documentary *Louisiana Story,* about the arrival of the oil industry among the Cajuns, echoes some of the notions established by Longfellow's *Evangeline.* Set on Bayou Petit Anse, the film presents the Cajuns as inhabitants of the "forest primeval," living in harmony with nature, quietly paddling along the natural curves of the bayous, far from the hustle and bustle of the urban mainstream. Standard Oil funded *Louisiana Story,* in part, to vaunt the progress brought by the oil industry. In hindsight, the message is quite the opposite. Now as we watch the arrival of the noisy machines that violate the silence, cutting unnaturally straight lines across the swamp, we are aware of such pressing contemporary ecological issues as salt-water intrusion, siltation, and erosion.

In *Thunder Bay* (1953), James Stewart stars as an Anglo-American dreamer/adventurer who designs, builds, operates, and brings in the first successful offshore oil well in the Gulf of Mexico. Though similar to *Louisiana Story* in some ways, this film shows considerably less indulgence toward the resident Cajuns. When their sleepy fishing village is invaded by the slick aggressive oil men, they revolt, struggling haplessly and hopelessly against progress, which is eventually rammed down their ungrateful throats. The Cajuns are portrayed as ignorant and superstitious, not unlike the image developed in Flaherty's docudrama. They are also superstitious and naïve, assuaged in defeat by the discovery of the "golden shrimp" that are attracted to the new platform at night.

American Films of the 1970s

During the 1970s, something happened to change Hollywood's image of the Cajuns from idyllic, naïve swamp dwellers to hostile, cunning swamp stalkers. This may have had something to do with the concurrent shift that took place in the portrayal of Southerners (described by Kirby in *Media-Made Dixie)* from the romantic racists of *Gone With the Wind* to the violent racists of *Hurry Sundown* and *Mandingo.* The entire nation watched as the South publicly confronted its sins during the Civil Rights struggle, and the violence in the news was translated onto the silver screen.

Several other factors may have contributed to the emerging image of the violent Cajuns. The Council for the Development of French in Louisiana (CODOFIL), created in 1968, launched a campaign to preserve Louisiana's French language and culture after decades of neglect. This effort included a highly visible public relations campaign that called attention to the Cajuns as a cohesive and different ethnic group. The effort to preserve the group's native French language went against the nationalistic current that had characterized the first part of this century; perhaps best expressed by former U.S. Pres. Theodore Roosevelt when he said such things as, "There is room for but one language in this country and that is the English language," and again, "There is no such thing as a hyphenated American, no such thing as a French-American, or German-American or Spanish-American. Those who feel French or German or Spanish should go home." Cajun music contributed significantly to the movement at the 1964 Newport Folk Festival. By the 1970s, Cajun musicians were exporting their French waltzes and two-steps to enthusiastic crowds at college campuses and folk festivals throughout America. The Cajuns had become a highly visible minority celebrating its difference.

Les Blank's 1971 documentary *Spend It All* portrayed the Cajuns as a hard-living, hard-playing people who enjoyed a wonderfully exotic cuisine and danced uninhibitedly to intense, soulful music sung in French. Blank was obviously fascinated with the Cajuns, viewing them as a refreshing alternative to the bland, rootless American mainstream, and his films enshrine this fascination. His documentary technique was exciting and innovative. In the tradition of Michel Brault and Richard Leacock, Blank made ingenious use of the hand-held camera, following the action, surprising his audiences and himself with the spontaneous discoveries he made through the lens. Blank was based in California and his innovative documentary was certainly not unknown among filmmakers.

Spend It All intends to be non-fiction. Unlike Flaherty, who directed real people in composed scenes designed to recreate reality, Blank filmed what was actually happening in front of his camera without direction, a style in the film genre called "cinema direct." Yet, as in all documentaries, there is no purely objective truth here. Blank's interests and curiosity led him to point his camera in certain directions and not in others. Further, logical connections were discovered and created in the editing room. In the end, even non-fictional films are in no small way the result of the vision and understanding of the filmmaker. Blank's admiration for the earthy values he found among rural Cajuns is due, in part, to his own disenchantment with the American melting pot. Furthermore, if he made a film about the Cajuns, it was not to show how they are the same as everyone else, but how they are different. He had no interest in showing Cajuns going to work at ordinary jobs in ordinary cars on ordinary highways, or cooking on ordinary stoves in ordinary kitchens, or watching television or going to the bank, or shopping at Winn Dixie. In the end, he did not make a film about the Cajuns. He made a film about what he found unusual, exciting, and different about the Cajuns. Unfortunately, when audiences in Peoria, or Chicago, or Tallahassee, or Laramie view Blank's documentary, they see it as a film about the Cajuns. This is a problem common to documentaries, especially those filmed not in some aboriginal tribe where everything really is different, but in America were many things are similar: the eccentricities of a culture end up defining it.

In 1975, another documentary focused on rural and small-town Cajuns (in Mamou, Eunice, and Basile). *The Good Times Are Killing Me* was produced by TVTV, a group based in California and New York experimenting with the use of new highly portable television equipment, the first mini-cams. Their documentary was edited from hundreds of hours of relatively inexpensive videotape recorded with the help of community leaders such as Paul Tate, Revon Reed, and Dewey Balfa.

Local projections of raw footage drew praise from locals. The final version, however, portrayed the Cajuns as a strange tribe of vulgar, hard partying, drunks; the front line in a losing battle for cultural and ethnic survival in America. Nathan Abshire, an impoverished, alcoholic musician, embittered and despondent about his son's recent arrest for the burglary of a drugstore, is defined as "everybody's idol." Louis Landreneau is presented dressing as a woman, complete with brassiere, pantyhose, wig, and makeup, under the careful supervision of his mother, without explaining that he is preparing for his community's *Mardi Gras* celebration.

Cajun women finally appear on the screen, in a beauty shop scene set up by one of the women crew members with the assurance that the vulgar jokes they were telling would not be used in the documentary; they were. By the time the woman's husband heard the whole sordid conversation on television, the crew was safely back in California. The *Mardi Gras* celebration is eventually presented with no explanation other than the definitions gathered by the fascinated but unenlightened crew from drunken participants.

In the 1970s, several fictional movies echoed the presentation of the Cajuns in these and other documentaries. *Live and Let Die* (1973), from the same period, develops the Southern genre of the inept sheriff as in the *Smoky and the Bandit* movies and the *Dukes of Hazzard* television series. James Bond's pursuit of a heroin kingpin leads him, among other exotic places, into the Louisiana bayous where he encounters a fat, stupid Cajun sheriff who is baffled by the witty, sophisticated debonair Bond. *Casey's Shadow* (1977) featured a run-down Cajun horse trainer with few redeeming values. He abuses alcohol, his children, and eventually his prize racehorse in his attempts to win a million dollar race and a little pride. The influence of Les Blank's racetrack scenes from *Spend It All* are hard to ignore.

More importantly, in 1975, Walter Hill was involved in two movies that featured the Cajuns. In addition to portraying the New Orleans Creoles as decadent, eccentric, and sexually deviant, *The Drowning Pool* has Harper, played by Paul Newman, roam the "steamy back roads and bayous of Louisiana" where he encounters a few odd, exotic Cajuns who describe themselves as "coonasses." *Hard Times,* the story of a bare-knuckle fighter, contains an episode in which a Cajun goes back on a bet–not impossible, but highly improbable in a culture characterized by an abiding respect for the rules of the game. In a particularly revealing scene, on his way out of a bar, the fighter shoots a jukebox playing Cajun music.

American Films of the 1980s

In 1981, Hill took on the Cajuns head-on in *Southern Comfort.* In this film, a disparate troop of National Guardsmen on maneuvers in the Atchafalaya Basin "borrow" a few *pirogues* from a Cajun hunting camp to cross a channel that does not appear on their maps. When they are halfway across, the Cajuns appear out of the woods and call for their boats. One of the guardsmen sprays the Cajuns with blank machine gun fire for a joke. The Cajuns, however, are not in on his joke and return real fire, killing the sergeant in charge. The remaining guardsmen escape to the other side, but the Cajuns pursue them. Without their leader, the guardsmen are "lost in a malignant landscape, quarrel among themselves as they are relentlessly pursued by an enemy they can't see, don't know, or understand." ("Bayou Guardsmen," *New York Times* Sept. 25, 1981, C20:1)

Using South Louisiana as an obvious metaphor for Vietnam, *Southern Comfort* is a story about the ineptitude of these ill-trained American troops in a "foreign" and hostile environment. The guardsmen find themselves in a war with the swamp-wise Cajuns who are almost invisible, gliding effortlessly through the scenes while the guardsmen fumble, fall, and wander in circles. Even nature seems to act against them. Eventually, all are killed but for the two guardsmen who have protested their cohorts' behavior.

The Cajun French language has long been an important ethnic identity marker, one which has not always had positive connotations when juxtaposed with the Anglo-American mainstream. Though the plot in *Louisiana Story* is the product of Flaherty's own observations and imagination, the Cajun characters are played by real people. Consequently, their speech is natural and authentic, shifting from accurate Cajun French to accented English as spontaneously as in real life. Hollywood's treatment of language is another matter.

In *Thunder Bay,* Gilbert Roland as Teche Bossier sounds more like Maurice Chevalier than a Cajun, and Antonio Moreno as the aggrieved father sounds Hispanic. In *Southern Comfort,* however, language becomes a barrier, an irritant, and a problem. When the guardsmen happen upon a Cajun swamper in the course of their flight, some of them assume that he is one of those responsible for the death of their sergeant and capture him. (Like the stereotypes concerning Blacks, Asians, Hispanics, and some other ethnic groups, one supposes Cajuns must all look alike.) When he insists that he does not speak English, they torture him to force a confession.

The 1980s saw a new set of films with Cajun episodes or settings. Of these, *No Mercy* (1986), *Angel Heart* (1987), and *The Big Easy* (1987) use cultural markers such as language, music, and cuisine to define and set off the Cajun and Creole characters. In *No Mercy,* the French language intensifies the exotic, thus threatening nature of New Orleans and Algiers (not in northern Africa, but across the river) for Chicago cop Eddie Jillette on a quest to investigate and eventually avenge his partner's brutal murder by the villain Losado.

Losado is presented as a sort of French Creole Mafioso. His exclusive and abusive relationship with the sultry Cajun beauty Michelle is underscored by the fact that they speak (subtitled) French to each other. Jillette abducts Michelle and escapes with her into the swamp. They discover a camp where she teaches him to eat crawfish after which they fall asleep exhausted by their flight. They are awakened the next morning by two Cajuns bearing shotguns who have the following exchange, in flawless Cajun French: *"Tu veux la piquer?"* (You want to screw her?) *"Oui, dans la bouche."* (Yes, in the mouth.) Never mind the meaning. The lines are not even subtitled. They are threatening simply by virtue of the fact that Jillette can't understand them, confirming his boss's warning as he was leaving Chicago. Speaking a language other than English is a badge of non-standard ethnicity. Losado's French already set him off; the Cajuns' non-standard dialect is beyond the pale. Lack of understanding naturally leads to fear and hate.

Angel Heart is set among the Black and French Creoles of New Orleans, characterized, as usual, by a steamy decadence and voodoo. Director Alan Parker uses the standard stereotypes. It rains throughout the film, and the daughter of Angel, a Brooklyn private eye, turns out to be named Evangeline Proudfoot. She even reports to him that "Mama waited, Mama died," echoing the fate of Longfellow's heroine.

In one remarkable scene, Angel pursues the truth into Cajun country, encountering cockfights, horse races, and what we later learn is his own true identity. In a striking manipulation of another cultural marker, one of Angel's contacts is boiled alive in a pot of gumbo. He later declines an invitation to eat with his client Louis Cyphere explaining, "Cajun cooking kills me."

The Big Easy features Dennis Quaid as Rémy McSwain, a free-wheeling New Orleans Irish-Cajun cop whose accent bounces back and forth between suburban New Orleans chat (which sounds a little like Brooklynese) and Cajun English dialect à la Justin Wilson: "I was just passing myself down to get breakfast."

The accent is so inauthentic and implausible that it is difficult for many who live in South Louisiana to suspend belief enough to enjoy the film. In fact, many movie-goers from the area took to counting his mispronounced uses of "*cher / chère*." A series of strange murders eventually leads Rémy and assistant D.A. Anne Osborne to uncover a ring of corruption in the New Orleans police department. Osborne is "not from here," and Rémy undertakes to smooth her rough edges as soon as he meets her. They soon fall for each other despite their best efforts.

The Big Easy is a cinematic tourist brochure, with every image designed to remind viewers that they are watching a fad-fueled film about the Cajuns and New Orleans—the Big Easy, as compared to New York, the Big Apple. As Rémy discusses his plight with Assistant District Attorney Osborne in his kitchen, there is a "How to Eat Crawfish" poster conspicuously located on the wall behind them. On their first date, they eat at Tipitina's (actually a local dancehall), served by a Paul Prudhomme look alike, with zydeco music in the background.

Rémy's apartment is predictably strewn with bachelor clutter, but not just any clutter: Irma Thomas, Dr. John, and Cajun music records. On their way to talk to Daddy Mention, the leader of the Black Creole underworld, they cross a jazz parade. Osborne eventually tries Rémy for taking a payoff (despite the obvious conflict of interest). He beats the rap and his victory party includes Cajun music on the porch of his mama's house and dancing in the yard, along a bayou, of course. As he discusses strategy with his NOPD staff, he makes his points with a stuffed alligator.

Recent studies seem to show that violence functions in a similar way south of the South (Ancelet, Brasseaux) and that filmmakers similarly misunderstand its nature there (Allain). At first, the Cajuns were generally presented à la Longfellow as a pastoral people living a rustic but gentle life in the Eden of Louisiana, in an image *National Geographic* endorsed around the same time in articles about these anachronistic, isolated French-speaking swampers. In

1953, *Thunder Bay* portrayed the Cajuns as hostile but ineffective, backward, and even pitiful in their struggle against the arrival of the offshore oil industry in scenes that caricature Cajun dueling traditions. Then, things began to change. In *Easy Rider* (1969), it happens that the Southern rednecks who blow Captain America and his sidekick to smithereens for no real reason are Cajuns.

Television frequently recycles images with little room for subtlety. The violent Cajun on film becomes even worse on television. In the early 1980s, the Cajuns appeared in several weekly series, including *Knight Rider* and *Stunt Man,* both produced by Glen Larson with similar results. If films such as *Southern Comfort, No Mercy,* and *The Big Easy* were the result of second generation stereotypes, these television programs represent a third generation. The *Knight Rider* episode is typical. Knight and his talking computerized car go to South Louisiana to break up a drug-smuggling ring. They are assisted in their efforts by a hauntingly beautiful dark-eyed Cajun woman. Unbeknownst to her, her boyfriend (or spouse) is involved in the ring. When he learns that she is inadvertently working against him, he confronts her, demanding loyalty. She refuses, insisting on doing what is right, so he beats her up. She protests and his response is, "Well, you know how us Cajun men are." He knocks her out and leaves her for dead on the floor of the cabin, which he then sets afire. The revived *Mission Impossible* also gave similar treatment. Cajun country seems to provide an exotic alternative to Appalachia and the big city ghetto as a place for television heroes to solve problems.

Many cultures are used and abused by Hollywood. Yet, most have more than one perspective available. We know that New York is not all slums and bums because we occasionally see Rockefeller Center and Park Avenue. There is, however, a remarkable consistency in the portrayal of the Cajuns in film. Even Robert Flaherty's widely respected *Louisiana Story* presented the Cajuns as backward, isolated, and superstitious swamp dwellers with few indications of contemporary civilization. Flaherty's black and white documentary is not exactly a regular in the video store trade or on the cable systems. The problem is that many people are impressed, to an important extent, by what they see on television and at the movies. It is true that some people know better than to believe everything they see on the screen. But for others, this may be the only source of information about such matters, the only time the subject comes up. What does the general public know about the American Indians, or people in Appalachia, or the Inuits? More people likely saw *Witness* than read a carefully documented description of the Amish.

Nevertheless, no amount of complaining will resolve this issue. In fact, complaints are invariably ignored by media executives who cannot be bothered with such trivial concerns as accuracy. When the *Knight Rider* episode aired, a few dozen people I know joined me in complaining to NBC. We all received the same form letter explaining that we had misunderstood the intent of the program. One way for Cajuns (and other ethnic groups) to repair Hollywood's faulty image is to take the media into their own hands, to tell their own stories. This is, of course, difficult since television and film production is expensive. Cable and community access television have opened new opportunities, but generally do not reach beyond the region. South Louisiana has begun to produce its own interpreters. Some have learned to work with filmmakers; instead of simply giving an interview, they are positioning themselves as consultants. Some have begun to produce their own documentaries and films to define the people and the culture from the inside.

California-based record producer Chris Strachwitz teamed up with filmmaker Les Blank to produce a documentary on the history and development of Cajun music and zydeco called *J'ai été au bal*. Blank, who had always avoided narration in his documentaries, was talked into using it in this film. In fact, the very structure and movement of the film are based on the narration provided through interviews with insiders such as Marc Savoy, Michael Doucet, and myself. In a quest for accuracy, Strachwitz willingly subjected his project to constant editorial input from his major consultants.

I could continue with the other American films shot from the 90s on to today, but the Cajun characters are often very much based on the same stereotypes, including the recent Oscar-nominated movie *Beasts of the Southern Wild.*

Homegrown Cajun Films

WLAE public television in New Orleans aired *Cajun Crossroads,* a carefully documented local production by Karen Snyder, which is heavily based on interviews with the historians, linguists, sociologists, and folklorists who are just now discovering the nature of Cajun culture and who all served as editorial consultants on the project. *Cajun Crossroads* avoids the usual speed of media presentation, which tends to flit from one image to another, supposedly to keep the attention of the audience. This locally produced documentary dares to dwell on characters and issues long enough to present the culture in its complexity.

Some documentaries are not so much about the Cajuns as about facets of Cajun life. Filmmakers Patrick Mire and Charles Bush have produced two documentaries that represent a more unselfconscious look at Cajun folklife from the inside. Mire's *Anything I Catch: The Handfishing Story* explores the tradition of hand fishing and includes both exciting footage of this disappearing practice and engaging commentary about the relationship between natural and cultural resources. Going far beyond the portrayal of the country *Mardi Gras* as a mindless drunken spectacle, Mire's *Dance for a Chicken* traces the complex history of the celebration and shows the rich diversity of its contemporary versions as found in communities across South Louisiana, including the variety in songs and dances, costumes and masks, ceremonial begging traditions and ritual floggings. This fascinating documentary shows indirectly but effectively how communities define themselves through cultural expression.

Cajun filmmaker Glen Pitre's first films were in Cajun French, with local actors. An avid student of oral history, he sought inspiration in the stories of his own family and region. *Fièvre jaune* is the story of a yellow fever epidemic and the effect that the ensuing quarantine has on a close-knit family and community. *Huit piastres et demie* is a docudrama about a shrimpers' strike, ingeniously illustrating the oral history simultaneously from the two opposing points of view. Both stories are about confronting pressures that threaten to rip apart families and communities, reflecting the Cajuns' long history of surviving upheavals with a strong sense of social cooperation and solidarity.

These low-budget exercises eventually attracted the attention of Robert Redford's Sundance Institute and gave Glen Pitre the contacts and the momentum he needed to tackle a real commercial film. With outside support and outside funding came outside pressures. The project's title was eventually changed from the lyrical *Acadian Waltz* to *Belizaire the Cajun,* apparently because supporters wanted to capitalize on the popularity of Cajun cooking and music. The story is set in mid-19th-century Louisiana and features a *traiteur* (faith healer/folk medicine man) who is typical of the traditional trickster hero in Louisiana French oral tradition. In fact, the film owes much to folktale style and structure. Belizaire Breaux eventually breaks up a vigilante movement that is exiling "undesirable" Cajuns to Texas, and wins the girl and a bit of booty in the end, in the tradition of the folk hero. The story is told from the inside. It is not about a visitor among the Cajuns. It is not so much about the Cajuns. It is rather set among the Cajuns and consequently includes rich ones and poor ones, heroes, rascals, and villains. Like its predecessors, it is fundamentally about the preservation of community.

Cajun film director and scriptwriter Glen Pitre (right) with co-producer Allan Durand Jr., are on the set of Pitre's first feature film, Belizaire the Cajun, *filmed on location in St. Martinville, in June 1985.*

As a historical drama, however, *Belizaire* avoids the contemporary image problem. The story about being Cajun in today's world had not been filmed until recently when director Patrick Mire took on the challenge in his feature film *Dirty Rice.* Based on his own original screenplay, the film deals with the return of a young Cajun man to his family rice farm after learning about the wide world. There he faces the kinds of decisions that are the stuff of real-life dilemmas for many young Cajuns today who have to negotiate a place for themselves between the pressures of the past and those of the future. And again, it is a story about the preservation of the community and of social and culture values.

In a set of recent documentaries, including *I Always Do My Collars First* and *T-Galop,* Cajun filmmaker Connie Castille demonstrated a clear understanding of a principle suggested by Patrick Mire in *Anything I Catch: The Handfishing Story.* In order to balance the image of the Cajuns in film, we have to tell our own stories, but we don't have to tell the whole story in one film. These three films are most remarkable for their tight focus on a part of the cultural scene. Yet they all expose much more about the culture than that tight focus. Ironically, perhaps focusing on too much has typically ended up caricaturing the whole, while focusing on a more manageable part has ended up exposing much more.

Conclusion

The image of the Cajun in film is obviously faulty. Three factors could help rectify this image problem. One involves developing an informed public in South Louisiana. Sometimes in our haste to entertain visitors, we create a poor long-term impression, representing ourselves as carefree party animals interested in little more than *laisser le bon temps rouler*. Another involves telling our own stories from the inside. We have many interesting stories and many great storytellers; we know the subtleties from the stereotypes. We just need to start developing them ourselves. Still another involves working more closely with outside filmmakers to provide accurate information about ourselves. It is unlikely that filmmakers who have presented this area poorly in the past did so because they had it in for us. In most cases, any errors they may have made were based on misunderstandings and misinformation, coupled with a desire for the sensational. We should not neglect to consider the impact of these films on our cultural and social ecology. The state's film commission is in a position to do more than recruit film projects wholesale. We try to entice film crews to come to Louisiana because they spend lots of money on hotels, meals, and production support. But do we really want to be in the movies at any cost?

Bibliography

Edward D. C. Campbell, *The Celluloid South: Hollywood and the Southern Myth* (Knoxville: University of Tennessee Press, 1981); C. Paige Gutierrez, *Cajun Foodways* (Jackson: University of Mississippi Press, 1992); and Jack Temple Kirby, *Media-Made Dixie: The South in the American Imagination* (Baton Rouge: LSU Press, 1978).

Movies

Belizaire the Cajun, director Glen Pitre, Côte Blanche Productions, 1985; *Deliverance*, director John Boorman, 1982; *Dirty Rice*, director Pat Mire, Attakapas Productions, 1998; *Dedans le sud de la Louisiane,* director Jean-Pierre Brunot, 1973; *Evangeline,* director Edwin Carewe, 1929; *Fièvre jaune*, director Glen Pitre, Côte Blanche Productions, 1978; *Gone with the Wind,* director Victor Fleming, 1939; *The Good Times Are Killing Me,* director Paul Goldsmith, TVTV, 1975; *Huit piastres et demie*, director Glen Pitre, Côte Blanche Productions, 1980; *Hurry Sundown*, director Otto Preminger, 1967; *In the Heat of the Night,* director Norman Jewison, 1967; *Live and Let Die,* director Guy Hamilton, 1973; *Louisiana Story,* director Robert Flaherty, Standard Oil, 1948; *Mandingo,* director Richard Fleischer, 1975; *No Mercy,* director Richard Pearce, Tri-Star, 1986; *Le son des Cadiens (en quatre parties),* director André Gladu and Michel Brault, Nanouk Films, 1976; *Southern Comfort,* director Walter Hill, Goldwyn, 1981; *Spend It All,* director Les Blank, Flower Films, 1971; *Tarzan of the Apes*, director Scott Sidney, 1918; *Thunder Bay,* director Anthony Mann, Universal, 1953.

Visual Arts of the Cajuns of South Louisiana

Mary Broussard Perrin

Acadians the world over have come to the visual arts via a long and difficult road. When Joseph *dit* Beausoleil Broussard brought the largest group of Acadians to the Louisiana wilderness of the Attakapas Territory, these pioneers began carving out settlements along the waterways of Bayou Teche in the midst of a devastating smallpox epidemic. Early renderings of the shelters that the early settlers managed to build show them to be simple palmetto huts. No doubt the able-bodied women immediately began performing the necessary domestic arts of, among other things, basket-making, soap and candle making, and later, spinning, weaving, and sewing. The survivors and their descendants later built simple wooden cabins insulated against the harsh semi-tropical climate with *bousillage*, a mixture of mud and Spanish moss. They built *pirogues* (a type of canoe) and rafts for transportation on bayous and rivers, and crafted tools and metal implements such as hinges and kitchen utensils. Farm buildings were constructed, and during times of prosperity, the *cabines* might have expanded to include outdoor kitchens.

There was little time left in a day to dabble in the finer arts–considered frivolous by most because they couldn't be eaten, slept on or under, worn, or used as shelter. During this time period, which lasted approximately two centuries, most Acadians had little extra time or money, and could only continue to practice, and even excel at, the survival arts as described above. It was only after this period of establishing new homes, farms, and permanent communities was successfully underway that the early settlers' descendants could begin to dream of having the luxury and the means of being educated in and creating visual arts. It was only after the Acadians–now known as Cajuns–gained a measure of equality with their non-Acadian peers in the mid to late 20th century did they dare to put themselves and their art out into the world.

Eight Visual Artists

George Rodrigue

Our book's cover artist George Rodrigue (1944-2013) was born and raised in New Iberia, Louisiana, in the heart of Cajun country. Rodrigue began painting in the third grade while bedridden with polio. Later, through his studies at the University of Louisiana at Lafayette followed by the Art Center College of

Design in Pasadena, California, he obtained a foundation that spawned one of the greatest success stories in southern art. He is now the subject of 12 books published nationally and internationally, as well as numerous museum exhibitions including retrospectives at the Dixon Gallery and Gardens Museum in Memphis, Tennessee, in 2007, and the New Orleans Museum of Art in 2008, both of which broke attendance records for living artists or contemporary shows.

He is best known for his iconic Blue Dog series of paintings, which catapulted him to worldwide fame in the early 1990s. Originally derived from the legend of the *loup-garou* (a Cajun werewolf), Rodrigue has sent the Blue Dog on a 25-year odyssey of exploration of and commentary on life at the turn of the 21st century. Prior to this, he had already won local acclaim for his rich depictions of images from his Cajun heritage–spreading moss-draped oaks, swamps, and scenes of music, food, festivals, and his own Cajun people.

Rodrigue exhibited his original paintings and silkscreens in his New Orleans, Lafayette, and Carmel, California, galleries. In New Orleans, he purchased and renovated a 200-year-old French Quarter building adjacent to St. Louis Cathedral, providing him more than 4,000 square feet of exhibition space.

Through his George Rodrigue Foundation of the Arts, Rodrigue raised $2.5 million benefiting post-Katrina New Orleans through sales of his relief prints. In early 2013, he held his fourth annual statewide art contest for high school juniors and seniors, a contest that has attracted 1,500 applicants since 2010 and granted over $150,000 in scholarships, art supplies, and other assistance. Today, the foundation's primary focus is to expose children to education in the visual arts in the hopes of inspiring an early and on-going creative passion similar to Rodrigue's own.

According to his son Jacques, his father said that if he had not been from the Acadiana region, he probably never would have been an artist. It was his Cajun culture and heritage that inspired him to paint.[1] Rodrigue passed away on December 14, 2013, at the age of 69.

Photo©George Rodrigue foundation

George Rodrigue, The Aioli Dinner, *oil on canvas, 48" x 36", 1971.*

George Rodrigue in his studio with a canvas depicting his iconic Blue Dog.

Elemore Morgan Jr.

Elemore Morgan Jr. (1931-2008) has been acknowledged as the leading contemporary Louisiana landscape painter for many years. He was especially renowned for his *plein air* landscape paintings done in the heart of the rice-growing region of southwest Louisiana. Many of Morgan's landscapes were done in acrylic on oddly shaped Masonite panels, cut to fit his vision of the land, and which he felt were integral to the design and composition of his works. Possessed of an amazing ability to transmit what is real and true about the southwest Louisiana landscape, Morgan communicated in his vibrant, color-saturated paintings the intense heat and overbearing humidity of the rice fields of Acadiana.

Morgan was born in Baton Rouge in 1931. After serving in the Air Force during the Korean War, he graduated from the Ruskin School of Fine Art in Oxford, England. He returned to Louisiana, and in 1968 became a professor of Fine Art at the University of Southwestern Louisiana, where he taught until 1998. Morgan's teaching skills were legendary. He was demanding, requiring a great deal of studies for his projects, yet his critiques were as gentle as the man himself. Generations of students remember him with the highest respect and appreciation.

In 2006, Morgan was given a major retrospective at the Ogden Museum of Southern Art, entitled *Art and Life in Louisiana: Elemore Morgan Sr. and*

Elemore Morgan Jr., which included the pioneering Louisiana photography work of his father.

Morgan received a Krasner-Pollock Foundation grant in 2007, which allowed him to travel to New York City where, again working in the open air, he completed multi-paneled paintings of the Manhattan skyline. Near the end of his life he also completed several Crescent City riverscapes. Morgan passed away in 2008 at the age of 76.

Photo©Elemore Morgan Jr. estate

Elemore Morgan Jr., June Rice, acrylic on masonite, 45" x 37-1/4".

Photo©Elemore Morgan Jr. estate

Elemore Morgan Jr., Early Barn, acrylic on masonite, 48-1/4" x 56-1/2", 2007.

Troy Dugas

The unique collages of Troy Dugas (b. 1970), purposeful and deliberate, are made from vintage product labels purchased in unused bundles. The material is cut or shredded, then arranged onto flat surfaces (paper, canvas, or wood) to produce artwork that appears woven. Repetition, pattern, precision, and scale are used to distract from the original purpose of the label to advertise. The essential elements of color, shape, and line are utilized in a new way, and the altered context of the source material provides new meaning. Aesthetic sensation and contemplation is substituted for the immediacy of the graphic label. According to Dugas, there is a certain mischievous pleasure in the process of this transformation, and at the same time, a kind of meditation. The images take on a spiritual quality but have no defined religious affiliation, only the wandering spirit of a scavenger creating his own myths.

Dugas, born in Rayne, received a BFA from the University of Southwestern Louisiana in 1994. He moved to New York shortly after graduating and earned an MFA from Pratt Institute. He lived and worked there until returning to Louisiana in 2002. He experienced a tremendous amount of growth as an artist living in New York, and worked as a successful designer in the fashion and television industries for many years. For the last decade, he has dedicated himself to the development of his art, receiving awards from the Pollack-Krasner Foundation and the Louisiana Division of the Arts. His work is included in many private and public collections such as the Frederick Weisman Foundation in California and the West Collection in Pennsylvania. Troy is represented by the Arthur Roger Gallery in New Orleans, the McMurtrey Gallery in Houston, and the Barbara Archer Gallery in Atlanta.

Troy Dugas, product labels on paper, 60" x 60", 2012.

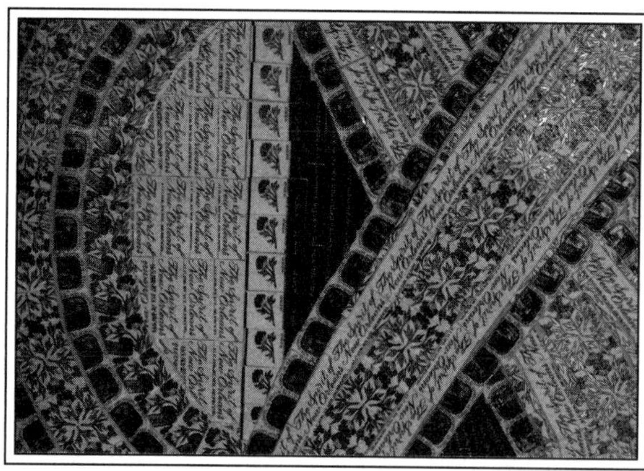

Herbsaint *detail, 2012*

Debbie Fleming Caffery

Internationally renowned photographer and New Iberia native Debbie Fleming Caffery (b. 1948) graduated from the Academy of the Sacred Heart in Grand Coteau, Louisiana, and went on to obtain a Bachelor of Fine Arts degree from the San Francisco Art Institute. Known world-wide as a documentary photographer and photography teacher, she is the recipient of numerous awards, including a Guggenheim Fellowship, the George Soros Foundation's Katrina Media Fellowship, the Museum of Photographic Arts of San Diego's Lou Stoumen Award, and the Louisiana Endowment for the Humanities' Michael P. Smith Documentary Photography Award. Her early work on the Louisiana sugar cane harvesting resulted in a book, *Carry Me Home*, published by the Smithsonian Press, and was the subject of a one-person show at the Smithsonian's National Museum of American History in Washington, D.C. Her other books include *Polly and The Shadows*, published by Twin Palms Press; *The Spirit and The Flesh*, published by Radius Books; and *Collection L'Oiseau Rare, Filigranes Edition*, France.

Her work has been exhibited internationally and is in the permanent collections of the Museum of Modern Art, New York; the Whitney Museum of American Art, New York; the Metropolitan Museum of Art, New York; *Bibliotheque Nationale*, Paris, France; the City of Paris; *Fond Nationale D'Art Contemporain*, Paris, France; *Museem Fur Kunst und Gewerbe*, Hamburg, Germany; the New Orleans Museum of Art; the Ogden Museum of Art, New Orleans, Louisiana; Harvard University, Boston, Massachusetts; Tulane University, New Orleans, Louisiana; the Elton John Collection; and the Boston Museum of Fine Arts.

Especially interesting to Louisiana Acadians are Caffery's works centering on the sugar industry of Louisiana. Since the early 1970s, she has photographed workers in the sugar cane fields and sugar mills of her native state. She is represented by the Gitterman Gallery, New York; *Camera Obscura Gallery*, Paris, France; and the *Box Gallerie*, Brussels, Belgium.

Debbie Fleming Caffery, Mary Van's Camp, *silver gelatin print, 20" x 24", 1987.*

Debbie Fleming Caffery, Papa, *silver gelatin print, 20" x 24", 1987.*

Lou Blackwell

A Louisiana native, Lou Blackwell (b. 1948) has called Acadiana home for the last 30 years. She received her art education at Newcomb College of Tulane University, the University of Louisiana at Lafayette, the Santa Fe Art Institute, the Vermont Studio Center, and Vermont College of Norwich University, where she earned an MFA degree in 2000.

In recent years, Blackwell has been honored with a Visual Artist Fellowship from the Louisiana Division of the Arts; a public art commission from the Joan Mitchell Foundation and the Arts Council of New Orleans; first prize at the Southern Open, a regional biennial sponsored by the Acadiana Center for the Arts, Lafayette, Louisiana; solo exhibitions in New Orleans and Lafayette; and a Chevron Foundation grant.

A conceptual artist, Blackwell is inspired by current events and questions how our actions affirm or contradict the American values we espouse. She works in both two- and three-dimensional media, allowing the topic of inquiry to suggest the materials and means of expression.

Over the last decade, no event has done more to test the mythology of American exceptionalism and invincibility than the tragedy of Hurricane Katrina. For a series of digital collages, entitled *Broken Rainbow*, she paired news media photographs of New Orleans in Katrina's wake with iconic imagery from Michelangelo's 16th-century frescoes for the Sistine Chapel. Both sources depict the failure of a civilization while simultaneously celebrating individual acts of courage, empathy, and resilience. The layered narratives, both ancient and modern, merge to create a third context where Old Testament heroes share pictorial space with contemporary actors, affirming the universality of man's experience.

Lou Blackwell, All Aboard, *a panoramic view of a 2,500 square foot banner mural on Poydras at Carondelet St., New Orleans, Louisiana, commissioned by the Joan Mitchell Foundation and the Arts Council of New Orleans for Art in Public Places, 2008-2010.*

Lou Blackwell, Instruments of Passion, *archival print on matte paper, 30" x 36", 2008.*

Mary Beyt

Mary Beyt (b. 1959) is a native and current resident of Lafayette who lived and worked as an artist in New York City for 20 years. She considers herself a visual storyteller, with her paintings being the portals for the narratives that are non-linear, abstracted, and self-referencing. Bits and pieces of her subconscious dance or march across the canvas; images, often mythical, botanical, and/or anatomical in nature appear, reappear, and morph. That change, she says, is reassuring.

Beyt wears many hats: in addition to being a painter, she is a curator at the Acadiana Center for the Arts and a sought-after interior designer. Holding a BFA from Washington University in St. Louis, as well as MA and MFA degrees from Yale School of Art and Architecture, Beyt has exhibited widely across the United States and Europe as well as far-away destinations such as Hong Kong.

Besides numerous group exhibitions, she has also had several solo shows in New York, Los Angeles, California, and Louisiana. She has been included in several prominent exhibitions including the San Francisco Museum of Modern Art; the Wexner Center for the Arts in Columbus, Ohio; and the Ogden Museum of Southern Art in New Orleans. Beyt is in the permanent collections of the Whitney Museum of American Art, New York; the Norton Foundation; American Express; and the Progressive Corporation; with critical discourse published in Art Forum, the *New York Times*, the *Los Angeles Times, The New Yorker, Time Out, Flash Art*, the *Boston Globe*, the *Miami Herald, The Times-Picayune, Gambit Weekly*, and others.

Mary Beyt, The Repair, *acrylic on canvas, 16" x 20", 2008.*

Photo©Gene Beyt

Megan Barra

A lifelong resident of Lafayette, Louisiana, Megan Barra (b. 1959) received a BFA from the University of Louisiana at Lafayette. Inspired by both graphic design and vintage quilts, her current medium of choice is fabric. Silk guitars, horns, accordions, and fiddles, along with crabs, snakes, and coffee cups are fashioned into patchworks reminiscent of the Louisiana culture in which she is immersed. Music and the men and women who play it, along with the Louisiana landscape, provide rich material for Barra to draw from. Her silk fabric compositions are hand-sewn, sometimes imprinted with original text and images, and finished on a 1901 Singer treadle sewing machine. Barra's work has been exhibited in galleries and museums in South Louisiana, Quebec, and France.

As a designer, she has worked in a variety of media and in collaboration with painters, photographers, illustrators, and printmakers. Barra has been named Art Director of the Year by the Acadiana Advertising Federation eight times, and has had her work selected to appear in such prestigious publications as *The Art Directors Club of New York*, *Graphis Book Design*, *Graphis Poster*, *The Society of Illustrators Annual*, *Communication Arts*, and the American Association of Museums *Museum News*. In 2001, her design for Sonny Landreth's CD *Levee Town* was nominated for a Grammy Award in the "Best Recording Package" category.

"I owe a great debt to the many teachers and artists who've inspired me," Barra says, noting especially Elemore Morgan Jr., Darrell Bourque, Sonny Landreth. "Louisiana is home to such an incredibly deep and rich culture. Our music and cuisine are great examples: it seems people here are always combining different elements to create new concepts and express new ideas." It is the same with visual artists.

Barra's work is defined as much by its daring and passion as it is by its beauty and restraint. As an artist and designer, she powerfully arranges and re-arranges imagery to vividly express intangible emotions, observations, and responses. Barra designed the cover of this book and artfully created the numerous maps found herein.

Megan Barra, Festivals Acadiens et Créoles, *silk composition, 22" x 28", 2012.*

Photo©Megan Barra

Megan Barra, New Orleans Horns, *silk composition, 13" x 19", 2008.*

Camille Comeaux

Camille Comeaux (b. 1996) is one of Acadiana's top up-and-coming photographers. Currently, and at just 17 years of age, she already has a national award under her belt. An image Comeaux submitted as a high school junior during a Savannah College of Art and Design (SCAD) Summer Seminar program won an honorable mention in a world-wide photography competition sponsored by SCAD. Comeaux, currently a senior at Lafayette High School, opened her own business, Camille Comeaux Photography, at age 15 by taking creative senior pictures of her older graduating schoolmates. The business has since expanded into other types of photography such as photojournalism, and numerous images have been published.

Comeaux became interested in photography at age 13 when she began taking images of wildlife in the marshes of Vermilion Parish, Louisiana, while hunting with her father. She has obtained a good deal of hands-on experience as a photographer for her high school yearbook and by taking photographs through her company for business brochures and websites, magazine, and newspaper articles, and two published books. She also documents mission trips she participates in to Honduras and Panama, and is well-known for taking photographs of people in their natural element.

Camille Comeaux, Man vs. Wild, *photograph, 8" x 10", 2011.*

Camille Comeaux, The Mission, *photograph, 8" x 10", 2011.*

The visual arts are at last flourishing in the Acadiana region of Louisiana. Cajun artists have had the opportunity to be educated in the arts both in the U.S. and abroad. Prestigious awards, festivals, and exhibitions proclaim their talents. Museums and art connoisseurs from New York, Washington, and Los Angeles to France, Germany, and Hong Kong collect their work. Young Cajun artists, such as Camille Comeaux, who utilize their unique Cajun culture to sustain and inspire them, will ensure that Acadiana will be infused with the visual arts for years to come.

Endnotes

1. Kris Wartelle, "Retrospective examines Rodrigue's life, career," *The Daily Advertiser*, January 23, 2014, p.1.

Four Generations of Visual Arts in Acadie

Herménégilde Chiasson

It is true that there are several Acadies, but everyone agrees that they all originated in the same place, a northern area where the severe climate caused many difficulties and political tensions resulted in tragedies that we are still trying to deal with. For practical purposes, we will call this original Acadie, where we still live, Northern Acadie to distinguish it from the southern locale that we increasingly call "Tropical Acadie."

The history of Acadian art is difficult to describe because, up until the 1970s, there was little of what would qualify as art in today's terms. It is interesting to note that the early period of the colony in 1604-1605 was characterized by a cultural vibrancy that would not last long. The first play written and performed in North America was produced in Port-Royal. The playwright was a young lawyer named Marc Lescarbot, who would also author a collection of poetry called *Les Muses de la Nouvelle-France*, considered the first literary work to be published in North America. Port-Royal was also the birthplace of the Order of Good Cheer, which could be considered the first social club in North America. There was obviously a quality of life in the young colony that goes beyond the simple survival that we generally associate with this type of venture.

However, for visual representations we must wait for Samuel de Champlain's books or his embellished maps to be published in order to have an idea of what the French thought of their new land. These engravings are certainly the first historical images of the continent to appear, and so are extremely significant. But can they be considered works of art? There follows a huge gap, for we have no more images documenting what was happening in Acadie.

We do, however, have images that could qualify as a "flashback" to an event considered central to defining present-day Acadie: the mass expulsion that took place in the middle of the 18th century that affected the whole colony and devastated an area that would then disappear from geographical maps. This imagery represents the Expulsion in various forms depending on the originator's point of view.

In 1847, Henry Wadsworth Longfellow published *Evangeline*, a work that would give a face, prominence, and a legend to the Acadian people. The poem enjoyed widespread popularity, ensuring the author's reputation and inspiring many anglophone and Québécois illustrators and artists who would give a face to the famous heroine and the event that served as a backdrop to her story. The resulting images have become icons of Acadian history, often created by artists recognized in art history. The portraits of Evangeline by James Faed, Frank Dicksee, Henri Beaux, and Louis-Philippe Hébert are works that represent the spread of ideas in the history of art. It would be a long time before Acadian artists would give their own versions of this story. In 1997, on the 150th anniversary of the poem's publication, Luc Charette, then director of the *Université de Moncton* art gallery, called on notable contemporary Acadian artists for a response, a sort of visual commentary, to this great moment in the formation of the Acadian identity.

Evangeline is a significant event that paralleled the development of education, with St. Joseph College in Memramcook blazing the trail. This is also the era of the first artists who produced work we still have today. Most of them (mainly women) were educated in a variety of places, but mainly in the United States. One such case is Philomène Belliveau (1852-1940), who gave us charcoal and pastel portraits of the day's notables, including Father Camille Lefebvre, founder of St. Joseph College, and Pascal Poirier, the first Acadian appointed to Canada's senate. Philomène Belliveau, Léon Léger (1848-1918), creator of many high altars in Acadian churches, and later respected artist Jeanne Léger (1895-1978) all went to Boston for training that would enhance their reputations in the area. Alma Buote (1894-1966), from Prince Edward Island, would also attend the Fashion Institute of New York, and Edouard Gautreau took correspondence courses from the Federal Art School of Minnesota.

However, the artists who would leave their mark on modern Acadie were trained in Quebec in the 1950s. Claude Roussel (b. 1930) and Roméo Savoie (b. 1928) enrolled in the same year in the now defunct Ecole des beaux-arts de Montréal. In 1956, Roussel finished his training in sculpture and teaching, and Savoie did the same in architecture.

Back in Northern Acadie, Claude Roussel would start as curator of Fredericton's Beaverbrook Art Gallery. In 1963, Father Clément Cormier, founder of the *Université de Moncton*, convinced him to become an artist in residence at the brand new institution where he would give the first art classes in an academic context. In 1965, Roussel would also set up the first art gallery on the university campus devoted to exhibiting professionally trained Acadian artists. His initiative would grow to impressive proportions, especially when he founded the visual arts department in 1972, which has produced 300 graduates.

In the mid-1960s, Roméo Savoie left a brilliant career as an architect to devote himself entirely to painting and pursuing a career that would make him one of the best-known Acadian artists. Initially influenced by the American abstract expressionists, over the years he has shifted his interest to works where the materials, texture, and gesture are more related to European artists such as Cy Twombly, Antoni Tapies, and Anselm Kiefer.

Along with these two major Acadian artists, we must mention another Quebec-trained artist: Sister Marie-Hélène Allain, who, following the Notre-Dame-du-Sacré-Coeur congregation's long association with the arts, has produced impressive work in sculpture. There is a spiritual dimension to her work that Rodolphe Caron accurately captured in his 2008 documentary on her work, *Marie Hélène Allain en dialogue avec la pierre*. We must not forget the work of Georges Goguen, a mainly self-taught artist whose paintings reveal contemporary influences touching on American modernism as defined by such artists as Jackson Pollock and Frank Stella.

These four artists are part of the first generation of artists with advanced training to face the challenges of the visual arts sector. Three other generations of artists follow them, artists whose challenges and methods are defined not only by their times, but also by a special dynamic that, because they were trained in part at the university, makes them Acadian artists.

The second generation began this route with Herménégilde Chiasson (b. 1946), trained first in Moncton and then in Europe and the United States. The multi-talented Chiasson—writer, filmmaker, and leading figure in theatre—produced or participated in more than 150 exhibitions. He was originally inspired by conceptual art, but his latest work has mainly been in painting and engraving. Yvon Gallant (b. 1950) developed a unique style and a body of work spanning traditional Acadian art and modern exploration. His sense of color and the high profile he enjoys have made him one of the mainstays of this generation.

Luc Charette (b. 1952) began his career as a sculptor but moved to art forms focusing on video and performance. He has recently returned to painting. Paul-Edouard Bourque (b. 1956) is undoubtedly one of the most prolific and creative artists in terms of conceiving images. His composite paintings are often inspired by music and found photographs. Guy Duguay's (b.1955-d. 1996) brief career gave rise to profuse production in areas as varied as print-making, painting, and ceramics. Roger Vautour (b. 1952) produces paintings in which textures, colors, and designs inspired by his roots in a marine environment helped create work that is exceptionally coherent. Jacques Arseneau (b. 1956), trained in Moncton and Paris, is without doubt the artist that has made the largest contribution in the field of engraving. He currently teaches at and is head of the visual arts department at the *Université de Moncton*.

Ghislaine McLaughlin's paintings juxtapose personal images with images that stimulate reflection on the position of women in today's world. Giselle Ouellette, who teaches painting at the university, works on elements from the natural world around her, increasing their impact by reducing them to their simplest forms. The work of another professor, Lise Robichaud, expresses a variety of concerns by drawing on biography, the landscape, and the environment.

Other artists from this generation include Giselle Léger-Drapeau, Georgette Bourgeois, Pauline Dugas, and Raymonde Fortin, who have contributed significantly to painting. In other areas, we should mention sculptors Anne-Marie Sirois and her playful work; Denis Lanteigne and his socially significant installations; and Jean-Yves Vigneau with his work featuring widely diverse themes and materials. Paul Babin's paintings, the textile work of Marjolaine Bourgeois, and Ronald Goguen's photos also figure in this generation.

The third generation of artists, also trained at the *Université de Moncton*, often put their predecessors' concerns behind them to focus on more experimental and often ephemeral art forms. Daniel Dugas is an Acadian artist whose work goes beyond sculpture to installations, performances, and videos—disciplines that have made him a nomadic, unpredictable artist. His method is followed by a group of younger artists who gather at the Galérie Sans Nom and Imago Print Shop.

Trained in sculpture, Mathieu Léger has since turned to photography, installation, and performance art. He has also travelled extensively, participating in numerous artist residencies around the world. Jennifer Bélanger records childhood and adolescence in painting and prints. Mario Doucet—a multi-disciplinary artist who has also worked in music, film, and video—creates paintings in which the history of Acadie, among others, is interpreted in a fanciful, playful way. Angèle Cormier crafts works where the informal aspect of her images often resembles installation.

Bélanger, Doucet, Léger, and Cormier have joined forces to create the group Taupe, focusing on media and computer art to manipulate visual elements we often take for granted. This third generation of artists has also contributed to more traditional disciplines, but in a completely personal and often experimental way: painters George Blanchette, André-Allan Phelps, Michel Robichaud, and David Toussaint; engravers Carole Deveau and Gilles Leblanc; sculptors Gerry Collins, Joël Boudreau, and Diana LeBlanc; and photographers Pierre LeBlanc, Marc-Xavier LeBlanc, and Julie D'Amour-Léger.

The fourth generation, currently in their 20s, follow the previous generation's direction. We find a mix of techniques, proposals, sources, and aesthetic choices similar to what is now called postmodernity. This term, which is often used to describe the artwork of the generation influenced by the Internet, certainly belongs in this category, because these artists don't fit into any movement and often work as individuals rather than representatives of a specific artistic trend. Artists such as Maryse Arsenault, Alexandre Robichaud, Dominick Robichaud, Jessica Arseneau, Mario LeBlanc, Rémi Belliveau, Angie Richard, and Alisa Arsenault, for example, are just starting their careers, but the originality of their work indicates that Acadian art is alive and well with a bright future.

Observing the vibrancy of the last 50 years, we realize how the university has been a mechanism not only for visual arts, but also for the whole Acadian cultural field, particularly in Moncton, home base for several organizations promoting this culture. Institutions such as the Galérie d'art Louise-et-Reuben-Cohen on the university campus, the Centre culturel Aberdeen, Galérie 12, and the Galérie Sans Nom are proof of creative activity in the visual arts never before seen in Northern Acadie.

The university has also opened a door to the world for its body of artist professors who have energized the milieu with new ideas and new methods. A good example is Francis Coutellier, who has been teaching ceramics, painting, and photography for many years now and who, aside from his work as an artist and head of the visual arts department, has helped organize several exhibitions and established many institutions to promote visual arts.

There is also André Lapointe, who is the prime mover behind Moncton's Symposium d'art nature—a unique event attracting artists from around the world—in addition to the great demand for his sculpting. Julie Forgues, currently teaching photography, is another example of artists whose activities go beyond the simply practical. Many other artists have stopped by the university during its 50-year history. Although their stays may have been brief, their presence greatly influenced the development of an institution that, from the very start, has prided itself on its modernity.

In light of this too-short and unfair overview, it is obvious that art is thriving in Northern Acadie. We must thank the artists, who had the courage to stay in an environment that is not always receptive to art forms that are not only unusual but often provocative. But it is true that the nature of all socially engaged art is to make us think about the issues of the society to which we belong and to which we all contribute.

The cultural environment here is no different from that found anywhere else in the world in that it is not easy to be an artist, to uphold aesthetic requisites while searching for creature comforts. Artists take on a multitude of jobs while coming up with ingenious ways to function in a familiar, inspiring, or hostile environment. This is why it is difficult to be an artist and live up to one's own aspirations.

Acadians from Maine Visit Cajuns in Louisiana

Gisèle Faucher

"I wasn't certain what to expect. Would it be a culture shock? Would it be like visiting another American city with a diverse ethnic population? No, it wasn't. In Lafayette, I felt like I met extended family," said Anna-Sophie Faucher, a student at Madawaska High School in Madawaska, Maine.

Indeed, the small group of Maine students who visited southern Louisiana during a recent February school vacation (and not just to get away from the piles of snow and cold weather in northern Maine!), were welcomed with open arms and a very warm, "*Bienvenue chez nous*" (Welcome to our place.)

Cédric Gendreau, a student, commented that he expected Louisiana to be a lot like his home in Maine, but without the regular presence of the Canadian border. "I thought to myself that maybe they would have a lot of the same traditions that we have over here. Maybe we share some culture—and I found out that we do. The Cajun musicians jamming at the Blue Moon Saloon sang mostly French songs, but in New Orleans, I was astonished because French-speaking people were very scarce."

I am a chemistry teacher from northern Maine's St. John River Valley and decided to bring a group of French-speaking students to Louisiana. Why? I may be a science teacher, but my roots are French, perhaps more *Brayon* (a cultural mix of Québécois and Acadian), but nonetheless, I have grown up as an Acadian in northern Maine.

Being bilingual has been a great asset throughout my life—it has helped me with my education, in my travels, and has opened many doors of opportunity. I was fortunate that my high school years came after the years when speaking French in school was forbidden in Maine, and a time when Acadian French was falsely labeled as "not correct" because of the regional accent and dialect.

I never suffered the embarrassment and stigma that I wasn't as bright as anybody else because English was my second language and the French I spoke wasn't "standard." I never had to copy hundreds of times on a blackboard, "I will not speak French in school." Other Acadians just a few years older than me had to do this, when teachers enforced a Maine law aimed at assimilating the heritage-language-speaking Acadians so that they would acquire English skills. In fact, in the mid to late 1970s when I was in secondary school, a new pride was developing and programs pushing for the reacquisition of Acadian

French were offered in our St. John Valley schools. This timing in my upbringing is key to my having a very positive attitude and appreciation for being bilingual.

I am thankful that the stigmatization of speaking French did not deter my parents, who were from both sides of the border (an American father and a Canadian mother), from making French the language of our home, and to my grandparents who weren't deterred by the actions of the Ku Klux Klan targeting the textile-working French Catholics of central and southern Maine in the 1920s.

Yet today, in our families and schools, I see fewer and fewer students using French. Our heritage language has diminished considerably, and groups such as the *Association française de la Vallée Saint-Jean* are working hard to encourage people to speak French to the younger generation, to continue offering French programming in schools, and to stress that being bilingual can complement rather than threaten English language acquisition.

As a science teacher, I am aware of both the cultural and physiological benefits of being bilingual. Learning languages can help the human brain develop, especially when the person is young. Moreover, I want to encourage the next generation to appreciate and maintain the gift of their heritage language. It is in this vein that I continue to work with students, in school and in the community, to promote retention of our heritage language and culture.

Student Cédric Gendreau echoed these sentiments, "I like having an Acadian heritage because I think there is so much that people don't know about us. If you go somewhere else in the country and you ask them what the Great Deportation is, often, they won't know. I'm an Acadian and I will teach the French language to my future children. I hope to continue the traditions that we have here in northern Maine."

When our group of students and staff first began planning our trip to Louisiana last autumn, one of our goals was to visit a newly-created Acadian youth group, the *Fédération des jeunes francophones de la Louisiane* (FJFLA), so that we could learn from their experience in forming our own Acadian youth group. Our vision for the youth group was to create a mechanism whereby all U.S. St. John Valley schools (located in Fort Kent, Frenchville/St. Agatha, Madawaska, and Van Buren) would be represented by a group of young leaders who would promote the Acadian language and culture. As an enticement to become part of the initial group, we proposed traveling to meet our students' peers in Louisiana so they could experience first-hand how similar or different young Cajuns might be from themselves.

We were told, "If you want to visit some French parts of Louisiana, you have to go to Lafayette Parish" ("parish" is the equivalent of "county" in Maine), so our planned journey to Louisiana centered on the Lafayette area, with short excursions to Baton Rouge and New Orleans.

We knew we'd be on a limited budget, so we sent out an email to a few contacts we had been given and simply stated, "*La visite vient!*" (Company is coming!). We asked if anyone could connect us to families who might consider allowing our students to experience home stays. It was not long before the emails started pouring in: "We'll take you for one night;" "Come stay on our farm;" "The Blue Moon Saloon will put you up for two nights." This was soon followed by advice on what activities to do, what to visit, and which schools to contact. The only thing these friendly folk knew about us was that we were Acadians from northern Maine who wanted to experience Acadiana, and they opened their doors wide. What a fantastic show of hospitality and a great first impression of our Cajun cousins!

The students from Maine, all bilingual and with the majority having French as their first language, were well versed on their Acadian heritage, thanks to their French teachers Mr. Cur Soucy and Mrs. Debbie Nadeau who also covered the Acadians' history in addition to language instruction in school. However, what they did not expect were their counterparts in Louisiana being so well informed about Acadie, and in fact they commented that they felt the general population in Louisiana seemed to be more familiar with their Acadian heritage than the general population in Maine.

A few of the Maine students had also heard about the Royal Proclamation of 2003 by Queen Elizabeth II acknowledging the illegality of the *Grand Dérangement* (the expulsion of Acadians from maritime pre-Canada in the mid-18th century). They were thrilled to be in the presence of its original petitioner, Warren Perrin, dressed as historic Acadian leader Beausoleil Broussard, standing in front of a copy of the Royal Proclamation in the Acadian Museum of Erath, Louisiana. He explained how he persuaded Queen Elizabeth II, in her capacity as Queen of Canada, to issue a royal proclamation acknowledging the historical fact of the Great Upheaval and consequential suffering experienced by the Acadian people.

Maine students expressed a desire to have had more time to examine the many artifacts contained within the museum. However, the Museum's *Living Legends* segment that followed Perrin's depiction of Broussard's life ended up being a major highlight of their trip to Louisiana. Dr. Glynn Granger, a local physician, shared his life story of growing up Cajun French and struggling to learn English. He spoke of his childhood experiences as the son of a sharecropper and his determination to succeed, ultimately graduating valedictorian of his high school class.

Even as a young man, Dr. Granger was renowned for his grit and wit as he attended medical school and became a surgeon whose Cajun French heritage proved invaluable for Cajun French patients. The students from Maine later described having goose bumps and being brought nearly to tears by Dr. Granger's life story.

"Our generation needs to hear more of these living legend life stories," said student Alexis Cyr: "*On a une histoire à raconter.*" (We have a story to tell.)

When we visited Church Point High School in Acadia Parish, the Madawaska students spoke in French about their lives as young Acadians in Maine and were confronted with a language barrier because their Louisiana peers did not speak French fluently. When the Maine students spoke more slowly, several of the Cajun students could pick out vocabulary words and get the gist of what was being said. Even though the language proved troublesome, the culture was definitely not! French teacher Valérie Broussard Boston's students had prepared traditional Cajun foods, including *la galette du Roi* (King's Cake). They explained and acted out, in costume, the community tradition, *Courir de Mardi Gras.*

Our students also discovered that Louisiana adults, when asked if they understood/spoke French, would respond "*un petit peu*" (a little bit), just as many older Acadians do in the St. John Valley, yet it was evident that they knew more than they admitted to and were perhaps merely shy about using a different accent, or still feel the stigma of speaking a French that is not "correct."

Overall, the populations of French-speaking young people in Louisiana and Maine are gradually decreasing, but as we continued to speak in French, and the Cajuns realized that we spoke in French just like them, it put a smile on their faces. "Some were very surprised to hear us young people speaking French," said Cédric Gendreau.

Alexis Côté, another Madawaska student, commented, "Everyone in Lafayette and Acadia Parish seems to be proud to be Acadian, the young and the old. Here in Maine, the older people are proud, but the younger people are not as enthused at being Acadian as the younger people in Louisiana. If it weren't for our French teachers in school, I don't think I'd know as much about the Acadians."

Another of the highlights experienced by our students was Cajun and zydeco music with traditional dancing. The teenagers who hosted our students were determined to show the Maine students (and chaperones!) how to dance à la Louisiane. The Maine students felt right at home as if they had known these Louisiana teenagers all their lives. Seeing all generations dancing at Randol's Cajun Restaurant in Lafayette made our students wish for a similar venue back in Maine.

On comparing Cajun and Acadian food, the Maine students expressed that Cajun foods were spicier and included much more seafood (crawfish!). "Even the chocolate at Avery Island had Tabasco sauce," exclaimed one student. Having had a cooking lesson to make *poulet étouffé* (a type of chicken stew), another student added, "But some of their food is the same, just with different names."

When asked by one of our home-stay hosts what stood out as the biggest highlight, the host was touched when the response was "the feeling of family and how welcoming everyone has been."

When both sets of students were asked if it would be good for more youth exchanges to occur in the future between the two Acadian communities, the resounding response was, "Absolutely! We need to stay connected more than every five years during the World Acadian Congress *(Congrès mondial acadien)*. It helps, but we need to meet more often. There is so much more we can learn from each other. We are very much the same and share a lot: our fears, our disappearing language, our traditions, and our cultural pride."

Madawaska's students are looking forward to reconnecting with their Louisiana counterparts during the *Congrès mondial acadien 2014*, especially at the *Grand rassemblement jeunesse* (Grand Youth Rally), the key event for the youth of Acadie, where francophone youth from most Atlantic Canadian Provinces, Maine, Louisiana, France, and Belgium will gather to celebrate their common heritage.

In addition, everyone agrees that Madawaska would truly enjoy hosting Cajun students from Louisiana in the future, to share with them our piece of Acadie. *La porte est ouverte et nous voulons de la visite!* (The door is open and we want company!)

Finally, one principal benefit of meeting young people in the future was given by Madawaska student Alexis Côté: "We need to meet more young dancers!"

The Métis of Mi'kmaq and Acadian Origins

Marie Rundquist

In the book *We Were Not the Savages*, historian Daniel Paul states: "The Mi'kmaq, who had been living in northeastern North America for approximately 10,000 years, were willing partners of the French. These Europeans treated the Mi'kmaq with respect as human beings. They ate their food and were quite willing to learn about their culture and adapt to their ways while enjoying their hospitality. Consequently, French settlements in Acadie (Nova Scotia) did not encounter any organized resistance from the Mi'kmaq. Many factors account for this state of affairs, but the prime reason probably was that they did not display an overwhelming desire to covert the Aboriginal communities completely to their cultural values."

The Mi'kmaq land, described by Paul as "vast," was situated in most of today's three Maritime Provinces, the southern section of the Gaspé Peninsula in Quebec and in northern Maine. While it is difficult to assess exactly in what areas the "earliest people" were, as observed by author Stephen A. Davis, in *Mi'kmaq People of the Maritimes*, the shell middens of the Maritime coastal areas, dating from the Middle to Late Ceramic period, serve as an archeological record of their existence, with the discarded, calcium-rich shells protecting the food, bones, and tools layered among them against decay.

Photo©Marie Rundquist

In Maine, at the head of the Damariscotta River is the Whaleback Shell Midden. On a river where salt water mixes with fresh, the historical presence of the Native community is still felt here. Each layer preserves a record of a time, a culture, and a people.

Historian Daniel Paul also states that during the Acadian Deportations from 1755 until 1763, hundreds of Acadian fugitives hid with their allies the Mi'kmaq in Kejimkujik in today's central area of mainland Nova Scotia.

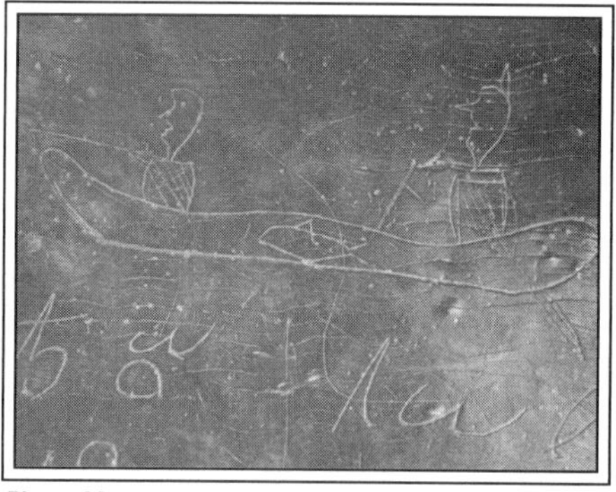

Photo©Marie Rundquist

Ancient petroglyphs (carvings in stone) articulate the long history, spirituality, and material culture of the Mi'kmaq, and may be viewed in Nova Scotia at the Kejimkujik National Historic Site and National Park in escorted tours.

In 1605, the French Europeans settled Port Royal (today Annapolis Royal, Nova Scotia) in the Mi'kmaq territory called *Kespukwitk* (Land Ends). Aged near 100 years, Membertou, the *Sagamore* (Chief) of this territory, welcomed the French to live among his people. The St. Jean-Baptiste church parish registers in Port Royal reveal the marriages of Mi'kmaq and French Acadians of Port Royal and the baptisms of their descendants. It must be noted that 150 years later in 1755, the Acadians and Mi'kmaq who were bilingual spoke one other's language, not English. The two peoples were friends, allies, and family.

Photo©Marie Rundquist

The Chief Membertou memorial at Port Royal (Annapolis Royal), Nova Scotia.

The Mi'kmaq also lived in today's Gaspé Peninsula in Quebec, and their territory was called *Kespek* (Last Land). In a garden at *Listuguj* First Nations Reserve (next to Pointe-à-la-Croix, in Gaspésie, Quebec) stands a statue of Saint Anne.

A narrative commemorating the baptisms of Chief Membertou and his family in 1610 is inscribed on the statue's base in three languages: Mi'kmaq, French, and English. A link between Chief Membertou's 17th-century Mi'kmaq settlement at Port Royal, Nova Scotia, and a 21st-century First Nation community in Quebec is thus carved in stone.

Photo©Marie Rundquist

In the 1687-88 Gargas Census at La Have (near today's Bridgewater), Native Americans numbered four times the French. Then at the 1708 Census, the Acadian surname Meuse stands out among the Mi'kmaq listed at La Have.

A path at Petite-Rivière, through a farmer's field, leads to a granite monument on a Mi'kmaq French burial ground. The names of Mi'kmaq and Acadian ancestors, who lived here 400 years ago, are engraved upon the stone's surface.

Photo©Marie Rundquist

The majority of people living at *K'chibouktouk* meaning Great Harbour (in today's Halifax) were Mi'kmaq who spent summers there. The 1687-88 Gargas Census reported 33 Mi'kmaq living in seven *wigwams* (huts), with one family listed as Acadian. When in 1749, the British arrived and built Halifax as their new Nova Scotia capitol, the Mi'kmaq stopped coming here.

Photo©Paulette Thériault

A traditional Mi'kmaq woman's hat worn at the Membertou 400 Celebration, held in 2010 at Halifax, Nova Scotia.

In the 17th century, Mi'kmaq were hunting, fishing, and trapping all along Newfoundland's southern coast, according to historical records. That the Mi'kmaq occupied the island from prehistoric times is a long-standing belief. The 1857 Newfoundland census records have Mi'kmaq families living in Acadian St. George's Bay, and in Codroy River, Grandy's Brook, Conne River, Bay d'Espoir, and in the Bay of Exploits.

Photo©Peggy Bennett

Pictured is the Stephenville Crossing at K'taqmkuk, in the area of St. George's Bay in Newfoundland, where Acadians and Métis still live today.

In 1713, the French started building the Fortress of Louisbourg (in today's Cape Breton, Nova Scotia) on the Mi'kmaq lands of *Unama'kik* (Land of Fog). Navigable waters, abundance of fish and shellfish, a good water supply, and habitable sites made this a perfect location for Mi'kmaq summer villages. They include *Oegogmog* and *Moglagatig*, both located at the mouths of rivers with notably high fish spawning runs. Subsequently, the fishing port grew to become a major commercial port and a strongly defended French fortress. By 1745, Louisbourg was the most extensive and expensive French fortification constructed in North America. During the French regime, Mi'kmaq continued to live in the area with the Acadians and French.

Photo©Edward Nowicki

Geganisg *(Remarkable place) is today's Ingonish in Cape Breton, and one of the most beautiful places in North America.*

Accounts describe how the beloved Father Pierre Maillard in the 1750s, who served the Mi'kmaq on *Epexiwitk* (Lying in the Water) on today's Prince Edward Island, engaged elder Mi'kmaq shaman Arguimaut and Acadian interpreter, Barthelemi (Petit Pas) Petitpas, in planning for a feast. The Shaman directed Petit Pas to instruct the young men of his village to gather supplies from the Acadian settlement of Port La Joie (today's Prince Edward Island capitol, Charlottetown).

Photo©Peggy Bennett

Shown is the island of Epexiwitk *(renamed Isle St. Jean, and then Prince Edward Island), where Mi'kmaq have dug clams for thousands of years.*

The Mi'kmaq had flourished, living a prosperous and contented life, but after the British arrived and started deporting the Acadians in 1755, the Mi'kmaq were hunted down by the military and the mercenaries. After the Treaty of Paris in 1763 when French America was lost, the British government placed the Mi'kmaq into native reserves across the Maritime Provinces and in the Gaspé Peninsula. They forced them to learn English, thus causing them over the years to forget most of their Mi'kmaq and French languages. Thrown into isolated and often small reserves, even with signed treaties, they were refused access to most of their ancient fishing and hunting grounds.

Today, many Acadians retain Mi'kmaq blood in their DNA, including the Meuse (Muise), and d'Entremont families, who live in the Cape Sable area of the Municipality of Argyle, in Nova Scotia. You can still see today the Mi'kmaq traits in many Acadian faces here.

Photo©Paulete Thériault

The British referred to the Mi'kmaq and Métis Acadians of Cape Sable Island as "Cape Sables."

During World War II (1939-1945), many children at the Gesgapegiag Reserve (near the Acadian village of Bonaventure, in Gaspésie, Quebec) grew up without fathers, as Mi'kmaq men joined the military and served in the war effort. Emile Broome and his siblings were among the Mi'kmaq children who lived on the reserve (formerly named "Maria") and attended school there. In 1945, Emile and his family moved to the United States where they lived in Van Buren, Lewiston, and Bangor, Maine before settling in New Hampshire. Emile Broome traces his Acadian–Mi'kmaq family lines through his mother, the late Marie Dubé, maternal-line descendant of Marie Christine Aubois (listed as "Marie Sauvagesse," native of Acadie in the marriage record of daughter Anne Roye) and Jean Roy *dit* Laliberté of Port Royal. His family lines from his mother's side also include such familiar Acadian names as Roy, Clemenceau, Doiron, and Gallant. The Broome surname is among the earliest records for the Mi'kmaq in Gespe'gewa'gi. This territory is situated in the actual region of northern New Brunswick and the Gaspé Peninsula.

Photo©Edward Nowicki

Cyrile Broome, Emile's uncle, features among the Mi'kmaq World War II veterans honored for military service. His name is listed on this monument at the Gesgapegiag Mi'kmaq Reserve.

The Métis Today

Métis is a term used to describe people of mixed native and European origin. Almost half of the Acadians, whether those deported or those having been obliged to migrate, have Mi'kmaq in their bloodlines. The Métis Acadian/Mi'kmaq are not only situated in the northeastern part of the continent, but also in Louisiana and in Texas where they migrated.

Today, there are 30 federally recognized First Nations Mi'kmaq reserves. Of these, 27 are situated in the Canadian Atlantic provinces, two in the Quebec Gaspé Peninsula, and one in Aroostook County in Maine. The Mi'kmaq also recognize that many members of their communities have mixed Acadian bloodlines. Frank Meuse Jr. (an Acadian surname) is the Chief of the Bear River First Nation, in Annapolis and Digby Counties in Nova Scotia.

Photo©Marie Rundquist

A "Medicine Trail" behind the Bear River First Nation Heritage and Cultural Centre leads to a Mi'kmaq wikwam *(hut), made from sections of bark lashed together. Indigenous plants featured in the Mi'kmaq medicine tradition, grow naturally along woodland paths behind the Centre. The Mi'kmaq's knowledge of medicinal plants saved numerous Acadian lives in the 17th and 18th centuries.*

In 2009, Nova Scotia's first Métis judge Pierre Leon Muise, from Quinan, was sworn in to office at the Digby Justice Centre. On the occasion Leland Surette, spiritual leader of the Kespu'kwitk Métis Council, addressed all, telling of the joy of the aboriginal community in having one of their own appointed to such an honorable position. "Today, the aboriginal community rejoices as our people, and especially our youth, have yet another prestigious role model to look up to." said Surette, who presented Muise with feathers from an eagle and a great horned owl. Judge Pierre Muise, who is bilingual and conducts some trials in French, serves in Digby, Annapolis Royal, and Yarmouth in Nova Scotia.

Outside the Mi'kmaq reserves are active Métis associations that have been created in the last 20 years. They include the Confederacy of Nova Scotia Métis with memberships with regional Councils such as the We'kopekwitk Métis Council (Truro), Yarmouth & District Métis Council (Yarmouth), Kespu'kwitk Métis Council (Tusket), the Annapolis Valley Métis Council (Annapolis), and Eldawik Métis Council (Halifax). Other independent Métis groups include the very active Association des Acadiens-Métis Souriquois (Saulnierville, N.S.), New Brunswick Woodland Métis Tribes (Moncton, N.B.), L'Alliance Premier Peuple de la Côte-Est (St-Isidore, N.B.), Eastcoast Maritime Métis Council / L'Alliance Premier Peuple de la Côte-Est (Lamèque, N.B.), and l'Union Métis Est-Ouest des Maritimes (Shédiac N.B. and Rigaud, Quebec).

The Métis in Western Canada scored a major breakthrough in 1982 when the Constitution Act recognized that they have special rights that must be protected. The extent of these rights is still in dispute. The Métis people of Mi'kmaq and Acadian bloodlines are still trying to have their status recognized on the East Coast of Canada.

Paul Comeau Tufts, co-founder and past-president of the Association des Acadiens-Métis Souriquois (AAMS) stated: "In the context of the Canadian Constitution Act (1982), and in the context of the 'Powley Criteria' as established by the Supreme Court of Canada in 2003, the constitutional rights claimed by the Métis in Eastern Canada are being denied by the testimonies of certain historians in the courts. Sections 35 (1) and (2) of the Canadian Constitution Act indicate that the existing aboriginal and treaty rights of the aboriginal peoples of Canada are hereby recognized and affirmed; and in this Act, the 'aboriginal peoples of Canada' include the Indian, Inuit, and Métis peoples of Canada." However, in 2003, the Supreme Court of Canada established the Powley Criteria that describe the qualifications required in order for a Métis community to be recognized as a "rights-holder" in the context of the Canadian Constitution. The most significant criteria indicate that a contemporary community, that is seeking recognition as a Métis rights-holder, must self-identify as a Métis community and show that it is the continuation of a historical Métis community that existed in a particular area, as an identifiable Métis community, with a unique and distinct culture, prior to the time of effective political and legal control by Europeans. Therefore, the following discussion will focus on the controversy associated with ascertaining the presence or absence of qualifying "Métis Communities" in Acadie.

Other historical factors place the Acadian-Métis in a separate category: The mixed-blooded people of Acadie, with French and Mi'kmaq bloodlines, were identified as either Acadian or Mi'kmaq depending on the communities in which they lived. Historical events indicate that generally the British made a distinction between the Acadian and the Mi'kmaq communities. They considered most Acadians to be related to the Mi'kmaq as "half breeds" with French and Mi'kmaq bloodlines. However the British dealt with the Acadian communities differently than with the Mi'kmaq communities. For example, the Acadian communities containing Mi'kmaq bloodlines were deported (beginning in 1755) while the Mi'kmaq communities containing French bloodlines were not; the British dealt with the Mi'kmaq communities via warfare, scalping proclamations and treaties of "Peace and Friendship." Despite historical claims that no Mi'kmaq people were deported, it is however certain that Mi'kmaq bloodlines and some Mi'kmaq people, who were living as members of the Acadian community, were also deported as recently proven by the science of DNA testing, combined with painstaking research of the records–a technique called "genetic genealogy." Similarly, it is probable that some mixed-blooded Acadians succumbed to the scalping proclamations, even though these proclamations were not aimed at the Acadian communities.

In 2013, the Metis and non-status Indians scored a major victory when the Federal Court recognized them as "Indians" under the Constitution. On April 17, 2014, the federal government's appeal, has largely upheld a landmark ruling that could extend Ottawa's responsibilities to hundreds of thousands of aboriginal people who are not affiliated with specific reserves and have essentially no access to First Nations programs, services, and rights. If the federal government appeals again, the case would go the Supreme Court. The Congress of Aboriginal People in Canada also supports the Métis' demands.

The Association des Acadiens-Métis Souriquois *(AAMS), with a membership of 900 Métis mostly from Clare, Argyle, and Yarmouth municipalities in Nova Scotia, participated at the Canada Day Celebrations at the Wedgeport Tuna Museum in Nova Scotia. From left to right: Alan Comeau, June Comeau, Kendra Jacquard, John Deveau, Paul Tufts, Don LeBlanc, Joseph Jacquard (current president), and Gerald Amirault.*

BIBLIOGRAPHY

Daniel N. Paul, *We Were Not the Savages* (Halifax: Nimbus Publishing Ltd, 1993); Paul D. Tufts, *l'Association des Acadiens-Métis Souriquois* (AAMS); Patricia Nietfeld, "Determinants of Aboriginal Micmac Structure" (University of New Mexico, 1981); Ruth Holmes Whitehead, *The Old Man Told Us*, (Halifax: Nimbus Publishing Limited, 1991), p.94; Bernard Gilbert Hoffman, "The Historical Ethnography of the Micmac of the Sixteenth and Seventeenth Centuries" (University of California, 1955); "The History of Newfoundland Mi'kmaq," Ralph T. Pastore Archaeology Unit & History Department Memorial University of Newfoundland, c. 1998; Article contributed by Mikmaw Elder, Dr. Daniel N. Paul, "On the road again: Pubnico's, Cape Sable Island," Halifax Herald, August 7, 2003; and Stephen A. Davis, *Mi'kmaq: Peoples of the Maritimes* (Halifax: Nimbus Publishing, 1997.

BLACK CAJUNS

Charles Larroque

Louisiana residents now have the option of purchasing a personalized license plate that says either, "I'm Cajun ... and proud," or, "I'm Creole ... and proud." It is for a good cause: the teaching of French in the schools. However, driven home will surely be some thorny questions of ethnic identification.

Our history is a colorful mosaic. Two-and-a-half centuries removed from the forest primeval, one ethnic reality of South Louisiana is that for practically every white family with a Cajun surname in Louisiana, there is a black family with the same name. It is an old story that began well before vanity license plates.

From the early days of the colony, Louisiana was a center of diaspora: African slaves poured in through the port of New Orleans, Indians were enslaved and/or removed, and expelled Acadians adopted the swamps and prairies as sanctuary. Folks isolated themselves for protection. However, in order to adapt and survive, ethnic groups mingled much like the Acadians did with the native people in Acadie.

The resulting cross-pollination was grounded primarily by the cultural elements of religion (Catholicism), some form of French language, family values, music, dance, and especially food. But the great American melting pot in Louisiana had to cook down these ingredients in a *roux* of generational struggles before any distinct ethnic identities could be served. The resulting dish was a culturally rich and exotic *mélange* that has become the unique Louisiana "Cajun-Creole" brand—for better or for worse—with stereotypes and misconceptions often filed under the woefully dismissive expression "Cajun mystique."

The peculiar institution of slavery must have seemed very peculiar to the first Acadians who had little stomach for the indentured servitude they left back in Europe. But in colonial Louisiana and on into the early 19th century, failing to keep up with the Joneses (or in this case, the white Creole planters) meant getting yoked with socio-economic and even cultural inferiority. Thus, it was that a substantial number of upwardly mobile Cajuns in the cotton and sugar producing regions came to own slaves. It must have felt no less peculiar to witness free people of color owning slaves.

And the *roux* thickens.

While there were instances of blacks adopting the white master's surname in order to grease the skids of struggle in the pre-Civil War South, more prevalent was the actual mixing of the races in antebellum Louisiana. No doubt relations were had, both voluntarily and involuntarily. These were times of great turmoil in a very young and mostly unsupervised country. Notwithstanding the economic success of some Louisiana Acadians, the dreadful effects of diaspora weighed heavily upon many Cajuns and Africans, with the most common of denominators being socio-cultural isolation.

Here was the nexus of one more "creolization" process in its myriad manifestations, where the best of all available resources blended together in a syncopated celebration of resilience and survival. Those who dwelled there were far from the poet's "Eden" of Louisiana, but there must have been a certain sense of freedom in the disenfranchisement of the underclass. Think Br'er Rabbit thrown into the briar patch. The planter surely had his skeletons in the closet; but in the chifforobe of the *Cadien* and the *Créole*, one would likely find only sharecropper's overalls, a wedding dress, or an old pair of boots ... but no hidden skeletons.

Around the time of post-Civil War Reconstruction, Louisiana went from a multiracial to a biracial society. This was the beginning of the collective amnesia, for some, brought on by trauma. For others, forgetting was like a balm. Folks were now separate in society but equal in fear and derision. White Cajuns distinguished themselves from their "country Cajun" relations; free people of color distinguished themselves from the "less bright" on the color palette. The French word *Nègre,* historically a term of endearment for many white Cajuns, now became lost in a poorly translated culture only to be found as a crude slur in *Américain* (English). Even the word "Cajun" at one time was a fighting word among people of both persuasions. But the pecan does not fall far from the tree.

While Cajuns were shedding stigma along that long, hard slog toward cool, black was becoming beautiful. Civil Rights kicked in and there was a definite shift toward black ethnic identification. However, from jazz to jambalaya to French black blues, Louisiana's Afro-Caribbean beat had over the years become the *sui generis* of the state's brand, now with "Creole" as a cultural bridge between the old multiracial and the new biracial society of Louisiana. Today, one's last name might be Cormier, Sonnier, Senegal, or Zeno, and if they identify with African-America, in Louisiana they almost certainly identify themselves as Creole.

Then Cajuns "came out of the closet" and all was cool. Or was it? The commodification of the Cajun culture back in the 1970s received a massive bump from European and Canadian *Francophonie* while the Creole (i.e. black) cultural economy lay fallow on the Louisiana prairie in the shadow of the "Cajun is hot!" phenomenon. Look into the kitchen of most any Cajun restaurant. No one is beating on the pots and pans making a *tintamarre*. Chances are the cooks do not fit the standard Cajun phenotype, yet they are Arceneauxs, Heberts, Thibodeauxs, and even Broussards. They might speak the French of Beausoleil, the *courri vini* of the islands, or even *la langue de Molière*. They mostly do not know about *poutine râpée* or the *Congrès mondial acadien* (CMA), but are eager to find out.

Blood is thicker than *roux* and, indeed, *ensemble on est capable* (together we are able). "Creole Cajuns" are still standing tall, thanks to the wide shoulders of all their ancestors. Perhaps they are waiting for their own *tintamarre*—waiting to let the world know that they are still out there—and that maybe it is time to come out of the woods. Perhaps some will be driving with both Cajun and Creole prestige license plates on their vehicles: one for the back saying where they have been, and one in the front for where they are headed.

III

Remarkable Acadie

THE LANDSCAPE OF GRAND PRÉ, UNESCO WORLD HERITAGE SITE

Ronnie-Gilles LeBlanc and A.J.G. Johnston

Photo©François Gaudet

World Recognition

The Landscape of Grand Pré was inscribed on UNESCO's World Heritage List in 2012. The site, measuring 12 square kilometers (five square miles), is located next to the town of Wolfville on the Bay of Fundy's Minas Basin in Nova Scotia. It is a treasure protected for all of humanity.

UNESCO World Heritage Sites are recognized as having Outstanding Universal Value (OUV) for humanity as a whole. This means they have cultural and/or natural significance that is so exceptional it transcends national boundaries and is of common importance for present and future generations everywhere. The essence of the Outstanding Universal Value of this remarkable agricultural and symbolic landscape is captured below.

The Landscape of Grand Pré is an exceptional living agricultural landscape, claimed from the sea in the 17th century and still in use today applying the same technology and the same community-based management system. Grand Pré is also the iconic place of remembrance of the Acadians who lived in harmony with the native Mi'kmaq people before the Expulsion, which began in 1755. Its 20th-century memorial constructions form the center of the symbolic re-appropriation of the Acadians' lands of origin, in a spirit of peace and cultural sharing with the local area community.

The Official Statement by UNESCO

> *The Landscape of Grand Pré: Situated in the southern Minas Basin of Nova Scotia, the Grand Pré marshland and archaeological sites constitute a cultural landscape bearing testimony to the development of agricultural farmland using dykes and the aboiteau wooden sluice system, started by the Acadians in the 17th century and further developed and maintained by the Planters and present-day inhabitants. Over 1,300 hectares (3,212 acres), the cultural landscape encompasses a large expanse of polder farmland and archaeological elements of the towns of Grand Pré and Hortonville, which were built by the Acadians and their successors. The landscape is an exceptional example of the adaptation of the first European settlers to the conditions of the North American Atlantic coast. The site—marked by one of the most extreme tidal ranges in the world, averaging 11.6 meters (38 feet)—is also inscribed as a memorial to Acadian way of life and deportation, which started in 1755, known as the Grand Dérangement.*

The Acadians at Grand Pré

Since the 1680s, when a small group of Acadian settlers from the Port Royal area first arrived in the Minas Basin area and called the vast wetlands *la grand pré* (the big meadow), the human history of Grand Pré has been linked to its natural setting and the exceptional fertility of this land by the sea.

The earliest settlers were isolated. They were a long way from home and were mostly ignored by the various French and British authorities who administered the area. The settlers developed close relations with the local Mi'kmaq, the indigenous people of Nova Scotia—not just at Grand Pré, but elsewhere in Acadie—as they came to grips with the natural setting and began to claim fertile land from the sea by building dikes. All of these factors contributed to their developing a new and distinct identity. Though French by birth, over the course of the second half of the 17th century they came to see themselves as belonging to l'Acadie, as being Acadiens and Acadiennes.

During the roughly 70 years before their forcible removal in 1755, the Acadian community of Grand Pré introduced an environmental management approach that had been applied elsewhere in Acadie. Acadians took European practices, developed for wetlands and saltpans, and adapted them to the much different environment in Acadie.

Faced with the highest recorded tides in the world, the Acadians at Grand Pré worked for three generations to transform over 1,300 hectares (3,212 acres) of tidal marsh into farmland. The farmland was then—and remains today—some of the finest farmland in North America.

The Deportation at Grand Pré

The events that occurred at Grand Pré in 1755 were among the earliest of the Acadian Deportation. Most importantly, they were recorded by some of the key British participants. The records provide a detailed historical account of the events and their impact on the Acadians, and also set the context for later depictions of Acadian culture. They also provide later Acadians with a snapshot of a transformative event in their cultural history. The following information comes from the two most important sources: the journals of Lt.-Col. John Winslow and of one of his junior officers, Jeremiah Bancroft.

Lt.-Col. John Winslow of Massachusetts was the officer in charge of rounding up and deporting the Acadians from Grand Pré. He arrived on August 19, 1755, with about 300 New England provincial soldiers. He gave no indication of what was to happen, but gave the impression he was there on a routine assignment. His first act was to establish a secure base of operations, because his force was greatly outnumbered by the 2,242 Acadian men, women, and children living in the Minas Basin area, one of the largest Acadian settlements.

For his stronghold, Winslow chose the area around the Grand Pré parish church, Saint-Charles-des-Mines. His soldiers erected a palisade around the priest's house, the church, and the cemetery, and his troops pitched their tents within that enclosure. So as not to upset the Acadians unnecessarily, Winslow informed community leaders they should remove the sacred objects from the church before it became a military base. By early August 1755, the parish priests of Saint-Charles-des-Mines, and of neighboring parishes had already been arrested and brought to Halifax to await their deportation to Europe.

As August 1755 came to a close and September began, the Acadians of Grand Pré and other nearby villages were harvesting crops from the dike land and cultivated upland areas. This harvest, although the Acadians could not know it, would be their last in Grand Pré.

On September 4, 1755, Lt.-Col. Winslow issued a call for all men and boys aged ten and older to come to the parish church at three o'clock the next afternoon to hear an important announcement. A similar ploy was used by Capt. Alexander Murray to call Acadian males of the nearby Pisiquid region to come to Fort Edward (today Windsor, Nova Scotia) on the same day at the same time. In fact, the British had used a similar ruse on August 11 in the Chignecto area to attract and imprison some 400 Acadian men in Fort Beauséjour (today near Sackville, New Brunswick), renamed Fort Cumberland after its capture, and Fort Lawrence (today near Amherst, Nova Scotia). Winslow and his men had witnessed this just before their departure for Grand Pré.

On September 5, 5,418 Acadian males of Grand Pré proceeded to their parish church—now surrounded by a palisade and controlled by armed soldiers—to hear the announcement. Once they were inside, Winslow had French-speaking interpreters tell the assembled men and boys that they and their families were to be deported. Included in the announcement was this statement:

> *that your Lands and Tenements, Cattle of all Kinds and Live Stock of all Sorts are Forfeited to the Crown with all of your Effects Saving your money and Household Goods and you your Selves to be removed from this ... Province.*

Jeremiah Bancroft, one of Winslow's junior officers, records in his journal that the look on the Acadian faces as they heard the announcement was a mixture of "shame and confusion ... together with anger." He added that the "countenances" of the Acadians were so altered they could not be described.

The removal of the 2,242 people who lived at Grand Pré and in the neighboring villages proceeded neither quickly nor smoothly. Winslow had to cope with a shortage of transport ships and provisions. The men and boys spent more than a month imprisoned within either the church of Saint-Charles-des-Mines or on the transports anchored in the Minas Basin before the rest of the population was forced on board the ships. Winslow described the scene of the first contingent of young men, marching from the church along the road beside the dike land to what today is known as Horton Landing. He wrote:

> *[they] went off Praying, Singing, & Crying, being Met by the women & Children all the way ... with Great Lamentations upon their knees praying.*

On October 8, 1755, the mass embarkation of the men, women, and children to the waiting ships began, with small boats setting off from Horton Landing. Those who lived at Grand Pré and Gaspereau went first. Winslow recorded that:

> *[the inhabitants left] unwillingly, the women in Great Distress Carrying off Their Children in their Arms, Others Carrying their Decrepit Parents in their Carts and all their Goods moving in Great Confusion and appeared a scene of Woe and Distress.*

Acadians lived together in large, extended family units. Although Winslow gave orders that families were to be kept together, this often proved impossible in the confusion and because of the small size of the ships. Friends, relatives, and neighbors were separated, never to see each other again.

On October 19 to 21, the soldiers compelled families from outlying communities to assemble at Grand Pré in preparation for their eventual loading on board transport ships. This group of Acadians numbered about 600, from 98 families. While they waited for the transports to arrive, they lodged in the now-empty Acadian homes near Winslow's camp, along the upland area by the reclaimed marsh. These families were deported to the Anglo-American colonies just before Christmas 1755.

The Grand Pré Acadians were deported to five of the Anglo-American colonies, including Massachusetts, New York, Connecticut, North Carolina, and South Carolina. In the coming decades, thousands of Acadians would land at ports around the world, only to depart again in search of a place from which they could one day return to their homeland in Acadie. Out of this Odyssey was born the Acadian Diaspora.

Grand Pré becomes the Township of Horton

In 1760, New England Planters settled at Grand Pré, renamed the Township of Horton, and took over the lands once farmed by the Acadians. Then, as now, the transformed marsh was the primary focus for the area's inhabitants. Like the Acadians before them, the New England planters developed their own strong connections to the land and their rural way of life. While they expanded the dike land created by the Acadians, some of the most important features of the original diked area remain in place.

Creation of a *lieu de mémoire*

In the early 19th century, certain individuals and organizations began to commemorate the bygone Acadian presence at Grand Pré. Two major forces were at work. One related to the historical, literary, and artistic works that linked Grand Pré more than any other pre-1755 Acadian village to the Acadian Deportation. The other was the Acadian Renaissance that began in the latter half of the 19th century throughout the Maritime Provinces of Canada. Together, the two forces combined to overlay the agricultural landscape with a symbolic landscape.

At the beginning of the 20th century, individuals such as John Frederic Herbin and Fr. André-D. Cormier, private companies such as the Dominion Atlantic Railway and the *Société nationale l'Assomption* (today *Société nationale de l'Acadie),* and the Acadian community transformed Grand Pré into a historic site and a major tourist attraction in North America. The commemorative monuments, buildings, and gardens they created were a symbolic reclaiming of the Grand Pré area by the descendants of the people who were forcibly removed in 1755. As a result, for people of Acadian descent, Grand Pré became the most cherished of all their historical sites.

Today, Grand Pré National Historic Site, located at the heart of the Landscape of Grand Pré World Heritage Site, commemorates the former Acadian settlement, the Deportation, and the Acadians' continued attachment to their ancestral homeland.

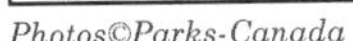

Photos©Parks-Canada

On July 28, 2005, the Deportation Cross at Grand Pré was relocated and rededicated as part of the ceremonies commemorating the 250th anniversary of the Acadian Deportation. The monument is located on the shore where the Acadians from Grand Pré were forced onto British ships and deported in 1755.

Sources and Acknowledgements

Published with the permission of Parks Canada (www.parkscanada.gc.ca/grandpre). The Landscape of Grand Pré can be seen at www.landscapeofgrandpre.ca. The official statement by UNESCO was taken from the UNESCO site (whc.unesco.org/en/list/1404/).

THE ACADIAN ABOITEAU: A CULTURAL AND ECONOMIC KEYSTONE

Whitney P. Broussard III

One could reasonably argue that it was the Acadians' water management expertise and keen agrarian capacity that eventually led to their deportation. The earliest European inhabitants of the Northeast, the Acadians quickly realized the potential of the fertile coastal lowlands and efficiently organized a land reclamation that was unprecedented for its time. This massive effort would eventually convert the higher fringes of tidal salt marsh around the Bay of Fundy into fertile fields of hay and grain, enough to support a growing and independent society. Such bounty was sought after with jealous eyes, for the Acadians' fields were among the most productive in the New World.

The shaded area depicts the wetlands surrounding La Rochelle, France, circa 1600.

Many of the early Acadians came from the French farming region of Poitou. Surrounded by extensive wetlands, these immigrants of La Rochelle and surrounding communities brought with them several generations of advanced knowledge of agricultural land reclamation techniques, including the use of dikes for salt production. In Acadie, they would find over 35,000 hectares (86,000 acres) of fertile salt marsh, fed twice a day by the highest tides in the world. Acadian villages reaping the benefits of both systems soon grew at the edge between upland and marshland. Early settlers accompanying the Acadians criticized them for such a focus on the seemingly barren salt marshes. The European paradigm of progress at that time was an agricultural economy built on the rich soils of the forest. Most settlers would cut down such forests and convert them to farm fields. The Acadians, however, would reclaim salt marshes for farm fields, and do so with impeccable efficiency. The Acadian fields would eventually become prized possessions and the envy of two warring nations.

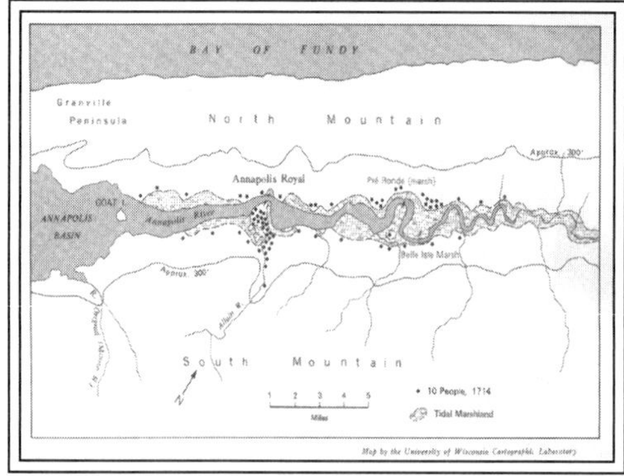

Acadian marsh reclamation started in Port Royal, Acadie's first permanent European settlement. Note the location of the farms at the edge of the marsh as well as the linear alignment of homesteads up the river.

Illustration©A. H. Clark Acadia 1968

Aboiteau

The concept was simple: build a dike on an elevation contour just a few feet above the peak elevation of the highest tide, thereby separating the highest salt marsh from the bay's influence. The impounded salt marsh would eventually freshen with rainwater, and the soils would soon be amenable to agriculture. To prevent flooding the newly impounded fields with excessive rainfall, a sluice was built at a location where the naturally draining tidal creek would have crossed the dike. To prevent saltwater tides from entering the field through the sluice, a one-way flap gate was built into the sluice that allowed free-flowing freshwater to exit the diked land while denying saltwater tides from entering. The combination of such a dike, sluice, and flap gate is known as an *aboiteau* (plural *aboiteaux*).

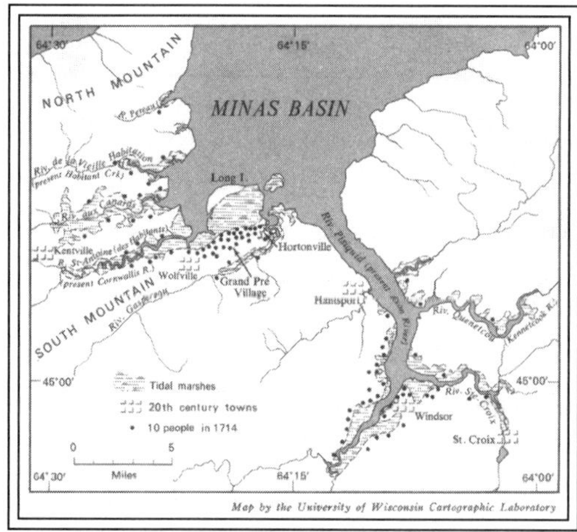

Marsh reclamation fueled the growing village of Grand-Pré, ideally situated atop the upland terrace above a vast lowland marsh that would become one of Acadie's largest reclamation projects.

Illustration©A. H. Clark Acadia 1968

Dièreville, a writer and surgeon from Normandy, visited the Port Royal area from September 1699 to October 1700 and succinctly described how the Acadians went about creating farm fields from coastal wetlands:

> *It costs a great deal to prepare the lands, which they wish to cultivate. To grow wheat, the marshes, which are inundated by the sea at high tide, must be drained; these are called lowlands, and they are quite good, but what labor is needed to make them fit for cultivation! The ebb and flow of the sea cannot easily be stopped, but the Acadians succeed in doing so by means of great dykes, called* aboiteaux, *and it is done in this way: five or six rows of large logs are driven whole into the ground at points where the tide enters the marsh, and between each, other logs are laid, one on top of the other, and all the spaces between them are so carefully filled with well-pounded clay, that the water can no longer get through.*
>
> *In the center of this construction, a sluice is contrived in such a manner that the water on the marshes flows out of its own accord, while that of the sea is prevented from coming in. An undertaking of this nature, which can only be carried on at certain seasons when the tides do not ride so high, costs a great deal, and takes many days, but the abundant crop that is harvested in the second year, after the soil has been washed by rain water, compensates for all the expense.*[1]

Painting©A. Vienneau. Nova Scotia Museum.

Portrait of an Acadian community repairing an aboiteau, *a dike and sluice structure that made agriculture possible in the marshland environments surrounding the Bay of Fundy. Note the location of the sluice at the lowest point in the landscape, which allowed rainwater to drain out of the protected lands.*

Marsh Grass Sods, a Sluice, and a Flap Gate

The dike was constructed with marsh grass sods and marsh mud. Sods of marsh grass were precisely cut for the steep outer face of the dike. It was important to keep the roots alive so that a new above-ground plant cover would develop on the outside of the dike to hold the soil in place and stabilize the dike.

The sods were cut into bricks about four inches (10 cm) wide, and the grass side was cut at a 30-degree angle. An elder artisan usually completed this part of the process. Digging marsh mud and filling the internal spaces of the dike was less precise and usually completed by a younger apprentice. The filler mud was removed from a site next to the dike to form a ditch called the "borrow pit." The grass sods were arranged into bottom rows for each side of the dike, and the filler marsh mud was thrown between the sod rows and tightly packed down by foot. When the filler mud reached the height of the bottom sod row, the next layer of sod was placed on top, like bricklayers building a wall, while filler mud was placed and packed inside. The process continued until the dike reached the planned height, which was always several feet above the highest tides.

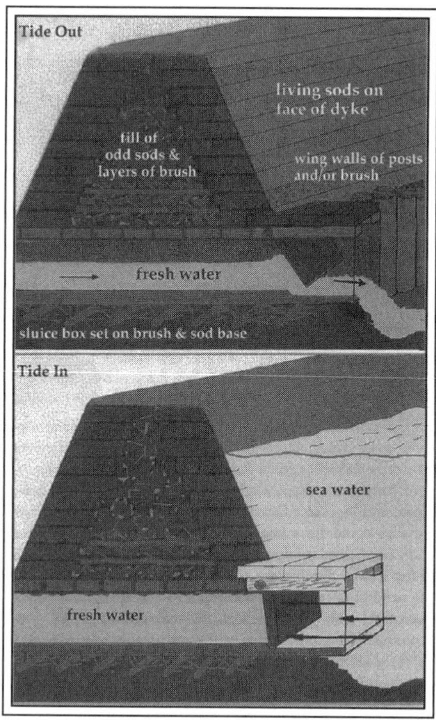

Illustration©J.S. Bleakney Sods, Soil, and Spades 2004

Cross section of a sluice inserted into a dyke. The aboiteau *consists of a sluice to channel rainwater out and a sluice door (one-way flap gate) to prevent seawater from entering.*

Dikes prevented tidewater from flooding the protected land twice a day, but rainwater had to drain off the fields and into the sea so as not to flood the newly impounded land. To accomplish this goal of keeping the tides at bay while allowing the rainwater to drain to the sea, the Acadians built a sluice under the dike at the lowest point of the landscape, usually where the dike crossed a tidal creek. The sluice was placed on a bed of brush beneath the dike to prevent settling, and then covered with sod. Although simple in design, these labor-intensive structures worked remarkably well.

Photo©W. Broussard

A modern drainage canal at Grand-Pré runs through a sluice (under the photographer) on its way to the sea.

The sluice was hand-hewn from a single large log and shaped into a trough using a hammer and chisel. It was capped with planked boards pegged to the top of the open log. This would keep the filler sod from falling into the trough. The carved-out area of the trough was enlarged at the seaward edge of the sluice, creating a ridge in the walls of the trough. A winged flap was hung from divots in the top of the trough, just seaward of the ridge. This arrangement would allow the flap to open seaward when pressure from falling rainwater pushed the flap open. When pressure from rising tidewater pushed the flap landward, the ridge would hold the flap in place and prevent the waters from entering the sluice and the protected lands behind the dike. The result was a fertile agricultural field on the inside and a saltwater marsh on the outside.

A modern tidal creek on the seawater end of a modern sluice at Grand-Pré. Note the pronounced mudflats as opposed to the fertile fields just up creek in previous photo.

Photo©W. Broussard

Agriculture and Subsistence

Marsh reclamation for agriculture was a grassroots, additive process stimulated by population growth and the need for additional land. Land reclamation peaked as young couples emigrated to the Minas Basin and Beaubassin. There was little interest in clearing the upland forests because of the low agricultural potential.

The Acadian farms gradually moved from self-sufficiency to commercial viability by raising more livestock than was needed for the number of family members. Archaeological studies indicate that the Acadians ate few fish, preferring domesticated animals instead. Wheat and hay were the primary crops made available for commercial endeavors. Other crops included corn, oats, beets, chives, salad greens, turnips, onions, carrots, flax, and hemp. The diked land was for cattle and sheep. Pigs were kept in the forest, and orchards were in the hills.

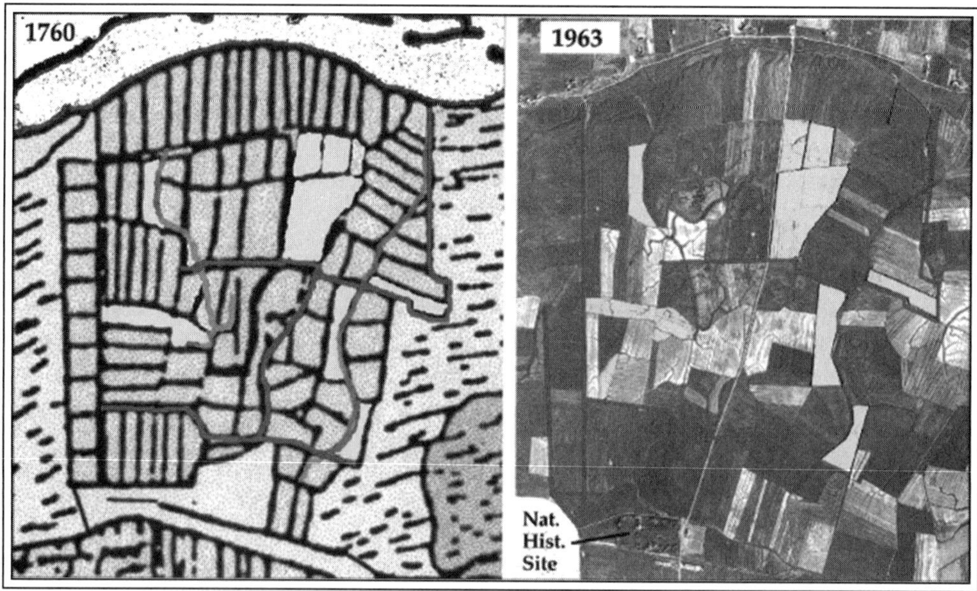

Illustration and Photo©J.S. Bleakney Sods, Soil, and Spades 2004

This reconstruction of the 1760 field patterns at Grand-Pré (left) aligns well with the land patterns in a 1963 aerial photograph (right) of the same area. Very little has changed in over 200 years demonstrating how well the Acadians originally placed their fields, drainage canals, and aboiteaux.

The fields of the Acadians produced an abundant harvest equal to any agricultural system of the day, and the legacy of the original Acadians can be seen in the lay of the land today. Three hundred years later, the benefits of their hard work live on. Many of the original 17th-century fields were simply consolidated, as is the general trend in modern agriculture, but the original dikes and sluice gates remain relatively in place.

Photo©R. E. Turner

Highway sign marking the Avon Causeway, a modern infrastructure built across the Avon River in Windsor, N.S. The causeway also serves as a dike and aboiteau *protecting farmland from high tides while allowing floodwaters to exit the system when necessary.*

Water Management Today

Modern-day Acadians still employ a sophisticated style of water management in both Acadie and Louisiana's Acadiana. Enlarged *aboiteaux* systems built with modern machinery protect larger tracts of agricultural land in Nova Scotia and New Brunswick. Some of these protected lands, however, have not been farmed in recent years, and environmentalists have called for a rehabilitation of the land back to a more natural, tidally-influenced salt marsh system. To accomplish this goal, smaller sluice and flap-gate systems have been replaced with very large open culverts to allow the tides to move freely into and out of the protected land. Much as the *aboiteaux* freshened and domesticated these fertile lands for subsistence farming, the open culverts are allowing the salty wilderness to settle back into its natural state.

Photo©R. E. Turner

A modern corrugated aluminum oval culvert which replaced a smaller wooden culvert (insert bottom right) where a causeway crosses Cheverie Creek, N.S. The newer culvert allows tide water to flow upstream and downstream without inhibition. This restoration technique is being increasingly used to restore abandoned agricultural fields in an effort to restore pre-settlement marsh conditions.

It is worth noting here that water management practices in Louisiana's Acadiana are strikingly similar to those of Acadie. Many Acadians found a new home in the low coastal lands of South Louisiana, which have a similar rise in elevation from the Gulf of Mexico to the higher grounds of the Cajun Prairie.

There is extensive documentation of the Cajuns' settlement patterns along the higher grounds of Bayou Teche, the Chenier ridges, and the tall grass prairies. Soon the bounty of the marsh, swamp, and bays would stimulate settlements deep in the heart of these wet places. Even today, however, it is hard to deny that similar water management practices are found in Louisiana, especially with the use of one-way flap gates to control salinity or water levels in coastal ponds, pastures, habitat management areas, and agricultural rice fields.

Indeed, one of the oldest approaches to restoration and preservation of Louisiana coastal wetlands is called structural management, in which levees, weirs, and gates are used to do just that. While there is no documentation from the late 18th century of any Acadian-style *aboiteaux* in Louisiana with a hand-hewn sluice and flap gate, the odds of an archeological find is highly likely and worth further investigation. A physical discovery notwithstanding, the history of water management in Louisiana today has undeniable ties and cultural roots in the lineage of the Acadian people, and there is no single legacy that exemplifies this connection more than the concept of an *aboiteau*.

Acknowledgments

This project would not have been possible without the contributions of R. Eugene Turner, Melissa Baustian, Jennifer Lasseigne, and Russell Fielding, who, together with the author, researched, co-authored, and produced a museum exhibit to fulfill the requirements for a graduate course instructed by Dr. Turner at Louisiana State University in 2006. The work is now on exhibit in the Acadian Museum of Erath, Louisiana. Funding was provided by the Department of Education through a grant, "Restoring the North American Ecological Landscape," and by the Louisiana Endowment for the Humanities.

Bibliography

A.H. Clark, *Acadia: The Geography of Nova Scotia to 1760* (Madison: University of Wisconsin, 1968); J.S. Bleakney, *Sods, Soil, and Spades: The Acadians at Grand-Pré and Their Dykeland Legacy.* (Montreal: McGill-Queen's University Press, 2004).

Endnotes

1. Sieur de Dièreville, *Relation of the Voyage to Port Royal in Acadie or New France*, trans. C. Webster and ed. J. C. Webster (Toronto: The Champlain Society, 1933), 94.

EVANGELINE: THE ICON WHO JUST WON'T DIE

Joseph Yvon Thériault

Considering that those in Acadian circles have dreamt of doing away with Evangeline for at least 50 years now, she just seems to refuse to die even though she has been dismissed as "fakelore," a fanciful invention or as the true story of Acadians truncated into a simple romance. She has been seen as an American, meek and childless and nothing like real Acadian women, and also as an instrument of Acadian nationalist élites in the Maritime Provinces at the end of the 19th century, as well as Cajun élites in Louisiana at the beginning of the 20th century who were trying to establish a cultural domination over their French-speaking communities.

But nothing has really worked; she is still around. She is present in the visual productions of artists like Herménégilde Chiasson of New Brunswick and George Rodrigue of Louisiana. She is a character who is found—sometimes explicitly, sometimes in disguise—in contemporary literary works of Antonine Maillet or Claude Lebouthillier in the north, or of James Lee Burke or Tim Gautreaux in the south.

In St. Martinville, Louisiana, in the heart of bayou country, people continue to visit her statue as personified by the Mexican film star Dolores del Río, who played her in the Hollywood production of 1929. Since the 1930s, a monument of Evangeline still reigns at Grand-Pré, in the middle of a commemorative park and landscape that was recognized in 2013 by UNESCO as a World Heritage Site. Academics such as Maria Hebert-Leiter (*Becoming Cajun, Becoming American: The Acadian in American Literature from Longfellow to James Lee Burke,* LSU Press, 2009), and the author of this text, Joseph Yvon Thériault (Évangeline: Contes d'Amérique, Quebec Amérique, 2013), continue to study the influence of this poem on the identity that is being built by the descendants of those who were expelled from French Acadie in 1755.

In the beginning, Evangeline was an American icon born from the pen of Henry Wadsworth Longfellow in his poem *Evangeline: A Tale of Acadie* (1847). Longfellow, along with Ralph Waldo Emerson, his friend Nathaniel Hawthorne, and other writers were working together to create stories and images that would shape the identity of the young American Republic. In the latter half of the 18th century, at the time of the War of Independence, Evangeline traveled across what would become the new American frontier—Ohio, the western plains, Mississippi, Louisiana—searching for her lost lover. Her life came to a sad end in 1794 with the Quakers in Pennsylvania, in Penn's city where the American Declaration of Independence had just been signed. It was the most-read poem in English-speaking American schools at the turn of the 20th century, but Evangeline's star would dim slowly, just as the image of the author did, under the combined assaults of the advent of literary modernism and the rejection of romanticism.

Evangeline would begin to fade from the American imagination at the same time as she was being reclaimed by two different groups in America: the former French Acadie in the north, and southwestern Louisiana in the south. Evangeline would be at the heart of each groups' quest for a new identity.

In Acadie, it was Pamphile Lemay's 1864 translation in Quebec that popularized the heroine. As a result of the poem, the deportation would become the center of a nationalist interpretation of the history of French-speaking Catholics who were living on lands from which, in the middle of the preceding century, an attempt had been made to banish their ancestors forever.

The figure of Evangeline, competing with Our Lady of the Assumption, patron saint of the Acadians—as evidenced by the site of Grand-Pré where the two statues vie for attention—would mark the difficult path taken by a story between the Acadian tragedy and the desire to rebuild society. This nationalist configuration would hold for a century, and would be the origin of an Acadian society organized by and through institutions that were mostly Catholic: parishes, convents, schools, newspapers, and national associations.

It is at the beginning of the 1960s, under the influence of a growing welfare state, that this Acadie would be called upon to modernize. In the ensuing criticism of the (traditionally) economically and culturally backward character of the Acadie of the preceding century, Evangeline was taken to task by artists as well as writers and historians. If Acadian society was lagging behind, it was largely because the figure of Evangeline was so central to old Acadian nationalism. More "Acadian" figures were needed—Louis Mailloux, *Pélagie-la-Charrette*—to represent an Acadie that was more combative but also more individualistic.

In Louisiana, it was after the Civil War that the great American poet's work would enter the universe of the Cajuns. Until then, they had been looked down upon by the dominant white Creoles, as well as by white Americans and black populations. They were considered to be poor white Catholics, not very industrious, prone to violence, fond of revelry, speaking an old French-American patois, and living in socioeconomic conditions much like those of former black slaves ("white niggers").

The True Story of Evangeline (1907), by Judge Felix Voorhies, would, by making Evangeline the ancestor of Cajuns in Louisiana, Acadianize them. They would thereafter be able to define themselves, in the tradition of American democratic romanticism, as a gentle people of noble French heritage. This new outlook would allow them to disassociate themselves from the white Creoles (fallen after the Civil War) and the black populations. The romance of Evangeline would open, via the path of Acadian ethnicity, the way to the Americanization of these poor French-Catholic whites from the south.

Just as their counterparts in the north had done, the Cajuns in 1960s Louisiana would question the importance that the popular icon had acquired. It was mostly her non-authentic character that they didn't like—too "American," and not really a true Cajun heroine. If anti-Evangeline rancor came about at the same time that the Cajun awakening was beginning—the movement that aimed to revive the French language in Louisiana—it was because the French language that they were trying to restore was not the old language of France but rather Cajun French. Evangeline was too closely associated with the attempts of the "Genteel Acadians" of the preceding period, the group that had tried to ennoble Cajuns by sanitizing their language and their customs.

In the end, it would be a truly Cajun culture that would affirm itself, less linked to language and more to land, and less based on history and more on cultural ecology. Evangeline, irreducibly linked to the French and Acadian identity of Cajuns, would have difficulty finding her place in this new landscape of identity.

In spite of anti-Evangeline anger, in spite of the desire to get rid of her, to forget her, Evangeline is still around. As we have mentioned, she is an icon who just won't die. Why is she so resilient? It is because Evangeline, in the Acadie of the north as well as in Cajun country in the south, is closely associated with the birth and the formation of the identity of these groups. It is her tale that has contributed to the shaping of the idea that an Acadian nation was born from the ashes of the Deportation upon the soil of old French Acadie; it is her tale in Louisiana that has created the borders of an imaginary Cajun country based on those of the old French Creole and black populations. Every time that someone tries to knock Evangeline off her pedestal, it is that identity that is being shaken.

Evangeline will fade away completely only when the historical communities that she has helped build have also disappeared, or have themselves been merged with another identity.

BEAUSOLEIL BROUSSARD, ACADIAN HERO

Dianne Marshall

From an idyllic rural setting near Port Royal came a man whose impact on his community and the world at large can still be felt today, three centuries later.

Joseph Brossard (later spelled Broussard) was a small boy in 1710, when the British took control of Port Royal and renamed it Annapolis Royal for their queen. Despite his youth, he could not help but be aware of the negative impact this was having on the adults around him. From his father, François, a community leader, he soon gained a deep mistrust of the British occupiers, and an appreciation for the need to protect, defend, and fight for the rights of the Acadian people. As a teenager, the exuberance of youth took over and Joseph, who was becoming known as Beausoleil for the village near the family farm, became a very willing and enthusiastic thorn in the side of the British authorities.

The British Council didn't quite know how to contend with the young rascal who was brought before them numerous times, and on at least one occasion for having participated in a Mi'kmaq attack on Fort Anne. They let him go with a warning, however. To do anything else would have simply inspired other young Acadians and their Mi'kmaq friends to carry out more raids. Joseph began to feel the power of resistance.

By 1730, both Joseph and his best friend and confidant—his brother Alexandre—had wives and children to support. To get away from British control and influence, they relocated to an area north of the Bay of Fundy known as Chipoudy, where their older brothers had settled several years earlier. There, they founded a new village they called "Beausoleil" and settled happily into family life, with the British at a comfortable distance, and their Mi'kmaq friends and allies close at hand.

Things began to change, however, when a new priest Jean-Louis LeLoutre arrived on the scene in 1738. LeLoutre was unlike any other priest they had ever met. Devout Catholics, Acadians had enormous respect for priests—many of whom were in the employ of the French authorities at Quebec and charged with the task of provoking anti-British sentiments among them. This priest was different. He encouraged unrest like no other had ever done, and his influence was soon felt across the region.

The seeds of resistance that had been sown in Annapolis Royal when he was just a young man began to grow again in Beausoleil's heart and mind. It was his destiny to fight for his people the Acadians, and fight he would. The village of Beausoleil, which started out as one of several farming communities, took on a new role—as the headquarters of a resistance movement that would leave its mark on the history of Acadie and the world beyond for generations to come.

With the encouragement of LeLoutre, the Broussards, their Mi'kmaq friends, and several other resistance families in the region came into the employ of the French fortress of Louisbourg. Theirs was a common goal: to drive the hated British out of Acadie using any means necessary. Though there were other pockets of resistance across the region, Beausoleil's force was the most active. Under his direction, bands of fighters carried out land raids from Nova Scotia to Massachusetts wreaking havoc on countless British farms and villages. As an incentive, the French authorities at both Louisbourg and Quebec offered a bounty of 100 *livres* (Acadian currency) for each English scalp that they brought back.

In frustration, the governor of Massachusetts, William Shirley, issued a scalp bounty of his own, although his soldiers were no match for experienced wilderness fighters like Beausoleil and his men. Shirley began lobbying the British government to create a military base on the Atlantic coast of Nova Scotia to counter the influence of Louisbourg. Britain's role in the War of the Austrian Succession, however, took precedence over colonial concerns, and Shirley's pleas went unanswered.

Unfortunately for Louisbourg, France was in a similar position, and its resources were becoming seriously depleted. In 1746, Shirley and the other New England governors took matters into their own hands. They organized a civilian force which, with the help of a British fleet that happened to be in the vicinity, launched a successful assault on Louisbourg. Two years later, after Louisbourg was returned to France under the terms of a treaty, Britain turned its attention to Shirley's suggestion and in June 1749 a British expedition, under the command of Col. Edward Cornwallis, arrived at the bay of Chebookt (Chebucto) to found the new settlement of Halifax.

Cornwallis, concerned by reports of resistance attacks, invited Acadian deputies from across Nova Scotia to meet with him. He advised them that peaceful co-existence was his goal, provided of course that Acadians took an oath of allegiance to the British Crown—something that several generations before them had refused to do. Beausoleil did not sit idly by while this meeting was going on, however. Unknown to Cornwallis, one of the deputies sitting at his table was Alexandre Broussard who later reported to Beausoleil and LeLoutre on his observations of the strengths of the British garrison at Halifax. The resistance movement had a new target.

Louisbourg and Quebec provided the resources, but for the most part, Beausoleil planned and executed the entire operation. Acadians, Mi'kmaq, and French soldiers, often disguised as Mi'kmaq, combined to make a fearless fighting force.

Several horrific attacks at the outskirts of Halifax left the settlers terrified and the military unable to do anything but put up more defences. A ten-foot palisade surrounded the settlement, and anyone who dared venture beyond did so at their own great peril. The market for British scalps was a lucrative one. In short order, Cornwallis and his Nova Scotia Council put a similar bounty on Mi'kmaq scalps.

Cornwallis returned to England in 1753, and his successor Hopson stayed for just one year. Both governors believed that Acadians who signed the oath should be allowed to live in peace on their own land, because as farmers they were essential to the survival of the colony. Each, in turn, had adamantly refused to go along with Gov. Shirley's suggestion that the entire Acadian population should be rounded up and deported from Nova Scotia.

In 1754, Charles Lawrence took an entirely different position on the matter. Lawrence, an experienced soldier, was well aware of the impact that Beausoleil was having on the British ability to settle Nova Scotia. Despite the fact that most of the Acadian people had taken a neutral position, Lawrence considered each and every one an enemy. In June 1755, the capture of two French ships bound for Louisbourg–the *Alcide* and the *Lys*–gave him the excuse he needed to put an end to what he considered "the Acadian problem." In its hold was a cargo of 10,000 scalping knives, with a manifest indicating that many were to be delivered to Beausoleil.

In July 1755, Lawrence wrote to Britain to seek approval of his plan to drive every Acadian out of Nova Scotia and to then recruit English-speaking Protestant farmers to take over their lands. In September, even though he had not yet had a reply, Lawrence put his plan in motion. A few weeks later, orders arrived from Britain that he was not to carry it out, but it was already too late.

All over the territory, Acadians were being rounded up. Smoke from their burning farms stretched across the Bay of Fundy, and though some managed to seek refuge in the forest with their Mi'kmaq allies, thousands of others were suffering terrible losses at the hands of British soldiers. In May of 1756, ongoing tensions between the two countries resulted in Britain formally declaring war on France.

Still, the resistance continued. In a captured enemy ship that had been outfitted as a privateer, Beausoleil Broussard led countless attacks on British shipping both in the Bay of Fundy and along the Atlantic Coast, particularly at the approaches to Halifax Harbour. And on more than one occasion, his privateer rescued Acadian prisoners from the holds of ships bound for distant ports, and transported them safely to Louisbourg. Across Nova Scotia, British forts or soldiers on patrol were fair game, and the relentless assaults by resistance fighters began taking a serious toll on their morale. The mere mention of Beausoleil was enough to strike fear in the hearts of even the strongest among them.

Louisbourg and Quebec were actively supporting the resistance and still paying handsomely for British scalps, and so in the spring of 1758 the British launched a major assault. Under the command of Gen. Jeffrey Amherst, tens of thousands of British troops set out from Halifax for Louisborg and the French fortress was quickly brought under British control. A year later Gens. Wolfe and

Montcalm met on the Plains of Abraham, and although Wolfe died in battle, by the end of the summer Quebec had also fallen to British forces.

During the bitter winter that followed, the loss of their primary sources of supplies left the resistance fighters unable to feed their families, and rather than see them starve in the forest, Beausoleil and other leaders made the difficult decision to surrender to the British. Hundreds of men, women, and children were marched to Halifax, where they were confined to a prison camp on Georges Island.

Charles Lawrence, who had since become governor, died in October 1760, and was replaced by Gov. Jonathan Belcher who feared that Beausoleil would break free from the island camp, find his house, and kill him in his sleep. So Beausoleil was transferred miles away to another prison at Fort Edward in Windsor, where he would have no influence over the other prisoners on Georges Island–or so Belcher thought. It soon transpired, however, that Beausoleil Broussard was quite able to get messages to and from the island camp, and as there was little point in keeping him at Fort Edward, he was returned once again to Georges Island.

The Acadian prisoners were provided with little in the way of rations, and forced to live in an open field without shelter. Nearby, a barracks housed French prisoners of war, but no such accommodation was made for the Acadians. Over the next few years, many of the old and very young joined far too many others in an unmarked mass grave.

Five years after the fall of Quebec and the end of war in North America, the resistance fighters and their families were still confined to Georges Island. Montague Wilmot, who had succeeded Belcher as governor, had no interest in releasing them.

The British government, however, was of a different view. The continued incarceration of Acadians on Georges Island was politically embarrassing, and Wilmot was given a direct order to let them go. Seeing an opportunity to get his people safely away on their own terms, Beausoleil proposed hiring a ship to transport Acadians to Saint-Domingue (now Haiti). As it was deemed far enough away from Nova Scotia to discourage their return, Wilmot readily agreed.

In 1764, the great Acadian hero Beausoleil Broussard led 200 of his followers away from their homeland to Saint-Domingue, then on to Louisiana where they arrived in February 1765. They had found freedom once again in the place they named "New Acadie" and Beausoleil was named Commandant of the Acadians in the Attakapas Territory. Unfortunately, on October 18, 1765, just eight months after arriving in Louisiana, Beausoleil died in an epidemic, as did many other newly-arrived Acadians, including his brother Alexandre. Yet, his courageous resistance against injustice makes him, even after 250 years, the most respected Acadian hero of all time.

Folk Healing and the Traiteurs of South Louisiana

Mary Broussard Perrin

Folk healing has taken on many forms in the Acadiana region of South Louisiana. The term *traiteur* in the Cajun and Creole French dialect of Louisiana refers to a man or woman who practices what is sometimes called faith healing. This tradition of folk healing goes back countless generations in the rural marshes and prairies of the Cajuns, Creoles, and Native Americans of South Louisiana, back to a time when physicians were virtually non-existent, deemed too expensive or too impersonal, or, with the lack of decent roads and transportation, nearly impossible to get to.

Traiteurs did not advertise their practices. People from surrounding communities knew who these healers were simply by word-of-mouth communication, and there were often lines of people outside their doors waiting to be treated. Starting in the 1960s, however, with the advent of readily available western medicine and the means to obtain it, the tradition began to die out, especially in urban areas. Nevertheless, in the early part of the 21st century, there are still *traiteurs* known to be steadily practicing their healing arts mostly in the rural areas and villages of the 22-parish region now known as Acadiana.

According to staff members at Vermilionville Living History and Folklife Park in Lafayette, Louisiana, interest in the practice has spiked. A recently initiated speaker series held there, *Healing Traditions of Acadiana*, has received an excellent response from the community. Many calls came in after the first lecture in 2013 by *traiteur* Allen Simon, with callers wanting to be put in touch with a healer (which the facility is not allowed to do). The intense response has been surprising, and a theory has not yet been proposed to explain this level of interest. It was at first thought to be merely increased interest in a cultural tradition, but the calls do not bear this out.

Although there are fewer *traiteurs* now than in days gone by, several of them still spend a part of each day performing their healing rituals. In the past, some *traiteurs* employed native-plant-based medicinal remedies to treat an ailment, others used a combination of medicinal remedies with secret prayer rituals, and some even used "white magic," but today, most Cajun healers use only Christian prayers to heal their patients, sometimes with the addition of the laying on of hands. And despite the advent of the 21st century, most healers still recite their prayers in the centuries-old Cajun French of their ancestors, although a few of the prayers are thought to be in unknown Native American dialects that the *traiteurs* of today still use but cannot translate.

It is possible, however, that the Native American prayers are also Christian. May Gwin Waggoner says in her book, *Le Plus Beau Pais du Monde: Completing the Picture of Proprietary Louisiana, 1699-1722,* that the Jesuit priests from France were known to have been in the Louisiana Territory as early as the 17th century, and as part of their mission likely converted a significant number of the aboriginal people they encountered to Christianity.

The traditional method a *traiteur* uses for healing is to say a series of three prayers three times, then, if the situation does not improve in a timely enough fashion, two more series will be recited, making a total of 3 + 3 + 3. The number three is important, as three is known as the number of wholeness or completeness, as in the three persons that make up the one God of Christianity. Some *traiteurs* use their prayers to treat only specific ailments, such as sunstroke, warts, or shingles, while others treat a wide range of physical and even mental problems. These prayerful rituals are simple and time-honored, and *traiteurs* are usually careful to not transgress the teachings of their ancestral religion, the Catholic Church. This contrasts with Louisiana Voodoo, which is centered in the city of New Orleans, away from the Cajun bayous.

Since the *traiteurs'* prayers have been passed down orally, traditions vary. One striking variation is the method by which the "gift" of healing is passed down. In one tradition, an older man passes it down to a younger woman and an older woman to a younger man. In another, it is passed down to members of the same sex within a family. Some practitioners believe that they lose the gift when they pass it down, and therefore they often refrain from doing so until they are very old or very sick. This belief sometimes causes the line to die out within a family if the *traiteur* dies unexpectedly.

Traditionally, the healer must wait to be asked to perform a healing ritual unless he or she perceives that the need is great. Their rituals have traditionally been performed by one Catholic for the benefit of another, but are said by some to be effective regardless of faith—or even in the absence of it. There are even cases of animals being successfully treated for various ailments and wounds.

Another widely held custom is the practice of not accepting payment for a healing ritual, the belief being that it is not the *traiteur* but God who is doing the healing; the *traiteur* is merely a conduit. Gifts may be accepted but are never required, and, if given, the *traiteur's* spouse is the preferred recipient. Some healers will accept payment if it is offered, but within the *traiteur* community, these practitioners are not held in very high esteem.

Traiteurs once widely used native-plant-based medicinal remedies in addition to prayer, but now the tradition focuses mostly on prayer. However, to commemorate this former tradition, there exists in Lafayette the unique, international award-winning Jardin du Traiteur (Healer's Garden). This medicinal plant-based demonstration garden is a joint venture of the Lafayette Parish Master Gardeners Association and Vermilionville Living History and Folk Life

Park, and contains varieties of medicinal plants documented as having been used in the area for more than 100 years. The Master Gardeners' *Jardin du Traiteur* tour guides, who volunteer at Vermilionville for "culture days," are often astounded at the depth of knowledge exhibited by some of the local visitors who tour the garden. They are the repository of the area's native medicinal plant knowledge that is increasingly being lost to modern society.

In South Louisiana, the coexistence of conventional medicine and the healing rituals of *traiteurs* offers patients a range of resources for treating illness. *Traiteurs* and their patients, as well as many doctors, do not view the two systems as conflicting. If a *traiteur* becomes ill, he might go to a doctor, but he might also perform his healing rituals on himself, perhaps employing herbal remedies, or even request a treatment by another *traiteur.*

A good example of this way of thinking is Allen Simon (b. 1936), a well-known and sought-after *traiteur* who grew up one of 11 children in Meaux, Louisiana, and who now lives in nearby Maurice. As a child, going to a traiteur to heal an ailment was all his large family could afford, and in addition, getting to a doctor by mule and wagon on often muddy roads would have been a big undertaking for them. There was, as he says with the humor for which he is known, no "high-speed transit" available to the Simons.

Today, Simon has a lively healing practice himself, but since 2001, he has also been volunteering his healing services regularly at Our Lady of Lourdes Medical Center in Lafayette. He feels that conventional medicine has its place, but his faith in the prayers he uses is just as strong. He believes that human beings have been blessed with a body designed for healing itself and maintaining its natural state of health, but he states, "Sometimes it just needs a little kick-start." If, for personal reasons, a patient does not want to tell him what his or her ailment is, Simon says he does not need to know; he is one of a handful of *traiteurs* who does not specialize in certain ailments, but instead treats the whole person since he believes that all parts of the body work together. Simon also volunteers his time as a docent and popular speaker on folk healing at Vermilionville. He usually presents his talks before a full house.

Allen Simon (right) at a 1994 Acadian Museum of Erath event near Lake Peigneur, a once pristine area now the focus of controversy pitting residents against a company which uses the salt dome beneath the lake as a natural gas storage facility; at left is D.L. Menard of Erath, Louisiana, twice Grammy-nominated Cajun musician; and Jim Viator, cultural activist, actor and singer. Simon and Menard are both Acadian Museum of Erath Living Legends.

Traiteuse is the female form of the Cajun French word *traiteur*. Helen Boudreaux is a 74-year-old Cajun *traiteuse* and Catahoula native who now lives in Butte LaRose. She has eight children, 23 grandchildren, and 12 great-grandchildren. A well-known and award-winning Cajun singer-songwriter and former over-the-road/line-haul truck driver, Helen has lived among *traiteurs* all of her life. Her gift of healing, she said, was passed down to her from her Tante (Aunt) Eunice when Helen was 52 years old. She never thought she would ever become a *traiteuse* because, she explained, "that was something that only happened to other, very special people." But no one else wanted Eunice's prayers, and even though Helen had never seen or heard the prayers, she accepted them. "This was a gift from God," she states, "they came to me at a time when I was prepared to share."

Helen believes most of the prayers she uses in her healing rituals are hundreds of years old. She has met Acadian *traiteurs* in Canada who use some of the exact same prayers that she uses. Helen has binders, notebooks, and loose papers filled with healing prayers, nearly all of them handwritten in phonetic French, except for the few that appear to be in a Native American language. It is probably, she says, Atakapa-Ishak and/or Chitimacha, from two of the tribes of Native Americans who have resided in the Acadiana region for eons, although the Atakapas have now all but died out. She neither questions their provenance nor understands their meaning, but she knows what ailments they treat and she simply takes them on faith. She uses them because, she says, they work.

She insists, like the majority of *traiteurs*, that there is never to be any money changing hands for the prayers she offers up in her healing rituals. It is not she who does the healing, she states gently, it is God. She does not advertise her services; requested prayers come from recommendations spread by word of mouth. And, unlike many *traiteurs*, she will pass on her prayers to anyone she feels she can trust and who she knows will use and honor them, especially for their own family. Helen is intensely spiritual and, like most Cajuns, family-oriented.

Seated at front right is traiteuse *and Acadian Museum of Erath Living Legend Helen Boudreaux at a Vermilionville Folk Life Park speaker event in Lafayette. Helen and Velma Johnson (left) spoke on "Healing Traditions of Acadiana." In rear are Lafayette Parish Master Gardeners Maryann Armbruster (left) and fellow* traiteuse *Mary Broussard Perrin, co-chairs of Vermilionville's* Jardin du Traiteur *(Healer's Garden).*

Ray and Brenda Comeaux Trahan both in their late 60s live just south of Lafayette. The Trahans are both *traiteurs,* a rather unusual phenomenon. Natives of Indian Bayou, they have been married for 48 years and have two sons and six grandchildren. They are deeply involved in the Cajun culture. Brenda was director of the Acadian Memorial in St. Martinville for ten years and has taken on other cultural projects both large and small, and too numerous to mention. She is a certified mental health professional in the area of geriatrics and holds a master's degree in Interpersonal and Public Organizational Communications. Her soft voice and petite appearance belie the strength, determination, and amazing work ethic she possesses.

Brenda was first exposed to *traiteurs* in childhood, first while watching her parents use the services of the local Cajun faith healers for their ailments, and then being brought to one for her own occasional nosebleeds and seeing them stop immediately. Because of her positive experiences, Brenda always believed in the phenomenon. It was a natural extension of their culture and was always a part of her life.

In her 40s, Brenda began working for a mental health clinic, serving patients in a five-parish area because of her ability to use Cajun French to evaluate the mental status of elderly nursing home residents. Eventually, after working with two elderly female patients for a time, they disclosed to her that they were both *traiteuses.*

She questioned them about what it was like to be a *traiteuse* in their former days and wanted to know if their prayers were effective. They told her that parents would bring their children to them if it was not a serious disease, and at times, the parents themselves also asked to be treated, and yes, it would work. In return, the adults would often bring her chickens, eggs, or fruits and vegetables as offerings, but money never changed hands.

The local people believed in it, they told her, and it was a very powerful feeling to know that God was using them to heal people. Brenda's conversations with the old women were all conducted in French, and after she gained their confidence, both of them passed their prayers on to her –one treated anything involving body heat, such as sunstroke or fever, and the other treated for bone and joint problems such as back aches, broken bones, sprains, etc.

Both elderly women mentioned, however, that any injury could be treated, if the injured person asked for healing. Brenda says all of the prayers were, of course, in very old Cajun French but that one of the prayers she was given was in a language that sounded African or some other strange dialect with which she was not familiar. She also says that, along the way, she has learned that she has what she calls the "healing touch" –her hands get hot when she touches the afflicted area. She used this gift most recently when her 14-year-old grandson was hospitalized for several weeks with a serious injury incurred while playing football. His grandmother's warm touch gave him much comfort and relief, and aside from the hospital health professionals, she was the only person whom he allowed to touch him. Therefore, she was "on call" more or less 24 hours a day for several weeks.

These days, she says, she gets a request for treatment only every five to six months. She sees the tradition in great decline since she was a child, but possibly there are more requests in rural areas than in metropolitan Lafayette where she lives. Now that there is an increased interest in the Cajun culture and a demand for *traiteurs* to give talks about the practice and its history, people seem to be gaining interest again.

Brenda's husband, *traiteur* Ray Trahan, is heavily involved in the *Louisiane-Acadie* Cajun culture also, often working hand in hand with his wife on projects. After graduating from USL in accounting, he went to work for the State of Louisiana Revenue Department and retired after 34 years of service as a Regional Director. But along the way, Ray has immersed himself in the culture and traditions of Acadiana, as director of the Acadian Memorial Festival, grand master of *l'Ordre du Bon Temps*, president of the *Confederation des Associations des Familles Acadiennes* (CAFA), president of the Trahan Family Association, president of Louisiane-Acadie, and serving in other capacities as well.

Like Brenda, Ray first encountered *traiteurs* as a boy in Indian Bayou. He played basketball in his youth and had frequent sprained ankles. The morning after these incidents, with his ankle "swollen like a little pig," his parents would take him to a *traiteur* to be treated, and by the next game, he was running up and down the court as if nothing had ever happened.

Later in life, his mother became a *traiteur*, and when he was in his 50s she passed the "gift" down to him. He has specific prayers, which he recites in both French and English, for warts, heat strokes, and sprains, but will treat any ailment if requested to do so. When asked if he feels the person must be a believer to be treated, his answer is that if a person asks for treatment, he assumes such a request implies belief, but, "if they don't ask, then I might gently allude to the fact that I am a *traiteur* and see if he or she asks me to treat him or not." Like most *traiteurs*, he occasionally treats a person without their knowledge, if he feels the need is great.

Right now, like the knowledge and use of Cajun French in Louisiana, the tradition of *traiteurs* is at a critical point–still alive, but seemingly dying out. The interest in both is reviving but the actual practice is fading. There are very few young speakers of true Cajun French or a younger generation interested enough in learning the *traiteur's* healing rituals to bring the practice into the future.

In the opinion of UL Lafayette anthropology professor Dr. C. Ray Brassieur, the modern complexities of our day-to-day lives are such that they form an impediment to possessing the simple faith that is required to carry on the traditions of the *traiteur*. And the Roman Catholic faith that is common to nearly all *traiteurs* is also loosening its hold on the young. But as long as doctors are unable to cure all illnesses, and a belief in God persists, there will be a need for alternative treatments, perhaps one that Cajun faith healers will continue to be able to fill.

Shown are traiteurs, *leaders in the promotion of Cajun culture, and Living Legends Brenda and Ray Trahan during a snowfall in 2008.*

BIBLIOGRAPHY

Daigle, Ellen M. *Traiteurs and Their Power of Healing: The Story of Doris Bergeron*, (www.louisianafolklife.org); Brasseaux, Carl A. *Acadian to Cajun: Transformation of a People, 1803-1877.* (Jackson: University Press of Mississippi, 1992); Rushton, William Faulkner, *The Cajuns: From Acadia to Louisiana* (New York: Farrar Straus Giroux, 1979); Ancelet, Barry Jean; Edwards, Jay; Pitre, Glen *Cajun Country* (Jackson: University Press of Mississippi, 1991).

Cattle Culture in Louisiana and Texas

Thomas L. Linton

Long before "Mr. Dunson," played by John Wayne, envisioned the Red River D brand in the iconic movie *Red River*, the Acadians and their descendants were engaged in the cattle industry. In the early 18th century, while they were still in Acadie, they were providing provisions for the sailing ships that docked in the well-protected harbors in the bays of Chignecto and Cobequid and in the basins of Minas and Annapolis, all part of the Bay of Fundy. Prior to immigrating to Louisiana, the Acadians also raised cattle in their villages in the Bay of Fundy, situated between present day Nova Scotia and New Brunswick.

The cattle industry in Acadie can be dated back to 1739 when the Chignecto Bay area's first cattle brand was recorded in the French brand book. In Louisiana, the industry traces its origin with the signing of the Dauterive Compact in New Orleans on April 4, 1765. It was there that French infantry captain Antoine Dauterive entered into an agreement with Commandant of the Acadians Joseph Beausoleil Broussard and seven other exiled Cajun families to "share crop" cattle. However, the Acadians turned aside from the agreement and obtained their cattle from Jean-Baptiste Grevemberg.

Thus, though the Dauterive Compact was not honored, it had the effect of drawing the Beausoleil-led Acadians to the Attakapas Territory. Later, after resettling on the Cajun prairies of South Louisiana, some Acadians exported their cattle industry to southeast Texas. In his book *Cajun Country* (1991), Dr. Barry Ancelet states that Acadians raised cattle on small ranches (*vacheries*). The majority of those who developed the cattle industry in southeast Texas were of South Louisiana origin: White (LeBlanc), Cade, Butler, Campbell, Dick, Coward, and Perkins, to name but a few.

Back in Louisiana, in the *Brands of the Attakapas and Opelousas Districts, 1760-1888*, more than 27,000 brands were listed. Sen. Bill Jones, in his book *Louisiana Cowboys* (2007), writes that on November 16, 1769, when Spanish Gov. Alejandro O'Reilly sent envoys Kelly and Nugent out to explore the southwest prairies of Louisiana, they reported that the Acadians were beginning to prosper as ranchers. They found over 2,000 head of cattle at the Opelousas Post alone.

According to historian Dr. John Mack Faragher in *The Great and Noble Scheme* (2005), the Acadians were also practitioners of the cattle drive. "The sons of Alexandre and Joseph Beausoleil Broussard were soon 'driving' cattle to the cattle markets in New Orleans just as their father had driven cattle to ports in Acadie on the northern coast of Chignecto." They established both farms and ranches, constructing their homesteads along the banks of the rivers and bayous that laced the open grasslands of the two districts. The westward movement of the Cajuns toward Texas began as early as 1780, and Cajun settlements reached the Louisiana-Texas border region by the late 19th century.

According to Bona Arsenault in his book *History of the Acadians* (1988), Acadians became prosperous by raising livestock. This provided them with the funds necessary to acquire slaves, who often took the surnames of their masters. Dr. Thomas J. Arceneaux, dean of the agriculture department at the former Southwestern Louisiana Institute (now the University of Louisiana at Lafayette), located the succession of Pierre Arseneaux, who was born in Beaubassin, Acadie, in 1731. When he died in Louisiana in 1793, he owned 16 slaves on his large farm near present-day Carencro, Louisiana. The estate documents on file in the courthouse of St. Martinville also prove that he owned 400 head of cattle.

Before the late 1770s, no legal commerce existed between the Spanish colonies of Texas and Louisiana. Instead, there were instances when Texas Native Americans stole cattle from missions and drove them to the Acadians. When the viceroy lifted the trade embargo between the two Spanish provinces in 1778, Francisco Garcia left San Antonio in 1779 with 2,000 steers, bringing them to beef-starved New Orleans. Garcia's drive was the first to travel the route that is still known today as the Old Spanish Trail. At that time, Cajun cowboys used natural levees along Louisiana's coast for driving longhorn cattle to market.

In 1817, James Taylor White (LeBlanc) moved to Texas from Louisiana with a small herd of cattle. White built a house at Turtle Bayou in what is today's Chambers County, Texas, even before Stephen F. Austin received his charter to bring to Texas the "Old Three Hundred," 297 grantees of families and partnerships of any married men who purchased 307 parcels of land. This established a large colony in Texas, and White became known as the "Cattle King" of southeast Texas. By 1840, he owned 10,000 head of cattle and 45 horses.

In only a few short years, White would retrace his original steps along the Opelousas Trail into Louisiana, but this time taking with him a large herd of his cattle to sell in the lucrative market that existed in New Orleans and up the Mississippi River. The route that he and others took along the Opelousas Trail never received much attention from historians or Hollywood, despite the fact that these eastern cattle drives occurred 70 years before the cowboys of the Chisholm and Goodnight-Loving Trails moved cattle from Texas to northern markets in Abilene and Dodge City, Kansas.

Today, the spread of farms growing sugar cane, rice, and other crops has reduced the economic importance of cattle rearing in many ways. Yet, the old-style cattle rearing is still visible along the nonagricultural coastal marsh regions of southern Louisiana. In 2013, the 39th *Festivals Acadiens et Créoles*, held in Lafayette's Girard Park, celebrated the theme "Cajun and Creole Cowboys."

Gone to Texas

Ryan Bernard

I should have realized God didn't want me to leave Louisiana when He destroyed our TV antenna in the summer of 1957. Up until Hurricane Audrey hit, I was watching New Yorkers like Steve Allen and Sid Caesar, beamed across 60 miles of swamp and sugarcane fields, all the way from NBC in Baton Rouge. After the 100-mph winds twisted our outdoor antenna into a pretzel, WBRZ became too fuzzy to watch, and we had to amuse ourselves with local fare like *Meet Your Neighbor* on KLFY in Lafayette.

But even God could not overcome the influence of my mother, a New Yorker shipped to Louisiana on the "Orphan Train" in 1919 at the age of three. Despite a sometimes loving, sometimes stern upbringing by her Cajun parents, something in Mom's DNA gave her an enormous urge to roam. Most Cajun families were content to visit places like Baton Rouge, Lake Charles, and New Orleans. Instead, Mom had us on the road each summer, traveling to places like Washington, D.C., Los Angeles, Miami, and Texas—which is where I finally ended up somehow.

You have to understand how un-Cajun the whole Texas thing seemed to me when I was growing up. The boots, the twang, the oily music, the preening, and the braggadocio—it was all just the opposite of how God intended humans to be. Yes, Hank Williams sang a song called "Jambalaya," but the rest of them could go jump in a bayou. And the names they called us—particularly "coonass"—were insulting. Texas was the embodiment of everything that I found despicable in the world. If you had told me I would end up here, I might have called it quits right then and there.

Somehow that all changed when I graduated from the University of Southwestern Louisiana with a degree in English/Journalism and couldn't find a job in Lafayette. There were only a few spots for reporters at *The Daily Advertiser*, and to get one you had to wait until the current job holder quit or died. My older brother, a chemical engineer for Conoco, had already moved to Houston, and his apartment was a convenient place to crash in the spring of 1972. I only planned to stay a couple of weeks, maybe a couple of months ... at most, a couple of years. Little did I realize I would still be here among the skyscrapers 40 years later.

Looking back on the sweep of history, I realized that in the 1940s my parents made the same journey that I did, long before I was born. Soon after marrying, they found themselves in Texas, searching for work. My dad, Reuben, a seventh-generation descendant of the original Acadians, took a job as a timekeeper at the Texaco refinery in Port Arthur, and they lived in a rented apartment over a store, with a bed sheet for curtains. By the late 1940s, however, they had inherited a 150-acre farm south of Erath, Louisiana, and the lure of the land pulled them back to a life growing cotton, corn, and sugar cane.

A good number of other Cajuns wound up in places like Houston, Austin, and Dallas in the same way. There are plenty of names like Broussard, Boudreaux, Landry, and LeBlanc in the Houston phone book. The towns between Houston and the Louisiana border—Dayton, Winnie, and Beaumont—are peppered with mailboxes and street signs sporting Cajun names. Just a few miles east of Houston, you begin to see crawfish ponds gleaming in the Texas sun.

Years ago, the phrase "Gone to Texas" (or "GTT") was often written on abandoned houses by people leaving to find jobs or escape debt. After Davy Crockett narrowly lost an election in Tennessee, he supposedly said, "You may all go to hell, and I will go to Texas." Of course, we all know what happened to him.... Remember the Alamo?

There are many who left Louisiana looking for jobs but then came back, preferring a life closer to home, the way Cajuns are supposed to live. A friend of mine had it both ways: living in an apartment in Houston for 20 years, but keeping a fully furnished home south of Erath and making the four-hour trip back home on weekends. The bridge over the Sabine River at Orange, Texas, is loaded with Cajuns zipping along at 80 mph who are making that weekly pilgrimage.

Some who left never returned. The oil industry scattered many to the North Sea, the Far East, and Africa, where my best childhood friend met his wife, an Irish lass. A true citizen of the world, he lived for years with his family in the country north of Dublin. But then his heart gave out and he ended up buried in a Celtic graveyard on a low hill overlooking the Irish Sea.

This is the fate that haunts me and the other wanderers, too: that we may all someday be buried in strange places where nobody remembers our names. How ironic, that after the *Grand Dérangement* left our ancestors wandering the globe, Louisiana itself was—for some of us—just another way station on that endless journey. You can still hear the pain and suffering of the Acadian Diaspora in the wail of the fiddles and the sad cadences of old Cajun songs. There is no sound on earth quite as sorrowful as this.

"How can you live there?" old friends ask me. Houston is okay, as cities go, but to understand how I feel about it you also have to understand how I grew up: sitting on a branch in a pecan tree, waiting to see when the next car would come rattling down the gravel road. Or wandering barefoot through forlorn pastures, dodging errant cow pies and dreaming vividly about the future.

Back in the hot Louisiana sun, as a child neck deep in cornstalks, I always swore I would someday work in a cool, air-conditioned office. That's when God played another cruel joke on me. Once I had my college degree and office job, He said: "Let there be air-conditioned tractors with Internet and GPS." If this had happened 20 years earlier, I might still be plowing the fields, basking in the sun, and feeling that dark, rich loam sifting between my toes.

You might still recognize pieces of the old me if you spent time following me around this city of four million. Cajun friends tell me they hate the freeways, and frankly so do I. To get across town, I will always choose a deserted two-lane back street over a 24-lane expressway. I do eat foreign foods like enchiladas, barbecue, sushi, and masala. But over the years I have perfected a gumbo recipe that I will put up against any other in the world, just the way I would have done if I had never left Louisiana. I have also discovered that I must eat at least one plate of fried catfish every month, or else something dies inside my soul.

And still I go home. After all these years, I still drop by to see my old classmate Russell Suire, *Le Barbier d'Erath* (the barber of Erath), whenever I am in the old hometown, just to hear his delightfully off-color jokes and keep up with the latest gossip. Ironic that he is a barber, since we are now both as bald as crab apples.

Our old farmhouse is still there amid the cane fields, though we have others farming for us now. The twisted antenna behind the house is long gone. In her later years, before she went into assisted living, Mom had Internet and a cable TV that could bring live feeds all the way from Borneo. Speaking of Mom, she's a celebrity now. At 97, she is known as the last living Orphan Train rider in Louisiana. Every month a newspaper or TV reporter stops by to interview her, and all of her bingo partners go gaga when she gets her picture in the paper. Grand Central Station is holding its 100th anniversary this year, and I am told that somewhere inside that enormous cavern there may be a video playing of her.

As for me, some lazy summer afternoons you can still see me alone in my Japanese car, roaming the Acadiana back roads around Henry, Bancker, Bayous Tigre and Dugas, reminiscing about the old times, seeking out the weathered cemeteries and the ruins of long-lost barns and farmhouses, remembering the old French people who lived here during my childhood, and the way the world used to be.

A few years ago, another hurricane came and washed away the old homesteads, pulling graves right out of the soil and wiping the land clean of its memories. As I wander here among this ruined landscape, far from traffic, a sad video runs inside my head, reminding me of everything we have lost. That old world, with its gentle French *patois* and all of its peace and quiet, is long gone—but still lives on, deep down inside of me.

Meanwhile, back in Houston, life is good, despite the traffic and all the noise. I did marry a gorgeous Texas girl, and we raised two beautiful daughters who think of this place as their home. They don't have a stake in the old country like I do, but at least they appreciate where I come from.

The good news is that they really like my gumbo. Of all the things I've done as a husband and a father, that complex *mélange* of shrimp, oysters, and crabmeat sometimes seems to be the one thing holding us all together. When we all sit around the table sipping that sublime broth, our eyes really glow. Somehow, in the steam that rises from the bowl, you can glimpse all the mysteries of the past. Like the Holy Eucharist, this has become our Communion.

The Bernard family is shown seated (left to right): Paul Bernard, Mary Dinkins, parents Alice Bernard and Reuben Bernard (now deceased), Kaye Bernard; standing (left to right) Glenn Bernard, Lola Doucet, Connie Babin, and Ryan Bernard.

IV

Dignity of a People

Revisiting the Royal Proclamation on Its Tenth Anniversary

Warren A. Perrin

After the supportive editorial noting the tenth anniversary of the Queen's Royal Proclamation, many have asked me to provide more information about the document. To afford the public access to all my files and materials dealing with the effort to resolve the Petition successfully, I donated over 500 items on December 9, 2013, to the UL Lafayette Special Collections, University Archives and Acadian Manuscripts Collection. The public may view them by making an appointment with the Dr. Bruce Turner, the Assistant Dean of Special Collections.

Some background is necessary to explain the genesis for launching "The Petition to Obtain an Apology for the Acadian Deportation" in 1990 which resulted in the Queen's Royal Proclamation of 2003. During World War II, "War Relocation Camps" received over 110,000 Americans of Japanese heritage who lived on the Pacific coast of the United States. Pres. Franklin D. Roosevelt authorized their internment with Executive Order 9066, issued February 19, 1942, which allowed local military commanders to designate "military areas" as "exclusion zones," from which "any or all persons may be excluded." This power was used to declare that all people of Japanese ancestry were to be excluded from the entire Pacific coast, including all of California and much of Oregon, Washington, and Arizona, except for those in internment camps.

In 1944, the Supreme Court upheld the constitutionality of the exclusion orders. In 1980, Pres. Jimmy Carter conducted an investigation to determine whether putting Japanese Americans into internment camps had been justified by the government. He appointed the Commission on Wartime Relocation and Internment of Civilians (CWRIC) to investigate the camps.

The commission's report, named "Personal Justice Denied," found little evidence of Japanese disloyalty at the time and recommended the government pay reparations to the survivors. They recommended a payment of $20,000 to each internment camp survivor. In 1988, Pres. Ronald Reagan signed into law legislation that apologized for the internment on behalf of the United States government. The legislation said that government actions were based on "race prejudice, war hysteria, and a failure of political leadership." The government eventually disbursed more than $1.6 billion in reparations to Japanese Americans who had been interned.

When I read about the apology to the Japanese Americans, I was struck by the parallels between their treatment and that of the Acadians by the British government and Crown. I delved into legal and historical records, and the more I researched, the more I became convinced that we had to address the issue in some way.

One night I was reading *The Magic Rug of Grand-Pré,* a children's book about the Acadians, to my then-eight-year-old son, Bruce, and he asked me what our ancestors had done to deserve to be exiled and whether they were "pirates and criminals." I was stunned. He was right in observing that history had judged them as such–forever.

While doing research, I read the book *Dead Certainties: Unwarranted Speculations* by the Columbia University historian Simon Schama, which brilliantly underscores the abyss between the knowledge of an historical event and the resulting historical interpretations. Further, I noted that in his 1847 epic poem *Evangeline* the American poet Henry Wadsworth Longfellow referred to the Acadian Deportation as an "exile without end." This had to be challenged in some way in order to bring about a symbolic end to our exile. Being an attorney, I found the legal system to be the best way to correct the injustice, so I drafted the Petition.

My Petition requested the following: 1) restoration of the status of "French neutrals," 2) an inquiry into the Deportation, 3) an official end to the Acadian exile by a declaration annulling the Order of Deportation, 4) an acknowledgement that tragedies occurred that were contrary to existing law, and 5) a symbolic gesture to memorialize the "end of the exile." These were essentially the very same unmet demands made of the British Crown in 1760 by the Acadians who had been exiled to Philadelphia, Pennsylvania, which was my primary inspiration for launching the Petition.

What was achieved? When first contacted, the British Crown and government had absolutely no desire to acknowledge, or even discuss, the history of the Acadian Expulsion. Indeed, for the first ten years the government spokesperson, Helen Mann, British Vice Counsel, publicly denied that the British government was even talking or negotiating with me.

A major breakthrough occurred in December 1992 when the British Crown, through their Houston attorney, offered me a settlement to end the Petition: they would pay one million dollars to fund an endowed professorship at UL for the study of Acadian history. In order to discuss the details with university officials, the British sent Dr. Robert M. Lewis, lecturer on American history of the University of Birmingham, England, to Lafayette, Louisiana, where meetings were held with UL Lafayette Vice Pres. Dr. Gary Marotta. I rejected the offer of settlement because it was conditioned upon the requirement that the resolution would forever remain confidential and secret. Ultimately, however, the British Crown did indeed, for the first time, acknowledge the historical misdeed.

Importantly, the proclamation, an act of contrition, declared a closure to the century-long debate over whether the Acadian Deportation was justified. It is telling that no one now argues that the ethnic cleansing carried out by the

British was "unfortunate but necessary" as British defenders had argued for centuries. The salient point: the Acadians of that period were vindicated and, it is submitted, a historical wrong was symbolically rectified.

The Royal Proclamation was signed on December 9, 2003. The matter was satisfactorily resolved because there was a guilty consciousness about it that began when British officers, upon learning of their orders, were dismayed at the inhumanity of their duties (we know this from their diaries), and because the proposed justifications did not prevail in the long term. The better part of British tradition overcame the worst part–the imperial violence against many during its colonial history.

Although the proclamation does not contain the word "apology" per se, one must consider not the letter but the spirit of the Royal Proclamation, as well as the context in which the document was hammered out over 13 years of careful diplomacy. Similarly, just because the United States Constitution does not explicitly ensure the right to vote, or to privacy, this does not mean they are not implied therein. (See: www.usconstitution.net.)

Most critics complain that the Royal Proclamation does not go far enough or award financial responsibility. From the beginning, I made it abundantly clear that seeking compensation for the clear harm and damages caused by the extirpation of the Acadians was not a goal of the Petition. The language of the Royal Proclamation is clearly remorseful because it is the entire reason for having been drafted and signed–to express regret for the tragic event; particularly poignant are the following words by Queen Elizabeth II:

> *Whereas on 28 July 1755, the Crown, in the course of administering the affairs of the British colony of Nova Scotia, made the decision to deport the Acadian people;*
>
> *Whereas the deportation of the Acadian people, commonly known as the Great Upheaval, continued until 1763 and had tragic consequences, including the deaths of many thousands of Acadians–from disease, in shipwrecks, in their places of refuge and in prison camps in Nova Scotia and England as well as in the British colonies in America;*
>
> *Whereas we acknowledge these historical facts and the trials and suffering experienced by the Acadian people during the Great Upheaval.*

The Queen of England does not grovel, but this is obviously an expression of sincere remorse. The definition of an apology is, "an offering of remorse or regret." As such, the language of the Royal Proclamation completely satisfies one of my primary demands. One of the things actually not sought in the Petition turned out to be one of the most phenomenal results: the queen established July 28th as an annual Day of Commemoration of the Great Upheaval.

How was the Royal Proclamation accomplished? Our negotiations did not achieve all of my demands. But, as an attorney who is often engaged in intense arbitrations and mediations, I can assure you that the best solutions are often the ones in which both sides make concessions. In June 2001, a general assembly of the *Société nationale de l'acadie* (SNA), the umbrella organization of the three million Acadians in the world, voted to join me in negotiating the final terms of the Petition. In October 2001, as part of an inquiry, Acadian historians were asked to opine on the merits of the Petition. The officials of the SNA prepared well and established a commission made up of four imminent historians and legal advisors. A total of 140 submissions were made, with only three dissensions.

Public support for the Petition was extremely beneficial, and it came from many quarters. My presentation in 1993 on the Petition at the World Human Rights Conference in Caen, France, brought much-needed and helpful press from all over the world, especially the British magazine *The Economist* ("Sorry isn't enough," July 25, 1998). We obtained resolutions of endorsement from many sources, including the United States Senate, the state of Louisiana, the state of Maine, the American Legion, and the 1994 *Congrès mondial acadien* (CMA), where I was invited to deliver an address on the Petition to an enthusiastic audience.

In 1997, I was kindly invited by French Pres. Jacques Chirac to accompany the French delegation to the World Francophone Summit in Hanoi, Vietnam. While there, the SNA officials, including Françoise Enguehard, arranged a meeting with Canadian Prime Minister Jean Chrétien, who pledged his support. In August 1999, Stephane Bergeron, member of the Canadian Parliament, came to Louisiana for the *Congrès mondial acadien* and became an ardent supporter of the Petition. On October 27, 1999, he was the whip of the *Bloc Québécois* party and introduced a resolution calling on the queen to respond favorably to the Petition.

Others who aided the effort were Quebec Premier Bernard Landry (of Acadian descent), Jean-Robert Frigault, Viola LeBreton, Paul Arsenault, Richard Laurin, Chris d'Entremont, Wayne d'Entremont, Paul d'Entremont, Gerard Johnson, André Forcier, Vera Petley, Jean-Marie Nadeau, Judge Allen M. Babineaux, Mark Babineaux, Phillip Gustin, Gale Luquette, Michel Roux, John Hernandez Jr., John Hernandez II, Kermit Bouillion, Pat Mire, Zachary Richard, Michel Cyr, Clive Doucet, R. Martin Guidry, Ray and Brenda Trahan, James H. Domengeaux, Michelle LeBlanc, Paul Surette, Daniel Paul, Marc Belliveau, Patrick O'Keefe, Jean Ouellet, Dr. William Arceneaux, Louis Koerner Jr., Louisiana Gov. Kathleen Babineaux, Judge Michel Bastarache, M.P. Howard Crosby, Sen. Gerald Comeau, Prof. Michel Doucet, Prof. Fernand Landry, Prof. Yvon Fontain, Prof. Pierre Arsenault, Brian Comeaux, David Marcantel, Dr. David Cheriamie, Dr. Shane Bernard, Dr. Barry Ancelet, Roger Leger, Dr. Carl Brasseaux, Ron Thibodeaux, René Babineau, Louise McKinney, Wilfred Doucette, and Yvon Godin. I will forever be indebted to them, and many others, for their dedicated backing.

According to Euclide Chiasson, then president of the SNA, and Denis LaPlante, then director of the SNA, initially the Liberal Party of Canada was not in support of the Petition, but with the leadership of Minister of Heritage Sheila Copps (who has some LeBlanc ancestry), Prime Minister Jean Chrétien brought the motion to his cabinet. Minister Stéphane Dion, who was recruited by Chrétien to handle the national unity file, had done his research and was convinced that the Petition was legitimate and sound. The legal staff at the Privy Council (his department) was initially against the Petition but reluctantly relented because Minister Dion also had convinced his colleagues and the premiers of the three Maritime Provinces in which important Acadian populations live. Therefore, Chrétien's motion on the proclamation passed unanimously.

With critical help from Chrétien, the terms were finally approved by Adrienne Clarkson, the Canadian governor general and representative to the Queen. This approval occurred with much effort and give-and-take by all parties, and I am proud of the results, as can be all descendants of the Acadian exiles.

In 2010, the Louisiana Bicentennial Commission was created to mark the 200th anniversary (in 2012) of Louisiana's attainment of statehood as the 18th state in the Union. Through education and celebration, the commission's goal was to commemorate the Bicentennial in varied ways including the publication of a book containing photographs of the most precious and tangible pieces of Louisiana's history. The Royal Proclamation is featured on page 144 of the bicentennial book *Being Louisiana: 200 Years of Statehood,* (Baton Rouge, LA: Bicentennial Commission, 2012) edited by Jennifer Ritter Guidry.

During his tenure as president of the *Société nationale de l'Acadie*, Euclide Chiasson led the project to obtain apologies from the British Crown for harms inflicted on Acadians during the Deportation. Since the Repatriation of the Constitution (from Britain) in 1982, Canada became officially independent from the British Crown, so that those apologies had to come from the Canadian government.

Euclide Chiasson asserted that it was Hon. Stephane Dion, then Federal Minister of Intergovernmental Affairs, who, once convinced of the just cause of the Acadian demand, shepherded the project in Ottawa. Chiasson was dismayed that the headline in the news media stated that the SNA had not succeeded in getting the proper apologies. He stated: "In the diplomatic world, even more so when it concerns the Crown, the expression of an apology is not an acceptable practice. At the very start, the federal government made us understand this. The equivalent is a recognition of the harm inflicted upon the Acadians, and this is what this Royal Proclamation affirms." In an interview by Jean Saint-Cyr in *Acadie-Nouvelle* ("Euclide Chiasson: *Bâtir et développer l'Acadie moderne,*" February 4, 2014, page 12), Euclide Chiasson's pivotal role in obtaining the Royal Proclamation was discussed.

I believe this quote by Gilbert K. Chesterton is germane: "A stiff apology is a second insult.... The injured party does not want to be compensated because he has been wronged; he wants to be healed because he has been hurt."

On January 25, 1993, I presented my "Petition for an Apology for the Acadian Deportation" at the World Human Rights Conference at the Mémorial de Caen museum and war memorial in Caen, Normandy. The memorial officially opened in 1988 and is dedicated to the history of violent conflict in the 20th century and particularly World War II. Helping to prepare me for the event was Michel Doucet, an Acadian law professor at the *Université de Moncton.* From Dieppe, New Brunswick, he was then working in Paris and was in charge of the Democratic Process and Human Rights Promotion Program of the *Agence internationale de la Francophonie*, the *Secretariat* for the various bodies of *La Francophonie.*

Bruce Perrin (top), Warren and Mary's son, with the two Michel Doucet girls, Marie-Michèle (front), and Véronique. Marie-Michèle is now completing her PhD in history at the Université de Montréal, *and Véronique (middle), is finishing a post-graduate degree in business. Bruce, a UL graduate in French, is currently public relations director for Prejean's, the world-renouned Cajun Restaurant in Lafayette.*

On March 11, 2005, Dr. John Mack Faragher of Yale University launched his book A Great and Noble Scheme *in Lafayette by making a presentation at UL Lafayette. Faragher wrote of the Petition: "In 1990, Warren Perrin, a Louisiana attorney and a Cajun descendent of Acadian exiles, delivered a Petition to the British government seeking from Queen Elizabeth an official apology for what had been done to the Acadians in 1755. He took up the cause after one of his sons [Bruce] asked him what their ancestors had done to deserve expulsion from their homeland. 'I wasn't able to tell him,' Perrin later recalled. 'Like most Cajuns at the time, I knew very little about our history.' He began to read, and the more he read, the more incensed he became. 'It is the defining event in our history,' he concluded, 'a precursor to what we now call ethnic cleansing.'" Following the presentation he, along with Dr. Carl Brasseaux, were the guests of the authors at a dinner party held at their Lafayette home. Pictured here, left to right, are Director of the Living Legends program of the Acadian Museum, Kermit Bouillion, Faragher, and Perrin.*

On August 9, 2001, Warren A. Perrin met with representatives of the Société national de l'Acadie (SNA) *to discuss joining efforts to obtain a resolution of the "Petition to Obtain An Apology for the Deportation." Shown at that historic meeting at the home of Denis LaPlante in New Brunswick are, left to right, Perrin, Euclide Chiasson (president of the SNA), Denis LaPlante (director of the SNA), and Richard Laurin, Acadian travel promoter and tour organizer.*

Photo©Philip Gould, photographer

In 1990, Attorney Warren A. Perrin filed a "Petition for an Apology for the Acadian Deportation" on behalf of all Acadians against the British Crown and government for wrongs occurring during the Acadian exile. On December 9, 2003, Queen Elizabeth II's representative Adrienne Clarkson, the governor general of Canada, signed the Royal Proclamation with which Perrin is shown in 2003. The document is in the Canadian archives, but a facsimile is on display at the Acadian Museum of Erath.

The Protection of Minority Rights in Canada

Michel Bastarache

My contribution to this book will be to provide a description of the role of the judiciary in protecting minority language communities, in particular the Acadians, who have greatly benefited in that regard since the adoption of the Canadian Charter of Rights and Freedoms in 1982.

As we all know, Acadie was definitively ceded to England in 1713. Normally, according to international law, this was a conquest, which means that all of the private laws then applicable in Acadie should have been preserved until changed by new legislative institutions. But this was not the case. In fact, England used a legal fiction; they considered Acadie to be uninhabited and introduced all of the laws of England as of 1719. At that time, the legislative power that had been given to the governor by virtue of the royal prerogative was suspended and a local assembly was called to exercise legislative powers.

The effect of this was to exclude all Acadians from social and political life, even though they formed the great majority of the population, because the introduction of English law in the colony also meant an introduction of all the anti-Catholic laws that created legal incapacities for them. Among these laws were the Conventicle Act of 1664 and the Parliamentary Test Act of 1678. Simply put: all private French laws were abolished, and the Catholic population was from that point on without legal status and without a knowledge of the law that was to affect it in the future.

The 1713 Treaty of Utrecht did not protect the Acadians. The seigneurial régime introduced by the French to regulate private property was tolerated for a time, but in fact inhabitants were invited to move to Cape Breton, which remained under French rule. A letter from Queen Anne guaranteed property rights and permitted the practice of the Catholic religion. But soon thereafter, Gov. Cornwallis limited the scope of that promise by decreeing that the right to leave was limited to one year, and that all property of those who left would be confiscated. He also indicated that property rights were protected only so long as the property owners were willing to swear allegiance. Modern authors who have studied this have all concluded that the decisions of Govs. Cornwallis and Murray were unconstitutional under British law.

In practice, the British first tolerated the refusal to swear allegiance in order to preserve social peace. They worried about an uprising, given the percentage of the population that was Acadian. In 1730, however, Gov. Philipps persuaded the Acadians to swear allegiance by guaranteeing their neutrality. In 1749, the system collapsed. From then on English legislation would be applied strictly. The Acadians could not hold any public office. An order of mobilization canceled the guarantee of neutrality. State religion was imposed. Members of the Catholic Church were prevented from teaching or performing any public act.

All this was illegal because it was contrary to the promises of Queen Anne, but no tribunal was formed to hear a case and secure the application of the rule of law. All of the boats belonging to Acadians were confiscated, as well as their arms. In 1755, the order to swear allegiance was reimposed. This was also illegal since the Acadians were British citizens. Then came the Deportation order, which itself was illegal because it was contrary to British public law, and also because it was passed without the vote of the Assembly.

After the Deportation and the return of the Acadians, which began in 1758 and continued until 1784, very repressive local legislation was adopted and implemented. The Royal Commission given to Cornwallis extended the application of anti-papist English legislation to the colony without further legislation. This meant that the deportees were not legally permitted to return to their lands or to recover their property.

Those who found refuge in what is now New Brunswick were considered to be illegal aliens. New laws were adopted that created further legal incapacities for Catholics. They could not hold any lands and all of their belongings could be confiscated. Residence in the territory was subject to swearing allegiance. The papist clergy was expelled. An act adopted in 1759 abolished all subsisting property rights of Acadians.

The repressive regime began to dissipate as of 1783. In 1784, New Brunswick was created and it adopted its own laws beginning in 1786. In 1791, New Brunswick abolished Nova Scotia laws still in force, but continued to apply English statutes through reception, including the anti-papist legislation. The government was effectively in place around 1773, with Nova Scotia laws being enforced in the interim.

Catholics continued to be forced to swear allegiance in order to hold lands and seek public office. Moreover, they were prevented from marrying because the Anglican religion was the only one with public recognition. In 1791, marriage was authorized. In 1810, Acadians were allowed to vote, and in 1829 they could hold a public office. In 1834, Catholic priests could marry Catholics.

With regard to education, the situation and legislation were very complex; I will not deal with the issue except to say that the correspondence between school and religion created an impossible situation for Acadians because they were Catholic. This began in 1802. In 1816, all education in French was prohibited, though it was sometimes tolerated and more often hidden from the authorities. In the Constitution Act of 1867, religious instruction was guaranteed under Section 93. Acadians believed this would protect them, but an unrealistic and historically unfounded decision of the Judicial Committee of the Privy Counsel in London quashed that expectation. Parliament had been given the authority to legislate for the protection of the minority, but Canadian Prime Minister Wilfrid Laurier refused to act, seeking a political compromise. French language education continued on a small scale without legal status or public funding, more often hidden from the authorities. The same situation prevailed in all three Maritime Provinces.

At the national level, certain language rights were entrenched in the constitution of 1867, but they applied only to some federal institutions and the province of Quebec. For the general population, language rights would have to wait for the adoption of the Official Languages Act of 1969, which would have very little impact on the Acadian population.

Real progress came with the adoption of the Canadian Charter of Rights and Freedoms in 1982 and the new Official Languages Act in 1988. At the provincial level it took a long time for progress to occur, and it was uneven between the three Maritime Provinces.

In Nova Scotia, progress was limited to liberalization of the education system in 1885 and 1902, then a reduction in services in 1914 and 1926, and then some progress again in 1939 and 1941. Real change resulted in 1981 from the adoption of the recommendations of the Royal Commission of 1974, and especially from federal funding. It is section 23 of the Canadian Charter of Rights and Freedoms that provided the means for progress, because it gave access to the courts to force the provinces to provide minority language education. Civil actions were brought in every province and all were successful. In Prince Edward Island, the same slow course prevailed: the first reform was instituted in 1971, and the right to French language education was recognized in 1980. Here again, judicial decisions made the difference.

In New Brunswick, the situation was rather different. The Common Schools Act adopted in 1871 was totally inapplicable in francophone regions, for it abolished church-run schooling and replaced it with government-run "common schools." This gave rise to the armed uprising of Caraquet in 1875. A constitutional action questioning the validity of the Act was eventually rejected by the Judicial Committee of the Privy Council in London. What followed was a period of extreme instability, which forced the government to compromise in 1875, but without amending the legislation.

In 1928, there was a formal recognition in provincial regulations of the illegal language régime in education: this was meant to guarantee the status quo. Teaching in the French language was recognized for a few teachers who had attended the Normal School in 1947. The Byrne Commission of 1960, created by Premier Louis Robichaud, produced the Great Reform of 1963, which itself lead to the new design of school districts in 1966. The school crisis was unabated however, and conflicts arose in Fredericton, St. John, Moncton, Grand Falls, and Campbellton. A new inquiry was ordered in 1972, to be followed by still another in 1973.

In 1975, a new Education Act was adopted. But there was still conflict, and a further inquiry in 1978 gave rise to another reform in 1979—one that coincided with the creation of the University of Moncton and the community colleges, and introduced parallel school boards. One of the most significant institutional reforms, however, occurred internally within the civil service, especially after the adoption of the Official Languages Act of New Brunswick in 1969. After 1973, all legislation was adopted in both official languages. In 1976, the right to receive a trial in one's own language was recognized. That right was still subject to discretion; it was modified after amendments to the Criminal Code and the Official Languages Act of New Brunswick. This Act was replaced in 2003 and modified in 2010 and 2013. The adoption of an Act recognizing the equality of official language communities in New Brunswick in 1981 gave rise to a constitutional amendment in 1993.

There is obviously, even today, a major difference between formal legal equality and true equality. We all recognize nevertheless that they are very few examples in the world of a small people that has known such a spectacular Renaissance. We have celebrated the 400th anniversary of the founding of Acadie with full recognition by the federal and provincial authorities, in a spirit of cooperation and pride that is manifested on radio and state television. That accomplishment is marked by events demonstrating mostly that Acadians have found their place in our modern society, without having to renounce their culture or their language. It is obviously more important for the Acadian population to mark this anniversary by affirming its existence and recognizing the fact that it fully intends to promote the development of the country through the principles of liberty and equality.

What does all this have to do with the judiciary? We must in fact realize that the world has changed and that the role of the judiciary is much more important; it is the means to ensure the rule of law and control over government action. If minorities could be ignored in the past, their protection is now one of the founding principles of the constitution and a source of public law. This means that the judiciary has the responsibility of protecting minority rights as part of the mandate to build a just society.

The recent debate concerning the appointment of judges to the Supreme Court of Canada has provided an illustration of the change in the role of the judiciary, and more importantly in their power to create law in areas that relate to the economic and social policies of the country. The extent of the power of judges is under scrutiny, but more so their power to decide on the scope of their interventions. There has been a fundamental change in our legal culture. For many, this illustrates our acceptance of a new form of democracy.

There is something unique about our understanding of democratic principles when considering the powers of judges in interpreting the Constitution. It is our new idea of the delegation of powers. Our political and legal institutions are not all dependent on elections: consider the senate. Criminal law is created by our elected representatives, but no one would leave its application to the result of a vote. Today, we accept that the minorities must be protected from the abuses of the majority. In Canada, there is no outcry because of the enlargement of the role of judges, but there is concern about the appointment of judges. Those who are entrusted with the definition of our democratic values should be surely more independent, more accountable, and chosen differently if speaking of the Supreme Court of Canada especially.

Modern democracy needs a strong judiciary to guarantee respect for the Constitution, including the Canadian Charter of Rights and Freedoms. The judiciary must therefore reinforce its mechanisms to dispel the idea that decisions can be arbitrary, especially when they are controversial or unpopular or go against the clear objectives of Parliament or provincial or territorial legislatures. We must insist on respect for those characteristics of the judicial system that provide for decisions that are not subjective, but grounded in rules of interpretation and principles of great importance.

In essence, the question is about constitutional review and, to a degree, judicial review. These notions are the most important ones to characterize changes in our legal system over the last few years. In Canada, constitutional review has existed for a long time and has been implemented without problem with regard to the division of constitutional powers and, in the early years of the Constitution, with regard to the conformity of national laws with imperial legislation.

But the Charter of Rights and Freedoms has changed everything in the eyes of the general public. Decisions interpreting a vague document which leaves a large degree of maneuverability for judges have given rise to a new national debate. Judges now often decide cases on the basis of general principles of law, new sources of law, even historical, cultural, and social considerations, institutional arrangements, and social values. Anyone who knows the constitutional history of this country recognizes that the Judicial Committee of the Privy Council was as staunch an advocate as the modern courts in defining constitutional powers and their division between the two orders of government. But today there are many more decisions to be made because of the creation of a large number of new individual rights, and because of the wider possibility of attacking decisions of the public administration.

This has left the public with the impression that courts should now rule on all of the important questions affecting society. Pressure groups more frequently choose to take court action rather than face parliamentary committees. Why? Because they believe that judges make the law and that their independence plays in their favor. This has left many with the impression that the courts have given themselves a mandate to control all legislative action and all government decisions substantially, and not just with regard to natural justice.

The real question is that of establishing the norms and values that must guide the legal process. It is true that under the common law system judges have always had the ability to develop the law without creating concern within the community. Without this concern, one would have expected a different system where judges would simply interpret the law. But that distinction has largely disappeared today. The common law has lost ground in Canada, but the discretion of judges has not diminished because they now apply a contextual approach to legislative interpretation. This has resulted in a very liberal and evolving interpretation. One would have thought that Section 33 of the Charter, which authorized Parliament and other legislatures to withdraw Charter protection for some laws for a limited time, would have reassured those worried about judicial powers. But this does not seem to be the case. The importance of the Charter has made governments reluctant to invoke Section 33.

When all is considered, it comes down to a matter of legitimacy. We want to know how far the interpretation of the law can be used to create new law, and what criteria apply in this case. If we accept that our constitutional law is a "living tree," according to the formulation of Lord Sankey, and that there are a number of norms that must be constantly adjusted to meet with the evolution of social and moral values, it is nevertheless certain that the courts are not entitled to rewrite the Constitution and that they must, with regard to general statutes, defer to the will of Parliament and legislatures. The symbolic value of the Charter, the very importance of the fundamental principles of law and the culture of rights that has become part of our system, however, have infused all exercise of statutory interpretation.

The issue is of importance because there is no consensus concerning the choice of the forum to determine the moral values of our society or the sharing of responsibility with regard to their implementation. In a country like ours, it is difficult for some to accept that the undefined, underlying principles of the Constitution, those that result from the interpretation of the preamble, authorize the Supreme Court to fix its own limits. Many would consider interpretation to be its true role. But then, some would argue that the rule of law is the primary consideration and that it must reflect our vision of social justice and moral values, something more compelling than supremacy of the law.

To conclude, let me simply say that the fundamental values that were used in the interpretation and implementation of language rights in the last few years have had a real impact on minorities in general and Acadians in particular. The cases of Mahé, Arsenault-Cameron, and especially Beaulac, have contributed in a significant way to the development of *francophonie* in Canada. To the Acadian people, this development was not like one resulting from protests. Still, the fight for true equality is not over.

Louisiana Interest in French Turns into a Growing Business

Marsha Sills

In Arnaudville, Louisiana, students and tourists have been flocking to the small Acadiana town to soak up the French language and culture. In Vacherie, Louisiana, a rural community between Baton Rouge and New Orleans, employees of a plantation home offer tours in French. And across South Louisiana, scholars say, a younger generation is finding pride in a language that has been in a deep decline in the state named for a French king.

For those struggling to revive the language in Louisiana, the cause is morphing from education initiatives to a focus on business. "We have tens of thousands of students who are taking French as a second language, and nearly 4,000 in French immersion learning environments," said Joseph Dunn, former executive director of the Council for the Development of French in Louisiana (CODOFIL), the state agency charged with developing the language. "We've got to be looking to create opportunities for them so they are eventually anchored in this linguistic identity."

"Forty years ago, about one million people in Louisiana could speak French fluently. Today, CODOFIL estimates about 150,000 people in Louisiana are fluent in the language. The decline is due in large part to natural attrition–the deaths of people who spoke French as their primary language at home. The state's declaration of English as the legally-recognized language, and attempts by educators in the 1920s to punish children who spoke French on school grounds, led to the social and economic decline of French," Dunn noted.

In 1968, the state created CODOFIL. It promotes French education and recruits native speakers from francophone countries to teach in Louisiana classrooms. CODOFIL also plays a part in developing Louisiana French immersion teachers. In the past two years, the agency broadened its efforts to include economic development and tourism in French.

Dunn pointed to his former workplace–Laura Plantation–as an example of how the French language boosts the economy. Located in the St. James Parish community of Vacherie, the plantation home attracts about 15,000 to 20,000 francophone visitors annually and maintains at least four French-speaking tour guides on its roster to handle the demand for tours in French, according to Jay Schexnaydre, assistant manager of Laura Plantation. "Those tourists are spending $20 to tour the plantation, and while in the area they will likely tour other sites, eat at local restaurants or stay overnight at local accommodations," Schexnaydre said.

Focusing on the economic angle, CODOFIL is launching a *Franco-responsable* program, encouraging French speakers who own businesses or provide services to do business in French. The program–its name means *French responsible*–is designed to encourage French speakers to take responsibility for promoting the language in their daily lives and at work.

Participating businesses will be identified with a *Franco-responsable* sticker. The program, still under development, is an update on a program initiated about 30 years ago that identified businesses with another sticker: *Ici on parle français* or "French is spoken here."

The goal, Dunn said, is to create a statewide database accessible to tourists and Louisiana residents. "It's important and essential for the people in Louisiana who speak French to take personal and professional responsibility for their linguistic identity," he said. "French is spoken across the state. We want to begin to build that network."

The new CODOFIL initiative is encouraging to business owners like Lori Johnson Walls, owner of *Johnson's Boucanière* in Lafayette. The small restaurant and meat store is an homage to her family's grocery store and meat market, Johnson's Grocery in Eunice, started by her grandfather, who spoke little English.

Her father, Wallace Johnson, as a young boy would take care of the English-speaking customers in his family's store. Johnson, now 85, learned English before he started school for practical reasons–to play with "the little American boy" who lived near his house. It was also for practical reasons that he and his wife did not teach French to their daughter. "When we wanted to say something we did not want her to hear, we said it in French," Johnson said. Walls matched her dad's smile. "They spoke French a lot around Christmas," she said. Walls learned French in school and can understand conversations better than she can speak the language. Her dad is the resident-speaker in the shop, conversing with French-speaking customers, both locals and tourists, who visit. "We're about continuing the Cajun tradition, and the language is another way to show commitment to those traditions," Walls said. Johnson said he's not worried about the decline in French speakers. He said he still hears the language spoken between Lafayette and his hometown of Eunice.

Scholars such as Thomas Klingler and Amanda LaFleur sense a renewed advocacy for the language–among both old and young Louisiana French speakers. "The inter-generational transmission of the local Cajun and Creole French language at home is certainly in decline and very furiously threatened, but we are also witnessing, currently, a real enthusiasm for the maintaining of French, largely among the younger generation who did not learn the language in the home, but in school and in immersion programs," said Klingler, an associate professor of French and head of the French and Italian department at Tulane University.

Klingler and LaFleur, who is coordinator of Cajun studies at Louisiana State University, have both taken groups of their students for field experiences in Arnaudville, a town of about 1,100 some 30 miles north of Lafayette, to document native speakers' dialects and stories and to learn more about cultural traditions. A group of French speakers there is marketing Arnaudville as a place for tourists and university students to experience the language and culture.

In Arnaudville, the *Franco-responsible* movement is in place and it is encouraging locals to speak *en francais.* "Many French speakers in Louisiana are not quite aware of the potential positive effect that speaking French in their public lives can have on the cultural and economic well-being of the area," said LaFleur.

And the more the language is heard, the easier it will be for even the most timid of speakers to begin practicing what they know, she said. "It's sometimes tough to overcome what we call the '*honte*' factor, a sort of shyness that comes from not being quite convinced that our French is 'good enough,' " LaFleur said. "But most things worth doing involve sticking our necks out."

Acknowledgement

This article was originally titled "Interest in French Turns into a Growing Business," and was published in *The Advocate*, on July 16, 2013.

The Birth of the Fédération Acadienne du Québec

Roger Léger

For as long as long as we can recall, there have been associations of Acadians in Quebec. This includes Montreal, Gatineau, Quebec, Trois-Rivières, and Montérégie on the North Shore; and in the lower St. Lawrence district, the Gaspésie Peninsula and Îles-de-la-Madeleine. These groups would survive a decade or two then cease to exist, along with their founders. However, the main problem was that these scattered associations and committees were completely unconnected and were only concerned with "local issues." In 1980s Montreal, there were three Acadian associations: *Les Acadiens en ville,* the *Comité universitaire acadien de Montréal*, and *Le regroupement des Madelinots* in Verdun.

I first had the idea of creating an association for Acadians from all over Quebec in 1987 when I attended a formal assembly in Quebec City. Present were activists for the French cause in America, there to honor the work of the illustrious Acadian Émery LeBlanc.

What struck me at the time was that there were no Acadians in Quebec that evening to specifically honor this eminent Acadian. I wondered why Acadians here did not celebrate their own, and it was at that moment that I realized there was no official Acadian representation for the North American continent. There was, of course, the *Société nationale de l'Acadie* (SNA), but this organization was only for Acadians in the four Atlantic provinces. It seemed a good time to start organizing Acadians across North America, much like the Jewish people have done in many countries around the world.

That evening in Quebec City a concern occurred to me that took a few weeks to figure out. My brother Yvon, author of *L'Acadie de mes ancêtres* (1987), which I had just published, had been recounting the story of Acadie to me for years, particularly the Léger and Gallant family histories. Although a New Brunswick Acadian by birth, I became Québécois through necessity in the 1940s. Because I had spent my adolescence and young adulthood in Quebec, I completely embraced the Quebec cause. I nonetheless recognized the need for Acadians to become organized in Quebec and elsewhere and to put a stop to the insulting custom of calling Acadians "francophones outside Quebec." There were thousands of Acadians living in every province across Canada, so it seemed appropriate to create Acadian associations "where numbers warrant."

Accordingly, September and October 1987 were devoted to putting together the new *Fédération acadienne du Québec* (FAQ). Through my brother Yvon, who was familiar with *Les Acadiens en ville* and the members of the *Comité universitaire acadien de Montréal*, we could rapidly reach and attract a few hundred Acadians in the Montreal area. During these two months, I wrote up the general by-laws, went through the incorporation process, held meetings for the temporary committee that had been formed, and coordinated the usual activities required for founding a new corporation.

At the beginning of October 1987, I organized a promotional tour with my brother for his book *L'Acadie de mes ancêtres* in Quebec and New Brunswick, which would culminate with a book launch at the Monument Lefebvre in Memramcook, New Brunswick. During this trip, I wanted especially to meet with the SNA to inform them that Acadians in Montreal were creating the FAQ and that we wanted to join them.

I met with Jean-Marie Nadeau, then secretary-general of the SNA, in his office in Shédiac. He told me my request was not permitted, because the SNA was open only to Acadians from the four so-called Maritime Provinces. They had also received a request from Louisiana Cajuns four years previously, which had unfortunately also been refused. So how could we bring together Acadians spread out all over the world? It seemed a natural route to follow.

After this surprising meeting with the SNA, I returned to Montreal somewhat disappointed. After all the preparatory work was done, the inaugural meeting of the FAQ was held on November 20 at the Dominican Fathers' residence on Côte-Sainte-Catherine in Montreal, with about 80 people attending. As the founder of FAQ, I willingly accepted the nomination as its first president. When the *Semaine de l'Acadie* was organized at the same place in October 1988, the FAQ already boasted more than 200 very enthusiastic members.

The original group that formed the Fédération acadienne du Québec *in 1988, left to right, are (first row) Judge Marcel Trahan, Dr. Ephrem Robichaud, Huguette Froment, Roberte Arsenault, Émérentienne LeBlanc-Tremblay, Diane Leclerc, and Louis Morais; (second row) Donat LeBlanc, Judge Roger Vincent, Roger Léger, Jean-Guy Blanchard, René Robichaud, Bernard Tremblay, Paul Arsenault, and Yvon Léger.*

The FAQ executive of 2009-10, seated left to right, are Al Samson, Jacqueline Mallet (president), Rachel Benoit, and Donald Hebert; (standing) Georges LeBlanc, Robert Larose, Sylvain Gaudet, and Claude Lamouche.

Over 35 years, during which five people have succeeded me as president, the *Fédération acadienne du Québec* has organized numerous dinners, conferences, and meetings. The jewel in our crown, however, is undoubtedly the creation of the *Méritas Acadien* award, conceived in 1989. Jacqueline Mallet, the very devoted president who succeeded me, organized the *Méritas* for nearly 20 years.

Throughout the years, many Québécois celebrities with Acadian roots have received the *Méritas*, including Antonine Maillet (author), Viola Léger (actress), Bertin Nadeau (businessman), Jean Béliveau (hockey player), Michel Robichaud (fashion designer), Edith Butler (singer and musician), Pierre Bourque (mayor of Montreal), Réjean Thomas (doctor), Gérald LeBlanc (journalist), Nérée DeGrâce (painter), Phil Comeau (film director), Zachary Richard (singer and musician), Bernard Landry (premier of Quebec), Marcel Léger (former president of the FAQ), Isabelle Cyr (actress), Monsieur Pointu (fiddler), Abbé François Lanoue (historian), Marie-Jo Thério (singer and musician), Rachel Léger (director of the *Biodôme*), and Patsy Gallant (singer).

Despite such success, however, the FAQ has not met all of its goals–especially that of uniting all Acadians in Quebec–but today there are a dozen Acadian associations solidly established in almost all areas of Quebec. The *Coalition des organisations acadiennes du Québec* was created in August 2007 as an umbrella group, and, in June 2012, the first-ever Quebec assembly of Acadians, *le Ralliement Acadien,* was held in the Saguenay region, bringing together Acadians from all over Quebec and neighboring provinces. My original dream finally came true, thanks to the hard work of many devoted and proud Acadians.

I would like to conclude this trip down memory lane with my thoughts and my take on the future. I am Acadian by birth and Québécois by adoption. Above all, I am a North American francophone who is trying to forge links with other francophones in North America. I can only envision a future for French America that is based on greater cooperation among its different francophone communities—a future that I believe should take shape alongside the *Centre de la Francophonie des Amériques* (CFA), recently created to fill the void left by the *Conseil de la vie française en Amérique* (CVFA), which ended in September 2007.

In 2002, I suggested that the CVFA create a *Coalition des Francophones d'Amérique*, bringing together local representative associations such as the SNA

(Maritime Provinces), MNQ (Quebec), CODOFIL (Louisiana), *Fédération des Alliances françaises* in the United States and Canada, and all other francophone delegations. This would include Acadians in Canada; Cajuns in Louisiana and Texas; Québécois; franco-Ontarians; francophones from Western Canada and the American Midwest; franco-Americans in New England; and those in the cities of Boston, New York, Miami, Los Angeles, and San Francisco. These people should band together as the Jewish people have learned to do so well.

Through the 1990 American census and the 1991 Canadian census, 20 million people in North America self-identified as having French origins, five million of whom still speak French. We must take a pro-active stance to this reality, see beyond our local borders, and act locally and globally. These are my thoughts as I take stock of the past and my various activities in francophone North America.

In October 1988 in Montreal the Semaine de l'Acadie *was held, which was a regional predecessor of the* Congrès mondial acadien. *Left to right, are Acadian music stars Angèle Arsenault, Édith Butler, novelist Antonine Maillet, and author Roger Léger.*

ASSOCIATIONS

Fédération acadienne du Québec (federationacadienneduquebec.com)

Coalition des organisations acadiennes du Québec (acadiensduquebec.org).

Against the Wind and Water in Louisiana

Natial Perrin d'Augereau

This is my story about Hurricane Rita that devastated southwest Louisiana on September 24, 2005. I wrote it 12 days after the hurricane hit. I apologize if some of the details don't seem to make sense, but I had hoped that through writing it, a healing process could begin for me since I was having trouble sleeping at night. I had to write it.

I was very critical of the people who stayed in New Orleans when Hurricane Katrina was approaching on August 28, 2005. How could people be so stupid as to put themselves in harm's way! Now *we* were under a mandatory evacuation order for Hurricane Rita–the fourth-most intense Atlantic hurricane ever recorded, the most intense tropical cyclone ever observed in the Gulf of Mexico–and what did we do? We stayed home, of course. After all, I had always bragged about how I knew that we could live for at least two weeks off the food that I have stored.

We live on what is considered a "high hill" in Louisiana–at least 12 feet above sea level–and my house is three steps high! No flood could ever reach my doorstep. My husband David had made a wonderful electrical generator after Hurricane Andrew that could power the whole house. It had worked fine for Hurricane Lily in 2002. He had lots of diesel. This hurricane was supposed to hit in the Galveston area, and we lived five miles south of Abbeville, Louisiana, which is about 225 miles east of Galveston. Surely the winds couldn't be too bad here. I told my friends that we were staying because we weren't worried about strong winds, and we were prepared to be self-sufficient after the storm hit, even if there was some flooding.

This picture, taken on March 7, 2011, shows the house owned by Natial Perrin d'Augereau's mother. The house was elevated nearly ten feet, but d'Augereau's mother never went back home. She passed away six months after Rita.

My 87-year-old mother's house is a few miles south of mine, and the Vermilion Bay is just a few miles south of hers. My brother, a recent Katrina evacuee, had been staying with her. That Friday night, my niece Angie had invited her father and grandmother to spend the night with her family in Lafayette, 45 miles inland. Momma had asked me to pick up her car and drive it to my house – just in case it would flood. You see, Momma remembered well that, in 1957, when she was nearly nine months pregnant with me, there was a horrible flood at her home following Hurricane Audrey, which had come ashore at Johnson's Bayou. Water had almost entered her back door, missing by mere inches. Nearly 750 people lost their lives in that hurricane.

My daughter Jessica drove me to pick up Momma's car. I thought about the safe in her house, which had some important documents in it. We always left it cracked open so that we didn't have to actually use the combination to open it. I thought that maybe I should at least go in and close the safe. I chuckled to myself when I saw that Momma had carefully placed many of her shoes and her good suitcase on the bed – just in case there might be some flooding.

Another thought: maybe I could go to the store one more time. I had three loaves of bread, five gallons of milk, six dozen eggs, at least 15 gallons of water, and there was a full tank of gas in my van. I concluded that should be enough for my family of seven people, including one three-month-old baby.

The wind started to blow late in the day on Friday.

But this wasn't going to be too bad: The air conditioner was running constantly so we wouldn't be too uncomfortable when the power went out. We had the TV going from the Weather Channel to ABC to CBS–what's this? It's not going to hit near Galveston? Closer to the east, near the state line. Hmm... that was a little worrisome.

We lost our electricity at about 11:00 p.m. that night. Each of us had a flashlight nearby. It was kind of fun for a little while. My husband David couldn't go out to start the generator in the rain, so he just went to bed. One by one the kids fell asleep, but I couldn't stop going from window to window to check out the wind and to see if the water was rising; there's a canal in our backyard. I was carrying around my battery-operated radio, which also caught local television stations. Now they were saying it would probably come ashore near Cameron. Then, well, maybe Johnson's Bayou. That didn't sound good for us. No hurricane had come ashore in that area since the deadly Audrey, and this storm was much bigger and stronger than Audrey. I finally fell asleep close to daybreak.

When we woke up, we checked for damage. Things looked pretty good. Even though we must have had close to 100 mph gusts of wind, there wasn't one large branch in our yard; Hurricane Lilly had taken care of all the weak branches three years ago. All our structures looked fine. The only apparent damage was a couple of broken birdhouses. The water was over the banks of the canal, but it had been this high before. As the weathermen liked to say, it looked like we had dodged the bullet. I called a few people from my home phone at about 8:00 a.m. that morning and told them we were okay. David went out and started the generator. I cooked a big breakfast.

Don's Boat Landing was totally rebuilt from the devastation caused by Hurricane Rita (shown) in 2005, and then again by Hurricane Ike in 2008. It is once again open for business–once again a testament to Cajun people's fortitude. Located on the Boston Bayou in Henry, Louisiana, Don's Boat Landing features entertainment and fishing tournaments on scheduled weekends.

When we are flooded in, it's always fascinating to watch the water. Our backyard canal flows to the Vermilion River, then to Vermilion Bay, and finally out to the Gulf of Mexico. At about 9:30 a.m., I noticed that there was a really strong current in the canal. It's fun to watch branches and barrels and whatever else float on by. But wait–the water was starting to come up some more. This must be that surge we were told about. I warned David to check to see if there was anything important on the floor of what we call the "shell shack" behind the house, because it's lower. It looked like water was going inside that building. That had never happened before. My nine-year-old son, Joey, was having fun floating on an old tire in the backyard. The water was in my chicken yard now, and the current was strong. It looked like duckweed was collecting around the fence, and I later learned that there were millions of fire ants floating in it. The water was inching its way up my backyard.

Heather Bouillion Foster pictured on September 14, 2008, at Lake Peigneur after Hurricane Ike came ashore on the Louisiana and Texas border.

Ella Mae Broussard Perrin and director Warren A. Perrin pictured at Lake Peigneur.

David went to his big shop on the opposite side of our house and across from a large cow pasture. When I looked out the front door, I noticed that water was starting to fill the pasture behind the shop. This, too, had never happened before. I could see David trying to raise things up. I slipped on some boots and, in just that little amount of time, the water was almost touching the slab of his shop. When I offered to help, he said there was no point; he just had too much stuff to move. Water began to completely surround us at an incredible rate of speed. I could see my neighbor, Christine, in her yard in the distance, and all we could do was look at each other. Christine and her family soon left their house in a truck with high tires, fully expecting to find water in their house when they came back. Fortunately, it missed them by inches.

Ella Mae Broussard Perrin and Henry L. Perrin pictured on November 30, 1989, on their 50th wedding anniversary.

I walked back to my house just ten minutes later, and by now the water was over my ankles on the long driveway. And the water was still rising. I tried not to cry, but I don't handle emergencies very well. I brought my two young children into my bedroom and asked them to pray a rosary with me. I told them that if it was part of God's plan that we die that day then we would die, but Jesus had the power to calm the sea, and he had the power to stop this water from rising. After we had finished saying our rosary, we checked, and the current didn't seem as strong.

David had pulled our aluminum flat boat near the house and started the motor running just in case we might need it. Our small herd of cattle made its way to the small patch of visible land, which was just outside my yard. My cousin Mark's cattle across the canal weren't as lucky as mine. They were standing in water up to their necks. Several times they had attempted to swim to us, but they would get scared and turn back. It was so sad to hear them crying all night and day, but there was nothing we could do for them. Fortunately, they all seemed to have made it through the night in decent shape.

Photo©Bobby Mallet Jr.

On September 25, 2005, the day after Hurricane Rita struck at Sabine Pass, Bobby Mallet Jr. took this photograph of cows on the porch of Dale and Michelle Reaux's home in Boston, Louisiana, a rural hamlet just east of Henry, in southern Vermilion Parish. The couple had prudently built their house on high ground to escape possible flooding but they never thought to protect it from cows trying to escape drowning. The photo has been widely disseminated. The image conjures up the old expression "when the cows come home."

All afternoon I kept my eyes on that water level. My nephew-in-law called and offered to send someone to rescue us. My daughter Jennifer called from Lafayette and offered to do the same. I told them that the water would have to come up another three feet before it would come into our house. I reassured them that we had a working boat and promised that we would find a way out if it got too bad. There was a call for boats to help rescue people in low-lying areas. Helicopters started flying over us. David said that he waved off at least five helicopters during that day and the next; I flagged off two. We must have been a sight for the people in those helicopters. We had less than an acre of dry land, and here we were with small children playing in the yard! My daughter Janine said that she couldn't wait to tell her friends that a helicopter tried to rescue her. I told her that some of her friends probably were being rescued by helicopter right this very minute. I was right.

At some point Saturday, David reminded me that there were probably thousands of homes with water in them, including my mother's home in the nearby small settlement of Henry. David and my son John David planned on going by boat the next day to check on the house.

When I wasn't watching the water, I was watching television. When we saw the first aerial footage of Vermilion Parish, we saw Momma's house. It's easy to spot her big red barn. There was no land visible around the house. I told my family about seeing it so they could watch.

Flooding of the Perrin farm where Ella Mae Broussard's garden had been located for over 65 years.

A large snake shown taking refuge from the storm's floodwaters in Perrin's garage.

This photo, taken on April 6, 2011, shows Ella Mae Broussard Perrin's restored and expanded garden. The beloved garden is now maintained by her family.

As of that night right before bedtime, we weren't sure if the water was finished rising. It was only four inches below a dangerous level for our water well, and about a foot below a dangerous level for our generator. David and my son John David shut the generator off for the night. They had a tough time fighting off those horrible fire ants. Now, the ants were making nests everywhere in our backyard.

Sunday morning, my neighbors Buffy and Tommy went by boat to check on their house. Tommy told us he had been to Henry, where Momma's house is. When we explained where the house was, he said that he thought there was water halfway up the windows. David and John David left our house soon after by boat and were able to go all the way to Momma's and tie up to her mailbox. The water had indeed been halfway up her windows. There had been at least six feet of water outside her house, and four feet of water and mud inside.

The strangest thing they found, even before getting out of their boat, was another aluminum flat boat tied to the gutter on the front of the house and hanging about three feet off of the ground. When I called and mentioned the boat to my niece Rebecca, she commented that she thought someone was shown on a television clip being rescued from off of the roof! That all made sense.

Following Hurricane Rita, Tyler and Brooke Domingues are shown on a tractor owned by their cousin Corbet "Little Jim" Domingues Jr., a sugarcane farmer, on Aurelien Road in Henry, Louisiana.

By Monday morning the water had nearly receded. We loaded up the small generator, the pressure washer, a blower, a big tank of water, and a tractor and drove to Momma's in Henry. Just a few minutes after we arrived, a truck towing a boat trailer drove up. I regret not getting the name of the man, but he told us that the boat was his. The water had risen so fast the night before that his car had quickly gone under water so, fearing for their lives, he quickly put his family and the family next door in his boat and tried to navigate it to the nearest town to safety. But he hit something with his boat in the dark and his motor went underwater and wouldn't run after that. He was able to grab onto the nearest solid object which happened to be a tree in my mother's front yard. While they were there, he said, two alligators were circling them. One of them was about 12 feet long. They were able to get to the house, tie their boat to the gutter and climb onto the roof. They stayed clinging to the roof in the wind and rain until a helicopter spotted them early the next morning. A total of nine people were rescued from Momma's roof!

The next thing we did when we arrived at Momma's for cleanup was try to figure out what furniture could be saved, then I started pushing mud off the patio. There were three to four inches of that muck everywhere. David cleaned the furniture with the pressure washer and we put it on the clean patio. My niece brought Momma to see the house. It was very difficult to enter; you had to wear boots, and everything inside had been tossed around like a whirlpool had been in there. My niece took some of Momma's pictures and also the soggy contents of the safe back home with her to try to dry them out. Apparently, the safe was designed for fire, not flood.

Photo©Bobby Mallet Jr.

Ben Vaughn in front of St. John Catholic Church in the tiny hamlet of Henry, Louisiana. The small parish, established in 1895, raised $400,000 in order to restore, elevate, and maintain their beloved church after the hurricane.

Photo©Joey Hebert

St. John Church in Henry was lifted by Devillier House Movers. The money was donated by people from the parish, the state, and the nation. During the work, mass was held in the Henry Elementary School gym. The elementary school across the street was not so lucky; the only building that survived was the gym. The school was never rebuilt.

I drove a little farther down the road to our church. There had been about four feet of water in there, too, but the mud was not as bad as it was at Momma's. It looked like the floor support beam had popped up into the center aisle the entire length of the church. Much of it will have to be rebuilt. I hope we can rebuild; unfortunately, much of the Henry community consists of elderly people, and I'm pretty sure most of them do not feel strong enough to rebuild their homes. Many of their homes literally floated away. I drove through Henry yesterday morning before daybreak. I could find only two houses that looked like there were people inside.

I rode around one day with a couple of cameras and took a lot of pictures. Janine, Joey, and I checked out the cemeteries where we have family members buried. None of our tombs were affected, but many other tombs had popped up and floated away. Some stayed right next to the original location, but some were off in the distance, just barely seen.

What happened to Henry is sad, but the devastation didn't only happen there. So many rural and urban communities all along the Gulf Coast were hit hard by Hurricane Rita. Fortunately, there seems to be no loss of life in Louisiana.

(editor's note: the final death toll from Hurricane Rita is 120, with most of them occurring in Texas. Of that, Louisiana had a single fatality in Calcasieu Parish.)

Momma wants to go to a nursing home now. We're trying to talk her into assisted living. She has been saying for a couple of years that she wanted to go. Some of her former neighbors are living there already. I think that her garden was the main reason she stayed home. Her garden is destroyed now, covered with marsh grass and debris.

We keep going back and forth with each other about what should be done with her house. We'll probably try to restore it, but we may just get discouraged by the overwhelming need to be done. We may not even be allowed to rebuild it at the present height. Whatever building we may do there in the future, I'm pretty sure we'll have flood insurance to cover future damages.

Two days later: If you have been affected by either of the recent hurricanes, I highly recommend that you write your own story and send it to friends. This has been a healing process for me. I have slept through the past two nights.

Photo©Warren Perrin

Today St. John's Church is beautifully restored, and a tribute to the determination of the Cajuns not to leave their communities after any kind of "storm." This photograph of St. John the Evangelist Catholic Church was taken on September 22, 2012, after it was restored and raised. As Dr. Barry Ancelet said, "This building is a testament to the dedication of Cajuns wanting to remain on the lands that were settled by their ancestors."

LOSING LOUISIANA

Katy Reckdahl

Because of a slow-moving disaster caused by sinking land, climate change, and oil exploration, Louisiana's coastal families must now choose between leaving their homes for higher ground or staying where generations of their families lived, on land so precarious that the next hurricane could wash them away.

Every morning, inside his house perched on 11-foot stilts, the Rev. Roch Naquin, an 80-year-old Catholic priest, wakes early. He walks to his small prayer room, where a Native American dream catcher gets equal billing with crosses and images of Catholic saints. Then he lights incense and picks up his eagle feather for his prayer ritual. The Rev. Roch Naquin begins his morning prayers with a blessing at his home on Isle de Jean Charles. He burns sage, sweet grass, and tobacco to bless the four corners, the heavens and the earth.

Rev. Roch Naquin

Photos©Kathleen Flynn

Facing east, he waves the incense away with the feather and asks God for protection from "evil forces," three of which he names: "hurricanes, high tides, and strong winds." Then he faces each of the other compass points – south, west, and north – and repeats his plea. "We thank you for the many gifts you give to Mother Earth," he says. "Protect us."

Naquin is praying not only for himself, he says, but for everyone on Isle de Jean Charles (in Terrebonne Parish), the Gulf Coast barrier island he calls home. Here climate change, oil exploration, and coastal erosion have turned a once idyllic island community into a thin strip of land ready to give way to the sea. It's come to the point that residents and scientists alike fear that one more big storm could put Isle de Jean Charles underwater. Worries are at their worst during the Atlantic hurricane season, which starts every year in June and continues until the end of November.

The community of Isle de Jean Charles

Photos©Kathleen Flynn

Over the past 80 years alone, experts estimate that about 1,900 square miles of Louisiana coastal land have washed away. The state loses a football field-sized area of land every 45 minutes. Flooding has increased markedly, causing residents to raise their homes again and again. Many homes are now set on stilts more than 13 feet in the air.

But elevated houses only postpone what now seems inevitable: the complete disappearance of South Louisiana's small coastal fishing communities, most of them populated by families who have spent their lives pulling shrimp, crabs, and oysters from the water that now threatens to submerge them.

This land seems almost sacred for its longtime residents, whose descendants found it a safe haven long before Thomas Jefferson purchased it for the United States. Some families, like the residents of Isle de Jean Charles, can be traced back to Native Americans trying to avoid federal reservations or to fleeing African slaves. Others were exiled Acadians, now called Cajuns.

Cajun Reggie Dupré, who manages a levee district in Terrebonne Parish in the hardest-hit area of the coast, recounts the tale of his Acadian ancestors. They departed France in the 1600s, he said, and settled in Acadie, which booted them out when they refused to sign a loyalty oath to the King of England. When their boats landed in Spanish-ruled New Orleans of the 1760s, they were given land grants by the Spanish. Eventually they bonded with the other exiles in this region, on bayou-land once perceived uninhabitable.

But soon, the exiles may have to pick up and move again.

"My ancestors have been here for eight generations, but I don't think that Terrebonne Parish has eight generations left," said Dupré, former chair of the Louisiana Senate's natural resources committee. Dupré's work protecting the area with floodwalls, pumping stations, and elevated highways delays his homeland's demise, but not for long. "I'm buying maybe three or four generations; 100 or so years," he said.

The timeline is much shorter for the parish's most fragile areas, like Isle de Jean Charles, which maybe has 20 or 25 years left, based upon what Dupré has seen over the past 15 years, he said. Other locals predict ten years before the island is uninhabitable; some say five is more realistic.

"It kills me to see what has happened," said Dupré, whose dad ran the community grocery store nearest to the island, in Pointe-aux-Chênes, and whose stepfather was part of the island's Naquin family. "In my lifetime, I have witnessed a thriving community and culture reduced to a small community on life support."

Dupré himself moved inland recently to the town of Bourg, which is on the area's highest ridge, about ten feet above sea level. Still, his family isn't out of danger, he said. "Where I live in Bourg, it might be 40 years until my children have problems."

Windell Curole, who manages a levee district in Lafourche Parish, can't stand in his yard and look at the Mississippi River without marveling at the river's vast drainage basin. "Every drop of water that falls from western New York to Montana all the way into Canada goes right past my house on Bayou Lafourche," he said.

Along with the water came the sediment that made South Louisiana. "I say that we live in the re-united states," Curole said. "Because other states sent us every bit of soil we sit on."

Here, where the Mississippi empties into the Gulf of Mexico, the river dropped its load of heavy clay and silt, creating five north-south land ridges. They're like terrestrial fingers that reach into the gulf with wetlands in between, said Sherwood "Woody" Gagliano, a coastal scientist.

Residents like Dupré say that Isle de Jean Charles is also part of that hand, part of a sixth finger running east-west between the first and second terrestrial digits. "It's the first finger to be diminishing," he said.

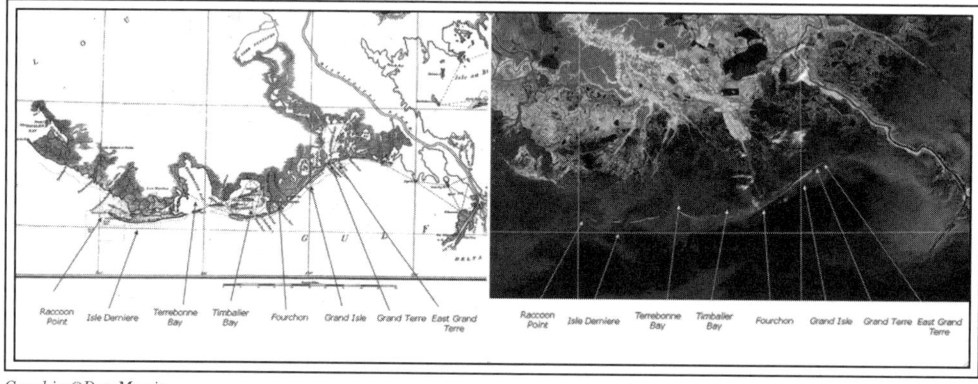

Graphics©Don Morris

All around it, the coast is vanishing quickly. A coastal map made by the National Oceanic and Atmospheric Administration (NOAA) in the 1960s, compared with a recent satellite image, shows how massive segments of Louisiana land are now underwater.

Even towns once well shielded from the sea face water at their doorsteps, said lifelong resident Patty Whitney, environmental advocate for Bayou Interfaith Shared Community Organizing. "We didn't move to the coast," she said. "The coast moved to us."

Oil and gas companies have played a significant role in destroying that marshy buffer by digging 10,000 miles of pipeline access canals far inland, killing marsh plants. Without plant roots, the soft, silty soil is washed away by what locals refer to as "the saltwater." That loss is compounded when a hurricane makes landfall, tearing away land in big chunks.

Sea-level rise, which Dupré refers to "as the new boogeyman," accelerates each of the other factors threatening the Isle de Jean Charles, said Louisiana scientist Virginia Burkett, chief scientist for Climate and Land Use Change at the U.S. Geological Survey and a lead author of the coastal chapters of the 2007 Intergovernmental Panel on Climate Change report. That panel won the Nobel Prize.

The root of rising sea level is a shift in climate, but that's not really discussed on the Isle de Jean Charles, said Albert Naquin, chief of the island's Indian tribe. "Climate change–that's not part of the island people's vocabulary," he said. "We hear it on the news, but that is about as far as it goes." But climate change is quickly putting its stamp on the area. Steep sea-level rise is expected to continue beyond the end of the century, at a rate that hinges on how fast the earth's ice sheets decline, Burkett said. The result could be a sea that is one to four feet higher than it is now.

On Isle de Jean Charles and all along the Mississippi Delta region of the Gulf Coast, the sea will rise even farther over the land, because sinking land–called subsidence–that's "the controlling factor" in this area. Curole sees about three feet of subsidence to each foot of sea level rise, he said.

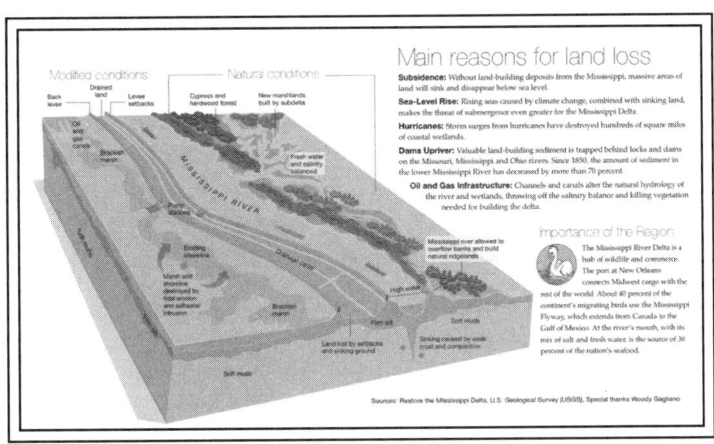

Graphics©Don Morris

Every year, this delta land used to be replenished by sediment and freshwater left by the flooding Mississippi River. With the river blocked in by levees, the land is left without nutrients that historically helped it survive. And because of soil geology–what Gagliano calls "the pile of soft, oozy sediment ten miles thick"–the land is relatively weak and unable to support itself. So, it settles on subtle fault systems that further submerge the land. Oil and gas extraction causes even further compaction.

NOAA measurements along the Louisiana coast have found, so far this century, 3.2 feet of "relative rise"–sea-level rise combined with subsidence, said NOAA's Tim Osborn. That spells disaster for the most at-risk areas, such as Isle de Jean Charles and other communities in Terrebonne Parish, where 80 percent of the land is at or below two feet of elevation, he said.

"Terrebonne Parish and Isle de Jean Charles face a serious challenge, likely one of the greatest in the nation and world," Osborn said. But no help is coming from Washington, D.C. Last year, as Congress approved its water resources bill, it left out Louisiana's $13 billion, 98-mile federal flood protection plan, called Morganza to the Gulf, despite its approval by the U.S. Army Corps of Engineers earlier this year after more than 20 years of development and discussions.

Also, under a reconfigured federal flood-insurance program, some residents may see their premiums rise by thousands of dollars every year. Someone who owns a modest house in Pointe-aux-Chênes might pay $28,000 a year in flood insurance alone, said Whitney, the environmental advocate, who calls the change "evacuation order by default." "They didn't come out and say, 'You can't live here anymore,'" Whitney said. "But if I live on the coast and I can't get flood insurance, then I can't get a mortgage. And if I own a house, I can't sell it. So I'm in a house that I can't sell, I can't afford, and I can't insure."

Whitney has tried to talk to her children about moving elsewhere, she said. "How do you let your kids get a 30-year mortgage here? It's frightening." But her children resisted the idea of pulling up roots after hundreds of years here. "It's our home," she said. "We have a deeply ingrained attachment to this place."

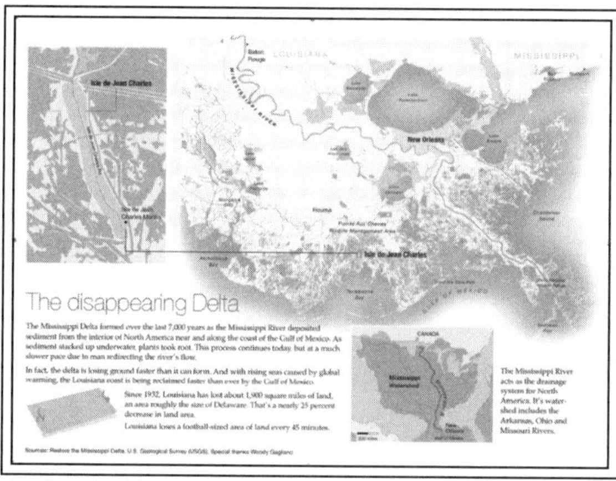

Graphics©Don Morris

Memories are now submerged. Once a peninsula formed as part of the river's sprawling delta, the fast-eroding Isle de Jean Charles has basically become a barrier island on the frontlines for any hurricane that strikes this section of the coast. The plight of the island's plucky residents inspired the Oscar-nominated film, *Beasts of the Southern Wild* (2013), which was set on the fictional "Isle de Charles Doucet." But despite its recent moment of fame, there's no solution in the offing. Even if Congress eventually approves it, the island will not be protected by any of the 98 miles of earthen levees planned as part of Louisiana's massive Morganza to the Gulf of Mexico Hurricane Protection Project. The Army Corps of Engineers determined it wasn't cost-effective.

Rev. Roch Naquin is frustrated by the decision. But he hasn't lost faith. "There's never anything you can't pray for," he said. So every day, as he goes through his morning devotions, he asks for a slowing of the coastal erosion that eats away at his backyard. Still, he's a pragmatist. "I just pray to preserve what we got," he said. "But I don't expect that this place will be rebuilt like it was."

When Rev. Naquin stands on his back deck today, he sees a growing expanse of blue saltwater. But when he was a child, no water was visible from his family's house, which stood about 50 feet from where he lives now. Instead he recalled long rows of garden vegetables and woods of oak trees as far as the eye could see. The forest and the freshwater marshes that nourished the trees also protected island residents from hurricane-force winds and storm surges.

At one time he had been able to walk through half a mile of woods from his house to trap mink and gather stove wood. But the forest is no more. "Now, people fish there," he said. "What were once canals became so wide, there was no way to close them." Like other island residents, Naquin is well aware that the beloved Isle de Jean Charles may soon become too sunken to be habitable. And if it became necessary, he would leave. "Some say, 'They'll have to drag me out,'" he said. Not Naquin. "I won't be extremely stubborn," he said. "But this is home. As long as I can possibly stay here, I will."

Naquin was a young adult by the time Isle de Jean Charles was officially linked to nearby Pointe-aux-Chênes by a raised, two-lane ribbon of highway called Island Road. Before the road was completed in the early 1950s, the easiest way to travel was by boat.

Island road

Photos©Kathleen Flynn

Roch Naquin's younger cousin, Albert Naquin, recalls how every Sunday his family would row to church. On the way, they'd pass a boat dock for the Humble Oil & Refining Company, which later became Exxon Mobil. Almost without fail, Albert Naquin said, a large, powerful speedboat would leave the dock as his family approached in their small vessel, sending what seemed like a terrifying wake of water their way. "Each time, I thought, 'They're going to sink us,'" he said, covering his eyes at the memory.

Albert Naquin

Photos©Kathleen Flynn

The story could be a parable to illustrate the island's eventual fate. But it's just one in a string of narratives about a childhood where families threw nets into the water whenever they wanted crabs or shrimp, about an island where most residents are third and fourth cousins–with last names like Dardar, Naquin, Chaisson, and Billiot. They're descendants of intermarried Native Americans and Frenchmen who settled the island in the early 1800s.

Children from the island attended Indian-only schools until the district was integrated in the late 1960s; most dropped out by about the seventh grade and began working on boats, fishing, crabbing, shrimping, and harvesting oysters, like their ancestors had done before them. Money was always tight–according to official standards, the income of most everyone on the island was far below the poverty line. But seafood was plentiful, and each house was backed by a large garden that was fenced in from the cows that roamed the island and were called by name at milking time. Like many residential lots in this part of Louisiana, the lots begin with solid, arable land, used for houses and gardens, and are backed by marshland where trappers snare raccoon, otters, and mink.

Like his grandfather, uncle and brother before him, Albert Naquin now serves as chief of the island's Biloxi-Chitimacha-Choctaw tribe, and he peppers his stories with Choctaw words and phrases spoken in French, his first language.

He describes what he's seen first-hand, the irreversible damage caused by oil companies, which indiscriminately dug networks of canals totaling an estimated 10,000 miles, bringing saltwater far inland and killing freshwater marshes and even solid, centuries-old oak trees. As a result, every hurricane that makes landfall here now rips acres of soft land from the shoreline.

"This area has the worst rate of erosion anywhere on the planet. And Isle de Jean Charles just happens to sit in the middle of it," said Reggie Dupré, of the Terrebonne levee district.

Without plants and roots, the land once built by delta silt simply melted away or was torn away by the storms, said Albert Naquin, who is 66. During his lifetime, he has witnessed literally a sea change, which leaves his part of the world much more vulnerable to hurricane winds and storm-surge waters.

The effects are felt much farther inland, in places like New Orleans, a two-hour drive from here. That's because, when a hurricane makes landfall, the earth it hits–in this case, the coast's few remaining barrier islands–act as a natural buffer, a speed bump. "But the speed bump is wearing out," Naquin said.

A half-century ago, the canals seemed like a modern convenience when oil and gas companies began cutting them through the freshwater marshlands near Isle de Jean Charles. "When the canals first opened, I felt like they were helping us," Albert Naquin recalled. Thanks to the saltwater mixing with the freshwater, his father's oyster beds were closer to home, in the brackish water they need. His mother took home bounteous harvests from her garden planted in the rich dredged soil that was piled next to the water. And the water was now conveniently close. "Mama would finish with the garden and start fishing. It felt like a godsend."

Small boat in canal

Photos©Kathleen Flynn

Across the water in the town of Pointe-aux-Chênes, on what the Naquins call "the land," Alton Vernon, 58, stood recently on the edge of blue water, now wider than a football field. When he was a child this bayou, Bayou Pointe-aux-Chênes was so narrow and shallow that his father would have to climb up on the bank to pull his family along in the pirogue, a flat-bottomed boat.

Tillman Naquin, 67, who lives on a high hill near Island Road, remembers when nearby Lake Tambour was a freshwater lake. The land around it has now been eaten to a lace of what it was, and the lake is "part of the saltwater," he said. Everyone in the area has similar illustrations of land that became water, of places remembered but now submerged.

And then there are hurricanes. But Isle de Jean Charles was not always on the front lines. Instead it was protected from the Gulf by a fairly substantial barrier island, Timbalier, where Albert Naquin remembers scaling large hills of sand before a large canal was dredged right through it. He's since watched Timbalier nearly vanish. Reports note that the island lost half its width between 1978 and 1988 and, without intervention, it will completely disappear by 2055.

As recently as a half-century ago, Isle de Jean Charles was five miles wide and ten miles long; it's now about a quarter-mile wide and two miles long, Chief Naquin says. The population has also dropped, from a high of more than 350 people to about 75 now, living in about 25 homes. Every home faces toward the long main road that runs down the center of the island. Their backyards, which run all the way to the water, were once vast but now are shrinking.

In recent years, many–including the chief himself–moved off the island because of flooding. Floodwaters were once rare but are now commonplace on the slender slip of land, especially when hurricanes come, pushing storm-surge water in front of them. The island's small protective levee was built eight feet high but has sunk to four in some sections, and is sometimes even overtopped by a high tide.

Roch Naquin's tidy house was built in 1957 on two-foot-high cement blocks on land that already stood two feet above sea level. "It was just fine until Hilda in 1964," he said.

Island residents like to drop hurricane names into their conversations easily, much the way New Yorkers speak of subway stops. Residents believe that the groundwork for Hurricane Hilda was laid by Hurricane Audrey, which hit the area hard in 1957, tearing away acres of marshland weakened by newly dug canals.

Storms in 1974 and 1985 brought more flooding. "It was Carmen, then Juan, then we put the house on eight-foot blocks," Roch Naquin said. But that wasn't enough. He was dry during Andrew, which flooded other island homes and got close enough to his floor to put sea grass on the cables underneath. But Lili, in 2002, put a few inches of water in the house so he raised it to the present 11 feet. He fears that new federal flood maps will soon determine that even 11 feet is not enough to keep his house dry.

A generation ago, the region learned a hard lesson as a result of what Curole terms "Leave it to Beaver syndrome," which attracted many South Louisiana residents to houses built on ground-level slabs. But in recent years, flood-control officials like Dupre and Curole have had widespread success pushing, as Curole says, "elevation as a salvation from inundation." On Isle de Jean Charles, at least half of the homes stand on concrete stilts. Still, elevation and adaptation can only go so far in the hardest-hit areas, where both homes and fishing grounds have been destroyed, leaving communities fragmented, said Kristina Peterson, head of the Lowlander Center.

On Isle de Jean Charles, for example, Peterson said, residents have been "valiant" in trying to adapt, by attending meetings, elevating homes, evacuating during storms, and finding other work besides fishing and crabbing. But it seems as though all of it has ultimately been for naught, she said, because residents haven't been able to convince federal agencies to halt erosion or promote widespread restoration. "The next adaptation may be relocation," she said.

That idea is almost unthinkable to Maryline Naquin, 68, who has never lived off the island, unlike some of her relatives who spent some time in the military and worked other jobs that took them away from home. "It's the only home

I've known," she said. She lives with her granddaughter Erin Naquin, 24, in a house that now stands 17 feet off the ground. One of a handful of young people who live on the island now, Erin Naquin says that she thrives on the peace and quiet and likes being able to go crabbing off the side of Island Road whenever she feels like it.

There's only one downside to island life, Erin said. "Hurricanes." And to truly understand the history of hurricanes on the island requires only a walk across the street, she said, to talk to her grandmother and her uncle.

In one of four family houses clustered on this end of Isle de Jean Charles, Maryline Naquin was spending a breezy day on the screened porch with her older brother, Wenceslaus Billiot, a spry 86. It seems like a typical Southern small-town scene, except the porch that spans the front of Billiot's house stands 13.5 feet off the ground.

Wenceslaus Billiot

Photos©Kathleen Flynn

First built in 1960, the house was raised to its current height not long after Hurricane Lily's storm surge flooded it, Billiot said. Every wall in the house is filled with pictures of children and grandchildren. He created a special little kitchenette in the back where he can cook and look out at the water. As children, they weathered storms within their homes on the island, he said. "But we didn't have too many hurricanes when I was younger," said Billiot, one of the island's oldest residents, along with his wife, Denecia, who's 88. These days, they'll leave for a few days, then return quickly, because on the island, the water comes fast, then recedes. "It don't stay long," Billiot said. That's better, they say, than low-lying areas on the land, where the land's natural basins flood and stay flooded.

Billiot was born in 1926, only one month after a particularly bad storm that blew through before storms were given names. He remembers only a few other unnamed storms, one in 1933 and another in 1942. But the storms have gotten more ferocious and more frequent, he said, as he and his sister tick off the familiar litany of names: Audrey, Hilda, Betsy, Juan, Andrew, Lili, Katrina, Rita, Gustav, Ike, and–last year–Issac. With each storm's name, he gives quick descriptions of the damage: "some wind; a few feet of water; a lot of water; a lot of wind; and plenty, plenty water."

A visitor cannot leave Isle de Jean Charles around sundown without seeing a white-haired figure in shrimp boots tossing a circular cast-net into the water, with hopes of snaring shrimp. Edison Dardar's mother gave birth to him on a boat. Today, 64 years later, he still is drawn to the sea every day. When he wakes, he looks out his window, straightens his tousled hair with his fingers and says one thing. "I'm going to go fish," he said.

Edison Darder

Photos©Kathleen Flynn

Twenty years ago, after Hurricane Andrew pushed Dardar's house to the middle of the road, he and his wife built a new one on the same lot, raised up 12 feet. They plan to stay there, no matter what. "We're never going to move," said Dardar, 64. "I was born and raised here. The water is all I've ever known."

His family on the island used to be much bigger–at one time they occupied four houses in a row here. But one by one they left, tired of fighting floodwaters and increasingly fearsome hurricanes. Even his son now lives across the water, on land.

For most of their lives, Dardar and his wife stayed even if a storm threatened from the Gulf. These days, in his one concession to change, Dardar leaves. He lashes down anything loose on his property, boards up his windows, and drives with his wife 45 minutes to the city of Houma, which stands on higher ground.

Unlike some other parts of Louisiana, residents of Isle de Jean Charles can't evacuate at the last minute, because Island Road isn't high enough. At least a full day, maybe two, before a hurricane's projected landfall, Dardar and all of his longtime neighbors pack their cars and leave the island along the narrow causeway. Soon afterward, waves cover the road.

ACKNOWLEDGEMENTS

Courtesy of *The Weather Channel.*

Visiting Post-Deportation Acadian Cemeteries in Nova Scotia

Sally Ross

In 1755, an estimated 6,000 Acadians were deported by the British from mainland Nova Scotia. Hundreds more were imprisoned while others were able to flee to safer locations. By the mid-1760s, Acadians were permitted to return to what had been their homeland, provided they took the oath of allegiance to the King. Unable to resettle their fertile ancestral farms, which had already been given away to Protestant settlers from New England, they were forced to start clearing the land and rebuilding all over again in distant corners of the province. Victims of mistrust, they were obliged to settle in small groups geographically remote from each other. As a French-speaking minority, they found themselves marginalized from every point of view. As Roman Catholics, they were subject to numerous restrictions.

Influenced by the availability of land and the development of the fisheries, Acadians settled in eight main regions of the territory covered by present-day Nova Scotia and Cape Breton Island. Settlement after the Deportation was a slow process that took place over a period of several decades and started at different times in different places. In every case, however, a network of family ties created a tight-knit community bound by a common language and culture.

Little by little, missions and parishes were established to serve the spiritual needs of a growing population. As the number of families increased, early chapels with an adjoining graveyard were gradually replaced by larger churches in more central locations. By the 1950s, there were about 40 parishes or missions in Nova Scotia inhabited primarily by Acadians.

Photo©Nova Scotia Archives

There is no written or archaeological evidence that Acadians in Port Royal, Grand-Pré or elsewhere used stones to mark their graves. The oldest Acadian gravestones in Nova Scotia are located in Chéticamp. This hand-carved block of local sandstone is dedicated to Jean LeLièvre who died in 1817.

Since the traditional Acadian grave marker had always been a wooden cross, old post-Deportation Acadian cemeteries generally have no visual evidence of the first two generations of parishioners. For example, take the case of the cemetery beside Sainte-Anne-du-Ruisseau Church in southwest Nova Scotia: the oldest gravestone is that of Ambroise Potier, who died in 1854. It is made of white marble and bears a sculpted *fleur-de-lys* cross, the monograph *IHS*, and the traditional request for prayers of intercession, *Priez pour l'âme de...* ("Pray for the soul of..."). Ambroise was a third-generation Potier (Pothier) in Sainte-Anne-du-Ruisseau parish. His grandfather Dominique Potier, who had been imprisoned in both Fort Cumberland and Fort Edward during the Deportation years, was the first of the family to obtain land in this area. He was buried in this cemetery in 1818 at the age of 87, though no grave marker can be found for him. The first two generations of Potiers are thus part of the invisible Acadian heritage of this cemetery.

White marble gravestones were used in both Catholic and Protestant cemeteries in Nova Scotia between 1845 and 1920, but they were a luxury that most Acadian families could not afford. Any spare money a family had would be used to pay for masses for the repose of the soul of the deceased. It is not surprising, therefore, that for several generations the most common grave marker was a wooden cross inscribed with the name of the deceased, his or her age, and the day and year of death. Two of the oldest and most elaborate Acadian wooden crosses in Nova Scotia, which were erected in memory of Simon and Scholastique Doucet (who died in 1910 and 1909, respectively), are located in the little inland community of Quinan, not far from Sainte-Anne-du-Ruisseau. According to a document in the local archives, they have been painted regularly by members of the family.

Photo©Nova Scotia Archives

Traditionally, Acadians used a simple wooden cross to mark their graves. These lovely wooden crosses in Quinan in southwest Nova Scotia date from the early 20th century. They are dedicated to the memory of Simon and Scholastique Doucet. The crosses are repainted regularly by descendants of the Doucet family.

In addition to wooden crosses, Acadians made large wooden monuments designed to resemble marble gravestones. The oldest one is dated 1897 and is located in Saint-Pierre cemetery in West Pubnico. A slightly newer one with a French inscription is located in Saint- Michel cemetery in the village of Wedgeport, which was settled in the late 1760s by Acadians who had come back to Nova Scotia after having been deported to the Boston area. It is dedicated to Charles Boudreau, who died in 1904.

A number of Acadian cemeteries in Nova Scotia contain beautiful metal crosses. The largest and most spectacular one marks the grave of Adrien C. Amirault, who died in West Pubnico in 1909. An inscription on the back indicates that it was made at the Bélanger foundry in Montmagny, Quebec. In all likelihood, it was transported by train to the railway station in Pubnico Head and then taken by ox-drawn cart to its final destination.

Photo©Nova Scotia Archives

This superb cast iron cross, decorated with fleurs-de-lys and scallop shells, is dedicated to the memory of Adrien C. Amirault who died in West Pubnico in 1909.

Cemeteries are sacred places of commemoration, but they are also windows on the past. Walking through any post-Deportation Acadian cemetery in Nova Scotia, one can discover innumerable tributes to a past that has long since disappeared. In the old Sainte-Marie cemetery in Church Point, established around 1790, there are a number of very unique slate gravestones like the one dedicated to Joseph Dugas, the first Acadian born in Clare. A plain granite stone dating from the early 20th century is particularly striking because it reflects a reality that is impossible to imagine nowadays. It was erected in memory of Anselme (1844-1899) and Charlotte (1834-1900) Comeau by their seven daughters, who all became nuns in the religious order of the *Petites Soeurs de la Sainte Famille*, which provided the housekeeping duties for the *Collège Sainte-Anne*, founded by the Eudist Fathers.

To find the oldest Acadian gravestones in Nova Scotia, one must travel all the way to the parish of Saint-Pierre in Chéticamp in northern Cape Breton Island. Because there is an abundant supply of carvable sandstone all along the coast, gravestones appeared much earlier than in other Acadian areas. The 14 founding fathers of Chéticamp received a large land grant in 1790. Although there are no gravestones bearing their names, they are all buried in the old cemetery on a plateau in the Cape Breton Highlands. The oldest legible stone in this cemetery bears a simple cross on a triangular base, and is dated 1817. The initials JLL are inscribed which stand for Jean Lelièvre, a fisherman from the Isle of Jersey who converted to Catholicism. Another hand-carved stone dated 1842 commemorates Nectaire LeBlain (LeBlanc), the infant son of Lazare LeBlanc and Henriette Chiasson.

Photo©Nova Scotia Archives

This beautiful hand-carved sandstone monument is located in Saint-Joseph-du-Moine, near Chéticamp. It was erected in memory of Thomas Chiasson who died in 1893 at the age of 89. The background has been painted black. The three Acadian parishes in northern Cape Breton Island are the only ones in Nova Scotia that developed a tradition of grave stone carving.

The vast "new" Saint-Pierre cemetery (opened in 1854), also located high up on a plateau, offers an awe-inspiring sight. According to an inventory done in the early 1980s, there were over 2,000 gravestones, 99 percent of which had an inscription in French. The exceptionally high percentage of inscriptions in French is no doubt due to the fact that carving was done locally for almost 150 years. The three Acadian parishes in the Chéticamp area (Saint-Pierre, Saint-Joseph, and Saint-Michel) are the only ones in Nova Scotia that developed a tradition of gravestone carving.

Photo©Georges Arsenault

This is a view of the magnificent Saint-Pierre Cemetery located in the highlands above the village of Chéticamp in northern Cape Breton. Until the 1950s, the majority of gravestones in this area were carved locally from the sandstone that can be found along the coast. Most of the inscriptions in this vast cemetery are in French.

Until recently, grave markers without a cross, a sacred heart, praying hands, or some other religious symbol were extremely rare. Nowadays, Acadians prefer to decorate their gravestones with symbols of work or pleasure. On the grey or black granite rectangles that populate the modern sections of Acadian cemeteries, one can see sandblasted or laser-engraved images of everything from lobster traps to bingo cards. The grave marker of Ronald à Gonzague Landry (1955-1997) illustrates this modern preference for non-religious decorations. Ronald was a well-known young artist who worked in Petit-de-Grat, a fishing village that began as one of the main outports of the fortress of Louisbourg in the early 1700s.

Photo©Nova Scotia Archives

Many Acadians nowadays prefer to have their gravestones decorated with images of work or pleasure, as opposed to religious symbols. Ronald à Gonzague Landry was a young artist from Petit-de-Grat who died in 1997. In addition to the French words for "long live the French language and culture," his gravestone shows an artist at his easel, a brush, and a palette.

Photo©Nova Scotia Archives

This touching monument decorated with seashells and beach glass is dedicated to the infant child Kelvin Joseph Marchand who lived for barely a month in the winter of 1956. It is located in Louisdale, Cape Breton Island. Concrete grave markers start appearing in Acadian cemeteries in the 1920s. They were more long lasting than wood and less expensive than marble or granite.

Photo©Nova Scotia Archives

This unique slate stone is located in Sainte-Marie Cemetery in Church Point. It commemorates Joseph Dugas who was the first Acadian born in Clare municipality, a region in southwest Nova Scotia. According to the inscription, he died on October 9, 1858, at the age of 92. This gravestone was erected a long time after his death.

To stroll through the Acadian cemeteries of Nova Scotia is to commemorate a people and reconnect with history. Every grave marker forms part of Acadian religious and cultural heritage, whether it is a hand-made labor of love decorated with seashells and beach glass or a noble column of pink granite erected in memory of an Acadian politician.

Governor Lawrence's Devils —The John Winslow Story in Acadie

A.M. Hodge

One of my Acadian friends, a Comeaux, said his grandmother spat every time the name of Lt. Col. John Winslow was mentioned in her home. I was amazed that his name had such power some 250 years after the events that made him infamous to the descendants of the 12,000 Acadians exiled from Nova Scotia in 1755. John Winslow is remembered vividly, while the other names in the pantheon of English perpetrators may not come as quickly to mind. That would include Charles Lawrence, Charles Morris, William Shirley, Robert Monckton, John Handfield, Alexander Murray, and Abijah Willard, to mention a few. Of them, John Winslow is the only one who left a detailed journal, and he is the only one immortalized in infamy in Henry Wadsworth Longfellow's epic poem *Evangeline.*

Thomas Chandler Haliburton's books on the history of Nova Scotia brought to light John Winslow's journal of 1755, then housed in the Massachusetts Historical Archives, three quarters of a century after the deportations. There were neither copies of Lt. Gov. Lawrence's correspondence after 1754 archived at Halifax, nor any sign that Col. Monckton ever kept a journal, only copies of letters from them kept by Winslow. By 1884, however, copies were made of Lawrence's correspondence after 1754 and these were placed in the records at Halifax, Nova Scotia.

In 1930, historian John Clarence Webster mentioned in the introduction to his book *The Forts of Chignecto* (1930) that Robert Monckton's *Journal of the Expedition of 1755* had been discovered a few months earlier. In the same year, Webster mentioned seven journals, including Winslow's, that had come to light during the previous century that had added to our knowledge of the expulsions. Webster cited officer Abijah Willard's journal as having provided the only record made at the time of the atrocities committed against the Acadians.

In researching my book, *Acadia Lost* (2012), I delved into John Winslow's history and his 18th century world. I placed Winslow in the third rank of my pantheon of perpetrators above Handfield and Murray, who played the same role as Winslow. The two governors, Lawrence and Shirley, and the surveyor Charles Morris, who drew up the deportation plans, reside in my top rank. I saw Morris as cunning Vulcan hammering out the fiery fate of unsuspecting innocents, playing to Lawrence's commanding Jupiter, and encouraging Massachusetts Gov. Shirley's silver-tongued Mercury. I put Monckton in the second rank as their ferocious Mars.

Gov. Shirley asked his friend, Lt. Col. John Winslow, to raise 2,000 troops after the decision was made to drive the French out of Acadie (Nova Scotia). Their initial objective was to take Fort Beauséjour (on today's Nova Scotia/ New Brunswick border), and to push the French back to Ile Royale (Cap Breton) to Ile St. Jean (Prince Edward Island) and to Canada (Quebec).

In June 1755, Monckton, commanding a fleet of 31 transports and three warships carrying 270 British regular troops and 2,000 New England militia, arrived at Fort Beauséjour. The fort fell two weeks after the siege. The British had come primed for a lengthy siege. Now the timing, Morris's plan, and New England manpower all came together in the perfect storm, resulting in the Acadian deportation, which left an entire people broken apart and stranded on alien shores.

A few weeks after Fort Beauséjour became Fort Cumberland, Monckton summoned Winslow for a private conversation about orders he received from Gov. Lawrence. The historian John Mack Faragher in his book, *A Great and Noble Scheme* (2005), describes John Winslow's reaction: "Winslow seemed genuinely surprised by what Monckton told him. 'As to the Inhabitants commonly called the Neutrals at Chignecto [border area of present day Nova Scotia and New Brunswick] the point seems to be settled with them and they are to be removed.... The Inhabitants throughout the Province it is supposed will suffer the same Fate, although not equally guilty of open violence.'"

Lt. Col. Winslow took on his assignment but had no enthusiasm for it. I believe his attitude toward the Acadians differed from that of Monckton and Murray because he saw them as human beings, not as enemy aliens. Major Alexander Murray commented in a letter to Winslow, "You know our soldiers hate them and if they can find a pretense to kill them, they will." As for Major John Handfield at Annapolis Royal (Nova Scotia capitol until 1749), he had an Acadian wife, Elizabeth Winniet. Of the four officers charged to implement the first series of expulsions, he was the only one who had to deport his wife's relatives.

The Acadians had been the butt of reprisal raids for decades–blamed, but blameless for the death and destruction brought by French-instigated incursions into New England. The Acadians were relatively easy for English bounty hunters like Benjamin Church to get to. They had only to sail east, bypass Maine (then a part of Massachusetts), and head straight up the Bay of Fundy until they reached places like Beaubassin and Grand-Pré.

A century's worth of ministerial thundering from New England's Protestant pulpits had conditioned the English to fear their French neighbors to the north. Long before the siege at Fort Beauséjour in 1755, Acadian farmers were falsely seen as an enemy who could rise to arms and turn on their English neighbors. That year, 300 Acadians who had abandoned the cloak of neutrality by participating at Fort Beauséjour's defense, compelled to do so by the French commander of the fort, made it easy for the British to label an entire people as an army willing to serve French interests; it served their own long-term interest. It mattered nothing if many more Acadians still held to their oaths.

There was no Acadian public relations machine to counter the propaganda the British advanced against them in the guise of a mountain of evidence, which became the final rationale for their deportation. When British Gen. Edward Braddock was killed while attacking a French fort in the wilderness of western Pennsylvania, it induced a hysteria that set the match to years of collected tinder. Though no Acadians were involved, the wheels ground into motion for the Acadians to be exiled.

Massachusetts men were responsible for producing the plans, militia, and transports that provided the logistics. Governor Shirley sent John Winslow to Nova Scotia as a symbol of Massachusetts' shared responsibility to drive out the French. Lawrence had not received permission for the expulsion from the Lords of Trade in London, England. But neither he nor Shirley hesitated to work their joint will on the innocent Acadians.

John Winslow may have been unsettled by the reprehensible nature of the mission imposed on him by Lawrence's orders, but he could no more have entertained a passing thought of refusing Shirley's request or of disobeying Lawrence than an Acadian farmer could resist a boundary dispute. Each was who he was, soldier and farmer, defined in blood and bone.

The British had already collected their hunting guns, but if words were weapons, the Acadians were still armed. In the aftermath of the expulsions, one of the Acadians' great strengths in exile was their ability to fill the dockets of English courts to petition justice for reasons ranging from an old man deprived of his daily ration of milk to parents grieved by their sons being taken from them, leaving the family without their support.

More often than not the Acadians got the relief they sought, but their victories seem like bandaids applied against a mortal wound. We have to go all the way back to the Romans to find a conquering nation with a policy that left a conquered people in place when they expanded their empire. All the conquered had to do was worship the emperor as a god, be counted in the census, and pay their taxes.

What if the Acadians had been willing to swear their allegiance to the British Crown by taking the full oath in 1727 when Ensign Wroth held all those neighborhood barbecues to encourage them to sign? The Roman way was not the British way, and the British were not likely to treat the Acadians any differently or better than they had already treated the Irish, the Scots, or the French; sooner or later something was bound to happen. Lack of resources prior to 1755 was the only thing that kept the British from doing anything earlier. Paul Mascarene, a Huguenot who served the British in Nova Scotia prior to retiring as governor in 1749, had written to the Lords of Trade in London as early as 1720 to argue for the removal of the Acadians.

Monckton, as the ranking officer of the Regulars and therefore commander, handled the most intransigent of the Acadians, the men who resisted siege with the French at Fort Beauséjour. Monckton was young, ambitious, unafraid to use brutal force, and soon had rebellion on his hands. Winslow asked for more soldiers at Grand-Pré because Monckton's difficulties made him nervous, as he had three times the number of Acadian prisoners as he had armed soldiers to guard them. The transports finally arrived from Boston and took Monckton's charges to the farthest corners of the Anglo-American colonies, some all the way to Georgia. Winslow, Murray, and Handfield then carried out their orders and expelled the rest of the habitants they had captured in nine British American colonies south, excluding Virginia, which refused their disembarkation and had them sent to England.

While the deportation of the Acadians was about removing a group disloyal to the British Crown, there is no denying that the fertile dike lands at Grand-Pré and elsewhere were also extremely important to the British plans for settlement. The acting governor of Nova Scotia, Charles Lawrence, offered the following opinion on October 18, 1755, in a letter to the Lords of Trade in London: "As soon as the French are gone, I shall use my best endeavors to encourage People from the Continent to settle their lands ... and the additional circumstances of the Inhabitants evacuating the Country will, I flatter myself greatly hasten this event, as it furnishes us with a large quantity of good Land ready for immediate Cultivation."

The land stood empty for many years but for wandering animals and escaped Acadians who went into hiding with the Mi'kmaq. The English burned most of the farms to make sure the Acadians would not return. The Canadian Charles Deschamps de Boishébert ranged around to rescue fugitive Acadians and direct them to refugee camps he had established in Miramichi and Restigouche. He and Acadian resistance fighter Joseph Beausoleil Broussard plagued the British, forcing them to send armed guards out with details of woodcutters searching for firewood. Monckton sent out details of his own–soldiers in no mood to take prisoners. They combed the forests, searching for refugees and anyone aiding them.

By the end of 1755, the Massachusetts militia had all left Nova Scotia, leaving behind the men who enlisted with the officers of the Regulars, who went up and down the lines of militia waiting to board ships bound home to Boston. Much to Winslow's chagrin, they recruited many of his men. John Winslow returned to his farm in Marshfield, Massachusetts. In 1756, Governor Shirley again asked Winslow to serve, this time at Fort Frederick, New York. Shirley was about to be replaced in his role as commander by Lord Loudon, a Scot with a reputation for being the most arrogant, irascible aristocrat in the British stable of formidable characters.

Winslow and the other New England officers learned that in May of 1756, a royal order was issued that "all general and field officers with provincial commissions were to take rank only as eldest captains when serving in conjunction with the regular troops." In effect, by the stroke of a pen, the entire New England militia could be put under the command of a major of the Regulars. Because of the storm of protest that arose among the militia officers–and Winslow's opinion about it, which he shared with Shirley–Lord Loudon summoned him to Albany, New York, to discuss the issue. Winslow brought some of his officers along. Loudon gave them his ultimatum. Shirley had encouraged Winslow to work in harmony with Lord Loudon. Winslow served during 1756 at Lake George, New York, where the English army faced a French force holding the opposite shore until both forces withdrew to winter quarters in November.

Winslow's ambition had been to achieve a command rank in the British Regulars and be given charge of his own regiment. He worked hard to promote himself with influential people, even using agents in London to lobby for him to achieve it. But he returned to Marshfield in 1757, with his ambitions "frustrated at the peak of his career." Again he became the town's representative to the Massachusetts legislature. In 1762, he was appointed Chief Justice of the Court of Common Pleas in Plymouth County.

According to the *Journal of Abijah Willard 1755* (Collections of the New Brunswick Historical Society No. 13, 1930), Willard returned home to Lancaster, Massachusetts, and "On April 19, 1775, while riding at Beverly he met the minute men who were hurrying to fight at Concord and Lexington. This decided him to go to Boston to join the British. He was appointed by General Gage as captain of the 'Loyal America Associates' of Boston. Henceforth Willard's life was cast with the British. He never saw his home in Lancaster again, for he was proscribed and banished and his estates were confiscated." Abijah Willard moved to St. John in New Brunswick and died there in 1807. When Washington and his army stood with mounted cannon on Dorchester Heights in March 1776, they exchanged fire with the British for several days before Richard, Admiral Lord Howe, decided it was time to weigh anchor and leave Boston for Halifax, Nova Scotia. His ships were loaded with Loyalists from the very colony, and perhaps even the very families, that provided the militia that exiled the Acadians from Nova Scotia two decades earlier.

According to Cynthia Hagar Krusell in *The Winslows of Careswell in Marshfield* (2012), John Winslow died in 1774 before the War of Independence began, scion of a family that had already produced two governors of the Plymouth Colony. He probably lived out his remaining years happier as a judge in the service of his neighbors than as a general of British troops. John Winslow's son, Dr. Isaac Winslow, "... was highly esteemed among the people of Marshfield and was especially respected for his experimental work with smallpox. Despite his Tory sympathies neither his home ... nor the Winslow House were confiscated by the Great and General Court of Massachusetts as were other Tory homes in the area. According to tradition this was because of the high regard for Dr. Winslow held by the local community."

In Marshfield, Massachusetts, the still-standing Winslow House mansion is listed on the United States National Register of Historic Places. Virtually untouched by modernization, it was built in 1699 and occupied by the Winslow family of governors, generals, doctors, lawyers, and judges. It survives as an example of how some well-to-do landed gentry, particularly those loyal to the king, lived in the years prior to the American Revolutionary War.

Acknowledgements

Thanks the Historic Winslow House for the information they provided.

ACADIAN REFUGEES OR PRISONERS IN ACADIE—1755-1765[1]

Ronnie-Gilles LeBlanc

Very little is known about the history of the Acadian families who stayed in mainland Acadie[2] between 1755 and 1765. Most studies of Acadian history treat the matter in a rather summary, if not superficial, fashion. They tend to concentrate on the fate of the families who were deported to the Anglo-American colonies and Europe during the same period. However, it is one of the most crucial aspects of Acadian history because the families who stayed behind form a significant portion of the ancestors of the Acadian community of the Gulf of St. Lawrence and the Atlantic region, in other words contemporary Acadie, including the Acadian communities of Louisiana and Quebec.

The capture of Fort Beauséjour and Fort Gaspareau in June 1755 was the death knell for France's dream of an empire in Acadie, and it also had disastrous consequences for the Acadian community where the British caused destruction and deported the population. In the summer of 1755, on the eve of the Deportation, there were approximately 14,100 Acadians: 6,345 in English Acadie (mainland Nova Scotia); 2,897 in the Beaubassin region and along the Shepody, Petitcodiac and Memramcook Rivers in French Acadie, for a total of 9,242 people. Except for settlements in the areas of Cobeguid, Tatamagouche, Cape Sable, and a few families in the regions of Pisiquid, Les Mines, and Port Royal, most the of Acadian population was deported from English Acadie between October and November 1755. That represented a total of about 5,056 people (Merligueche: 50; Pisiquid: about 1,100; Les Mines [Grand-Pré and Rivière-aux-Canards]: 2,242; Port Royal: 1,664) along with 1,014 people deported from Beaubassin and the three rivers of Shepody, Petitcodiac, and Memramcook. Consequently, out of a population of 9,242 people, about 6,070 were deported to the Anglo-American colonies in the fall of 1755. Where did the other 3,172 people go—in other words, the people who were not captured or deported by the colonial authorities of Nova Scotia?

For the most part, these people had to find refuge in existing settlements on Isle St. Jean and Isle Royale or in the neighboring forest, hardly an obvious choice for a society of peasants or a sedentary population that subsisted primarily from produce of the land. It is the story of these families that we shall trace in the following pages, stressing the role of two Acadian leaders at the time: Joseph Broussard *dit* Beausoleil and Joseph LeBlanc *dit* Lemaigre.

Refugee Families

Let us begin with the settlements in peninsular Nova Scotia (English Acadie). We learn from Fr. François LeGuerne that "only about 30 families from Port Royal were able to escape, the majority of them fled into the woods with the inhabitants of Cape Sable, others stayed in the woods nearby." He also notes that in Les Mines, ten or 11 families hid in the woods waiting for the opportunity to escape. The Cape Sable region had not yet been targeted by the British authorities during the first phase of the Deportation. Most of the families from Port Royal who found temporary refuge there in the fall of 1755 left the region in the spring of 1756 and made their way to the Petitcodiac River, where they arrived in the summer of 1756 at the same time as families from Les Mines. According to Fr. François LeGuerne, there were about 50 or 60 families from Port Royal who went first to the Petitcodiac in mid-August 1756 before going to Cocagne and then to the Miramichi. These families from Port Royal thus found their compatriots who had escaped deportation on board the *Pembroke*.

The fate of the families from the Tatamagouche and the Cobeguid regions was somewhat similar except that they took refuge on Isle St. Jean (present-day Prince Edward Island) to be close to relatives who had already taken refuge there in the 1750s. A few individuals from Les Mines and Port Royal seem to have stayed in Nova Scotia to lead a war of resistance against the British forces.

About two-thirds of the population in the Beaubassin region and along the Shepody, Petitcodiac, and Memramcook Rivers escaped deportation—in other words about 1,883 of the 2,897 people enumerated between the autumn of 1754 and the winter of 1755, just before the fall of Fort Beauséjour. Of this number, about 500 from the Beauséjour and Tintamarre region went directly to Isle St. Jean under the direction of Fr. LeGuerne in November 1755. They were mainly the wives of the men who had been deported without their families.

In fact, the women had refused to join their husbands, on the advice of Fr. LeGuerne who had assured them that their husbands would come back for them, even if they were deported. Thus 300 families from the Tintamarre, Memramcook, Petitcodiac, and Shepody Rivers escaped deportation in the fall of 1755, some of whom went to Isle St. Jean. Consequently, there were still 250 families remaining by the end of the fall of 1755. In the summer of 1756, there were about 1,000 people in the area of the Shepody, Petitcodiac, and Memramcook Rivers without counting the 50 or 60 families who had just arrived from Port Royal and Les Mines, along with about 30 others who had returned from South Carolina where they had been deported without their families, including Beausoleil and his brother Alexandre Broussard, with his son Victor.

In the meantime, the French authorities had to feed the refugee families not only on Isle St. Jean but in Cocagne. During the winter of 1755-1756, the cattle that had been taken from the British soldiers in the Beaubassin region provided enough nourishment for the refugees in Cocagne. Despite a blockade by the British that began in the spring of 1756, the fortress of Louisbourg was spared a famine thanks to the cattle that the Acadians had taken from Nova Scotia to Isle St. Jean and then to the fortified town. An officer estimated that 4,000 head of cattle had been retrieved in this way.

To complicate matters, the harvest in 1756 was completely destroyed by high winds on Isle St. Jean and in Canada (today the province of Quebec) where the situation was equally serious. In addition to being deprived of food from France, Louisbourg could no longer depend on Canada. The governor of New France (i.e. Louisiana and all the territory situated between the Gulf of St. Lawrence and the Rocky Mountains), Pierre de Rigaud de Vaudreuil de Cavagnial wrote to the minister indicating that he had told the governor of Isle Royale (present-day Cape Breton), Augustin Drucourt about "the desperate shortage of rations and that he must try to ask you for some." One can easily imagine the desperate situation in which Acadian refugees found themselves in 1756.

If famine was widespread in Canada, the refugees were the first to feel the effects because they were entirely dependent on help from France, especially since there were already shortages in the Cocagne refugee camp by the winter of 1756. In fact, that is why the French evacuated 230 people in the spring to Isle St. Jean which, in turn, sent some to Quebec. These are the difficult circumstances the refugees found themselves in during the summer of 1756, while the governor of New France was still awaiting news from France regarding what to do with them. What in fact could be done with all these people?

Camp d'Espérance

The former commander of Camp d'Espérance, Captain Charles Deschamps de Boishébert, declared in 1763 that it was he who first ordered the Acadian refugees to move to the Miramichi and that Gov. Vaudreuil agreed. That is probably accurate, but this is what Vaudreuil says regarding the matter:

> *All the Acadians sent deputies to me who informed his honor the Intendant and myself that Miramichi is the only place where they can go in order to survive next winter. Fishing there is productive and providing help is sent from Quebec, they hope that they can sustain themselves rather than what one could provide them at the St. John River because of the problem of transportation via Témiscouata. We agreed to their demand. I gave the order to Mr. de Boishébert to let all the Acadians in Cocagne and the families that he was unable to support in the St. John River area go to the Miramichi and to get them to build warehouses to receive and store the supplies that his honor the Intendant plans to send there.*

Photo©Parks Canada

Island of Boishébert (Beaubear) on Miramichi river in New Brunswick

Photo©IR Walker

Monument of the Acadian Odyssey *at the site of the refugee camp,* Camp d'Espérance *(Camp of Hope).*

Thus, by the end of the summer of 1756, the refugee camp on the Miramichi River (Camp d'Espérance) was starting to take shape at a time when New France and the colonies of Isle Royale and Isle St. Jean were experiencing a famine. However, Acadians were not the only refugees there. There were also aboriginal families, allies of the French, and men who had been called upon to fight the British in exchange for their livelihood. Like the Acadian refugees, the aboriginals had to obey the king since they were dependent on him.

By the winter of 1755-1756, at the refugee camp in Cocagne, there were a number of Maliseet and Abenaki families who had followed Boishébert after he withdrew from the fort in Ménagouèche at the mouth of the St. John River in the summer of 1755. The men had participated in Boishébert's campaigns at the Petitcodiac River and around the Isthmus of Chignectou in the fall of 1755. It was the aboriginal warriors who retrieved from the British the cattle that had been confiscated from the Acadians during the preceding summer and fall, which enabled them to feed their own families as well as the Acadian families. But by the winter of 1756-1757, this source of food was no longer available.

By the fall of 1756, famine had hit Camp d'Espérance on the Miramichi River. As promised, Intendant François Bigot sent from Quebec a ship loaded with provisions for the Miramichi even though there was still a famine in Canada. Unfortunately, this ship had to put into port on the way because of head winds. Boishébert had also turned to Isle St. Jean for help, but Commander Gabriel Rousseau de Villejouin could do nothing since the colony was already reduced to its last supplies. Consequently, the misery was so great at Camp d'Espérance that at the beginning of the winter, Boishébert was obliged to reduce the ration for the Acadian refugees, the aboriginal families, and the garrison.

Even though 40 head of cattle had been received from Petitcodiac to feed them, the supply of fish was totally depleted. Within a very short time, there was no bread and people were forced to eat the skins of the cattle that had been killed the previous year, along with the small supply of seal oil that was left. When these provisions were exhausted, the infants and the elderly were probably the first to die. In desperation, the Acadians revolted and took up arms to force others to give them the food they suspected was being kept in reserve. Boishébert intervened and asked them what they were planning to do, to which they replied: "Prolong our days!"—a response that broke his heart and moved him to such an extent that he had half of his own food sent to them immediately. He hired those who still had the strength to make sleds to pull the weakest across the snow to the Pokemouche River, located about 26 leagues, or about 100 kilometers (62 miles), away. The strongest came back with some fish, probably eels, to feed the starving in Camp d'Espérance.

By repeating these trips, they managed to survive the winter, but by late March the ice had become too thin so it was no longer possible to reach Pokemouche. The reserves of fish or eels were quickly consumed. The refugees were then forced to turn to the remaining beaver pelts and finally were reduced to eating deerskin shoes. Boishébert, who said, "the officiers, soldiers, and the Acadians weakened and languishing on the ground," could do nothing but await death. Then, in early May 1757, a ship loaded with supplies came through the ice from Quebec.

Exactly how many people were in Camp d'Espérance in the Miramichi during the winter of 1756-1757 and how many died? Based on information from official documents, approximately 1,250 Acadian refugees started the winter of 1756-1757 at the camp. In his manuscript on the misery of the Acadian families who had taken refuge in the Miramichi, Placide Gaudet estimates that 400 people died. The official correspondence provides a similar figure. If there were 400 deaths in Camp d'Espérance, then one must conclude that of the 1,376 Acadian refugees present in the fall of 1756, only about 976 were still alive in the spring of 1757, of which 120 made their way to Quebec. That leaves approximately 856 people who remained in Acadie, a figure which coincides more or less with the numbers in the official documents. Thus, about one-third of the Acadian refugees in Camp d'Espérance died in the extreme conditions that prevailed during the winter of 1756-1757.

After the fall of Louisbourg in July 1758, the fate of Camp d'Espérance was sealed forever. In fact, the commander-in-chief of the British army in North America, Gen. Jeffrey Amherst, ordered Brig.-Gen. James Wolfe to lead an expedition against the settlements in the Miramichi, Gaspé, and neighboring posts. In accordance with these orders, Wolfe commissioned Col. James Murray to lead an expedition of about 800 men against the settlements in the Miramichi. He arrived there on September 15, 1758, aboard the *Juno* under the command of Captain John Vaughan.

The captain was concerned about the location of his ship, which, along with the fire ship *Aetna* and six other vessels, were transporting the troops. They were at the mouth of the Miramichi Bay where they were exposed to offshore winds that could blow them into the shore. Captain Vaughan urged Murray to act as quickly as possible. With 300 of his men, Murray led an attack against the Mi'kmaq mission. When he learned that there was another settlement on the opposite shore of the Miramichi, at Baie-des-Ouines, Murray sent troops there immediately in order to destroy the post. In fact, he had burned the church (present-day Burnt Church) and the dwellings of both the Mi'kmaq and the Acadian refugees at the Mi'kmaq mission.

Beausoleil had taken refuge with his family and his son at the Caches River in Néguac (today known as *la hêtrière à Beausoleil* or Beausoleil's beech grove) not far from the Burnt Church, but they were not detected by the British. Murray stated: "That Ten Leagues up the River there was another Settlement very considerable of neutrals and some Family's who had fled from the Island of St. John's since the taking of Louisbourg. That the whole were in a starving Condition, had sent away most part of their Effects to Canada, and were all to follow immediately as they every Hour expected the English, & besides could not subsist since they could not now be supported by Sea as they formerly were before Louisbourg was taken." It is interesting to note that Acadians from Isle St. Jean had already taken refuge in the Miramichi when families, who had remained on the island, were being assembled to be deported to France: 3,100 people were thus deported in October 1758.

Murray would have liked to have attacked Camp d'Espérance, but after consulting with Captains Vaughan and Bickerton, he decided to abandon the idea and ordered his men back on board ship. Visibly distraught and fearful for the safety of their vessels, the commanders weighed anchor on September 18 and the small squadron sailed back to Louisbourg, leaving Camp d'Espérance intact.

That did not prevent the Acadians from continuing to put up a resistance against the British, mainly by raiding commerce. Acadian privateers came into action by attacking the supply ships of the British flotilla that had come for the siege of Quebec in the fall of 1758. Their activities lasted until at least the fall of 1761, creating considerable inconvenience for the movement of the British merchant ships. However, the Acadian privateers did not always have the advantage. In October 1760, 47 Acadians armed a schooner as a privateer ship and after a successful prize off Gaspé, it chased a British frigate which caused it to go aground near Shippagan (at present-day Saint-Simon). Most of the Acadian boats were between 15 and 20 tons, consequently they were not able to inflict as much damage on the British merchant navy as the larger and much faster ships.

In the spring of 1759, the transit camp established in the Miramichi by Captain Boishébert was moved to the Restigouche by his successor, Lt. Jean-François Bourdon de Dombourg. He was followed there by the families from Isle St. Jean and the refugee families in the Miramichi. The camp was located near the present-day National Historic Site of the Battle of the Restigouche (across from Campbellton) at a place known at the time as Petite-Rochelle. At the Battle of the Restigouche in early July 1760, the British were unable to capture the camp but they destroyed the three French ships that had taken refuge there and the village further downstream on the Restigouche River. This village, identified by a British officer as Petite-Rochelle, included about 150 or 200 dwellings and harbored primarily refugee families from the Miramichi, Richibucto (including Lemaigre's family), and other locations in the southern part of the Bay of Chaleur.

In fact, these families had made their way there when hearing the news of the arrival of the French ships in June 1760 and were still there in October of the same year when the commissary Bazagier made a list of the people at the Restigouche post. He counted a total of 881 people: 230 from Isle St. Jean and 22 from Richibucto (families from Port Toulouse, including Lemaigre's who settled there after the fall of Louisbourg in 1758). The other people came from Camp d'Espérance, Caraquet, Shippagan, and other refuge sites. In addition to the 881 refugees in Restigouche, there were another 485 living in Richibucto, Camp d'Espérance, Caraquet, and Shippigan—the only sites mentioned by Bazagier.

The following year, the camp in Restigouche was completely deserted. The families from Isle St. Jean appear to have gone back to the island and the remaining 708 refugees spread out around the Bay of Chaleur, at places like Bonaventure (the founding families of this region), Nipisiguit (present-day Bathurst), Caraquet, Shippagan, and also in the Miramichi. In fact, in early August 1760, according to Pierre du Calvet, there were 24 families, including the founding families of Néguac (the Breaus and the Savoies) who were neighbors of Beausoleil and his son Joseph. Unfortunately, Calvet's census does not include the refuge sites of Richibucto or Buctouche.

In October 1761, the commander of Fort Cumberland (formerly Fort Beauséjour), Captain Roderick MacKenzie organized an expedition against the posts of the Acadian refugees in the Miramichi and the Bay of Chaleurs. Since they had been left to their own devices and without supplies, the Acadians offered little resistance and surrendered to Captain MacKenzie and his troops. The latter took 187 men, women, and children back to Fort Cumberland. They were joined by 63 others who took shelter in the fort for the winter. The remainder of the families had to make their way there in the spring of 1762. A number of refugees were transferred to Fort Edward, no doubt to repair the dikes and *aboiteaux*. This included Beausoleil and his son Joseph who were captured after MacKenzie's expedition, probably in the winter of 1762. These were the last Acadians to surrender and thus among the most battle-hardened of the Acadian resistors.

Prisoners in Halifax

By October 1761, privateers sailed directly from Baie Verte to Halifax. These were captains or owners of ships that were still armed (like Lemaigre and his sons Alexandre and Paul). They were there on May 17, 1762, when Gov. Jonathan Belcher and his council resolved to seize the ships of these Acadian partisans who were to be disarmed and imprisoned. These Acadian families, unlike the other families who had preceded them in the Halifax region, had not yet been interned on Georges Island, located in the middle of the harbor.

Photo©Government of Nova Scotia

Georges Island, situated in the middle of the harbor of Halifax, Nova Scotia, was used for detaining Acadian prisoners. The island was named after George II of Great Britain.

Photo©Société national de l'Acadie

The Monument of the Acadian Odyssey *facing Georges Island prison.*

In fact, Acadians were probably imprisoned on this island as early as the fall of 1749 and the winter of 1750. In July 1755, about 80 deputies from Port Royal, Rivière-aux-Canards, Grand-Pré, and Pisiquid were incarcerated in the cells of Georges Island by Gov. Charles Lawrence and his council. Two months later, they were escorted back to their respective villages to join their families before being deported to the Anglo-American colonies. In November 1755, about 50 people, or eight Acadian families, from Merligueche (present-day Lunenburg), were deported to North Carolina from Georges Island.

In the summer of 1756, a group of Acadian women and children from the Beaubassin region were part of the refugee families from Isle St. Jean who were to be transferred to Quebec. According to a French officer stationed in Louisbourg: "A boat with 150 Acadians that left Isle St. Jean for Canada was captured by a warship off Gaspé. The poor Acadians were taken to Georges Island in Halifax where they stayed for several months, sleeping outdoors and in most cases with nothing to cover themselves with, because their clothes had been taken when they were captured. They sent them to us at the beginning of November in exchange for sailors taken by our privateers."

A number of other families and individuals, for the most part from Cape Sable, stayed on Georges Island before being deported in November 1758 and in November 1759. Right after the fall of Louisbourg, in addition to the refuge areas in the Gulf of St. Lawrence, the British launched punitive expeditions in November 1758 against the settlements in Cape Sable, on the St. John River, and the Petitcodiac River. As a result, 68 Acadian men, women, and children, along with the missionary Jean-Baptiste de Gai Desenclaves, were captured and taken to Halifax where they arrived in early November 1758. At the very beginning of 1759, after being detained for two months, all these people and other Acadians who had been captured during the expeditions on the St. John and the Petitcodiac Rivers were deported to France aboard cartel ships that arrived in Le Havre in early February 1759. However, that was not the end of the story for the Acadians of the Cape Sable area.

In fact, in September 1758, the Acadians still present in this region addressed a letter to the governor of Massachusetts, informing him that there were 40 families that included 150 individuals who were ready to surrender due to the great distress in which they found themselves. Before the British authorities had time to act, since they had not received a response from the governor of Massachusetts, these Acadians sent several representatives to Halifax in the spring of 1759 to make their offer of surrender to Lawrence. At the end of June, Captain Joseph Gorham and his Rangers (militia hired to hunt and fight the families of Acadian resisters) brought back to Halifax about 152 people that Lawrence put on Georges Island "as being a place of the most security" to join a half a dozen Acadian prisoners captured the previous winter on the St. John River. After several months of detention on the island, these Acadian families were deported in early November 1759 to England from where they were transported to Cherbourg, France.

Not long after the departure of the vessel transporting the deportees in November 1759, a group of about 300 Acadians from the St. John River were transported to Halifax aboard two schooners and kept on Georges Island. These families had come back from Canada where they had taken refuge starting in the fall of 1758 and where they had obtained a pass or authorization from Brigadier Robert Monckton to return to their dwellings, after signing the oath of allegiance following the fall of Quebec. In November 1759, when they arrived at Fort Frederick, that the British had built on the ruins of the fort abandoned by Boishébert at the mouth of the St. John River, the 300 Acadians were stopped immediately and escorted to Halifax as prisoners of war in early January 1760, prior to their deportation to England.

Another group of Acadian families from the Petitcodiac and Memramcook Rivers, and refuge sites on the east coast of present-day New Brunswick (Buctouche et Richibucto), arrived in Halifax in the summer of 1760 to surrender. The group was comprised of about 300 individuals. During the November 1758 expedition on the Petitcodiac River, all the villages had been burned, leaving the inhabitants in distress. Beausoleil had already taken refuge in the Miramichi where he had gone to have a wound to his heel treated. He had been wounded at the battle of the Cran, near present-day Riverview, in early July 1758.

Less than a year later, the same scenario played out on the St. John River. After a siege of several months, the town of Quebec fell in September 1759. The infamous storm took place on November 3 and 4, 1759, which essentially sounded the death knell for the Acadian resisters on the Petitcodiac. The marsh that they had dried and diked at considerable pain and effort was now inundated, thus compromising any attempt of reconstruction for the inhabitants whose dwellings had been completely destroyed the year before. Since the remaining 190 inhabitants found themselves deprived of everything and incapable of surviving the fast approaching winter, their representatives, along with those of the Memramcook River, went to Fort Cumberland to surrender to the British. Commander Joseph Frye agreed to feed one-third (63) of them during the winter; the others would have to wait until spring to come to the fort.

By November 18, 1759, the Acadian refugees in Buctouche, Richibucto, and Miramichi began negotiations with Frye that led to their capitulation. However, at the beginning of the winter of 1760, the news of the arrest of families from the St. John River caused these Acadians to renounce their commitment to go to Fort Cumberland, despite having promised to do so. The British authorities took offense to this and would not give up until all these Acadian rebels had surrendered.

In the meantime, by the fall of 1759 and especially during the winter and spring of 1760, the Mi'kmaq and the Maliseet started surrendering to the British authorities on the advice of their missionaries Fr. Pierre Maillard on Isle Royale and Isle St. Jean, Fr. Charles Germain at the St. John River, and Fr. Jean Manach on the east coast of present-day New Brunswick. The British authorities could only rejoice at this new development because they would no longer have to fear attacks by aboriginals on their settlements that were due to be established by the spring of 1760 with the arrival of colonists or Planters from New England.

However, the damage to the dikes and *aboiteaux* caused by the storm on November 4, 1759, meant that sea water flooded the Acadian marshes, rendering them useless for farming. In addition, the Acadians were the only ones who were able to remedy this unfortunate situation. Thus, from one day to the next, the precarious state of the Acadian community changed radically. The very people who had put up a fierce resistance to the British for the last five years were now greatly needed.

The families from Petitcodiac and Memramcook (including the families of Alexandre Broussard, his sons, and his brother Joseph Beausoleil's sons) were transported from Beauséjour to Pisiquid in the summer of 1760. From there, they walked to Halifax where they were kept on Georges Island while awaiting deportation with the Acadian families from the St. John River. In all, there were about 600 people in Halifax, about 500 of whom were on Georges Island from the winter of 1760 until the spring of 1761.

During the winter of 1761, Fr. Jean Manach, among others, was incarcerated on the island while awaiting deportation to England via New York. However, the situation changed after the arrival of the engineer John Henry Bastide at the end of May 1761. He came to direct the work on the fortifications in Halifax; a number of Acadian men were hired as carpenters. Bastide actually asked for 150 men, whereas Gov. Belcher wanted 120 others to go to help the Anglo-American settlers repair the dikes and *aboiteaux* in the Minas area. That represented a significant number of men who could leave Georges Island where they were incarcerated in order to work in the town or in the countryside. Unfortunately, this apparent calm did not last long because another event happened that was to disturb the peace and cause panic in Halifax.

It was with great consternation, at the beginning of July 1762, that the British authorities learned that the French had invaded Newfoundland and now controlled the port of Saint John. Considerable panic took over Halifax at the arrival of this rather alarming news for the local population and the colonial authorities. A war council sat secretly on 12 occasions between July 10 and August 17, 1762, in order to prepare Halifax harbor in the event of an attack by the French, an idea that was deemed absurd by Gen. Amherst, who wrote to Belcher on July 29, 1762, indicating that he feared nothing for Halifax which was well-defended by 1,500 men, in addition to the militia, adding that Nova Scotia "is the only province [in Canada] that is provided with a proper defense."

By July 10, the council had already decided that the Acadians prisoners would be housed and guarded as a single group by the commander in chief, Col. William Forster, to prevent any crimes and to have them ready for departure at first notice. On July 13, 1762, in accordance with the decision taken by the war council the previous day, Belcher decreed martial law and summoned the militia from King's County to escort the Acadians who were working in the marshes in the Minas, Pisiquid, and Port Royal areas.

By July 20, around 130 Acadian prisoners arrived in Halifax under escort to join the 785 or so Acadian men, women, and children. Some 80 of these were from Fort Edward including Beausoleil and his son Joseph. Thus, 915 people (400 of them being men capable of bearing arms) were guarded night and day in open barracks by the militia or the townspeople—a very difficult task since these barracks were the only place in the town that could be used for so many people. According to Belcher, "We are destitute of the means, Confinement is the first which offers itself to consideration, but here is no other than of their ordinary abode, the Barracks." In addition, it was feared that in the event of an enemy attack, these Acadian prisoners could set fire to the town and join the enemy.

Things stayed that way until August 1762 when they were all embarked onto seven ships bound for Boston. It was during the meeting of the governor's council on July 26, 1762, (almost seven years to the day that a similar decision was made by the council on July 28, 1755) that the decision was made to deport all these people to Massachusetts, not only because of their influence on the aboriginal population, but also their arrogance and impertinence. On July 30, 1762, the war council ratified the decision made by the governor's council on July 26, 1762, and decided that the Acadians would be deported to Boston where they would remain at anchor awaiting Gen. Amherst's decision on their fate. On August 12, 1762, the Assembly expressed its position by a memorandum to Belcher on the behavior of the Acadian prisoners in Halifax putting forward a justification for deporting them out of the province of Nova Scotia.

Fr. Pierre Maillard died on August 12, 1762, the same day the 915 or so prisoners were embarked. This number included Lemaigre and all of the other Acadian prisoners in Halifax, in addition to the 130 men who had been escorted from Port Royal, Minas Basin, and Pisiquid (among whom was the other resistance leader Beausoleil and his son Joseph) who were to be deported without their families.

Fr. Pierre Maillard, who had negotiated peace on behalf of the Mi'kmaq in 1759 and 1760, now enjoyed the favor of the British authorities. During one of the meetings of the war council on or before July 30, 1762, when asked about the loyalty of the Acadians, he supposedly responded that one could only trust a handful of the Acadian prisoners in Halifax. Was it because of his opinion that the decision was made to deport the 915 or so Acadian men, women, and children, despite the Gen. Amherst's opinions to the contrary? Whatever the case, Belcher informed the war council about Gen. Amherst's correspondence regarding the Acadian prisoners and the aboriginals, who according to him, presented no danger to the safety of Nova Scotia. The decision remained unchanged, especially after the news that some of the settlers or Planters in the Minas or Horton region (present-day Grand-Pré) had deserted fearing an imminent attack by the French.

The seven ships transporting the Acadians left Halifax on August 18, 1762, and reached their destination one week later on August 25. The authorities in Nova Scotia had given the order to Captain James Brooks, commander of the convoy, to go to Boston and await the orders of Gen. Amherst regarding the fate reserved for these Acadian prisoners of war. Not long after their arrival, the authorities in Massachusetts refused to allow the Acadians to disembark; only reluctantly did they permit the sick passengers to disembark. Out of compassion, Gov. Thomas Pownall would have allowed everyone to disembark, but the Assembly was of a different opinion since there was no question of receiving any more Acadians from Nova Scotia, and since there were already deemed to be too many in Massachusetts, which had welcomed many more than the other Anglo-American colonies since 1755.

The seven ships remained at anchor for a month with their human cargo while awaiting a decision on the deportees. Even with the approval of Gen. Amherst that these Acadians could be placed in temporary installations and his assurance that that he would assume the entire cost of their upkeep, the Assembly still refused to receive them in their territory. In the end, Captain Brooks had to face the facts and weigh anchor. It is not hard to imagine the consternation among the colonial authorities in Halifax when they saw the seven ships back in their berths at the beginning of October, nearly a month and a half after departing with these dangerous Acadian men and women.

Since the British had succeeded in taking back Saint John's (Newfoundland) from the French, any threat of an attack on Halifax had vanished, so these families must have been housed in the barracks where they had been prior to their departure. It is obvious that these 915 people were not kept on Georges Island while awaiting deportation to Boston. If they had been, how could they have set fire to the town? It could well be, however, that they were taken to the island just before they were embarked in early August 1762, but no mention is made of this in the official documents. We can assume that some of them were kept on the island after their return from Boston, but it cannot be confirmed. Nevertheless, it is possible that Beausoleil and Lemaigre were interned there while waiting to be deported to England where their presence is noted in the winter of 1763.

In the summer of 1763, just after his return from Europe, Joseph Broussard *dit* Beausoleil, the famous leader of the Acadian resisters was arrested in Pisiquid with compromising documents in his possession. Included was a letter from de La Rochette, secretary or emissary of the ambassador of France in London, the Duke of Nivernais, inviting the Acadians in North America to move to French territory and encouraging them to sign their names on subscription lists that could be sent to him through an intermediary in London. This letter reached Joseph LeBlanc *dit* Lemaigre via Acadians in Philadelphia who, in turn, had received it from Acadian refugees in England just before they left for France in March 1763. After he was arrested, Beausoleil was taken from Pisiquid to Halifax where, along with Lemaigre, he was summoned by the governor's council of Nova Scotia to explain himself. Beausoleil and Lemaigre might have been incarcerated on Georges Island while awaiting the interrogation by the members of the council in August 1763, but once again there is no specific mention of this and we know nothing more of the affair.

To Stay or To Leave?

Such were the circumstances when Col. Montague Wilmot arrived in Halifax. He was already familiar with the Acadian prisoners because he was the commander of Fort Cumberland in 1756-1757, when the Acadian resisters were very active in the Isthmus of Chignectou region. Unfortunately, as governor of Nova Scotia, his attitude regarding the Acadian community was not much better than that of his predecessors, Charles Lawrence and Jonathan Belcher. Like them, he wanted at all cost to get rid of the Acadians. However, if they were going to be permitted to settle in the colony, Wilmot demanded Lord Halifax to only allow them to settle in small groups in settlements that were already established and in areas where they would have as few contacts as possible with the Native people. He even suggested sending them to the Carribean islands that had been won back from the French at the end of the war, because in his opinion "the further they are distant, the greater our safety." The British authorities, on the other hand, considered that the Acadians no longer represented a threat to the internal safety of the colony and, like Gen. Amherst, said it was better to let the Acadians settle in Nova Scotia where they could become "good subjects."

In the meantime, the Acadians living in exile in the Anglo-American colonies and in Nova Scotia (including Halifax), responded in large numbers to the invitation issued in the spring of 1763 to move to France. Obviously, not all the families responded to the call, but we can assume that the majority of them did. Moreover, at the bottom of the list of Acadians in Halifax, dated August 12, 1763, is the following statement: "There are still many families dispersed along the seacoast who will be of the same feeling whose names are not written here."

In any case, the majority of Acadian families detained as prisoners in Halifax subscribed to this list, namely 161 families, or 711 individuals, out of a total of 232 Acadian families of the 1,056 who were present in Halifax and vicinity. These figures are based on a count sent by Wilmot to Londres, in the spring of 1764. In addition, 76 Acadian heads of family sent a request to Wilmot on May 12, 1764, reiterating their wish they had expressed two weeks earlier on April 29, 1764. Because they recognized no other sovereign but the king of France, they asked to be provided with supplies and ships that would enable them to move to France or a French territory. Since the war was over, in their opinion, they were no longer prisoners of war and should enjoy the freedom of going to the country of their choice, like the Acadians incarcerated in England who went to France or those in Carolina who went to Cap-François in Saint-Domingue (Haiti).

At the same time, Wilmot received an answer from Lord Halifax who agreed with him, that the Acadians who decided to stay in Nova Scotia should be dispersed in small groups around the colony. According to him, it would not be better to let them settle in Canada because of the proximity to Nova Scotia and that, in addition, the islands in the Carribean recently conquered from the French were going to be sold at public auction, and would thus not be available for Acadians. Finally, Lord Halifax added at the end of his letter, that the king of England considered that the Acadians had the same status as his other Catholic subjects in North America, and that they just had to take the oath of allegiance in order to settle and enjoy the same rights and privileges as other British subjects. On the other hand, as British subjects, one could not forbid them from leaving the colony or British territory if that was their wish. Apparently, Lord Halifax encouraged Wilmot to do everything in his power to prevent the Acadian families from moving to foreign territory following solicitations or secret maneuvers of a foreign power, namely France.

The royal instructions of July 20, 1764, were similar to this; consequently, Wilmot submitted them to the members of the council of Nova Scotia, who immediately prepared the text of the oath of allegiance offered to the Acadians and also a list of places where they could settle. However, the majority of the Acadian families refused this offer and decided to leave Nova Scotia. Since the British authorities refused to pay their passage out of the colony, these families chartered ships to take them directly to Cap-François on the island of Saint-Domingue (Haiti) and from there to the Mississippi in route for Illinois, where they planned to settle under the leadership of Beausoleil. Thus, starting in late November 1764 and during the winter of 1765, about 600 men, women, and children left Halifax aboard chartered vessels headed for the island of Saint-Domingue where some families stayed, but most left in the spring of 1765 to settle in Louisiana.

After the departure of these Acadian families in the fall of 1764 and the winter of 1765, a number of other families stayed in the Halifax area before dispersing to various locations in Nova Scotia, including Arichat, Chezzetcook, and Sainte-Anne-du-Ruisseau, and to Acadian settlements in present-day New Brunswick, most notably to Cocagne, after staying on the island of Miquelon (near Newfoundland). In fact, a number of families that had taken refuge on Isle St. Jean or been incarcerated in Fort Cumberland, in addition to families from the Halifax area, went to the French archipelago. Among them was the Lemaigre family who ended up moving to Belle-Île-en-Mer in France, whereas other families put down roots on the island of Miquelon where their descendants live today. Finally, about half of the families imprisoned in Halifax went to settle in Louisiana: in St. Martinville, St. James, and Opelousas.

Over half of the households or individuals who stayed in Camp d'Espérance in 1756-1757—many of them later imprisoned in Halifax—decided to stay in Acadie where they were among the pioneers in most of the villages or regions settled in the 1760s and 1770s. The other families and individuals settled primarily in Louisiana, but also in France and in Quebec, where their descendants are still very numerous today.

Endnotes

1. This article is a condensed version of two studies the author devoted to families who were refugees or prisoners in Acadie during this period: "*Les réfugiés acadiens au Camp d'Espérance de la Miramichi en 1756-1761 : un épisode méconnu du Grand Dérangement*" in *Acadiensis*, Vol. XLI, No. 1 (Winter-Spring 2012), pp. 128-168 and "*Les Acadiens à Halifax et dans l'île Georges, 1755-1764*" in *Port Acadie*, No. 22-23, (Fall 2012-Spring 2013), pp. 43-76. For the translation by John Estano deRoche of the latter article, see the web site of the Amis de Grand-Pré: "Acadians in Halifax and on Georges Island, 1755-1764": www.rootsweb.ancestry.com/~nsgrdpre/documents/dossiers/menudossiers.html (consulted March 13, 2014). For further information regarding sources, please consult these articles which also provide detailed tables. The author wishes to thank Anselme-Chiasson of the *Centre d'études acadiennes* and the genealogist Stephen A. White who provided access to his manuscript for the *Dictionnaire généalogique des familles acadiennes*, an indispensable tool for completing these articles.

2. That is to say, Nova Scotia (English Acadie) and French Acadie or the present-day province of New Brunswick. This excludes Isle Royale (Cape Breton Island) and Isle St. Jean (Prince Edward Island) which were under French administration until 1758 when the civilian and military populations were deported to France. Some of the families who escaped deportation from these two French island colonies found refuge in French Acadie and were later imprisoned in English Acadie.

ACADIAN EXILES IN ENGLAND

Richard Holledge

As former U.S. Defense Secretary Donald Rumsfeld said when questioned about the looting in Baghdad during the Iraq conflict: "Stuff happens, and it's untidy, and freedom's untidy, and free people are free to make mistakes and commit crimes and do bad things."

If "free people" were changed to "powerful people," that infamous outburst would be pretty much what the British Prime Minister, the Duke of Newcastle (1754-1756), would have said if he had been asked about the expulsion of the Acadians.

In his book *Crucible of War* (2000), an account of the battle for power between France and Britain in North America, American historian Fred Anderson described the expulsion as "chillingly reminiscent of modern ethnic cleansing operations...." But imagine the world in 1755: War had already broken out in America between France and Britain, but in the summer of 1756 Britain and Prussia took up arms against France, Russia, and Austria in what was to become the Seven Years' War. In this, the first global war, battle was waged in Europe, the West Indies, India, the Philippines, and of course in North America. The stakes were enormous. Britain was taking the first steps in its quest for world domination.

What were they to do with a few French-speaking citizens in one of Britain's colonies who refused to declare their allegiance to the crown, spoke a different language, and followed the Catholic faith? Swat them out of the way; what else?

The Acadians sailed into the British ports at a time when the war was not going well for the British. Within weeks of the declaration of war in May 1756, Adm. John Byng lost Minorca to the French. And in America during the previous year, Gen. Edward Braddock perished while on a failed expedition to capture Fort Duquesne, in present-day Pittsburgh.

Considerable unrest was to be found at home, which would come to characterize life in Britain for the duration of the war. Bread riots were a testament to the plight of the starving populace. The imposition of the Enclosure Acts drove country folk off their traditional common lands, which were to be given to new landlords. Millions of acres of land were swallowed up by the rich, forcing hundreds of thousands to flee to the cities, where they lived in poverty. It is unclear whether the attack on an Acadian wife by these down-and-outs, as portrayed in the 2012 book *The Scattered*, actually occurred, but it is possible to imagine the resentment of this angry underclass at these "French" interlopers–especially because the Acadians were given a better allowance to live on than they were.

Their resentment does not justify the crimes against this small band of humanity, but it does help to explain them, and it helps to explain why the story of their time in England has remained untold–not just because the exiles were unwanted, but because there were events, quite apart from news from the battlefront, which capture the imagination more so than the arrival of a hundred disease-ridden foreigners.

Much bigger news at the time were the exploits of the French privateer François Thurot, who terrorized the northwest coast of England, or the story of a press gang attempting to seize the crew of a whaling ship, only to be fought off by the harpoon-wielding whalers. Similarly, in Bristol, local history records show how, in the year before, the water in the Hotwell spa became red, and a well in a field near Clifton Church, belonging to a Mr. John Harrison, turned black as ink. Bristol also found "great success" against privateers in 1756, when the French ship *Belliqueux*, with 64 guns and 415 men, was seized by the *Antelope* upon entering the Bristol Channel by mistake.

But when it comes to the Acadians, who died by the score, the vicar of St. John, in Bedminster, a suburb of the city, found time to record only the names of two victims who died: Anastasie Boudreau, aged nine, on June 30, 1756, and Marie Scannat, identified as a "French Neutral," on July 3rd.

Reeling from the effects of the tsunami caused by the earthquake in Lisbon in late 1755, the citizens of the seaside city of Southampton had other matters to occupy their interests—they were not very concerned by the eyesore of Acadian arrivals begging in the streets. Much more exciting were sightings of the British royalty, who visited because they were told the salt water there had healing properties, and would protect them against rabies and other diseases.

When the city of Liverpool published the compendious book *Liverpool 800,* in 2007, to celebrate its long and intriguing history (maybe even illustrious, if so much of the city's wealth had not been derived from a booming slave trade of the mid-18th century) there was not a single mention of the Acadian tragedy. It has taken the work of Acadian scholars to find, in London's Catholic Record Society, the briefest of references to a handful of baptisms and marriages in the parish church of Woolton, a Liverpool suburb.

Trivial matters of passionate concern, the atrocious conditions of the poor, and the horrors of the war—all of these things made the plight of the Acadians a matter of little consequence, and today it remains a hidden shame. I have met only one Brit who has heard of the Acadians, and while I tell the story, my listeners' eyes glaze over until the payoff: "The Acadians settled in Louisiana and became known as Cajuns." Then they are interested.

Even the Acadian scholars have struggled to come out with anything like a full picture. When I was looking for background for my novel *The Scat-*

tered (2012), I found precious few facts relating to the time in England, only the compendious research into family trees by the likes of Stephen White, Paul Delaney, Naomi Griffiths, and Dorothy Vyner.

Even though some of the Acadians were beginning to be accepted–in Bristol, for example the *Journal* newspaper reported that, "during their abode here, by their industry and civil deportment, they have gained the esteem of us all" –at the end of the war they were sloughed off just as carelessly as they had been in Acadie seven years before.

Call it *realpolitik*, condemn Britain and France for their casual cruelty, rail at man's inhumanity if you will, but sadly, the lesson is: Powerful people have always done bad things. Stuff has always happened.

Letter by Joseph LeBlanc —A Prisoner in England

Jean-François Mouhot

In an article published in 1994 by the Canadian revue *Acadiensis*, the Louisiana historian Carl A. Brasseaux regretted that, after many years of research and in spite of frequent references to such exchanges in contemporary documents, he had never found correspondence between Acadians in the period directly following the *Grand Dérangement*. Brasseaux, after a long search for these "ghostly letters" (*lettres fantômes*) concluded: "There are no extant copies of letters between Acadian exiles." ("Phantom Letters: Acadian Correspondence, 1776-1784," *Acadiensis*, XXIII, 2 [Spring 1994], pp. 124-132).

Correspondence Between Acadians

Yet, many letters between Acadians have surely been preserved and 15 missives have just been re-edited in the same revue.[1] The published body is mostly made up of nine letters of the d'Entremont family, sent from Cherbourg and Saint Servan (suburb of Saint Malo) to Nova Scotia between 1764 and 1784. Despite their great interest, these letters are little known by researchers working on the exile period. Because of the limited space in the revue, it was not possible to publish long excerpts of the correspondence. However, one of the edited letters sets up an as-yet-unedited confrontation with the "genealogical declarations" of the Acadians at Belle-Île-en-Mer.

A Letter From a Certain LeBlanc

The document re-transcribed below was written by one of the Acadian prisoners in England shortly after the Deportation. This relatively brief letter has very little information about its provenance. We correctly read that it was written by a certain Joseph LeBlanc from Liverpool on September 21, 1757, and that it was addressed to a person named Charles, whom the author addresses as cher frère (dear brother).

His principal message is the death of Joseph's wife. Many questions arise: Who is the real author? There are many named Joseph LeBlanc and their identification is not always easy. The most famous among them is probably the one called "Le Maigre" (the thin one), deceased at Belle-Île, and to whom the *Dictionnaire Biographique du Canada* has dedicated a biography.

Where is the addressee of the letter (Charles) when the letter is sent? Who is the wife of Joseph LeBlanc who just died and who is not named in this letter? Reconstituting the sequence of events has been a real detective story. First of all, this letter, from all evidence, was intercepted and kept by the British authorities who controlled the letter exchanges. The Acadians in Liverpool in fact complained in 1763, that "the commissioner [Langton] opens all the letters that they write or receive."[2] The author, Joseph LeBlanc, was at the time in Liverpool, one of the places where the Acadians from the region of Minas, were sent after having been refused in Virginia.[3] We know that most of the Acadians repatriated from England to France after 1763 settled at Belle-Ile-en-Mer. Among these are found at least four males named Joseph LeBlanc. It has been possible to retrace the journey of the author of our letter thanks to the depositions given a few years later in 1767 during the reconstitution of the civil status of the Acadians settled at Belle-Île-en-Mer (a reconstitution aimed at making up for the loss of the parish registers).[4]

Among the four "Joseph LeBlancs" mentioned in the depositions, only one, residing at Kerledan, parish of Sauzon at Belle-Île, matches all of the information contained in the letter, having: (a) a brother named Charles, (b) a wife deceased in Liverpool in 1757, and (c) two children living at the time of the death of their mother. No confusion is possible among the individuals when Joseph notes that his ex-father-in-law lives in the village of Borderhouat (commune of Locmaria, near the point off Kerdonis), and the declarations of this latter corroborate those of Joseph.

Date Error

In his own declaration of March 7, 1767, Joseph declares, "born at Minas, parish of Saint-Charles, 27 January 1730 of René Leblanc and Anne Landry, of said place" (Casgrain, *Collection de documents inèdits*, op.cit., tome III, p. 48). After listing his ancestral genealogy all the way to the ancestors who came from France, he verifies the names of his brothers and sisters, and gives the spouse of each as well as the places to which they were deported in 1755.

Of the six brothers and sisters, five were transported to Boston with their spouses; two to the Carolinas; one to Philadelphia, and two to England (Joseph, the deposer, to Liverpool, and Charles, the addressee of the letter, to Southampton).[5] Thus, it would seem likely that the latter is the place where Charles is living at the moment and where Joseph writes to him. Therefore, we have now answered one of our opening queries.

As he goes on with the deposition, Joseph attests that in 1750 he married Marguerite Trahan (born in 1731), who bore two children, in 1752 and 1754. Joseph then declares that his wife, "died in Liverpool on December 13, 1757." However, this last date is probably incorrect [6]

First of all, the date of the letter (September 21, 1757) re-transcribed further on is evidently incompatible with the testimony; or the date of the letter (at the time of the events) is less apt to be wrong than a declaration relying on memories already ten years old: historians know well that one should not always rely on human memory on this subject. See the analysis and examples by Annette Wieviorka, *L'ère du témoin [The Era of the Witness],* (Paris: Hachette, 2002), regarding the loss of memories of those imprisoned in concentration camps.

Furthermore, the declaration of Pierre Trahan (the ex-father-in-law of Joseph), on February 11, 1767, agrees on all points with that of Joseph except for the date of Marguerite's death. Pierre Trahan declares that he had a daughter, Marguerite, born at Pigiguit in August 1731, "married to Joseph leBlanc, of the village of K(er)ledan, Parish of Sauzon and deceased at Liverpool in the month of July 1757,"[7] which seems this time perfectly compatible with the date of the letter.

Finally, Joseph declares that he remarried Anne Hébert in Liverpool on January 28, 1758. Yet, it seems unlikely that Joseph would have remarried a mere one month after the death of his first wife. Thus, it is more likely that Marguerite would have died in July, or at the end of the summer (Jean Tarrade [art. Cit.p.17] is amazed at the "speed record" of the remarriage of Joseph Leblanc, without noticing that there is probably an error in dating, as we have just pointed out). Could it be that Joseph, ten years after the event, has forgotten by about six months the exact date of his first wife's death? Would he not at least remember if his spouse died in the winter or the summer? It is more probably an error of one of the copiers of the registers or an error during the transcription by Casgrain. It should be possible to verify the originals at the *Archives Départementales* of Morbihan at Vannes.

The Addressee of the Letter

Joseph finally does give some indications about his brother, Charles, to whom he addressed the letter cited below. Charles, born in 1717, married Anne Boudrot who also died at Southampton in August 1756. Remarried in the same city to Magdeleine Gautrot, Charles, at the moment of his brother's declaration in 1767, is living in Saint-Malo with his family.

Jean-Marie Fonteneau notes that Joseph Leblanc, of Kerlédan, left Belle-Île-en-Mer headed for Poitou in 1773, then embarked for Louisiana in 1785. [See *Les Acadiens: citoyens de l'Atlantique* (*Rennes: Éditions Ouest France*, 2001), p. 490]. In the embarkation lists published by Gérard-Marc Braud, Joseph Leblanc, 54 years old (in fact 55, since we have seen that he was born in January 1730), is listed as embarking on *Le Bon Papa* with Anne Hébert, his wife (49 years old), and their four children. [See *De Nantes à la louisiane, l'histoire de l'Acadie, l'odyssée d'un people exile* (*Ouest editions*: 1994, Annexe V), p. 127s.]

His brother Charles obviously followed the same path: Gérard Marc Braud has the couple, Charles LeBlanc and Madeleine Gautrot, staying in Saint-Servan until 1773, then from there going to Châtellerault. The family of Charles LeBlanc stayed in Nantes, undoubtedly from 1775, then boarded the ship *Le Saint-Rémi* with their one surviving daughter, Marguerite Geneviève, on June 27, 1785. Thus, the two brothers were able to end their separation which began in 1773 in Poitou and then stayed together at least until their common departure (although on different vessels) for Louisiana.

Transcription of the Letter

Liverpool, September 21, 1757

To Charles LeBlanc
My dear brother, I tell you these words to tell you that my very dear wife has left this world to pass to the other world. I will tell you that she had been sick eight weeks; she died of the tropics [trospisque].[8] *But she received all the aid that a dying person can receive at death. As for me, I am in good health as well as my two children. I beseech you to pray for her and to commend her to all our good relatives and friends. Give my regards to Uncle Charles Richard as well as his wife. Give my regards to aunt Marguerite Commo and all her family. Give my regards to Jean Jacques Terriot and his brother Olivier and all the French neutrals*[9] *in general. I remain in grief your servant and brother.*
(Signature) Joseph LeBlanc

Conclusion

Even if many shadows of doubt hover over this correspondence,[10] the combination of resources has allowed us to know a little more about the persons and the places linked to this little known letter, and to correct an obvious error contained in the declarations of the Acadians at Belle-Île in 1767.

Acknowledgement

The article was originally published under the French title *Lettre d'un prisonnier*, in the Paris periodical *Les Amitiés Acadiennes, no 112, June 2005.* It was translated to English by C. Mel Surette.

Endnotes

1. Jean-François Mouhot, *« Des Revenantes' ? À propos des 'Lettres fantômes' et de la correspondence entre exilés acadiens (1758-1785) », Acadiensis, XXXIV, 1 (Fall 2004), pp. 96-115.* An addenda "about the transcription of a letter from Jean-Baptiste Semer to his father, written from Louisiana in 1766, will likewise be published in the next issue of *Acadiensis.* The totality of the letters will likewise be reproduced in the annexes of my doctoral thesis, *Les Acadiens refugiés en France (1758-1785): l'impossible réintegration?* (provisionary title), *Institut Universitaire Européen*, Florence, Italy, nearing completion with commentaries that could not be reproduced in the article, for lack of space. [Editor's note: the book was published in 2009 and Mouhot has obtained his PhD].

2. *"Mémoire sur les Acadiens"* de La Rochette ou du duc de Nivernais, *alors ambassadeur de France en Angleterre, Archives Nationales de France* (ANF), Colonies, C 11 D, vol. 8,

folios 242-251, février 1763. Copies of this *mémorial* are found in many other archival deposits.

3. Cf. Ernest Martin, *Les exiles Acadiens en France au XVIIIième siècle et leur établissement en Poitou*, Paris, Hachette, 1936 (re edited in facsimile, Brissaud, Poitiers, 1979), p. 37 or Jean-Marie Fonteneau, *les Acadiens citoyens de l'Atlantique*, Rennes, *Éditions Ouest France*, 2001 (1996), p. 190 and ff.

4. The declarations of the Acadians were published in a collection of Father H.R. Casgrain, *Collection de documents inédits sur le Canada et l'Amérique*, published by *le Canada-Français*, Quebec, Demers, 1888-1891 (tome II pp. 170-194 ; tome III pp. 5-59 and 88-134), followed by comments by Rameau de Saint-Père (tome III); for a succinct analysis of these genealogies, cf. Jean Tarrade, *La longue errance des Acadiens après le Grand Dérangement (1755-1785), Bulletin de la Société des Antiquaires de l'Ouest,* série 5, tome 7, trimestre 1, (1993): pp. 2-19.

5. Many authors have already been surprised by the amazing circulation of information between Acadians that allowed them to know precisely where the members of their dispersed family were located. Dr. Carl A. Brasseaux (art. cit.) theorized that the information was carried by various letters swapped among the poor exiles. In the case of Belle-Île, it is verified that many Acadians who came from Saint-Pierre and Miquelon rejoined their families settled on the island of Morbihan in 1767. That is the case for Joseph Leblanc *dit* Le Maigre, who wrote a *mémoire* to the minister on June 26, 1767 (Joseph Leblanc *dit* Le Maignre, to the Secretary of State of the Navy, the duke of Praslin, June 26, 1767, AN, Colonies C 11 A vol. 105 Fol 577-579. This is also the case for Jean Arseneau and Michel Boudrot, who had gone from Miquelon to Nantes on the vessel *Les Deux Amis.* These individuals undoubtedly brought much new and "fresh" information to the Acadians at Belle-Île (Michel Poirier, *Les Acadiens aux îles Saint-Pierre et Miquelon, 1758-1828:* Three Deportations 30 Years of Exile, *Éditions d'Acadie*, 1984, p. 63, note 53).

6. Rameau, in his commentaries (Collection of unpublished documents, op. cit.), believes that the declarations about facts before 1713 "are the translation of hesitant memories, and sometimes altered by the purely oral transmission. Once compared to censuses, to the registers of Port Royal and other authentic documents that we have of this period, we find, in the declarations made at Belle-Île, confusion of dates, of facts dénigrés, a few contradictions, and some omissions, that teach us to accept them only with the benefit of inventory." Yet, he thinks that, "it is not the same about information provided about the dispersion of Acadians, their transportation to England, and the United States, on their captivity in English ports, as well as the genealogy of their families from 1714 until the proscription. There we recognize certain and clear deposition of personal witness about facts that the declarer has himself seen." (p. 137, tome III). We can tell in the case of Joseph Leblanc that these affirmations need to be nuanced! Marguerite Daligaut (Marguerite Daligaut, *Les Acadiens prisonniers en Angleterre, Société historique acadienne* [Cahiers], 34, pp. 160-2) has taken the time to systematically compare the burial registers of Acadians in England found and published by Régis Brun (Regis Sygefroy Brun, *Le séjour des Acadiens en Angleterre et leurs traces dans les archives britanniques, 1756-1763, Société historique acadienne* [Cahiers], IV, 2 [1971]: pp. 62-8) and the later oral declaration of the Acadians of Belle-Île-en-Mer. In general, there is great agreement between the two lists, with differences at times of 15 days. None of the dates of the two lists agree exactly, but this is probably due to the fact that the "register of burials" of Penryn gives the date of burials while the Acadians in their declarations more likely give the date of death. In general the dates are relatively close to one another, but the errors in the declarations are evident in certain cases like the declaration

of Charles Granger, who appears in the list published by Brun as buried October 12, 1756, while the family at Belle-Île-en-Mer declares his death on September 29 (yet, it is not very likely that the body would have been kept that long). An error as flagrant as that of Joseph Leblanc seems to be a particular case. It should also be noted that Régis Brun unfortunately did not find in the death records of Liverpool information that would have allowed us to know with certitude the date of the death of Marguerite Trahan, the wife of Joseph Leblanc.

7. Ibid., tome III, p. 7

8. In spite of researching many dictionaries (Littré, *Dictionnaire de l'Académie* [1762], *Dictionnaire de Trévoux*, *Encyclopédie*, or *Dictionnaire raisonné des Sciences, des Arts et des Métiers* [Diderot], *Dictionnaire Historique de la langue française*, Petit Robert, *Larousse Médical and Longman Dictionnary of Contemporary English*), I did not succeed in identifying this word. It could be a reference to a sickness or "*tropical*" fevers (trospisque=tropiques); *L'Encyclopédie* has an entry at "*fièvre tropique*" of chevalier de Jaucourt. Joseph Leblanc may be referencing this illness or perhaps hydropsy (Swelling caused in certain body parts by fluids that gather and spread according to the *Dictionnaire de l'Académie*). It should be noted that the Acadians shortly after the deportation suffered from a violent epidemic of smallpox, at that time called "*petite vérole*" or smallpox in English. It could be that Marguerite Trahan died from this illness.

9. The text reads "nutrie" which is closer to the pronunciation of neutral than of "neuter." We know that the Acadians were often identified by the expression "*Français neutres*" or "French neutrals." The insistence on the term *neutral*, that is likewise found in other letters is extremely interesting as well as the association with the term *French*.

10. The original of this letter is found in London at the Public Record Office (PRO), Admiralty, Med. In Letters, 122. The Center of Acadian Studies at the University of Moncton (New Brunswick) has a copy (CEA, A6-1-1). A transcription appeared, without indication of its source in a publication from Poitou in 1930: Alfred de Curzon, *Les Acadiens à Liverpool, La Grand' Goule* (Poitiers, 1930), pp.5-6. The writing was modernized except for the surnames.

Letter by Jean-Baptiste Semer to his Father in France

Jean-François Mouhot

Letter From Jean-Baptiste Semer From New Orleans, Louisiana to his Father in Le Havre, France, April 20, 1766.[1]

In a recent issue of the Canadian journal *Acadiensis*, several letters exchanged between Acadians just after the Great Deportation were published.[2] Recently, I had the good fortune recently to discover a copy[3] of a letter—to my knowledge previously unpublished—whose existence was well-known to historians, but which was thought to be lost.[4] This letter was written in April 1766 by Jean-Baptiste Semer, an Acadian recently settled in Louisiana, to his father Germain Semer, a refugee in Le Havre in France. Given its importance for our knowledge of the beginnings of the Acadian settlement in Louisiana, it seemed appropriate to publish the complete transcript here. A number of indications in the letter suggest that it was probably not the first exchange between father and son. Indeed, Jean-Baptiste had already received a letter from his father just before his departure from New Orleans for Attakapas in April 1765. It is also possible that Jean-Baptiste had already sent a first letter to his father, since the father knows where to write to his son and Jean-Baptiste gives few details on the beginning of his journey. Moreover, Germain has a fairly precise knowledge of the previous peregrinations of his son, since he gives an account of them to Mistral, the superintendent of the navy in Le Havre. In a report accompanying the copy of Jean-Baptiste's letter, Mistral conveys some pieces of information to the minister:

An Acadian named Germain Semer who, among those who reside in this port, is regarded as a man of good sense and level-headed, and whose advice they consequcntly follow, came to me to pass on a letter he received from his son, now living in New Orleans. This son stayed in Acadie with the English during the whole period of the war and was among those who in peacetime went from Acadie to St-Domingue to settle at Moule [Mole] St. Nicholas where the intemperate climate not suiting them and causing the death of many of them,[5] Messieurs the governors and intendants of Saint Domingue decided to send the remainder of these Acadians to New Orleans, perhaps even by order of M. le duc de Choiseul. This letter, of which I have the honour to send you an enclosed copy, has made a very deep impression on the man named Germain Semer, as well as on some other Acadians whom he has told about it, and the former came to me to ask permission to go with his family to rejoin his son, provided however that the King was willing to pay the cost of their passage which it is impossible for them to provide for ... I made it known to them that New Orleans belonging today to the King of Spain, I could not grant them permission to go there even at their own expense without your orders. If you don't see, Monseigneur, any drawback to this emigration ... it would be easy with little expense, made once forever, to get them to the Mississippi ... Until you have honoured me, Monseigneur, with your orders on this matter I will not let any of these Acadians leave for this Spanish colony.[6]

Therefore, a previous correspondence had no doubt been established between father and son. It is possible that a letter had been sent from Saint-Domingue before the arrival of the group of Acadians, including Jean-Baptiste, in New Orleans in February, 1765.[7] Germain Semer's subsequent journey can be retraced thanks to research published by G.M. Braud on the Acadians of Nantes.[8] Following the refusal of the minister Praslin in 1766 to let the Acadians depart for New Orleans, Germain Semer and his family resided in Le Havre until 1773 or 1774, then, along with the other Acadians, proceeded on to Chatellerault (Poitou, France), attracted by the offers of the Marquis de Perusse des Cars. Like many of these same Acadians, the Semer family later moved on to settle in Nantes, in 1776.[9] He practiced the trade of carpentry there and resided at the *Hôpital du Sanitat*. Sadly, he was unable to realize his wish of rejoining with his son in Louisiana, as Germain Semer passed away and was buried on December 14, 1782, at the Hotel Dieu of this city.[10]

A copy of the letter written by the man named Jean-Baptiste Semer, to the man named Germain Semer, his father, former inhabitant of Acadie, residing in Le Havre, France, dated New Orleans, Lousiana, April 20, 1766.[11]

> *My very dear father, at the time of my departure for Attakapas,*[12] *I had the honour of receiving yours*[13] *in New Orleans, where I had gone down with about 30 of our Acadians who came to return the King's boats, which had been loaned to us to take our material and our families. We had left last year in April from here [from New Orleans] to go there [to Attakapas] and illnesses having overcome us this last summer, we were in no state to row them [*sic, "ramer" *used here, probably for "ramener," to bring back] until now, but we were once again given others added to those we prepared up there and we are leaving again with our supplies and munitions and other provisions we have made. I gave your letter to the holy hospitaller, Mother Madeleine, who has done a thousand kindnesses for all of us so that she again has the one [kindness] to reply to you, which she does while assuring you, my very dear father, that it is not for want of natural [affection] for you and my very dear mother that I have not had the honour of telling you our news, but the Attakapas are 60 leagues from here and our letter-writers are dead. I will forget myself even sooner than forget you both, the kindnesses that you have done for me are always in my thoughts and I never miss offering them to God in my prayers for your dear preservation and ask of you also the same in return and the continuation of your friendship to both of us and to please me by giving me your*

dear news as often as possible. I will tell you then my very dear father that I arrived here in the month of February 1765 with 202 Acadian persons, including Joseph Brossard,[14] *called Beauplaisir* [sic]*, and all of his family, la Greze and Catalan,*[15] *all coming from Halifax and having passed by the Cape.*[16] *Beausoleil led and paid the passage for those who didn't have the means. After us, there arrived yet another 105 in another ship and then 80, 40, some 20 or 30, in 3 or 4 others. I believe there are about 5 to 600 of us Acadian persons counting women and children. We the first ones have been sent 7 or 8 men to look over the land and locations in order to find a suitable site and we have been told that at Attakapas there were magnificent grasslands with the finest soil in the world.*

M. Aubry[17] *who commanded through the death of M. d'Abbadie*[18] *favored us as much as was possible for him but he has not quite been the master not being assisted by the Ministers of finance. Finally, while we were here we were given a pound and a half of bread and meat for women who were pregnant or nursing and to the disabled at the King's hospital, in sickness, and starting from [?] bread that is, flour for the men equivalent to the rice and "mahy"* [sic, *for "mais," or corn] for the women and children. We went to Attakapas with guns, powder and shot, but as it was already the month of May, the heat being so intense, we started the work in too harsh conditions. There were six plows that worked; we had to break in the oxen, go 15 leagues to get horses. Finally, we had the finest harvest and everybody caught fevers at the same time and nobody being in a state to help anyone else, 33 or 34 died, counting the children. Those who started again wanted to go and work in their wilderness and they fell ill again, but we came down in the month of February 1766 of this year and here we all are, thank God, very well and hoping for a very fine harvest this year, with God's help, having cleared a great deal. We have only to sow and we already have oxen, cows, sheep, horses and the finest hunting in the world, deer, such fat turkey, bears and ducks and all kinds of game. We saw it on the end of our gun. There are several since the death of Beausoleil who came down from Attakapas, among others those of the Rivière de Saint-Jean, and went to settle along the Mississippi river on the German side where the latter have already started a settlement.*

We lack only the good missionaries like we had in Acadie for here there are only a very few Capuchin Fathers. There was a gouty one here that had gone up with us but he was forced to go back down. There is a Spanish governor who likes us very much, who has just arrived with two very zealous Capuchin fathers, but they know only Spanish. We are waiting for others. The land here brings forth a good yield of everything anyone wants to sow. Wheat from France, corn and rice, sweet potatoes, giraumont,[19] *pistachios, all kinds of vegetables, flax, cotton. We lack only people to cultivate it. We produce indigo, sugar, oranges, and peaches here grow like apples in France. They have granted us 6 arpents to married people and 4 and 5 to young men, so we have the advantage, my dear father, of being sure of our land, and of saying I have a place of my own. Wood is very common here, and we do a good trade in it, for construction and for the building of houses at the Cape and other islands. A person who wants to devote himself to property and make an effort will be comfortably off in a few years. It is an immense country; you can come here boldly with my dear mother and all the other Acadian families. They will always be better off than in France. There are neither duties nor taxes to pay and the more one works the more one earns without doing harm to anyone. The religious from here who are Ursulines and who, although they teach the young girls at home, are also responsible for the care of troops at the hospital, have done a great deal of good for all of our Acadians; the girls come there to be taught and they do about an hour of catechism every day at the hospital for the boys of whom they have got more than 40 at various times to make their first communion. This is, dear father, a detailed account of the advantages that we have here and which everyone is very happy about. They promise us missionaries very shortly. There are around 60 families 15 leagues from us, settled at Appellonsa*[20] *who are very happy there.*

The new governor[21] *is coming up to do a tour of all the posts, to build churches and fortify the forts because at the last peace treaty we ceded to the English a large part of the country and we are expecting Spanish troops soon to fortify all the places that France has given away to the Spanish; thus we have a good country. The governor is a man of great distinction, of great piety, who isn't married, who is of superior talent, understands all sorts of languages. We hope for a great deal from his disinterested administration, which is coming from Peru, and has given to poor communities and to shamefully poor people all that it had, having salaries in this place of thirty thousand piastres per year. He was forced to borrow in Havana while coming here. He is a man of rare merit in every respect.*

Lacking paper, I can only assure you of the profound and obedient respect with which I am, my very dear father and mother, your very humble, etc...

(Signature) Jean-Baptiste Semer

Acknowledgement

This letter was originally published in French under the title *Lettre de Jean-Baptiste Semer, de La Nouvelle-Orléans, à son père, au Havre, 20 avril 1766,* in the Canadian journal *Acadiensis, Journal of the History of the Atlantic Region,* XXXIV, 2, spring 2005. It was translated in English by Bey Grieve.

Endnotes

1. This letter was first published in French in the Canadian journal *Acadiensis, Journal of the History of the Atlantic Region*, XXXIV, 2, spring 2005. I wish to warmly thank Bey Grieve for his translation.

2. Jean-François Mouhot, "*Des Revenantes? A propos des "Lettres fantômes" et de la correspondance entre exilés acadiens* (1758-1785)" *Acadiensis*, XXXIV, 1 (Automne 2004).

3. The letter was copied in 1766, by the Department of the Navy so that the Minister of the Navy Praslin, could peruse it. It is this copy—and not the original, which has probably been destroyed—that I had the good fortune to rediscover. It is hard to assess the possible changes made to the original by the copyist. Nevertheless, the precision of the facts mentioned in the letter (and their agreement with what historians have been able to piece together about the Acadien settlement in Louisiana) leads one to think that only stylistic or grammatical touching up has been done to the text, even if one can't exclude the possibility that certain parts perhaps too critical of the conditions of life in France (for example, the passage concerning the "duties and taxes to pay") might have been watered down by order of Mistral, superintendent of the navy in Le Havre. We should also remember that the original letter was not written directly by Semer—who obviously doesn't know how to write—but by "the holy hospitaller, Mother Madeleine."

4. The existence of this letter was until now known only through an allusion of the Minister (Praslin to Mistral, September 13, 1766, *Archives Nationales de France*, Colonies, Series B, vol. 125, folio 450). Praslin summarized in a few words the remarks of Jean-Baptiste Semer and forbade the Acadiens to immigrate to Louisiana. We find a transcription of Praslin's missive in Carl A. Brasseaux, "Phantom Letters: Acadien Correspondence, 1776-1784," *Acadiensis*, XXIII, 2 (Spring 1994): pp. 124-32. Ernest Martin returns to this letter after having written "From 1766 on, an Acadien from Louisiana having written to his parents, repatriated to Le Havre, says how happy he was there, all the refugees of the port had asked to be transported to this land of plenty." (*Les Exilés Acadiens en France au XVIIIe siècle et leur établissement en Poitou*, Paris, Hachette, 1936 p. 87). Brasseaux also refers to this letter in his book *The Founding of New Acadie: The Beginnings of Acadien Life in Louisiana, 1765-1803*, (Louisiana State University Press, 1987) p. 60; in the same book p. 73 and following, the historian tells about the arrival of a group of Acadiens in Louisiana—led by Joseph Brossard [Broussard]—including Semer; the information that he gives corroborates what we find in this letter. Brasseaux alludes again in a general way to the correspondence sent from Louisiana to France (constantly citing Praslin's letter of September 1766) in "A New Acadie: Acadien Migration to South Louisiana, 1764-1803," *Acadiensis*, 15, 1 (1985): pp. 123-32 (p. 129). In this same article, speaking of "letters from Attakapas Acadiens [sent] to relatives in France," Brassaeaux affirms that "none of these letters has survived" (p. 29).

5. Several contemporary memoirs corroborate these remarks. Thus, a "Summary of the difficulties that afflict the commerce of Saint-Domingue," written from the Cap [Français] (cf. note 29 below) by an anonymous author on April 2, 1765 states: "The settlement of Moule [Mole] Saint-Nicolas by Acadien emigrants [is] viewed here as impracticable because of the insalubrity of the air [these families here having almost all succumbed]" (*Archives Départementales* of Gironde, France, C4328). Concerning the passage of Acadiens to Saint-Domingue, see particularly Gabriel Debien, "The Acadiens in Santo-Domingo: 1764-1789," in:

Glenn R. Conrad, *The Cajuns: Essays on their History and Culture* (Lafayette: University of Southwestern Louisiana, 1978), pp. 21-96. This last article contains numerous documents translated into English.

6. Mistral to Praslin, to Le Havre, August 12, 1766, *Archives Nationales de France, fonds marine*, B3 568, f° 317. Until now, we didn't know the response (negative) of Praslin to this request. On the arrival of the first Acadiens in Louisiana, see the works and articles of Brasseaux previously cited.

7. Carl A. Brasseaux, "A New Acadie," art. cit., p.125.

8. Gérard Marc Braud, *Les Acadiens en France: Nantes et Paimboeuf, 1775-1785. Approche Généalogique, Ouest Edition*, 1999 (p. 233).

9. For further details, please see my doctoral dissertation, *Les Acadiens réfugiés en France (1758-1785): l'impossible réintegration?* PhD. Thesis (History), European University Institute, Florence, January 2006.

10. According to G.M. Braud, Germain Semer was born about 1720 at Petcoudiac (a village situated approximately at the present site of Moncton, New Brunswick, Canada) and married Marie Trahan, born about 1725 at Rivière-aux-Canards (Acadie) and died on October 25, 1776, Nantes, Hopital du Sanitat. G.M. Braud specifies that they had several children, but curiously doesn't mention Jean-Baptiste. Here is the list of the Semer children indicated by Braud: Madeleine, born around 1748; Marie-Claire, married to Jerome-Dominique Doulle; Marie-Francoise, born around 1762, Le Havre de Grace, Notre-Dame (Seine-Maritime) parish; married May 30, 1785, Chantenay, St. Martin, to Joseph Boudreau; Grégoire-Dominique, born about 1768. "Grégoire and Marie-Françoise are announced as leaving on l'*Amitié* (n°10) but Marie-Francoise gets married three months before the departure of the ship and will not follow up on her plans. As for her brother, did he leave alone? We don't know points out G.M. Braud. In the lists published by Guy Bugeon and Monique Hivert-Le Faucheux (*Les Acadiens partis de France en 1785 pour la Louisiana: listes d'embarquements*, Poitiers-Rennes, (tapuscrit), 1988) we find a number of Semers on board the *Amitié*; notably, n°10; "Semer, Gregoire (Ropemaker, 16 years old) and his sister Francoise, 24 years old" (p. 37).

11. Attached to Mistral's letter of August 12, 1766. *Archives Nationales de France, fonds marine* B3 568, folio 319ss. [Writing and punctuation partly modernized]

12. District of Louisiana west of New Orleans, on the Bayou Teche. The principal Acadien settlements are: Breaux Bridge; Lafayette; Broussard; St. Martinville; New Iberia; and Abbeville.

13. I received the honour of your letter...

14. On this individual, see the *Dictionnary of Canadian Biography Online* (http://www.biographi.ca).

15. Non-identified individual.

16. The Cap-Haitien, north of the present state of Haiti (formerly Cap-Français, in Saint-Domingue).

17. Charles Philippe Aubry, last French governor of the colony.

18. Jean-Jacques d'Abbadie, governor of Louisiana from 1763 to 1765.

19. "Giraumont or Giraumon: kind of zucchini of America, also called zucchini of Saint-Jean or Iroquois pumpkin" (*Dictionnaire de l'Academie*, 1762)

20. Opelousas Territory, more upstream on the Bayou Teche.

21. Antonio de Ulloa, first Spanish governor of the colony (1766-1768). The visit of Ulloa to the Acadiens is recalled in Brasseaux, "A New Acadie", art. cit., p. 126. The "*bonne entente*" between the Acadiens and the governor was to be of short duration; Ulloa's wish to disperse the Acadiens to secure the Louisiana Territory rapidly gave birth to conflicts which led to the revolt of October 2, 1768 (ibid. p. 128).

NOVA SCOTIA FARM UNITES TWO FAMILIES IN SEARCH OF THEIR PAST

Dean Jobb

On a hot and sunny summer day in 2013, about 30 people gathered in a farmer's field at the eastern end of Nova Scotia's scenic Annapolis Valley to search for their roots. It was no ordinary family reunion and more than a chance to swap genealogical information–they came to help a team of archaeologists uncover their family's history. Thibodeaus and Thibodeauxs from as far away as Louisiana, Texas, California, Arkansas and nearby Maine and New Brunswick took part in an archaeological dig on the site of Village Thibodeau, a community their ancestors founded more than three centuries ago near the present-day town of Windsor. It was a rare chance for members of an Acadian family to connect with their tragic past.

"It's an experience to stand on the native land from which your ancestors were deported," said Don Thibodeaux, a retired accountant from Baton Rouge who has made several pilgrimages to this farm and was soon on his hands and knees, scraping away dirt in search of artifacts. "It's heart-moving and it's emotional."

Photo©Sara Beanlands

Archaeologist Sara Beanlands believes this building, which once stood on the site excavated in the summer of 2013, was home to both the Thibodeaus and her New England ancestors, the Shaws.

Remnants of Village Thibodeau are buried under rolling fields that overlook the muddy St. Croix River in the community of Poplar Grove, about a half-hour's drive from the Grand-Pré National Historic Site and its memorials to the Deportation of 1755. For seven generations, this has been Shaw land–now owners David and Allen Shaw brothers and descendants of New England Planters who arrived from Rhode Island in 1760, operate farms on the property. But before the Acadians were marched into exile, this was Thibodeau land. Pierre Thibodeau, a member of one of Acadia's founding families, settled here in 1690.

Remarkably, for 300 years and counting, these fertile fields have been home to only two families–one Acadian, the other Canadian; one of French descent, the other, English.

And two people on opposite sides of Acadian history–a Thibodeau and a Shaw–have brought them together.

Dick Thibodeau (left) of Maine, who in the 1980s discovered the pre-deportation village of his Acadian ancestor Alexis Thibodeau, joined archaeologist Sara Beanlands for a television interview during the dig.

Photo©Dean Jobb

Dick Thibodeau of Kennebunk, Maine, located to Village Thibodeau in the mid-1980s after devoting many summer vacations to the quest. Armed with a crude map of the area drawn the year after the Deportation, he followed a sharp bend in the river to a site marked "Vil. Tibodeau." It was the Shaw farms, where the occasional discovery of French coins and local landmarks known as French Orchard Hill and the Old French Road had long pointed to the area's Acadian past. It was years before Sara Beanlands, a teenager at the time, learned of Dick Thibodeau's visit, and the discovery kindled her passion for history. They teamed up, gathered evidence of the possible locations of homesteads on the property, and presented their findings when Nova Scotia hosted the CMA in 2004. More than 100 Thibodeau descendants attending the conference were invited to tour David Shaw's farm, cementing the bond between the families.

Archaeologist Sara Beanlands, who organized the dig on the farm that unites the Thibodeaus with her family, the Shaws, holds a fragment of a plate that dates to the 1770s and was likely used by her New England Planter ancestors.

Photo©Dean Jobb

Sara Beanlands, now a professional archaeologist, invited the Thibodeaus back in July 2013 to help excavate a hilltop she is convinced was once the site of an Acadian farmhouse. Family lore says a house was standing on this spot when the Shaws arrived in 1760–a Thibodeau home that escaped destruction during the Deportation–and the newcomers moved in and expanded it over the years. The building, later used as a barn, is gone, but was still standing when Dick Thibodeau found the site.

"When you think about the long history between the Thibodeaus and the Shaws," Beanlands noted, "it's quite fitting that at some point we actually lived in the same home." The dig uncovered shards of china and other artifacts dating to the Planter era. But as the Thibodeaus and the archaeologists overseeing their work probed deeper, they found nuggets of hardened clay mixed with grass–the tell-tale material Acadians used to insulate the walls of their houses. It offered strong evidence that Beanlands is right, that the site was once home to both families.

"Without Sara, none of this would have happened," Dick Thibodeau said as he watched distant relations huddle over the rectangular trenches and use trowels to carefully scrape away the dirt of the centuries. He may have been the first to pinpoint the village's location, he said, but "Sara picked up the ball and carried it."

Photo©Dean Jobb

Therese Thibodeau (right), of Kennebunk, Maine, wife of the site's discoverer, Dick Thibodeau, showed off fragments of china she discovered during the archaeological dig at Village Thibodeau in July 2013.

While other Thibodeaus who took part in the dig had no direct connection to the site, Dick Thibodeau's ancestor, Alexis, lived on this land. He was among those deported to Pennsylvania, where many exiles died of disease or hunger. His branch of the family migrated to Quebec before settling in Maine. "Here we are, back together, on the land of our ancestors," he said.

Gisèle (Thibodeaux) Lavoilette and sister Yvonne Thibodeau, both from New Brunswick, worked their section of trench alongside Irving and Doris Thibodeaux of Morse, Louisiana. "As soon as we see each other, it's just like family," Lavoilette explained of the instant rapport among Thibodeaus scattered across North America. "It's a special thing."

Photo©Dean Jobb

Yvonne Thibodeau (left) and Gisèle Lavoilette, both from New Brunswick, screened a bucket of soil to ensure that tiny artifacts were not missed.

Photo©Dean Jobb

Yvonne Thibodeau (left) and Gisèle Lavoilette worked their portion of trench alongside Irving and Doris Thibodeaux of Morse, Louisiana.

Artifacts found at the site and on an adjacent hilltop, where another Acadian house once stood–everything from buttons and rusted nails to a large chunk of a broken iron cauldron–provide fresh insights into how the Acadians lived. Some of the fragments of their everyday lives were destined for a display case at the nearby Avon River Heritage Museum.

Dick Thibodeau put a lost Acadian village back on the map and built an online community of descendants to spread the word about the site. Sara Beanlands unearthed evidence of a past that two families share, and her aunt and uncle, David and Joanne Shaw, have welcomed countless Thibodeaus to their farm. And Don Thibodeaux, Gisèle Lavoilette, and other Thibodeau descendants have a tangible connection to a family history marred by tragedy, yet infused with hope, endurance and survival.

"It's a very fulfilling thing," said Don Thibodeaux, "to come home."

Photo©Dean Jobb

Thibodeau descendants surrounded archaeologist Sara Beanlands during a break from the dig. "Without Sara, none of this would have happened," said Dick Thibodeau, standing at left. "She's a very special individual."

Photo©Dick Thibodeau

Sara Beanlands (center) took members of the Thibodeau family on a tour of her family's farm near Windsor, Nova Scotia, during the Congrès mondial acadien 2004.

V

Acadian Regional Histories

ACADIANS IN NEW BRUNSWICK

Maurice Basque and Marc Robichaud

The colony of New Brunswick was officially created in 1784, following the arrival of thousands of Loyalists who were fleeing their homeland at the time of the American Revolution. The territory which became the province of New Brunswick had previously been part of Nova Scotia, but the new Loyalists wanted their own province, and pleaded their case that they should have one in return for their loyalty to the British Crown. On the other hand, the territory already had a long and rich history. At least three large aboriginal groups had inhabited it for millennia, and still do: the Mi'kmaq, the Wolastoqiyik (Maliseet), and the Passamaquoddy. These were the First Nations who had welcomed the earliest French pioneers at the very beginning of the 17th century, at the St. Croix Island trading post in 1604. St. Croix marked the beginning of the Acadian adventure.

While the history of the Acadian colony in the 17th century unfolded mainly on peninsular Nova Scotia, in villages such as Port-Royal, Grand-Pré and Beaubassin, there was, nonetheless, a small French presence in the area which became New Brunswick. Fur trading posts would be established at the mouth of the Saint John River, in the Miramichi region, as well as on Miscou Island, and at the mouth of the Népisiguit River. French military authorities would construct small forts on the banks of the Saint John, such as the one found in Jemseg. The first Acadian families would also settle in the region called Trois-Rivières, along the Memramcook, the Petitcodiac and the Chepoudie Rivers. An Acadian village would be built in Chepoudie near the end of the 17th century and the beginning of the 18th century.

The Treaty of Utrecht, in 1713, would completely transform the geopolitical profile of the region that would become Atlantic Canada. France surrendered Acadie, including peninsular Nova Scotia as well as Newfoundland and the immense territory around Hudson's Bay, to Great Britain. It retained Île-Royale (Cape Breton Island), where the imposing fortress and the city of Louisbourg would be built shortly afterwards. It also kept Île Saint-Jean (today's Prince Edward Island).

Meanwhile, New Brunswick was a contested territory, as both Paris and London would lay claim to it, but in reality it belonged to the French until the Seven Years' War. New Acadian settlements would appear in the Trois-Rivières region, in Memramcook, and on the banks of the Petitcodiac, where Dieppe and Moncton now stand. A larger Acadian settlement would be founded in Sainte-

Anne-des-Pays-Bas (today's Fredericton). The Mésagouèche River, which now forms the boundary between Nova Scotia and New Brunswick, was at this time the border between what historians label English Acadie and French Acadie.

Once the French military forces built Fort Beauséjour and Fort Gaspereau, in 1751, Acadian families were spurred to leave Nova Scotia and seek the protection of Fort Beauséjour. One of the great architects of this evacuation was a French abbot, Jean-Louis LeLoutre, who had dreamed of rebuilding a new French Acadie, in close co-operation with the military authorities of Louisbourg and Quebec, and with the support of the Court of Versailles and the help of Mi'kmaq allies. It bears noting that LeLoutre himself, in complicity with the French military and the Mi'kmaq, had ordered the Acadian village of Beaubassin burned in 1750. Hundreds of Acadian families were thus forced to retreat to the French side of the Mésagouèche River, which was under the protection of the far-off King Louis XV of France, known as "*le Bien-aimé*" or the Beloved.

But the promises of French military protection would no longer hold up in 1755: at that time, Fort Beauséjour was captured by the British during an expedition from Massachusetts. A short time later, on July 25, 1755, the Nova Scotia Council ordered the deportation of Acadians from the region, starting precisely with those living in the Isthmus of Chignectou. Several Acadian families who had settled in New Brunswick would be captured by British troops or the militia from New England, and deported to the Thirteen Colonies, the British territory along the Atlantic coast that would become the future United States of America.

Thousands of other Acadians would take refuge in the Miramichi region, in what was called Camp Espérance. Others would flee to Shippagan, Miscou, Caraquet, and the surrounding areas, and some families would push on as far as the St. Lawrence Valley, where they would become the first Acadian pioneers in Quebec. The Expulsion would leave deep scars on the territory and on the collective memory of the Acadian people, who would never be able to forget the destruction of Sainte-Anne-des-Pays-Bas in 1759, or the battles against the British by Acadian resisters on the banks of the Petitcodiac, to name but two incidents. Finally, at the Battle of Restigouche in 1760, the French, supported by the Acadian and Mi'kmaq militia, fought and lost their last battle against the British. After the fall of Quebec and Montreal, the Treaty of Paris confirmed in 1763 that Great Britain would rule Canada, including Acadie. France would be left only the tiny archipelago of the Saint-Pierre and Miquelon Islands.

Colonial Acadie may have existed and then been wiped from the map, but the same cannot be said of the Acadians, who proved to be extraordinarily resilient. Particularly after 1764, when the British authorities granted them permission to settle or return to the Maritimes, they worked tirelessly to rebuild a new Acadie in three large areas: southeastern, northeastern, and northwestern New Brunswick. Despite the arrival of new English-speaking pioneers, including the Planters and the Loyalists, Acadians formed a population of a few thousand at the beginning of the 19th century, living in Memramcook, Bouctouche, Néguac, Tracadie, Shippagan, Caraquet, Népisiguit, and Saint-Basile. Despite the fact that New Brunswick was officially established by Loyalists in 1784, Acadians gradually and quietly started to have a voice in its affairs. In 1810, the province passed a law allowing Catholics to vote in elections for members of the Legislative Assembly, but it was not until 1846 that a prosperous farmer from the Memramcook Valley named Amand Landry would become the first Acadian elected to a seat in the provincial legislature.

For Acadians in New Brunswick, the first half of the 19th century was characterized by diligent efforts to regain their previous status and way of life. Before 1755, the Acadian people had consisted mainly of successful farmers. But things were much different afterwards. The best farmland, along the Saint John River, for example, was occupied by the Planters and Loyalists.

Acadian farmers in the areas of Madawaska and the Memramcook Valley were better off, however. It is no coincidence that these regions were home to the first Acadian MLAs (Members of the Legislative Assembly) and the first colleges and convents, such as the Saint-Thomas Seminary in Memramcook, founded in 1854; the Madawaska Female Academy in Saint-Basile, in 1857; and the *Collège Saint-Joseph* in Memramcook, in 1864. In the tiny coastal villages in northeastern New Brunswick, and especially on the Acadian Peninsula, Acadian families cobbled together a meager existence from fishing, a bit of farming, and working in lumber camps.

At the time, the economies of many local communities on the shores of the Gulf of the St. Lawrence were dominated by large Anglo-Norman fishing companies, based out of Jersey, to which a significant portion of these Acadian families were indebted. This situation would persist until the beginning of the 20th century. Already, in the early years of the 19th century, two strata of Acadian society had emerged. One, in Madawaska and the southeastern section of the province, was better positioned to take its place in the new provincial economic structures. The other, on the Acadian Peninsula, was hit hard by the increasing capitalism, which could rightly be qualified as brutal.

Nonetheless, two things remained constant in Acadian society. The first was the strong influence of the Catholic clergy, mainly from France and Quebec, and the second was the survival of the French language, which managed to stand up against the arrival of more and more newcomers from the British Isles, especially the thousands of Irish Catholics fleeing the devastating Potato Famine in their homeland in the 1840s. Among the Irish immigrants, numerous Catholic priests would take up leadership roles in the ecclesiastical structures of New Brunswick, to the great detriment of the first-generation French-Canadian priests. The latter, including Antoine Gagnon, an abbot from the province of Quebec, or the young abbot Marcel-François Richard, from Saint-Louis-de-Kent, New Brunswick, who became extremely vocal, demanding that Catholic dioceses which were mainly Acadian be placed under the supervision of a bishop who was Acadian, or at least a francophone. They received no response to their grievances for many years. The first Acadian bishop in New Brunswick was not appointed until 1912, in the diocese of *Saint John*; this was Fr. Édouard-Alfred LeBlanc, an Acadian abbot from the Baie Sainte-Marie region in Nova Scotia.

In the second half of the 19th century, there was a reawakening in Acadian society in the Maritimes. This rebirth has been called the "Acadian Renaissance" by many historians. Starting in the 1860s, a small but mighty Acadian elite, composed of members of the clergy, merchants, teachers, lawyers, doctors, and politicians, insisted more and more strongly that Acadians be considered full members of New Brunswick society, on equal footing with their Catholic and Protestant English-speaking neighbors.

The founding of the *Collège Saint-Joseph de Memramcook*, in 1864, directed by priests from the Order of the Holy Cross who had come from Quebec, was a major contributing factor to the Acadian rebirth. Another was the first Acadian newspaper, *Le Moniteur Acadien*, which was started in Shédiac in 1867 and which gave rise to other newspapers in the years that followed, such as Bathurst's *Le Courrier des provinces maritimes* in 1885, Moncton's well-known *L'Évangéline* in 1905, and Edmundston's weekly newspaper, *Le Madawaska*, in 1913.

The compelling debates around the Confederation of Canada in 1867 would make it possible for members of the Acadian elite to hone their skills in federal politics, given the fact that the first French-speaking Member of Parliament from New Brunswick, Auguste Renaud, was elected that year. One of the most important leaders of the Acadian Renaissance, writer and scholar Pascal Poirier, would become the first Acadian senator in 1885, while Pierre-Amand Landry, who became the first Acadian lawyer in New Brunswick, in 1871, would be appointed judge in 1890, making him the first Acadian to hold this position in the Provincial Court.

The Acadian Renaissance was not simply a series of new gains and victories for the Acadian elite, however. Acadians would also witness major setbacks, such as the law on non-sectarian schools, the Common Schools Act, passed by the government of New Brunswick in 1871, which caused ripples that were felt at the Parliament in Ottawa and would end, at least in part, in the unfortunate incident known as the "Louis Mailloux Affair," in 1875.

The Common Schools Act had a considerable and deeply-felt impact on the way Catholic schools evolved in the province. Some had to close their doors due to a lack of public funds. This was what happened to the *Académie de Madawaska* in Saint-Basile, which closed in 1873. One of the strategies the Catholic leaders in the province devised to deal with the law was to call on well-established women's religious orders in Quebec to establish convents in New Brunswick, in order to take charge of existing educational institutions or to start new ones, such as those that were started by nuns in Bathurst, Bouctouche, Caraquet, Memramcook, Saint-Basile, Saint-Louis-de-Kent, and Tracadie. The village of Saint-Louis-de-Kent would sponsor an initiative, under the guidance of Fr. Marcel-François Richard, to open a college for boys in 1876. Néguac would try to do the same in the 1880s, but would not have the same success. Moreover, certain notable Acadian figures would use the provisions of the Common Schools Act to have schools built and funded by the public purse, as they did with the "superior school" in Petit-Rocher, built in 1888.

The 1871 act would serve as a catalyst, propelling a number of Acadian leaders onto the provincial stage to fight for the French language and Acadians in general to have their rightful place. Their speeches could be heard at Acadian National Conventions, the first of which was held in Memramcook in 1881. The national symbols adopted at these conventions—the Feast of the Assumption, as the Acadian national holiday; Our Lady of Assumption as the Patron Saint of

Acadians; the gold *stella maris* on a red, white, and blue background as the flag; *Ave Maris Stella* as the anthem—were tangible demonstrations of the desire to proclaim a unique French-language identity in the newly-formed Canadian Confederation, an identity distinct from the largest francophone group, the French-Canadians. New Acadian infrastructures would be established: schools, convents, newspapers, and associations such as the *Société Mutuelle l'Assomption*, founded in 1903, and so forth. Acadian society, at least in terms of its elite, now had a stronger voice in the discussions, debates, and conversations about the important issues of the day.

The First World War, from 1914 to 1918, would shake Acadian society to the core, just as it would the Canadian population as a whole. Many Acadians would fight in the war, and Acadian women would serve as nursing officers ("bluebirds"). Newspapers from this period, such as *L'Évangéline*, overflowed with articles describing the numerous activities organized in Acadian villages to support the soldiers and the war effort in general. In a way, the first global conflict brought Acadian society into modernity.

Soon there were new forms of transportation and communication, such as the automobile and the radio. This technological revolution would not be entirely positive, though, because it would lead to a large mass of Acadians leaving the area for the United States and the central and western Canadian provinces in search of work. Jobs had disappeared from the Maritimes because of profound changes in the regional economy. In terms of language, this movement to what was often called "the States," as well the migration to urban centers which were primarily English-speaking–such as Moncton, Saint John, and Fredericton–weakened the francophone foundations on which Acadian society was built. In the years to come there would be a growing tendency for Acadians to slip into English as their usual language. Their struggle against the threat of English assimilation has certainly not yet been won.

Acadians in Prince Edward Island

Georges Arsenault

At first glance, a visitor to Prince Edward Island would never guess that a quarter of the Island's population is of Acadian or French ancestry. Its inhabitants, including Acadians, are seldom aware of this fact themselves. Over the years, numerous marriages into the dominant population of British origin, the decline of the French language, and the Anglicization of many family names have camouflaged an important part of the island's Acadian heritage. It is not evident to most people that familiar island surnames such as Perry, Deagle, Myers, Burke, Peters, and Wedge were once—in most cases—Poirier, Daigle, Maillet, Bourque, Pitre, and Aucoin.

The Acadians are the descendants of the French colonists who settled in Acadie in the 1600s. This French colony then roughly covered the Maritime Provinces, the eastern coast of Maine, and part of the Gaspé peninsula. The colonists, most of whom originated from the western part of central France, settled mainly around the Bay of Fundy, where they diked and drained the marshlands for arable soil, farming the land and raising livestock.

The Acadians were eventually able to reach a certain degree of prosperity despite the fact that they were living in a politically unstable colony. Situated between New England and New France, and close to some of the world's richest fishing grounds, Acadie was a strategic territory for both Britain and France. As a result of the continuing battles between the two superpowers, the Acadians lived alternately under French and British rule.

In 1713, according to the Treaty of Utrecht, France was forced to hand over to Great Britain its colonies of Acadie and Newfoundland. To offset its losses and to protect its important cod industry, the French government decided to develop Cape Breton Island (renamed Île Royale) and Prince Edward Island (then called Île Saint-Jean).

The task of bringing settlers to colonize Île Saint-Jean was given to an entrepreneur from Normandy, the Comte de Saint-Pierre, who founded the *Compagnie de l'Île Saint-Jean*. In the spring of 1720, the Company sent to the island some 200 French settlers and fishermen. Upon their arrival, fortifications were built at Port-la-Joye near present-day Charlottetown, which was chosen as the administrative capital of the colony.

Most of the colonists were brought, however, to the north shore of the island, closer to the cod-fishing grounds where the settlement of Havre Saint-

Pierre (St. Peter's Harbor) was established in honor of the company's founder. Throughout the French period, Havre Saint-Pierre was the island's most important settlement.

The first Acadian families came to the island in 1720, the same year the French settlers arrived. French authorities in fact encouraged the Acadians, living under British rule in Nova Scotia since 1713, to move to French territory.

One of the first Acadian families to settle on Île Saint-Jean was that of Michel Haché (*dit* Gallant) and Anne Cormier. They are the ancestors of all the Hachés and Gallants in North America. They settled at Port-la-Joye, where Michel was harbor master. The surname Gallant is one of the most common family names on the island today. Another frequently occurring Acadian family name is Arsenault. The first members of that large family came to the island in 1728, and settled on the shores of Malpeque Bay.

The colony of Île Saint-Jean never really prospered. As a result of financial problems, the *Compagnie de l'Île Saint-Jean* abandoned the island in 1724, and many colonists left. Acadians were hesitant to abandon their rich farmlands in Nova Scotia, which were under British rule, for a new beginning on Île Saint-Jean, a French possession. But in 1735, 15 years after its founding, the colony's population was made up of only 432 persons, 162 of whom were Acadians. The French-born settlers, mainly oriented towards the fisheries, would, however, eventually be outnumbered by Acadian families who did continue to cross over from the mainland in small numbers.

A drastic change occurred in 1749 when a sudden shift in British policy with regard to Nova Scotia triggered another wave of immigration to the island. Protestant settlers loyal to the British Crown were brought to Nova Scotia, new fortifications were raised (including the Halifax citadel) and Acadians there were pressed into taking an unconditional oath of allegiance to the English Monarch or face expulsion from their lands.

Many Acadians living in Beaubassin, Pisiquid, Grand-Pré, and Port-Royal became concerned about their safety and moved to Île Saint-Jean. Within five years, the population of the colony jumped from 735 to 2,223. It also increased significantly when the Deportation began on the mainland in 1755. It is estimated that the island population of French origin was 4,250 in 1758.

The years between 1749 and 1758 were very difficult ones for both the Acadian refugees and the early settlers. Various disasters destroyed the crops, cattle were lost through sickness and lack of fodder, and seeds were difficult to obtain. The colony was most often on the brink of famine. A letter written in 1753 by the parish priest of Point Prime, Abbé Jacques Girard, well illustrates the conditions under which many people were living: "Our refugees do not lose courage, and hope by working to be able to live; but the nakedness which is almost universal and extreme affects them sore; I assure you they cannot protect themselves from the cold, either by day or night. Most of the children have so few garments that they cannot cover themselves.... Not all are reduced to this extremity, but most of them are in great need."

On Île Saint-Jean, any hopes the Acadians had of living peacefully were shattered when the fortress of Louisbourg on Île Royale was attacked by British troops in the summer of 1758. The French capitulated, thereby forfeiting Île Saint-Jean as well, with disastrous results for the Acadians. Soldiers were sent to the island with orders to deport the inhabitants to France. More than half of those who were deported died by drowning or disease during the voyage, and many others died in poverty in the months following their arrival in France.

Later in the fall, some 3,000 Islanders were rounded up and crowded onto ships that set sail for Europe. Of those remaining, an estimated 1,100 of the islanders managed to escape deportation by fleeing to the Bay of Chaleurs region and to Quebec, but many died there of sickness and starvation. Only a few families managed to remain on the island.

Obviously some Acadian families later came back to the island; some returned just a few years after their expulsion by the British. Many of them had been recruited as fishermen by British entrepreneurs, while others returned to rejoin members of their families. They arrived from New Brunswick, the Magdalen Islands, and the French islands of Saint-Pierre and Miquelon, and a few of them arrived from France. By 1798, 116 Acadian families were living on the island in three clan-like communities: Malpeque in Prince County, Rustico in Queen's County, and Fortune Bay in King's County.

In the 50 years that followed the Deportation, Acadians sought not only to rebuild a homeland, but also to reunite a society scattered throughout the world. Those who came back to establish themselves on what the British now called St. John's Island still suffered innumerable hardships, this time caused by the land tenure system.

In order to stay on Prince Edward Island, the Acadians, like other settlers, were forced to become tenants to British landlords. Relations were somewhat strained between the Acadians and their landlords since they were often unable to pay the rent and in some cases were victims of dishonest practices. Under such circumstances, they were forced to resettle several times, thus splitting the Acadian population into small groups scattered over the island and the mainland. The moves from one area to another weakened the demographic and geographic concentration of the Acadian community, which was gradually surrounded by, and even intermingled with, people of another culture and language.

However, until the middle of the 19th century, the entire Acadian population on the island succeeded quite well in closing itself off from outside cultural influences, despite the fact that it was broken up into small farming and fishing communities relatively isolated from one another. They remained deeply attached to the Roman Catholic Church, their language, their traditional dress, and to their festivals such as *Chandeleur* (Candlemas), *Mi-Carême* (Mid-Lent), *Mardi Gras* (Shrove Tuesday), and other celebrations, some of which have been kept alive to this day.

Important changes began to take place in the island's Acadian community in the 1860s. It was a period of Acadian renewal, which expressed itself throughout the Maritime Provinces. A number of institutions were founded to further the development of the Acadian community. In Rustico, Fr. Georges-Antoine Belcourt and his parishioners created the Farmers Bank of Rustico, a precursor to the Credit Union and *Caisse Populaire* movements in North America. At the same time, convent schools were opened in a few Acadian parishes on the island. During this period, young Acadian men began to enter politics, business, and the professions.

But in order to integrate themselves into the island's dominant anglophone culture and society, Acadians had to master the English language. In the 1860s and 1870s, the island government even passed several amendments to the School Act, forcing Acadian schools to anglicize the teaching program.

The cultural isolation of the community was quickly eroded. Acadian leaders soon realized that this rapid integration into mainstream society was being done at the risk of completely banishing both the French language and Acadian culture from the island landscape, a peril which was also felt in the other Maritime Provinces. As a result, an Acadian nationalism movement was born. Important conventions were held to find ways to preserve and stimulate the Acadian identity. One such convention was held in Miscouche in 1884, where the Acadian flag and anthem were selected.

Among many local initiatives was the 1893 publication of the island's first French-language newspaper, *L'Impartial*. That year, an Acadian Teachers' Association was organized to promote the teaching of French in the public school system. At its 1919 annual convention, the *Société Saint-Thomas-d'Aquin* was created to promote the development of the Acadian community, in particular by overseeing the formation of Acadian leaders through higher education.

Today, many organizations on the island have as their mandate the promotion and development of the French language and the Acadian culture. However, the *Société Saint-Thomas-d'Aquin* is recognized as the principal voice of the island Acadian community. It has been instrumental in setting up many projects and institutions that have given dynamism and visibility to the island Acadian community.

A few examples of the vibrant Acadian presence in Prince Edward Island today are the weekly newspaper, *La Voix acadienne*, published in Summerside, the French-language school and community centers, the *Collège Acadie Î.-P.-É.*, the Acadian Museum in Miscouche, the *Festival acadien* in the Evangeline Region, and the numerous musicians and singers, such as Angèle Arsenault from Egmont Bay and Lennie Gallant from Rustico.

Although Acadians on the island have not had an easy time preserving their language and culture, they have won a number of significant battles over the past few decades. In 1979, for example, there was only one French-language school on the island, and it was located in the heart of the Evangeline Region. Today there are six schools, scattered from one end of the island to the other, where children can receive their education in French.

The forces of assimilation will never disappear, but federal and provincial laws now ensure that the French language is better protected than it was in the past. According to the 2011 federal census, 3.8 percent of Islanders (2,465) have French as their mother tongue. However, 12 percent (17,000) have claimed a knowledge of the French language.

In the year 2020, Prince Edward Island, Canada's smallest province, will be celebrating the tricentennial of an Acadian and French presence. After 300 years of surviving against all odds, Island Acadians have every reason to be proud of their accomplishments and confident that they will celebrate other cultural milestones.

Photo©Georges Arsenault

The annual Acadian Festival and Agricultural Exhibition of the Evangeline Region is the biggest Acadian celebration in the province. The agricultural exhibition was started in 1903, whereas the Acadian Festival portion was inaugurated in 1971. The mass celebrated aboard fishing boats is one of the popular activities.

Photo©Georges Arsenault

The Notre-Dame-du-Mont-Carmel church was built in 1898. The Mont-Carmel parish is one of the island's most francophone parishes. Most of the Acadian parishioners are Arsenaults, Aucoins, Bernards, Gallants, Poiriers, and Richards.

Photo©Sylvia Arsenault Collection

In 1917, the Honorable Aubin-Edmond Arsenault (1870-1968), a lawyer and judge born in Abrams Village, became Premier of Prince Edward Island. He is the first Acadian to become the premier of a Canadian province.

Acadians in Nova Scotia –from 1764 to the Present

Marie-Claude Rioux

In 1755, prior to the beginning of the Deportation, over 15,000 Acadians lived in the current territory of Nova Scotia. In 1763, only 1,500 Acadians remained in the province, most of whom were refugees or prisoners who had been liberated. Starting in 1764, the deportees obtained permission to return to the former territory of Acadie. This did not come without its challenges. Land, once occupied by these first pioneers, was taken by Planters: anglophone immigrants from American colonies. Acadians were therefore reduced to settling on infertile land, where families were isolated from each other. They then turned to the sea to provide for their subsistence. Today, 35,000 proud Acadians of Nova Scotia speak French as their first language, of the some 100,000 Acadian-origin inhabitants in the province.

Rural Acadian Communities

Par-en-bas (Municipality of Argyle)

It was in 1653 that Charles de la Tour, governor of Acadie at the time, granted land to Philippe Mius d'Entremont, thus also awarding him the title of baron. The barony of Pobomcoup, later to become Pubnico, was born. One hundred years later, the area's Acadians did not escape the Deportation. However, contrary to other Acadians who saw their land confiscated, the families of the deportees returned to the area they once occupied, starting in 1767 and settling on the west side of the harbor. West Pubnico is the oldest Acadian village to still be occupied by Acadians. Nova Scotia's only *Village historique acadien de la Nouvelle-Écosse*, the *Musée Acadien,* and the Genealogy Research Centre have been established there for those who would like to retrace their Acadian roots.

The Par-en-Bas area is characterized by a complex network of straits, inlets, and islands and give each of its villages a distinct personality. In neighboring villages close to Pubnico, are the Wedgeport Tuna Museum, the spectacular Sainte-Anne-du-Ruisseau wooden church and in Tusket, Canada's oldest courthouse.

Baie Saint-Marie (Municipality of Clare)

In 1768, the government of Nova Scotia granted its first concessions to its Acadian inhabitants, who then settled between the towns of Saint Bernard and Church Point. By the mid-1770s, some 30 families were already established in this area. The towns of Petit-Ruisseau and Meteghan (Mi'kmaq name meaning Blue Rock) would later be founded by the area's second generation of Acadians. By 1850, the area would stretch to Salmon River.

With a coastline covering a distance of close to 40 kilometers and including 15 villages from Saint-Bernard to Salmon River, St. Mary's Bay and its surroundings is the largest Acadian area of Nova Scotia, with a population of 8,800 inhabitants. Today, the Meteghan port possesses a large dock, where it is not unusual to see up to 100 boats moored. Canada's largest fishing business held by the same family, Comeau's Sea Foods, has its head office in Saulnierville. *Université Sainte-Anne*, Nova Scotia's only French language university, has its main campus and head office in Church Point. The Église Sainte-Marie, the tallest wooden building in North America, and the excellent Acadian Museum, *Le Rendez-Vous de la Baie* are also in Church Point.

In addition to its Acadian heritage buildings, you'll discover many art galleries as you visit the area, while tuning in to CIFA community radio, broadcast throughout southwestern Nova Scotia. During the summer months, many festivals are held, including *Musique de la Baie,* the *Festival de la parole* and the *Festival acadien de Clare*, which was founded in 1955, and is the oldest Acadian festival in the world.

Chéticamp (Cape Breton)

A fishing outpost originally occupied by Jersey Islanders starting in the late 1760s, Chéticamp was founded in 1785 by its first permanent inhabitants. In 1790, 14 Acadians were awarded a first concession of 7,000 acres. Starting in 1915, Cheticamp's Acadians worked to develop one of the strongest cooperative movements in Nova Scotia.

A picturesque village bordering the Cape Breton Highlands National Park and the Gulf of Saint Lawrence, the natural beauty of the Chéticamp area cannot be overstated. Its Acadian villages bear evocative names like Petit-Étang, Grand-Étang, Terre Noire, Saint-Joseph-du-Moine, Collet-à-l'Orignal, and Anse-du-bois-marié. *Les Trois Pignons* cultural center is home to the CKJM community radio station, a hooked rug museum, and genealogical center. Chéticamp also offers unique cultural events, including the *Festival de l'Éscaouette,* a carnavalesque atmosphere during mid-Lent, and numerous plays.

Isle Madame (Cape Breton)

Attracted by the abundant fish and game in the area, the French, Basques, and English have been frequenting Isle Madame seasonally for a very long time. In 1767, France invited the Acadian Deportation victims in the Saint Pierre and Miquelon archipelago to leave. Some went to France and others chose to return to Acadie, where the Halifax government offered them land in the Isle Madame area.

Located southwest of Cape Breton, Isle Madame is in fact made up of a series of islands and islets: Petit-de-Grat, Arichat, Martinique, Samson's Cove,

Boudreauville, Cap-La-Ronde, D'Escousse, Petite-Anse, and Poirierville. Isle Madame is the perfect place for long bike rides, shellfish harvesting, beach walks, and seabird watching along the Cap Auguet Eco Trail. *La Picasse* is a cultural and community center that houses a café, an arts and crafts shop, and a regional library. The Ardoise and Petit-de-Grat Acadian festivals offer numerous summer activities.

Pomquet

This town was founded in 1774 by five families of Acadian refugees from Saint-Malo, France: the Broussards, Doirons, Duons, Lamarres, and Vincents. Between 1789 and 1792, other Acadian families—the Boudreaus, Landrys, Melansons and Rosias—joined the founding families.

Today Pomquet is characterized by its provincial nature park and beach—the warmest in Acadie of Nova Scotia—and a series of 13 dunes measuring four kilometers (2.4 miles). Numerous bird species, some of which are rare, like the piping plover, as well as minks and even bears reside here. Among the area's attractions are the *Chez Deslauriers* heritage home, an interpretive centre and Église Sainte-Croix, built in 1861.

Cities with an Acadian Presence

Halifax

Founded in 1749, Halifax is the provincial capital and the Atlantic Province's biggest city. Over 10,000 Acadians live in Halifax, which also hosts other francophone communities: Québécois, Europeans, and a large Lebanese population.

Halifax is home to Canada's most important naval base, due in part to its having the second largest ice-free natural harbor in the world, making it a strategic point for international trade. The city has many important historical sites, including the Nova Scotia Legislative Assembly, where Canada's first assembly of elected representative was held in 1758. The Canadian Museum of Immigration, at Pier 21, celebrates the historic contribution of the city as a port of entry for newcomers to Canada. There is also a museum dedicated to nautical themes called the Maritime Museum of the Atlantic.

The *Maison acadienne* houses several provincial Acadian organizations, including the *Fédération acadienne de la Nouvelle-Écosse*, the *Conseil jeunesse provincial*, the *Fédération culturelle acadienne de la Nouvelle-Écosse,* the *Fédération des femmes acadiennes de la Nouvelle-Écosse*, the *Fédération des parents acadiens de la Nouvelle-Écosse* and the *Regroupement des aînées et aînés de la Nouvelle-Écosse.* Located not far from the *Maison acadienne,* the *Conseil communautaire du Grand-Havre* offers programs, services, and community activities to francophones in the area. A mere 30 minutes from Halifax are the Acadian villages of West Chezzetcook and Grand-Désert, which also has an Acadian museum.

Sydney

Founded in 1785 by Colonel Joseph Frederick Wallet DesBarres, a Swiss Huguenot, Sydney was the capital of the British colony of Cape Breton, between 1784 and 1820. During the Second World War, Sydney was a very important port, its coal and steel greatly contributing to the Allied war effort. Every year, North Sydney welcomes many cruise ships and is the home port for a ferry that crosses between Nova Scotia and Newfoundland. The *Centre scolaire communautaire Étoile de l'Acadie* is used as a francophone gathering place in this second-largest Nova Scotian city.

Located 50 km (30 miles) from the city, Fort Louisbourg is a National Historic Site of Canada. Taken by the English in 1758, the 18th-century French fortress was rebuilt and showcases inhabited houses and cultural activities during the summer months.

Other Towns

Bridgewater (once Cap de la Hève) was the first area to be identified and documented by Samuel de Champlain, in 1604. Truro (formerly Cobequit) was originally a small Acadian agricultural community that became an important rail hub starting in the mid-17th century. At Annapolis Royal (formerly Port-Royal), you'll be able to visit the Port-Royal Habitation, a National Historic Site of Canada, that is a reconstruction of the first French colony in North America. Close to Wolfville is Grand-Pré, a National Historic Site of Canada. It is by far the most famous of Acadian sites, and offers visitors the opportunity to learn more about the Acadian Deportation. While gathering in the commemorative church, visitors can admire its beautiful bronze statues, including one of Evangeline. This place of memory for Acadians was recognized as a UNESCO world heritage site in 2012.

Acknowledgements

Written in cooperation with the *Fédération acadienne de la Nouvelle-Écosse.*

ACADIAN MIGRATIONS TO QUEBEC —1755 TO THE PRESENT

André-Carl Vachon

Epic legends tell of Acadians walking distances of more than 500 kilometers (310 miles) in the years following the Deportation to take refuge in Quebec. Is this fact or fantasy? How many Acadians sought a safe haven in Quebec? Did they only settle within the borders of what is now Quebec in the decade after the Expulsion?

In this article, I will discuss the different waves of Acadians moving to Quebec, starting in 1755 and continuing up to the 20th century. I will be reviewing the history of Acadian migration over three periods: the refugees arriving in Quebec between 1755 and 1763; the deported Acadians who emigrated to the Province of Quebec from 1766 to 1775;[1] and the migrations of Acadians in the 19th century and into the 20th century. I will present only the major waves of Acadian settlement in this article; it would be impossible to account for all the individuals or small family units who moved to Quebec during these periods.

Acadian Refugees 1755 to 1763

Starting in the fall of 1755, a few months after the deportations began (1755, 1756, 1758, 1759, and 1762), exiles landed in the port of Quebec City. The first refugees were from Île Saint-Jean (Prince Edward Island). Were they Acadians? Actually, no; there was only one Acadian, Catherine Doiron, wife of François Turcot, a Frenchman from Anjou, as well as her niece, Marguerite Nogues, wife of Jean Nogues and daughter of Magdeleine Doiron (an Acadian). The other refugees had been born in France and in Switzerland. In April 1756, this first group of refugees moved to the first *petite Cadie* ("Little Cadie")[2] settlement, located in south of Saint-Charles-de-Bellechasse, where the town of Saint-Gervais would later be located.

In a letter dated August 6, 1756, from the Governor General of New France, Marquis Pierre de Rigaud de Vaudreuil de Cavagnial, we can read that the only area where Acadians could find refuge was the *Camp d'Espérance* in Miramichi (in what is now New Brunswick). In another letter written the same day, we learn that, as an exception and as relief for the population suffering from famine, a number of Acadian families had relocated to Quebec. In a letter dated August 7, we discover that Gov. Vaudreuil had given the order to send

Acadians, unable to take care of themselves, to Quebec City. In other words, the governor had authorized Acadians to take refuge in Quebec.

Three groups of Acadians arrived in the port of Quebec in 1756, on the approximate dates of June 22, August 17, and October 18. They were all from Île Saint-Jean. Each group consisted of about 200 Acadians. Fr. Jean-Baptiste de La Brosse, a missionary working in Acadie, accompanied the last group. On October 26, some families of the Lejeune clan were sent on to the Île d'Orléans.

In 1757, six convoys of Acadians found refuge in the port of Quebec: on or about June 13, 120 Acadians arrived from the Miramichi. On July 10, approximately 200 more arrived from Sainte-Anne-des-Pays-Bas, via the Miramichi with about 160 more arriving on August 18, accompanied by a Spiritan priest, Fr. François Le Guerne. On October 16, 150 Acadians arrived, likely from the Miramichi, along with Charles Deschamps de Boishébert, an army officer. On October 20, 125 more Acadians arrived from Île Saint-Jean, with another 137 to 150 arriving later on November 8.

Other Acadians traveled by canoe up the Saint John River (in what is now New Brunswick) until they reached Lake Témiscouata, made a portage, returned to their canoes and continued paddling up the river to Trois-Pistoles (or Rivière-du-Loup). They took up residence in the area from Trois-Pistoles to Montmagny. This was the case of the Jean-Baptiste Raymond family from Kamouraska, who had been on the *Pembroke*, the only boat to escape the Expulsion.

The Acadian exiles were impoverished, lacking everything from food to clothing to supplies. They had fled with the bare minimum and some also suffered from smallpox. From November 1, 1757, to March 1, 1758, no fewer than 335 Acadians were buried in *Notre-Dame-de-Québec*. Between 1756 and 1759, 488 Acadians in Quebec City lost their lives,[3] dying of malnutrition, exhaustion, exposure to the cold, or smallpox. Acadians caught smallpox through contact either with the passengers, (who were French military men), sailors travelling on the *Léopard* (1756), or British soldiers from Halifax, the location of an epidemic in 1757.

On May 30, 1758, an entry in the Marquis de Montcalm's journal tells us that the Abenaki found nine Acadians who had been deported to Massachusetts, and that the Abenaki had taken the Acadians with them. In the spring of 1759, a group of a dozen Acadian families from the Saint John River Valley found refuge in the Kamouraska area. This brings the total of Acadian exiles living in Quebec to approximately 200, including 25 families who settled in the region between Trois-Pistoles and Montmagny. Then, on May 30, 1759, Montcalm wrote in his journal that three Acadians and a Frenchman managed to escape to Montreal after a 25-day journey on foot from Boston. These refugees confirmed the rumor that the British were planning to invade Canada. A few months later, on July 5, 1759, 21 Acadian women landed safely at the port of Quebec.

In 1759, Acadian refugees living in Quebec began to move to different locations, and several of them left the port of Quebec. They had different reasons for leaving: Acadians settled in and around Trois-Rivières and Montreal, especially in L'Assomption, in compliance with the orders given by Gov. Vaudreuil on April 1, 1759. This is how the second and third "Little Cadies" were founded, in Saint-Jacques-de-la-Nouvelle-Acadie (Saint Jacques) and Sainte-Marguerite (Saint-Grégoire-de-Nicolet).

Another reason for Acadian mobility was Gen. Monckton's authorization, issued in November 1759, for approximately 200 to return to Sainte-Anne-des-Pays-Bas, in what is now Fredericton, New Brunswick, in the French colony of Acadie. Unfortunately, those who returned were imprisoned by the British authorities as soon as they arrived.

After the Deportation from Île Saint-Jean (Prince Edward Island) in 1758, several residents of Malpeque fled and took refuge in Petite-Rochelle (today's Pointe-à-la-Croix, Quebec), in Miramichi, and elsewhere. After the Battle of the Restigouche and the fall of Petite-Rochelle (October 24, 1760), the Acadian population numbered 1,003 persons and 170 families, the majority of which surrendered to the British on October 29. However, approximately 100 Acadians fled to Bonaventure, the town that became the fourth "Little Cadie." Later, several of them settled in Tracadièche (what is now Carleton).

The following year, 17 Acadian exiles left Boston for the Magdalen Islands. Col. Richard Gridley was granted the concession of the islands in 1761 in return for services rendered[4] to the British Crown during the Seven Years' War. He brought with him 22 people in his employ, including 17 Acadians.

These pioneers had to adjust to harsh conditions on the islands: they were completely isolated during the five months of winter while ice separated the islands from the mainland. They had to establish the foundations of a local economy by developing and trading an available maritime resource: the walrus. Indeed, walrus fat was a very lucrative commodity at the time, as it could be melted and made into an oil used as lamp and lantern fuel.

In 1763, the British and the French made peace; France ceded the Magdalen Islands, which became part of Newfoundland. On August 3, 1765, Gridley's people had to pledge allegiance to King George III. In return, they asked Gridley to have a priest brought over to the islands. They would have to wait nine years before Fr. Leroux arrived.

In 1764, an Acadian refugee family, who had moved to Quebec some years before, established the foundations of the fifth "Little Cadie" in Petite-Rivière-de-Montréal, where the municipality of L'Acadie (amalgamated into Saint-Jean-sur-Richelieu) now stands.

A thumbnail sketch of the Acadians who arrived in Quebec during this first period, between 1755 and 1763, shows us that approximately 1,850 Acadians sought refuge in Quebec. Between 1756 and 1759, 488 Acadians died in Quebec City, including 335 who succumbed to smallpox and famine during the winter of 1757-1758. About 200 of the survivors returned to their homeland in 1759. By the end of this period, the colony was home to approximately 1,162 Acadians.

Acadian Deportees Emigrating to the Province of Quebec 1766 to 1775

Between 1760 and 1766, no Acadians came to Quebec. After that time, everything changed. On March 1, 1765, Gen. James Murray offered Acadians, who had been deported to New England the opportunity to move to the Province of Quebec. Only in the next year, however, did the first contingent of 40 Acadians arrive in Quebec, on September 1, 1766. A second contingent of 90 Acadians arrived on September 8, 1766, and a third, of 68 Acadians, on September 25, 1766. The following year, two groups of approximately 200 Acadians arrived in Quebec, in May, and another 240 in August. Most settled in Montreal, Assomption, Saint-Denis-sur-le-Richelieu, Saint-Ours, and Trois-Rivières.

In the spring of 1768, a group of 80 Acadians, unable to afford the fare to sail to Quebec City, voyaged up the Hudson River in small boats, using the portage routes to Lake Champlain and the Richelieu River, and settled in the fifth "Little Cadie" in Petite-Rivière-de-Montréal (the village of L'Acadie, part of Saint-Jean-sur-Richelieu).

Six years passed before another group of Acadians arrived in Quebec, in April of 1774. They were 81 Acadians from the Brittany area of France, and they settled in Paspébiac, on the Gaspé Peninsula. Charles Robin had recruited them to come and work in the fishing industry.

To summarize the settlements in this period: approximately 800 Acadian deportees from New England and France came to live in the Province of Quebec between 1766 and 1775. The Acadians from the Magdalen Islands are not counted in this figure, because the islands were not handed over to the Province of Quebec until May 1775.

Migrations of Acadians in the 19th and 20th Centuries

The first migration of Acadians was in 1793. The second group of about 250 Acadians, from the St. Pierre and Miquelon Islands, came to the Magdalen Islands. Accompanied by Abbé Jean-Baptiste Allain, they sought to escape the French Revolution.

Later, the search for new habitable lands motivated Acadians from Quebec to move around. Good farmland was becoming harder to find in the old seigneuries of New France, so a number of Acadians from the Bécancour region moved to the Eastern Townships of Quebec, despite the fact that this area was reserved for anglophones. With a migration starting in 1808, they founded towns and villages such as Saint-Louis-de-Blandford, Princeville, Victoriaville, and Plessisville. Over the same period, Acadians living in the Beauce and Bellechasse regions left for Sherbrooke and its surrounding area.

A million French-Canadians and Acadians from Quebec immigrated to the United States, again because of the lack of available land and in order to improve their economic situation. Many of those who emigrated in the period between 1830 and 1930 went to work in textile factories. This number does not include the many Acadians from the Maritimes who went directly to the United States.

Many Acadians, especially those who lived in the Richelieu region, joined in the struggle of the Patriotes during the Lower Canada Rebellion in 1837 and 1838, in the hopes of improving their rights and living conditions.

A few years later, for the first time in the history of Acadians in Quebec, one of their own was appointed bishop: Jean-Charles Prince was named Bishop of Martyropolis in 1844. In 1852, he became first bishop in the diocese of Saint-Hyacinthe. Jean-Charles was the brother of the founder of Princeville, Pierre Prince.[5]

In 1847 and 1848, a shortage of food incited the Acadians from the Magdalen Islands to find yet another home. A certain number of them settled in Bay St. George, Newfoundland. The next year, Nicolas-Tolentin Hébert, an Acadian abbot, recruited families from Kamouraska and L'Islet counties to come and settle in the Lac-Saint-Jean region. This is how the municipality of Hébertville came to exist.

In 1853, the governor passed a law ending the monopoly of the Hudson's Bay Company on the north shore of the St. Lawrence. In doing so, he made it possible for people to move into the area and for other companies to compete in the fishery trade in the Minganie, such as Charles Robin and Company, LeBoutillier Brothers, the William Fruing Company, and John & Elias Collas Co.

Thereafter, representatives of the different companies came to stay on the North Shore every spring, returning to their villages on August 20 or thereabouts. Some of these companies remained there permanently. From 1854 to 1865, many Acadians emigrated to the North Shore (120 families) as well as to Anticosti Island. The latter had come from Newfoundland, the Magdalen Islands, Nova Scotia, and even New Brunswick. Together, they founded more "Little Cadies," notably Natashquan and Pointe-aux-Esquimaux (Havre-Saint-Pierre). Others went to the Outaouais region to work in lumber camps or in forestry.

In 1860, through the influence of Abbé Georges-Antoine Belcourt, 12 Acadians from Rustico, Prince Edward Island, accepted the invitation to obtain land and to live in the Matapedia Valley, in the Gaspé. This is how a new "Little Cadie" was established in 1870; it was called Saint-Alexis-de-Matapédia. Two years later, another Acadian, Dominique Chiasson, founded Sept-Îles on the North Shore.

In 1875, in order to stem the exodus of Québécois and Acadians from Quebec, the government introduced a policy of repatriating francophones who had emigrated to the United States, prioritizing the settlement of specific remote areas.

Ten years later, Acadians from Natashquan were invited by Abbé François-Borgia Boutin to go to Beauce, and there they founded Saint-Théophile. Despite their important role in building this new "Little Cadie," however, these Acadians ended up looking for another place to live, because the rocky terrain was difficult to farm. At about the same time, Acadians from the other end of the province, Joliette, left for Témiscamingue and established the village of

Béarn. In 1896, Acadians from the Magdalen Islands travelled to the Matapedia Valley with plans to start a village in Lac-au-Saumon. This was despite the fact that as of 1895, they could once again own the land they had lived on, the first time this was possible since their ancestors had arrived in 1761.

At the beginning of 1910, several Acadians from the Magdalen Islands and the Gaspé Peninsula, settled in Verdun, on the island of Montreal, and lived there for ten years. Abbé Joseph-Arsène Richard assisted and served them there.

Between 1914 and 1939, Acadians from New Brunswick and various other areas in Quebec moved into the Saguenay-Lac-Saint-Jean area, especially in Kénogami (a municipality amalgamated into Jonquière in 1975), to work at Price, Alcan, and other factories. In 1927, there were 223 families from Acadie and the Gaspé.

The migration of Acadians from the Magdalen Islands continued until 1941. One group went to Neepawa Island, near Sainte-Hélène-de-Mancebourg, in the Abitibi, and the next year another group went to Roquemaure. Even a group of Acadians from Campbellton, New Brunswick, was recruited to settle the Abitibi region.

In 1960, an Acadian museum was created in Bonaventure, to preserve and promote Acadian heritage in Quebec. In 1987, the *Fédération des Acadiens du Québec* organization was established. The next year, a survey by the Léger & Léger firm revealed that there were one million Acadians (according to their surnames) in Quebec, out of a population of seven million. As proof of the importance of Acadian ancestry, a dozen Acadian organizations joined together to form the *Coalition des Organisations acadiennes du Québec* in 2007.

To summarize, the two centuries discussed in this article are marked by Acadians' desires for a better life and living conditions. At the heart of these migrations and settlements is a search for good land and a good job—both a way of putting food on the table. The shortage of food and overpopulation on the Magdalen Islands pushed Acadians to leave their homes on the islands in the hopes of improving their living conditions. The Acadians moved to chase the American dream in the new industrial age.

Conclusion

Acadians chose Quebec as a safe haven and a hospitable environment. Moves in the first decade after the Expulsion were characterized by Acadians who came to find a temporary refuge until they could return to Acadie. Later, events such as the Fall of New France and the invitation of Gen. Murray in 1765 changed the course of history. Quebec became the preferred destination for Acadians looking for a new home. In the 18th century, approximately 2,270 Acadians came up the St. Lawrence River to Quebec, while another 200 travelled up the Saint John River by canoe to Lake Témiscouata, then made the portage on foot before taking up their canoes and paddles again to go to Trois-Pistoles (Rivière-du-Loup). They settled mainly in the area between Trois-Pistoles and

Montmagny. Another 80 Acadians travelled up the Hudson River in small boats, portaging to Lake Champlain and the Richelieu River. Finally, approximately 100 Acadians came from Eucharistic to live in Bonaventure.

In the 19th and 20th centuries, several hundred Acadians from the Maritime Provinces chose Quebec as their new homeland, often moving to the North Shore, Anticosti Island, the Gaspé Peninsula, the areas of Saguenay-Lac-Saint-Jean, and Abitibi-Témiscamingue. Moreover, a number of people from the Magdalen Islands did the same, this time in order to escape famine and over-population on the islands.

By becoming more familiar with this chapter of history, we can better understand why it is that, according to a Master's thesis at *Université du Québec à Montréal* (UQAM), one out of every two Québécois has at least one Acadian ancestor.[6]

ACKNOWLEDGEMENTS

I am indebted to Pierre-Maurice Hébert who inspired me to further explore the history of Acadians in Quebec.

BIBLIOGRAPHY

Josée Bergeron, *Contribution différentielle des ancêtres d'origine acadienne au bassin génétique des populations régionales du Québec* (Master's thesis, *Université Laval*, November 2005, 103 p.); Pauline Carbonneau, *Découverte et peuplement des Îles de la Madeleine* (Rosemère, Humanitas, 2009, 260 p.); John A. Dickinson, *Les réfugiés acadiens au Canada, 1755-1775* (Canadian Studies/ *Études Canadiennes*, Issue 37, December 1994, p. 51-61); Pierre-Maurice Hébert, *Les Acadiens du Québec* (*Éditions de L'Écho, Montréal*, 1994, 478 p.); André-Carl Vachon, *Les déportations des Acadiens et leurs arrivées au Québec: 1755-1775* (*Tracadie-Sheila, La Grande Marée Ltée*, 2014).

ENDNOTES

1. See the in-depth study on the Acadians who arrived in Quebec between 1755 and 1775 in the third chapter of: André-Carl Vachon, *Les déportations des Acadiens et leurs arrivées au Québec. 1755-1775*, Tracadie-Sheila, La Grande Marée Ltée, 2014.

2. Translators' note: "*Petite Cadie*" refers to an Acadian settlement in Quebec. In this article, I use the term "Little Cadie," in the same way that "Little Italy" refers to the Italian section of Montreal.

3. John A. Dickinson, «Les réfugiés acadiens au Canada, 1755-1775," *Études Canadiennes/ Canadian Studies*, Issue 37: December 1994, 58.

4. Pierre-Maurice Hébert, *Les Acadiens du Québec*, Éditions de L'Écho, Montréal, 1994, p. 127.

5. Pierre-Maurice Hébert, *Les Acadiens du Québec*, Éditions de L'Écho, Montréal, 1994, p. 186.

6. "Our findings show that the Acadian founders and their descendants left traces in all regions of Quebec. Depending on the region, between 46 and 100 percent of the subjects had at least one Acadian founder in their family tree." Josée Bergeron, *Contribution différentielle des ancêtres d'origine acadienne au bassin génétique des populations régionales du Québec*. (Master's thesis, Université Laval, November 2005), 2.

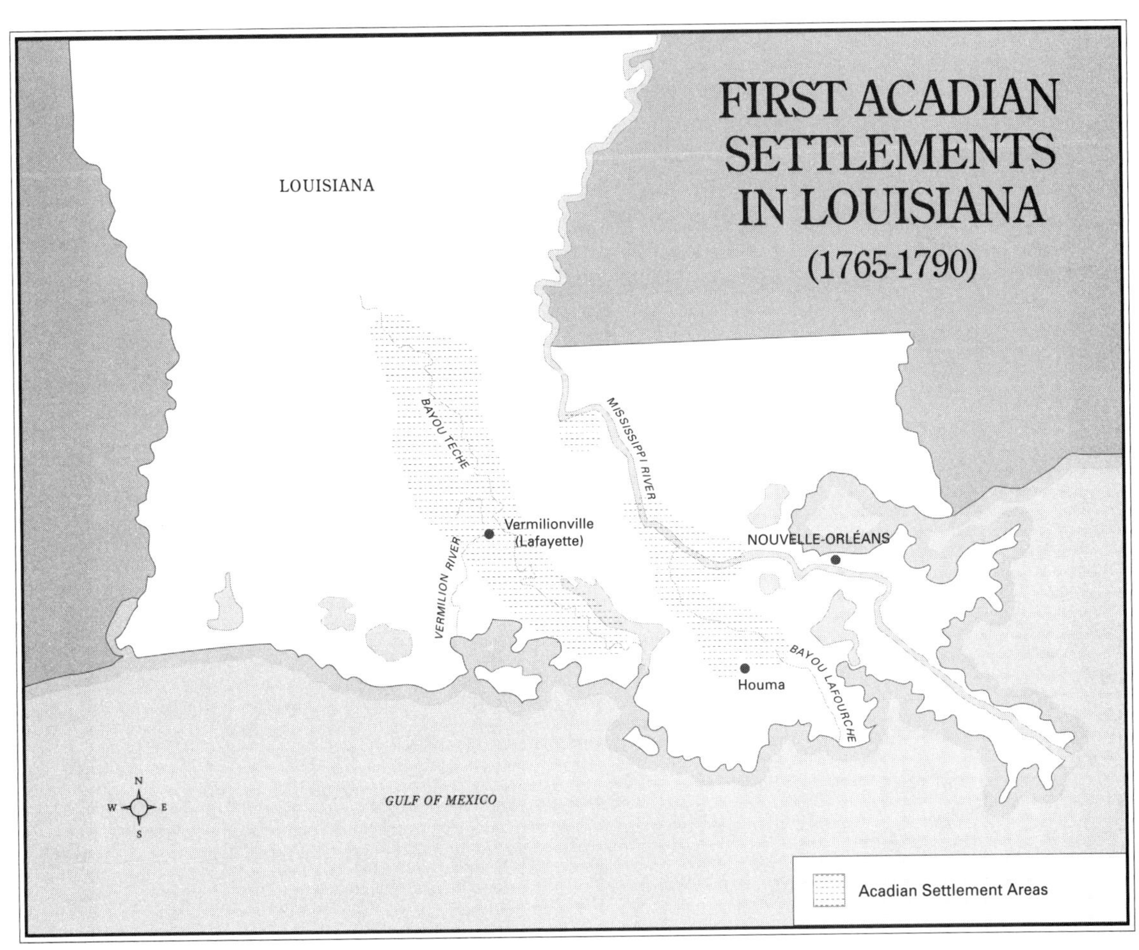
FIRST ACADIAN
SETTLEMENTS
IN LOUISIANA
(1765-1790)
LOUISIANA
BAYOU TECHE
MISSISSIPPI RIVER
Vermilionville
(Lafayette)
VERMILION RIVER
NOUVELLE-ORLÉANS
BAYOU LAFOURCHE
Houma
GULF OF MEXICO
N
W
E
S
Acadian Settlement Areas

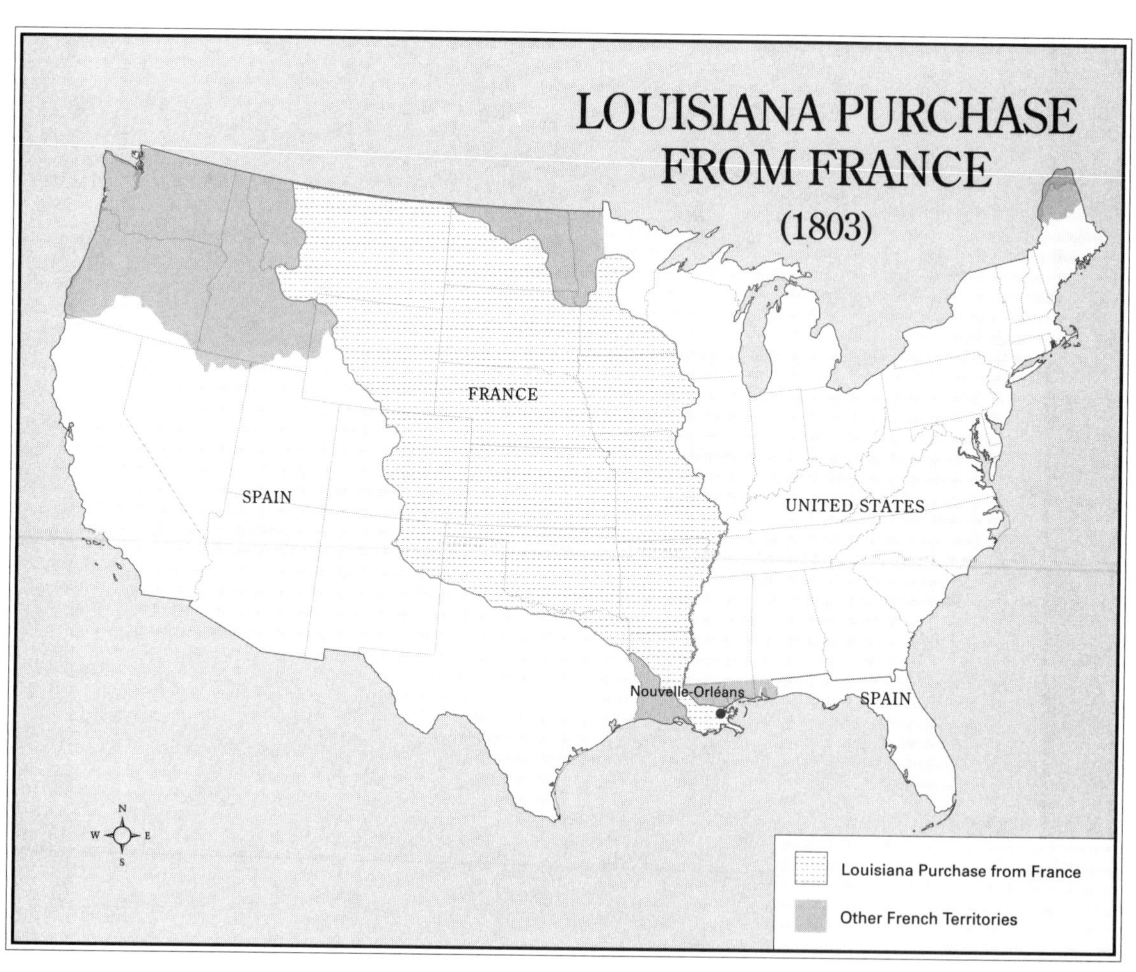
LOUISIANA PURCHASE FROM FRANCE
(1803)
FRANCE
SPAIN
UNITED STATES
Nouvelle-Orléans
SPAIN
N
W
E
S
Louisiana Purchase from France
Other French Territories

The Cajuns in Louisiana

Warren A. Perrin

On November 3, 1762, the Treaty of Fontainebleau transferred the French Louisiana colony from France to Spain, causing much chaos and conflict for the newly arriving Acadians. In February 1764, the first 20 Acadians to reach Louisiana came from New York via Mobile. Larger groups were to follow later, but this group was made up of four families—Poirier, Richard, Cormier, and Landry. The first child to be born of Acadian parents in Louisiana was most likely François Poirier, son of Jean Poirier and Madeleine Richard. He was baptized on March 6, 1765.

These four families settled along the Mississippi River above New Orleans. In 1776, a church was built and became known as the church of St. Gabriel. It is one of the oldest churches in the Mississippi River Valley. Its ecclesiastical records go back to 1767. The Maryland Acadians deposited the *St.-Charles-des-Mines* Catholic Church registers from Grand-Pré at the St. Gabriel Catholic Church in 1776 where they remained until the 1950s when the Baton Rouge Catholic Diocese was created and the registers moved to the diocese archives. This area was referred to as Cabannocé and was located where St. James Parish is located today. Governmental relations with the Acadians at this time were still amicable.

Photo©Kermit Bouillion

Presenting the Louisiana Acadian flag to King Juan Carlos of Spain (right) are, left to right, Lynn Breaux, Dorothy Broussard, and A.J. LeBlanc.

In the late 1760s, the previously harmonious relations between Acadian and Spanish officials ended when a series of disputes developed over where the more recently arriving immigrants were allowed to settle. These new families wanted close proximity to their already established Acadian brethren, but instead they were required to establish a series of new settlements along the Mississippi River in present-day St. James Parish.

Fearing Indian and British encroachment along its eastern borders (along the river), Louisiana's first Spanish governor, Gov. Antonio de Ulloa, decided to use the immigrants in these settlements in the defense of the colony. However, inexplicably, no government objections were made when the 200 Maryland Acadians and the 80 late-arriving Halifax Acadians all settled in the Cabannocé Post.

The caretaker French government soon came to realize the difficulties keeping Acadian families from trying (and often succeeding against all odds) to reunite their scattered relatives in the region, which they called *Nouvelle-Acadie* (New Acadie). Yet, continuing settlement disputes reached a crescendo after a group of Acadians were ordered to settle to the north, near present-day Vidalia, Louisiana. This forced settlement resulted in some Acadians becoming active participants in the ouster of Gov. Ulloa in the New Orleans Rebellion of 1768. In 1769, the Spanish regained control over their colony by the return of Gov. Alejandro O'Reilly, who permitted the Acadians to reunite along the Mississippi River in present-day Ascension and northern Assumption parishes.

In 1770, a group of 30 Acadians finally arrived in Natchitoches, Louisiana, after having been through a 15-month ordeal which began when their ship was blown off course during a violent storm, forcing it to land in Spanish Texas and compelling the ragged group to spend some time there before having to walk more than 400 miles to reach Louisiana. These Acadians settled in St. Landry and Iberville Parishes.

In April 1976 at Lake Peigneur are four generations of a Cajun family from Erath, Louisiana. Left to right: Kermit Bouillion, Allison Bouillion (baby), Mavely Aucoin Bouillion (Kermit's mother), Aline Bourque Aucoin and Alexis Aucoin (Kermit's grandparents, who only spoke French). Kermit Bouillion, a descendant of both the Acadian and Spanish settlers of Louisiana, is Director of the Living Legends program of the Acadian Museum of Erath and a member of the Lafayette Parish School Board representing District Five.

Descendants of the Acadians: Charles Broussard, B.J. Landry, and Rose Broussard in Lafayette, Louisiana.

Unlike most Acadians, the first group that settled in the Attakapas Territory of South Louisiana were never exiled to the British colonies. In 1755, they were captured and imprisoned by the British while waiting for the ships used in the deportation to arrive. On October 1, 1755, 86 of these Acadians managed to escape by digging a tunnel under the fort and organizing an unrelenting Acadian resistance. The leaders of these militant escapees were Pierre II Surette and Joseph Beausoleil Broussard.

The British viewed the Acadians who avoided deportation as threatening because they carried out an unbridled insurgency aided by the Mi'kmaq Native Americans. According to Diane Marshall in *Heroes of the Acadian Resistance* (2011), hundreds of them died—including nearly all of the children of the insurgents—during the brutal winter of 1757 while at a refugee camp in Miramichi, *Camp de l'Espérance* (Camp of Hope). Marshall states that among the dead were Beausoleil's wife Agnes and Joseph Surette, the younger brother of Pierre. The Acadians, who were struggling to survive at the refugee camp, found their insurgency hopeless after the fall of Quebec in 1759 during the French and Indian War (1756-1763), and some of them surrendered and were imprisoned for four years on Georges Island in Halifax harbor, Nova Scotia. Their remarkable story was the subject of the books *Acadian Redemption* (2005) and *Une Saga Acadienne* (2009) by the author.

Beausoleil descendant and Mi'kmaq activist Joseph Bernie Wayne David (d. 2012) of Vermilion Parish, Louisiana, playing a song he wrote, La Valse de Anne Marie, *in the Grand-Pré Memorial Church.*

After the war was ended between the British and French by the Treaty of Paris on August 18, 1763, the Beausoleil-led Acadians petitioned Gov. Montague Wilmot of Nova Scotia to be allowed to depart from their prison on Georges Island. With unrest in the area, the problematic Acadians were allowed to charter a ship for Saint-Domingue (today Haiti) in the Caribbean and leave behind them the lands which they and their ancestors had occupied for 160 years.

Upon arrival in Saint-Domingue, they learned that the Acadians who had arrived earlier were either deceased, near-death, or destitute. These earlier arrivals had been recruited from the British colonies to come to the French island to build a naval base in the tropical jungle, but they were inadequately supplied and over-worked. Therefore, the Beausoleil-led Acadians—consisting of 60 families—resupplied and went on to Louisiana.

On February 28, 1765, Commissaire-Ordonnateur Denis-Nicolas Foucault reported that the first large group of 193 Acadian refugees had landed in New Orleans, Louisiana. Over the next five years, about 800 Acadians arrived from Maryland and Halifax, Nova Scotia. In 1785, seven vessels brought 1,600 Acadians to Louisiana from France in the last major wave of French immigration to the Mississippi Valley.

In the mid-1960s, in Erath, Louisiana, with their dog, are Acadian descendants Freddie Suire, a fiddle player, and his wife Adia Suire.

As part of the Treaty of Paris, Louisiana had recently been transferred by France to Spain. According to historian Dr. Carl Brasseaux in his book *Scattered to the Wind* (1991), the colonial caretaker administrators in New Orleans, moved by pity, mobilized what limited resources were available and provided each Acadian family with a grant of land, seed grain for six months, a gun, and crude land-clearing equipment.

The government also provided to them a former Army engineer, Louis Andry, and on April 7, 1765, he led them to the Attakapas Territory and aided them in their settlement. Andry had been directed to prepare a map, showing the location of the new settlement, but unfortunately it was never done, and as a result, the locations of the first Acadian settlements are unknown.

This is a photo of Beausoleil descendants Theogene and Victorine Broussard of Vermilion Parish, the great-great-grandparents of author Warren A. Perrin. The Broussards settled in south Vermilion Parish, and in the mid-19th century used an aboiteau-*like structure to reclaim marshlands for agricultural use.*

New Orleans needed a supply of meat, so on April 4, 1765, the Acadians negotiated and executed a "sharecropping" cattle contract with Jean Dauterive, owner of a large ranch near New Iberia. However, due to some unknown problem, instead of working with Dauterive, the Acadians purchased their cattle from Jean-Baptiste Grevemberg shortly after their arrival at Fausse-Pointe. Their cattle rearing operations proved successful and soon they were self-sufficient.

Nelwyn Hebert, a founding member of the New Acadie Project committee. She is also an educator and leader in the unique culture of Iberia Parish, which was settled by both Acadians and Spanish. Hebert co-authored the book Iberia Parish *(2012), which chronicles how the two groups of pioneers that came to the area worked together for their mutual benefit.*

On April 24, 1765, Gov. Charles-Philippe Aubry reported that, "I have sent them to the Attakapas District." In 1765, after the Beausoleil-led Acadians arrived in the Bayou Teche area of the Attakapas Territory, they established three settlements somewhere at or near present-day St. Martinville and Loreauville. The New Acadie Project, an ongoing archeological work led by University of Louisiana at Lafayette Professor Dr. Mark Rees, is attempting to locate the sites of these first three Acadian settlements.

On April 8, 1765, Beausoleil Broussard was given the title Captain of the Militia and commandant of the Acadians in the Attakapas Territory by Aubry on behalf of the colonial Spanish government, which granted Acadians their land.

Sadly, Beausoleil, referred to as an "Acadian Chief," never lived to see his dream of a New Acadie fulfilled. He died on October 20, 1765, likely in a smallpox outbreak only eight months after his arrival. About 30 percent of the

Acadians also died in the epidemic in the first year of their arrival. Researcher Donald Arceneaux found that between May 16, 1765, and November 24, 1765, Fr. Jean Francois performed 41 burial rites—all Acadians.

From these burial records, it is known that the Acadians had divided themselves into three "camps" upon arrival in the Bayou Teche region. The first Acadian child born in the Attakapas Territory was Marguerite Anne Thibodeaux, daughter of Olivier and Madeleine Broussard. Madeleine was the daughter of Alexandre Broussard, Beausoleil's brother. Marguerite Anne Thibodeaux was born May 10, 1765, baptized May 11, and died just five days later on May 16, 1765, the same day as her mother.

After all of this tragedy, one group of the Beausoleil-led Acadians left the Attakapas and joined other Acadians who had established themselves on the Mississippi River. By the 1770s, another group also departed and settled along the Vermilion River in Prairie de Vermilion in extreme south Louisiana, on the edge of the wetlands and prairies of modern-day Acadiana. The Acadians, as seen, did not have an easy time settling in their New Acadie.

Pictured in the 1890s are the Boudreauxs, an early Cajun pioneer family in Vermilion Parish–said to be "The most Cajun place on earth."

Early settlers quickly acquired survival skills—treating illness with native plants, weaving palmetto leaves into hats and baskets, farming local vegetables—from helpful local Native American tribes like the Opelousas, Attakapas, and the Chitimacha. Acadian men wore knee-length *braguettes* (pants), *cotonnade* (cotton) shirts, and *capots* (coats). Male footwear was the *quantiera*, moccasin-type leather boots that reached to the knee.

Shown is the Germain Bergeron house. According to LSU Professor Dr. Jay Edwards, this is the oldest known Acadian-style house in Louisiana, which he says dates to the late 1700s because of the Norman truss construction within the attic. The house is now on display in the LSU Rural Life Museum in Baton Rouge, which is directed by David Floyd.

In 1800, Napoleon Bonaparte took Louisiana from Spain and offered to sell it to the fledgling United States. Seizing the opportunity to expand his country, U.S. President Thomas Jefferson agreed to the Louisiana Purchase in 1803. Thus, all of the colonial Louisiana Territory—which stretched from the Rocky Mountains to the Mississippi River and from Canada to the Gulf of Mexico—joined the United States. Historian Dr. Shane K. Bernard has observed, "As Louisiana residents, the Acadians suddenly became 'Americans,' at least in a legal sense."

The largest group of French to come to Louisiana was called the "Foreign French" (1820-1860), including the family shown here. About 550,000 of these immigrants came through New Orleans. They intermarried with Acadians and prospered because of their skills as carpenters, tradesmen, and farmers, and were responsible for the emergence of French journalism, opera, and theatrical productions.

Louisiana was the first true "melting pot" in North America. The Acadian influx into Colonial Louisiana was so large that it eventually engulfed not only many colonists who were already in the colony when the Acadians arrived, but also the later arrivals. The Spanish colonists never came in sufficient numbers to retain a separate ethnic identity. After the first few generations, the Spanish began intermarrying with the Acadians. Even the German Coast families, the French Creoles at Pointe Coupée, and the French from Mobile and Fort Toulouse intermarried with the Acadians, as did later arrivals from France, Ireland, Scotland, upper Louisiana, and other parts of the United States. In summary, all Acadians who came to Louisiana eventually became Cajuns along with anyone having at least one Acadian ancestor.

Resettlement to Louisiana in the mid-19th century was caused by European political instability, which created widespread famine in France, thus stirring waves of migration in the 1820s. These people—mostly craftsmen and small businessmen—became storeowners, shoemakers, and mill workers.

In 1900, Dr. Raphael Sagrera is shown at the Dyson Cotton Gin in Pecan Island.

Shown is the first-place winning float—La Fête—*in the children's parade at the 1950 Dairy Festival in Abbeville. Note the Catholic Church and rectory in the background, evidence of Spanish architecture in the area. By 1950, the Cajun culture had advanced to such a degree that Cajun crafts, music, and storytelling were incorporated into the festival.*

In the late 1770s, nearby New Iberia was settled by 16 families brought from Malaga, Spain, to Louisiana by Gov. Bernardo de Galvez, the Spanish governor of Louisiana. Since the Acadians had already been in the region for about ten years, they helped the Hispanic pioneers to adapt to the conditions of south Louisiana. They intermarried, and today many in Louisiana with Spanish surnames—like Miguez, Goutierrez, Gary, Romero, Blanco, Mendoza, Viator—speak French and consider themselves to be Cajun.

Shown is the Raphael Semmes Segura family, early settlers of the wetlands in South Louisiana, having a meal in the hotel at Chenier Au Tigre in southern Vermilion Parish. Like many early settlers, their principal occupations were hunting, trapping, and fishing.

The cultural transformation was determined by the capacity of the Acadians to adapt, and by the willingness of other cultures to be assimilated. This interaction contributed to the distinctiveness of the Cajuns.

The wetlands, a haunting and mysterious place, seemed alien at first, but its abundant wildlife and vegetation proved nurturing. The Atchafalaya Basin, located in south central Louisiana, is the largest wetland region and swamp in the United States. The area and its environs is a combination of wetlands and river delta area where the Atchafalaya River and the Gulf of Mexico converge. In 1984, the Atchafalaya National Wildlife Refuge was established to improve plant communities for endangered and declining species of wildlife and waterfowl.

From the beginning of Louisiana's statehood in 1812, there were legal requirements of the formerly French Louisiana colony to conform to the language and culture of the rest of the United States. The Enabling Act of the United States Congress (Act of Congress Feb 20, 1811, c. 21, 2 U.S. Stat. 641) dictated that after statehood, Louisiana was required to conduct its judicial and legislative written proceedings in English. Louisiana's Constitution of 1812 was published in both French and English, but the English version was required for statehood. Louisiana's legislature continued to publish its session laws in English and French until 1867.

Another important change took place at the end of the Civil War in 1865 when the elite urban population, understanding that their future would be as English-speaking Americans, began sending their children to English-language schools. In the late 1800s, the arrival of Anglo-American farmers from the Midwest sent the same message to francophone citizens: that their future was tied to the English language. In 1907, President Theodore Roosevelt stated that the United States had room for but one language: English.

In 1916, English-language education became mandatory in the southern part of Louisiana in an effort to force French-speaking Cajuns and Creoles into the American mainstream. The Louisiana constitution of 1921 codified the law thereby prohibiting the speaking of French in public schools or buildings. However, the law (Louisiana Revised Statute 1:51) allowed for documents to be in either French or English. French-speaking students were punished for speaking their native tongue. According to Dr. Barry Ancelet, "several generations of Francophone first-graders were forced to wet their pants at school because they could not ask permission to go to the restroom in English. Thus began an association that their native language and culture was a social stigmatization." It is for this reason that many parents of those generations chose not to speak French to their own children.

Appreciation for the French heritage of Louisiana began in the 1940s when Louisiana soldiers in World War II discovered that their French language had value as interpreters in provincial France and other Francophone countries. In 1955, local political leaders used the 1955 bicentennial of the Acadian exile as a rallying point for the revitalization of ethnic pride: Cajuns had survived the worst. Their culture and language were injured but still alive. The Louisiana Constitution of 1974 adopted a progressive equal protection clause: "the right of the people to preserve, foster, and promote their respective historic linguistic and cultural origins." (Art. XII, Sec. 4).

Fifty years ago, Congress passed the 1964 Civil Rights Act, a landmark law that banned racial discrimination in public places. The new recognition of minority rights worked to inspire Cajun leaders to launch their own initiative for cultural and linguistic rights. James R. Domengeaux, a former state legislator and United States Congressman of ethnic French descent, was the driving force behind the creation of the Council for the Development of French in Louisiana (CODOFIL).

A semi-retired attorney at the time, Domengeaux began his crusade for restoring French in Louisiana after Sen. Edgar G. "Sonny" Mouton Jr., of Lafayette obtained passage of an "urge-and-request" resolution for Louisiana school boards to help reverse the decline of the use of the French language within the state. Domengeaux traveled around Lafayette and neighboring parishes to gain support for his campaign to make Louisiana a bilingual state through French language education.

By the spring of 1968, Domengeaux had gained enough interest from the public—and support from officials such as State Sen. Dudley J. LeBlanc—to present his plan to the legislature. Legislators voted unanimously to create CODOFIL, and the measure was signed into law in July 1968, by Gov. John J. McKeithen. Today, the organization is led by its fourth President, Dr. William Arceneaux, and its Executive Director, Charles Larroque. CODOFIL plans to expand the development of professional and economic opportunities for French-speaking Louisianians.

Louisiana Today

Inspired by the first *Congrès mondial acadien* held in New Brunswick, Canada in 1994, along with the threat of the elimination of CODOFIL, *Action Cadienne* was created in 1996 by several Louisiana activists, including Earlène Broussard, Richard Guidry, Mark Babineaux, Zachary Richard, Del Guillory, Brenda Mounier, Mike Landry, and Mary and Warren Perrin. CODOFIL, with Earlène Broussard as its director, and the author as its third president, was instrumental in launching the organization. Zachary Richard became the first president of the non-profit organization, as well as its *porte parole* (spokesman).

Founding members of this grassroots organization chose to prioritize the support and growth of the French immersion programs and the teaching of Cajun-Acadian history in the schools. Among other activities, *Action Cadienne* organized several town hall meetings in different communities to support French immersion. The French immersion program in St. Landry Parish resulted from one of these meetings.

Due to the group's efforts, Acadian history is now taught to many Louisiana students. Public concerts were held in the beginning to raise awareness, as well as money and membership. Members spearheaded an educational forum on French immersion during the *Congrès mondial acadien* held in Louisiana in 1999.

In 2000, *Against the Tide (Contre Vents, Contre Marées)*, an award-winning Pat Mire film, was produced by *Action Cadienne*, to cinematically explain the Louisiana Acadian story. Many people were motivated by *Action Cadienne*'s activities, which were key to distributing funds donated by people from all over the world for French immersion programs adversely affected by Hurricanes Katrina (2005) and Rita (2005). Their principal legacy remains one of bringing many people together in numbers and in ways that had never happened previously.

Shown at a news conference and reception held at the CODOFIL office in Lafayette on June 7, 1996, are, left to right, Zachary Richard, president of Action Cadienne, *Warren A. Perrin, president of CODOFIL, and Lynn Breaux, chairman of the Lafayette Hospitality Committee.*

The first French immersion school program began in Baton Rouge at *La Belle Aire* Elementary School in 1984. There was only one class of students in the program, who began in kindergarten and continued through fifth grade. When the class of students moved on to sixth grade in 1986, immersion no longer existed in any form in Baton Rouge. However, the following year the Calcasieu Parish School Board, under the guidance of Supervisor Anthony Zaunbrecher, began a program which continues to this day.

According to world language specialist Nicole Boudreau of the Lafayette Parish School System, for a program to be considered French immersion, the students must spend at least 60 percent of their school days studying math, science, history, and sometimes, even physical education, in French.

With the success of this program, other parishes soon followed; St. Martin, St. Landry, and Assumption all have well-established programs. In 1992, Lafayette Parish began French immersion programs in three elementary schools: Prairie, Myrtle Place, and S.J. Montgomery. Not only do those schools still have the innovative French immersion classes, but they have further expanded to three other schools and to the middle and high school levels, as have the other parishes. Lafayette Parish is the only parish that has so far tried it at the high school level.

Today, French immersion is also flourishing in Iberia, East Baton Rouge, Jefferson, and Orleans parishes. In the state of Louisiana, there are presently 30 schools with a combined enrollment of over 4,000 students. Immersion programs are growing at the rate of four percent per year. Since the beginning of the program, it has been estimated that over 20,000 students have been educated in French immersion.

Many of the first students are now young professionals working in fields such as law, government, business, music, and education. Some of the graduates of the highly acclaimed program have become French immersion teachers, and others are ensuring that their children become bilingual by putting them in the classes. In 2013, Sen. Eric Lafleur and Rep. Stephen Ortego co-authored a bill requiring a school system to establish an immersion program if at least 25 parents committed to enrolling their children in the kindergarten program and teachers were available through CODOFIL to serve the program.

The Louisiana Acadian flag was unveiled February 22, 1965, by, from left to right, Dr. Thomas Arceneaux, State Comptroller Roy Theriot Sr., and Judge Allen Babineaux, and made official by the state of Louisiana in 1974. The Louisiana Acadian flag was designed by Arceneaux, and features three silver fleurs-de-lys on a blue field, symbolizing the Acadians' French heritage; a gold castle on red, symbolizing Spanish rule; and a gold star on white, representing Our Lady of the Assumption, patron saint of the Acadians.

Acadiana is the name now given to the traditional 22 parishes in the Cajun homeland, which in 1971 the Louisiana state legislature officially recognized for its unique Cajun and Acadian heritage (per House Concurrent Resolution No. 496). The term was coined by accident around 1960 and soon took on a life of its own.

The term "Acadiana" is often mistakenly applied only to Lafayette Parish and several neighboring parishes, usually Acadia, Iberia, St. Landry, St. Martin, and Vermilion parishes. Sometimes the list also includes Evangeline and St. Mary parishes. This eight-parish area, however, is actually the "Cajun Heartland, USA" district, which makes up only about a third of the entire Acadiana region; the entire Acadiana region actually consists of the parishes of Acadia, Ascension, Assumption, Avoyelles, Calcasieu, Cameron, Evangeline, Iberia, Iberville, Jefferson Davis, Lafayette, Lafourche, Pointe Coupée,

St. Charles, St. James, St. John the Baptist, St. Landry, St. Martin, St. Mary, Terrebonne, Vermilion, and West Baton Rouge.

However, historian Dr. Shane K. Bernard notes that, "Apparently in order to appease ... [certain] border parishes, the legislature designated the 22 core parishes as 'The Heart of Acadiana,' thereby implying the existence of a larger, more nebulous 'Acadiana.' The legislature further clouded the region's makeup by including an unspecified number of other, unnamed parishes 'of similar cultural environment' in the Heart of Acadiana. Regardless, once the resolution had been approved, the 22 core parishes immediately shortened their designation to 'Acadiana' and ignored the legislative clause including other parishes in the region."

The moniker "Acadiana" is now part of the names of many businesses, schools, and associations. The creation of the unique cultural designation for the region has become a rallying point of pride for all of the Cajuns residing within the state.

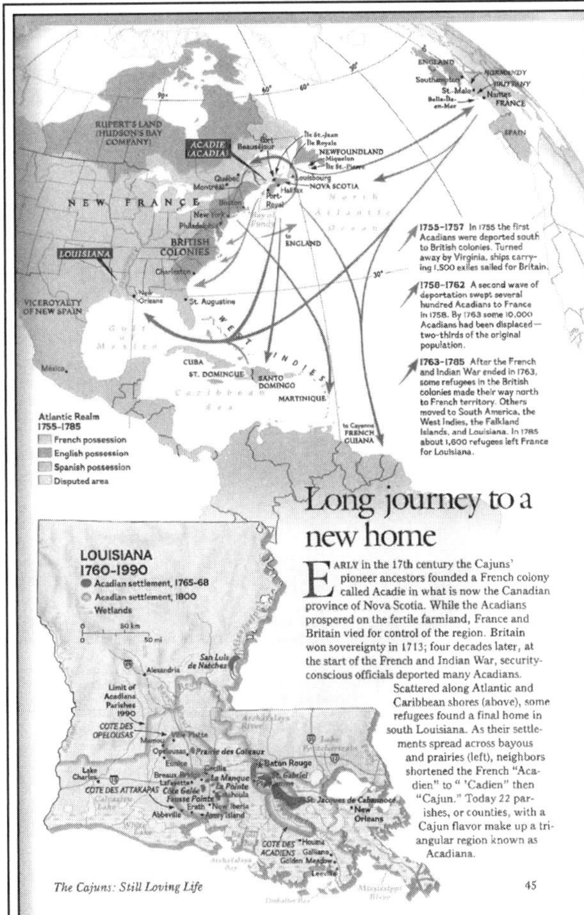

Long journey to a new home

EARLY in the 17th century the Cajuns' pioneer ancestors founded a French colony called Acadie in what is now the Canadian province of Nova Scotia. While the Acadians prospered on the fertile farmland, France and Britain vied for control of the region. Britain won sovereignty in 1713; four decades later, at the start of the French and Indian War, security-conscious officials deported many Acadians.

Scattered along Atlantic and Caribbean shores (above), some refugees found a final home in south Louisiana. As their settlements spread across bayous and prairies (left), neighbors shortened the French "Acadien" to "'Cadien" then "Cajun." Today 22 parishes, or counties, with a Cajun flavor make up a triangular region known as Acadiana.

The Cajuns: Still Loving Life 45

This chart shows the general Acadian diaspora (top) and where the Acadians settled in Louisiana (bottom). It appeared in the October 1990 issue of National Geographic Magazine *in an article by Griffin Smith Jr., called "The Cajuns: Still Loving Life."*

The Cajuns' well-practiced talent for adaptation to circumstances has served them well. One of the best examples was their response in 2005 to Hurricanes Katrina and Rita, which devastated New Orleans and most of coastal south Louisiana in a three-week span. How beleaguered citizens created their own salvation when their institutions failed them is the subject of the book by Drs. Barry Jean Ancelet, Marcia Gaudet, and Carl Lindahl, *Second Line Rescue: Improvised Responses to Katrina and Rita* (2013). The authors state that, "The vernacular responses and solutions recorded in this book are rooted in south Louisiana's cultural historical background. It is no accident that those who improvised jazz, blues, second lines, Cajun waltzes, and zydeco two-steps also improvised to get people off of their roofs. In addition, the *Mardi Gras*, with its longstanding tradition of carnivalesque, is all about subverting ineffective authority to accomplish what must be done."

On December 1, 2005, three months after Hurricane Rita flooded the area, Acadians from Canada met with Vermilion Parish teachers and principals to offer financial assistance to help with French education programs. Representatives of the Société nationale de l'Acadie *held a meeting at the Acadian Museum of Erath to discuss the needs of the schools damaged by Hurricane Rita in Vermilion and Iberia parishes. The organization raised $184,000 to help support the teaching of French and the beginning of a French Immersion program in Vermilion Parish. Shown here are (front row) Charlotte Waguespack, principal at Henry Elementary; Elizabeth Gremillion, principal at Dozier Elementary; Lynn Moss, principal at Erath Middle School; Rachelle Dugas, director* Société Nationale de L'Acadie*; (top row) Gerald Boudreau, vice-president of* Société Nationale de L'Acadie*; Ron Miguez, operations manager for the Acadian Museum of Erath; Warren A. Perrin, president of CODOFIL; Michel Cyr, president of* Société nationale de L'Acadie*; Zachary Richard,* Solidarité Acadie-Louisiane*; Roland Pautz, supervisor French teachers of Vermilion Parish; O.J. Dore, supervisor for the Vermilion Parish School Board; and Ray Trahan, representative of* Louisiane-Acadie.

At the front corner of the Acadian Museum of Erath are bronze sculpted busts of local men who died while in service to their country: At the left is First Lieutenant Brandon Dronet, who was killed in a helicopter crash in 2006 in northern Africa while training pilots for Operation Iraqi Freedom. At the right is Private Farrell Vice, who was in the U.S. Army and awarded the Silver Star for acts of valor in Vietnam after he was killed during combat in 1969.

Photo©Stacy Bodin

The Acadian Museum of Erath, located at 203 S. Broadway Street in Erath, was established in 1990. The museum houses over 5,000 artifacts of Acadian and Cajun history. The Acadian Museum of Erath contains three rooms: the Erath Room, the Acadian Room, and the Prairie Bayou Cajun Room. Located next door to the museum is *Le Café du Musée*, owned by Sonny Moss.

Left to right in 1993 are Jim Landry, owner of CathLan Landscaping Services of Abbeville, and Warren A. Perrin, chairman of the Acadian Museum of Erath. Landry donated the materials and labor for the preparation of a flower garden to enhance the historical marker in the Town of Erath, which memorializes the first Acadian prairie settlement in the area in the 1780s. The historical marker is situated on the northern shoulder of Louisiana Highway 14, west of Erath.

PERRIN BROUSSARD FAMILY PHOTOS

Photo©Preston Broussard

Shown in 1980 at the Broussard family reunion held at the Vermilion Parish Boathouse in Abbeville, Louisiana, are (left to right) sisters Rose Broussard LeBlanc, Nolia Broussard Thibodeaux, and Letia Broussard Perrin, three of the eight descendants of Aristide and Leontine Broussard.

Shown on September 4, 2013, near his camp on the Boston Canal south of Erath is Lafayette attorney Jean Ouellet, who had just finished a successful alligator hunting expedition with members of the Stelly family on family-owned marshlands in southeast Vermilion Parish. Ouellet, a native of Quebec City, Canada, and a descendent of Acadians, is a good example of Cajun assimilation. He is married to Rebecca Perrin Ouellet, daughter of Warren and Mary Broussard Perrin and a ninth-generation descendent of Beausoleil Broussard.

Henry Perrin (left) and his father Andrew Perrin are shown on November 11, 2012, duck hunting on wetlands in southern Vermilion Parish acquired by their ancestor Aristide Broussard during the late 19th century.

On November 12, 2012, Nicolas Ouellet, a tenth-generation descendant of Beausoleil Broussard, is shown on the boat owned by his father, Jean Ouellet, returning to their camp on the Boston Canal after a successful duck hunt.

Dawn breaking over duck decoys floating near Lake Cock in southern Vermilion Parish.

Pictured in 2013 is Perrin (center) with some of her grandchildren, (front) Louis Perrin and Nicolene Perrin, and (back) Lily Ouellet and Henry Perrin. Not shown is grandson Nicolas Ouellet.

On March 27, 2014, the third grade class of Ascension Episcopal School in Lafayette presented the play Louisiana Day. *The students performed the French song brought to Louisiana by the Acadians, La Rose Au Bois. The students also chose a popular fairytale and altered it, giving it a Cajun twist. Then they wrote and illustrated their very own book. Shown here is the Perrins' granddaughter Lily Ouellet, nine, who dedicated her book to her grandparents.*

Acknowledgements

This article was written in collaboration with Drs. Carl Brasseaux, Shane Bernard, and Barry Ancelet.

Bibliography

Dr. Barry Jean Ancelet, Jay Edwards and Glen Pitre, *Cajun Country* (University Press of Mississippi, 1991); Dr. Shane K. Bernard, *The Cajuns—Americanization of a People* (Jackson, University Press of Mississippi, 2003); Dr. Carl A. Brasseaux, *Scattered to the Wind: Dispersal And Wanderings of the Acadians, 1755-1809* (Lafayette, LA: Center for Louisiana Studies, 1991); Dr. Laurence Powell, *The Accidental City* (London, Harvard University Press, 2012); and Zachary Richard, Sylvain Godin, and Maurice Basque, *Histoire des Acadiennes et des Acadiens de la Louisiane* (Lafayette, LA: UL Lafayette Press, 2012).

Cajuns in Texas

Kathey King

The ancestors of the people we now call Cajuns originated in eastern Canada in the colony of Acadie (now Nova Scotia) over 2,000 miles from the state of Texas. After being deported by the British in the mid-1700s, many of the Acadians eventually migrated to New Orleans in Louisiana.

As Acadians arrived at the port of New Orleans they regrouped and moved westward toward the prairies and bayous of South Louisiana. After the Louisiana Purchase of 1803, new English-speaking neighbors corrupted the pronunciation of "Acadian" into "Cadian" and then to "Cajun." This area eventually became the 22-parish area now called Acadiana, a designation approved by the Louisiana Legislature in 1971 in recognition of the uniqueness of the Cajun culture.

Louisiana Cajuns began their move to east Texas as early as the 1840s. As noted by Dr. Barry Ancelet in his book *Cajun Country* (1991), horses and cattle were primarily of Spanish origin, and the Cajuns developed a relationship with Texas, then a part of the Spanish territory of Mexico, as a source for livestock as well as the methods and equipment to handle it. At first, Cajuns who immigrated made their livelihood as farmers in Jefferson County, Texas, on the west side of the Sabine River, which is today's Texas/Louisiana border. During the late 1800s, the expanding rice cultivation in southeast Texas and the need for additional labor lured more Cajuns to the area.

Expansion of the Southern Pacific Railroad from the Sabine River to Houston brought even more immigrants from Louisiana, and ultimately many of the Southern Pacific Railroad workers moved permanently to Houston. In the *Handbook of Texas Online,* it is noted that a community called Frenchtown, a neighborhood of four square blocks in Houston's 5th ward comprised of 500 French, Spanish, and African descendants from Louisiana, was organized in 1922.

Many of the occupants of Frenchtown were employed by the Southern Pacific Railroad in skilled and semiskilled jobs such as mechanics, carpenters, bricklayers, and sawmill workers. Frenchtown was made up of French-speaking Catholics with a rich Creole culture distinguished by its colorful patois, unique cuisine, and zydeco music. According to Roger Wood in *Texas Zydeco* (2006), the musical genre known as zydeco, a blend of Cajun, blues, and rhythm and blues performed by these African American Creole French, was popularized and named in the Frenchtown area of Houston where these families settled to seek a better life. There are alternate theories that zydeco was born in Louisiana; however the music does not belong to any one state but to all of the people of the upper Gulf Coast region. The area between Houston and Lafayette is known by many as the "Zydeco Corridor."

Our Mother of Mercy Catholic Church in the Frenchtown area of Houston.

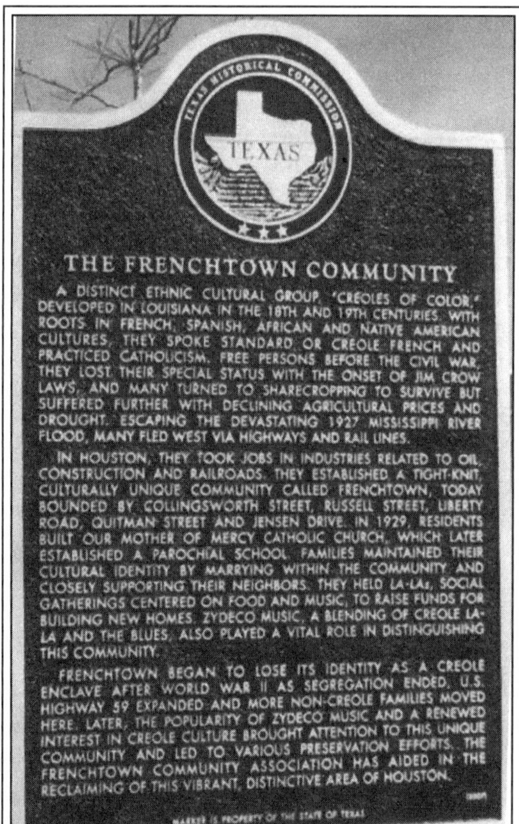

The Frenchtown historical marker.

The Louisiana Cajuns generally stayed within their own communities and trusted only each other due to the trials and tribulations endured during and after the expulsion of their Acadian ancestors from Nova Scotia. This social attitude built a wall of self-protection between the Cajuns and the outside world. They developed their own form of French, known as Cajun French, generally a mixture of Acadian French, Creole French, and English. Although their language created a common bond among the Cajuns in Texas, it also served to isolate them from their Anglo-American neighbors. As they moved further westward, Cajuns began to assimilate into the existing societies, slowly resulting in the relaxing of this isolation. Clearly, the Americanization of the Cajuns took place more easily in Texas than it did in Louisiana.

A primary catalyst in bringing the culture of Cajun Louisiana into the homes and offices of Texans was the increase of the Cajun population. Their exciting and alluring lifestyle, with emphasis on the love of family and an amazing work ethic, was accompanied by laughter and fun. Spicy Cajun food and music also captivated their Texas neighbors.

The discovery of oil in east Texas at Spindletop near Beaumont on January 10, 1901, was a turning point for the state and the United States as a whole. The new oil field produced more than 100,000 barrels of oil a day and soon gave rise to what became known as the Texas Oil Boom. Although the production of oil would not remain at this level, drilling around Spindletop would continue until the mid-1930s, encouraging more Louisiana Cajuns to immigrate to Texas.

From the 1950s until 1975, sulfur mining replaced oil drilling as the area's largest employer. Both oilfield work and sulfur mining required a hard-working labor force, and both paid good wages. Ironically, during this same period, oil was discovered off the coast of Louisiana and resulted in many Anglo-Americans moving into Louisiana to help develop that important facet of the "oil patch."

During the first two decades of the 20th century, many new oil and gas refineries were built in the three-city area in east Texas now called the Golden Triangle, an area encompassing Beaumont, Port Arthur, and Orange. These industries provided an ever increasing number of jobs that attracted many more Cajuns to Texas. Numerous new communities sprang up in this area with the largest portion of the population coming from southwest Louisiana where many Cajuns had been trapped in a system of tenant farming going back to the Reconstruction Era. As more industries expanded and developed, additional opportunities were made available for Cajuns in south and east Texas.

When a hurricane hit the upper Texas coast in 1915, many Cajuns left Louisiana to take advantage of immediate opportunities in rebuilding the infrastructure. The next sizable influx of Cajuns was the United States' entry into World War I with its resultant increase in the growth of oil refineries and shipyards in the Golden Triangle region. During the postwar period, the shrimp industry provided another important source of employment for Cajuns. The lure of better fishing off the Texas Gulf Coast brought many Cajuns to the coastal cities from Freeport to Harlingen.

In 1894, the American sulfur industry was born in Louisiana when a rich deposit was found in a swampy area of Calcasieu Parish near Lake Charles in western Louisiana. Extracting sulfur was difficult until Dr. Herman Frasch, a German-born chemist and engineer, found a method to permit the sulfur to be pumped to the surface and hardened. This new method was utilized in the Louisiana mine from 1895 until 1924.

Oil exploration in 1901 and 1908 resulted in the discovery of important sulfur deposits in Brazoria County, Texas, located on the Gulf Coast area around Bryan Mound. Patents belonging to Dr. Herman Frasch, who virtually monopolized sulfur production in the huge mine at the town now known as Sulphur, expired in 1912, and opened the door for new sulfur ventures and the additional employment that came with them.

On November 12, 1912, the Freeport Sulphur Company began production at the Bryan Mound facility. This was the first sulfur mine in Texas, and only the second in the world to utilize the Frasch process. Experienced drillers looking for work were recruited. A migration of Cajun recruits flocked to the new Texas town of Freeport. On the 1920 and 1930 census records for Brazoria County, approximately 60 to 70 percent of the people in the town were of Cajun heritage and worked for the company.

At one point, approximately 90 percent of all the sulfur produced in the world came out of Brazoria County, Texas. Production eventually slowed, and the Bryan Mound facility was closed in 1935 after producing five million tons of sulfur. Back in 1923, the company had leased another mine at Hoskins Mound and ran that operation until the mid-1950s. When Bryan Mound closed, employees were sent to Plaquemines Parish, Louisiana, where the Freeport Sulphur Company had acquired the sulfur rights for Lake Grande Ecaille. It was in this area where the town called Port Sulphur was developed, that the growth of the sulfur industry in Louisiana began.

Even with the loss of a number of families in the Texas town of Freeport, the influence of Cajun culture would remain strong through the 1990s. Many of the sons and daughters of the first generation of Cajuns in Freeport married local Anglo-Americans and reared their families in this multi-cultural area; this intermarrying hastened the Cajuns' assimilation. In the late 1940s, a church was erected for the large contingent of Catholics, mostly with Cajun backgrounds. Children growing up in the area did not speak the traditional Cajun French and were raised like any other Texan child in the area. Even though the Americanization of the Cajun culture brought basic changes in lifestyle, many of the values and traditions were retained and embraced, especially the Catholic religion and Cajun food and music.

According to Dr. Shane Bernard in his book *The Cajuns–Americanization of a People* (2003), World War II brought South Louisiana civilians into contact–and sometimes conflict–with different peoples and cultures. Anglo-American GIs and oilfield workers with their families moved into formerly insular regions. Other Cajuns left Acadiana to take jobs in east Texas where, despite their frequent trouble with the English language, they worked in shipyards, refineries, and defense factories. The Hackberry Ramblers, a popular

Cajun string band from Cameron Parish, hosted their own live music program on KPLC radio in Lake Charles, Louisiana, located about an hour from the Texas-Louisiana state line. The band received letters from fans throughout east Texas requesting traditional Cajun songs in French like "Jolie Blonde." Ultimately, the Ramblers mirrored the on-going Americanization process, for despite their Cajun roots the band embraced Anglo-American western swing music, a genre popular in neighboring Texas.

Cajun culture, primarily the cuisine, continues to have a profound impact on Texas. Spicy and tasty gumbo, *boudin*, smothered okra, jambalaya, crawfish, and other delightful Cajun dishes are a wonderful addition to traditional Texas beef dishes. Cajun restaurants with a wide variety of spicy Cajun offerings can be found in practically every city in Texas. Boiled crawfish and Louisiana music, both Cajun and zydeco, are regularly featured at county festivals and private celebrations.

By the latter part of the 20th century and into the 21st, Cajun professionals in petroleum, telecommunications, and construction began a different kind of migration. For the first time, it was white-collar experts and not laborers who were leaving Louisiana. In fact, during the 1990s, Louisiana had a net loss of population. Today Cajuns living throughout the country have assimilated into every society in the United States. In some Texas counties Cajuns make up more than 30 percent of the population. As shown on the chart from the 1990 and 2000 census, there are more people of French Canadian/Cajun descent in Harris County, Texas, than in Orleans and Lafayette parishes in Louisiana. Some estimates say that 375,000 people of Cajun heritage live in Texas.

Note in the chart below that Houston has more Cajuns than New Orleans, which, although it has many French Creoles, is not a Cajun city. – RP

Texas county	1990 census			2000 census	
	French Canadian* (including Cajun)	French (all, including French Canadian/Cajun)	% of total pop.	Acadian/Cajun	French (all, including French Canadian/ Cajun)
Jefferson	39,263	66,446	27.8	2,203	25,830
Orange	15,783	26,483	32.9	1,598	12,202
Liberty	3,488	7,769	14.7	128	3,453
Hardin	3,402	7,685	18.6	346	4,197
Chambers	3,233	5,349	26.6	174	2,160
Jasper	1,949	4,059	13.1	276	1,826
Tyler	771	2,329	14.0	53	1,178
Newton	1,009	1,817	13.4	108	921
Sabine	481	1,162	12.1	18	569
Harris (Houston)	59,345	192,019	6.8	2,619	97,433
Dallas	17,001	88,216	4.8	483	45,323
Tarrant (Ft. Worth)	13,690	67,991	5.8	•578	39,539
Bexar (San Antonio)	12,780	51,735	4.4	415	32,142
Travis (Austin)	8,096	34,155	5.9	706	26,794
TEXAS total	**264,986**	**965,448**	**5.7**	**15,276**	**552,959**
Louisiana parish	**1990**			**2000**	
Orleans	13,818	66,927	13.4	826	30,514
Lafayette	99,107	138,041	83.8	5,145	53,689

**In 1990 totals, the bureau included Cajuns with French-Canadians. Source: adapted from the U.S. Census 2000 and 1990.*

1990 and 2000 census population chart.

According to some authorities, the decline of the French language will hasten the loss of the Cajun culture. Others suggest that contemporary Cajuns will help save the culture and retain some of their identity by participating in preservation groups, attending Cajun festivals, listening to Cajun music, and researching and saving family histories. Even though present-day Cajun descendants do not always practice the traditional folkways of their forebears, the culture can still be embraced and passed on to the next generation in an updated and innovative form.

Texas owes a great deal to the Cajuns and their culture. Without their aggressive work ethic, Texas oil fields might not have developed to a world-class level. Without gumbo, crawfish, and Cajun music, our enjoyment of life would lack diversity. In many ways, the Cajuns' contributions to the Texas economy and culture have enriched the lives of all the citizens of Texas.

Acadians in France –from 1758 to the Present

Warren A. Perrin

Prior to 1758, no Acadians had been deported directly to France although some made the journey on their own, but when Fortress Louisburg fell to the British, over 3,500 Acadians on Île St. Jean and Ile Royale (today Prince-Edward Island and Cape Breton), were deported to France. Their numbers were reduced when two of the ships (the *Violet* and the *Duke William*) sank en route, drowning 700 Acadians. Hundreds more perished on other ships during the voyage, or soon after arriving in France. The ships carrying deported Acadians arrived at the French port towns of Saint-Malo, Le Havre, Cherbourg, Brest, and Boulogne-sur-Mer. One group arrived at Boulogne-sur-Mer when their deportation ship was blown off-course in a storm. Only 179 survivors made it to that port.

When Quebec fell in 1759, hundreds of prisoners of war were sent to France, including many Acadians. In 1763, after the Treaty of Paris ended the Seven Years War, 753 more Acadians who had resided at Falmouth and Southampton, England, since 1756 would later join the Acadians in France in 1763 in Morlaix and Saint-Malo. [See Richard Holledge's article on page 254].

Generally, in France, they all lived in poor conditions in coastal cities, although several attempts were made to settle them elsewhere. When the opportunity came to leave France in 1785, over 1,600 of them elected to migrate to Louisiana.

The Acadians mainly settled in small towns around the Saint-Malo area in 37 different communities such as Chateauneuf, Chateau Malo, Corseul, Dinan, Parame, Piouer, Pleslin, Pleudihen, Langrolay, Bonaban, La Gouesnière, Pleurtuit, Ploubalay, Saint-Briac, Saint-Cast, Saint-Coulomb, Saint-Enogat, Saint-Lunaire, Saint-Jouan des Guerets, Saint-Méloir des Ondes, Saint-Servan, Saint-Suliac, Taden, Tremereuc, and Trigavou. But some Acadians were also at Cherbourg, Boulogne-sur-Mer, La Havre, Brest, Rochefort, and other coastal cities.

The post-Deportation French stratagem for dealing with the Acadians within their midst was thoroughly laid bare by Brigham Young University historian Dr. Christopher Hodson, a specialist in the early modern French empire, in his book *The Acadian Diaspora: An Eighteenth Century History* (2012). The French government thought the Acadians would eventually blend in with the populace, but it did not turn out that way. They went on government welfare at six *sols* a day. The Duc de Nivernois, charged by the French government to look into the fate of the Acadians, proposed a settlement plan that might have worked but was instead ignored by the government.

The Acadians became a pawn in internal government affairs. A number of plans were considered, none of which were favorable to the Acadians, and a few were even attempted, but generally they called for settling the Acadians on poor land or in French colonies with terrible climates. For example, French Minister of Foreign Affairs Etienne François duc de Choiseul had the job in 1762 of populating French tropical colonies, so he pushed the Acadians to move there. He convinced several hundred to go to French Guiana. After struggling with disease and hot weather, the poorly supplied survivors eventually returned to France. The same failure occurred when Acadians tried to colonize the Falkland Islands.

In 1765, Etienne-Francois again tried to settle some 78 Acadian families on Belle-Île-en-Mer, a French island off the coast of Brittany, but after seven years the colony failed due to livestock epidemics, crop failure, drought, and local resistance. Some moved back to Saint-Malo and Morlaix, and some later moved to Nantes. Some Acadians remained on the island, however, and, because of its isolation, most of the *Bellilois* today have Acadian blood, and some have retained Acadian names.

Clearly, the French government had varying viewpoints about the Acadians. At times they intended to reward the Acadians for their patriotism, as the Acadians expected. But at other times they were considered ungrateful peasants who should just try harder to blend into French society. By 1772, the Acadians had resorted to direct appeals to the king. Acadian representatives apprised the king of their plight and requested permission to go to Spain. The new King Louis XVI was moved and directed that a place be found for the Acadians, not in Spain, but in France. LeMoyne, the head of the navy, ordered a census of Acadians be taken in 1772, which found 2,566 Acadians in France distributed as follows: 1,727 in Saint-Malo, 228 in Cherbourg, 179 in Morlaix, 166 in Le Havre, 103 in Belle-Île-en-Mer, 79 in Rochefort, 42 in La Rochelle, 27 in Lorient, 10 in Bordeaux, three in Paris, and two in Boulogne.

In 1772, the Marquis Perusse des Cars gave the Acadians some of his land to farm in the province of Poitou, ironically the same area where many of their ancestors had come from over a century earlier. But the 1,472 Acadians who migrated there found the soil sterile and, at first, no housing.

By 1775, *La Ligne Acadienne* was constructed, a long, straight road where simple houses were ultimately built for them for which they were charged unduly high rent. Consequently, most Acadian settlers eventually decided to abandon the area, and almost all moved to Nantes in four convoys. Only 160 Acadians were left in the Poitou area by the following year, but their descendants today still remember their Acadian roots. For the next ten years, Nantes would have the largest concentration of Acadians in France.

According to historian Gérard-Marc Braud, President of *France-Louisiane* and author of *From Nantes to Louisiana* (1999), there were 2,000 Acadians in Nantes in 1775. Louisiana had been transferred from France to Spain in 1763, but many French officials remained in the struggling colony, and they encouraged immigration. By now the successful resettlement of Acadians in Louisiana, which had begun in 1764, was well-known by Acadians everywhere, so interest began to build among the Acadians in France of migrating there to join their brethren who were regularly sending them letters extolling the opportunities afforded by the bayou state. [See the Semer letter on page 263]. Although their main concern for the next decade was providing basic sustenance for themselves, a small group of 22 Acadians did get permission to sail to Louisiana in October 1777, thus creating more interest in a trans-oceanic migration.

In about 1783, a Frenchman named Henri Peyroux de la Coudreniere returned to France from Louisiana. With the help of the Acadian cobbler Olivier Theriot, he worked to recruit Acadian pioneers to move to Louisiana. At first, France was not cooperative—after all, Louisiana was now a Spanish colony—but they finally came to an agreement in late 1784, and the following year about 1,600 Acadians sailed for Louisiana in seven ships. Six of them left from the Nantes/ Paimboeuf area. Another ship, *La Ville d'Archangel*, sailed from Saint-Malo.

As stated by Gérard-Marc Braud, many among these Louisiana-bound emigrants did not know America; only a third had been born on that continent. The population that left France in 1785 was predominantly a younger one, and passengers over 60 were rare (there were only eight). The majority of the group was under 20, and many were young children; thus, the majority knew Acadie only through the stories of their parents. The ships' lists seem to indicate that the Acadians left in family groups—sometimes three generations. There were also some Acadians at Saint-Malo and Nantes who made their way to the island of Guernsey and then on to Prince Edward Island and Nova Scotia. However willingly they all went, once again some families were unfortunately separated because some members married to French citizens remained in France. Also, women without children tended to stay in France.

There were still thousands of Acadians in France after the last of the seven ships left for Louisiana. Once the French government saw the migration's success, it stopped the emigration of any more Acadians, so that those who remained were there to stay. Nevertheless, during the ensuing years, there is anecdotal evidence that a few Acadians journeyed to Louisiana, Quebec, and other places of re-settlement to join their families, but they have not been documented.

Today in France

Those Acadians who stayed in France became largely assimilated into French society. However, today there are still some areas, such as the Poitou-Charente region and the island of Belle-Île-en-Mer in Brittany, where you can find French people who will readily and proudly tell you that they are of Acadian descent.

Today, there are many Acadian associations presently active in France. Paris has two important Acadian associations. In 1976, the *Amitiés Acadiennes (today Amitiés France-Acadie)* was founded by the passionate, dedicated, and wealthy Parisian Philippe Rossillon (1931-1997). Today, this association is the umbrella group of all Acadian associations in France. The group organizes trips and student exchanges with Acadie (mostly to the Canadian Maritime provinces), and promotes Acadian cultural events in France. It offers professional study grants, the annual *Prix France-Acadie* in literature, and the *Prix du meilleur mémoire de maîtrise* on an Acadian subject. It also publishes a news bulletin on Acadian activities in France and in Acadie. The other Paris-based association is the *France-Louisiane/Franco-Américanie*, which does similar work but only with the Cajuns in Louisiana.

There are also many associations in parts of France, mostly in the regions of Poitou-Charentes, Brittany, and Normandy. In Brittany, they include *Belle-Île-Acadie* on the island of Belle-Île-en-Mer, and *Bretagne-Acadie-Louisiane* in Nantes and Saint-Malo. In the Poitou-Charente region, they include *La Maison de l'Acadie* in Loudun; *Les Cousins Acadiens du Poitou,* and *La Ligne Acadienne,* all in Archigny; *Chatellerault-Québec-Acadie* in Chatellerault; and *Falaise-Acadie-Québec* in Falaise. In Normandy, the association is called *ACA-NAMI (Amis du Canada et de l'Acadie),* located in Saint-Ouen de Tilleul. Also, an association in Aquitaine is *Béarn-Acadie-Nouvelle-France* based in Escout.

Les Cousins Acadiens du Poitou is one of the favorite pilgrimages for Acadians visiting France. This Acadian farm museum organizes ceremonies yearly on August 15, National Acadian Day.

The association *Falaise-Acadie-Québec* was created in 1987. It regroups friends of Acadie, descendants, and historians. Its library has one of the most important documentation files on French America, including files on the Mi'kmaq Amerindian nation. It also administers the *Musée de la chapelle,* built in 1648, in the *Château de Falaise.* Here, Louis de Gannes served mass as a young man, and then later became a major of troops in Port-Royal, Acadie. De Gannes was also the father of the first two Acadian priests, Louis Joseph DeGannes, born in 1704, and Pierre DeGannes, born in 1705. His other son Michel was a major in the Louisbourg fortress.

There are presently five festivals in France that include Acadian activities such as arts and music in their programming. These festivals include *La Semaine Acadienne* in Saint-Aubin-sur-mer, Normandy; the *Festival Les Cousins d'Amérique* in Loudun, Poitou-Charentes; *Les Francofolies de La Rochelle* in La Rochelle, Poitou-Charentes; the *Festival Interceltique de Lorient* in Lorient, Brittany and *Les Nuits Cajun* in Saulieu, Bourgogne.

Bibliography

Gérard-Marc Braud, *From Nantes to Louisiana* (*Éditions La Rainette Inc.*, 1999); Christopher Hodson, *The Acadian Diaspora: An Eighteenth Century History* (Oxford University Press, 2012); Ernest Martin, *Les exilés acadiens en France au XVIIIe siècle et leur établissement en Poitou* (*Geste Éditions*, 2012); André Magord, *Le fait acadien en France* (*Geste Éditions*, 2010).

ACADIANS IN THE LOUDUN AREA OF POITOU, FRANCE

Michèle Touret-Bodin

Several of the first families to settle in Acadie in the 17th century were from Loudun in the Poitou region, which includes La Chaussée and Saint-Jean de Sauves. They became Acadians, and many of the Acadian exiles in the 18th century came back to the Poitou region. In addition to the settlers, many dignitaries from this region were involved in the founding of Acadie. The early history of Acadie runs parallel to the history of France, and its destiny is closely linked to the political events of the time.

After Port Royal was established in Acadie in 1605 by Dugua de Mons, it was burned to the ground in 1613 by British troops led by Samuel Argyle. Acadie was occupied by England for 20 years thereafter. However, in 1627, King Louis XIII of France negotiated the Treaty of Saint-Germain-en-Laye, and Acadie was handed over to France. The Prime Minister, Cardinal de Richelieu, then decided to reorganize the French Marines, and proceeded to develop the French colonies in Acadie and Quebec. He created the Company of One Hundred Associates, a trading company that was able to finance maritime equipment and expeditions to America. Cardinal de Richelieu owned numerous seigneuries land held by a grant from the King of France in Richelieu as well as in Loudun, where his Coussay-en-Mirebalais castle was located.

At the Cardinal's side was his cousin, Isaac de Razilly, Knight of the Sovereign Military Order of Malta and his adviser on maritime affairs. This great naval captain was renowned for his expertise in combat and maritime expeditions. He was born in the castle of Eaux-Melles, very close to Loudun, where he completed his schooling.

The castle in which Isaac de Razilly was born.

The coat of arms of Isaac de Razilly.

In 1632, King Louis XIII and Cardinal de Richelieu commissioned Seigneur de Razilly, accompanied by geographer Samuel de Champlain and his cousin Seigneur Charles de Menou d'Aulnay, to develop a new settlement in Acadie. With a company of "300 elite men" (according to Théophraste Renaudot's *La Gazette*) the new governor left for La Hève (now La Have, Nova Scotia). He opened the first school for the settlers' children as well as those of the aboriginal population in the area. Richelieu's contribution, although rather brief in duration (he died in 1636), was decisive in the colonization of Acadie.

Portrait of Menou d'Aulnay from 1642.

His captain, Seigneur Charles de Menou d'Aulnay, then took charge and continued to expand the French presence in Acadie. He decided to enhance the value of land around Port Royal, and recruited new farmers. His mother, Nicole de Jousserand, owned an important feudal estate, the Seigneurie d'Aulnay, located near Aulnay, Martaizé, and Chaussée in Poitou. In 1643, she left as an inheritance to her son the right to manage the land and farmers who lived on the estate. Several farmers set out on the long journey to Acadie, attracted by the promise of land and the possibility of becoming landowners.

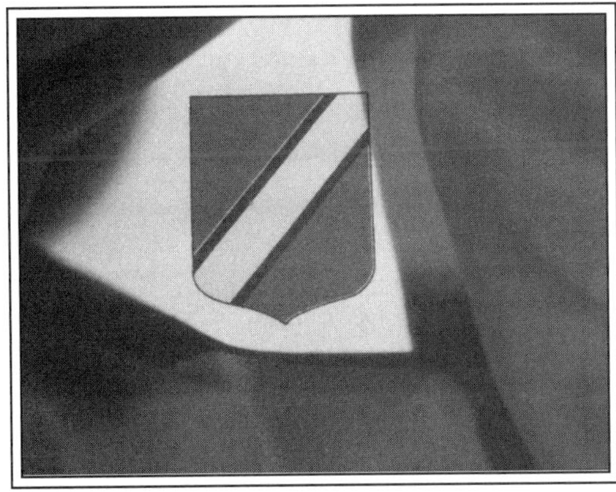

Coat of arms of Menou d'Aulnay.

In order to assist Charles de Menou d'Aulnay, Seigneur [Martin Le Godelier], owner of the estate of La Chaussée, joined him. An expert in agriculture, he wanted to share the benefits of his experience. He left La Chaussée with his son René and some farmers. Unfortunately, he died a few months after landing in Port Royal.

The Estate of Martin Le Godelier, in La Chaussée.

Church in La Chaussée from the 17th century.

These three French noblemen from the Loudun region, accompanied by several settlers from the area, set off from the old country to help build the New World. These men, women, and children who would settle in Acadie came from the villages of Oiron, Brie, Martaizé, Aulnay, Guesnes, Angliers, and La Chaussée.

According to research published in the thesis by ethnologist and genealogist Geneviève Massignon, "*Les parlers français d'Acadie*" (French spoken languages in Acadie), several families from different villages in the Loudun region were among the pioneers who settled Acadie. For example, Massignon found in the La Chaussée parish archives information about Madeleine and Andrée, two daughters of Vincent Brun and Marie-Renée Brault, who were baptized in the church in La Chaussée in 1645 and 1646, respectively. The family settled in Port Royal and three other children were born in Acadie. Madeleine married Guillaume Trahan (his second marriage) and was the ancestor of all the Trahans in America and elsewhere.

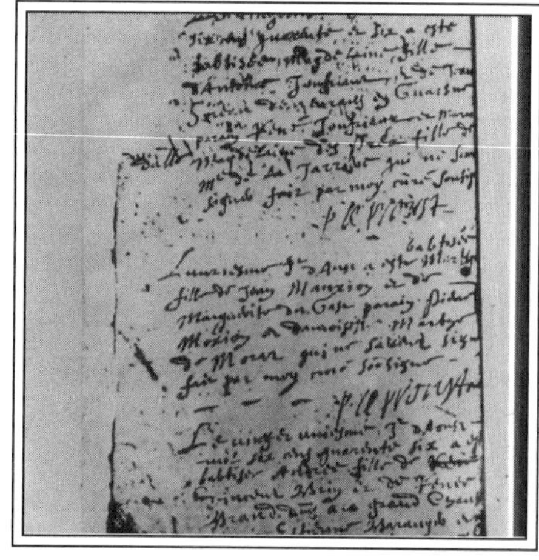

Baptismal certificate of Andrée Brun, found at the Archives Départementales, *La Chaussée.*

The Loudun region shares its heritage and its bond with Acadie. For this reason, *La Maison de l'Acadie* association has been working for 30 years on the documents uncovered and studied by Geneviève Massignon. In particular, thanks to private archives, it was recently discovered that Etienne Robichaud (Rébéchau) and his family lived and worked in La Chaussée.

La Maison de l'Acadie à *La Chaussée, in Poitou.*

Located near the church in La Chaussée, *La Maison de l'Acadie* is a place of memory and history, where Acadians from all over the world are welcome to learn more about their own family history. The facility has been called "the little house with a big heart," and feels less like a museum than a gathering place in which friends can meet for the first or hundredth time. The members of the association that run the museum are all volunteers who wish to give visitors there the sense that they are coming home.

Open to the public from July 1st to August 31st every year, the museum collects, displays, and makes available information about the families from the Loudun region who left for Acadie in the 17th century. The mission of the museum association includes conducting genealogical research on families from Loudun as well as organizing presentations and exhibitions related to Acadian history. *La Maison de l'Acadie* belongs to the network of regional associations affiliated with the *Amitiés France–Acadie*. These associations organize dinner shows and performances of Acadian music. On August 7, 2013, at the last concert given by Angèle Arsenault, she performed her trademark song *Grand-Pré*. The popular singer died in February 2014.

The *Cousins Acadiens du Poitou* is an association founded in 1980 to organize gatherings for the descendants of Acadians living in Poitou and to encourage exchanges between the families of this region and those of historical Acadie in Canada and in Louisiana. Its Acadian genealogical service responds to requests from families to conduct research tracing the history of their Acadian ancestors. Since it began, the association has seen a marked increase in interest in heritage and history, and its program has evolved to include the study and presentation of Acadie's rich and unique heritage, largely through the *Musée des Huit-Maisons*, located in Farm No. 10 in Archigny, which was donated by Mme. Gabrielle Papuchon Bernard.

Thereafter, Farm No. 6 in Archigny was restored to its original state. The association set aside one room for a library of references on Acadie and another for archives, and there is a large room that is used for lectures and exhibitions. These two buildings, Farm No. 10 and Farm No. 6, are classified as historic monuments.

Every year on August 15th, the *Cousins Acadiens du Poitou* celebrates the Acadian national holiday at the *Musée des Huit-Maisons* in Archigny. This social event has become very popular. Parents and children share a meal and listen to Acadian and Cajun music. A new show is planned and presented every year. Other activities include a dinner and dance, where all those who love Acadie, whether or not they are descendants of this "country without borders," can enjoy themselves. The Acadian Museum of Archigny welcomes visitors from March until October and invites them to discover the origins and the story of the Acadian people. The association also takes part in different events organized in the region, such as fairs and heritage celebrations. Through its affiliation with *Amitiés France–Acadie*, it is also able to participate in international projects with the different Acadian areas of the world.

ACADIANS IN BELLE-ÎLE-EN-MER, FRANCE

M.M. Le Blanc

In France, there exists an island in southern Brittany so small that it is not found on many maps, yet this island was once destined to play an important role not only in the history of Europe but also of America. Belle-Île-en-Mer would be for nearly four centuries the center of many issues, particularly for the Acadians. Nothing predestined Belle-Île-en-Mer and Acadie to merge under any circumstances, but history forever united these two distant lands after the Acadians were expelled from their homeland during peacetime and condemned to the tragedies and humiliations of the 1755 Deportation and Exile.

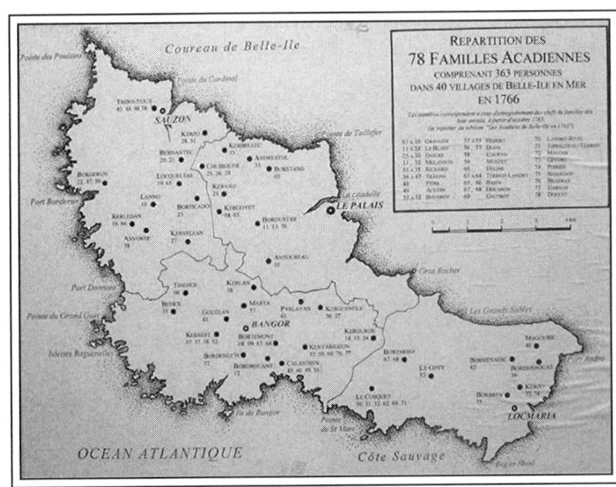

Map of Belle-Île-en-Mer, showing how land was divided.

Beginning in the 17th century, the development of marine traffic off the European coast and further out in the Atlantic gave Belle-Île-en-Mer an importance that it did not have before. Attacks on the island by Dutch and English ships were incessant, with some leading to successful landings that were quickly repressed. Belle-Île-en-Mer's attraction for conquest was further strengthened during the reign of Louis XV, which coincided with England's rise as the superior maritime power. In France's disastrous Seven Years War against England, Belle-Île-en-Mer suffered assaults and the disgrace of defeat. Yet this same war, so fatal to France's American colonies, brought Belle-Île-en-Mer and Acadie together.

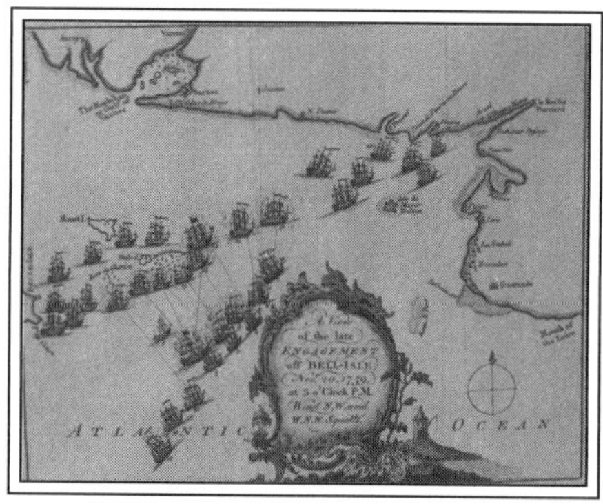

Battle during the Seven Years War.

In the famous 1759 Battle of Quiberon, fought near Belle-Île-en-Mer, France lost its finest vessels to the English ships that awaited them off the southern coast of the island. Under King George III, Belle-Île-en-Mer finally fell into British hands on June 3, 1761. Although not a poor island, Belle-Île-en-Mer is small and has limited resources and, had the British occupation's two-year interruption of crops and livestock continued, its inhabitants would have faced starvation if not for a peace treaty. The Treaty of Paris, signed on February 10, 1763, returned the Acadians imprisoned in England to France. However, King Louis XV did not know quite what to do with these Acadians. They presented a significant problem. Their faithfulness to king and religion after years of banishment and wandering made it impossible to leave them destitute. Locating them, however, was another question.

After a ruinous war and an unfavorable treaty, France's finances were grave. Its single source of wealth was land, so the Acadians were finally repatriated to France after their seven-year imprisonment in English ports. In May of 1763, four English ships carried 394 Acadians to Saint-Malo and 384 to Morlaix where they were forced to stay, not knowing their future, but finding a good number of their fellow citizens there and settling in these host cities.

The Duke of Choiseul suggested the availability of Acadians to work the lands of those who would accommodate them. As the Receiver of the King's Domain of Belle-Île-en-Mer, Francis Kermaquer knew the island's general economy would improve with more families, given that the British occupation had driven out many locals, leaving their farmlands abandoned. Abbé Jean-Louis Le Loutre had been introduced to the Duke, who obtained official status for him as an advocate for the Acadians and an ambassador for France.

Abbot Jean-Louis Le Loutre, friend of the Acadians.

Abbé Le Loutre, from Morlaix, had previously been sent to Acadie as a Catholic missionary priest. He had fought alongside the Acadians at Fort Beauséjour, escaping through the woods to Quebec. After setting sail for France, his ship was captured and he was imprisoned on the British island of Jersey for eight years until his release in 1763 via the treaty. He had returned to Paris where he learned of the projects concerning the Acadians, and was introduced to the Duke as the one person who could convince them of the plan, as he had the respect and admiration of the Acadians and was well-known. Le Loutre became both an ambassador and an official advocate for the Acadians, giving him the credibility and authority needed in the negotiations.

While Belle-Île-en-Mer measures only 86 square kilometers and was unable to absorb all the refugees, relocating a contingent would solve part of the problem. Based on the available farmland, it was decided that about 77 families could be established on the island. The resettlement project was finally accepted on October 25, 1763, five months after the Acadians had arrived in France.

Grain Warehouse of the Seigneurie on Belle-Ile-en-Mer

King Louis XV abandoned his royal domain at Belle-Île-en-Mer and presented the land to French citizens for cultivation. Having the Acadians on Belle-Île-en-Mer was the opportunity to "downsize" a somewhat utopian project—a division of the island into as many parts as there were families of Belle-Islanders and Acadians. For the first time in France, a farmer could own the land he cultivated and, even more extraordinarily, his children could inherit his land and property.

Le Loutre could not count on the alliance and sympathy of Gov. Warren, the king's commander on Belle-Île-en-Mer, who saw the arrival of the Acadians only as a large working population able to increase the economy of the island. Also going against Le Loutre were the heads of the island's four communes, as well as all the Belle-Islanders themselves, who could not understand why he would give their land to the Acadian "strangers." Still, he went to Morlaix to meet and identify Acadian families willing to settle permanently in Belle-Île-en-Mer; 77 families agreed, so he announced their impending arrival.

The baron Richard-Auguste de Warren, governor of the island.

To accomplish the lot division, a full survey of the land in each municipality was undertaken. Engineers, auditors, and surveyors arrived on the island in 1763 and finished their work in December 1766, but not without great difficulty. The result was the first *cadastre* in France, a significant legal document of land ownership.

Previously in June 1763, one month after their arrival in France, three heads of Acadian families in Morlaix and Saint-Malo came to Belle-Île-en-Mer to examine the possibilities of establishment there. These patriarchs, Joseph-Simon Granger, Honoré LeBlanc, and Joseph Trahan, all from the Minas Basin in Acadia, remained the spokespersons and negotiators for the Acadians during the later settlement procedures. In their negotiations, these Acadians were aided by Le Loutre. Nevertheless, another dispute arose.

The Acadian leaders proposed the creation of a new commune so they could all live together. However, Governor Warren and the inspector Isambert both thought it was better to scatter them throughout the four existing communes of Belle-Île-en-Mer so they would become part of the indigenous population. This forced separation was the solution that was approved.

Le Loutre had encountered another problem when he met with the original families who had agreed to move to Belle-Île-en-Mer. Now, only 57 families were willing to relocate from the welcoming city of Morlaix, so Le Loutre went to Saint-Malo, which had received a much larger number of Acadian families, and there he had no trouble finding additional families for a total of 78. Thus, with his full quota, Le Loutre returned to Belle-Île-en-Mer to welcome them.

The first Acadian family arrived from Saint-Malo on September 24, 1765: Armand Granger, his wife Marguerite Terriot, and their three children, all born in Rivière-aux-Canards in the Minas Basin of Acadia. Other Acadians arrived on Belle-Île-en-Mer, some in small groups and many by the boatload. Those from Saint-Malo embarked at Auray, and those from Morlaix traveled from one port to another until they reached Belle-Île-en-Mer.

Commorative sign on the Rue de la Manutention, reading, "In September 1765, the first Acadian arriving on Belle-Ile were lodged in the 'Magasin de la Seigneurie.'"

The last convoy reached the port of Le Palais on Belle-Île-en-Mer under the high walls of the Citadel on October 30 during a storm of such unusual violence that it was talked about for years after. In total, 78 Acadian families consisting of 373 persons of all ages, were finally settled in Belle-Île-en-Mer, but housing was scarce. Before the war in 1761, the island had almost 1,800 homes, but only two years later, after the British occupation, there were fewer than 700 habitable abodes. Upon arriving, they saw work had been delayed and, though the surveys were completed, the lot divisions had not yet been made. The Acadians immediately set out to build new houses and buy materials and animals.

With winter on its way, the decision was made to house the immigrants temporarily in warehouses used to store grain and in former military barracks. The Acadians were directed to arrange themselves into the available spaces. It may not have been what they had imagined, but Warren, who in the almost daily mail he sent to his many correspondents (now kept in the French departmental archives of Vannes), referred optimistically to the successive arrivals of Acadians as people who were "robust, well-made, healthy, and courageous."

On November 28, 1765, Le Loutre and Isambert established a list called the "State of Acadian Families Coming to Belle-Île-en-Mer," containing 363 names that included heads of families, wives, children, dependent minor orphans, and widows. Despite the years in exile, families remained extremely united, from a Terriot and six sisters married to Granger brothers and cousins, to LeBlancs comprising 14 heads of families.

Most of the Acadians who arrived were from the Minas Basin and were all related. Of the heads of families, 22 were born in La Rivière-au-Canards, 18 in Grand-Pré, 22 in Pigiguit, four in Port Royal, two in Cobequid, and one in Beaubassin. The LeBlanc families had 57 members, Granger had 46, Trahan had 49, Terriot had 27, and Daigre had 21. Among the 78 heads of families, 67 were married, and all were born in Canada except eight. Of the 67 wives, only three were born outside Canada. The list included 211 children, of which 95 were born in Canada and were at least ten years old, and 116 born outside Canada who were under nine years of age. The mortality rate of newborns among the Acadians was low.

The 78 families were to be divided into 13 brigades of six families each, and then to be sent to 40 different villages. The brigades were based on kinship ties, and were carefully supervised by Le Loutre and Isambert to avoid suspicion of injustice or favoritism.

Le Loutre supervised the construction of small houses 27 square meters in size, each with low, narrow openings, built with local shale, covered with thatch or slate, and appended to each other, a style still used in Belle-Île-en-Mer today. In February 1766, the successful integration of the Acadians with the Belle-Islanders produced its first "mixed" marriage between Lawrence Babin, an Acadian born in Grand-Pré, and Françoise Carrière of Le Palais, Belle-Île-en-Mer.

At long last, by December of 1766, the final lot divisions had been made. Contracts to permanently transfer the divided lots, the famous "*afféagement* contracts," were signed. While the lots could be handed down to descendants, they could not be sold until they had been worked for ten years, so no lots could be sold before January 1, 1776.

An Acadian house on Belle-Île-en-Mer.

A judgment dated January 12, 1767, required the reconstruction of the legal status of the Acadian families of Belle-Île-en-Mer, a completely original idea of returning their lost roots by taking oral statements of the families and recording their marriages, baptisms, and burials. The ruling gave the precise procedures for the implementation of this important work, supervised by Le Loutre. He brought the notary Auray, the heads of the four communes, and four Acadian witnesses. The work consisted of interviewing heads of households about their ancestors, and was completed within one month. Though there are some omissions and errors, the statements are surprisingly accurate for over 800 people, particularly as to specific dates. It was as though each Acadian had brought a small diary on which was noted the day of his grandmother's death or his sister's wedding or the birth of his fifth grandson.

Within ten years, 22 heads of families had left their lands on Belle-Île-en-Mer and moved away, leaving only 64 Acadian families—450 souls in all—on Belle-Île-en-Mer. Several families who had left settled in Nantes on the mainland. About 125 Acadians of Belle-Île-en-Mer left for Louisiana, not due to a failure of their situation but to the impossibility of all of the members of a large and growing family living together on one small lot.

A wedding in 1976 shows the Granger and Thomas families.

A Granger family gathering in 1907.

To celebrate 200 years of an Acadian presence on Belle-Île-en-Mer, in 1966, the *Association Belle-Île Acadie* invited many prominent Acadians, including those from the Canadian Maritime Provinces and a delegation from Louisiana led by Sen. Dudley J. LeBlanc. It was the beginning of a rebirth of Acadian life on Belle-Île-en-Mer through exchanges with other Acadians.

On National Acadian Day on August 15, 2012, Ray Trahan and Brenda Comeaux-Trahan, from Lafayette, Louisiana, stand in front of the Acadian Monument on Belle-Île-en-Mer.

Belle-Île-en-Mer today maintains the memory of the Acadians, not as a historical park or an island museum, but as an entire landscape steeped in 250 years of Acadian presence, with commemorative plaques and preserved original homes. In effect, the disastrous Treaty of Paris allowed Belle-Île-en-Mer to regain its place in the kingdom of France. The island would have stagnated for decades had the Acadians not provided an economic balance. The Acadian history of Belle-Île-en-Mer has found its place in the history of France.

Bibliography

Danielle Blancaneaux and Maryvonne LeGac, directors of the *Association Belle-Île-Acadie* wrote the original article *Les Acadiens de Belle-Île-en-Mer*; and Jean-Marie Fonteneau, *Les Acadiens du Canada à Belle-Île-en-Mer* (2004).

Acadians in St. Pierre and Miquelon, France

Françoise Enguehard

The archipelago formed by the Islands of Saint-Pierre and Miquelon is located only a few nautical miles from Newfoundland, in the middle of Atlantic Canada. Ideally situated near the fishing banks and on the route from the Old World to the Gulf of Saint Lawrence and New France, these islands were at the heart of the turbulent history of French North America. They were passed back and forth between France and England at the whim of wars and peace treaties before finally being returned to France in 1816. Today, Saint-Pierre and Miquelon are the only concrete vestige of New France, the only French soil in North America. Although little known, their Acadian history is one of the cruelest chapters of the *Grand Dérangement.*

The Islands of Saint-Pierre and Miquelon were frequented first by Portuguese and then by French seasonal fishermen, who settled on a temporary basis while cod fishing and then returned to Europe in the fall. Joas Alvarez Fagundes passed by in 1520, and then Jacques Cartier in 1536. When returning from his second voyage to Canada, Cartier found "several ships there, from both France and Britain."

Gradually, by the end of the 17th century, a permanent settlement developed on Saint-Pierre and Miquelon that was placed under the responsibility of Plaisance, the headquarters of the French colony in Newfoundland. In 1713, after the signing of the Treaty of Utrecht, the inhabitants of the archipelago, like those of Plaisance, were ordered to move to Isle Royale (today Cape Breton Island), which they did, although it appears that some of them preferred to remain in hiding, and even welcomed into their midst a few Acadians who came over from Cape Breton. For 50 years, the archipelago remained under British rule, during which time the Acadians began the long calvary of the Deportation (1755-1763) and France lost Isle Saint-Jean, Louisbourg, and Isle Royale (1758).

In 1763, the Treaty of Paris brought an end to the Seven Years' War and, although France lost Isle Royale, it managed to regain Saint-Pierre and Miquelon. Before the treaty was officially signed, King Louis XV had worked at repossessing the archipelago. The title of governor of Saint-Pierre and Miquelon was granted to Sire Dangeac, and that of captain of the infantry to the Baron de l'Espérance, from Plaisance and Port Dauphin (Isle Royale) respectively. In his instructions, the king indicated that he expected many Acadians would want to leave the New England colonies, but that as few as possible should be welcomed because "too large an influx could cause jealousy in the neighboring English settlements."

Needless to say, the news of the return of the Islands of Saint-Pierre and Miquelon to France spread like wildfire among the Acadian deportees. Hardly had Dangeac set foot on the archipelago with over 100 recruits from France when a group of 116 Acadians arrived. They came from Boston, Roxbury, Charlestown, Savannah, Tinten, and a number of other villages; there were only four family names: Hébert, Vigneau, LeBlanc, and Sire (Cyr). That was far more mouths to feed than the food and supplies allotted by Versailles could handle.

But it was obvious that Dangeac, like the Baron de l'Espérance, was reluctant to enforce the orders from Versailles with regard to the Acadians. The first winter was so harsh that the new arrivals took refuge on the island of Langlade, where the terrain offered better protection against the elements and wooded areas provided a source of heat. They built "huts made of fir posts stuck in the ground, with no sheathing, a thatched roof and a chimney made with a *torchis* of hay and clay." During this time, a plan was made in Versailles to move the Acadians in France and those on the archipelago to Cayenne (French Guiana).

In August 1764, a second group of Acadians arrived on the archipelago from Chedebucto, Pointe de Beauséjour, and Beaubassin. There were 110 with surnames such as Laforest, Boudreau, Vigneau, LeMale, Chiasson, Bourgeois, Cormier, Bertrand, Comeau, Arsenau, Lapierre, Deveaud, Boudret, Dousset, Renaud, Poirier, Oncle, Brand, Gaudet, Hébert, Mirat, LeBlanc, Pire, Sire, and Gautier.

As Michel Poirier indicates, in all likelihood these people were brought to Saint-Pierre and Miquelon on board the *St-Jacques*. This was a ship belonging to Jacques Vigneau, the representative of the first group of Acadians who had arrived the previous summer, who wanted to reunite members of his family, including his brother Joseph. All these poor people came to settle on Miquelon, where Gov. Dangeac and the Baron de l'Espérance attempted in vain to persuade them to leave for Cayenne. The Acadians replied politely that they were grateful to the king for his offer but that "no matter what proposal we receive [...] and no matter what threats are used to entice us, we prefer life above all; never will we accept to leave this climate."

In October 1765, 111 more Acadians arrived from Isle Saint-Jean and Halifax, and then 72 others who had embarked at Beauséjour, supposedly to go to Halifax. As if by chance, their ship stopped over in Miquelon, but the passengers did not want to leave. It was a lot of people, too many for a tiny colony in such a precarious situation.

In August 1766, Versailles sent word that these Acadians could not stay and that they must return to France; otherwise they would receive no food after the month of May. The Acadians refused to move, so the king decided to send all the Acadian families to France.

Gov. Dangeac's sadness is apparent in his letter to Versailles: "Here I am, close to the end of the departure of these inhabitants from these islands," he wrote. "It gives me great pain and embarrassment and it is without question costly to have to tear these miserable souls from their settlements after they have sacrificed the fruit of all their labor for several years to build them and are forced to abandon them just when they were beginning to take advantage of them."

Next came a period of movement back and forth between France, Saint-Pierre, Miquelon, Acadie, and America. While some Acadians crossed the Atlantic to go to Nantes, Saint-Malo, Lorient, Brest, or Rochefort, others left for Prince Edward Island, Quebec, Louisiana, and New Brunswick. That is how 24 families from Miquelon ended up founding Cocagne, where they obtained the first land grants given to Acadians.

Six months later, for reasons unknown, the Duke of Choiseul changed his mind and allowed the Acadians who had been forcibly removed to France to leave for Saint-Pierre and Miquelon—and nearly 200 of them did. However, the following year, everything was so scarce that some of them asked to return to France. Acadians were arriving in the archipelago, whereas others were leaving for Acadie to be with relatives who were more comfortable.

Over the years, in spite of everything, the fate of the Acadians on Miquelon improved; according to the 1776 census, there were 649 residents (Acadians) and 129 overwintering (fishermen from France who spent the winter with the inhabitants in order to be able to start fishing in the spring), 107 houses, 64 barns, 222 head of cattle, 73 horses, and 106 sheep, in addition to stages and boats for the fishery.

The tranquility that the Acadians had hoped for did not last long. With the arrival of the governor of Newfoundland in Saint-Pierre and Miquelon in 1778, the inhabitants found themselves once again forced to leave. They arrived in France, where they waited five years before the archipelago was returned yet again to France by the Treaty of Versailles in 1783. In all the French ports where they had taken refuge, the Acadians registered to return "home." Unfortunately, only 240 people were given permission to return that year. In fact, since everything had to be rebuilt (the English had taken what they wanted and burned the rest of the settlements), the king allowed passage only for strong men able to rebuild. In the years that followed, other Acadian families returned and started fishing and farming again, so that by the 1790s some of them were prosperous and could hope to live in peace at last.

That was not taking into account the French Revolution, which was being felt on Saint-Pierre by 1790; a constitution club was created, causing quarrels and skirmishes between the inhabitants that took the life of a young girl, who was killed by a stray bullet. Much to the despair of the Acadians on Miquelon, this agitated political situation lasted until 1793.

On April 12th of that year, a group of about 250 or 300 of them left Miquelon for the Magdalen Islands and Isle Madame with their priest, Fr. Allain. In the end, it was a wise move, since on August 26th, the English landed on the archipelago and took possession of it. They deported the population of Saint-Pierre but allowed the Acadians on Miquelon to stay, hoping to take advantage of the profits from their fishing and farming. It is not surprising that the Acadians decided to pack their bags and once again go back to France, where misery awaited them.

In 1816, the Acadians were finally able to return once and for all to the Islands of Saint-Pierre and Miquelon. Some of them (such as Marguerite Vigneau, wife of Alexis Poirier, who was born in Grand-Pré and experienced six deportations) saw their life in exile finally come to an end. The 1818 map of Miquelon indicates 48 dwellings belonging to, among others, Poiriers, Costes, Vigneaus, Moutons, Doucets, Boudrots, and Beliveaus. Their descendants are still proudly there today, some on Saint-Pierre but the majority on Miquelon, where the Acadian heritage is celebrated.

Over the centuries, Acadian names that date back to the early days have more or less disappeared, replaced by Basque surnames such as Detcheverry, Etcheverry, and Orsini. Nevertheless, almost all the residents of Miquelon have Acadian blood. They participated enthusiastically in the events celebrating the 400th anniversary of Acadie in 2004, they maintain strong cultural, sports, and trade relations with the Acadians on the Magdalen Islands, and they erected an Acadian Odyssey monument in the center of their village. Their cultural association, *Miquelon-Culture-Patrimoine*, continues to forge firm ties with the Acadie of New Brunswick and encourages the preservation of traditions. In the cemetery of Miquelon (alongside many Mi'kmaq and near the grave of Anne-Claire Dupont de Renom, wife of the Baron de l'Espérance), lie many Acadians whom Acadian tourists come to visit with heavy hearts.

For a long time, the Acadians of Saint-Pierre and Miquelon have been the forgotten people of Acadie, a regrettable fact, because their epic was one of the cruelest. As Fr. Anselme Chiasson states in the foreword to Michel Poirier's book *Les Acadiens aux îles Saint-Pierre et Miquelon*: "The history of all the Acadians is marked by manhunts, imprisonments, and the Deportation, but the history of the Acadians of the Islands of Saint-Pierre and Miquelon is by far the most tragic. Even if they were deprived of their rights, Acadians elsewhere had a relatively peaceful life after the Treaty of Paris, whereas the Acadians of Saint-Pierre and Miquelon were stripped of their possessions, imprisoned, and deported many times right up until 1816. Their misery and their suffering dragged on for over a half a century. And worst of all, history has not told their sad odyssey."

Photo©Jean-Christophe L'Espagnol/AFP

The town of Saint-Pierre, on the island of same name. This French town has a population of 6,100 inhabitants.

Photo©Office du tourisme, Saint-Pierre

The island of Saint-Pierre. The town harbor faces a few other islands.

Photo©Remi Guillot

The town of Miquelon on the island of Miquelon, is situated a few miles from the island of Saint-Pierre. The mostly Acadian population is 700 inhabitants.

Photo©Evangeline Richard

The welcome sign includes the Acadian flag.

BIBLIOGRAPHY

Michel Poirier, *Les Acadiens aux îles Saint-Pierre et Miquelon* (Moncton, NB: *Éditions d'Acadie*, 1984); and Jean-Yves Ribault, *Histoire des Îles Saint-Pierre et Miquelon (la vie dans l'archipel sous l'ancien régime)* (*Saint-Pierre: Imprimerie du Gouvernement*, 1962).

ACADIANS IN THE MAGDALEN ISLANDS, QUEBEC

Pauline Carbonneau

Photo©Tourisme Iles de la Madeleine

Ile du Havre-aux-Maisons.

"The Iles de la Madeleine [Magdalen Islands] descend deep into the oceans of the past," wrote Gaspasian Antoine Bernard in his book *Histoire de la survivance acadienne* [History of Acadian Survival] published in 1935. In fact, Amerindians first visited this archipelago in prehistoric times, and the Mi'kmaqs continued to travel to the Magdalen Islands from the Maritimes before and after the Conquest. The Vikings may also have landed here, but there is no evidence to prove this.

Jacques Cartier was the first to leave written descriptions of his two visits to the Islands in 1534 and when he returned to France in the spring of 1536. The Basques and the Bretons hunted walrus and seal throughout the archipelago. Under French rule, as of 1653, land grants and fishing rights were given to the Magdalen Islands by either the King of France, the Governor of

Quebec or, later on, the Governor of Louisbourg in Acadie. The first person to claim these rights was Nicolas Denis; neither he nor those who were granted the archipelago following him were able to populate the Magdalen Islands.

It was only during the English rule that Acadians came to settle in the Islands around 1761. They worked for Richard Gridley, a colonel from Boston who had received temporary permission to hunt and fish on the Islands for service rendered to the British Crown. Almost all of them came from Saint-Jean Island (now Prince Edward Island), having probably escaped the 1758 Expulsion.

Among those hired were ten Arseneaus from Malpèquc, four Boudreaus (Budero) from Saint-Jean Island and Cape Breton, three Hachés (Gallant) from Saint-Pierre-du-Nord and Tracadie, two Poiriers from Malpèque, Jean Chiasson from Saint-Pierre-du-Nord, Charles Doucet (Ducette) and Félix Desroches (De Ruche) from Malpèque. It seems those engaged worked on the Islands in the summer and returned to their families in winter. They pledged allegiance to the British Crown on August 3, 1765, before F. Allwight, representing Richard Gridley in the Islands.

According to oral tradition, expatriates from Petite-Rochelle (near Ristigouche where the Acadians that fled through the woods had taken refuge) had come to work for Gridley, but their names do not appear on the list of those employed. The names Jean Cormier and Charles Dugas are mentioned. The latter did not stay in the Islands but returned to Baie-des-Chaleurs to become one of the founders of Tracadièche, known today as Carleton-sur-Mer in Quebec.

With the help of his lieutenant, Jonathan Thompson, Gridley built a fishery at Pointe à Sauvage, that is, buildings for rendering seal and walrus blubber and curing fish.

The First Families

According to oral tradition, Gridley's lieutenant Jonathan Thompson urged some of those hired to bring their families to live on the Islands. It is difficult to confirm where these families came from as most couples who had been married at Saint-Jean Island or Cape Breton had fled to Miquelon (a French island near Newfoundland) or elsewhere before settling in the Magdalen Islands.

Among these were six Boudrot families: François "Manne" and Jeanne Landry, François and Marie Boudrot, Joseph and Louise Arseneau, Joseph "Castor" and Marguerite Chiasson, Charles and Marie-Madeleine Chiasson and the family of their son Louis and Louise Dugas. Pierre Cormier and Isabelle Chiasson along with Jean Cormier, who married Marie Boudrot in Havre-Aubert in 1775, also settled in the Islands. Jonathan Thompson also allowed them to cross the Islands to find suitable land to settle on.

According to my father, Pierre-Cornélius Carbonneau, all the first Boudrot families settled in Havre-Aubert except for Joseph (Manne), one of his sons, along with Antoine Arseneau, who chose Havre-aux-Maisons. The Pierre and Jean Cormier families and Antoine Etcheverry would set up in Havre-Aubert. Amand Chiasson and Pierre Lapierre chose to stay on in Bassin. However,

François, one of Pierre Lapierre and Cécile Blanchard's sons, went to join the Acadians of Havre-aux-Maisons.

Arrival of the Saint-Pierre and Miquelon Acadians

The giant wave of Acadians who arrived in the Magdalen Islands came from Miquelon where many had fled following the Expulsion. Researchers are divided on the date of their arrival. Paul Hubert, author of *Les Îles de la Madeleine et les Madelinots* published in 1926, states that residents left Saint Pierre and Miquelon following the September 22, 1792, proclamation which forced them to take the constitutional oath and would arrive in the Islands two days later. The Acadian priest Jean-Baptiste Allain led about 250 people. According to historian Michel Poirier, himself from Miquelon, about 300 left the archipelago on April 12, 1793, with Abbé Allain. About 250 reached the Magdalen Islands; the others sought refuge at Isle Madame in Cape Breton. Parish registers were not kept until July 28, 1793, with the baptism of Françoise Anne Bourg (Bourque), daughter of Joseph Bourg and Madeleine Haché. A little later, many more Miquelon residents came to the Islands when the English took the archipelago on May 14, 1793.

Most of the Vigneau, Bourgeois, Bourg, Hébert, Devost, Cyr, Gaillardé, Briand and Cormier families, along with a few bachelors, settled in Havre-Aubert. The Greniers, Bourgeois, Vigneaus and Arseneaus chose Ile d'Entrée [Entry Island], later occupied by the English from 1822 on. Settlers from Miquelon also chose Havre-aux-Maisons Island because of the natural harbours that could shelter fishing boats. The Thériault, Cormier, Poirier, Richard, Cyr, Basque and Turbide Acadian families elected to live here. Few Acadians from Miquelon settled in Étang-du-Nord, the main Island. We have been able to trace Joseph Boudrot, Joseph, Joseph and Pierre Gaudet and François Petitpas from this group.

Photo©Tourisme Iles de la Madeleine

Ile du Havre-Aubert

Photo©Tourisme Iles de la Madeleine

La Grave.

Acadians From the Maritime Provinces

Starting in 1805, many Acadians from the Maritime Provinces, mainly from Cape Breton, would choose to live in the Islands. This included Paul Landry, who came from Arichat, Isle Madame. Once in the Islands, he married Marguerite Boudrot, daughter of Louis and Louise Dugas, one of the first families to put down roots in the archipelago. The following year, 1806, Charles Leblanc d'Arichat married Marguerite Cormier, daughter of Jean and Marie Boudrot, who had settled in the Islands before the Miquelon Acadians arrived.

Next, around 1826, would come the Pierre Molaison family and François-Xavier Forest, who was only four years old. Somewhere around 1830, one of Antoine Etcheverry's nephews, Jean Chevarie, and a few years later another Jean Chevarie, from Saint-Jean Island, arrived. Starting in 1833, the Isidore, Polycarpe, Jean-Baptiste, William and Charles Chiasson families left the Maritimes to settle in the Islands. Around 1834, Raymond Bourgeois and his family left Chéticamp for the Islands. The Poiriers, Longuépées, Bourques, Fougères, Doucets, Gallants, Daigles, Mius (Miousse) and another Arsenault and de Lapierre family would later join the community. The Aucoins, Costes (Decoste), Benoits, Le Jeunes and finally the Blaquières from Rustico, Prince Edward Islands, would arrive around 1926.

Acadian Emigration from the Magdalen Islands

In the mid-19th century, Magdalen Island settlers began to leave. They did not depart because of the limited space or lack of natural resources, but rather because of the impediments to owning their land and the shameless exploitation of some foreign companies to whom they tried to sell their fish.

After the massive influx of settlers from Miquelon, Acadian families in the Magdalen Islands managed to survive by fishing and subsistence farming on small pieces of land not occupied by the first families. Following a long journey to lands from which they were often expelled, the Acadians thought they could finally live in peace. But this peace was short-lived: five years after the wave of settlers from Miquelon, Isaac Coffin received letters patent from the British Government conferring ownership of the Magdalen Islands. He quickly started demanding rent for the bits of land the Magdalen settlers thought they owned. Despite the desire to own their land, some preferred to simply leave the Islands. They were also exploited by the merchants who had taken over the archipelago's economy.

Around 1805, some families went to Saint-Grégoire (today Bécancour, Québec) where many Acadian refugees settled. In 1848, the first group emigration, led by Abbé Alexis Bélanger, was to Newfoundland, where the Havre-aux-Maisons families set up in St. George's Bay.

From 1845 to 1872, more than 125 Magdalen fishing families emigrated to various villages on Quebec's North Shore. From 1855 to 1861, 21 families, the majority from Havre-Aubert, settled in Natashquan. Famous singer Gilles Vigneault's great grandfather Placide Vigneau was among them. In 1857, a group from Havre-aux-Maisons, led by Firmin Boudreau and his wife, Pélagie Cormier, founded Pointe-aux-Esquimaux (now Havre-Saint-Pierre). In 1858 and following years other Magdalen families would join them. Many descendants of the Magdalen Island Acadians settled on the North Shore, particularly in the cities of Baie Comeau and Sept-Îles. Around 1874 and following years, Magdalen Islanders travelled to fish off Île d'Anticosti and many brought their families with them. Others worked in logging.

Fishing did not bring the expected earnings on the North Shore, so many families in Natashquan and the surrounding areas moved to Beauce, particularly to Saint-Théophile. In 1896 and later, Magdalen Island Acadians received government aide to join other Maritime Acadians and colonize the Matapédia Valley. The Magdalen Islanders settled mainly in Lac-au-Saumon in Quebec. In 1899, five families left Havre-aux-Maisons to found Baie Sainte-Anne in New Brunswick with other Acadians.

Unhappy with the salaries offered in the pulp and paper plants on the North Shore, the Magdalen Islanders left Clarke City to work in the Saguenay. The city of Kenogami was founded in 1912-1913, and in 1925 there were more than 140 families from the Magdalen Islands in the city. When Alcan started making aluminum in Arvida, several families left the Islands to work there. Backed by the experience they acquired in the Saguenay, Magdalen Islanders went to work in factories in Mauricie and the Quebec City area.

Magdalen Islanders were also drawn to the United States immediately following World War II to work in the textile mills. Among them were Alphonse Boudreau and his wife Vénéda Doucet, who settled in Rhode Island and who are grandparents to Dennis Boudreau, well-known genealogist and author of the *Dictionnaire généalogique des Îles de la Madeleine, 1760-1948.*

In the 1940s, overpopulation and extreme poverty forced many Magdalen Islanders to leave and colonize the La Sarre area in Abitibi, in northern Quebec. They would settle particularly at Île Nepawa and Roquemaure.

However, the bulk of the Magdalen Islander Acadian emigration was to the Montreal area, where the majority would settle in the Verdun-Côte Saint-Paul sector and later LaSalle and the South Shore.

Conclusion

Other nationalities settled in the Magdalen Islands, but were eventually absorbed by the Acadian population to form one of the most "Acadianized" groups on the North American continent. Magdalen Islanders are Acadian and their racial behavior is proof. Although civilly, politically and religiously part of Québec, their national holiday is not Saint-Jean-Baptiste as celebrated by all Quebeckers, but the Assumption on August 15, and their national anthem is *Ave Marie Stella.*

Nouvelle-Acadie,
Acadian Mosaic in Lanaudière, Quebec

Alexandre Riopel

Almost four years after the *Grand Dérangement*, in 1760,[1] a first group of Acadians settled along the banks of the Assomption River, in Saint-Pierre-du-Portage-de-l'Assomption (currently L'Assomption). Some in the group were refugees from the Beaubassin and Menoudy parishes, in what is now Nova Scotia. A small group stood out within this first unit of immigrants. In fact, some of them had taken part in the takeover of the *Pembroke* vessel out of Port-Royal that was to deliver the 232 people on board to North Carolina.[2] Fleeing the English, most of these newcomers passed through Quebec.

The risks of being captured by the English, combined with the smallpox epidemic and famine affecting people in the winter of 1757-1758, pushed many to pursue their route to the southwest, along the north shore of the Saint Lawrence River, a journey during which many perished. Some 1,900 Acadian refugees found protection in the Saint Lawrence Valley, representing six percent of the population of New France.[3] Of this number, 16 families and 11 individuals finally settled in Portage, totalling 84 people.[4] Their migration was primarily the result of an individual itinerary.

Conditions That Led to the Arrival of Acadians in Quebec

The signing of the Treaty of Paris in 1763 marked the end of the Seven Years War. As a result, Acadians were authorized to leave the American colonies. Many decided to settle in the province of Quebec. In exchange for an oath of allegiance to the British Crown, they would be able to continue their French traditions, including the practice of their native language and religion. It was from this perspective that, starting in 1765, Gov. Murray offered land to all immigrants who wanted to populate the colony and contribute to stimulating the economy. Finally, in September 1766, a Royal Proclamation recommended that the Lords "accommodate the Acadians so that they settle on the ungranted lands of their seigneuries.... It is ordered that they be provided with provisions for one month, outside the *Magasins du Roi*, to sustain them until they are able to provide for themselves."[5] The Sulpicians answered the call, and a colonization plan was set in motion. Three weeks later, the first deportees were reported in L'Assomption.

Proprietors of the Saint-Sulpice seigneury (where Saint-Pierre-du-Portage was located), the Sulpicians assigned a surveyor to Ruisseau Saint-Georges, and then to Ruisseau Vacher in 1769. The foundations were laid for the future Saint-Jacques Parish. Several *Messieurs de Saint-Sulpice* had been missionaries in the Minas Basin (Grand-Pré, Pisiguit, Cobequid) and Port-Royal areas prior to the deportation, which could explain the sympathy they felt for the exiles. Of the seven main *cadies* of Quebec, the Lanaudière region seemed to be the only one to receive such thoughtful support from a religious organization. The Sulpicians granted them fertile land, offered them work, and brought in an attentive priest. In the middle of a famine, each family received considerable food supplies and farming tools.

Second Phase of Acadian Colonization

Starting in 1766, a true Acadian migration flow was taking place in the Saint-Pierre-du-Portage (L'Assomption) area. It marked the second phase of Acadian colonization in the sector, and was the result of presentations made to the governors of Boston and Quebec by Acadians posted in New England. After several of them had attempted in vain to reach France[6] and the island of Saint-Domingue (Haiti),[7] many took steps to settle in Quebec.[8] Starting in 1766, some 890 Acadians traveled by ship to Quebec, leaving—for the most part—Massachusetts and Connecticut.

In spite of his demanding pastoral duties, the Portage parish priest, Jacques Degeay, went to the capital to welcome them. He took 11 families and one widow under his wing, for a total of 80 people.[9] Several of them were associated with the Landry family. For these family units and the ones that would follow, the decision to migrate, as well as the choice of location, seemed to be the result of a collective initiative. Encouraged by an effective communications network, a migration route was established. Important contributors, the Sulpicians provided them with a geographic area where they could rebuild a prosperous agricultural community, thus preserving their Acadian identity.

Étienne de Montgolfier, superior of the Montréal Sulpicians and vicar general, was present when they arrived in Saint-Pierre-du-Portage. In partnership with Bishop Jean-Olivier Briand, they ensured that many Acadians remained in the seigneury. These newcomers were housed in the buildings of the Sulpicians and with Acadian families already settled in the area. The warehouses of the merchants Antoine Laroque and Germain Leroux were transformed into makeshift shelters. After the winter, the settlers progressively settled along the Achigan and Saint-Esprit rivers—close to the Saint Lawrence River, in Saint-Sulpice and Repentigny, but primarily in the territory of the future Saint-Jacques Parish.

Arrival of a Third Group; Importance of Family Migrant Networks

In 1767-68, several Acadians who had been temporarily housed in Portage migrated some 15 kilometers north to start clearing the ranges in Petit Saint-Esprit and Ruisseau Saint-Georges, and their concession. Time was short: stimulated by the presence of family migrant networks, a third group of Acadians had just arrived. By far the largest, this 1767 group included 41 families, totalling 223 people.[10] Most of them arrived from Massachusetts (Boston, Salem, Waltham) and Connecticut (Pomfret Center, Norwick, New London).

The following year, seven other families and six individuals were added to their numbers.[11] As with their predecessors, these 51 deportees were mostly poor and many were sick. The commitments undertaken by the neighboring merchants were at their height.[12] Considering that their living conditions were deplorable, Degeay, the parish priest, contacted Gov. Carleton in 1768 to ask for his help.[13] Everything would indicate that it was in 1769 that the first houses were raised in Ruisseau Saint-Georges. The opening of a sawmill in Ruisseau Vacher during the spring of 1770 facilitated building in this sector.

Odilon Forest surrounded by his children, sons-in-law, grandchildren, and neighbors, the day before his house was demolished. The Acadian-style dwelling was built in 1772 in the Bas-de-l'Église Nord (Ruisseau Vacher) area.

Photo©Louis-Beaulieu Fontaine, 1905, Coll. François Lanoue

The arrival of the Acadians did not stop here. With Fr. Degeay weakened by disease, a new player entered the scene to lend a hand. Recently ordained, it appears that Jean-Baptiste Bro was sent to New England in the fall of 1773.[14] His mission: convince his compatriots to settle in the seigneury of Saint-Sulpice.

A Rivière-aux-Canards native, Bro would have been present in the Grand-Pré church when the deportation decree was ordered. He returned from this mission accompanied by several families. In November 1774, Abbé Bro succeeded Fr. Degeay. During this same year, the parish of Saint-Jacques-de-la-Nouvelle-Acadie was officially established. Its name was chosen in memory of Degeay, who had been so committed to the Acadian cause. It would later be named Saint-Jacques-de-l'Achigan, then Saint-Jacques.

Photo©unknown photographer, ca. 1940, Coll. François Lanoue

A Port-Royal native, Charles Forest was deported with his family to Boston. Upon return from exile, he married Isabelle Dugas on February 4, 1771, in Saint-Pierre-du-Portage. Owner of one of the biggest houses in Ruisseau Vacher, Jacques Degeay, the parish priest, chose the location to celebrate the first Mass in June 1772. The temporary chapel was used until the rectory in Saint-Jacques was built in 1775. The house was taken down in 1946.

Photo©unknown photographer, Coll. Réjeanne Plouffe

Wayside cross erected to commemorate the first Mass celebrated at the house of Charles Forest by Abbé Jacques Degeay in June 1772. On September 5, 1920, a commemorative monument was added to the cross in memory of the event. It is found opposite the Forest house at 2145 Bas-de-l'Église Nord. This photo was taken the day before the monument's inauguration on September 4, 1920.

Profile of the Migrants of Nouvelle-Acadie

Some 607 Acadians settled in L'Assomption and Saint-Jacques between 1760 and 1784, for a total of 117 families and 24 individuals.[15] The 84 refugees from the first colonization wave represented 14 percent of all Acadians who settled in L'Assomption Parish.[16] Among these first arrivals, there appear to have been greater numbers of widows and persons who remarried.[17] As for deportees, there were 519 individuals, distributed over 101 families and 12 individuals; 60 percent of them, or 354 people, settled in L'Assomption between 1766 and 1768.[18] Of these, 24 of them had spent a decade in France. Many of the immigrants were from Port-Royal and, to a lesser degree, Grand-Pré. There were few kinship ties between the refugees and deportees.

Located in what is now the Nova Scotia peninsula, these parishioners were under the control of the English until 1713. Although they lived in an environment with almost no French immigration and with a limited religious presence, the Acadians preserved their cultural unity. Through their resilience, they were able to adapt and make the most of the situation that was imposed upon them. During the *Grand Dérangement*, they were dispossessed of most of their belongings, yet what probably pushed them to leave New England was a life without the sacraments of the Catholic religion. United by descent, origin, faith, experience, and attachment to family, 82 percent of the Acadians registered in L'Assomption and Saint-Jacques permanently settled in Nouvelle-Acadie (526 people, including 102 families and 23 individuals).[19]

The demographic vitality of this community was impressive; 66 percent of the newcomers were children and young singles.[20] Contrary to what was described in several monographs, it appears to have been rare for members of the nuclear family to be separated, or at least they were reunited with each other. In all, 326 immigrants living in the area were born in Nouvelle-Acadie.[21]

Of the 89 families in this group, 82 were interrelated. The multigenerational Dugas-Robichaud-Mireault-Forest-Hébert kinship group from Port-Royal alone united 41 families (211 people). Originally from Grand-Pré, the Landry-Dupuis group brought together 12 families (57 people), the Bourgeois-Richard group was made up of 48 people, and the Landry-Robichaud group was 43. The arrival of this founding people doubled the population in L'Assomption, whereas that of Saint-Jacques was mostly made up of Acadians.

In spite of the many ties uniting them, some 15 families (77 people) continued on, after having spent a few months in Portage.[22] Located on the south shore of the river and close to Montréal, the La Prairie area and to a lesser degree Acadie were key destinations.

Strong feelings of identity were forged. Another dozen Acadian families,[23] from Carleton, in the Gaspé Peninsula, further strengthened this unity at the beginning of the 19th century. Over the course of the following centuries, as a result of interregional migration, the descendants of some of these same ancestors had considerable influence on genetic groups in the Quebec regions of Témiscamingue (Béarn), and Outaouais (Masham), as did others in Ontario (Sturgeon Falls, Embrun). During the 19th century in northern Lanaudière, they contributed to the colonization of Sainte-Julienne, Rawdon, Chertsey,[24] Saint-Gabriel-de-Brandon, Saint-Donat, Saint-Côme, and particularly Saint-Alphonse-de-Rodriguez. It was in this area that author Gabrielle Roy's mother, Mélina Landry, grew up. Seeking land or work, other families settled in Montréal, Manitoba, and the United States. For the Lanaudière region as a whole, anthropologist Sylvain Gaudet identified 59 Acadian surnames.

Today, an analysis of ascending genealogies reveals that Acadian-origin founders represent 18 percent of Quebec's ancestors.[25] For most of the 1,459 Acadian unions, Acadian development took place in seven regions: Magdelan Islands (17.6 percent), the Gaspé Peninsula (13 percent), southern coast (12.5 percent), Lanaudière (11.5 percent), Bois-Francs (10.8 percent), Richelieu (7.3 percent), and Mauricie (7.3 percent). These *cadies* brought together close to 80 percent of Quebec's Acadian pioneers. In the Lanaudière region, 73 percent of the population has at least one Acadian ancestor.[26] In the parish of L'Assomption alone, 82 couples were married, whereas in Saint-Jacques the number was 66. They join Havre-Aubert (183), Bécancour (84), and Carleton (77) as the parishes where the greatest number of marriages between Acadian founders was celebrated.[27]

Social and Economic Affairs at the Time of the Mills

From an economic standpoint, agriculture was the main source of household income at the beginning of the 19th century. Sawmills and flour mills were at the heart of the seigneurial system, and were a very important place of exchange. Millers were recognized as being excellent managers, and several Acadians were specialized in this field. In 1755, in Minas Basin alone, there were 12 mills for milling grain and sawing wood.[28] Once he arrived in Quebec, Simon Savoie was seen as a pioneer. Starting in 1760, he worked in Saint-Sulpice, and then the following year in Achigan (L'Épiphanie). In Saint-Jacques, Amable, Préjean assumed the role of miller starting in 1770.

Joseph Dugas and Pierre LeBlanc were trusted confidants of the Sulpicians.[29] The former was a miller born in Port-Royal, who was in charge of the large Archigan mill. Important to the region, this building—which was also used as a manor—brought in important revenues to the seminary of St-Sulpice. At the same time, his brother, Claude, was responsible for the lower mill. As for Pierre Leblanc, he ran the mill located close by. At the beginning of the 19th century, Pierre's father, Basile LeBlanc, took a managing role at the parish's second flourmill. Another of his sons, Jean-Édouard, and his grandson, Séraphin, would take over. Séraphin would later donate land for the construction of L'Épiphanie church.

The development of the Saint-Sulpice seigneury was a success. In 1815, the surveyor general of Lower Canada, Joseph Bouchette, stated the following: "More than three-fourths of this seigneury is well cultivated, and for the goodness of its soil, the quality of the timber, and state of improvement, is not surpassed by any that surround it."[30] The commercial and industrial importance of the L'Assomption region was undeniable. There were dozens of merchants and artisans. Many warehouses and vast stores for wheat were located in the area. It was one of Quebec's key places of trade. Other mills were built to meet overseas (Great Britain, the Antilles), trade (fur trading company, Outaouais logging camps) and local orders.

It was within this context that in 1787 a windmill was built in Saint-Roch-de-l'Achigan, a parish independent of L'Assomption and Saint-Jacques. Acadians Charles Chamberland and his son Michel operated the mill[31] for close to two decades. The family would then be associated with the history of the windmill and that of the watermill in Petite ligne, Saint-Jacques. Julien Poirier's son, Odilon, followed by his grandson, Gédéon, would later take over. Acadians were experts in the art of operating mills, from one generation to the next.

As for the women in the Saint-Jacques area, in addition to working on the farm, they became specialists in a new domestic art, that of making woven sashes. An accoutrement that was specific to the traditional dress of French Canadians starting in the last quarter of the 18th century. The fur traders appreciated its use to support their backs. The *L'Assomption* sash featured bright patterns and was the most popular. Another was called *L'Acadienne*.

The merchant Laurent Leroux, who hosted Acadian families in L'Assomption, held the monopoly on sashes used by the North West Company for trade. Around 1830, Salomon Bélanger settled in Ruisseau Saint-George and became the representative for the Hudson Bay Company. He was the official supplier of Assomption Belts, North West Belts, and North West Caps.[32] After his death in 1863, the branch was taken over by Joseph Dugas, and was prosperous until the late 19th century. Destined to disappear in the early 20th century, the technique was documented and taught by reputable craftswomen, including Élisabeth Mireault and Marie Gaudet.

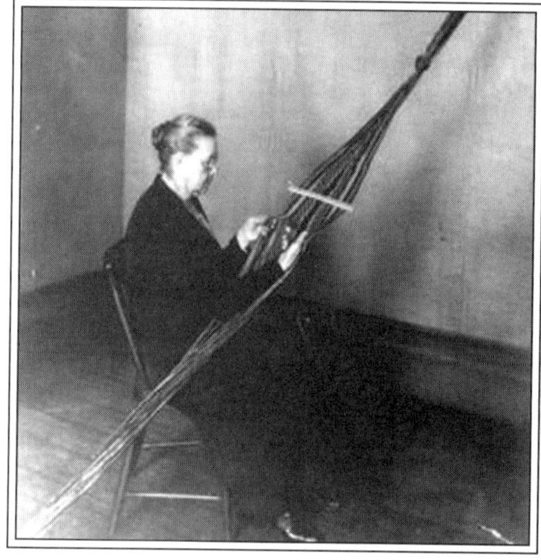

Photo©unknown, 1933, CCDMD, Coll. Denis Chabot

Mme Napoléon Lord (Élisabeth Mireault, 1866-1943), a talented woven sash maker, contributed to carrying on the traditional finger-weaving techniques.

The Acadian Elite

An integral part of parish life, the Acadians of Saint-Jacques occupied certain key roles within public institutions governing community life. Land needed to be cleared, and transportation and communications facilitated. The population was ever-growing, and land concessions became increasingly less frequent. Starting in 1794, a contingent of Acadian families settled along the Ouareau River.

Lacouareau, the future parish of Saint-Liguori, was taking shape. In 1817, three influential men built a sawmill in Montcalm (Saint-Liguori), along the Rouge River. These were second cousins Firmin *dit* Philémon Dugas, Isaac Dugas, and Pierre Richard. The millers of Achigan would have a new generation of young workers; Firmin was Claude's grandson and Isaac that of Joseph. Five years later, Firmin also built a flour mill.

Meanwhile, in 1819, the Sulpicians erected a windmill along the Ouareau River. A bridge was built. The town center of Saint-Liguori took shape around these infrastructures. Attracted by the quality of the surrounding forests and prairies, the Braults, Bourgeois, LeBlancs, and Richards also started operating mills in the sector. When the municipality was officially established in 1855, five sawmills, three flour mills, and one carding mill were in operation.

The mills played both an economic and social role. They were used as a place of assembly, of trade, and as a public area. Through their professionalism, good civic activities, and their roles in social and economic affairs, millers accumulated public offices. The many ties Acadian millers forged with local and regional representatives elevated their social status over several generations. This facilitated the integration of Acadians in the region.

Saint-Liguori village. The bridge can be seen in the foreground and the Sulpicians' mill (when it was the property of the Richard family) in the background to the left.

Photo©Pierre-Fortunat Pinsonneault, ca. 1900, Coll. of the photographer

As for justice, various public positions contributed to maintaining order. One of the most prestigious was that of militia captain, since its role was that of liaison between local administration and government. In addition to being a war leader in time of crisis, the captain enforced municipal by-laws and saw to the orderly functioning of public works.

The duties of an individual within the militia were dependent on social recognition. In Acadie, the militia was generally the reserve of British citizens while Acadians were excluded. The Quebec Act of 1774 provided new definitions in their favor, however. It was greatly appreciated, since the militia corps was the first identifying factor for institutional stakeholders prior to 1840. In the region, this honor went, in turn, to the following men: Honoré Thério (1776);[33] Jean Mireau (1810); Joseph Bourgeois (1812); Pierre Dupuis Jr. (1812); Julien Poirier and his son Odilon (1827); Joseph Dupuis (1828); Pierre Richard (1828); Isaac (1828) and Hyacinthe Dugas (1847); Antoine (1847) and Séraphin LeBlanc; Isaïe, Ludger; and Jean-Baptiste Forest. As a major, J. Bourgois (1827), J. Poirier (1847), and I. Dugas (1847), all influential figures, even had a battalion under their command. However it was Firmin *dit* Philémon Dugas who reached the highest rank when he was named lieutenant-colonel (1863).

Michel Prévost, who was captain of the 1st Battalion of L'Assomption (1794), inspired many. By the War of 1812, the Acadians had gained a reputation as excellent militiamen in spite of their small stature, and were the first to volunteer to fight the Bostonians. Prévost had to stand up to his staff to keep these brave men under his command. Another feat of arms: it was under the orders of Captain Euclide Dugas (son of the merchant Joseph) that the Saint-Jacques company participated in a Fenian raid in 1870.

Lastly, parish growth led to the establishment of socio-cultural facilities; churches and schools needed to be built and managed. These projects were under the wing of parish trustees, school trustees and *marguilliers*. Acadian surnames were common on these committees. Educational and religious fields were popular. In Saint-Jacques alone, seven teachers had already been working since 1831.[34]

Many priestly and religious vocations resulted from this devotion: 134 priests,[35] 324 nuns, and 35 brothers.[36] *Les Dames du Sacré-Cœur* founded the first school for girls in Canada in 1842. In 1853, *Les Soeurs de Sainte-Anne* took over the vocation, founding their main convent. In the second half of the 19th century, most of the Ste-Anne sisters were of Acadian origin. They created several convents in Canada and the United States, including one in Victoria and another in British Columbia.

During the 1820s and 1830s, the civilian population mobilized in order to defend the cause of education and social progress. Political representation had to be reviewed. Many local elites supported the demands of the Patriot Party, whose goal was to obtain the sovereignty of the Assembly by limiting the governor's powers. However, regional institutional stakeholders were concerned about the party's movement to radicalize. Julien Poirier was an exception. Resuming an old strategy of neutrality, few Acadians were involved in Patriot committees. Yet, Saint-Jacques' parish priest wrongly thought that some would use parish corporation funds to finance the rebellion. The close ties between these local stakeholders, business partners, employers, and friends at the heart of the regional and provincial power structure probably explained their reticence.

Times were changing; the seigneurial system was abolished in Quebec in 1854, to be replaced by a municipal system. It was during this transition period that several parishes were created within the territory of Saint-Jacques: Sainte-Julienne (1848, 1855), Saint-Alexis (1851), Saint-Liguori (1852), L'Épiphanie (1853, 1854), and Sainte-Marie-Salomé (1888). Progressively, the municipal council would replace, notably, the parish corporation and corps of militia officers as the key institution in the community.

Despite this change in the type of governance, many influential men succeeded in getting elected as mayor or prefect of the county of Montcalm.[37] The confidence of citizens in Acadian-origin townsfolk went beyond the boundaries of the parish. Some were elected as representatives.[38] The Martin and Dugas families were represented by four of their family members.

Cooperation

The Saint-Jacques area was known for its woven sashes, but also for its maple products and cigar and pipe tobacco. This expertise was the result of locally-developed know-how. In 1864, François-Louis Genand, a Saint-Jacques physician, started the ball rolling by writing two articles on tobacco. Cultivating this plant out of pleasure, he was still able to win several prizes, including one at the Paris World Fair in 1867. Following in his footsteps, Médéric Foucher decided to enter the tobacco industry. For a century, several Acadiens cultivated this plant with seeds brought back from New England. The American Civil War (1860-1865) led to surging prices. Foucher wanted to develop the market in Canada, while taking advantage of Acadian know-how. He studied 22 tobacco varieties.

Photo©unknown, August 18, 1912, Coll. François Lanoue

Tobacco factory located at the end of Marion Street (today, Brault Street), in Saint-Jacques.

Along with his brother-in-law, Joseph-Odilon Dupuis (Nazaire's brother, both founders of the *Dupuis frères* department store), Foucher established tobacco factories, a business that proved to be profitable for the region. Between 1920 and 1930, ten such companies were operating in the sector. Several of them were founded on the principles of mutual support and cooperation. Up until 1911, Quebec was the biggest tobacco producer in Canada. Foucher and Dupuis were the fathers of tobacco cultivation in Canada. To this day, despite production being discontinued in the 1990s, tobacco kilns are still an integral part of the landscape.

Photo©Archives-HEC Montréal

Front cover of the Dupuis Frères catalogue from fall-winter 1932-1933. "Aidons-nous les uns les autres, la coopération est la clé du success" ("Let's help each other, cooperation is key to success"). *This maxim was typical of the "biggest French department store in America."*

United, many citizens of Nouvelle-Acadie (Saint-Alexis, Sainte-Marie-Salomé, Saint-Jacques and Saint-Liguori) adhered to the principles of the cooperative movement. In Bas-du-Ruisseau-Vacher (Sainte-Marie-Salomé-de-

Port-Royal), the second cooperative creamery was founded in 1883. In 1919, it was the county of Joliette's second *Caisse Desjardins* that was up and running. Neighboring towns followed in their footsteps.

Meanwhile, in Saint-Alexis, a mutual company providing insurance against fire, lightning and wind was created in 1905. It led to the creation of one of the biggest insurance companies, *Promutuel Lanaudière.* Other cooperatives would follow, particularly in the agricultural sector. In Saint-Jacques, the Joliette district's tobacco growers cooperative was to become the model for other cooperatives. In the 20th century, these were the types of initiatives that led to the area becoming one of the key cooperative centers in Quebec.

Photo©Archives-HEC Montréal

Second creamery in Quebec, at Saint-Marie-Salomé, founded only a few months after an act to protect butter manufacturers was adopted, in March 1883.

The Acadian Legacy

The poet Marcel Dugas was born in Saint-Jacques in 1883. This man of letters is considered to be one of the pioneers of literary criticism in French Canada. In his short story, *Adélaïde Lanoue,* he relates how, as a young boy, he liked to play in the sashes, woven at the general store of his grandfather, Joseph Dugas. A native of the same municipality, Judge Ludger-Urgel Fontaine *dit* Beaulieu, appears to have been one of the first to write about the situation of Acadians. In 1866, he published *Les Acadiens du district de Joliette.* Eight years later, his brother, Joseph-Octave Fontaine, gave a talk at the *L'Institut canadien de Québec* entitled *La corvée des fileuses (scène acadienne).*

In 1885, Ludger-Urgel Fontaine finally published *Voyage du sieur de Diéreville en Acadie.* Some of his writings such as *Rapport sur les Acadiens de la province de Québec (1880)* and *La succession Leblanc* were included in this re-edition. In 1816, a man by the name of Charles White (LeBlanc) died in Philadelphia without heirs. He was very wealthy. Difficult to separate truth from fiction, some claimed that the city had even been built on his fortune. Two delegations of the Leblanc family left Ste-Julienne in order to receive their share. Following a ruling of the American court of appeal, the first delegation was told in 1828 that the amount of $36,200 would be awarded to the first cousins of the Charles White family. The second delegation was to receive $17,000. However, they returned with empty pockets and many questions left unanswered.

Several Lanaudois of Acadian origin took part in the creation of contemporary Quebec: the strong man Louis Cyr, the historians Alphonse-Charles Dugas, Guy Courteau,[39] and François Lanoue; the administrator Yvan Forest, who had a brilliant career in the cooperative movement; professor emeritus of agriculture and food, Germain Brisson;[40] and lastly, the general secretary of the *Union Catholique des Fermières*, Marie Dupuis, which is also the name that designates the Joliette women's center. The most influential figure remains Bernard Landry, premier of Quebec from 2001 to 2003.

To this day, many residents of the Lanaudière region—and Nouvelle-Acadie in particular—are proud to boast of their Acadian roots.[41] The legacies are many, and living legacy is honored. Marc Brien,[42] from Sainte-Marie-Salomé, was an important bearer of tradition. He greatly contributed to the distribution and preservation of the Québécois and Acadian musical heritage. Thanks to Brien and people like him, traditional music groups (*La Volée d'Castors, Belzébuth, La famille Cantin* and *La Cantinière*) are more common in this area than in any other part of the province. This art represents a coming together of people united in song. Just as the Irish are a people united by music, so too are the Acadians.

At the same time, the mission of the organization *Les Petits Pas Jacadiens* is that of fostering, transmitting, promoting, and distributing traditional dance music. In the surrounding area, it is not uncommon to hear words pronounced as they were in the old country. Philippe Jetté studied the subject and published an article on nicknames in Nouvelle-Acadie. This ombudsman of living heritage, collector of memory, and cataloguer of traditional musicians is found alongside Andrée Mireault Foster[43] in a documentary by Phil Comeau, *Les Acadiens du Québec : Lanaudière mémoire vivante de l'Acadie.*

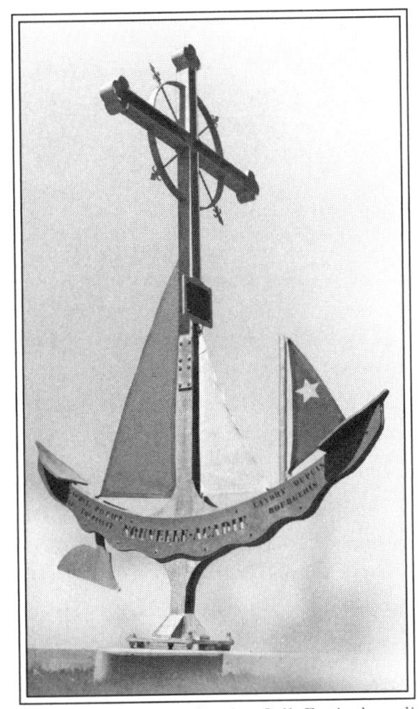

Photo©Jean-Philippe Gaudet, Coll. Festival acadien

Since 2001, the Festival acadien de la Nouvelle-Acadie *has been promoting Acadian culture in the Lanaudière region. In honor of the founding Acadians of Saint-Liguori, a memorial,* Le bateau-ancre *was inaugurated on November 18, 2012, in the presence of elected officials and many citizens. Among them was the festival's founder, the artist Gaston Gaudet, who designed the monument. Also participating were Cajetan Larochelle and the festival President Évangéline Richard.*[44]

Photo©Municipality of Saint-Jacques, August 12, 2013

On August 11, 2013, the inauguration of the 12th Acadian Odyssey monument commemorating the Grand Dérangement was held in Saint-Jacques. Left to right, Bernard Landry, 28th premier of Quebec; Jean Gaudet, monument representative; Pierre Beaulieu, mayor of Saint-Jacques; Paul Léveillé, Notre-Dame-de-l'Acadie parish; Serge Rivest, mayor of Saint-Liguori; Maurice Richard, mayor of Sainte-Marie-Salomé; Véronique Hivon, provincial minister for Joliette; René Légère, president of the Société nationale de l'Acadie; and Robert Perreault, mayor of Saint-Alexis. Seated is Manon Perreault, federal deputy member for the Montcalm district.

Proud and dynamic, the Acadian community is alive and well in the Lanaudière region. The epicenter of Acadian immigration in Quebec, this territory was a place of refuge for nearly 20 percent of Acadian immigrants. It is the largest in this regard, if the regions bordering the Atlantic Provinces are not included. Nouvelle-Acadie is one of the regions that best maintained the farming trade. Master millers, craftswomen who produced woven sashes, and tobacco producers were all bearers of this know-how. With its exceptional community spirit, it participated in the region's social development by establishing and managing parishes, schools, and municipalities. Culturally speaking, Acadie has remained strong through its language, songs, music, and writings. Lastly, by promoting cooperative principles, it enabled the economic development of not just Nouvelle-Acadie, but Quebec as well. The wealth of its heritage is vast. Conscious of its value, increasingly, this heritage is being preserved and showcased, for the joy of all.

Endnotes

1. According to the historian Christian Roy, it was in 1759 that the first Acadians arrived in L'Assomption, as he argued in Commission Des Fêtes Du 250E. Histoire de l'Assomption (L'Assomption, Quebec, La Commission des fêtes du 250e, 1967, p. 467-470). According to Marie-Thérèse Lagacé, however, the year 1760 appears to be the year of their arrival, as she argues in "Familles acadiennes de l'Assomption et de Saint-Jacques-de-la-Nouvelle-Acadie 1760-1784 : immigration et profil des migrants" (doctoral dissertation, Université de Montréal, 2006).

2. Among those who took part in the Pembroke revolt, in addition to Captain Charles Belliveau and the strong-man Louis Fontaine *dit* Beaulieu, were Charles Dugas, Denis Petiteau-Sincenne, Pierre Guilbeau, and Charles Mélançon. All these men have descendants still living in the Lanaudière region.

3. John A. Dickinson, "Les réfugiés acadiens au Québec, 1755–1775" (*Études canadiennes/ Canadian Studies*, 1994, Vol. 37, p. 56. and 60) and Marcel Fournier, *Les origines familiales des pionniers du Québec ancien* (2001, p. 3).

4. M-T Lagacé op cit, p.31.

5. Gazette de Québec, 15 Sept. 1766. Can. Arch. 1905, Vol. II p. 157.

6. M-T Lagacé, op cit, p. 47. In 1763, at the invitation of the Duke de Nivernois, Acadians of Massachusetts presented, in vain, a list of 1,019 people who were interested in leaving for France. Of them, approximately 160 went to L'Assomption.

7. Ibid. See French Nentrais, State of Massachusetts Archives, and Can. Arch. (1905) app. E. P. 148. In 1764, 406 people attempted to obtain a passport from the Massachusetts authorities and accept the invitation from the Count d'Estaing. A few years later, 140 of them were present in L'Assomption and Saint-Jacques.

8. M-T Lagacé, op cit, p. 49. On June 2, 1766, an application was made by 890 Acadians of Massachusetts. Of this number, some 30 families, approximately 180 people, would immigrate to L'Assomption.

9. Lagacé, op cit, p. 30.

10. Ibid.

11. Ibid.

12. Lise Saint-Georges, "Le village de l'Assomption, 1748-1791» (Master's Thesis in History, Université du Québec à Montréal, 1984, 145 p.).

13. Bona Arsenault, "Histoire des Acadiens" (*Les Éditions Fides*, 2004), 268.

14. Alphonse-Charles La Nouvelle-Acadie et messire Jean Bro, 1743-1824, second prêtre acadien et premier curé de Saint-Jacques-de-l'Achigan. Édition privée (Réjean Olivier) 1984, p. 72. (Louis-Guy Gauthier, Chronology).

15. M-T Lagacé. op. cit. p. 29. It is possible that other Acadians who do not appear in parish registers or notarial deeds were missed by the historian.

16. M-T Lagacé, op cit, p. III.

17. M-T Lagacé, op cit, p. 83.

18. M-T Lagacé op cit, p. 30 and 32.

19. M-T Lagacé op cit, p. III, p. 105.

20. M-T Lagacé op cit, p. 110.

21. M-T Lagacé op cit, p. 79-80 and 87 + author's research.

22. M-T Lagacé op cit, p. 76.

23. M-T Lagacé op cit, p. 29.

24. Nancy Gadoury, "L'encadrement du mouvement de colonisation dans le piedmont des Laurentides dans Lanaudière de 1810 à 1880" (Master's Thesis, Université du Québec à Trois-Rivières, 2004).

25. Josée Bergeron, Hélène Vézina, Louis Houde, et al, "La contribution des Acadiens au peuplement des régions du Québec" (*Cahiers québécois de démographie*, 2008, Vol. 37, No 1, p. 181-204).

26. Josée Bergeron, *Contribution différentielle des ancêtres d'origine acadienne au bassin génétique des populations régionales du Québec* (Ste-Foy: Université Laval, 2005, p. 69).

27. J. Bergeron, op cit, p. 50.

28. Alphonse-Charles Dugas, La Nouvelle-Acadie et messire Jean Bro, 1743-1824, second prêtre acadien et premier curé de Saint-Jacques de l'Achigan (Joliette, Édition privée, 2012, p. 51). Online (in French): http://collections.banq.qc.ca/ark:/52327/bs2242712

29. C. Roy, op cit, p. 483-484.

30. Joseph Bouchette. A topographical description of the province of Lower Canada. Embellished by several views, plans of harbours, battles, etc. (Printed for the author and published by W. Faden Geographer to His Majesty and the Prince Regent, Charing-Cross, 1815, p. 230).

31. Jean-René Thuot, La vie économique du territoire de L'Épiphanie, d'hier à aujourd'hui (Conference presented on July 11, 2004, in L'Épiphanie. p. 13).

32. Association des artisans de ceinture fléchée de lanaudière. Histoire et origines de la ceinture fléchée traditionnelle dite de l'Assomption (Les éditions du Septentrion, 1994).

33. Upon his return from exile in Bretagne in 1774, Honoré Thério joined the American revolutionaries to help them take Québec. The attack was aimed at garnering the support of Canadians in the War of 1812. It was unsuccessful.

34. Louis-Guy Gauthier, *De l'ancienne Acadie à la Nouvelle-Acadie : Saint-Jacques-de-l'Achigan en 1825.* (Éditions du pot de fer, 1991, p. XVII).

35. Ordained in 1847, Alfred Dupuis was the first priest from Saint-Jacques. He was director of the Collège de L'Assomption in 1860.

36. François Lanoue, "L'abbé Lanoue, mémoire vivante de Lanaudière" (Article: La famille Lanoue)

37. Acadian prefects in the County of Montcalm: Jean-Louis Martin (1861), Simon Richard (1881-1887), Louis E. Dugas (1912-1915), Lucien Martin (1915-1917), Joseph-Alcide Dupuis (1917-1918), Édouard Thibodeau (1919-1921), Jules LeBlanc (1923-1929), Gaspard Dupuis (1939-1940). Claude Lambert, Répertoire numérique des archives de la Corporation municipale du comté de Montcalm 1855-1950 (Joliette, Société de généalogie de Lanaudière, p. 71-75); Louis-Guy Gauthier, Saint-Jacques-de-l'Achigan, la population au 25 février 1861 (Saint-Jacques, Éditions du Pot de fer, 1989, p. I).

38. At the provincial level, there was Julien Poirier (1827- 1830), Firmin Dugas (1867-1874), Jean-Lois Martin (1861), his son Louis-Gustave Martin (1874-1878), his brother Joseph-Alcide Martin (1890-1892), Jean-Baptiste Richard (1881-1886), Ludger Forest (1886-1890), Joseph-Alcide Dupuis (1916-1917), and Gérard Martin (1962-1966). The elected federal representatives were Firmin Dugas (1871-1887), his son Louis-Euclide Dugas (1892-1900), and François-Octave Dugas (1900-1909), whose son, Lucien Dugas, was a provincial MP (1927-1936). He was named president of the Legislative Assembly in 1936.

39. His mother was Acadian: Marie Corinne Élisabeth Dugas, daughter of Euclide Dugas and Rose-Délima Brien.

40. His mother, Clara Gaudet, was Acadian.

41. In Sainte-Marie-Salomé, all the important anniversary dates of the Deportation have been celebrated with great pomp, including Bicentennial celebrations (1955), erection of the Acadian monument in memory of the 225th anniversary (1981) and the commemorative mass for the 250th (2005).

42. Fontaine descendant.

43. His mother was Thérèse Melançon-Mireault, who wrote *Le Bas du Ruisseau Vacher*: Sainte-Marie-Salomé (Sainte-Marie-Salomé, 1986).

44. Her mother, Fernande Desmarais Richard, wrote several books on the history of Saint-Liguori.

Madawaska Settlement in Maine and New Brunswick

Joseph Donald Cyr

The Madawaska Territory is the area of Northern Maine, Northwestern New Brunswick, and the western Gaspé region of Quebec known as Témiscouata. The region is defined by the Saint John River watershed and forests. It was first put on a map by Samuel de Champlain, in 1612, using information gleaned from the natives. Champlain saw it as a link between the two settlements then known as Acadie (now the Maritime Provinces) and Canada (now the province of Quebec). This vital link eventually became a land caught in a struggle between the British and French (and later American) empires as a source of materials to build navies. It became a land divided by the river that was also a link to economic markets.

When Samuel de Champlain first put the Madawaska/Témiscouata territory on a map, he envisioned a route between Port Royal, Acadie, and Quebec City, two French settlements that were built on fish, fur, and farming for the expanding French Empire, directly in competition with the British, who were established in Newfoundland and Hudson Bay.

The Massachusetts Bay Colony had once been claimed by Champlain, but the attack on Acadie's capital, Port Royal, by Argall in 1613 took away the southern reaches of Acadie and began 150 years of warfare that would gradually redraw Champlain's map into British possessions (and eventually become a boundary with the Americans).

Acadian settlements were not in competition with the native tribes. The Acadians built dikes in tidal marshes for farms and left the hunting grounds alone. The Malecite tribes in the region were settled into the Saint John River watershed and were trading partners with the French for the furs that were in such high demand in Europe. The trade followed the river systems, and the gifting that quickly evolved into trade also made the Malecites and French allies. They were also linked by the Roman Catholic religion, which helped forge alliances, and also by intermarriage, which would help define the two most important institutions in the lives of the people: the church and family.

Madawaska and Témiscouata were undeveloped. Whereas the territory was a vital link, its geography was very vague and maps of it were crude and misleading. Missionaries (even bishops) traveled through the region, but settlements were not established until the late 18th century, as a result of the birth of the United States, which would claim the region in order to obstruct the development of Canada. Once again, the people of the region found themselves in a dispute between two larger imperial interests.

Madawaska and Témiscouata were made *seigneuries* by the government in Quebec City in 1683. Development of these *seigneuries* was slow; in fact, little happened for the first century. The furs were becoming depleted because of the deep trading network with the Malecites that did not depend on a French presence in the region except for the itinerant missionaries, who sustained the links.

The tribes had a long history of military cooperation with the French, who were constantly raiding English settlements in New England, most notably in Maine. King William's War, Queen Anne's War, King George's War, and the Seven Years War had proven the value of alliances with the native tribes. The Saint John River watershed acted as a back door to the highlands that separated the waters from the ones flowing through the English settlements, allowing surprise attacks anywhere in New England, at will. At times, Maine was emptied of its population, but British persistence would eventually take bites into New France until it would all be consumed in the Seven Years War, which ended in 1763 with the Treaty of Paris, exchanging New France for the sugar islands of Guadeloupe and Martinique, as well as keeping the islands of St. Pierre and Miquelon, near Newfoundland, as a base for the French Atlantic fishery.

The Madawaska/Témiscouata region was also noted in the treaty, but it was not described with reliable geographic evidence. It noted that the British possessions of Nova Scotia, Massachusetts, and Canada would be separated by a line made from a northwest angle from the source of the Saint Croix River, which intersected the highlands that separated the watersheds of the Saint John and Saint Lawrence rivers.

Not knowing the division of the watersheds didn't seem too important at the time, because all of the involved parties were British colonies. The region remained undeveloped, but the river portage that ran from the Saint John River to the Saint Lawrence, either through the Madawaska River and Lac Témiscouata, or by way of the Saint Francis River and Lac Pohénégamook, was still utilized, and Acadians carried the mail for the British, as they had done for the French. This was the period when dispossessed Acadians came to occupy the Lower Saint John River Valley near the Malecite settlement known by the French as Sainte-Anne-des-Pays-Bas (now Fredericton, in New Brunswick) and by the Malecites as Aukupag (today Springhill, just north of Fredericton). Many of these settlers would eventually settle in the Madawaska Territory above Grand Sault (Grand Falls, New Brunswick). The great waterfall and gorge that necessitated a portage was out of reach of British ships.

American independence, legalized in the Treaty of Paris of 1783, would change the imperial ties in the region in many ways. British Loyalists from the former British colonies (which became the American Confederation) were forced to leave for loyal British colonies. One result was the birth of the colony of New Brunswick in 1784, when it was separated from the expansive colony of Nova Scotia. Nova Scotia was far removed by land from the new settlers on the Lower Saint John River, so the rapid rise in population necessitated the creation of the new colony of New Brunswick.

Acadian refugees had been squatting for at least a decade in the same region that was granted to the Loyalists. It was particularly important for the New Brunswick government to establish farms west of the Saint John River to the Massachusetts frontier that was known as the District of Maine. The eastern part of the District of Maine, from the Kennebec River, had been the western part of Acadie, scantily settled by the French, but held by the Passamaquoddy, Penobscot, Kennebec, and Abenaki tribes, who were allies of the French. New Brunswick's interest in establishing the Loyalists there was to prevent American expansion to the Lower Saint John River.

The 1783 Treaty of Paris borrowed the language for defining the border from the Treaty of Paris of 1763, still lacking reliable knowledge of the geography of the two watersheds. The Treaty's language seemed relatively unimportant when it defined the frontier between two British colonies, but became a future source of contention between two belligerent powers in North America: the Loyal British Colonies, and the United States, created from the American Confederation of States in 1789. The District of Maine started to petition Massachusetts for separation; a long process would result in the establishment of the State of Maine in 1820, because of dissatisfaction with Massachusetts sovereignty. Massachusetts had failed to protect the District of Maine in the wars since the 1690s.

The British and the Americans sent out a surveying party to establish the border line. They started at the head of the Grand lakes that formed the Saint Croix River. The Americans disputed which river was the Saint Croix, claiming Magaguadavic Lake as the source of the Saint Croix River, about 20 miles farther east, intersecting the Saint John River at Nackawic, New Brunswick. Evidence of the French Settlement of Saint Croix in 1604 was found, and the proper river was designated as the Saint Croix River. This was evidence of American aggressiveness in the question of the border. The British realized their mistake in approving the language about two watersheds in the two Treaties of Paris, and saw the probability of an American incursion bisecting their primary communication route between New Brunswick and Lower Canada (Quebec).

The surveying of the border was made more important by the War of 1812, which witnessed eastern Maine falling to the British. Massachusetts' indifference helped Maine's cause for statehood and demonstrated the importance of the Madawaska Settlement, which had been officially established by Acadian and Canadian families in 1785. British troops passed through the region on their way to the Great Lakes, where most of the battles were fought, but it underscored the vagueness of the boundary in the Madawaska Territory.

Ironically, the Acadians were loyal to Britain, probably because of the British holding deeds to their land. These Acadians were working the system to their advantage. They knew that they were being used by the British to establish British sovereignty in the disputed territory, but it worked well to get land in an isolated but important area, and allowed them to keep their extended families together and run their affairs without too much scrutiny from Fredericton (the new capital of New Brunswick in 1784).

The Madawaska Settlement was the result of 14,000 Loyalist settlers on the Lower Saint John River having grants to the land on which Acadian refugees were squatting. The Acadians' attitude about land tenure was quite cavalier, the result of their neglect by the Lords of Acadie, who were more interested in the fur trade than the development of the colony of Acadie. The lords were supposed to rent land to the Acadian people, provide services, and govern. The lords, who had been granted large tracts of land, failed to provide services and collect rent, and also left the small Acadian population to its own devices. So when Acadian refugees arrived on the lower Saint John River between 1754 and 1763, they cleared land in the lowlands they were so attracted to, because they resembled their holdings in Nova Scotia. When the Loyalists were granted the same land, the Acadians sought compensation for the improvements they had made in the decade or more that they were established there, as well as the granting of new lands in the northern part of New Brunswick: in the east at Caraquet and in the west at Madawaska.

The colonization of the Madawaska Settlement in 1785 was in a familiar territory. It was familiar in the sense that the lowlands of the Saint John River above Grand Falls were attractive to them. They were also known to them because couriers of messages between Acadie and Canada had taken note while passing through. There were Malecite villages that had had Catholic missionaries imparting the Sacraments in the region since 1651, so religious services were guaranteed, though intermittent, and serviced from the Bishopric of Quebec.

The families that settled in the territory might well have sent out "scouts" to claim portions of the land, putting up shelter to make way for the arrival of large extended and interconnected families, who had to immediately plant crops when they officially arrived at the end of June 1785. Some families from the Kamouraska region of what is now Quebec had also come to the Lower Saint John Valley and probably were gratified to be back up river, closer to their origins. In 1784, a fur trading post had been established at the Malecite village at Petit-Sault (Edmundston) by two half-brothers (Pierre Lizotte and Pierre Duperré) from the Kamouraska region before the official settlement of 1785.

This whole time period is foggy, with few records, but the Acadian settlers used the experience to take advantage of the many opportunities that resulted. They realized that there was no military salvation coming from France, which was aiding American independence at the expense of their enemy, the British. They realized that they could rely only on their own devices, and they had to work within the system they were forced into.

This, they did very well, taking advantage of the British desire to hold onto their "Canada Road," which linked New Brunswick to the City of Quebec, the capital of North America between 1763 and 1783. When they petitioned for land in the former Seigneurie de Madawaska, they did so in the region claimed but not occupied by the Americans. They also knew that they would be getting permanent deeds to their land and that they would dovetail their economy into the established British economy, fitting the British Navy with timber: pine for masts, spruce for spars, and tamarack for ships' knees.

When Maine achieved statehood, it fervently claimed land all the way to the Saint Lawrence River. Americans from the Kennebec region entered the Madawaska Territory in 1817 and established a lumber mill on the Miruimticook River at what is now Baker Brook, New Brunswick, and claimed American sovereignty in the region. These conflicting claims would result in the Northeastern Boundary Dispute as well as the Aroostook War, to the south.

These two separate issues, the border between Maine and New Brunswick, and the timber rights in the region of central Aroostook, were settled at different times (but were finalized in the Webster–Ashburton Treaty in 1842). By 1824, there was a "road" from Fredericton, New Brunswick, to the Saint Lawrence, connecting Fort Ingall on Lac Témiscouata with the Fort at Petit Sault (now Edmundston). The road from Bangor to Houlton, Fort Fairfield, and Fort Kent was functioning by 1839, connecting three forts on what would become the American side of the valley.

The Acadian settlers of the Madawaska Settlement were established at Saint Basile and expanded rapidly to Grand Falls along the lowlands and islands in the Saint John River. The first land grants were finalized in 1790, and new grants were pending. The founding families were large, interconnected, and rooted in long, narrow farm lots going back from the river. Each farm had river frontage and a place for a house above the flood plain, as well as pasture and woodland going over the hills to the interior. Later, in many places, a second, third, or even fourth rank of farms, marked by roads, "checker-boarded" their way into the interior.

The first families had the choice land and planned where their children would expand to. The problem was that Massachusetts had sold the interior land to pay its Revolutionary War debt, and that land was unavailable. Some squatting, evictions, and land sales resulted; this was a long and difficult process that was successfully and favorably finalized in the Maine Legislature by Peter Charles Keegan of Van Buren. The forests were harvested and the pine disappeared by the beginning of the 20th century, when the farmland dominated the landscape, which was much more cleared of trees than it is today.

The border dispute gathered steam gradually after the War of 1812. That war did not come to the Upper Saint John Valley, but it brought up the question as to where the border should be. The British opinion was that Britain had jurisdiction because of the well-established Acadian population with British deeds to their farms. For the British, the road to the Saint Lawrence was vital.

As the previously mentioned border survey team approached Mars Hill Mountain, in central Aroostook, they climbed and cleared the top to look for the highlands mentioned in the Treaties of Paris in 1763 and 1783. What they learned was that the mountain they were looking from was the highest land, unequaled to the north. The British took note that the real highlands were to the west, including Mount Katahdin. The British, knowing Maine was claiming all the way to the Saint Lawrence, sought to balance this with a claim to the highlands going west from Mars Hill. Those highlands separated river watersheds. The Penobscot and Kennebec rivers flowed south to the Atlantic, while the north slopes fed the rivers that defined the Saint John River watershed that flowed into the Bay of Fundy.

The result was two opposing views, each flawed, but each also partly fulfilling the treaty language. Washington and London had experienced the Revolutionary War and the War of 1812, and were not about to become embroiled again over "wasteland." In 1831 they asked the King of the Netherlands to arbitrate a solution, by finding the highlands. This he did, using maps of the region, and bisected it with a border following the Saint John River to the Saint Francis River, and up that river. The border then would traverse land to the south, working around the streams that emptied into the Saint John River, nearly to New Hampshire.

Neither side accepted the decision, saying that the highlands did not run down a river channel, so the dispute heated up. It was a kind of cold war, in the sense that casualties were due more to weather than to exchange of fire. Surveyors, census takers, and lumbermen were arrested by low officials and released by higher officials, with London and Washington working the strings.

Eventually, Secretary of State Daniel Webster (formerly a powerful senator from New Hampshire) was asked to negotiate with Alexander Baring, Lord Ashburton from England, who had lumber investments in Maine and New Brunswick. Daniel Webster was his lawyer in Washington, guarding Ashburton's interests. At the time, this was seen as an advantage rather than a conflict of interest, and Webster knew Ashburton's interests very well.

Those interests were further complicated when Ashburton, owner of Baring Bank in London, married the daughter of Sen. Bingham of Pennsylvania, the founder of the Second National Bank of the United States. Powerful international interests were at play, and Bingham owned a sizable amount of land in Maine. The result was that both sides won, no matter what the outcome of the dispute was.

The treaty followed the line set by the King of the Netherlands except that Maine lost land on its western boundary, where streams were bisected by a straight line. The boundary was fixed all the way to Lake in the Woods, Minnesota. Webster lied to the senate and failed to inform Maine and Massachusetts of the final language before it was railroaded through the U.S. Senate by a large majority. Maine and Massachusetts were irate, as was New Brunswick, which saw 2,000 loyal British subjects (Acadians with British deeds) on the south bank of the Saint John River given to the Americans. The Madawaska Territory was divided by an international boundary. Maine offered its new citizens American deeds to their formerly British land.

After Canadian Confederation in 1867, New Brunswick and Quebec had to establish a boundary as well. They resorted to a commission that determined from testimony that the identity of the Madawaska Settlement was Acadian, so they chose to stay with New Brunswick rather than Quebec, fixing the boundary south of Ville-Dégelis, separating Madawaska from Témiscouata.

With the political boundary fixed, the church was also partitioned, resulting in the ecclesiastical separation of the valley. It was started by a group of Americans in the Grand Isle area that came to be known as the Carmelists, because their chapel, built at the foot of Mount Carmel in 1847, was not being adequately served by the parish of Saint Basile across the river. The Bishops of Boston, Quebec, and New Brunswick each exercised jurisdiction and supported each other by each naming the others as co-vicars general. The people of the region petitioned whomever they felt would grant their requests. Bishops Fenwick and Fitzpatrick of Boston visited the region in 1846 and 1848, respectively. They approved and dedicated the third parish on the American side. The first parishes had been Saint Bruno in Van Buren and Sainte Luce in Frenchville, both established in 1826, but they didn't get resident priests until a decade later.

The Mount Carmel chapel was served by Fr. Henri Dionne, of Frenchville, and later his replacement, Fr. Sweron, a priest from Belgium. The movement to separate was justified by the political division that had taken place in 1842. Other problems included the difficulty of crossing the river at freeze-up and ice-out times; the discount on American money; and the uncooperativeness of Fr. Langevin, pastor of Saint Basile, in providing baptismal, marriage, and burial information to the State of Maine.

The Carmelists petitioned Pope Pius IX in Rome. The result was that in 1864, the Pope answered by attaching the American side of the valley to the newly created Diocese of Portland, Maine. The chapel at Mount Carmel lasted only a score of years and was moved to what is now Lille in 1870. Because the erection of a new parish in Saint David was close to Mount Carmel, a new location was selected halfway between Van Buren and Saint David that would better serve the community.

The economy in the Madawaska Settlement was quite prosperous by colonial standards and was tied to Fredericton, because the river, which provided the only access to markets, made that a necessity. Local stores, which acted as credit managers, outfitted lumbering operations with provisions. The accounts would be settled at the end of the season, after the lumber had been floated down to Fredericton. Sawmills were abundant and developed in each locality to supply local needs.

After 1842, the economy prospered and villages grew into towns, defined by the location of churches. Getting to mass by horse and wagon took time, and business in the village would be the main activity after mass. Stores were located near the church, for this reason. The villages were not clusters of houses; rather, they were strung out along the river. Farms had divided lengthwise back from the river, so houses were closer together, with extended family close by. When there was a need, abundant manpower was available, drawing from family. The roads that had developed as a result of the border dispute were used for commerce. When the railroads came to the region, commerce picked up. The Canadian Pacific Railroad came to Edmundston in 1878. Fraser Paper was founded in 1916.

The American side of the valley developed quickly, with the establishment of a Normal School to train teachers in 1871, headed by Vital Cyr of Saint David. Classes were in English. The school shifted between Van Buren and Fort Kent annually until it was permanently established in Fort Kent in 1886; this was done because Saint Mary's College was established in Van Buren by the Marist Fathers in 1887. The curriculum in Van Buren was in French and English. The Convent of the Good Shepherd Sisters was established there in 1891, to educate females.

The result was that by 1870, Van Buren was the first town on the American side to really look like a town, with a business district that hosted many professions. Fort Kent soon followed. Madawaska developed after Fraser Papers was established and a bridge to Edmundston was built in the 1920s. The catalyst for development was the growth of convent hospitals and schools that went beyond the elementary level. A hospital was built at Eagle Lake in 1905. In 1897, the Little Franciscans of Mary were settled in Wallagrass, near Fort Kent, and later in Fort Kent itself. The Missionary Sisters of the Our Holy Rosary were established in Frenchville in 1898.

The Daughters of Wisdom were in Sainte Agathe, where they had a boarding school and hospital in 1904; the parish having been established in 1889. The Daughters expanded to Lille and Edmundston, where they established high schools. The schools, convents, and hospitals were more numerous on the American side, but the most important convent was in Saint Basile in 1873, where the Sisters of Saint Joseph established the largest convent in the region, with a hospital and college for women. The sisters started a brickyard that sold bricks as well as produced them for the immense building they erected following the destruction of the wooden convent by fire.

The railroad arrived first on the Canadian side, but its arrival on the American side a quarter of a century later brought access to the huge city markets of the northeastern United States, for potatoes which became the cash crop and brought prosperity. There were many farms, operated by huge families. The area became prosperous enough to replace nearly every church between 1900 and 1920, some because of fire, but most because of an increase in population. In 1900, the population of the American side was 16,000, the same as in 2010. The Canadian population was 14,000, but grew greatly in the 20th century and is now the most developed part of the valley.

Potato farms and mills brought employment to every town. Van Buren/ Saint Léonard was a focal point because the largest mills were there, and the pulp that was floated down the river in the spring drives was sorted there. It was also a transportation terminus, beginning in 1878, with four railroads that connected the valley with the rest of the continent, and major roads that connected the valley with Campbellton, New Brunswick, and Bangor, Maine. The railroad bridge in Van Buren was a vital link and brought enough commerce to necessitate a U.S. Consulate in Saint Léonard. Bridges were built in Van Buren/Saint Léonard, Edmundston/Madawaska, and Fort Kent/Clair. The potato industry in Aroostook grew to become the leading producer in the world until water projects in the far west of the United States during the Depression turned desert into potato land in Idaho and it developed into a competitor.

There was a secret economy in the region as a result of American Prohibition that involved smuggling liquor on a massive scale. Although national Prohibition was established after World War I, it had been instituted in Maine in 1851, so there was much experience smuggling from Canada, where liquor sales were legal. Bootlegging was also an expanding secret industry. This resulted in tightened controls at the boundary, which served to divide the valley further, but the general population, being Roman Catholic, could not understand why communion wine could be legal and general sales of alcohol, illegal. Internal Revenue agents lost the uphill battle until Prohibition was repealed during the Great Depression.

The Depression was more seriously felt on the American side of the valley, but the valley managed to fare better than most parts of the United States. Large extended families were a support system in a region where firewood and farm products were abundant. Farming offered work, and the region resorted to survival methods practiced in earlier times. Most were poor in money, but managed to survive by growing their own food and foraging the wilderness.

Today, the Trans-Canada Highway serves the region, passing through on the same route as the Canada Road since 1612. It has brought much development on the Canadian side, with the expansion of the paper mill and the development of the Edmundston campus of the *Université de Moncton*, which grew out of the "College Saint Louis." The region is still perceived by outsiders as a backwater, however, and is now beginning the initiative to look at itself as a cohesive international and interprovincial territory, divided by differing law codes, language, and attitudes; but better off cooperating economically, despite the differences.

The identity of the region differs from village to town to city. Some identify historically as Acadian, others, more of a mix of French Canadian and Acadian. Some are Scots-Irish and Native Americans. Others see themselves as American and Canadian. For some, identity is tied to language; for others, it is tied to blood relations. It doesn't seem practical to identify the whole region with any one group because the percentages of each differ by geography. Making it a melting-pot identity doesn't serve either, because it isn't the general reality. It is a complex question that is probably best dealt with in each locality.

The mystique of the Acadians as a nationality in exile has been in the public imagination since it was branded by railroad tourism efforts when they first came to the region in the late 19th and early 20th centuries. The region certainly has a colorful history that is well-tied into the large events of the past four centuries, and tapping into that heritage history is a strategy for future development. No other region shares this particular situation. The Territory of Madawaska–Témiscouata is a singular definable area, removed, yet centered, with a unique adaptation to a complex history that needs to be revealed as the resilient and peaceful outcome of a turbulent time.

Acadians of Eagle Lake, Maine, learned to make snowshoes from the local Mi'kmaq, so they could hunt and trap in the winter. Left to right are Edmund Thériault, working with his children Brian and Louise.

Lionel Doucette, from Saint-David, Maine, plays his fiddle in front of a traditional fence.

BIBLIOGRAPHY

Thomas Albert, *Histoire De Madawaska: D'Apres les Recherches Historiques de Patrick Therriault, et Les Notes Manuscrites de Prudent L. Mercure* (Quebec: Imprimerie Franciscaine Missionnaire, 1920); William David Barry, *Maine: The Wilder Half of New England* (Thomaston, Maine: Tilbury House Publishers, 2012); Beatrice Craig and Maxime Dagenais, *The Land in Between: The Upper St. John Valley, Prehistory to World War I* (Thomaston, Maine: Tilbury House Publishers, 2009).

PUBNICO—OLDEST PRE-DEPORTATION ACADIAN VILLAGE IN NOVA SCOTIA

Bernice d'Entremont

Pubnico is the oldest pre-deportation Acadian region in Atlantic Canada still occupied by Acadians. The settlement of Pubnico was originally named Pobomcoup and was part of the Cape Sable region. Though the Acadians were deported in 1756 from Buttes-de-Sable (Sandy Hills), they came back in 1766 to the Barrington area the following year and settled on the other side of the harbor from their original lands. This Acadian area is unique in history: it began in 1653 as a barony founded by Sieur Philippe Mius d'Entremont; Philippe is the ancestor of all the d'Entremonts in North America.

Philippe Mius d'Entremont was born in 1609 in Normandy, France. Married to Madeleine du Tillet in 1649, he sailed to Acadie accompanied by his wife and their daughter, Marguerite. On July 17, 1653, while the area was under the command of Gov. Charles de Saint-Etienne de La Tour, d'Entremont received land measuring 2.5 miles of coastline by nine miles inland on the east side of Pubnico harbor. He was also given the title of Sieur d'Entremont, Baron de Pobomcoup, and lieutenant-major and troop commander. In 1670, he was promoted to king's prosecutor-general in Acadie and followed the governor in his travels for the next 18 years, only stopping at age 89 when infirmity compelled him to relinquish his post. Philippe then moved to Grand-Pré to join his daughter, Marguerite, and died two years later, in 1700, at age 91, "with all his teeth."

Philippe Mius d'Entremont

Sieur Phillippe Mius d'Entremont, or his son Jacques I Mius d'Entremont of Pobomcoup, could have built the manor house at the center of the barony. Jacques I Mius d'Entremont married Anne de Saint-Etienne de Latour in 1677. Their eldest son, Jacques II Mius d'Entremont, married Marguerite Amireau (Amirault), who bore him four sons: Jacques III, Joseph, Paul, and Benoni and three daughters: Marie, Anne, and Marguerite. When deportations started in this area, the family members would travel to various destinations.

In the spring of 1756, a first group of 72 Acadians from the Cap Sable area were captured and deported by the English to Massachusetts. Jacques II was deported on the ship *Vulture* along with his family, which included his wife, three sons, and two daughters. Arriving in Boston, they were then sent to Walpole in late November 1756.

The fourth son, Jacques III, escaped this first deportation, only later to be deported on November 3, 1759, to England, then France. The family manor house of the barony was burned to the ground in 1758 by the British. Jacques was placed aboard the *Mary the Fourth* along with his wife, but a storm postponed their departure for a week. They arrived in England seven weeks later, on December 29, and then proceeded on to Cherbourg, France, on January 14, 1760.

In Massachusetts, Jacques II found himself in exile and living in miserable conditions, housed in a small shanty, clothed in rags, and barely able to provide food for his family. Ironically, while they were restrained from moving about, his sisters, who had married high-ranking, wealthy French officers, were enjoying a very comfortable life at the Louisbourg Fortress in Île Royale (today Cape Breton). Another sister, Anne Mius d'Entremont, was living in southwestern France, previously married to one of the former governors of Ile Royale.

The current governor, Augustin de Drucourt, was implored by Jacques' sisters, sons-in-law, and nephews to write to Thomas Pownall, governor of Massachusetts, to send their brother back to Nova Scotia. Pownall replied from Boston, dated November 10, 1757, "I would feel happy if I had the power to give you a proof of my good will with regard to your demand concerning Monsieur de Pocomcourt (Pobomcoup). Even though he is a subject of His British Majesty, but, since his is old and French by birth, and of those who are more inclined towards their native land, I will willingly give him permission to depart from here; that is why I have given orders to look for him; he is from this town and I was not able to have him leave on this voyage, nevertheless, he will reach you by the first occasion that I will have, and for that, I will send him to Halifax."

Sadly, Jacques II never made the return trip to Halifax, and less than a year later, died in Walpole on July 28, 1759, at the age of 79 and was buried in Roxbury. Of all the Acadians who were sent into exile, he was the only one who had efforts made on his behalf to return him to Nova Scotia. The rest of the family in Massachusetts returned from their exile on August 23, 1766.

The *Boston News-Letter* announced that Captain Amiro (Amirault) had left Boston harbor for Quebec. Among the numbers leaving with Captain Amiro were Marguerite d'Entremont, widow of Jacques II, and her children, as well as the families of Charles Amirault, Abel Duon, and Charles Belliveau.

While en route to Quebec, they stopped in Halifax, Nova Scotia. There they met an English officer who recognized them and greeted them heartily; apparently before the Expulsion this officer had been taken prisoner in a battle, and one of the d'Entremonts had saved his life. When he learned where they were going, he told them to settle in Nova Scotia, and he would send a Catholic priest to them. They continued on to Buttes-de-Sable (today Villagedale). The following year, they decided to go back home to Pubnico. Disappointed to find the land already taken where the d'Entremont manor once stood, they moved on to the facing-side of the harbor.

The d'Entremont family, eight in all, settled in West Pubnico. They were Paul, Benoni, sister Marguerite (not yet married), Anne d'Entremont and husband Abel Duon (d'Eon), Joseph and wife Agnes Belliveau and two children, and their mother Marguerite Amirault, widow of Jacques II d'Entremont. All were given grants by the governor of Nova Scotia in 1771 and 1784. The Amirault and Belliveau families settled on the east side of the harbor, while the d'Entremont and the Duon took up residence on the western side. Since then, other family names added to the population, include Surette and LeBlanc.

The Documentation Center of the *Musée des Acadiens des Pubnicos* (founded in 1994) keeps the original deeds of land grants and eight original letters written between 1764 and 1775 from Cherbourg by members of the d'Entremont family, most of them written by Marguerite Landry, wife of Jacques III d'Entrement to their close relatives who returned to Pubnico. Even a hundred years ago, some people from Pubnico were still corresponding with descendants of these exiled Acadians in France.

The jewel of the *Musée* on permanent exhibition is a rare original *aboiteau* found in 1990 on an eroding beach on Île-de-Grave (Double Island). An *aboiteau* is an Acadian farmer's trademark used to reclaim land from the sea; earthen dykes made to isolate areas of reclaimed salt marshes from repeated inundation by the tides. Into the base of each dyke an *aboiteau* is added, a wooden sluice fitted with swinging doors that allows excess fresh water to drain from the land, but which shuts down at twice-daily high tides to prevent re-entry of salt water on to the farmlands.

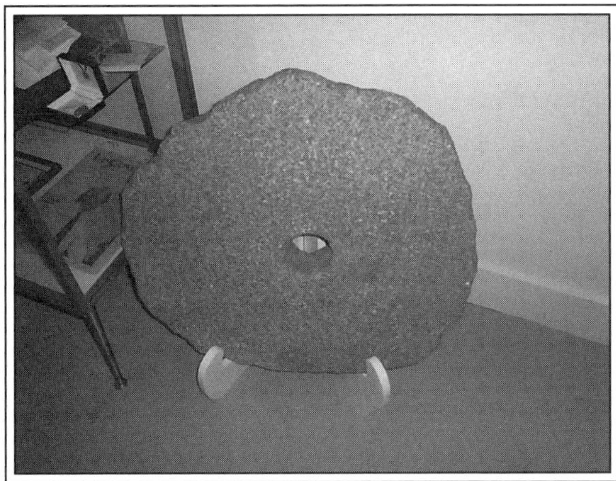

This stone is an old gristmill discovered in East Pubnico in 1997. Welsh archeologist Christine Yeats noticed it in a brook, and Pubnico history enthusiasts Réal d'Entremont and Ted d'Eon pulled it from the tidal pool. It is almost certainly from the mill that was part of the barony of Pobomcoup. Sieur de Villebon's writings of 1688, recorded that there were 80 bushels of wheat to be milled at the d'Entremont grist mill.

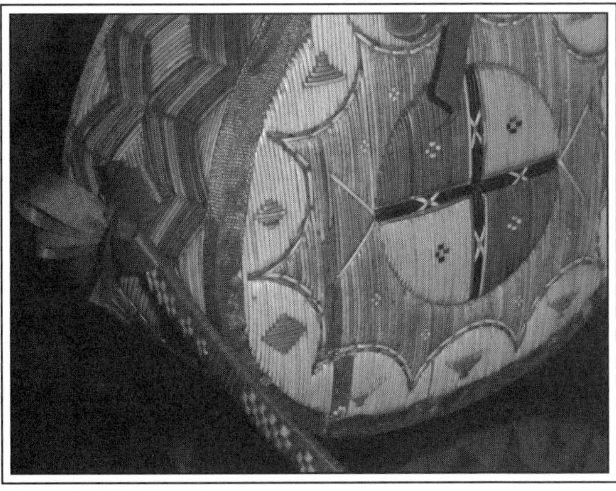

This quillwork basket was crafted in the late 19th century by local Mi'kmaq Amerindians, who were the first occupants of this area; marriages between the Mi'kmaq and early Acadians are recorded in the parish registers and confirm that a close relationship was maintained between the two peoples. The son of Philippe Mius d'Entremont, Philippe Mius-d'Entremont dit *d'Azit, married two Mi'kmaq women, becoming the progenitor of the Métis Meuse and Muise families.*

A Few Personalities from Pubnico

Benoni d'Entremont (1745-1841) was born in nearby Cape Sable (Barrington today) and was deported with his family to Massachusetts in 1756 at the age of 11. Ten years later, after his return from exile, he was involved in the civic affairs of Yarmouth County. In 1780, he became the first Acadian magistrate and justice of the peace in Nova Scotia, and the first assessor, then treasurer, for the Municipality of Argyle.

In 1799, Benoni d'Entremont built the first house made of boards in Pubnico (picture shown), which is still standing today. If, at this time, a man's wealth was measured according to the property he owned, d'Entremont was a rich man. In 1813, Benoni was appointed a justice of the Inferior Court of Common Pleas for the County of Yarmouth.

Benoni owned the ship *Bonaventure*, in which he made frequent voyages between Halifax and the French islands of St. Pierre et Miquelon (near Newfoundland) to buy and sell liquor. France, which owned the islands, did not have alcohol prohibition. In 1781, on his return from St. Pierre et Miquelon, his ship was attacked by pirates off the coast near Lockport. The pirates sent Benoni and his sailors ashore at Lockport, retaining only the pilot of the ship, Captain Kinney. That night, under the cover of darkness, Benoni and his crew, with loaded guns, started to row toward the *Bonaventure* with muffled oars. Boarding the vessel firing their guns and making a tremendous noise, they ran to the stairway leading to the hold where they found the pirates gloriously drunk and making no resistance. They nailed shut the sliding door leading to the hold, imprisoning the pirates within. From there, the vessel was brought to shore at Lockport to the sound of cheers from the villagers. The pirates were brought before the magistrate for trial. Many people who had suffered in the past from such privateers wanted the pirates hanged, but Benoni "with true Acadian preference for milder punishment," according to one report, said that they had been punished enough already by the loss of their firearms, and requested that the pirates be let free, telling them to make their way back home and never come back.

Simon d'Entremont (1788-1886) was an Acadian politician. Elected in 1836 in Argyle Township, he is the first Acadian deputy to sit in the Nova Scotia legislature. He refused to take the heretical oath of allegiance to the British Crown and was reported to have said, "I would rather swallow a dogfish, tail first." Lt. Gov. Sir Colin Campbell saw to it that from that day forward the ordinary oath of fidelity to the law of the country would be used. Having done so, d'Entremont entered the chamber with acclamation from his colleagues, who admired his courage. It was also a victory for other minorities who would eventually serve in the provincial legislature. The Acadian people consider d'Entremont's actions a legendary symbol of liberty. He died in East Pubnico on September 6, 1886, at age 98, having fathered 18 children with two wives.

Henri Léander d'Entremont (1862-1944), a historian and collector, opened the first Acadian Museum in East Pubnico. Most of that first collection is now held by the Musée des Acadiens des Pubnicos et centre de recherche.

Père Clarence d'Entremont (1909-1998) was a priest who became a renowned historian and genealogist. His many publications, papers, and books form the core of the archives located in the Musée des Acadiens des Pubnicos.

Désiré d'Eon (1905-1996), an educator, founded the French newspaper Le Petit Courrier *in 1937. Still today, it is the oldest and only French language weekly provincial newspaper, now called* Le Courrier de la Nouvelle-Écosse.

Conclusion

The Acadians of Pubnico remain attached to their region, their children, and their future. The Philippe Muis d'Entremont heritage is rooted in the families of Pubnico, most of whose ancestors have been here since the 1650s. Though the baronial manor has disappeared, it lives on in the hearts and minds of the people who like to think that Baron Philippe Mius d'Entremont and his wife would be pleased to learn that the French language and Acadian culture is still thriving in this area.

Acknowledgements

Thanks to historian and genealogist Coral d'Entremont, for his collaboration as research fact-finder.

Bibliography

Clarence J. d'Entremont, Histoire du Cap-Sable de l'An Mil au Traité de Paris (1763); Archival collection of Clarence J. d'Entremont, Musée des Acadiens des Pubnicos.

Memramcook, Cradle of Acadie in New Brunswick

Gérard LeBlanc

Memramcook is often referred to as the "cradle of modern Acadie." Such an assertion is based on the fact that, after the *Grand Dérangement* of 1755, a large number of Acadians settled in Memramcook from where, later on, their descendants moved on to establish new communities and thereby contributed greatly to Acadian survival. The first Acadians arrived in the Memramcook region at the beginning of the 18th century and settled along the marshes bordering the Memramcook River and the eastern shore of the Petitcodiac River. Just prior to the events of 1755, Memramcook had a population of about 250, while the neighboring region of Beaubassin numbered close to 3,000 people.

A large number of the Acadians of the greater Memramcook region were not deported in 1755. Some proceeded to the northern regions of present-day New Brunswick, while others hid in the surrounding forests. Condemned to a perilous existence, the latter eventually became prisoners either by being captured by English soldiers or by surrendering to them in order to avoid death by starvation.

Once prisoners, these Acadians from Memramcook and elsewhere were detained in the English forts of the Maritime region: Fort Cumberland (previously Fort Beauséjour), Fort Edward in Windsor, Fort Anne in Port-Royal (Annapolis), and Georges Island in Halifax.

Some ten years after the disastrous events of 1755, the English authorities, somewhat less belligerent and more tolerant, allowed the Acadian prisoners to leave the forts, but prohibited them from returning to their original lands. Despite this warning, one of the first groups of Acadians to leave decided to settle along the marshes on the west side of the Memramcook River in areas later known as La Montain, McGinley's Corner, and Old Shediac Road. Among this group were five brothers, surnamed Richard and nicknamed "Leplate" after the Leplate River in Prince Edward Island where their ancestors had resided. Along with these brothers the group also included a Richard cousin and two sons of Jacques Léger.

Around 1770, another group of Fort Edward Acadians arrived in Memramcook and settled south of Village-des-Leplate in the region of modern-day Saint Joseph. This group was comprised of two clans, the Belliveaus and the

Gaudets. Pierre, the elder of the Belliveaus, was nicknamed "Piau," and as a result this settlement eventually came to be known as Village-des-Piau.

Along with the Belliveaus and the Gaudets, this group of Acadian settlers included Bourgeois, Girouards and LeBlancs, most of whom were related by marriage. At about the same time, farther downriver in the region known today as Cormier's Cove, other Acadians settled along the marshes—Landrys, Goguens, and the two sons of Pierre Bastarache. These pioneers of Village-des-Leplate, Village-des-Piau, and Cormier's Cove are the ancestors of a large number of Acadians in Memramcook, southeastern New Brunswick, the Maritime provinces, and elsewhere in Canada and the United States.

As these Acadians were settling on the west side of the Memramcook River, another group, comprised mostly of people from Fort Edward, settled on the opposite side of the river at a place once called Pointe-à-l'Ours (Bear Point). These Acadians were Dupuis, Landrys, Bourgeois, Saulniers, Breaus, LeBlancs, and another member of the Richard family. Residing in the greater region of present-day College Bridge, these pioneers of Acadie also have a long line of descendants today in Memramcook and elsewhere.

At the same time as the Memramcook River marshes were attracting Acadians, other Acadians chose to settle along the marshes on the east side of the Petitcodiac River. This region, later known as Gautreau Village, was first settled by Cyprien Dupuis and others who came from Turtle Creek (Fourche-à-Crapaud) around 1775. A few years later, two brothers, Pierre and Jean Gautreau, joined Dupuis, and these three Acadians became the patriarchs of this village. Many Acadians who live there today are descendants of the first inhabitants of the Petitcodiac.

At about the same time, two more settlements were established as more Acadians chose to settle along the Petitcodiac. Around 1780, Belliveaus, Bourgeois, and LeBlancs (all brothers-in-law) settled in a region later known as Belliveau Village. To the south of this locality, Gaudets, Boudreaus, Gautreaus, and Bourgeois also settled along the marshes of the Petitcodiac in regions which became known as Boudreau Village and Beaumont. Some 20 years after the arrival of the first settlers along the Memramcook River, another group of Acadians arrived in the region and took up residence in the Cormier's Cove-Taylor Village area. These new settlers, the Cormiers, Landrys, Ouellets, and Vienneaus, had left their village along the Saint John River in the Fredericton area after having been displaced by the Loyalists arriving from the New England states.

With time, other Acadians joined those already settled in Memramcook. Some, victims of the Expulsion, were coming back from Quebec or from the New England states, while others came from Nova Scotia, mainly from the Menoudie area. Memramcook's growth took place at a fairly rapid pace, and soon the increasing population requested the presence of a permanent priest in the region.

The Croix de La Montain *is located on the grounds where the first Saint-Thomas de Memramcook church was erected about 1781.*

As a result, in 1781, the Bishop of Quebec decided to erect a parish in Memramcook dedicated to Saint Thomas. At the time, this parish covered a region extending from Richiboctou to Menoudie in Nova Scotia. Its first pastor, Thomas Leroux, settled in the Village des Leplate (La Montain) area, where a small rustic chapel had been erected. In 1786, Leroux reported that there were 160 families in his parish comprising a total of 960 persons.

The first Acadians arriving in Memramcook after being freed from the English forts were not able to become title holders of the lands they were clearing, these being part of large plots granted to English officers and administrators. At first, the Acadians were not bothered by the owners, but eventually, in order to remain on their land, they had to sign leases obliging them to pay a rent consisting mostly of farm products. However, in 1786, the grant holder on the eastern side of the Memramcook River was deprived of his title by the government, thus enabling the Acadians of that region to purchase their land from the government.

Such was not the case for the Acadians living in the region between the Petitcodiac and the Memramcook rivers, a triangular-shaped region sometimes referred to as La Pointe. Formerly owned by Joseph Goreham, this large grant was purchased by Joseph Frederick Wallet DesBarres in 1775, and from 1784 onward these Acadians had to sign leases that they considered unfair. Claiming that DesBarres was not respecting all the clauses of the agreements, they became involved in a long legal proceeding that was not settled until 1842 when the New Brunswick government forced the DesBarres family to sell the lands which they had long occupied and tilled to the Acadians.

As these legal proceedings were taking place, the inhabitants of La Pointe were disturbed by the fast-growing population of greater Memramcook. During these years, many Acadians from Memramcook decided to leave and settle elsewhere—some being apprehensive with respect to the land titles and others feeling the shortage of land available along the marshes—thereby settling the villages of Barachois, Aboujagane, Cap-Pelé, Grand-Digue, Bouctouche, and Richibuctou, just to name a few.

The first wave of emigration took place around 1786. The five Richard brothers, their namesake cousin, and some Legers, all original settlers of the Leplate Village, as well as some Babineaus, settled in the Richibuctou area, thus becoming the ancestors of almost all the present-day families of Kent County bearing those family names. Around the same time, some LeBlancs and Bastaraches also left Memramcook to settle along the Bouctouche River. Other Bastaraches and some Saulniers migrated farther north to the Tracadie area. In the following years, many other Acadians from Memramcook would follow their example and move out to the coastal areas of New Brunswick.

In 1810, Fr. Ciquard, pastor of Memramcook, indicated that there were 158 families in his parish—about the same number as in 1786—thus corroborating the above exodus and, according to the priest Antoine Gagnon, by 1821 the population of Memramcook had reached 1,309.

Erected in 1842, the Sainte-Anne chapel is located at Beaumont on an old Mi'kmaq reserve. Still in use on occasion for the celebration of the mass, it is also the site of musical events during the summer months.

After the settlement of the land conflict in 1842, Memramcook underwent some noticeable growth. In 1840, the parish priest Ferdinand Gauvreau had already initiated the construction of the present-day stone church along with the *Sainte-Anne* chapel on the Mi'kmaq reserve in Beaumont. The stone church was not completed until 1855 by the new pastor, Fr. Lafrance. When he arrived in Memramcook, the parish had a population of 4,000. It was Lafrance who founded the first college in Memramcook, naming it *Séminaire Saint-Thomas.* The college closed in 1862 and was re-opened under the name *Collège Saint-Joseph* in 1864 by Camille Lefebvre of the Holy Cross Congregation.

Fr. François-Xavier Lafrance arrived in Memramcook in 1852 where he founded a college named Séminaire Saint-Thomas. In 1855, he completed the interior of the stone church which had begun construction in 1840 under Fr. Ferdinand Gauvreau.

Saint-Thomas de Memramcook, a stone church whose construction began in 1840, was completed in 1855 with the official opening taking place on August 15, 1856. Renovations were later carried out in 1879 and 1934.

Fr. Camille Lefebvre of the Holy Cross congregation arrived in Memramcook in 1864 where he founded Saint-Joseph's College.

The 1881 commemorative sculpture by local artist Monette Léger was unveiled in 2006 to mark the 125th anniversary of the first Acadian National Convention in Memramcook.

In 1881, the first National Convention of the Acadian people took place in Memramcook, organized mainly by the first graduates of Saint Joseph College. Its president, Memramcook native Pierre-Amand Landry, had been one of the first to enroll at the college. Fr. Lefebvre, aided by Landry, provided the impetus to education in Memramcook and Acadia, spending over 30 years in Memramcook as pastor of Saint Thomas Parish and as superior of the college which he had founded. In 1896, the alumni of Saint Joseph College erected in his honor the Monument Lefebvre, a stone building consisting of a museum, lecture rooms, laboratories, and a theatre recognized today for its excellent acoustical qualities.

Monument-Lefebvre *was built in 1896, one year after the death of Fr. Camille Lefebvre, in memory of the 30 years which he gave to the Acadian population.*

After Fr. Lefebvre's death in 1895, his congregation continued to serve the people of Saint Thomas Parish and maintained their role as educators at the college, which gained university status in 1923. In the 1960s *Université Saint-Joseph* was transferred to Moncton, where it became the *Université de Moncton.* The Holy Cross Fathers remained in charge of Saint Thomas Parish until the beginning of the 21st century (June 2001).

The Lefebvre statue was unveiled in honor of Fr. Camille Lefebvre during the celebrations of the 50th anniversary of Saint-Joseph's College in 1914.

Saint-Joseph's College burned to the ground in 1933.

Saint Joseph's College was rebuilt in 1934.

Many eminent people came from the college founded by Fr. Lefebvre. Placide Gaudet, whose father was a native of Memramcook, was a historian, educator and journalist and was recognized as the first Acadian genealogist. Sir Pierre-Amand Landry, born in Memramcook, was a lawyer, a politician, and the first Acadian to be named to the Supreme Court of New Brunswick; he was knighted in 1916. Pascal Poirier was an author, lawyer, and the all-time longest-serving senator of New Brunswick. André Bourque, Holy Cross Father, was a missionary, author, and well-known Acadian musical composer. Roméo LeBlanc, born in Cormier's Cove, was a member of Parliament, a federal minister, a senator, and the first Acadian to become governor-general of Canada.

Born in Memramcook, Sir Pierre-Amand Landry was the first Acadian to be appointed to the Supreme Court of New Brunswick, and he chaired the first Acadian National Convention held in Memramcook in 1881.

Born in Memramcook, Roméo LeBlanc had a distinguished political career as a Member of Parliament as well as holding a ministerial portfolio. After serving as a senator he was appointed governor general of Canada, the first Acadian to occupy that post. In 1999 he represented Canada in Louisiana for the Second Congrès mondial acadien and attended the LeBlanc family reunion in Erath.

For the "twinning" of Memramcook and Scott Louisiana, are Rose-Anna LeBlanc (left), of Memramcook and former teacher of French immersion in Lafayette, and then Mayor Hazel Myers of Scott. The 1996 twinning ceremony took place on August 15, the National Day of the Acadians.

Upon being liberated from the English forts, if a few Acadians had not dared to resettle on their original lands in Memramcook, this region would have probably been settled by English and Loyalist tenants, and Memramcook would not have evolved into the Acadian community which can today proclaim itself as the "cradle of modern Acadie."

Pomquet, Nova Scotia and Its Louisiana Connection

Sandra Pettipas Perro

The Acadian village of Pomquet is located in the County of Antigonish, Nova Scotia. This county holds the majority of Broussards still in Canada, who are all descendants of Joseph Beausoleil Broussard, the famous Acadian leader. This is unique because the majority of the Broussards now live in Louisiana, some 3,700 kilometers (2,300 miles) away.

Pomquet is home to about 900 inhabitants, most of whom descend from Acadian ancestry. It is nestled along the harbors of Pomquet and Monk's Head, and separated from Saint George's Bay by the barrier island that houses a unique and beautiful sandy beach.

The area is noted for its sense of community and connection to the land and water. Its beginning dates back thousands of years when the First Nations Mi'kmaq settled the land, making use of the richness of its harbors, bay, and forests. Its name, historically spelled Pomquette, is derived from the Mi'kmaq word "popumkek" possibly meaning sandy beach or a good place to land. Mi'kmaq artifacts have been found in several locations along its shores and oral history suggests the presence of at least two of their burial grounds: one at Pomquet Point and the other at Monk's Head, site of the first chapel in Pomquet.

Pomquet Beach

Acadians affected by the Great Expulsion of 1755 came to the area with other French settlers, starting in 1773. These were exiles from Saint-Malo, France, with transportation provided by merchants from nearby Jersey Island. The families first landed in the Acadian community of Arichat, in present-day Cape Breton, then traveled to Havre Boucher and Tracadie before continuing westward along the coastline to Pomquet Harbor. The 23 Mi'kmaq families living here aided them in surviving, as the two cultures had been friends and family for 150 years prior to their Deportation.

Initially, the Acadians subsisted mainly by fishing for flatfish (flounder), eels, and smelts from the harbor; trout and salmon from the river; and mackerel and lobsters from the bay. Being talented and prosperous farmers on their old lands taken by the British, they later used these skills to clear the land for growing crops and raising livestock.

The first Acadians to arrive in Pomquet were the Broussard, Doiron, Vincent, Duon (present-day Deon, D'Eon and DeYoung) families, as well as Louis Lamarre, a Frenchman. In 1789, 16 years after their arrival in Pomquet, these five families were issued land grants along the harbor by the Nova Scotia government. Their land was located along the creek near the present community hall.

Between 1785 and 1794, these families were joined by a second wave of exiled Acadians who had also made their way from Saint-Malo, France, and possibly related to the first group by marriage. The other Acadian families included Landry, Boudreau, Melançon, Daigle, Rosia (Rogers) and also Louis Morell from Quebec. In 1793, another 16 land grants were issued to both the first and second wave of settlers.

In 1817, two soldiers, Jean-Baptiste Rimbeau (Rennie) and Jean-Baptiste Vendome (Venedam), possibly from Belgium, were captured by the British during the Napoleonic Wars and imprisoned on Georges Island in Halifax harbor, where they later made their way to Pomquet. Other settlers arriving in the 19th century included families named DeKrauz (Cross) from Saint Pierre and Miquelon; Benoit from Tracadie, Nova Scotia; Jacquet/Deslauriers (Delorey) from Quebec via Tracadie; Wolfe from Chezzetcook, Nova Scotia; and other families of unknown origins including Philipart, Toupais, and Drouillet.

Today the school *École acadienne de Pomquet* provides Primary to Grade 12 education in French. The 19th century church Église Ste. Croix is built on a cliff in the center of the community, and nearby is the cemetery displaying the names of many of its founding families.

École Acadienne de Pomquet *(Pomquet School)*

Église Ste. Croix *(Pomquet Church)*

Along with the beach, the main attractions that bring most visitors to the area are the Pomquet Museum and *Chez Deslauriers*, which is a heritage home converted into an Acadian interpretive center. It provides historical information and features a tearoom and an outdoor stage. *Chez Deslauriers* property was originally a 1,000-acre tract granted to George H. Monk of the Royal Nova Scotia Volunteer Regiment in 1784. The house was constructed in the 1860s, and then later purchased by Femian Delorey (Deslauriers) and moved by a team of 20 oxen one kilometer (half a mile) to its present location. During the summer months, many activities take place here, including a traditional Acadian meal served every Friday at noon.

Chez Deslauriers

Over the years Pomquet has grown into a community with a strong sense of connection to the land and water. Although farming and fishing are still practiced, many residents have found employment in larger centers such as the nearby town of Antigonish. As a show of pride, every February Pomquet residents come together to celebrate their Acadian heritage at the annual winter carnival, *Carnaval d'hiver de Pomquet.* Here the Acadians display their national flag and dress in ancestral costumes. Included in the celebrations are musical events, dances, meals, mass, and sporting activities.

In 2004, during the third *Congrès mondial acadien* in Nova Scotia, the Broussards hosted an international family reunion in Pomquet, with nearly 300 in attendance. Among the highlights was the visit by Warren Perrin, a Cajun activist and descendant of Acadian leader Joseph Beausoleil Broussard, the courageous resistance hero during the Deportation years. Perrin spoke to the assembled of his 13-year struggle to obtain an acknowledgement from the British Crown for all of the wrongs committed during the deportation of the Acadians, with the appreciated help of Acadians from the north. The year prior, in 2003, a Royal Proclamation had been issued in Canada, on behalf of Queen Elizabeth II. Perrin is also author of *Acadian Redemption, from Beausoleil Broussard to the Royal Proclamation.*

A Catholic mass, celebrated by Fr. Pierre Baccardax, included the singing of traditional songs by the *Chorale acadienne.* A home-style Acadian meal was served, and then various Cajun/Acadian Broussard descendants played music, including famous Cajun Helen Boudreaux from Louisiana. Under the leadership of Shelia Broussard of Halifax, president of *La Famille Broussard Society,* the Broussard Family Reunion was a memorable and moving event that reunited Broussards from all North America.

Entertainment was provided by invited Cajun singer Helen Boudreaux

The local Acadian groups were the Benoit Family and Hank Boucher.

Charles Broussard (left) and Warren Perrin. Following Perrin's speech, Charles Broussard, vice-president of La Famille Beausoleil Association of Louisiana, *presented him with the 2004 Beausoleil Award.*

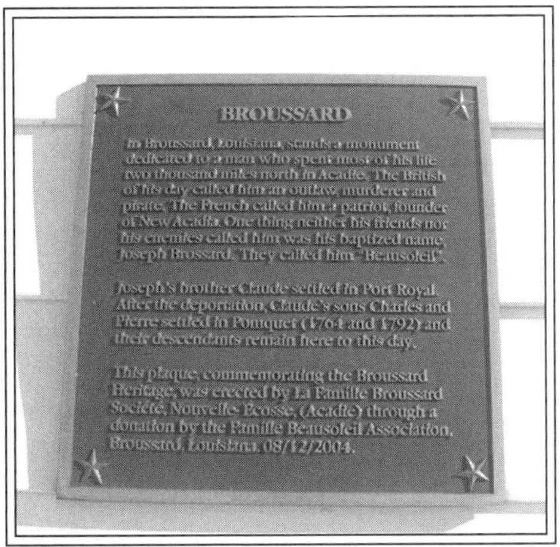

Plaque on Pomquet Church which reads, "In Broussard, Louisiana, stands a monument dedicated to a man who spent most of his life two thousand miles north in Acadie. The British of his day called him an outlaw, murderer, and pirate. The French called him a patriot, founder of New Acadia. One thing neither his friends nor his enemies called him was his baptized name, Joseph Broussard. They called him Beausoleil. Joseph's brother Claude settled in Port Royal. After the deportation, Claude's sons Charles and Pierre settled in Pomquet (1764 and 1792), and their descendants remain here to this day. This plaque commemorating the Broussard Heritage was erected by La Famille Broussard Sociéte, Nouvelle-Ecosse *(Acadie) through a donation by the* Famille Beausoleil Association, *Broussard, Louisiana, 08/12/2004."*

Bibliography

Sally Ross and Alphonse Deveau, *The Acadians of Nova Scotia* (Nimbus Publishing, 1992); Rev. D. J. Rankin, *A History of the County of Antigonish, Nova Scotia* (Toronto: MacMillian Company of Canada, 1929).

WEST CHEZZETCOOK OF HALIFAX COUNTY, NOVA SCOTIA

Judy Doucette Bellefontaine

Nestled amid the deep green fields and bright blue Atlantic waters of Chezzetcook Inlet along Nova Scotia's Eastern Shore is the Acadian community of West Chezzetcook, situated a mere 30 kilometers (20 miles) from Halifax, the capitol of Nova Scotia. Residents of West Chezzetcook sometimes refer to themselves as "Chezzetcookers." West Chezzetcook includes the residents of several other settlements that surround the inlet including Grand Désert, Head Chezzetcook, East Chezzetcook, Lower East Chezzetcook, and Conrad Settlement. Of these settlements, the two communities of West Chezzetcook and Grand Désert are inhabited by the largest number of direct descendents of the first French European settlers, the Acadians.

Canadians recognize that before all others, our First Nations peoples, the Mi'kmaq, were the first to inhabit these lands. The Mi'kmaq frequented these shores, especially during the summer months, making good use of the tidal flats, channels, lakes, and rivers that provided sustenance throughout the summer season.

Evidence has been found of the existence of a few Acadian families living in the Chezzetcook area as far back as the 1740s. The first permanent settlers of the West Chezzetcook/Grand Désert area occurred in 1764 following the release of fugitive Acadians who had been held captive in the British prison at Georges Island in Halifax harbor. A peaceful, contented, hardworking people, these Acadians faced many hardships and difficult situations, particularly in their efforts to acquire ownership of their lands. Family names of some of these early Acadian settlers that can still be found in the community today are Bellefontaine, LaPierre, Petitpas, and Roma. The local family name of Wolfe (of Alsatian descent) married with the original families and became Acadian.

The Acadians of this area made their living from farming, fishing, and forestry. At one time there was also an extensive shipbuilding industry and a brick-making factory. The world renowned clam flats of Chezzetcook Inlet were so fruitful that for many years a bountiful harvest allowed many families to be supported by the digging and processing of clams at a factory in Grand Désert. These clams were shipped to cities like Boston and others along the eastern coast of the United States. Many families added a small income to their daily lives by selling their products at markets in the cities of Halifax/Dartmouth. These products consisted of items such as fresh vegetables, eggs, wild berries, and clams.

In 1996, a group was formed to embark on an ambitious plan that would focus on economic development projects for the West Chezzetcook/Grand Désert communities. The group drew up a strategic plan with input from many community members, and then formed the West Chezzetcook/Grand Désert Community Interest Group.

After much community fundraising and support from various levels of government, one of the oldest homes in Chezzetcook was purchased from an original Bellefontaine family; the home was then transformed into the Acadian House Museum. The museum has since been expanded to include a cabano (clam shelling shed), an Acadian garden, *La Grange* (barn), *La Cuisine de Brigitte* (tea room), an outdoor clay oven, and a proposed community art gallery. The site is now called *L'Acadie de Chezzetcook.*

The Chezzetcook community found it nearly impossible to retain their French language, given the strong influence of the larger Anglophone population and the limited opportunity for schooling in French. Ronald Labelle, author of *Acadian Life in Chezzetcook (1987),* closed his book with this sentence: "In a very short time, unless the local population becomes conscious of the importance of preserving their cultural landscape, with its distinctive language, architecture and other traits, Chezzetcook will no longer exist as an Acadian community in Nova Scotia, and a unique element of Nova Scotia's cultural fabric will be lost forever."

The people of West Chezzetcook and Grand Désert were proud that Ronald Labelle saw the value of their communities and that he took great effort to document their history. Perhaps they viewed these closing words as a challenge, and through the hard work and dedicated efforts of the West Chezzetcook/ Grand Désert Community Interest Group, efforts were made in 1998 to establish a French language school in West Chezzetcook. This initiative was deemed to be impossible largely due to the regulation that at least one parent be fluent in French.

In a renewed effort to revive interest in our cultural language, volunteer classes were begun initially in *La Cuisine de Brigitte* tea room and then later in the upper level of *La Grange.* Interest grew exponentially, and another concerted effort was made to acquire a French language school. This second attempt was successful, and a former junior high school in nearby Porters Lake was refurbished and became the new French school named *École des Beaux-Marais.* The primary school was opened in the fall of 2011, and today some 80 students attend. As these young students age, it is hoped that secondary school classes will be added.

Should Ronald Labelle visit today, he would see a truly vibrant Acadian community that is well aware of and greatly treasures its unique cultural heritage.

MARYLAND ACADIANS

Gregory A. Wood

On July 28, 2013, the state of Maryland took a big step forward in acknowledging its supportive role in the *Grand Dérangement* with the placement of an official historical marker in the small Eastern Shore community of Princess Anne. There, in December of 1755, a number of Acadian exiles had been transported to the Manokin River shores to begin a very uncertain future in the colony. Thanks to the efforts of author Marie Rundquist—whose family has roots in Princess Anne and in the Acadian and indigenous peoples of Nova Scotia—and the efforts of state and local officials who supported her in seeking a tangible way of commemorating the Acadian presence in Maryland, the mid-summer weekend brought together scholars, supporters, civic dignitaries, and guests from Louisiana to discuss Acadians detained, not just on one side of the Chesapeake, but in all of Maryland.

The occasion also marked a major anniversary of these exiles in petitioning relief from their seven years of banishment. In July 1763, exactly 250 years ago from the time this article was written, some 810 detainees wrote the French ambassador in London, asking once again to be "counted as faithful subjects of His very Christian Majesty, the King of France and Navarre." That desperate appeal of "allegiance" may presently seem exaggerated since Acadians had really grown apart from France, becoming a distinct people in North America and finding opportunity, health, and relative wealth in the Maritimes not afforded to them on the European continent.

It is ironic that the Acadian story has been so undervalued by state historians for such a long time, because Maryland has accommodated many French-speakers of diverse color, nationality, and religious persuasion throughout her history. In 1529, the geographer Girolamo da Verrazano made Maryland's shores part of "Nova Gallia" in honor of his deceased brother Giovanni's flirtation with the Atlantic coast, and "Francesca," in the name of François I, five years earlier.

Maryland was even named after Queen Henriette Marie, wife of England's Charles I and sister of Louis XIII of France. Later, 17th and 18th century planters tilled southern Maryland lands; a Swiss, Francis Louis Michel, tried to promote colonization near alleged silver mines on the Potomac; Huguenots and Labadists lived side by side with a Catholic minority; and Frenchmen from Dijon and La Rochelle, like John Jarbo and James Richard, would become sheriffs of St. Mary's and Baltimore counties, respectively.

While the province certainly had to cope with constant and mostly unsubstantiated fears of French and Native American cooperation on its northern and western frontiers, and with a spirit of anti-Catholicism that marked the era, political and sectarian worries did not stop colonists from enjoying French language, arts, philosophy, and translated literary works. In time, Maryland became a formidable pro-Gallican region as America rose up against the mother country. She supplied French mercenaries and regulars during the Revolutionary War and continued to open her arms to *émigrés* escaping the radical changes in France after 1789 and to Saint-Domingan traders and refugees fleeing civil disorder in the Caribbean.

The Acadian plight in Maryland began in late November and early December 1755. Four ships from Nova Scotia via Boston entered the Severn River at Annapolis with over 900 passengers forced from their northern homeland. With such an intimidating number almost equal in population to the colonial capital, perplexed officials sought to distribute the exiles to various regions on both sides of the Chesapeake without the advice of the royal governor who was absent on business. Three ships were ordered to continue on to Patuxent, Choptank, and Wicomico river landings; some exiles were allowed to stay in Annapolis, while still others were transported the short distance north to Baltimore.

Caught off guard and hampered by limited resources, yet urged on by principle and the Oxford merchant Henry Callister, Maryland Protestants confronted a challenging political and moral dilemma. Maryland's neighbor, Virginia, viewed the situation in another light and sent her 1,200 Acadian exiles to England as quickly as weather permitted. Suffice it to say, the financial and psychological burdens were heavy for both exiles and colonists. It was no easy task to house, feed, clothe, and find suitable employment for such large families.

Xenophobia has unfortunately shown its ugly head at various times in the American experience, yet in May 1756, Maryland's lower house overwhelmingly approved, 25-7, for Acadians to stay in the province. Disenfranchised, influential Maryland Catholics such as Charles Carroll added a voice, if not a vote, and, with resigned planters, townsfolk, and Jesuit missionary assistance, dealt with the constant solicitation and a tenuous situation for well over a decade in an agriculturally dominant society. Initially, Acadians were restricted in their movement to a ten-mile radius and jailed when exceeding that limit without passes. In addition, there were some cases of indenture, a ban from viewing militia activities, and censuses required of area constables (which have not been found). An account of frigid winter temperatures inspired noted modern muralist Robert Dafford to portray Eastern Shore Acadians struggling in the snow.

Maryland records fail to provide much legislative detail about how closely exiles were supervised after 1758 or 1759 or how most dealt with other public and private assistance. Most early Acadians were nameless in Maryland documents until several years later. The best accounts deal with the Carroll family's correspondence involving the Anselme Manjeant family in Annapolis and private efforts in Europe.

As the Seven Years War dragged to a conclusion, exiles in Charles County and the Bohemia/Tuckahoe/Oxford area shed the veil of anonymity somewhat. Rev. George Hunter's Day Book, 1763-1768, records that Port Tobacco exiles on the Western Shore provided sewing, spinning, weaving, and milling, and that children benefitted from a "*school de la haute ville.*" Rev. Joseph Mosley's missionary journal from the Eastern Shore mentions a couple of instances involving charity, but it is best known for its specific records of eight Acadian marriages, two burials, and seven named (and several more anonymous) French baptisms. His last entry involving Acadians–the baptisms of Sarah and Rosanna Clemensau (Clementson)–dates from April 1773.

By 1763, exiles were identified with 11 areas: Annapolis, Baltimore, Upper and Lower Marlboro, and Port Tobacco on the Western Shore; Fredericktown and Georgetown in far northeast Maryland; and Newtown, Oxford, Princess Anne, and Snow Hill on the central and lower Eastern Shore. The vast majority of exiles preferred to be called "Neutrals;" only some exiles in Lower Marlboro used the label "prisoner of war." As a whole, Maryland colonists tended to agree that the Acadians thrust upon them were British by treaty, albeit potentially dangerous politically.

As Acadians became increasingly aware that the war-weakened French government had little influence left in North America, and could only help those caught up in ports in England and France, many found other means of escaping their destitution within a few years after the end of the French and Indian War (as the Seven Years War was known in North America). Unlike their compatriots in New England, the majority of Maryland Neutrals looked south for deliverance and accepted the offers of the new Spanish authorities in charge in Louisiana.

Ships left Maryland four times from various ports between the years 1766 and 1769. All in all, approximately three quarters of Maryland Acadians found their way to Spanish protection in New Orleans, Pointe Coupée, St. Gabriel, Cabannocé, and Natchez. The impressive Dafford tableau at the Acadian Memorial in St. Martinville, Louisiana, depicts, among others, Acadians from each of the four Maryland voyages: Joseph Landry (1766, Cabannocé Post); Anselme Blanchard and Elizabeth Brasseaux (1767, St. Gabriel); Augustin Boudrot, Alexis and Honoré Breau (1768, Natchez); and Olivier Benoît (1769, Natchitoches via Texas). Before the arrival of other Acadians from France in 1785, Maryland settlers accounted for the majority of exiles in Louisiana, and thanks to the Spanish authorities, their first years there are remarkably well-documented.

While Maryland's experience with her Neutrals has previously been judged to be lacking in specific detail, this historian's opinion is that some modern scholars have relied too strongly on just one article published over a century ago. In recent years, many archival centers have shared documents on microfilm, microfiche, and online, thus opening a larger window for patient, thorough research in history and genealogy. Truth be known, exile gave way to rebirth: many Acadians and their progeny stayed and eventually thrived in Maryland well into the mid-19th century. Here they chose a path different from their "cousins" who moved on to Louisiana. They quickly became more culturally, economically, and politically diverse than those under Spanish jurisdiction.

After their fellow exiles left for Louisiana, those remaining in the Maryland colony regrouped in Baltimore Town and were joined by the members of the Aucoin (Wedge), Bouton, Beausseron, Bujeau, Douaron (Gold), Pierre Douliard, Charles Thibodeau, and Louis Dechamp families from Philadelphia. With the exception of the LeBlancs (Whites) and Poiriers, who were the only ones left, coming from the previous assignment to the very small community of Baltimore in 1763, a completely different "French Town Quarter" developed. By the early 1790s Acadians occupied the southern end of Charles Street as it approaches the harbor, and owed their land acquisition principally to the efforts of Paul Gold.

Local censuses from that decade note the presence of, among others, Gauterots (Gutthrows), Babins, Germains, Grangers, Deschamps (Deshields), Celestins, Boudreaus, Chameaus, Dupuis (Wells), Mangeants, and a few Maffies (Murphys!), Paillottets, and Tilliards. Soon there were Jeaudains and Daigle (Deagles), and Anglo-Acadian couples surnamed Lockerman and Holmes. Early Acadians in Baltimore were mainly common laborers and those found in the seafaring and dry goods trades. Remaining families had fewer members than their Louisiana counterparts; some had ties with *Canadiens* and other ethnic communities, and the promise of the Chesapeake and a more urban setting rapidly moved them further from agriculture, a return to Acadie, another Romance language, and untamed waterways.

Americanization set in, and some exiles even joined the war efforts as artillerymen and privateers. Young Cyprien Dupuis (Wells) had been a member of the Sons of Liberty in the 1760s. All were asked to sign an Oath of Fidelity; a few declined (as they exhibited a continuing reluctance with oaths), and there is evidence of at least two deserters, Martin Gutro and Francis Deshields. These Baltimore Acadians had a different vision, and only much later would a Maryland Thibodeau or DeValcourt be drawn southward to Lafourche or St. Martinville.

It took time for the Catholic Church, meanwhile, to have a permanent ministry in Baltimore. A Belgian-born missionary, Bernard Diderick, aided this effort, from 1775 to 1782, though he turned out to be a source of great consternation for his fellow Jesuits and Acadian parishioners. Only in 1783 was an official parish registry begun. By 1805, St. Peter's Church in French Town had hundreds of baptisms bearing the names of new children of Acadian lineage, their parents and godparents, and that list grew tremendously until the mid-1820s. St. Peter's became, in reality, the first cathedral in the United States, losing its importance only when a new cathedral structure was finally completed in 1821.

French Town took a while to prosper. Officers from Rochambeau's army noted not only the poverty and unpretentious appearance of that neighborhood, but also the enthusiasm of the Acadians upon seeing fellow francophones. In time, economics would vastly improve, and Baltimore would have three distinct French quarters: French Town; a wealthier area around St. Mary's Seminary, established by Sulpician émigré priests, on Paca Street; and a decidedly West

Indian, Saint Domingan, section on Fell's Point, served by Sulpicians at St. Patrick's Church. By the 1790s, many women of Acadian heritage were known publicly as Betsy, Peggy, Polly, and Sally.

The use of Americanized names was not at all derogatory. It just showed that women of Acadian heritage were becoming more and more part of the American fabric and had adopted the English nicknames for their French names such as Elizabeth, Marguerite, Marie, and Sarah. There was ample opportunity to speak French on the street and in shops. French colonists who fled Saint-Domingue, and émigrés from France, also intermarried with Acadians, further enriching the diversity of Acadian descendants. Now there were families surnamed Carré, Chalumeau, Duchemin, Baroux, DeValcourt, Hermange, Glavéry, Gouvernet, Groc, Heuisler, Latruite, Nouvel, Piet, and Martiacq, to name a few.

Baltimore continued to grow rapidly, from a few hundred residents in 1752 to over 26,000 at the turn of the century. As a city below the Mason-Dixon Line, there was some evidence of Acadian slaveholding (at least 18 are noted in the 1800 U.S. census). Trade on the Chesapeake still lured Acadians to the water, but lumber, medicine, lodging, millinery, tailoring, jewelry, tutoring, and groceries were trades and professions also attached to Acadian heritage households.

Rose Landry, the widow of Capt. Joseph White (LeBlanc), joined fellow widow Elizabeth Seton in establishing the American Sisters of Charity in Baltimore in 1809. The War of 1812 brought members of the Barbine (Babin), Gold, Guthrow, Wedge, and Wells families to the defense of Baltimore. An Acadian middle class developed, and young men enrolled at the Sulpician-sponsored St. Mary's College until its closing in 1852. Religious ministry attracted some, such as Joseph Barry, Matthew Deagle, Oliver L. Jenkins, Francis Hermange (seminary only), and Jacob Walter.

As the elder exiles began dying off in their 80s and 90s,[1] the label "Acadian" became more and more a genealogical note. Examination of Baltimore City directories shows that French Town and South Charles Street held on, barely, through the first third of the 19th century as Acadians chose residences in other neighborhoods. Memories of the past would then have to be preserved mainly with members of families like Donaldson, Jenkins, Holmes, Honeywell, Fisher, Goulding, Riston, Rosensteel, Walter, Winn, and a few original exiles.

The population of Baltimore reached 100,000 by 1840. Because of its size and stature in American society, Baltimore is a treasure trove of records: tax, land, census, church (baptisms, marriages, burials, pew rents), and newspapers (articles, advertisements, *Baltimore Sun* obituaries), which have made the study of Acadian ancestry and influence in Baltimore in the 19th century a daunting, but pleasant, task. Descendants of Barbines, Deagles, Golds, Guthrows, and Wedges can easily be traced to the Civil War and after.

As a second century began with Acadian ties to Maryland, political passions and war were once again at center stage. Two of that era's more interesting personalities, James Ryder Randall and the Rev. Jacob Walter, were like bookends of the age. The celebrated Randall, born in Baltimore on January 1,

1839, a great-grandson of original exile Cyprien Dupuis (b. November 5, 1752) and Marguerite [Peggy] White (b. October 19, 1762 to Olivier and Marguerite Leblanc, aforementioned residents of Baltimore in 1763), penned perhaps the greatest anti-Northern poem of the Civil War.

In April 1861, Randall, then a professor at Poydras College, Pointe Coupée, Louisiana, wrote *Maryland, My Maryland*, which became the official state song. In its memorable nine verses, Randall's poem praises the great state leaders of the past and calls citizens to "burst the tyrant's chain" and spurn "the Northern scum." Not as well-known is Rev. Walter, a nephew of the Rev. Matthew Deagle, who, during his long tenure at St. Patrick's Church, Washington, D.C. (1860-1894), ministered to Mary Surratt, condemned to death as a conspirator in the Lincoln assassination. Walter believed a little too strongly in Surratt's innocence and was scolded by local Catholic Church, military, and federal authorities. A photo taken at Surratt's execution on July 7, 1865, shows him on the scaffold with Surratt! Fr. Walter's mother, nee Mary Deagle, unfortunately passed away a month later, at age 74, perhaps feeling the strain of her son's political and spiritual involvement in nearby Washington.

The 19th century was to end quietly for descendants of Acadians and others of French heritage. The century had begun with a recognizable and influential number of francophones, be they exiles from the Maritimes, political and religious émigrés from France, former colonists of the West Indies, or veterans of the American Revolution. For the Acadians especially, intermarriage, smooth integration into American life, expansion of American territory, death, and later removal to Louisiana, were all factors that contributed to the "disappearance" of a continuous, identifiable presence in Maryland beyond the year 1900.

The Baltimore press (notably the *Sun*) informed its public of the deaths of several Acadian descendants: Elizabeth Barbine (1866, age 75), Joseph S. Barbine (1874, age 58, pneumonia), Charles W. Gold (1867, drowning), Ann E. Guthrow (1874), John Honeywell (1894, age 79), Rev. Oliver L. Jenkins (1869, age 56, former banker, college president and seminary head), Sister Mary Samuel (Mary Caroline) Piet (1868, age 40), John Anthony Riston (1881, age 62), and Simon Wedge (1887, age 87). Yet, even in the last quarter of the 1800s, there is a Fr. Joseph Luke Barry, son of James Barry and Mathilda Wedge (Aucoin), at St. Joseph's Parish, Baltimore, ending 33 years of service in 1899 to churches spanning the state from Cumberland in the far west to Havre de Grace and other communities in the northeast. Fortunately, the Roman Catholic community and their institutions in Baltimore have remained strong to this day and proud of its historic French roots.

At the beginning of the 20th century, the Louisiana "cousins" are those who remain most interested in the Maryland Acadian experience. In 1936, on the eve of the Acadian National Holiday, a group of Louisiana Acadians, led by the inimitable Dudley J. LeBlanc, passed through Baltimore by train en route to Nova Scotia. The 63 travelers, 57 described as young women, were on an 18-day "pilgrimage retracing the steps of their ancestors." Welcomed by the Maryland Historical Society, the Society of 1812, the Association of Commerce, the French consul, and city officials, the group visited sites pertinent to the Baltimore Acadian experience and resource centers exhibiting documentation on general cultural life during that era. LeBlanc told the local newspaper that his great-great-grandfather Gilles had married a Maryland Acadian, although the Baton Rouge Catholic records now show that a marriage dates 13 years prior to his research account. (According to the records, the newspaper had quoted LeBlanc giving a marriage year as 1796, not 1783.) Nevertheless, the politician and future elixir king used his voyage of 1936 to publish his second edition of *The True Story of the Acadians* the following year.

Each generation since has tried to decipher Maryland's role in the exile and rebirth of the Acadian people. The research has been intriguing, challenging, and sometimes discouraging. Two decades ago, noted historian Naomi E.S. Griffiths even declared that "the story of the Acadians sent to Maryland dwindles into the occasional genealogical detail and the fate of the majority becomes, once more, a matter for conjecture." Fortunately, more detail in many areas has come to light and, eventually, it is hoped that additional historical markers in Maryland, perhaps in pivotal areas such as Baltimore's "French Town," Annapolis harbor, Port Tobacco, and Fr. Joseph Mosley's Tuckahoe Mission, will help enlighten future scholars, tourists, and people of Acadian heritage of Maryland's rich past.

Photo©Frick Gallery, New York

Thomas Courtney Jenkins, husband of Elizabeth Gold (Douaron), was married January 23, 1806, by Bishop John Carroll, St. Peter's Church in Baltimore. The Jenkins family had many connections with Baltimore Acadians. Jenkins was a prominent leather merchant.

Photo©Matthew Brady, 1861

Rev. Jacob Walter was a defender of Mary Surratt (Surette), suspected of being an assassination conspirator of Pres. Abraham Lincoln. Surratt owned a boarding house where John Wilkes Booth and the other conspirators were alleged to have had meetings. But at least one scholar has called this link uncertain. Other sources claim that eyewitnesses had identified Booth as Lincoln's attacker, and the detectives had information (a tip from an unnamed actor and a bartender) linking her son,

John Surratt Jr., to Booth. When confronted by investigators, Mary Surratt lied and told the detectives that her son had been in Canada for two weeks. She also did not reveal that she had delivered a package to the Surrattsville Tavern on Booth's behalf hours earlier. She was convicted by a military tribunal. On July 6, Surratt was informed she would be hanged the next day; she wept profusely. Surratt was joined by two Catholic priests, Revs. Jacob Walter and B.F. Wiget, and her daughter, Anna. Fr. Jacob Walter remained with her almost until her death. Surratt spent the night on her mattress, weeping and moaning, ministered to by the priests. On July 7, 1865, Surratt became the first woman to be executed in the United States.

Shown on July 28, 2013, following the dedication of the marker dedicated to the 913 Acadians sent to Maryland are, left to right, Marie Rundquist, Priscilla Breaux, and Frances Wilcox.

BIBLIOGRAPHY

Basil Sollers, "The Acadians (French Neutrals) Transported to Maryland," *Maryland Historical Magazine* 3 (March 1908, pp. 1-21); Carroll Letter Book (206), Maryland Historical Society, Baltimore; "Acadians' Descendants, On Tour, Visit Baltimore," *Baltimore Evening Sun*, August 14, 1936; Baton Rouge Catholic Church Records, Volume 2, 1770-1803; Naomi Griffiths, *The Contexts of Acadian History, 1686-1784* (Montreal: McGill-Queen's University Press, 1992, p. 117).

ENDNOTES

1. St. Peter's/Cathedral Records note the passing of Francis Lucas, age 103, on January 12, 1811, and Rose Jeaudain (or Dine), age 98, on March 21, 1821.

MICHIGAN ACADIANS

Martin Guidry

There are Acadian descendants in many of the United States. Many people do not know that there are also proud Acadians in Michigan. The LeBlanc family was one of the first Acadian families to arrive in Michigan, initially settling in 1760 in Michilimackinac, on the straits between Lake Huron and Lake Michigan. Within a generation they moved to Ecorse, south of Detroit. Today in Michigan, one finds concentrations of Acadian surnames in the Michigan counties of Monroe, Bay, Saginaw, Arenac, Alpena, Wayne, Houghton, and Dickinson.

Most Acadians in Michigan came from Quebec in the late 1830s and 1840s. This is because, during the Acadian deportations that started in 1755 and went on for eight years, thousands of Acadians escaped capture and fled through the woods to Quebec. More Acadians migrated to Quebec after the French and Indian War ended with the 1763 Treaty of Paris. Also, many of the Acadians exiled to Massachusetts and Connecticut migrated to Quebec and settled along the Saint-Lawrence River areas and around St-Jacques, in the Lanaudière region. Many of these Acadians would later come to Michigan.

Initially the Acadian migrants in Quebec stayed together and did not interact a great deal with the French Canadians, but over time, the two cultures became closer and intermarriages occurred. In Quebec, the Acadians worked hard clearing land, building homes, and tending to their growing families while primarily returning to farming, as they had done in Acadie. As families grew, land was subdivided amongst the many heirs, having the effect of decreasing production. Because of this, many young Acadian men began moving west to Ontario to acquire farmland or to work as lumberjacks in the timber industry.

With the Patriots' Rebellion of 1837 and 1838 against the British, and the collapse of family farms from subdivision and depleted soils, an exodus began of young Acadians and French Canadians to New England and Michigan for work opportunities. These new arrivals to Michigan, mostly from the general area of Montreal, joined the first French-Canadian migrants of almost a century earlier in lumbering, mining, and farming. Among the Acadians migrating to Michigan were the surnames Guédry (Guildry), Thibaudeau, LeBlanc, Hébert, Doiron, Breau, Brossard, Boutin, Bourg, and Cyr.

One of the early Acadians to reach Michigan, around 1840, was Jean-Baptiste Guildry (*dit* Labine), who settled in Monroe County. Born on July 31, 1825, in St-Jacques, in the Lanaudière region of Quebec, he was the great-grandson of Jean-Baptiste-Augustin Guédry (*dit* Labine) and Marie-Marguerite Picot, who had been exiled in 1755 to Boston, where their family lived until 1766. At this time they migrated to St-Alexis, near St-Jacques.

In Monroe County, Michigan, on November 7, 1848, Jean-Baptiste Guidry married the French-Canadian Edwidge Senever (*dit* Lemarbe) and they had 17 children over the next 28 years. A farmer, Jean-Baptiste moved in the early 1880s, with Edwidge and their large family, north to Pinconning, in Bay County, on the shores of Lake Huron. Here he purchased 60 acres of land in Section 16. As Jean-Baptiste's sons matured, they also purchased land in the area and became farmers. Jean-Baptiste died around 1888 and was buried in the Pinconning Cemetery. Many of his descendants still live in the Bay County area and continue to make their living in jobs associated with the land. On Jean-Baptiste's arrival in Michigan, the Guidry *dit* Labine surname was shortened to Labine, and about 1881 it became LaBean—likely the result of phonetic spelling by Anglophone government officials.

As happened in northeastern Maine and northern New Brunswick, where Acadians and French Canadians settled together, the two groups in Michigan eventually melded through intermarriage into one French-language population. Although the influence of the growing Anglophone population has caused much of the Acadian and French-Canadian cultures and French language to be lost, some elements have been retained. The Michigan French remain a mostly rural people working within the agricultural and blue-collar communities. The Catholic faith remains strong within the families and is often the center of social life in the community. They still celebrate several of the holidays of their ancestors, and have kept traditional meals of *tourtière* (meat pie), *cassoulet* (meat casserole), cheese soup, and *tarte aux mûres sauvages* (blackberry pie). Several local events have their roots in old Acadian/French-Canadian celebrations, and at times the old folktales and stories are still recited.

Today there is a resurgence of interest among the Acadian/French-Canadian people of Michigan to find their French roots through genealogy. *Michigan's Habitant Heritage*, the journal of the French-Canadian Heritage Society of Michigan, which meets monthly, provides informative research articles on Acadian and French-Canadian heritage, history, language, culture, foods, and families of Michigan. The Monroe County Historical Museum has many interesting displays on the Acadian and French-Canadian heritage of the area. Likewise, the Historical Museum of Bay County has galleries on the history and culture of that county. The genealogical societies of several other counties provide excellent resources and meetings to help Acadians and French Canadians reestablish their roots. Those most active include the Genealogical Society of Monroe County and the Pinconning Genealogy Group.

VI

EPILOGUE

TWENTY-FIVE YEARS OF DISCOVERING THE ACADIAN WORLD

Warren A. Perrin

CANADA

New Brunswick

During my first visit to New Brunswick in 1990, I came away with the impression that we were first and foremost all one family. This was reinforced with my meeting of the Cyr family in Moncton. Michel Cyr, an attorney in Moncton who later served as president of the *Société national de l'Acadie*, helped to welcome us during our first legal seminar hosted at the *Université de Moncton* law school in 1990.

Cyr invited Judge Durwood Conque, his wife Rusty, my wife Mary, and me to join his family in a traditional Acadian meal at their cottage in Cocagne. That evening we met his parents Léonide, lawyer, and Laetitia Cyr, director of French radio at Radio-Canada. Later, we met two of his sisters Isabelle, an actress and singer based in Montreal, and Myriam, an Acadian actress based in London and New York.

Myriam was subsequently chosen as female lead in Phil Comeau's first Acadian feature film *Jerome's Secret*, and she then came to Louisiana to star in Pat Mire's feature film *Dirty Rice* where she played the role of a Cajun woman named Helene who struggles to keep her family together. In 2003, Isabelle Cyr was the *maitresse de cérémonie* in Ottawa during the official presentation of the Queen's Royal Proclamation of the Great Upheaval. In 2005, Michel and I participated in the activities in Halifax, Nova Scotia commemorating the 250th anniversary of the Deportation.

Feeling a close connection to history in New Brunswick, I wanted to walk the land where my ancestors had also walked and lived, near Moncton. This included places like Chipoudie, Fox Creek, Saint-Anselme, Coverdale, Boundary Creek, Salisbury, and Le Coude. I am the eighth generation descendent of resistance fighter Joseph Beausoleil Broussard who lived in the upper Petitcodiac River area near Boundary Creek for nearly 30 years. In 1998, Acadian historian Paul Surette took an entire day to bring me to all of these places, and we documented the path we took with maps and photographs of the sites. For me, the occasion was a communion with my ancestors and it inspired within me, the desire to continue learning about and promoting our Acadian homeland–Acadie–and to keep our big family together forever.

In August 1990, the Centre international de la common law en français *hosted a group of Louisiana lawyers and judges for the first of many legal seminars at the* Université de Moncton *Law School. At the reception are (left to right) former Dean Yvon Fountaine, Judge Allen M. Babineaux, Fleurette Doucet, and Law Professor Michel Doucet, who was then director of the* Centre *and had organized the seminar.*

In August 1992, a delegation from Erath, Louisiana, "twinned" their town with Bertrand, New Brunswick. After the ceremony are, left to right, Judge Allen M. Babineaux, Edward Domingues, named a Living Legend of the Acadian Museum of Erath in 2005, and Rickey Domingues.

Antonio Landry (left), director of the Village historique acadien, Caraquet, New Brunswick, is presenting a poster to Warren A. Perrin (right) on August 14, 1992, for the Acadian Museum of Erath. As the mayor of Caraquet, Landry has embraced the importance of preserving the language and culture of his forebears, and has done so in practical ways. At the same time, he has promoted the essential importance of linguistic harmony, respect, and tolerance between New Brunswick's French and English-speaking citizens.

In 1993, Warren A. Perrin (right) presents a gift from the Cajuns of Louisiana to singer Donat Lacroix of Caraquet, New Brunswick. Lacroix, a well-known Acadian composer and musician, formerly a fisherman, sings haunting songs about the travails of a fisherman and of the sea's many moods. His popular song Viens voir l'Acadie *(Come See Acadie) is often mistaken for the Acadian national anthem. Perrin was in New Brunswick to discuss the progress of the Petition for a British apology for the Acadian Deportation with the members of the Francophone Section of the New Brunswick Bar Association at their annual banquet. The party following the banquet was hosted by Antoine Landry, a leader in the Acadian community for four decades.*

The Perrins hosted a group of Acadians from New Brunswick to attend the Mardi Gras *in New Orleans, Louisiana. Enjoying the Bacchus* Mardi Gras *Ball is former* Université de Moncton *Law Professor Pierre Arsenault.*

In February 1996, Louisiana filmmaker Pat Mire filmed Dirty Rice *near Eunice, Louisiana. For the female lead, Mire recruited an Acadian from New Brunswick, Myriam Cyr. During a break in the filming are (left to right) Pat Mire, Myriam Cyr, Ben Mouton, and Warren A. Perrin.*

Attending the Eighth Annual Judge Allen M. Babineaux Comparative International Law Symposium on August 11, 1998, are (front row) Aldéa Landry; Louise Aucoin, law professor at the Université de Moncton*; Lynne Castonguay, assistant director of the* Centre international de la common law en français *(CICLEF); (back row), Fernand Landry, director general,* 8th Sommet de la Francophonie 1999*; Judge Roger Savoie, of the Court of Queen's Bench of New Brunswick; Serge Rousselle, vice-dean,* Université de Moncton *law school; Chief Judge Ned E. Doucet, Louisiana Third Circuit Court of Appeal; John Hernandez, III, attorney and chairman of the symposium; Dean Michel Doucet,* Université de Moncton *law school; Roger Bilodeau, law professor at the* Université de Moncton*; and Warren A. Perrin, attorney and president of the Council for the Development of French in Louisiana (CODOFIL).*

In September 1998, the Université de Moncton *law school hosted the Eighth Annual Judge Allen M. Babineaux Comparative International Law Symposium. The merits,* vel non, *of the Petition was the subject of the lecture. Those in attendance included Ferdinand and Aldea Landry; Law Professor Louise Aucoin; Lynne Castonguay; Judge Roger Savoie; Serge Rousselle; and Dean Michel Doucet. Following the symposium, Acadian historian Paul Surette (left) took the author (right) for a tour of the Petitcodiac River Valley to see where the Acadian settlements were located in the mid-1750s, including the Beausoleil Broussard homestead.*

In August 2012, a delegation of Acadians from Memramcook were hosted for a tour of the Acadian Museum of Erath and a lunch at the Perrin farm. They were in Louisiana to participate in the celebration of the Festivals Acadiens et Creoles. *At the Perrin's farm house are (left to right) Raymond Gaudet; Donald O. LeBlanc, mayor of Memramcook; Warren A. Perrin; Dolores Breau; Claude Boudreau, director of* Monument-Lefebvre*; and Conrad LeBlanc, president of* Monument-Lefebvre.

Jean Gaudet, a cultural activist, visited the Perrin farm in August 2012. The Acadian tour group was provided a Cajun meal and music by Grammy-nominated musician D.L. Menard. Gaudet led a delegation of Acadians from New Brunswick to Lafayette, Louisiana to attend the Festivals Acadiens et Creoles.

In October 2012, Perrin hosted a dinner for his dear Acadian friends in Moncton, Viola LeBreton (right), who taught many children to appreciate their Acadian culture, and her daughter Julie Frigault (top). Julie has been involved throughout the years with many French youth organizations around Atlantic Canada. She lived in Louisiana until the age of four, then moved to the vibrant Acadian city of Moncton. From 2006-2011, Julie was a member of la Fédération des jeunes francophones du Nouveau-Brunswick *(FJFNB). During her last year of involvement, she represented the Acadian youth as vice-president and chaired the committee of the* Societé nationale de l'Acadie *as New Brunswick's youth representative. Today, Julie gives back to the community by working with FJFNB to bring students the same amazing experiences that she has enjoyed promoting Acadian culture.*

On August 26, 2013, a delegation of Louisiana officials visited the Centre communautaire Sainte-Anne *(CCSA) in Fredericton, New Brunswick, in order to seek information on creating a French international high school on the campus of the University of Louisiana, in Lafayette. Left to right, are Rep. Stephen Ortego; Executive Director of CCSA Thierry Arseneau; School Board Member Kermit Bouillion; and CODOFIL Board Member Warren A. Perrin.*

On August 25, 2013, Perrin was invited to make a presentation at the Monument-Lefebvre. *Left to right, are Rep. Stephen Ortego; Claude Boudreau, director of the* Société du Monument-Lefebre; *Georgette Bourgeois, Acadian artist; Perrin; and Kermit Bouillion.*

Nova Scotia

The Port-Royal Habitation, capital of Acadie (now Nova Scotia), was constructed in 1605. Samuel de Champlain was the architect of the project. In 1613, the fort of Port-Royal was destroyed by the British from Virginia. The capital was moved to the south side of the river and Port-Royal became the beacon for the pioneer families who left from France to settle there in the 1630s. Despite turmoil and suffering, these people survived, the colony prospered, and the area became known as the "birthplace of Acadie." Today, Nova Scotia has many Acadian regions, although isolated one from another, they are all inhabited by the descendants of determined Acadians who returned after the Deportation. Every time I return to Nova Scotia I feel like I have returned to my native land and I am reminded that I am a "child of Acadie."

In August 1995, Acadian leaders from Church Point, Nova Scotia, hosted the directors for a dinner during the French immersion program at Université Sainte-Anne. *From left to right, are Louise d'Entremont; Rector Harley d'Entremont of the* Université Sainte-Anne*; Denise Comeau; Sen. Gerald Comeau; Aurora Comeau; Mary Perrin; and Dr. Jean-Douglas Comeau, founder of the popular French immersion program and named a fellow of the Living Legends program of the Acadian Museum of Erath, Louisiana.*

Enjoying a picnic are the first Louisiana students with CODOFIL scholarships who attended the summer French immersion program at Université Sainte-Anne *in 1991. Left to right, are Rector Dr. Harley D'Entremont; Delia Comeau d'Entremont; Denise Douglas Comeau; Dr. Jean-Douglas Comeau, dean of immersion program; Amy Veasey, student from Lafayette; Jason, student from Baton Rouge; Aurore Comeau, administrative assistant to Dr. d'Entremont; Registrar Muriel Comeau; and Viola LeBreton. This social event was held at Sen. Gerald Comeau's house at La Butte, Nova Scotia. Over the years, more than 1,000 Louisiana students have spent summers at the French immersion classes at* Université Saint-Anne.

On May 31, 1995, this group of Acadian leaders in Halifax includes (left to right) Wayne Gaudet, minister for Acadian Affairs in Nova Scotia; Warren A. Perrin, then-president of CODOFIL; Paul Gaudet, executive director, Nova Scotia Office of Acadian Affairs; and Dr. Charles Gaudet, French education director of the Nova Scotia Department of Education. At the event, the Acadian Museum of Erath, Louisiana, received a photograph of the church at Grand-Pré.

In November 1996, the Perrins hosted a dinner in honor of then-Minister Allister Surette, responsible for Acadian Affairs in Nova Scotia. Today, he is the rector of Université Sainte-Anne *in Church Point, Nova Scotia. At Perrin's home in Lafayette are (left to right) Warren A. Perrin; Mary Perrin; Minister Surette; Living Legend Christy Dugas Maraist, former president of the Acadian Memorial Foundation Board; and Dr. David Maraist, who helped to draft the speech on the Petition for the 1994* Congrès mondial acadien.

On April 30, 1999, as a gift from Dr. Jean-Douglas Comeau, Warren A. Perrin was brought on a canoe trip to tour the interior of Nova Scotia by Acadian Métis guide Melbourne Muise. He is performing an ancient Mi'kmaq ritual before launching the canoes for the outing.

Accompanying Perrin on the trip was David Dronet, vice-president of the board of directors of the Acadian Museum of Erath, who is in the front of the canoe with Dr. Jean-Douglas Comeau (right).

On May 1, 1999, Université Sainte-Anne *bestowed an honorary doctorate degree to Perrin. During the ceremony, Perrin updated those in attendance on the status of the Petition. Following the ceremony, Perrin is being congratulated with Gérald C. Boudreau (right), then-registrar and general secretary at* Université Sainte-Anne. *Years later, Boudreau became co-chairman of the nominating comittee to designate The Landscape of Grand Pré a UNESCO World Heritage Site.*

In August 2001, the Perrins, along with their son Bruce Perrin, attended the French immersion program at Université Sainte-Anne. *The Perrins announced at the final ceremony of the session the donation of an annual scholarship to help fund the attendance of Louisiana students in the program. Left to right are Warren A. Perrin, Mary Broussard Perrin, Virginia Smith, and then-Rector André Roberge.*

In 2004, a Louisiana delegation was hosted by a large group of Acadians in Chéticamp (Cape Breton) where they were entertained at the huge stone church by local musicians, and the Perrins were presented with a hand-made Acadian flag, which is now displayed in the Acadian Museum of Erath. During the Congrès mondial acadien 2004 *in Nova Scotia are (left to right) Napoléon Chiasson,* La Société Saint Pierre*; Daniel Aucoin, coordinator of* Congrès mondial acadien 2004 *in Chéticamp; Kermit Bouillion, director of the Acadian Museum of Erath; Yvette Aucoin, President of* La Société Saint Pierre*; and Warren A. Perrin. Chéticamp is "twinned" with Delcambre, Louisiana. The Acadians of Chéticamp donated a hooked rug to the Acadian Museum of Erath.*

On July 28, 2005, as part of the festivities commemorating the 250th anniversary of the Deportation, there was an unveiling of the Great Acadian Upheaval Commemorative Project *monument at Halifax Harbor. From 1758 until 1763, approximately 2,000 Acadians were held prisoners on nearby Georges Island. Representing the Acadians of the North was May Bouchard (left), and representing the Acadians of the South was Warren A. Perrin (right).*

The following officials participated in the unveiling of the monument are shown, left to right, Dawn Sloan, municipal councilor for Halifax Regional Municipality; Warren A. Perrin, president of CODOFIL; Chris d'Entremont, Nova Scotian minister of Acadian Affairs, Napoleon Chiasson; Michel Cyr, president of SNA.; and His Honor Lawrence A. Freeman, husband of the Queen's representative from Nova Scotia, the Honorable Lt. Gov. Myra Freeman.

At the unveiling of the monument are, left to right, Warren A. Perrin; the Honorable Myra A. Freeman, Lt. Gov. of Nova Scotia representing Queen Elizabeth II; and May Bouchard of Pomquet, Nova Scotia.

A delegation of Louisiana Acadians was invited for the first time in 250 years to visit Georges Island where their ancestors were held prisoners for many years. Documentary footage was made of the emotional event. Left to right, are chef and filmmaker Ronald Gaspard; Acadian Museum of Erath officer Ron Miguez; author Dianne Marshall; and Warren A. Perrin.

In 2005, following a visit to a historic building are Warren A. Perrin; Aldric d'Entremont, warden of the Municipality of Argyle; Gordon Wood, of the Argyle Municipality Historical and Genealogical Society; and Chris d'Entremont, minister of Acadian Affairs for the province and member of the Nova Scotian Legislative Assembly representing the district d'Argyle. Perrin and a group of his friends had gone to Canada in a motorhome to promote his book Acadian Redemption (2005).

Prince Edward Island

Prince Edward Island is the smallest Canadian province in both land area and population. On my first sojourn there, we visited *Le Village de l'Acadie* in Mont-Carmel of the Evangeline region. While there, I was pleasantly surprised to attend a play with the name similar to my mother's nickname: Mae Mae (her name was Ella Mae Broussard). The play was called *La Cuisine à Mémé* (*Mémé* means grandma). The island has three informal names: "Garden of the Gulf," referring to the pastoral scenery and lush agricultural lands throughout the province; "Birthplace of Confederation;" and "Cradle of Confederation." On my first visit, I was awestruck by the beauty of the island so I gave it one more nickname: "Pearl of Acadie."

Bernard Léger, then a tour guide with Tours Acadie *in the early 1990s, leading a delegation of Louisiana lawyers and judges for a ten-day tour of the Acadian communities in the Maritimes, including Prince Edward Island.*

In August 1990, enjoying lobster on Prince Edward Island, are Chris and Mary Roy of Alexandria, Louisiana. They were members of the Louisiana delegation participating in the First Annual Allen M. Babineaux International Law Symposium.

Quebec

When I first went to Quebec I had no idea about the more than a million Acadian descendants who are part of this vibrant francophone community. Modern Acadie now consists mainly of communities in New Brunswick, Nova Scotia, Prince Edward Island, Maine, Texas, and South Louisiana, which we now call Acadiana. However, the importance of the Acadian immigration to Quebec is underestimated, most probably because many Acadians have blended into Quebec's cultural mosaic. I was impressed by the fervor the people have for their culture and French language.

This Acadian presence is strong and visible in several areas, such as Bonaventure and Carleton in the Gaspésie peninsula, Îles de la Madeleine (the Magdalen Islands), Nicolet and St-Grégoire de Bécancour (south of Trois-Rivières), L'Acadie and Saint-Jean-sur-Richelieu (south of Montréal), Launaudière (east of Montréal), Saint-Gervais and Saint-Charles (south of Québec), the Saguenay area, and most of the North Shore including Hâvre St-Pierre and Natashqhan. In 1988, it was estimated by *Sondage Léger* that today among Quebec's population about one million people carry an Acadian family name. In 2008, a study by Josée Bergeron for the *Université du Quebec* found that three million people in Quebec have Acadian ancestry, which would represent about half of the French-speaking population of the province.

Through my travels to Quebec, I have had the pleasure of meeting many Acadian descendants from all regions of Acadie. On my first visit I was hosted by Jean Ouellet, an attorney from Quebec City who I had met in 1993 at a human rights conference in Caen, France at the *Mémorial de la Paix*. He and my daughter Rebecca later married and I am now the proud grandfather to Nicolas and Lily Ouellet. We playfully called them "Quebec-Cajuns."

André Forcier, an honored Québec filmmaker whom we had hosted as a houseguest while he was in Louisiana filming *La Comtesse de Baton Rouge* (1997), was a loyal supporter of my Petition. In anticipation of an address on the Petition that I was invited to deliver to a group of lawyers in Montreal, he and his wife Linda Pinet translated the entire 45-page document into French. Although not of Acadian descent, he married Acadian Linda Pinet whose family was originally from Caraquet, and André is a dedicated promoter of Acadian culture. In 2013, he was named a Living Legend by the Acadian Museum of Erath. Forcier also co-produced in Louisiana a series called *Gumbo Oh La La* for TV5 with Charles Larroque, a Louisiana native and now director of CODOFIL. This award-winning series showcased French Louisiana and further strengthened our cultural connections.

Another energetic and dedicated promoter of the culture here is Paul Arsenault who is originally from Moncton, New Brunswick and lives in Quebec City. Arsenault has often helped me navigate my way around the cultural community and has introduced me to countless Acadians during my many pleasant visits. His latest book *The True Story of Ancestor Pierre Arsenault in Acadia* (2013) is written in French and English, and is available as an eBook.

Vera-Anne Petley, another wandering Acadian originally from Cap-Pelé, New Brunswick now living in Montreal, has been a very zealous and hard-working devotee to my work for many years. I first met Petley at the 1999 *Congrès mondial acadien* held in Louisiana. She was a tour operator at the time and brought 350 Northern Acadians to Lafayette that year for the event. Since then, she has been ardently promoting the reuniting of Acadians of the world. In 2012, she introduced me to the region of Lanaudière and to some of its most prominent Acadian citizens, like Évangéline Richard, president of *Festival Acadien de la Nouvelle-Acadie*, and her husband Raymond Gaudet.

Another contributor to the culture is André Gladu, an outstanding filmmaker with the National Film Board of Canada, who since 1971 has directed many films focused on Francophone topics, including some with Louisiana subjects such as: *Le son des français d'Amérique* (1974-1980); *Zarico* (1984); *On the Trail of Acadians in North America* (2004); and *Marron* (2005). These extraordinary films documented and captured the lives and essence of Québécois, Acadians, Métis, Créoles, and Cajuns.

In his work, Gladu was strongly associated with and committed to the Louisiana phenomenon and became long-time friends with professor Dr. Barry Ancelet of UL Lafayette and Léo LeBlanc of Moncton, who spent ten years in Lafayette as Quebec's cultural delegate to CODOFIL. LeBlanc was responsible for "discovering" Zachary Richard by sending him to perform at the *Quebec Winter Carnival* in the early 1970s where his international career was launched. Tellingly, Richard and his musicians arrived for the event dressed in summer clothing as they would have for any "normal" carnival. However, they were surprised to learn that the temperature in Quebec was at minus ten degrees Celsius (14 degrees Fahrenheit)!

In January 1995, the Perrin family celebrated New Year's Day in Quebec City, Canada. They are (left to right) Mary, Andy, Warren, Bruce, and Rebecca Perrin Ouellet. The family vacation gave Perrin the first opportunity to make an argument in favor of the Petition to leaders of the Acadian groups in Quebec.

At the Concord Hotel are Warren A. Perrin (left) and Roger Léger, founder of the Fédération acadienne du Québec.

Representing Louisiana at the Acadian festivities in Montreal in August 2000 are Warren A. Perrin, then-president of CODOFIL; Jean Bourque; Kermit Bouillion, director of the Living Legend program; and David Dronet, vice-president of the board of directors at the Acadian Museum of Erath. The Louisiana delegation was hosted by the Fedération acadienne du Quebec, *whose members donated several books to Louisiana schools. Vera-Anne Petley organized the National Acadian Day concert by* Grouyan Gombo *of Halifax (they perform authentic Cajun music), an exhibit by New Brunswick Acadian Pauline Bujold, and the* Tintamarre au Parc La Fontaine. *A crowd of over 3,000 attended the event on the National Acadian Day on August 15.*

On March 18, 2002, the Supreme Council for the French Language awarded Warren A. Perrin l'Ordre des Francophones d'Amerique *in Quebec City at* l'Hôtel du Parlement. *The award was presented to Perrin by Québec Premier Bernard Landry, himself of Acadian descent. Following the induction are (left to right), Linda Pinet, Perrin, and André Forcier of Montreal.*

In August 2005, at the 250th anniversary of the Deportation, Warren A. Perrin attended a promotion event for his book Acadian Redemption *(2005) in Montreal. Pictured following the event are chef/filmmaker Ronald Gaspard; Paul Arsenault, Acadian activist of Quebec; Perrin; Marie-Jo Thério, singer and actress; and Phil Comeau, Acadian filmmaker and book director.*

On August 7, 2012, for the first time, a Louisiana delegation attended the Festival Acadien de la Nouvelle-Acadie. *The event was held in a region composed of four Acadian municipalities near the city of Joliette: Saint-Jacques, Saint-Liguori, Sainte-Marie-Salomé, and Saint-Alexis. In front row, left to right, are Warren A. Perrin, chairman of the Acadian Museum of Erath and CODOFIL board member; René Gareau, city councilor of Sainte-Marie-Salomé; Robert Perreault, mayor of Saint-Alexis paroisse; Pierre Beaulieu, mayor of Saint-Jacques de Montcalm; Kermit Bouillion, Lafayette Parish School Board member for District 5; (second row, left to right) Chef Pat Mould, who prepared a Cajun meal for a festival event on August 8; Stéphane Malenfant, director of* Les fêtes gourmandes de Lanaudière*; Serge Rivest, mayor of Saint-Liguori; and (third row, left to right) Vera-Anne Petley, event chair from Montreal; Annette Coutu, president of the* Conseil de développement bioalimentaire de Lanaudière*; and Évangéline Richard, president of* Festival acadien de la Nouvelle-Acadie.

In August 2012, following the premier of Phil Comeau's film Les Acadiens du Québec, *a dinner was hosted by the* Festival Acadien de la Nouvelle-Acadie *at* La Maison de bouche *in Saint-Jacques, which is the birthplace of respected Quebec Acadian patriot, historian, and author, Abbé François Lanoue (1918-2010). Left to right are Warren Perrin, Vera-Anne Petley, former Quebec Premier Bernard Landry, Évangéline Richard, Raymond Gaudet, and Louis Duval.*

The representatives of Festival acadien de la Nouvelle-Acadie *present a donation to CODOFIL in 2012. From left to right are Louisiana Chef Patrick Mould; Warren A. Perrin; President* Festiveal Acadien de la Nouvelle-Acadie *Évangéline Richard; Annie Lemarbre; Pierre Beaulieu, mayor of Saint-Jacques; Vera-Anne Petley; and Serge Rivest, mayor of St-Liguori.*

In August 2013, Perrin (right) visited Saint-Jacques in the Lanaudiére region and stopped by the century-old grocery-house (the oldest in Quebec) known as Épicerie J. P. Gaudet owned by 93-year old Jean-Paul Gaudet (d. 2014). While there, they were entertained with traditional Acadian music performed by Phillip Jetté, Gaudet's grand-nephew, who played the accordion while "stepping." Jetté is a member of the traditional music group Belzébuth.

On September 10, 2013, Perrin hosted a lunch at Le Petit Extra *restaurant in Montreal for Dr. Joseph Yvon Thériault (center) and Roger Léger (right) in order to discuss Thériault submitting an article on* Evangeline: The Icon Who Just Won't Die *(see page 149)*.

Mary Perrin and Harlan Johnson, an artist from Montreal, at the Perrin farm on December 22, 2013. Harlan was in Louisiana to coordinate the participation of artists from Louisiana for an exhibition that is part of the program of the Congrès mondial acadien. *The show, entitled* Acadie Mythique, *will tour five art galleries in Acadie from 2014 to 2015. Five of the 17 artists are from the Acadiana region of Louisiana; the others are from Maine, Nova Scotia, New Brunswick, and Prince Edward Island. Co-curator for the exhibition is Mireille Bourgeois.*

In January 2014, at the Cinema on the Bayou Film Festival, *in Lafayette, Louisiana, film director Phil Comeau received the* Directors Grand Jury Award *for his feature film* Secretariat's Jockey-Ron Turcotte *on the life of Acadian jockey Ron Turcotte. Comeau (left) received the* Goujon Caille *(Spotted Cat Fish) award from festival artistic director Pat Mire and director Rebecca Hudsmith.*

France

The French colony of Acadie was pioneered mostly by settlers from the province of Poitou—a coastal region in southwestern France that suffered great hardships in the late 16th and early 17th centuries. In the 1620s, famine and plague followed a series of religious wars between Catholics and Protestants. When social tensions in France ripened, many people left for the colony of Acadie, which was founded by Pierre Dugua de Mons and Samuel de Champlain in 1604.

Most of the Acadians who had resettled 150 years later in the Poitou area during the Acadian Diaspora, moved to Nantes. In 1793, the 12 remaining families in Poitou composed of 73 people stayed in Archigny and became the owners of 17 farms, on what was called *La Ligne Acadienne*. This small group of settlers became immersed into the Poitou population and distanced themselves from their relatives who returned to Acadie or Louisiana. As time passed, they were assimilated into French culture, although their Acadian roots are still evident today.

On several occasions I have traveled in the Poitou area and it has always been a poignant and stirring experience. I loved seeing the many Acadian names on mailboxes along the rural route and knowing that the families that are living there are still in their ancestors' original dwellings. Meeting and getting to know locals such as Michele Touret-Bodin was very moving for me. Visiting this beautiful place reminded me that the "roots of Acadie" are in this region of France.

In June 1991, the Perrins accompanied a Lafayette dèlegation that went to Suresnes, France to participate in the unveiling of the impressive Robert Dafford mural Flying Violin *symbolizing the unity between the Acadians in France and those from Louisiana. Louisiana artist Dafford has executed several classic paintings depicting Acadian history in various parts of the world, including in Nantes. The unveiling ceremony, in the town square, shows (left to right) Jean-Louis Testud,* adjoint mayor *of Suresnes; Michel Tauriac (d. 2013),* France-Louisiane*; then-Lafayette Mayor Dud Lastrapes; Director of* Le Centre International de Lafayette *Phillip Gustin; and artist Dafford.*

In 1977, Michel Tauriac, along with two friends, founded an organization to promote closer relations between France and Louisiana, called France-Louisiane. *In November 1997, the 20th anniversary reception was held at the* Palais Luxembourg *in Paris. In attendance included members of the French senate, former counsel general of France in New Orleans,* Secrétaire Général de l'Assemblée des Français de l'Etranger à Paris, *and* Président de France-Louisiane *Michel Couthures (right); Mayor of Paris Jean Tiberi; and a Louisiana delegation composed of Peggy Fortier; Cathy Chasse; Beth Landry; Jean and Louis Koerner Jr.; Patricia Furgeson, representing the Houma Native Americans of Louisiana; Mademoiselle de Pusy La Fayette (the mother of Gilbert de Pusy La Fayette, the Marquis de La Fayette); and the Perrins. Representing the Acadians of France was Robert Piart of* Les Amitiés acadiennes. *Couthures is standing with the former President of* France-Louisiane *Claude Teboul (left).*

Dr. Christelle Roux, a native of Tours, France, now living in Buffalo, New York, and Mary Perrin (right) are pictured in the Perrin's home. Roux came to Louisiana in 1998 and was hosted by the authors. She obtained her doctorate degree from UL Lafayette and is a research scientist. The Perrins met Roux during a trip to France to "twin" the Acadian Museum of Erath with a museum founded by her uncle, Michel Roux.

On November 9, 1997, a "twinning" ceremony took place in France between the Acadian Museum of Erath and the Musée de Falaise-Acadie-Quebec *of Les Ormes, France. Representing the Acadian Museum of Erath were the Perrins, and representing the museum of France was the Chairman Michel Roux (shown). Other notables in attendance were Dr. Christelle Roux; les Ormes Mayor Guy Monjalon; Simone Epinet-Carrier; Michel Girault; and Serge Cothet. A delegation from France completed the "twinning" by visiting the Louisiana museum in 1999 and attending the* Congrès mondial acadien.

In Paris in 2011 are Mary Perrin (left) and Karel Roynette, a Parisian attorney and another member of the Perrin's extended family. After meeting at a reception hosted by the Versailles Bar Association, the Perrins invited Roynette to come to Louisiana. He ended up staying two years working for Perrin's law firm, Perrin, Landry, deLaunay, Dartez, and Ouellet. While in Louisiana, he obtained his LLM (Master's degree) in law from LSU Law Center in Baton Rouge, Louisiana. Roynette helped to translate Perrin's book Acadian Redemption *(2005) into* Une Saga Acadienne *(2009). Happily, he also met his future wife in Louisiana, Jamie Oplt. They were married in 2013 and now reside in Paris.*

In Paris in October 2012, student Marissa Seraphin enjoys a dinner with the Perrins. Like several other students from France, she was hosted by the Perrins for a summer in Louisiana and has become part of the Perrins' extended family.

In July 2012, Frenchman Laurent Meslier (right), discovered a dog tag near Omaha Beach that belonged to John Mack from Centerville, Louisiana. Meslier contacted CODOFIL in Lafayette and then through Lt. Gov. Jay Dardenne's office, they discovered that Mack had been drafted in 1942 and was a truck driver part of the invasion force that descended upon France, after the initial D-Day landing. Meslier donated the dog tag to Lt. Gov. Dardenne at a ceremony at the Memorial de Caen, the museum at the American Cemetery in Normandy. On Veterans Day 2012, the Louisiana Bicentennial Commission was headed by Lt. Gen. Russell L. Honore, and the dogtag was carried to the National World War II Museum in New Orleans, Louisiana, in the largest military parade in Louisiana's history.

On April 26, 2013, at a dinner sponsored by the Madrid Bar Association, are representatives of Francophone bar associations: (first row, left to right) Mrs. Yves Bonhommo; René Diederich, Bâtonnier *of Bar of Luxemburg; Dominique Attias, National Bar Association of France; (second row, left to right) Yves Bonhommo,* Bâtonnier *of Carpentras; Warren A. Perrin, chairman of the Francophone Section of the Louisiana Bar Association; and Dominique Borde, member of the Bar Council of Paris.*

UNITED STATES

Texas

For economic reasons, Cajuns have been migrating to Texas since the 1840s. In southeastern Texas, the area between the cities of Beaumont, Port Arthur, and Orange is called the Golden Triangle. Today, this area's population is composed of between 30 to 50 percent of Cajuns depending on the town. The neighboring 50 counties have up to 20 percent Cajuns. There are also large Cajun populations in the cities of Houston, Dallas, Austin, San Antonio, Galveston, and Freeport.

In Beaumont, Texas, in 2012, are (left to right) Warren A. Perrin; Brenda Mounier, retired French teacher from Lafayette; Clyde Vincent (d. 2014); Amanda Lafleur, LSU French professor; and Sable Thibodeaux, a native of Beaumont.

John Clyde Vincent, named a Living Legend by the Acadian Museum of Erath, is a Texas Cajun with a passion for his culture. He was born in Port Neches, Texas in 1925 to Léonce Vincent and Della LeBlanc who were both from Vermilion Parish. Vincent was a militant activist of the French language. A self-effacing, man, Vincent strived to keep the Cajun language and culture alive in an area of East Texas where Cajuns were at one time the object of scorn by the Dutch and attacked by the area Ku Klux Klan because they spoke French and were Catholic. The area of Port Neches where Vincent was born was called "Little Abbeville" due to many of its Cajun inhabitants from the general area of Abbeville, Louisiana. As president of Les Acadiens du Texas *for 30 of its 32-year history, he worked diligently to remain connected with his cultural links to Vermilion Parish.*

In 2012, Mary Perrin visited with her friend Carol Cascio (right), a native of Minden, Louisiana, who lives in Houston, Texas, with her husband Frank Cascio, a native of New Orleans.

Maine

The majority of the Acadians in Maine live in the Aroostook County, in the northeastern part of the state. They live in the St. John Valley, mostly along the river carrying the same name, which is the border with northwestern New Brunswick.

On February 22, 2014, in front of the Acadian Museum of Erath are (left to right) Gisèle Faucher, teacher at Madawaska High School in Maine, with students Alexis Côté, Cédric Gendreau, Alexis Cyr, Claude Gendreau, Anna Faucher, and Mary Perrin. [See their story on page 134].

Maryland

On July 28, 2013, at Manokin River Park, the Maryland Historical Trust unveiled a historical marker in memory of the 860 Acadians who were deported to Maryland in 1755.

The historic marker is shown in the background with the Perrins. This is the first public plaque to be erected in Maryland which commemorates the Acadian presence in that state.

At the unveiling of the historical marker are (left to right) Warren A. Perrin; Gregory A. Wood, author of Acadians in Maryland *(1995); R. Martin "Marty" Guidry, president of* Les Guidry d'Asteur, Inc.; *and Harold Breaux of Aberdeen, Maryland.*

Paul Rundquist is a Métis of Acadian and Mi'kmaq blood, National Archives and Records Administration (NARA) contractor, former intelligence analyst, 2009 University of Maryland Baltimore County (UMBC) graduate, and first-time candidate for Congressional election in Maryland's 2nd District in 2014. A proud member of the Association des Acadiens-Métis Souriquois *(AAMS) in Nova Scotia, Rundquist embodies our ancestors' indomitable spirit as he carries forth his ideals, his ancestry, and his generation into the 21st century.*

Massachusetts

In 1755, some 900 Acadians were deported to Massachusetts. After the Treaty of Paris in 1763, many returned north to their ancestral home, but some stayed and began a new life in the British colony. From 1850 to 1930, some 600,000 French Canadians and Acadians migrated to Massachusetts to work in the textile and shoe factories. Today, many Acadians still remain in contact with their cousins in Massachusetts.

In June 2009, Perrin was invited to make a presentation on Acadian history promoting his book Acadian Redemption *(2005) at the John Winslow House Museum in Marshfield, Massachusetts. He was the first Acadian to be invited to speak at the historic house. As part of the event, the group from Louisiana–Mary Perrin, Philip Andrepont, and Debby Andrepont–prepared a Cajun meal of jambalaya and provided Cajun music by now-deceased musician Bernie David.*

Louisiana and CODOFIL

In 1968 the state of Louisiana created the Council for the Development of French in Louisiana (CODOFIL), an important organization that helped to develop and strengthen the connections among francophones and Acadians of the world. Perrin served as its third president from 1994 until 2010, and he remains on its board of directors.

Philipp Gustin was a native of Belgium who came to Louisiana and served as director of CODOFIL during its formative years. Today, he serves as director of international trade and development for Le Centre International *of the Lafayette Consolidated Government. In July 1998, Rebecca Perrin Ouellet (left) is shown with Gustin. Ouellet, who attended the* Université Laval *in Quebec in 1995, later worked for Gustin. She is the daughter of the Perrins and is married to Quebec City native Jean Ouellet.*

Since 1968, CODOFIL has brought many teachers from francophone countries to teach French in Louisiana schools. During an Acadian Museum of Erath social at Lake Peigneur in 2002 are, left to right, Micheline Fleurant, a native from Haiti and teacher of French immersion at Evangeline Elementary in Lafayette; Mavely Aucoin Bouillion, and her sister, Mae Aucoin Delahoussaye; and Pierrette Dugas, born in Caraquet, New Brunswick, who was a French immersion teacher in Lafayette from 2000 to 2005.

On February 14, 1991, the Louisiana-Maritime Provinces Cultural Accords *were signed in Baton Rouge, Louisiana by, left to right, Jean-Robert Frigault, representing the Maritime Provinces of Canada; Dr. John Bertrand, then president of CODOFIL and BESE (Board of Elementary and Secondary Education); then Louisiana Gov. Edwin W. Edwards; and State Rep. Raymond "Lala" Lalonde.*

The First Four Congrès mondial acadien

1994 Congrès mondial acadien (southeast New Brunswick)

The first *Congrès mondial acadien* in 1994 in New Brunswick welcomed 300,000 Acadians. Those in attendance participated in 70 family reunions and 160 conferences, many of them dealing with the preparations for Acadie's 400th anniversary planned for 2004. This event was opened by Boutros Boutros-Ghali, United Nations Secretary General. In his address to the large gathering of Acadians, he stated that the world should look to the Acadian experience to learn how disputes among people can be resolved peacefully.

New Brunswick Acadians Jean Luc Chiasson and his wife Jocelyn Savoie came to Louisiana in 1993 and spent a year helping Louisiana prepare for the 1994 Congrès mondial acadien. *Chiasson (left) is pictured with Perrin in January 1994, after a successful duck hunt at Perrin's duck hunting pond in Vermilion Parish, Louisiana.*

A large delegation of Acadians from Louisiana attended the first Congrès mondial acadien. *The well-executed event was organized, in part, by Co-President Aldéa Landry, Families Chairman Michel Bastarache, and Correspondents Brigitte Robichaud and Antonine Maillet. Enjoying a banquet during the event in New Brunswick are Faye and Dale Broussard of Abbeville, Louisiana.*

1999 Congrès mondial acadien (South Louisiana)

In 1999, Louisiana hosted the second *Congrès mondial acadien*, called *CMA-Louisiane 1999*. Acadians from New Brunswick, Nova Scotia, Prince Edward Island, Quebec, France, Belgium, and Australia came to meet their relatives in the United States. The event attracted 250,000 visitors, including family reunions involving several thousand people.

A gala dinner was held in the honor of his Excellency the Right Honorable Romeo Leblanc, Gov. Gen. of Canada and his wife, Diana Fowler LeBlanc, in the Mardi Gras Ballroom at the Cajundome in Lafayette, Louisiana, on August 12. Shown are Leblanc (left) and Warren A. Perrin (seated at the head table) where they discussed the status of the Petition.

Jean-Robert Frigault was Director of Programing at the CMA-Louisiane 1999. Born in New Orleans and was raised in Tracadie, New Brunswick, he studied at Université de Moncton, *and then worked for the dailies* Globe & Mail, Le Devoir *and the* Select Newspaper *of Quebec. He represented the Maritime Provinces of Canada at CODOFIL from 1990-1996, and now works at CODOFIL in all matters dealing with francophone affairs.*

2004 Congrès mondial acadien (Nova Scotia)

Part of the huge crowd of Acadians attending the August 15 National Acadian Day ceremonies at Grand-Pré. Note in the upper left the historic church. The event celebrated the 400th anniversary of explorers Pierre Dugua de Mons and Samuel de Champlain's founding of Acadie.

2009 Congrès mondial acadien (northeast New Brunswick)

On the August 15 National Acadian Day, in Caraquet, a huge traditional Tintamarre *was held, gathering thousands of Acadians. A* Tintamarre *is a parade of Acadians making loud noises with improvised noisemakers.*

Left to right, are Stephen Ortego, now a Louisiana state representative; Erin Stickney, Vermilionville public relations and marketing coordinator; David Luke; Rocky McKeon, Cajun activist from Houma, Louisiana; and Line Gigault. In the background are Chris Stafford and Emile Ancelet of Lafayette, Louisiana.

In August 2009, on the yacht Oceana *which Warren A. Perrin and his friends brought from Miami to the* Congrès mondial acadien *in Caraquet, are (left to right) Perrin; archivist Donald Arceneaux; and New Orleans attorney Stuart Smith, owner of the yacht.*

Five World Francophone Summits

The idea of holding a biannual summit meeting of *La Francophonie* heads of state took shape long before the first meeting was held in Paris in 1986 under French sponsorship. Pres. Léopold Senghor of Senegal was among the first summit promoters in the early 1960s. Today, the international francophone organization is comprised of 57 countries with notable affiliation with French culture.

1997 Sommet de la Francophonie (Hanoi, Vietnam)

While attending the summit in Hanoi, Perrin met Thi Hien Tran, a native of North Vietnam who presently resides in Paris. She is an attorney and the author of Itinéraire d'une Vietnamienne–l'etudiante insoumise *(2009). A close friendship developed between the two families. According to Tran, "It's a shame that our countries once were at war. There is a profound friendship and respect between our families. Due to our relationship, I have gotten to know a different America, which I love." The Perrins invited Tran and her two daughters Patricia and Marissa to come and stay with them in Louisiana. Like many others who came to be hosted by the Perrins, they became part of the Perrin's extended family. Patricia, also an attorney, worked for Perrin's law firm from 1998 to 2000. While in Louisiana, she translated many of the English displays at the Acadian Museum of Erath into French. Pictured here in Paris in 1998 are (left to right) Thi Hien Tran, her daughter Patricia Rosochowitz, and Mary Perrin.*

Prime Minister Jean Chrétien of Canada (left); Liane Roy, then-president of SNA; and Warren A. Perrin, president of CODOFIL at the World Francophone Summit in Hanoi, Vietnam on November 16, 1997.

1999 Sommet de la Francophonie (Moncton, New Brunswick)

Boutros Boutros-Ghali (left), first Secretary-General of La Francophonie, *during the 1999 summit in Moncton, New Brunswick with Warren A. Perrin, who represented Louisiana and the United States at the World Francophone Summit. One reporter remarked humorously that Boutros Boutros-Ghali should have been renamed Boudreau Boudreau-Gallant! To highlight the key contribution of young people to the future of* La Francophonie *and of the world in general, the summit's main theme was youth.*

During the ceremony at St. Joseph's College, in Memramcook, including a presentation by President Jacques Chirac of France are (left to right) Warren A. Perrin, president of CODOFIL; Roméo LeBlanc, Gov. General of Canada; Brian Comeaux, director of the Congrès mondial acadien-Louisiane 1999; *and Dr. David Cheramie, director of CODOFIL.*

2006 Sommet de la Francophonie (Bucharest, Romania)

HSH Prince Albert II of Monaco (center) presented the pin of Monaco to Warren A. Perrin (left). Perrin in turn gave him an Acadian flag pin, which can be seen here on his shirt pocket. On September 10, 2008, Warren A. Perrin and Mary B. Perrin (right) hosted the Prince and his future wife Charlene Wittstock for a Cajun dinner aboard the yacht Oceana *in Monte Carlo. The Prince is an enthusiast of Cajun food and music.*

2008 Sommet de la Francophonie (Quebec City, Canada)

In 2008, at the World Francophone Summit in Quebec City are Stéphane Bergeron (left), a deputy (and later Minister) of the National Assembly of Quebec, and Warren A. Perrin. Stéphane Bergeron was a great supporter of the Petition.

2010 Sommet de la Francophonie (Montreux, Switzerland)

Attending the 2010 World Francophone Summit in Montreux, Switzerland are pictured (left to right) Julie LaFleur; Warren A. Perrin; Mary Perrin; Claude Teboul; Rep. Jack Montoucet; Sandra Montoucet; Lynn Dural; Philippe Gustin; and Lafayette City-Parish President Joey Dural. These members of the Louisiana delegation are with Teboul, former president of France-Louisiane, *at their Louisiana exhibit.*

Conclusion

In conclusion, we need to remember that Acadie ceased to exist in 1713, over 300 years ago, and yet the mythical place remains stronger than ever in our hearts. Why? Four centuries after our first ancestors arrived in North America, we have remained a separate people. We have not been compromised by the Information Age, but have benefitted from it.

Our people occupy positions in practically every field of human endeavor. Many have achieved glory and fame. We have found a place in modernity and we are confident in our future.

My personal experiences in various regions of Acadie have convinced me that the evolution of emerging cultures all over the world has been exacerbated by many variables, yet one factor remains constant: adaptation. It seems like we were always strangers in our own lands but we never forgot our pioneer forebears' great traits: determination, faith, knowledge, and skills.

As historian Dr. Carl Brasseux has observed, outsiders usually fail to view the Acadian culture in its totality and thus fail to comprehend its bewildering complexities. In reliving my travels in Acadie, it made me prouder more than ever of our Acadian heritage. I have always felt at home in any Acadian or Cajun area in the world where I have had the privilege to venture. I am confident that my grandchildren will continue celebrating their heritage, and I also remain chronically optimistic for a united and expanding Acadian world for many years to come.

AUTHOR BIOGRAPHIES

Dr. Barry Jean Ancelet, author and professor, was born in Church Point and lives in Scott, Louisiana. He has a Bachelor of Arts in French from the University of Louisiana at Lafayette, a Master's of Art in folklore from Indiana University, and a PhD in *Études Créoles* (anthropology and linguistics) from the *Université de Provence/Aix-Marseille I*, in France. Ancelet heads the Department of Modern Languages at UL Lafayette, serves as Folklorist and Research Fellow in the Center for Louisiana Studies, and holds the Willis Granger and Tom Debaillon/ BORSF Endowed Professor of Francophone Studies. He has written academic papers, published numerous articles and several books, and produced concerts, festivals, records, museum exhibitions, documentary films, and television and radio programs on various aspects of Louisiana's Cajun and Creole cultures and languages. Some of his publications include *Cajun Music: Its Origins and Development* (1989); *Capitaine, Voyage Ton Flag: The Traditional Cajun Country Mardi Gras* (1989); *Cajun and Creole Folktales: The French Oral Tradition of South Louisiana* (1994); and *Cajun and Creole Music Makers: Musicians Cadians Et Creoles* (1999). He has also contributed to the following publications: *One Generation at a Time: Biography of a Cajun and Creole Music Festival* (2007); *Cajun Country* (1991); and *Cadiens D'Asteur–Today's Cajuns* (1984). His poetry, under the name Jean Arceneaux, includes *Je suis cadien* (1994) and *Suite du loup* (1998). He also co-founded the *Tribute to Cajun Music* in 1974, which became the annual *Festivals Acadiens et Créoles* in Louisiana. Ancelet has received many recognitions including the *Ordre des Palmes académiques*, the *Ordre des Arts et des Lettres*, the *Ordre des francophones d'Amérique*, the *Américo Paredes* Prize, and in 2009 he was named "Humanist of the Year" by the Louisiana Endowment for the Humanities.

Georges Arsenault, author, folklorist, historian, and broadcaster, was born in Abram-Village, and presently lives in Charlottetown on Prince Edward Island. He has published extensively since 1980 on Acadian history and traditions. He is a seventh generation Prince Edward Island Acadian. His recent publications deal with Acadian traditions associated with Christmas, Mid-Lent, and Candlemas. He is also the author of the double language books *The Island Acadians, 1720-1980* (1989), *La Roche & Grand Ruisseau: An Illustrated History of Egmont Bay and Mont-Carmel* (2012), and *The Acadians of Summerside* (2013).

Michel Bastarache, lawyer, businessman, and retired Puisne Justice on the Supreme Court of Canada, was born in Quebec City, earned his Bachelor of Arts degree from the *Université de Moncton* in 1967, and received a *Licence d'études supérieures en droit public* from the University of Nice, France, in 1972. The following year, he was the General Secretary for the *Société des Acadiens et Acadiennes du Nouveau-Brunswick*. Returning to school, he received a Bachelor of Law degree and joined the *Université de Moncton* as a law professor, and was Dean of the Law School from 1980 to 1983. From 1983 to 1984, he was the Director General for the Promotion of Official Languages in the Department of the Secretary of State of Canada. From 1984 to 1987, he was the Associate Dean of the Common Law section of the University of Ottawa. He was appointed to the New Brunswick Court of Appeal in 1995 and then promoted to the Supreme Court in 1997. Bastarache retired from the Supreme Court in June 2008 and joined the Ottawa office of Canadian law firm Heenan Blaikie. In 2009, he was made a Companion of the Order of Canada, in recognition of "his lifelong commitment to the promotion of linguistic duality and the protection of minority rights, as a law professor and a Supreme Court judge."

Maurice Basque, historian, author and scientific adviser at the *Institut d'études acadiennes de l'Université de Moncton*, lives in Moncton, New Brunswick. He has published many articles and wide-ranging books on Acadian life. As co-author, Basque worked with Marc Robichaud on *Histoire de l'Université de Moncton* (2013), with André Duguay on *Histoire du drapeau acadien* (2013), with Zachary Richard and Sylvain Godin on *Histoire des Acadiennes et des Acadiens de la Louisiane* (2012), with Sylvain Godin on *Histoire des Acadiens et Acadiennes du Nouveau Brunswick* (2007), with Jacques-Paul Couturier on *Les territoires de l'identité, perspectives acadiennes et françaises, XVIIe-XXe siècles* (2005), with John G. Reid, Elizabeth Mancke and Barry Moody on *The Conquest of Acadia* (2004), and with Nicole Barrieau and Stéphanie Côté on *L'Acadie de l'Atlantique* (1999). He also wrote three books with the sociologist Greg Allain on Acadians living in the New Brunswick anglophone urban environments of Saint John, Miramichi and Fredericton. As sole author he wrote *Histoires de Tracadie-Sheila* (2010), *La Société Nationale de l'Acadie* (2006), and *Des hommes de pouvoir* (1996).

Judy Doucette Bellefontaine, retired civil servant, was born in Palmer Road, Prince Edward Island, and now lives in Victoria, British Colombia. Bellefontaine, one of 12 children, moved in 1954 with her parents Alice (Pitre) and John M. Doucette to the community of West Chezzetcook, Nova Scotia. Educated on the Island, Quebec, Nova Scotia, New Brunswick, and Ontario, she developed a deep love of history and her Acadian culture. Employed as a public servant in various federal departments, she retired as Staff Ombudsperson for the Department of Indian and Northern Affairs in 1995.

Ryan Bernard, writer and consultant, was born in Abbeville, Louisiana, and now lives in Houston, Texas. He attended Erath High School, Immaculata Seminary, Texas A&M University, and the University of Louisiana at Lafayette, where he graduated with a Bachelors degree in English/Journalism. Early in his career, he served as a magazine writer and editor and as a freelance reporter for publications such as *Business Week*, *Newsweek*, *The Washington Post*, and *The International Herald-Tribune*. Later, he was the author or ghostwriter of four books on IT and Internet technologies and has consulted for Fortune 500 energy and technology companies in the U.S., Canada, and Western Europe.

Dr. Shane K. Bernard, historian and author, lives in New Iberia, Louisiana. He has published several books including *Cajuns and Their Acadian Ancestors: A Young Reader's History* (2008), which was later issued in French translation as *Les Cadiens et leurs ancêtres acadiens: l'histoire racontée aux jeunes* (2013). He also published *Tabasco: An Illustrated History* (2007); *The Cajuns: Americanization of a People* (2003); and *Swamp Pop: Cajun and Creole Rhythm and Blues* (1996). His work has been published in periodicals such as *Louisiana History*, *Louisiana Folklife*, *Louisiana Cultural Vistas*, and the *New Orleans Time-Picayune*. Bernard holds degrees in English and History from the University of Louisiana at Lafayette, and earned a PhD in History from Texas A&M University. He also serves as historian and curator for McIlhenny Company, maker of Tabasco® brand products, and for Avery Island, Inc.

Dr. Darrell Bourque, poet and professor, lives in a rural area near Church Point, Louisiana. He is author of seven books of poems, including *Megan's Guitar and Other Poems from Acadie* (2013); *Holding the Notes* (2011); *In Ordinary Light: New and Selected Poems* (2010); *Call and Response* (2009); *The Blue Boat* (2004); *Burnt Water Suite* (1999); and *The Doors Between Us* (1998). He graduated from University of Louisiana and then received a Master's and a Ph.D. in Creative Writing from Florida State University. He is Professor Emeritus in English at the University of Louisiana at Lafayette, where he served as director of the Creative Writing and Interdisciplinary Humanities programs. He was appointed Louisiana Poet Laureate in 2007 and again in 2009. Bourque was named the 2014 Louisiana Writer Award recipient of the State Library of Louisiana.

Dr. Whitney Broussard III, a native of Lake Charles, Louisiana, is a research scientist in the Institute for Coastal Ecology and Engineering at the University of Louisiana at Lafayette. He received his PhD in coastal sciences from Louisiana State University for his research using Geographic Information Systems (GIS) to couple land use practices and water quality trends. He continues this work at UL Lafayette in an effort to improve our understanding of coastal resiliency and water management in the 21st century.

Dr. Joshua Clegg Caffery, musician, producer and professor, was born in Franklin, Louisiana, and now lives in Bloomington, Indiana. Presently, he is a visiting lecturer at Indiana University's Department of Folklore and Ethnomusicology. Previously he was the Alan Lomax Fellow in Folklife at the John W. Kluge Center in the Library of Congress in Washington, D.C. He is the author of *Traditional Music in Coastal Louisiana: The 1934 Lomax Recordings.* A founding member of the Red Stick Ramblers and a longtime member of the Louisiana French band *Feufollet*, Caffery was nominated for a Grammy award in 2009 for the album *En Couleurs.* He is the producer of the acclaimed collection of Cajun and Creole drinking songs, *Allons Boire un Coup* (2004) and he currently serves on the board of the Louisiana Folklore Society and as a Fellow of the Center for Louisiana Studies at the University of Louisiana at Lafayette.

Pauline Carbonneau left the Magdalen Islands for a career teaching on the mainland. After teaching in the Montreal area, she moved to Gaspé, where she was involved in the cultural aspects of her community while continuing her career in education. Although she retired from UQAM university as a lecturer in 2000, she continues to research and write about the history of her birthplace. Pauline Carbonneau is the author of *Découverte et peulement des Îles de la Madeleine* (2009).

Dr. Herménégilde Chiasson, writer, poet, playwright, filmmaker, and visual artist, lives just outside Moncton, New Brunswick. He has published over 25 books on poetry and theater and is author of some 30 plays. He has also made 15 documentary films and has produced over 40 solo visual arts exhibitions and 100 group exhibitions. He was president and founding member of several Acadian cultural institutions, and sat on the Canada Council for the Arts, chaired the *Association acadienne des artistes professionnel.le.s du Nouveau-Brunswick* and the board of directors of the Aberdeen Cultural Centre. Between 2003 and 2009, he was Lt. Gov. of New Brunswick. He is currently artist-in-residence at Mount Allison University and at *Université de Moncton* where he is also Art History professor. He has received honorary doctorates from universities of Moncton, Mount Allison, Laurentian, McGill, and St. Thomas. Chiasson is a member of the Order of New Brunswick, the Order of Canada, the Royal Canadian Academy, the Royal Society of Canada, and the French Order of Arts and Letters.

Phil Comeau, film director and writer, was born in Baie Sainte-Marie, Nova Scotia, and lives in Montreal. Comeau studied dramatic arts at the *Université de Moncto*n in New Brunswick, and cinema in Paris, France. He has directed over 100 drama and documentary films and television episodes in some 25 countries, of which a third are films on Acadians. His films have won more than 40 awards in Canada, the U.S., and in Europe. He has also written some 70 film scripts; published poems in *Plumes d'icitte* and *Éloizes*; written an Acadian French dictionary *Les mots acadjonnes*; and written articles for the Montreal magazine *L'Actualité*. For his contributions to Acadian culture and cinema, Comeau received the Order of Canada, *l'Ordre des francophones d'Amérique* in Quebec, *l'Ordre des arts et des lettres* in France, the *Prix Méritas* of the *Fédération acadienne* in Quebec, and the *Prix Grand-Pré* in Nova Scotia. Comeau has also received honorary doctorates from the *Université Sainte-Anne* and the *Université de Moncton*, both in Canada.

Don Cyr, lives in Lille, Maine. Cyr teaches History at the University of Maine at Presque Isle, and Art at the Maine School of Science and Mathematics. He has earned Bachelor's degrees in History, Art, and English, and a PhD in History. He is the founder and president of the *Association culturelle et historique du Mont-Carmel* that runs the Acadian museum *Musée culturel du Mont-Carmel*, in Lille. The Museum is a restored former Roman Catholic Church and has a huge collection of material on Acadian culture.

Natial Perrin d'Augereau, was born and raised in rural South Louisiana not far from Vermilion Bay, is a wife and the mother of five children. On the weekends, she can usually be found singing in one of the local churches or with the Cajun folk troupe *Renaissance Cadienne*. Following the Cajun tradition of self-sufficiency is not easy, but it is her goal.

Bernice d'Entremont, born in Pubnico-Ouest, Nova Scotia, is the program director at the *Musée des Acadiens des Pubnicos et du centre de recherche*. She enjoys promoting Acadian culture and heritage. While teaching adult literacy, she wrote many stories about historic Acadian events. In 2003, she was active in organizing the 350th anniversary of the arrival of Sieur Philippe Mius-d'Entremont, who founded the area in 1653. She also organized the Mius-d'Entremont family reunion at the third *Congrès mondial acadien* in Nova Scotia in 2004.

Françoise Enguehard, author and businesswoman, was born on the French islands of Saint-Pierre et Miquelon and moved 40 years ago to St. John's in Newfoundland in Canada. She has been a television and radio reporter for Radio-Canada in Newfoundland and Labrador, and past President of *la Société Nationale de l'Acadie* from 2006 to 2012. She now heads VIVAT Communications, a public relations and communications firm located in St. John's. For the past 30 years, she has been continuously involved in the promotion of Canadian and international francophonies.

Gisèle Dionne Faucher, teacher, was born in New Brunswick, raised in Madawaska, Maine, and studied in Montreal. She grew up in a francophone family with a Canadian mother and American father. A science teacher and educational leader at Madawaska High School, Faucher has always valued her French heritage and continues to encourage her students to appreciate and promote their French language and Acadian culture.

Martin Guidry, a retired Dupont chemist, lives in Baton Rouge, Louisiana. He has been researching Acadian culture, language, history, and genealogy for the last 40 years. Past president of the Acadian Memorial Foundation in St. Martinville, Louisiana, Guidry is president of *Les Guédry d'Asteur* (The Guidrys of Today), and he also publishes articles and delivers seminars on Acadian topics.

A.M. Hodge, author, is from Marshfield, Massachusetts. (A.M. Hodge is the penname for Anita Flanagan.) During the years her children were in school, her family lived in an antique house dated 1675, near the Winslow House in Marshfield. In a later visit to Grand-Pré, Flanagan sensed the fear, dismay, and anger that seemed to mirror what the Acadians felt when they were held by Winslow's troops preparing to be deported. Those experiences led her to write *Acadie Lost* (2012).

Richard Holledge, author and journalist, was born in England. He is a former newspaper editor and executive with several UK national newspapers including *The Times* and *The Independent.* He is a freelance journalist for *The Times, Wall Street Journal, International Herald-Tribune,* and the *Gulf News* of Dubai. The idea of writing *The Scattered* (2012), a novel based on the Acadian expulsion, came to him during a visit to the Tabasco works on Avery Island, Louisiana. The untold story of the Acadians' exile to England inspired him to write a fictional account based on the real character of Joseph "dit Jambo" LeBlanc.

Dean Jobb, writer and journalist, is the associate director of the School of Journalism at the University of King's College in Halifax, Nova Scotia. He also teaches investigative journalism and media law. He is the author of *The Acadians: A People's Story of Exile and Triumph*, published in the U.S. as *The Cajuns: A People's Story of Exile and Triumph* (2005). Among his other books are *Crime Wave* (2012); and *Bluenose Justice* (2002).

Dr. A.J.B. (John) Johnston, an author, lives in Halifax in Nova Scotia. He authored or co-authored 13 books and over 100 articles in scholarly journals, magazines, and newspapers. Among his history books, *Ni'n na L'nu, The Mi'kmaq of Prince Edward Island* (2013), *Louisbourg, Past, Present, Future* (2013), *Endgame* (2007), *Storied Shores* (2004), and *Grand-Pré, Heart of Acadie* (2004). Among his works of fiction are *The Maze* (2014) and *Thomas, A Secret Life* (2012). Johnson has been awarded France's *Ordre des Palmes académiques* in recognition of his many publications on the history of the French in Atlantic Canada.

Kathey King, genealogist, was born in Freeport, Texas. In 1966, she graduated from Texas Tech University with a degree in marketing. After working as a buyer for Foley's retail store in Houston, in 1976, she moved to Lafayette, Louisiana, where she opened an interior design shop. Moving to the Woodlands, Texas, in 1986 she continued her design business until her retirement. In 1999 she began doing genealogy research and has written books including *Hudiburgh Family, Broussard Family*, and *The Wilson Brothers of Fort Towson, Oklahoma*.

Charles Larroque, educator, writer, and documentary filmmaker, was born in Jeanerette and lives in Lafayette, Louisiana. He is the executive director of the Council for the Development of French in Louisiana (CODOFIL) in Acadiana, Louisiana. For the past 25 years, he has been involved in Louisiana's French linguistic and cultural revival. He has been named member of the *Ordre des Palmes Académiques* in France, for contributions toward the preservation of the French language in the U.S.

Gérard LeBlanc, editor, was born in La Hêtrière in the Memramcook Valley, New Brunswick. He has an Arts degree from Saint Joseph's and a Bachelor of Science degree in electrical engineering at UNB in Fredericton. He was commissioned for three years as an officer in the telecommunications branch of the Royal Canadian Air Force. He was an instructor in telecommunications systems technology at the New Brunswick Community College in Moncton. He is a member of the executive committee of *La Société historique de la Vallée de Memramcook* and is responsible for the publication of *Les Cahiers* and the Heritage Ecomuseum.

M.M. Le Blanc, lawyer, author and filmmaker, lives in New Orleans, Louisiana. Le Blanc is a descendent of author and Democratic Senator Dudley J. LeBlanc, known as "*Cousin Dud.*" She wrote and produced an award-winning film titled *Dudley, Father of the Cajun Renaissance Movement* (2010). As author, she also wrote the novel *Evangeline: Paradise Stolen* (2011), which won the Paris Book Festival's Best Historical Fiction award, the Best State Book by Louisiana Press Women, and finalist for Best New Fiction at the USA Book News.

Dr. Ronnie-Gilles LeBlanc, historian and author, was born in Moncton, Nouveau-Brunswick. He has a Master's degree in History from the *Université de Moncton* and holds a doctorate in history from Laval University. He worked as an archivist at the *Centre d'études acadiennes Anselme-Chiasson* at *Université de Moncton*, after which he became a historian at the Parks Canada Agency. LeBlanc is still active in his research on Acadian studies and authored many publications and articles on Acadian history, focusing on Acadie (Maritime Provinces) during the second half of the 18th century and also on Southeastern New Brunswick in the 19th century.

Stanley LeBlanc, genealogist, lives in Houston, Texas. He has a BA in history from UL Lafayette, and did graduate work in public administration at the University of North Texas and the University of Oklahoma. He is owner of the website (www.thecajuns.com) that is dedicated to Acadian and Cajun Louisiana genealogy, history, and culture. LeBlanc is a member of several genealogical societies, and a Fellow of the Erath Acadian Museum of Erath's Order of Living Legends.

Roger Léger, author and editor, was born in Scoudouc, New Brunswick. He completed his secondary and university studies in Quebec and Ottawa and then taught at the Royal Military College Saint-Jean. In 1987, Léger was the founding president of the Quebec Acadian Federation, an association that exists to this day. He produced a 13-episode TV series on the history of Quebec (1973). Léger edited the Report of the World Commission on Environment and Development in 1987, and he holds the rights to the French edition. He is working on publishing writings of the great Acadian historian Father Antoine Bernard. In collaboration with Guy Thériault, Léger translated and edited *Une saga acadienne* (2009) by Warren A. Perrin.

Dr. Thomas L. Linton, author, lives in Galveston, Texas. He has been a professor at Texas A&M University and holds a degree in Biology from Lamar University, a Masters in Zoology from the University of Oklahoma, and a PhD in Natural Resources Management from the University of Michigan. He is the author of *How the Parks of Galveston County Got Their Names* (2011) and has two books in draft, *Parking With Brigid in Texas Parks Built by the CCC* and *Cowmen and Cowboys of the Wild, Wild East*. He has had three series of articles that have been printed in four newspapers.

Diane Marshall was born in Nova Scotia. She is an author, policy analyst, and history columnist for CBC Radio 2's *Information Morning.* A descendant of the Gauthereau bloodline, she is very proud of her Acadian Heritage, which prompted her to write her bestselling book, *Heroes of the Acadian Resistance, The Story of Joseph Beausoleil Broussard and Pierre II Surette* (2011). Among her other books are *The Spear of Destiny* (2013); *True Stories of Nova Scotia's Past* (2012), *Sly Foxes, Wolves and Men* (2010); *Manifesting the Wraught* (2010); and *Georges Island – The Keep of Halifax Harbour* (2009). She recently released a Halifax guidebook to accompany her book *Harbour Hopper's Best Halifax Stories: Hangings, Explosions, Tunnels, Romance, Politics, Riots and More!* (2013).

Dr. Jean-François Mouhot, author, was born in France and now lives in Washington D.C. He completed his PhD in history at the European University Institute, Florence, in 2006. His research has focused on Acadian refugees in France, Britain, and Louisiana after the Deportations. His first book, *Les Réfugiés acadiens en France (1758-1785): l'impossible réintegration?* (2009), was re-published in 2012 and is currently being translated into English by UL Press in Lafayette, Louisiana.

Jean-Marie Nadeau is an Acadian activist, journalist, author and union advocate. Born in Baker Lake, he now resides in Moncton, New Brunswick. He writes a column for the weekly newspaper, *L'Étoile*, and the daily *Telegraph-Journal* since 2009. He was an editor and columnist for the daily *L'Acadie nouvelle* and served as president of the *Société de l'Acadie du Nouveau-Brunswick* (2008-2013); secretary general of the *Société Nationale de l'Acadie* (1984-1989), and provincial secretary of the *Parti acadien* (1974-1976). He holds a Bachelor's degree in Sociology from the former Collège de Bathurst and studied in Political Science at *Université d'Aix-Marseille*, in France. He helped conceive the idea for the *Congrès mondial acadien* and was founding president of the community radio station CJSE. Nadeau wrote four books including *L'Acadie possible: la constance d'une pensée* (2009), *Que le Tintamarre commence! Lettre ouverte au peuple acadien* (1992) and *Carnets politiques* (1966). He was awarded the *Prix France-Acadie* and the *Prix A.-M.-Sormany* for two of his books, and received Quebec's *Ordre des francophones d'Amérique* and France's National Order of Merit.

Mary Broussard Perrin, visual artist and former educator and gallery owner living in Lafayette, Louisiana, is a mixed media artist working in painting, photomontage, artist books and performance art. She earned a Bachelor of Fine Arts from the UL Lafayette and a Masters in Visual Art from the Vermont College of Fine Arts. She has work in the collections of the National Museum for Women in the Arts, in Washington, D.C.; the Ogden Museum of Southern Art, in New Orleans, a branch of the Smithsonian; the New Orleans Museum of Art; and the Louisiana State Museum.

Warren A. Perrin, lawyer and author, was born near Erath and lives in Layette, Louisiana. He holds a Juris Doctorate degree from Louisiana State University School of Law and is an attorney with the firm of Perrin, Landry, deLaunay, Dartez, and Ouellet. From 1994 to 2010, he was president of the Council for the Development of French in Louisiana (CODOFIL) and an adjunct professor at the University of Louisiana at Lafayette. He was a member of the board of directors of the *Congrès mondial acadien-Louisiane* 1999, president of the Lt. Governor's Task Force of *FrancoFête 1999*, and the founder of the Acadian Museum of Erath, Louisiana. Perrin represented Louisiana and the U.S. at the World Francophone Summits in Hanoi, Vietnam; Moncton, New Brunswick; Bucharest, Romania; Quebec City, Canada; and Montreux, Switzerland. He is the author of six books dealing with French culture, including *Acadian Redemption* (2004), the first biography of an Acadian exile and which reveals how he obtained a successful resolution of his "Petition for an Apology for the Acadian Deportation" from the Queen of England, resulting in the Queen's Royal Proclamation, signed on December 9, 2003. The book was translated into French as *Une Saga Acadienne* (2005). In 1999, French President Jacques Chirac bestowed upon Perrin the French National Order of Merit. He received an honorary Doctor of Laws at *Université Sainte-Anne* in Nova Scotia, Canada. In 2007, Perrin was inducted into the Louisiana Justice Hall of Fame and in 2012 he was named chairman of the Francophone Section of the Louisiana State Bar Association.

Sandra Pettipas Perro, educator, was born in Tracadie, Nova Scotia, and presently lives in Victoria, British Columbia. She received her Bachelor of Arts Degree from the University of Manitoba and her Deaf Education Certificate from Smith College in Northampton, Massachusetts. In addition to her career as educator for the deaf, she has written a book, *Getting To The Roots of My Family Tree* (1995, 2nd Ed. 2005), tracing various lines of her Acadian ancestors from France to various parts of Acadie and Louisiana. In 2011, in Bayou Lafourche, Louisiana, Perro was appointed member of the Circle of Distinction, by Les Guédry d'Asteur.

Katy Reckdahl is a New Orleans-based news reporter. She is a frequent contributor to the *New Orleans Advocate, The Times-Picayune, The New York Times, Christian Science Monitor,* and *The Daily Beast.*

Zachary Richard is a cultural activist, environmentalist, poet and singer-songwriter. He lives in Scott, Louisiana, and in Montreal, Canada. Among his 20 music albums to-date, many of his French language albums have won Gold records in Canada and in France. His major musical hit has been his Double Platinum album, *Cap Enragé.* For his music, he has received six Felix awards in Canada, and has been nominated for a Grammy Award. He also produced, in both English and French, the film *Against the Tide (Contre vents, contre marées)*, the story of the Cajuns in Louisiana. Recognized as a cultural activist, Zachary cofounded *Action Cadienne*, a volunteer organization dedicated to the promotion of the French language and the Cajun culture of Louisiana. Zachary Richard is Officer of the Order of Arts and Letters of France, and member of the Order of Canada; Order of La Plèiade, in France; and the *Ordre des francophones d'Amérique*, in Quebec. He has also received three honorary doctorates, bestowed by the *Université de Moncton* in New Brunswick, the *Université Sainte-Anne* in Nova Scotia, and the University of Louisiana in Lafayette. A celebrated poet with five published books, he was named Louisiana's French poet laureate in 2014.

Alexander Riopel, author and historian, lives at Saint-Jacques in Lanaudière, Quebec. He holds a Bachelor's degree in History and Social Studies Education. Specializing in material culture, his interest lies in the relationship between man and the object. He has a wide field of expertise, ranging from archival work to multimedia. Emphasizing the iconographic archives of his area, Nouvelle-Acadie in Lanaudière, he is the author of *Saint-Alexis, Montcalm 1852-2002, La MRC Montcalm, terre fertile en histoire 1873-1964*, and *Pour rendre le monde meilleur, la Caisse populaire Desjardins de la Nouvelle-Acadie 1919-2005.*

Marie-Claude Rioux is executive director of the *Fédération acadienne de la Nouvelle-Écosse* (FANE). A native of Shippagan, New Brunswick, she lives in Halifax, Nova Scotia. Having first taught French, she then occupied the position of executive director of several provincial organizations, including the *Fédération des parents acadiens de la Nouvelle-Écosse*, the *Association des juristes d'expression française de la Nouvelle-Écosse* and *Réseau Santé–Nouvelle-Écosse*. She also worked as coordinator for the *Coalition nationale des femmes francophones.* As a volunteer, Rioux served on the boards of various organizations, notably as president of the *Conseil communautaire du Grand-Havre*, president of *Femmes Équité Atlantique*, treasurer and vice-president of the *Société de presse acadienne*, and the *Fédération des femmes acadiennes de la Nouvelle-Écosse.*

Dr. Marc Robichaud, historian and author, lives in Moncton, New Brunswick. He is senior researcher at the *Institut d'études acadiennes* of the *Université de Moncton*. He has studied at *Université de Moncton* and McGill University in Montreal, where he received a doctorate in history. He has published various articles for *Acadiensis* and *Bulletin canadien d'histoire de la médecine*, and published the books *Histoire de l'Université de Moncton* (2013) with Maurice Basque; *Vivre sa santé en français au Nouveau-Brunswick: le parcours engagé des communautés acadiennes et francophones dans le domaine de la santé* (2011), with Sylvie Ladouceur and the collaboration of Maurice Basque; and *Des aboiteaux à la génomique et au-delà: histoire de la Faculté des sciences de l'Université de Moncton* (2009), with Charles L. Bourque and with the collaboration of Christine Comeau.

Sally Ross, historian, author and translator, was born and lives in Halifax, Nova Scotia. Educated in France, she has worked in the area of Acadian studies for over 30 years. She co-authored with Alphonse Deveau the prize-winning book *The Acadians of Nova Scotia* (1992). Her book *Les écoles acadiennes en Nouvelle-Écosse, 1758-2000* (2001) traces the Acadian struggles of French-language schools in Nova Scotia. She received a grant in 2003 to conduct field research in all of the post-Deportation Acadian cemeteries in Nova Scotia and has published numerous articles.

Marie Rundquist, author and businesswoman, lives in Maryland. A University of Maryland graduate, she is president and CEO of North Fork Technical Solutions. She wrote *Finding Anne Marie* (2006), which was published in English and French, and later *Revisiting Anne Marie* (2009) and *Cajun By Any Other Name* (2012). Marie's proposal to the Maryland Historical Trust led to the erection of the state's first "Acadians in Maryland" historical marker on July 28, 2013. Descendant of Native Americans and French-Europeans, she volunteers as Administrator of the Amerindian Ancestry out of Acadia DNA project.

Marsha Sills, journalist, was born near Alexandria, Louisiana, graduated from the University of Louisiana at Lafayette, and now lives in Lafayette. As a news reporter for the Acadiana Bureau of the daily Louisiana newspaper, *The Advocate*, she has been covering area news for almost 15 years. As a youth, she spent many weekends and summer days visiting her maternal grandparents in Iberia Parish.

Jeannita Thériault lives in Moncton, New Brunswick, and is editor for the French weekly *Le Moniteur Acadien*. She is an active member of the Board of Directors of *La Société du Monument Lefebvre* in Memramcook, New Brunswick. She has been a journalist for the daily newspaper *Le Matin*; the newsroom director and a reporter at radio *CHLR Les Aboiteaux* in Moncton; and executive member of the Canada Council for the Arts.

Dr. Joseph Yvon Thériault, author and professor, was born in Caraquet, New Brunswick and lives in Montreal. He is a professor of sociology at the University of Quebec in Montreal (UQAM) and Chair for research in globalization, citizenship, and democracy in Canada since 2008. From 1978 to 2008, he was a sociology professor at the University of Ottawa. After his studies at the *Université de Moncton* in Bathurst, he received a Masters in Political Science at the University of Ottawa, and a PhD in the Development of Sociology at the *École des Hautes Études en Sciences Sociales* (EHESS) in Paris, France. His best-selling book, a finalist for the Governor General's Prize, *Évangeline: contes d'Amérique* (2013), was translated into English. His other books include: *Faire société. Société civile et espace francophone* (2007); *Critique de l'américanité: Mémoire et démocratie au Québec* (2005), and *L'identité à l'épreuve de la modernité, Écrits politiques sur l'Acadie et les francophonies minoritaires* (1995). His book awards include the *Prix Richard-Arès* and the *Prix France-Acadie*. In 2004, Thériault was made a member of the Royal Society of Canada.

Dr. Jason Theriot, author and historian of Cajun culture, is a native of New Iberia, Louisiana and lives in Houston, Texas. He earned his PhD in history at the University of Houston and lives in the city with his wife and two "Texas Cajun" children. His most recent book, *American Energy, Imperiled Coast: Oil and Gas Development in Louisiana's Wetlands* (2014), explores Louisiana's energy and environment history. He is also an energy and environmental consultant and worked as an energy policy research fellow at the Harvard Kennedy School of Government studying energy and environmental policies in the Gulf of Mexico.

Michèle Touret-Bodin, theater director, lives in Loudun, France. She is the director of *La Maison de l'Acadie*, in La Chaussée, and also president of the Twinning Committee of Loudun, France, with Shippagan, New Brunswick. She produces plays on Acadian subjects including *Acadie Naissance d'un Peuple, Les enfants de la Nouvelle France, Les Engagés du Nouveau Monde,* and *Les Vents de la Liberté*. In 2003, she was appointed to the *Ordre des Arts et des Lettres* in France.

Alain Troubat, born in France, studied in Montluçon, France; Paris; and at the Grenoble Business School. Starting in the late 1950s, he served with the military in Algeria, worked at the paint factory founded by his grandfather, and later established several chemical companies aimed at the industrial, community and building sectors. He is passionate about the French settlement in North America.

André-Carl Vachon, author and teacher, lives in Montreal and is a descendent of the Acadian refugees of Quebec. He holds a Bachelor's degree in Religious Education from the *Université de Montréal* and studied history at UQÀM. Since 2009, he has been a teacher and community involvement counsellor at *Collège Jean-Eudes*. Vachon has written books including *Living in Society* (2009) and *Les déportations des Acadiens et leurs arrivées au Quebec de 1755-1775* (2014).

Dr. May Gwin Waggoner is an author, dance choreographer and retired professor. She was born in New York, raised in Mississippi, and now lives in Lafayette, Louisiana. After studying at Newcomb College of Tulane University, she learned French in Paris, France, and went on to serve as professor of French and Francophone Studies for 40 years at the University of Louisiana. Waggoner published eight scholarly works, critical editions, and creative works in the field of Louisiana history and literature. Her prize-winning French poetry has been published in the U.S., France, and Belgium and her work has been published by University of Illinois Press, University of Louisiana Press, and the *Presses Universitaires de Limoges* in France. As director of the Louisiana Acadian folklore troupe *Renaissance Cadienne*, she arranged 45 traditional dances and songs, produced three CDs, and toured the U.S., Canada, France, and Belgium. She was named a Living Legend by the Erath Acadian Museum and an Honorary Cajun by the Council for the Development of French in Louisiana (CODOFIL). Her most recent book of poetry is *Le Chant de l'arc-en-ciel: Poésies et Proses.*

Dr. Gregory A. Wood, author, lives in Olney, Maryland. Holding degrees from Notre Dame University in Indiana and Johns Hopkins University in Baltimore, he spent 40 years in foreign language education. He has frequently been involved in historical projects and has been supported along the way by the Maryland Bicentennial Commission and the National Endowment for the Humanities. He has written histories on *The French Presence in Maryland, 1524-1800* (1978) and *Acadians in Maryland in the 18th and 19th Centuries* (1995) as well as its companion supplement published in 1999. Recently he worked with Canadian and American sources in completing a volume on genealogy, celebrating the Acadian and Quebec roots on the maternal side of his family.

ACKNOWLEDGEMENTS

We would like to thank everyone who contributed articles and photographs to this book, and to the following individuals for their assistance in editing, fact checking, and providing information for the book: Sam Broussard, Will Bunch, Dr. Barry Ancelet, Rachelle Dugas, Jean-Robert Frigault,Thomas Guilhot, Charles Larroque, Stanley LeBlanc, Mitch Conover, Donald Arceneaux, Dr. Daniel N. Paul, C.M., O.N.S., Bruce Perrin, Mi'kmaq Elder Odelle Pike, Roger Léger, Philip Andrepont, Michelle LeBlanc, Chris Segura, Vera Petley, Evangeline Richard, Andre Andrepont, Christophe L. Pilut, Karel Roynette, Kermit Bouillion, Dr. May Waggoner, Kirby Jambon, Dr. David Cheramie, Dr. Chris Hodson, Dr. George Arsenault, Dr. Shane K. Bernard, Viola LeBreton, and Dr. Carl A. Brasseaux. Thanks also to Dr. Kimberly Gilmore and The History Channel, for their financial support for many Acadian Museum of Erath projects. A special thanks to Darylin Barousse, who for two years, coordinated all incoming articles and photos.

In an earnest attempt to include every Acadian community in our book, it was necessary for the directors to write the local history of some areas. If we have left out an area, please know it was not intentional. During this challenging two-year venture of compiling this complex work, we necessarily have had to rely on our contributors to credit their sources. However, in order to make this a more reader-friendly book and reach the largest number of people possible, we have tried to minimize the use of footnotes. Sources not footnoted are often cited within the text of the articles, or are noted in their bibliography.

Many of the facts contained in the recitations of the pre-and post-deportation histories of the Acadians in this book were either obtained or confirmed from the website Acadian-Cajun Genealogy & History, developed by the late Tim Hebert of Louisiana, who was in the Terrebonne Historical Society and the Terrebonne Genealogical Society and authored several books on Acadian-Cajun history and genealogy. We wish to also thank and acknowledge the following websites that provided some of the historical information contained in our book: *Université de Moncton*; *Société historique de la Vallée de Memramcook;* Winslow House Museum; Lucie LeBlanc Consentino's Acadian and French-Canadian Ancestral Home; and the Acadian Museum of Erath in Louisiana.

Doing both a French and an English version of this book simultaneously has proven to be quite challenging. But thanks to the excellent work of our superb translators things have run smoothly. The translators for articles from French to English included Jo-Anne Elder, Jacquie Dinsmore, Marie Blythe, and Sally Ross. The translators for articles from English to French include Claire

LeBlanc Lapointe, Réjean Ouellette, Colette Mallet, Anne Audet, Marie-Berthe Landry, and Marc-André Haché. Finally, thanks to Ryan Bernard for his quality work in assembling an excellent team of copy editors and proofreaders including Evan Bernard, Clarisse Burns, Jessica Fazio Martire, and Julie Carter, and thanks to Jennifer Ritter Guidry for her work on the final proofreading.

This is a non-commercial enterprise and profits from the sales of this book will be donated to the following Acadian museums as chosen by the authors of this book: Acadian Museum of Erath (Louisiana), Acadian Memorial (Louisiana), *Musée acadien de l'Université de Moncton* (New Brunswick), *Musée acadien du Québec à Bonaventure* (Quebec), *Maison de L'Acadie* (Loudun, France), *Musée acadien des Huit Maisons à Archigny* (Poitou-Charentes, France), *Musée acadien de La Société historique de la Vallée de Memramcook* (New Brunswick), *Centre d'interprétation acadien–Rendez-vous de la Baie* (Nova Scotia), *Musée acadien de l'Île-du-Prince-Édouard* (Prince Edward Island), *Musée culturel du Mont-Carmel* (Maine), *Musée des Acadiens des Pubnicos et le Centre de recherche* (Nova Scotia), *Musée acadien de la Société du Monument Lefebvre* (New Brunswick), *Association Belle-Ile-Acadie* (France), Acadian House Museum *L'Acadie de Chezzetcook* (Nova Scotia), *Chez Deslauriers à Pomquet* (Nova Scotia), *Bibliothèque Mikesell de l'Association française de la Vallée St-Jean* (Maine), *Festival acadien de la Nouvelle-Acadie* (Quebec), Avon River Heritage Society Museum (Nova Scotia), *Comité historique Soeur-Antoinette-DesRoches* (Prince Edward Island), and the *Musée du Madawaska* (New Brunswick).

Selected Bibliography

Akins, Thomas B. *Acadian and Nova Scotia: Documents Relating to the Acadian French and the First British Colonization of the Province, 1714-1758*, 2nd edition (Cottonport, LA: Polyanthos, 1972).

Akins, Thomas B. *Selections for the Public Documents of the Province of Nova Scotia* (Halifax, NS: Annand, 1869).

Ancelet, Barry and Morgan, Elmore, Jr. *The Makers of Cajun Music* (Austin: University of Texas Press, 1984).

Ancelet, Barry Jean, Edwards, Jay, and Pitre, Glen. *Cajun Country* (Oxford: University Press of Mississippi, 1991).

Ancelet, Dr. Barry Jean, Gaudet, Marcia, and Lindahl, Carl. *Second Line Rescue* (Jackson: University Press of Mississippi, 2013).

Arsenault, Bona. *History of the Acadians* (Ottawa, 1988).

Arsenault, Georges. *The Island Acadians 1720-1980* (Charlottetown: Ragweed Press, 1989).

Babineau, René. *Brief History of Acadia 1604-1988* (Copyright Printing, Inc., 1988).

Banville, Beurmond. "Acadians to get apology from Queen Elizabeth." *The Bangor Daily News,* December 5, 2003.

Basque, Maurice. "Conflits Et Solidarités Familiales Dams: Ancienne Acadie: L'Affaire Broussard De 1724." *La Société Historique Acadienne, Les Cahiers* 20:2, (*Avril-Juin* 1989).

Basque, Maurice. "Genre et gestion du pouvoir communautaire à Annapolis Royal au 18e siècle." *Dalhousie Law Journal*, 17:2 (Fall 1994).

Bernard, Antoine. *Le Drame Acadien* (Montreal: Le Clercs de Saint-Viateur, 1925).

Bernard, Shane K. *The Cajuns: Americanization of a People* (Jackson: University Press of Mississippi, 2003).

Bernard, Shane K. *Cajuns and Their Acadian Ancestors: A Young People's History* (Oxford: University Press of Mississippi, 2008).

Bourque, Darrell. *Megan's Guitar and Other Poems from Acadie* (Lafayette: UL at Lafayette Press, 2013).

Bradshaw, Jim. "Broussard Led Acadians to Attakapas Area." *The Daily Advertiser*, Supplement: History of Acadiana, March 20, 1999.

Bradshaw, Jim. "UL Lafayette Acquires 1755 Letter." *The Daily Advertiser*, October 20, 2001.

Brasseaux, Carl A. *Scattered To The Wind: Dispersal and Wanderings of the Acadians, 1755-1809* (Lafayette: Center for Louisiana Studies, 1991).

Brasseaux, Carl A. *In Search of Evangeline: Origins and Evolution of the Evangeline Myth* (Thibodeaux, Louisiana: Blue Heron Press, 1989).

Brasseaux, Carl A. *Acadian to Cajun: Transformation of a People, 1803-1877* (Oxford: University Press of Mississippi, 1992).

Brasseaux, Carl A. *The Founding of New Acadia: The Beginnings of Acadian Life In Louisiana, 1765-1803* (Baton Rouge: Louisiana State University Press, 1987).

Brasseaux, Carl A. *Lafayette, Where Yesterday Meets Tomorrow: An Illustrated History* (Chatsworth, CA: Windsor Publications, Inc., 1990).

Brasseaux, Carl A., Garcia, Emilio Fabian., Voorhies Jacqueline K. *Quest for the Promised Land* (Lafayette: USL Center for Louisiana Studies, 1989).

Brebner, John B. *New England Outpost: Acadia Before the Conquest of Canada* (New York: Columbia University Press, 1927).

Brenner, John B. "Canadian Policy Towards the Acadians in 1751." *Canadian Historical Review,* 12:3 (1931).

Broussard, Alton E. "Were Early Acadian Men Really the Docile Type?" *The Daily Advertiser*, November, 1977.

Broussard, Emery J. and Campbell, Lorraine. *Vermilion Historical Society, History of Vermilion Parish, Col. II* (Dallas: Taylor Publishing Co.).

Broussard, J. Maxie. "Minutes of Gathering." *Gazette Beausoleil* (Spring, 2004).

Broussard, James F. *Pour Parler Francais* (Boston: D.C. Health and Co., 1921).

Brun, R. "Amherst Papers" *la Societé Historique Acadienne* (Moncton, New Brunswick, 1970).

Calhoun, Milburn. *Louisiana Almanac* 1995-96 (New Orleans, Pelican Publishing, 1995).

Carman, Bliss. *The Vengeance of Noel Brassard: A Tale of the Acadian Expulsion* (Cambridge: The University Press of Cambridge, Massachusetts, 1919).

Chiasson, Fr. Anselme. *Chéticamp: History and Acadian Traditions* (St. Johns, Newfoundland: Breakwater Books Ltd., 1986).

Chandler, R.E. "End Of An Odyssey: Acadians Arrive In St. Gabriel, Louisiana," *Louisiana History XIV* (1974).

Chevrier, Cécile. *Acadie: Sketches of a Journey (La société nationale de l'Acadie,* 1994).

Clark, Andrew Hill. *Acadia: The Geography of Early Nova Scotia to 1760* (Madison: University of Wisconsin Press, 1968).

Clark, George Frederick. *Expulsion of the Acadians* (Brunswick Press, 1955).

Clermont, Ghislain, and Gallant, Janine. *La Modernité En Acadie* (Moncton: *Chaire d'études acadiennes,* 2005).

Comeaux, Malcolm L. *Atchafalaya Swamp Life: Settlement and Folk Occupations* (Baton Rouge: Louisiana State University Press, 1972).

Condow, James E. *The Deportation of the Acadians* (Parks Canada, 1986).

Conrad, Glenn R. *The Cajuns: Essays on their History and Culture* (Lafayette: Center for Louisiana Studies, 1978).

Conrad, Glenn R. *Land Records of the Attakapas District,* Volume 1, *The Attakapas Domesday Book: Land Grants, Claims and Confirmations in the Attakapas District 1764-1826* (Lafayette: Center for Louisiana Studies, 1990).

Conrad, Glenn R. *Dictionary of Louisiana Biography,* "Joseph *dit Beausoleil* Broussard" (Lafayette: Louisiana Historical Association and Center for Louisiana Studies, 1988).

Cormier, Clément. *"Jean-Francois Brossard (Broussard)," Dictionnaire Biographique du Canada,* Vol. III (Quebec: Université Laval, 1974).

Cougle, R. James. *Not By Choice: The True Story of the French-English Struggle* (Fredericton, NB: R.J. Cougle, 1992).

Daigle, Pierre. *Tears, Love and Laughter: The Story Of The Cajuns* (Ville Platte: Swallow Publications, Inc., 1987).

Daigle, Jean. *The Acadians of the Maritimes: Thematic Studies* (Moncton: University of Moncton, 1982).

Daigle, Rev. Msgr. Jules O. *A Dictionary of the Cajun Language* (Ann Arbor, MI: Edwards Bros., Inc. 1984).

Dainow, Joseph. *Civil Code of Louisiana* (St. Paul, MN: West Publishing Co., 1961).

Davis, Stephen A. *Micmac* (Four East Publications, 1990).

Davis, Stephen A. *Peoples of the Maritimes, Mi'kmaq* (Halifax: Nimbus Publishing Limited, 1997).

DeCard, Frank. *Louisiana Sojourns* (Baton Rouge: LSU Press, 1998).

Deveau, J. Alphonse. *Two Beginnings: A Brief Acadian History* (Yarmouth: Lescarbot Publications, 1992).

Davis, Stephen A. *Le Chef des Acadiens (*Yarmouth: *Les Editions Lescarbot,* 1980).

Domengeaux, James H. "Native-Born Acadians and the Equality Ideal." *Louisiana Law Review* 46:6, (July, 1986).

Doucette, Michel. *Le Congrès Mondial Acadien (Les Editions d'Acadie,* 1996).

Doughty, Arthur G. *The Acadian Exiles* (Toronto: Brooks & Co., 1920).

Dronet, Gen. Curney J. *A Century of Acadian Culture: The Development of a Cajun Community: Erath* (Erath: Acadian Heritage and Culture Foundation, Inc., 2000).

Dupon, Albert Leonce. "The Career of Paul Octave Hebert, Governor of Louisiana 1853-1856." *Louisiana Historical Quarterly,* XXXI.

d'Entremont, Clarence J. "The Baronnie de Pombcoup and the Acadians." *The Yarmouth Herald-Telegram,* 1931.

d'Entremont, Clarence J. *Historie de Pubnico dans Les régions acadiennes de la Nouvelle-Écosse (Centre Acadien, Université Sainte-Anne,* 1982).

d'Entremont, Clarence J. "*Histoire du Cap-Sable de l'An Mil au Traité de Paris (1763),*" West Pubnico Archives: *Les archives père Clarence d'Entremont.*

d'Entremont, Clarence J. "*Joseph Brossard (Broussard) dit Beausoleil," Dictionnaire Biographique du Canada,* Vol. III, De 1741 á 1770 (Toronto, Canada, 1974).

Faragher, John Mack. *A Great and Noble Scheme* (New York: W.W. Norton and Co. Inc., 2005).

Fonteneau, Jean Marie. *Les Acadiens du Canada à Belle-Île-en-Mer* (LePalais: Association Belle-Île Acadie, 2004)

Gendron, Gilbert. "The British Genocide of the Acadian People." *The Barnes Review* 3:10 (October 1997).

Giraud, Marcel. *A History of French Louisiana* (Baton Rouge: Louisiana State University Press, 1958).

Griffin, Harry Lewis. *A Brief History of the Acadians,* from an address delivered at a meeting of *France-Amerique de la Louisiane Acadienne* at the College of Sacred Heart, Grand Coteau, Louisiana, October 18, 1952.

Griffiths, Naomi E.S. "The Acadians of the British Sea-Port." *Acadiensis 4* (1976).

Griffiths, Naomi E.S. *The Acadians: Creation of a People* (Toronto, NY: McGraw-Hill Ryerson Ltd., 1973).

Griffiths, Naomi E.S. *The Contexts of Acadian History, 1686-1784* (Montreal: McGill-Queen's University Press, 1976).

Griffiths, Naomi E.S. *From Migrant to Acadian* (Montreal: McGill-Queen's University Press, 2005).

Haliburton, Thomas C. *An Historical and Statistical Account of Nova Scotia* (J. Howe, 1829).

Hannay, James, *The History of Acadia* (St. John, NB: J. & J. McMillan, 1879).

Hebert, Rev. Donald J. *Southwest Louisiana Records* (Eunice, LA: Hebert Publications), Volume 1A.

Henry, Jacques. "From Acadien to Cajun to Cadien: Ethnic Labelization and Construction of Identity." *Journal of American Ethnic History,* 17:4 (Summer 1998).

Henry, Jacques M. and Bankston, Carl L. II. *Blue Collar Bayou* (Westport: Praeger Press, 2002).

Herbin, John Frederick. *The History of Grand-Pré* (St. John, NB: Heritage Books, Inc., 1891).

Hirsch, Arnold R. and Logsdon, Joseph. *Creole New Orleans: Race and Americanization* (Baton Rouge: LSU Press, 1992).

Hodson, Christopher. *The Acadian Diaspora* (Oxford: Oxford University Press, 2012).

Hoffman, Gilbert Bernard, Ph.D. *The Historical Ethnography of the Micmac of the Sixteenth and Seventeenth Centuries* (Berkeley, CA: University of California, 1955).

Hoffman, Paul E., editor. *The Louisiana Purchase and Its People* (Lafayette, LA: Louisiana Historical Association and the Center for Louisiana Studies, 2004).

Houdlett, Jeffery. "The Cajun Connection." *Portland Magazine*, 19:4.

Ignatieff, Michael. "Truth, Justice and Reconciliation." *National Canadian Bar Association* 5:7 (Nov/Dec 1997).

Jen, Janet. *Acadiana Genealogy Exchange* 26 (April/July 1997).

Jones, Bill. *Louisiana Cowboys* (Gretna: Pelican Publishing Co., 2007).

Kennedy, W.P.M. *The Commission of Canada 1534-1937* (New York: Russell & Russell, 1973).

Lauriere, Emile. *La Tragedie d'un Peuple* (Paris: Bossard, 1922).

LeBlanc, Dudley J. *The Acadian Miracle* (Lafayette, LA: Evangeline Publishing Company, 1966).

LeBlanc, Dudley J. *The True Story of the Acadians* (Lafayette, LA: Evangeline Publishing Company, 1927 and 1932).

LeBlanc, Robert G. "The Acadian Migration." *Canadian Geographical Journal* 81 (1970).

LeBlanc, Ronnie Gilles *"Joseph Broussard dit Beausoleil." (Cahiers de la Societé historique Acadienne* 52, 1986).

Ledgard, Jonathan. "An Old British Crime: Cajuns' Belated Counter-Attack," *The Economist,* January 31, 1998.

Leger, Viola *News From the Senate* 1:3 (June 2004).

Ljunggren, David. "Canada acknowledges wrong done to Acadians deported in 1700s." *The Boston Globe,* December 11, 2003.

Longfellow, Henry Wadsworth *Evangeline: A Tale of Acadie, The Political Words of Henry Wadsworth Longfellow* (New York: Houghton Mifflin, 1886).

Mahaffie, Charles D., Jr. *A Land of Discord Always: Acadia From Its Beginnings to the Expulsion of Its People,1604-1755* (Camden, ME: Down East Books, 1995).

Marcantel, David. "The Legal Status of French in Louisiana." *Revue des Parlementaires de Langue Française (*Fall 1994).

Marshall, Dianne. *Georges Island: The Keep of Halifax Harbour (*Halifax: Nimbus Publishing, 2003).

Marshall, Dianne. *Heroes of the Acadian Resistance: The Story of Joseph Beausoleil Broussard and Pierre II Surette 1702-1765* (Halifax: Formac, 2012).

McCreath, Peter L. and Leefe, John G. *A History of Early Nova Scotia* (Tantallon: Four East Publications, 1982).

Murdock, Beamish *A History of Nova Scotia or Acadie* (Halifax: James Barnes, 1865), Vol. 1, Vol. 2.

Nietfeld, Patricia. *Determinants of Aboriginal Micmac Political Structure* (University of New Mexico, 1981).

Paradis, Roger. *Papers of Prudent L. Mercure Histoire du Madawaska* (Madawaska Historical Society, 1998).

Paratte, Henri-Dominique. *Peoples of the Maritimes: Acadians (*Toronto: Nimbus Publishing, 1998).

Paul, Daniel N. *Confrontation: Micmac and European Civilization* (Truro,NS: Confederacy of Mainland Micmacs, 1993).

Paul, Daniel N. "On the road again: Pubnico's, Cape Sable Island." *The Halifax Herald*, August 7, 2003.

Paul, Daniel N. *We Were not Savages: A Micmac Perspective on the Collision of European and Aboriginal Civilization* (Halifax: Nimbus Publishing Ltd., 1993).

Paul, Daniel N. "Mi'kmaq, Acadians: friends then and now." *The Halifax Herald*, June 9, 2004.

Perrin, Warren A. *Acadian Redemption* (Opelousas: Andrepont Publishing, LLC, 2005).

Perrin, Warren A. *Une Saga Acadienne* 1755-2003 (Quebec: *Editions* LAMBDA and Opelousas: Andrepont Publishing, LLC, 2009).

Perrin, William Henry. *Southwest Louisiana Biographical and Historical* (Baton Rouge: The Gulf Publishing Co., 1891, reprinted by Claitor's Publishing Division, 1971).

Plank, Geoffrey. *An Unsettled Conquest* (Philadelphia: University of Pennsylvania Press, 2001).

Poirier, Leonie Comeau. *My Acadian Heritage* (Hantsport, NS: Lancelot Press, 1989).

Powell, Laurence. *The Accidental City* (London: Harvard University Press, 2012).

Quinpool, John. *First Things in Acadia* (Halifax: First Things Publishers Ltd., 1936).

Reaux, Vita B. and John R. "Jean Francois Broussard and Catherine Richard." *Attakapas Gazette* 6 (March, 1971).

Rees, Grover, translation, "The Dauterive Compact: Foundation of the Cattle Industry." *Attakapas Gazette* 11 (Summer 1976).

Richard, Edouard. *Acadia: Missing Links of a Chapter in American History* (Montreal: J. Lovell, 1895).

Richard, Zachary, Godin, Sylvain, and Basques, Maurice. *Histoire des Acadiennes et des Acadiens de la Louisiane* (Lafayette: UL Lafayette Press, 2012).

Ross, Sally and Deveau, Alphonse. *The Acadians of Nova Scotia: Past and Present* (Halifax: Nimbus Publishing, 1992).

Rundquist, Marie. *Revisiting Anne Marie* (Pennsylvania: Infinity Publishing, 2009, 2012).

Rushton, William F. *The Cajuns* (New York: Farrar Strauss Giroux, 1979).

St. Martin de Tours Catholic Church, *Copie d'un vieux registre Archives,* St. Martinville, Louisiana.

Savary, A. W. *Supplement to the History of the County of Annapolis* (William Briggs, 1913).

Savoy, Ann Allen. *Cajun Music: A Reflection Of A People* (Eunice, LA: Bluebird Press, 1984).

Schlarman, James H. *From Quebec to New Orleans* (Bellville: Buechler Publishing Company, 1929).

Ségalen, Jean. *Acadie en résistance* (Morlaix: *Skal Vreigh-Montroules*, 2002).

Sills, Marsha. "Queen Elizabeth II offers apology for deporting Acadians." *The Advertiser,* December, 11, 2003.

Simmoneaux, Angela. "All in the family." *The Sunday Advocate,* Baton Rouge, Louisiana, February 28, 1999.

Sinnet, Fabien, and Mimeault, Mario, in collaboration with Ginette Roy. *Gaspé Through the Years* (Quebec: City of Gaspé, 2009).

Smith, Jr., Griffin. "The Cajuns: Still Loving Life." *National Geographic Magazine*, 178:4 (October 1999).

Smith, Phillip H. *Acadia, A Lost Chapter In American History* (New York: S.N., 1884).

Surette, Paul. *Petcoudiac: Colonisation et Destruction 1731-1755* (*Les Editions d'Acadie,* 1988).

Surette, Paul. *Atlas de L'Etablissement des Acadiens aux Trois Rivieres du Chignectou*, 1660-785 (*Les Editions d'Acadie*, 1996).

Thibodeaux, Ron. "Royal Regrets Offered for Acadian Expulsion." *The Times-Picayune,* December 11, 2003.

Tregle, Joseph G., Jr. *The History of Louisiana* (Baton Rouge: LSU Press, 1977).

Trenholm, Gladys. *A History of Fort Lawrence* (Sackville, NB: Sherwood Printing Ltd. 1985).

Trisch, Joseph Le Sage. *French in Louisiana* (New Orleans: A.F. Laborde and Sons, 1959).

Vermilion Historical Society. *History of Vermilion Parish, Vol. I* (Abbeville, LA: Taylor Publishing Company, 1983).

Vermilion Historical Society. *History of Vermilion Parish, Vol. II* (Abbeville, LA: Taylor Publishing Company, 2003).

Vulliamy, Ed. "Fire in the blood on the bayou," *London Guardian Observer,* February 13, 1998.

Ward, Roger K. "The French Language in Louisiana Law and Legal Education: A Requiem." *Louisiana Law Review* 57:4 (Summer 1997).

Webster, John Chance. *Acadia At The End Of The 17th Century* (Saint John: Tribune Press, 1934).

West, Robert. *An Atlas of Louisiana Surnames of French and Spanish Origin* (Baton Rouge: Geoscience Publications, LSU, 1986).

Wicken, William C. *Mi'kmaq, Treaties on Trial: History, Land and Donald Marshall Junior* (Toronto: University of Toronto Press, 2004).

Wilson, Charles Regan and Ferris, William. *Encyclopedia Of Southern Culture* (Chapel Hill: University of North Carolina Press, 1989).

Winzerling, Rev. Oscar W. *Acadian Odyssey* (Baton Rouge: Louisiana State University Press, 1955).

Winslow, John. *Winslow's Journals* (Collections of the Nova Scotia Historical Society, Boston, Massachusetts).

Wood, Gregory A. *A Guide to the Acadians in Maryland* (Baltimore: Gateway Press, 1995).